Koren Talmud Bavli

THE NOÉ EDITION

YEVAMOT

Steinsaltz Center

KOREN

תלמוד בבלי

KOREN TALMUD BAVLI

THE NOÉ EDITION

יבמות

YEVAMOT

Daf 53b through Daf 70a

COMMENTARY BY

Rabbi Adin Even-Israel Steinsaltz

EDITOR-IN-CHIEF

Rabbi Dr Tzvi Hersh Weinreb

SENIOR CONTENT EDITOR

Rabbi Dr Shalom Z Berger

EXECUTIVE EDITOR

Rabbi Joshua Schreier

STEINSALTZ CENTER

KOREN PUBLISHERS JERUSALEM

Supported by the Matanel Foundation

Koren Talmud Bavli, The Noe Edition
Vol. 14d: Tractate Yevamot, Daf 53b through Daf 70a
Paperback, ISBN, 978-965-7765-67-8

First Hebrew/English paperback edition, 2021

Koren Publishers Jerusalem Ltd.
PO Box 4044, Jerusalem 91040, ISRAEL
PO Box 8531, New Milford, CT 06776, USA
www.korenpub.com

Steinsaltz Center

Steinsaltz Center is the parent organization of institutions established by Rabbi Adin Even-Israel Steinsaltz

PO Box 45187, Jerusalem 91450 ISRAEL
Telephone: +972 2 646 0900, Fax +972 2 624 9454
www.steinsaltz-center.org

This book was published in cooperation with the Israel Institute for Talmudic Publications.

הִנֵּה יָמִים בָּאִים, נְאֻם אֲדֹנָי יֱהוִה, וְהִשְׁלַחְתִּי רָעָב בָּאָרֶץ,
לֹא־רָעָב לַלֶּחֶם וְלֹא־צָמָא לַמַּיִם, כִּי אִם־לִשְׁמֹעַ אֵת דִּבְרֵי יהוה.

Behold, days are coming – says the Lord God – I will send a hunger to the land, not a hunger for bread nor a thirst for water, but to hear the words of the Lord. (AMOS 8:11)

The Noé edition of the Koren Talmud Bavli
with the commentary of Rabbi Adin Even-Israel Steinsaltz
is dedicated to all those who open its covers
to quench their thirst for Jewish Knowledge,
in our generation of Torah renaissance.

This beautiful edition is for the young, the aged,
the novice and the savant alike,
as it unites the depth of Torah knowledge
with the best of academic scholarship.

Within its exquisite and vibrant pages,
words become worlds.

It will claim its place in the library of classics,
in the bookcases of the Beit Midrash,
the classrooms of our schools,
and in the offices of professionals and business people
who carve out precious time to grapple with its timeless wisdom.

For the Student and the Scholar

DEDICATED BY LEO AND SUE NOÉ

Steinsaltz Center

Executive Director, Steinsaltz Center
Rabbi Meni Even-Israel

Managing Editor
Rabbi Jason Rappoport

Senior Content Editor
Rabbi Dr. Shalom Z. Berger

Editors
Rabbi Joshua Amaru, *Coordinating Editor*
Amy Kaplan Benoff
Menucha Chwat
Rabbi Yoel Domb
Rabbi Yonatan Shai Freedman
Rabbi Alan Haber
Rabbi Tzvi Chaim Kaye
Catriel Lev
Elisha Loewenstern
Adina Luber
Rabbi Avishai Magence, *Content Curator*
Gavriel Reiss
Rabbi David Sedley
Shira Shmidman
Rabbi Michael Siev
Avi Steinhart
Rabbi Binyamin Zimmerman

Copy Editors
Aliza Israel, *Coordinator*
Bracha Hermon
Ita Olesker
Debbie Ismailoff
Shira Finson
Ilana Sobel
Deena Nataf
Eliana Kurlantzick Yorav
Nava Wieder

Language Consultants
Dr. Stephanie E. Binder, *Greek & Latin*
Rabbi Yaakov Hoffman, *Arabic*
Dr. Shai Secunda, *Persian*
Shira Shmidman, *Aramaic*

KOREN

Design & Typesetting
Raphaël Freeman, *Design & Typography*
Dena Landowne Bailey, *Typesetting*
Tani Bayer, *Jacket Design*

Images
Eliahu Misgav, *Illustration & Image Acquisition*

Introduction by the Publisher

The Talmud has sustained and inspired Jews for thousands of years. Throughout Jewish history, an elite cadre of scholars has absorbed its learning and passed it on to succeeding generations. The Talmud has been the fundamental text of our people.

Beginning in the 1960s, Rabbi Adin Even-Israel Steinsaltz שליט״א created a revolution in the history of Talmud study. His translation of the Talmud, first into modern Hebrew and then into other languages, as well the practical learning aids he added to the text, have enabled millions of people around the world to access and master the complexity and context of the world of Talmud.

It is thus a privilege to present the *Koren Talmud Bavli*, an English translation of the talmudic text with the brilliant elucidation of Rabbi Steinsaltz. The depth and breadth of his knowledge are unique in our time. His rootedness in the tradition and his reach into the world beyond it are inspirational.

Working with Rabbi Steinsaltz on this remarkable project has been not only an honor, but a great pleasure. Never shy to express an opinion, with wisdom and humor, Rabbi Steinsaltz sparkles in conversation, demonstrating his knowledge (both sacred and worldly), sharing his wide-ranging interests, and, above all, radiating his passion. I am grateful for the unique opportunity to work closely with him, and I wish him many more years of writing and teaching.

Our intentions in publishing this new edition of the Talmud are threefold. First, we seek to fully clarify the talmudic page to the reader – textually, intellectually, and graphically. Second, we seek to utilize today's most sophisticated technologies, both in print and electronic formats, to provide the reader with a comprehensive set of study tools. And third, we seek to help readers advance in their process of Talmud study.

To achieve these goals, the *Koren Talmud Bavli* is unique in a number of ways:

- The classic *tzurat hadaf* of Vilna, used by scholars since the 1800s, has been reset for great clarity, and opens from the Hebrew "front" of the book. Full *nikkud* has been added to both the talmudic text and Rashi's commentary, allowing for a more fluent reading with the correct pronunciation; the commentaries of *Tosafot* have been punctuated. Upon the advice of many English-speaking teachers of Talmud, we have separated these core pages from the translation, thereby enabling the advanced student to approach the text without the distraction of the translation. This also reduces the number of volumes in the set. At the bottom of each *daf*, there is a reference to the corresponding English pages. In addition, the Vilna edition was read against other manuscripts and older print editions, so that texts which had been removed by non-Jewish censors have been restored to their rightful place.

- The English translation, which starts on the English "front" of the book, reproduces the *menukad* Talmud text alongside the English translation (in bold) and commentary and explanation (in a lighter font). The Hebrew and Aramaic text is presented in logical paragraphs. This allows for a fluent reading of the text for the non-Hebrew or non-Aramaic reader. It also allows for the Hebrew reader to refer easily to the text alongside. Where the original text features dialogue or poetry, the English text is laid out in a manner appropriate to the genre. Each page refers to the relevant *daf*.

- Critical contextual tools surround the text and translation: personality notes, providing short biographies of the Sages; language notes, explaining foreign terms borrowed from Greek, Latin, Persian, or Arabic; and background notes, giving information essential to the understanding of the text, including history, geography, botany, archaeology, zoology, astronomy, and aspects of daily life in the talmudic era.
- Halakhic summaries provide references to the authoritative legal decisions made over the centuries by the rabbis. They explain the reasons behind each halakhic decision as well as the ruling's close connection to the Talmud and its various interpreters.
- Photographs, drawings, and other illustrations have been added throughout the text – in full color in the Standard and Electronic editions, and in black and white in the Daf Yomi edition – to visually elucidate the text.

This is not an exhaustive list of features of this edition, it merely presents an overview for the English-speaking reader who may not be familiar with the "total approach" to Talmud pioneered by Rabbi Steinsaltz.

Several professionals have helped bring this vast collaborative project to fruition. My many colleagues are noted on the Acknowledgments page, and the leadership of this project has been exceptional.

RABBI MENACHEM EVEN-ISRAEL, DIRECTOR OF THE STEINSALTZ CENTER, was the driving force behind this enterprise. With enthusiasm and energy, he formed the happy alliance with Koren and established close relationships among all involved in the work.

RABBI DR. TZVI HERSH WEINREB שליט״א, EDITOR-IN-CHIEF, brought to this project his profound knowledge of Torah, intellectual literacy of Talmud, and erudition of Western literature. It is to him that the text owes its very high standard, both in form and content, and the logical manner in which the beauty of the Talmud is presented.

RABBI JOSHUA SCHREIER, EXECUTIVE EDITOR, assembled an outstanding group of scholars, translators, editors, and proofreaders, whose standards and discipline enabled this project to proceed in a timely and highly professional manner.

RABBI MEIR HANEGBI, EDITOR OF THE HEBREW EDITION OF THE STEINSALTZ TALMUD, lent his invaluable assistance throughout the work process, supervising the reproduction of the Vilna pages.

RAPHAËL FREEMAN, EXECUTIVE EDITOR OF KOREN, created this Talmud's unique typographic design which, true to the Koren approach, is both elegant and user friendly.

It has been an enriching experience for all of us at Koren Publishers Jerusalem to work with the Steinsaltz Center to develop and produce the *Koren Talmud Bavli*. We pray that this publication will be a source of great learning and, ultimately, greater *avodat Hashem* for all Jews.

Matthew Miller, Publisher
Koren Publishers Jerusalem
Jerusalem 5772

Contents

For the vocalized Vilna Shas layout, please open as a Hebrew book.

Introduction to **Perek VI**

If brothers dwell together and one of them dies and he has no child, the wife of the dead man shall not be married outside of the family to one not of his kin; her brother-in-law will have intercourse with her and take her to him to be his wife and consummate the levirate marriage.

(Deuteronomy 25:5)

By Torah law it is the act of intercourse itself by which the *yevama* is acquired by the *yavam* in fulfillment of the mitzva of levirate marriage. Therefore, it is necessary to determine the exact parameters of the act defined as intercourse for this purpose; both the objective definition of the act as well as the required intentions of the parties involved. Must they intend that the act be for the sake of performing a mitzva, or for the sake of validating the legal transaction? Or are their intentions irrelevant?

The clarification of what is considered a sexual act is useful for other areas of *halakha* as well. With regard to forbidden sexual relations, which acts constitute full-fledged violation of a prohibition? What is the severity of the punishment for a given act? Furthermore, when does a forbidden act of intercourse disqualify a woman from marrying a priest? In the case of marriage, when is a marriage considered to be consummated? These issues are discussed at the beginning of this chapter.

The chapter then turns to address the details governing women disqualified from marrying priests, especially the High Priest. How do these disqualifications come about? Who is included in these categories? Finally, the institution of marriage is addressed, with a particular emphasis on the mitzva to be fruitful and multiply. What is necessary in order to fulfill this mitzva? Who is included in the obligation to have children?

These matters form the bulk of this chapter, but, as is the way of the Talmud, several secondary matters stemming from these primary questions are also discussed.

מתני׳ הַבָּא עַל יְבִמְתּוֹ, בֵּין בְּשׁוֹגֵג בֵּין בְּמֵזִיד בֵּין בְּאוֹנֶס בֵּין בְּרָצוֹן, אֲפִילּוּ הוּא שׁוֹגֵג וְהִיא מְזִידָה, הוּא מֵזִיד וְהִיא שׁוֹגֶגֶת, הוּא אָנוּס וְהִיא לֹא אֲנוּסָה, הִיא אֲנוּסָה וְהוּא לֹא אָנוּס. אֶחָד הַמְעָרֶה וְאֶחָד הַגּוֹמֵר – קָנָה, וְלֹא חִילֵּק בֵּין בִּיאָה לְבִיאָה.

MISHNA **One who had intercourse with his** *yevama*, **whether unwittingly,** i.e., he thought he was having intercourse with someone else, **or intentionally,**[N] i.e., he knew she was his *yevama* and nevertheless had intercourse with her without intent to perform levirate marriage; **whether** due to **coercion or willingly; even if he was unwitting and her** participation was **intentional, his** participation was **intentional and she** was **unwitting, he was coerced and she was not coerced,** or **she** was **coerced and he was not coerced; both one who** merely **engages in the initial stage of intercourse**[N] **and one who completes** the act of intercourse **has** thereby **acquired** his *yevama*.[H] **And** similarly, the Torah **did not distinguish between** an act of **intercourse** in an atypical manner, i.e., anal intercourse, **and intercourse** in a typical manner.

וְכֵן הַבָּא עַל אַחַת מִכׇּל הָעֲרָיוֹת שֶׁבַּתּוֹרָה, אוֹ פְּסוּלוֹת, כְּגוֹן: אַלְמָנָה לְכֹהֵן גָּדוֹל, גְּרוּשָׁה וַחֲלוּצָה לְכֹהֵן הֶדְיוֹט, מַמְזֶרֶת וּנְתִינָה לְיִשְׂרָאֵל, בַּת יִשְׂרָאֵל לְמַמְזֵר וּלְנָתִין – פְּסָלָהּ, וְלֹא חִילֵּק בֵּין בִּיאָה לְבִיאָה.

And so too, with regard to a man **who had intercourse with any one of those with whom relations are forbidden** [*arayot*] by **the Torah or** with those who are **unfit for him** even though they are not in the category of *arayot*, **for example, a widow with a High Priest; a divorcée and a** *yevama* **who performed** ***ḥalitza*** [*ḥalutza*] **with a common priest; a** ***mamzeret***, i.e., a woman born from an incestuous or adulterous relationship, **or a Gibeonite woman with an Israelite; the daughter of an Israelite with a** ***mamzer*** **or a Gibeonite; he has disqualified her** from marrying into the priesthood through this act no matter how it was performed, **and the Torah did not distinguish between** the act **of intercourse** in an atypical manner, i.e., anal intercourse, **and intercourse** in a typical manner.[H]

גמ׳ מַאי אֲפִילּוּ?

GEMARA The Gemara asks: **What is** the significance of the word **even** in the statement that begins with: Even if he was unwitting and her participation was intentional? Since the mishna has already said that there is no halakhic difference whether the act of intercourse was performed intentionally, what is added by that statement?

לֹא מִיבַּעְיָא קָאָמַר: לֹא מִיבַּעְיָא הוּא שׁוֹגֵג וְהִיא קָמְכַוְּונָה לְמִצְוָה, אִי נָמֵי הוּא מֵזִיד וְהִיא קָמְכַוְּונָה לְמִצְוָה, אֶלָּא אֲפִילּוּ הוּא שׁוֹגֵג וְהִיא מְזִידָה, דְּתַרְוַיְיהוּ לֹא קָמְכַוְּונִי לְשֵׁם מִצְוָה – אֲפִילּוּ הָכִי קָנָה. תָּנֵי רַבִּי חִיָּיא: אֲפִילּוּ שְׁנֵיהֶם שׁוֹגְגִים, שְׁנֵיהֶם מְזִידִים, שְׁנֵיהֶם אֲנוּסִים.

The Gemara answers: The mishna is stated in the style of: **Needless to say.** It is **needless to say** that if **he** was **unwitting and she intended** to fulfill **the mitzva,** or **alternatively, he** acted **intentionally** without intent to fulfill the mitzva **and she intended** to fulfill **the mitzva,** he has acquired her. **However, even if he** was **unwitting and she** acted **intentionally, where both of them did not intend to act for the sake of the mitzva, he nevertheless acquires** her. Similarly, **Rabbi Ḥiyya taught: Even if both of them** acted **unwittingly, intentionally,** or **were coerced,** he acquires the *yevama* through the act of intercourse.

אָנוּס דְּמַתְנִיתִין הֵיכִי דָּמֵי? אִילֵּימָא כְּשֶׁאֲנָסוּהוּ גּוֹיִם וּבָא עָלֶיהָ – וְהָאָמַר רָבָא: אֵין אוֹנֶס לְעֶרְוָה, לְפִי שֶׁאֵין קִישּׁוּי אֶלָּא לְדַעַת.

§ The Gemara asks: **What are the circumstances** the mishna is referring to when it mentions a man who **was coerced? If we say** that it is **when gentiles coerced him** by threatening to kill him if he did not have intercourse with her **and** he therefore **had intercourse with her, didn't Rava say that there is no** such thing as **coercion** of a man to have intercourse with a woman **with whom relations are forbidden,**[NH] **because there is no erection** of the male organ **without intent?**[B] Consequently, even if he acted due to the threat, his action is considered intentional.

אֶלָּא בְּיָשֵׁן – וְהָאָמַר רַב יְהוּדָה

Rather, the mishna must be referring to **one who was sleeping** and became erect, and his *yevama* drew him onto herself. **However, didn't Rav Yehuda say** that

NOTES

Whether unwittingly or intentionally, etc. – בֵּין בְּשׁוֹגֵג בֵּין בְּמֵזִיד וכו׳: *Tosafot* inquired why the mishna specified both the case of one who had intercourse intentionally and the case of one who had intercourse willingly. What is the difference between these cases? They explain that the term willingly indicates that one does so with intention to fulfill the mitzva, whereas the term intentionally means that one acts purposefully but without intent to fulfill the mitzva.

One who engages in the initial stage of intercourse – הַמְעָרֶה: This term is subsequently explained in the Gemara on 55b.

There is no coercion of a man to have intercourse with a woman with whom relations are forbidden – אֵין אוֹנֶס לְעֶרְוָה: The Ramban cites a dispute with regard to this principle. Some explain that if a man is threatened with death unless he engages in an act of forbidden relations, and he commits the act, he is punishable in court for the forbidden relations due to Rava's principle that there is no coercion of a man with regard to intercourse. Others say that the man is not punishable in court because he is considered to be coerced, despite the fact that, *ab initio*, he is obligated to give up his life rather than engage in forbidden relations. Rather, Rava's principle applies to a case in which a woman or a third person coerced him to engage in intercourse, but not under pain of death. In this case, Rava's principle determines that it is as though he intentionally committed the act and he is not considered coerced. Nevertheless, the Gemara did not explain that the case of coercion in the mishna is one where the man's life has been threatened, as, since he engages in the act of intercourse willingly but for a purpose other than the mitzva, it is no different from the case the mishna refers to as having intercourse intentionally. See also *Tosafot*.

HALAKHA

Any act of intercourse acquires a ***yevama*** – כׇּל בִּיאָה קוֹנָה בִּיבָמָה: If one has intercourse with his *yevama*, whether intentionally or unwittingly, regardless of whether either party was coerced or willing, he has thereby acquired her and they are married. Furthermore, it makes no difference whether it was a typical act of intercourse or anal intercourse, nor whether he completed the act or merely began it (Rambam *Sefer Nashim, Hilkhot Yibbum* 2:3; *Shulḥan Arukh, Even HaEzer* 166:7).

Prohibited and disqualifying intercourse – בִּיאָה אֲסוּרָה וּפוֹסֶלֶת: A prohibited act of intercourse is considered to have occurred as soon as the act has begun, regardless of whether the act was completed or whether it was a typical act of intercourse or anal intercourse. Furthermore, the woman is disqualified from marrying a priest regardless of whether she or the man engaged in the act intentionally or willingly, as long as she is at least three years old and he is at least nine years old (Rambam *Sefer Kedusha, Hilkhot Issurei Bia* 18:6; *Shulḥan Arukh, Even HaEzer* 6:9; 20:1, and in the comment of Rema).

There is no coercion of a man to have intercourse with a woman with whom relations are forbidden – אֵין אוֹנֶס לְעֶרְוָה: A woman who was coerced to engage in forbidden relations is exempt from all penalties. However, a man who is coerced is liable to receive punishment. Since Rava ruled that erection occurs willingly, he is not considered to have been coerced at all. The Ra'avad adds that even a man can be coerced and therefore exempt from punishment if he became erect while intending to have intercourse with his wife, and then someone forcibly coerced him to engage in a prohibited act of intercourse. The *Maggid Mishne* writes that even the Rambam would agree that in this rare case, the man would be considered coerced and would be exempt from punishment (Rambam *Sefer Nashim, Hilkhot Issurei Bia* 1:9).

BACKGROUND

Intentional erection – קִישּׁוּי לְדַעַת: The nerves that cause erection are usually activated voluntarily. Although it is possible that an erection could be caused by a kind of mechanical stimulation, the assumption here is that a man's desire is largely in control of these nerves, and emotional causes are the decisive factor in the arousal of erection. The conclusion implied by the Gemara that erections are necessarily intentional is to be understood in the sense that there has to be some cooperation on the part of the man for it to occur.

HALAKHA

A sleeping man has not acquired his *yevama* – יָשֵׁן לֹא קָנָה בִּיבִמְתּוֹ: One who did not intend to perform an act of sexual intercourse, e.g., one who was asleep, drunk, or completely unaware of his actions, does not acquire his *yevama* even if they did engage in sexual intercourse (Rambam *Sefer Nashim, Hilkhot Yibbum* 2:4; *Shulḥan Arukh, Even HaEzer* 166:8).

One who fell from a roof and was inserted into a woman is liable to pay four types of indemnity – נָפַל מִן הַגַּג וְנִתְקַע חַיָּיב בְּאַרְבָּעָה דְּבָרִים: One who fell from a roof due to the force of a normal wind and hurt someone is liable to pay four types of indemnity: Indemnity due to injury, pain, medical costs, and loss of livelihood. However, he is exempt from paying for the victim's shame (Rambam *Sefer Nezikin, Hilkhot Ḥovel* 1:12; *Shulḥan Arukh, Ḥoshen Mishpat* 421:11).

And if she is his *yevama*, he has not acquired her – וּבִיבִמְתּוֹ לֹא קָנָה: One who became erect while intending to have intercourse with his wife and then fell onto his *yevama* has not acquired her (Rambam *Sefer Nashim, Hilkhot Yibbum* 2:4; *Shulḥan Arukh, Even HaEzer* 166:8).

Sexual intercourse completes…but money or a marriage document do not – בִּיאָה גּוֹמֶרֶת...וְאֵין כֶּסֶף וּשְׁטָר: A *yevama* can be fully acquired by her *yavam* only through sexual intercourse, but not by other means that generally effect betrothal, i.e., money or a marriage document. However, the Sages decreed that one should not have intercourse with his *yevama* without betrothing her first (Rambam *Sefer Nashim, Hilkhot Yibbum* 5:9; *Shulḥan Arukh, Even HaEzer* 166:2, 170:2).

NOTES

Her brother-in-law will have intercourse with her, etc. – יְבָמָהּ יָבֹא עָלֶיהָ וכו׳: The Gemara here cites several expositions of this verse and attempts to demonstrate that only one *halakha* is derived from each expression in the verse. Some of these expositions, as well as additional ones, are also cited in the Jerusalem Talmud, but there the Gemara sees no reason to avoid using a single phrase as the source of multiple expositions.

יָשֵׁן לֹא קָנָה בִּיבִמְתּוֹ! אֶלָּא – בְּנִתְקַע? וְהָא אָמַר רַבָּה: נָפַל מִן הַגַּג וְנִתְקַע – חַיָּיב בְּאַרְבָּעָה דְּבָרִים, וּבִיבִמְתּוֹ לֹא קָנָה!

a sleeping man **has not acquired his *yevama*,**[H] as he did not intend to perform the act of intercourse at all? **Rather,** the mishna was referring **to one who was inserted** into his *yevama* by accident. But **didn't Rabba say:** One who **fell from a roof and was inserted** into a woman due to the force of his fall **is liable** to pay **four** of the five **types of indemnity**[H] that must be paid by one who damaged another: Injury, pain, medical costs, and loss of livelihood. However, he is not liable to pay for the shame he caused her, as he did not intend to perform the act, **and if** she is **his *yevama*, he has not acquired** her[H] in this manner.

אֶלָּא: כְּגוֹן שֶׁנִּתְכַּוֵּין לְאִשְׁתּוֹ, וּתְקָפַתּוּ יְבִמְתּוֹ, וּבָא עָלֶיהָ, שְׁנֵיהֶם אֲנוּסִים דְּבֵי רַבִּי חִיָּיא הֵיכִי דָּמֵי? כְּגוֹן שֶׁנִּתְכַּוֵּין לְאִשְׁתּוֹ, וּתְקָפוּהוּ גּוֹיִם וְדִבְּקוּם זֶה בָּזֶה, וּבָא עָלֶיהָ.

Rather, it is a case **where he intended** to have intercourse with **his wife** and became erect, **and his *yevama*** forcefully **grabbed hold of him and he had intercourse with her.** The Gemara further asks: If so, **what are the circumstances** of the case when **both of them were coerced** that was mentioned by **the school of Rabbi Ḥiyya?** The Gemara answers: It is a case **where he intended** to have intercourse with **his wife, and gentiles grabbed hold of him and pressed** him and his *yevama* **against each other, and he** thereby **had intercourse with her.**

מְנָא הָנֵי מִילֵּי? דְּתָנוּ רַבָּנַן: ״יְבָמָהּ יָבֹא עָלֶיהָ״ מִצְוָה. דָּבָר אַחֵר: ״יְבָמָהּ יָבֹא עָלֶיהָ״ בֵּין בְּשׁוֹגֵג בֵּין בְּמֵזִיד, בֵּין בְּאוֹנֶס בֵּין בְּרָצוֹן.

§ The Gemara inquires as to the source of these *halakhot*: **From where are these matters** derived? **As the Sages taught** with regard to the verse **"Her brother-in-law will have intercourse with her"** (Deuteronomy 25:5),[N] that this indicates that the act of intercourse in this circumstance is **a mitzva,** i.e., it is preferable to the alternative, which is *ḥalitza*. **Alternatively,** the verse **"Her brother-in-law will have intercourse with her,"** indicates that it does not matter how he had intercourse with her, **whether unwittingly or intentionally, whether** due to **coercion or willingly.**

וְהָא אַפִּיקְתֵּיהּ לְמִצְוָה! לְמִצְוָה מִ״וְּאִם לֹא יַחְפּוֹץ הָאִישׁ״ נָפְקָא, הָא חָפֵץ – יַבֵּם, וְכִי אֲתָא קְרָא – בֵּין בְּשׁוֹגֵג בֵּין בְּמֵזִיד בֵּין בְּאוֹנֶס בֵּין בְּרָצוֹן.

The Gemara asks: **Didn't you derive** from this phrase that the act of intercourse in this case is **a mitzva?** How can the same phrase also indicate that it does not matter what the intentions of the two parties were during the act of intercourse? The Gemara answers: The fact that it is **a mitzva is derived from** the verse: **"And if the man does not wish** to take his *yevama*" (Deuteronomy 25:7), which indicates that if he **wishes, he performs levirate marriage,** which is preferable to *ḥalitza*. Therefore, **when** the **verse** cited above **came,** it indicated that levirate marriage has occurred **whether** the parties acted **unwittingly or intentionally, whether** due to **coercion or willingly.**

תַּנְיָא אִידָךְ: ״יְבָמָהּ יָבֹא עָלֶיהָ״ כְּדַרְכָּהּ, ״וּלְקָחָהּ״ שֶׁלֹּא כְּדַרְכָּהּ. ״וְיִבְּמָהּ״ בִּיאָה גּוֹמֶרֶת בָּהּ וְאֵין כֶּסֶף וּשְׁטָר גּוֹמְרִין בָּהּ. ״וְיִבְּמָהּ״ בְּעַל כָּרְחָהּ. דָּבָר אַחֵר: ״יְבָמָהּ יָבֹא עָלֶיהָ״ בֵּין בְּשׁוֹגֵג כו׳.

It is taught in **another** *baraita* that the phrase: **"Her brother-in-law will have intercourse with her"** indicates that levirate marriage has been performed if they engage in **typical** sexual intercourse. The next phrase, **"and take her,"** includes even **atypical,** i.e., anal, sexual intercourse. The concluding phrase of the verse, **"and consummate the levirate marriage,"** indicates that **sexual intercourse completes her** acquisition, **but money and** a marriage **document do not**[H] **complete her** acquisition to him as his fully betrothed wife, in contrast to the regular *halakhot* of marriage. By emphasizing **"and consummate the levirate marriage with her,"** the verse teaches that he acquires her even if he acted **against her will. Alternatively: "Her brother-in-law will have intercourse with her"** indicates that levirate marriage has occurred **whether** the parties acted **unwittingly** or intentionally, whether due to coercion or willingly.

וְהָא אַפִּיקְתֵּיהּ לְכְדַרְכָּהּ! הַהוּא מִ״לְהָקִים לְאָחִיו שֵׁם״ נָפְקָא, בְּמָקוֹם שֶׁמֵּקִים שֵׁם. וְכִי אֲתָא קְרָא – בֵּין בְּשׁוֹגֵג בֵּין בְּמֵזִיד בֵּין בְּאוֹנֶס בֵּין בְּרָצוֹן.

The Gemara asks: **Didn't you derive** from this phrase that levirate marriage has been performed if they engage in **typical** sexual intercourse? How can it also indicate that it does not matter what the intentions of the two parties were during the act of intercourse? The Gemara answers: **That** *halakha* **is derived from** a different verse: **"To establish a name for his brother"** (Deuteronomy 25:7), which indicates that intercourse must occur **in the place where he establishes a name,** i.e., where it can lead to childbirth. Therefore, **when** the **verse** cited above **came,** it indicated that levirate marriage has occurred **whether** the parties acted **unwittingly or intentionally, whether** due to **coercion or willingly.**

גּוּפָא, אָמַר רַב יְהוּדָה: יָשֵׁן לֹא קָנָה בִּיבִמְתּוֹ, דְּאָמַר קְרָא ״יְבָמָהּ יָבֹא עָלֶיהָ״ עַד דְּמִכַּוֵּין לָהּ לְשֵׁם בִּיאָה. וְהָתַנְיָא: בֵּין עֵר [בֵּין יָשֵׁן! אֵימָא: בֵּין עֵרָה בֵּין יְשֵׁנָה.

§ The Gemara addresses **the matter itself** cited in the previous discussion. **Rav Yehuda said: A sleeping** man **has not acquired his** *yevama*, **as the verse states: "Her brother-in-law will have intercourse with her"** (Deuteronomy 25:5), which indicates that he does not acquire her **unless he intends** to act **for the sake of sexual intercourse.** Since a sleeping man does not intend to engage in sexual intercourse, he does not acquire his *yevama*. The Gemara asks: **Isn't it taught** in a *baraita* that one acquires his *yevama* through sexual intercourse regardless of **whether he** was **awake or asleep?** The Gemara answers: **Say** the *baraita* in the following emended form: **Whether she** was **awake or asleep.**[H] The woman's awareness is not a necessary component in order to perform levirate marriage.

וְהָתַנְיָא: בֵּין עֵר] הוּא בֵּין יָשֵׁן הוּא. בֵּין עֵרָה הִיא בֵּין יְשֵׁנָה הִיא! הָכָא בְּמַאי עָסְקִינַן – בְּמִתְנַמְנֵם. הֵיכִי דָּמֵי מִתְנַמְנֵם? אָמַר רַב אַשִׁי: נִים וְלָא נִים, תִּיר וְלָא תִּיר, כְּגוֹן דְּקָרוּ לֵיהּ וְעָנֵי, וְלָא יָדַע לְאַהֲדוּרֵי סְבָרָא, וְכִי מַדְכְּרוּ לֵיהּ מִדְכַּר.

The Gemara asks further: **Wasn't it taught** in another *baraita* that one acquires his *yevama* through sexual intercourse regardless **of whether he was awake or he was asleep** and regardless of **whether she was awake or she was asleep?** The Gemara answers: **With what are we dealing here** when the *baraita* says that a sleeping man acquires his *yevama*? It is referring to a man **who is dozing.** The Gemara asks: **What are the circumstances** of **dozing? Rav Ashi said:** One is **asleep but not asleep, awake but not awake, when,** if **they call him, he will answer, but he is unable to provide a reasonable** answer. **And when they** later **inform him** of what happened, **he remembers** it.

גּוּפָא, אָמַר רַבָּה: נָפַל מִן הַגַּג וְנִתְקַע חַיָּיב בְּאַרְבָּעָה דְּבָרִים, וּבִיבִמְתּוֹ לֹא קָנָה: בְּנֶזֶק, בְּצַעַר, בְּשֶׁבֶת, בְּרִפּוּי, אֲבָל בּוֹשֶׁת לָא מִיחַיַּיב, דְּאָמַר מָר: אֵין חַיָּיב עַל הַבּוֹשֶׁת עַד שֶׁיִּתְכַּוֵּין.

The Gemara returns to the statement of Rabba cited earlier in order to discuss **the matter itself** that Rabba addressed. **Rabba said:** One who **fell from a roof and was inserted** into a woman due to the force of his fall **is liable** to pay **four** of the five **types** of **indemnity** that must be paid by one who damaged another, **and** if she is **his** *yevama* **he has not acquired** her in this manner. He is liable to pay for **injury, pain, loss of livelihood,** and **medical costs. However, he is not liable** to pay for the **shame** he caused her, **as the Master said: One is not liable** to pay **for shame unless he intends** to humiliate his victim.[H] Consequently, one who fell from a roof accidentally is not liable to pay for the shame he caused the woman.

אָמַר רָבָא: נִתְכַּוֵּון לְהַטִּיחַ בְּכוֹתֶל וְהִטִּיחַ בִּיבִמְתּוֹ – לֹא קָנָה. לְהַטִּיחַ בִּבְהֵמָה וְהִטִּיחַ בִּיבָמָה – קָנָה, דְּהָא קָמְכַוֵּין לְשֵׁם בִּיאָה בָּעוֹלָם.

Rava said: If **he intended to press** his sexual organ **into a wall, and he** accidentally **pressed** it **into his** *yevama*, **he has not acquired** her, as he did not intend to engage in an act of sexual intercourse. However, if he intended **to press** his sexual organ **into an animal, and he pressed** it into **his** *yevama*, **he has acquired** her, **as he** at least **intended** to act **for the purpose of sexual intercourse in general,**[H] i.e., for some form of sexual intercourse.

״אֶחָד הַמְעָרֶה״. אָמַר עוּלָּא: מִנַּיִן לְהַעֲרָאָה מִן הַתּוֹרָה? שֶׁנֶּאֱמַר ״וְאִישׁ אֲשֶׁר יִשְׁכַּב אֶת אִשָּׁה דָּוָה וְגִלָּה אֶת עֶרְוָתָהּ אֶת מְקֹרָהּ הֶעֱרָה״ מִכָּאן לְהַעֲרָאָה מִן הַתּוֹרָה.

§ We learned in the mishna that **both one who** merely **begins the act of intercourse** and one who completes it has acquired the *yevama* through this act. **Ulla said: From where** is it derived that **the initial stage of intercourse** is considered an act of sexual intercourse **by Torah law? As it is stated: "And if a man shall lie with a woman having her sickness and shall uncover her nakedness, he has made naked** [*he'era*] **her fountain"** (Leviticus 20:18). The verse is referring to the first stage of intercourse, and **from here** it is derived that **the initial stage of intercourse** [*ha'ara'a*] is considered sexual intercourse **by Torah law.**

אַשְׁכַּחַן נִדָּה, שְׁאָר עֲרָיוֹת מִנַּיִן? וְכִי תֵּימָא: נֵילַף מִנִּדָּה – מַה לְּנִדָּה שֶׁכֵּן מְטַמְּאָה אֶת בּוֹעֲלָהּ!

The Gemara asks: **We have found** a source for this *halakha* in the case of **a menstruating woman,** the subject of the verse cited above. **From where** is it derived that the initial stage of intercourse is considered sexual intercourse with regard to **the rest of those with whom relations are forbidden? And if you say we should derive it from the** *halakha* with regard to **a menstruating woman, what** comparison can be made **to a menstruating woman,** concerning whom the *halakha* is more stringent than others with whom relations are forbidden, **in that she causes one who has intercourse with her to become ritually impure?**[H]

HALAKHA

Whether she was awake or asleep – בֵּין עֵרָה בֵּין יְשֵׁנָה: One who had intercourse with his *yevama* has acquired her regardless of whether she was awake or asleep (Rambam *Sefer Nashim, Hilkhot Yibbum* 2:3; *Shulḥan Arukh, Even HaEzer* 166:7).

One is not liable to pay for shame unless he intends to humiliate his victim – אֵין חַיָּיב עַל הַבּוֹשֶׁת עַד שֶׁיִּתְכַּוֵּין: One is not liable to pay for shaming another individual unless he intended to do so. One who unintentionally shames another individual is exempt from monetary liability (Rambam *Sefer Nezikin, Hilkhot Ḥovel* 1:10; *Shulḥan Arukh, Ḥoshen Mishpat* 421:1).

As he at least intended to act for the purpose of sexual intercourse in general – דְּהָא קָמְכַוֵּין לְשֵׁם בִּיאָה בָּעוֹלָם: If one intended to perform an act of sexual intercourse, and he happened to have intercourse with his *yevama*, he has acquired her. However, if he did not mean to engage in sexual intercourse at all and nevertheless had intercourse with his *yevama*, he has not acquired her, as stated by Rava (Rambam *Sefer Nashim, Hilkhot Yibbum* 2:4; *Shulḥan Arukh, Even HaEzer* 166:8).

A menstruating woman…causes one who has intercourse with her to become ritually impure – נִדָּה...מְטַמְּאָה אֶת בּוֹעֲלָהּ: One who had intercourse with a menstruating woman becomes a primary source of ritual impurity with the same *halakhot* as the menstruating woman herself. He transmits impurity to vessels or individuals that come in contact with him or carry him as well as to items that he causes to move. Additionally, if he sits or lies upon an item that is designated for this purpose, it becomes impure even if he did not have direct contact with it or cause it to move (Rambam *Sefer Tahara, Hilkhot Metamei Mishkav UMoshav* 3:1).

NOTES

It is within his power to increase – שֶׁכֵּן בְּיָדוֹ לְרַבּוֹת: The argument is that since this prohibition is stringent in that the number of individuals to whom it applies can be increased, perhaps it is also stringent with regard to the manner in which it can be violated. Therefore, it cannot be derived that if the initial stage of intercourse is considered an act of sexual intercourse in this case, it is always considered sexual intercourse (Ritva).

Let it come by deriving the *halakha* in any one case from two of the sources mentioned above – תֵּיתֵי חֲדָא מִתַּרְתֵּי: Rashi and *Tosafot* understood that the *halakha* is derived from the common denominator between two of the sources mentioned above. However, the *Tosefot HaRosh* apparently understood that the *halakha* with regard to some forbidden relations would be derived from one source, and that other *halakhot* would be derived from the other source. The *Arukh LaNer* notes that the *Tosefot HaRosh* must have had a slightly different version of the Gemara text, as the phrase: Let it come by deriving the *halakha* in any one case from two of the sources mentioned above, implies that both sources are needed to derive a single prohibition.

אֶלָּא: אָתְיָא מֵאֵשֶׁת אָח, דִּכְתִיב ״וְאִישׁ אֲשֶׁר יִקַּח אֶת אֵשֶׁת אָחִיו נִדָּה הִיא״, וְכִי אֵשֶׁת אָחִיו [לְעוֹלָם] נִדָּה הִיא? אֶלָּא: כְּנִדָּה, מַה נִּדָּה בְּהַעֲרָאָה – אַף אֵשֶׁת אָח בְּהַעֲרָאָה.

Rather, the *halakha* in other cases **comes from** a verse about **a brother's wife, as it is written: "And if a man shall take his brother's wife, it is impurity** [*nidda*]**"** (Leviticus 20:21). The word *nidda* generally refers to a menstruating woman, and so the Gemara asks: **Is his brother's wife always menstruating? Rather,** it means that the *halakha* with regard to her is **like** that of **a menstruating woman: Just as** one is liable to receive punishment for violating the prohibition against engaging in sexual intercourse with **a menstruating woman through the initial stage of intercourse, so too,** one is liable to receive punishment for violating the prohibition against engaging in sexual intercourse with **a brother's wife through the initial stage of intercourse.**

מַה לְּאֵשֶׁת אָח שֶׁכֵּן בְּיָדוֹ לְרַבּוֹת, דְּאִי בָּעֵי מְקַדֵּשׁ וְאָזֵיל כִּי אַלְפָּא!

The Gemara asks: **What** comparison can be made between **a brother's wife** and other women with whom relations are forbidden? The prohibition with regard to a brother's **wife is** more stringent in that **it is within his power to increase**[N] the number of women forbidden by this prohibition, **as, if he wishes, he can go on betrothing a thousand** women, all of whom would be forbidden to his brother. Consequently, the prohibition with regard to a brother's wife cannot serve as a model for other prohibitions.

אֶלָּא אָתְיָא מֵאֲחוֹת אָב וַאֲחוֹת אֵם, דִּכְתִיב ״וְעֶרְוַת אֲחוֹת אִמְּךָ וַאֲחוֹת אָבִיךָ לֹא תְגַלֵּה כִּי אֶת שְׁאֵרוֹ הֶעֱרָה״. אִיכָּא לְמִיפְרַךְ: מַה לַּאֲחוֹת אָב וַאֲחוֹת אֵם – שֶׁכֵּן אִיסּוּר הַבָּא מֵאֵלָיו!

Rather, the *halakha* in other cases **comes from** a verse with regard to **a father's sister and a mother's sister, as it is written: "And you shall not uncover the nakedness of your mother's sister nor of your father's sister; for he has made naked** [*he'era*] **his kin"** (Leviticus 20:19). The Gemara asks: **It is** possible **to refute** this source as follows: **What** comparison can be made between other women with whom relations are forbidden and **a father's sister and a mother's sister, which are** unique in that they are prohibited due to **a prohibition that comes on its own?** The prohibition with regard to a father's sister and a mother's sister does not stem from marriage, but from the biological fact that she is his father's or mother's sister. It is therefore dissimilar to prohibitions that result from marriage.

מֵחֲדָא לָא אָתְיָא, תֵּיתֵי [חֲדָא] מִתַּרְתֵּי. מְהֵי תֵּיתֵי? תֵּיתֵי מֵאֵשֶׁת אָח וַאֲחוֹת אָב וַאֲחוֹת אֵם – מַה לְּהָנָךְ, שֶׁכֵּן אֲסוּרִין מִשּׁוּם שְׁאֵר!

The Gemara states: The principle that the initial stage of intercourse is considered sexual intercourse **does not come from** any **one** of the sources cited above. **Let it come** by deriving the *halakha* in any **one** other case **from** the common denominator of **two** of the sources mentioned above.[N] The Gemara asks: **From which** two sources could this principle **come** to be derived? If you say it can **comes** to be derived **from** the combination of the source with regard to **a brother's wife and** the source with regard to **a father's sister and a mother's sister, what** comparison may be drawn from these cases, **which are** unique in that they are **prohibited because** they are **kin?**

אֶלָּא תֵּיתֵי מִנִּדָּה וַאֲחוֹת אָב וַאֲחוֹת אֵם – מַה לְּהָנָךְ, שֶׁכֵּן אִיסּוּר הַבָּא מֵאֵלָיו! אֶלָּא תֵּיתֵי מִנִּדָּה וְאֵשֶׁת אָח, דְּמַאי פָּרְכַתְּ?

Rather, let it come from the prohibition proscribing **a menstruating woman and** the prohibition with regard to **a father's sister and a mother's sister,** as a menstruating woman is not prohibited as a family relative. The Gemara raises a difficulty: **What** comparison may be drawn from these cases, **which are** each a **prohibition that comes of its own** accord, as neither one is created through marriage? **Rather, let it come from** the prohibition proscribing **a menstruating woman and** the prohibition proscribing **a brother's wife. As, what** can you say to **refute** this teaching? These two cases do not share any unique features that might be cause for stringency.

מַתְקִיף לַהּ רַב אַחָא בְּרֵיהּ דְּרַב אִיקָא: מַה לְּנִדָּה וְאֵשֶׁת אָח – שֶׁכֵּן אֵין לָהֶם הֶיתֵּר בְּחַיֵּי אוֹסְרָן, תֹּאמַר בְּאֵשֶׁת אִישׁ שֶׁכֵּן יֵשׁ לָהּ הֶיתֵּר בְּחַיֵּי אוֹסְרָהּ!

Rav Aḥa, son of Rav Ika, strongly objects to this: What comparison may be drawn based upon the precedent of **a menstruating woman and a brother's wife, which are** stringent in that **they cannot be permitted** to others for the duration of **the existence of the** factor **that renders them prohibited?** A menstruating woman is forbidden as long as she experiences a flow of menstrual blood, while a brother's wife is forbidden for the duration of the brother's lifetime. Can **you say** the same **with regard to a married woman, who can become permitted during the lifetime of the one who renders her prohibited,** i.e., if her husband divorces her?

אֲמַר לֵיהּ רַב אַחָא מִדִּפְתִּי לְרָבִינָא: אַטּוּ נִדָּה וְאֵשֶׁת אָח בְּחַיֵּי אוֹסְרָן הוּא דְּאֵין לָהֶם הֶיתֵּר, אֲבָל לְאַחַר מִכָּאן יֵשׁ לָהֶם הֶיתֵּר? נִדָּה

Rav Aḥa of Difti said to Ravina: Is that to say that **it is** only **during the existence of the** factor **that renders them prohibited that a menstruating woman and a brother's wife cannot be permitted** to others, **but afterward,** when the prohibiting factor has been resolved, **they can be permitted?** In the case of **a menstruating woman,**

Perek **VI**
Daf **54** Amud **b**

בְּיוֹמֵי תַּלְיָא מִילְּתָא. אֵשֶׁת אָח – בְּבָנִים תַּלְיָא רַחֲמָנָא.

the matter depends upon days, not blood. Although the flow of blood causes her to become impure, she remains impure for a full seven days regardless of whether she continues to experience menstrual bleeding for the duration of that time period. Similarly, in the case of **a brother's wife, the Merciful One makes** her forbidden status **dependent upon children,** as, if she has children she remains forbidden to her husband's brother even after her husband dies.

אֶלָּא פָּרֵיךְ הָכִי: מַה לְּנִדָּה וְאֵשֶׁת אָח – שֶׁכֵּן אֵין אוֹסְרָן מַתִּירָן, תֹּאמַר בְּאֵשֶׁת אִישׁ – שֶׁאוֹסְרָהּ מַתִּירָהּ!

Rather, the Gemara **refutes** the derivation in the following manner: **What** comparison can be drawn from **a menstruating woman and a brother's wife, which** are unique in **that** what **renders them prohibited does not render them permitted?** Each becomes permitted due to an external factor, i.e., the passing of seven days or the death of her childless husband. **Can you say** that the *halakhot* of these cases apply **to a married woman,** whose prohibited status is different **in that the one who renders her prohibited** to the rest of the world, i.e., her husband, has the capacity to **render her permitted** through divorce?

אֶלָּא אֲמַר רַבִּי יוֹנָה וְאִיתֵּימָא רַב הוּנָא בְּרֵיהּ דְּרַב יְהוֹשֻׁעַ: אָמַר קְרָא "כִּי כָּל אֲשֶׁר יַעֲשֶׂה מִכֹּל הַתּוֹעֵבֹת הָאֵלֶּה וְנִכְרְתוּ הַנְּפָשׁוֹת הָעֹשֹׂת" הוּקְּשׁוּ כָּל הָעֲרָיוֹת כּוּלָּן לְנִדָּה, מַה נִּדָּה בְּהַעֲרָאָה – אַף כָּל בְּהַעֲרָאָה.

Rather, the Gemara offers another source for the *halakha* that the initial stage of intercourse is considered sexual intercourse. **Rabbi Yona said, and some say** it was **Rav Huna, son of Rav Yehoshua: The verse states** at the end of the chapter on forbidden relations: **"For whoever shall do any of these abominations, the souls that do them shall be cut off"** (Leviticus 18:29). **All those with whom relations are forbidden are compared** to each other in this verse, and therefore also **to a menstruating woman,** who is mentioned in that chapter. Consequently, **just as** one is liable to receive punishment for having sexual intercourse with **a menstruating woman** from the time of **the initial stage of intercourse, so too,** one violates **all** prohibitions against engaging in forbidden relations from the time of **the initial stage of intercourse.**

וְאֶלָּא נִדָּה דִּכְתִיבָא גַּבֵּי אֵשֶׁת אָח לָמָּה לִי? לְכִדְרַב הוּנָא. דְּאָמַר רַב הוּנָא: רֶמֶז לִיבָמָה מִן הַתּוֹרָה מִנַּיִן? מִנַּיִן?! הָא כְּתִיב "יְבָמָהּ יָבֹא עָלֶיהָ"! אֶלָּא: רֶמֶז לִיבָמָה שֶׁאֲסוּרָה בְּחַיֵּי בַעְלָהּ מִנַּיִן?

The Gemara further asks: **But** if that is the source of this *halakha*, **why do I need** the term ***nidda*** **that is written with regard to a brother's wife?** The Gemara answers that it is needed **for that which Rav Huna** taught, **as Rav Huna said: From where in the Torah** is there **a hint to** the *halakha* of **a** ***yevama***? The Gemara expresses surprise: **From where? Isn't it written** explicitly in the verse **"Her brother-in-law will have intercourse with her"** (Deuteronomy 25:5)? **Rather,** Rav Huna meant to say: **From where** is there **a hint that a** ***yevama*** **is forbidden**[N] to her brother-in-law **in her husband's lifetime,** even after she is divorced from her husband?

הַאי – סְבָרָא הִיא, מִדְּאָמַר רַחֲמָנָא: לְאַחַר מִיתַת בַּעְלָהּ שַׁרְיָא – מִכְּלָל דִּבְחַיֵּי בַּעְלָהּ אֲסוּרָה!

The Gemara remains puzzled: No proof is needed for this *halakha* either, as **this is** based upon **logical reasoning:**[N] **From** the fact **that the Merciful One says** the woman **is permitted** to her brother-in-law **after her husband's death** it may be inferred **that in her husband's lifetime she is forbidden** to him.

NOTES

From where is there a hint that a *yevama* is forbidden – רֶמֶז לִיבָמָה שֶׁאֲסוּרָה: The Ramban poses a basic question: Since it is explicitly prohibited by the Torah for one to marry his brother's wife, and the Torah explicitly permits her to him in only one particular circumstance, i.e., levirate marriage, why would one think that the prohibition does not apply in any other case? He explains that one might have thought that it is permitted for one to marry her in a case of levirate marriage not because the mitzva overrides the general prohibition, but because the prohibition never applied at all as long as his brother did not have children. If so, the prohibition would not apply even while his brother was alive (see *Tosafot*).

This is based upon logical reasoning – הַאי סְבָרָא הִיא: This is not merely intuitive logic, as it cannot be determined that one is liable to receive capital punishment or *karet* on the basis of abstract logic alone. It refers to logical reasoning based upon a verse (Ritva).

וְדִלְמָא: לְאַחַר מִיתַת בַּעְלָהּ – מִצְוָה, בְּחַיֵּי בַּעְלָהּ – רְשׁוּת? אִי נַמִּי: לְאַחַר מִיתַת בַּעְלָהּ – אִין, בְּחַיֵּי בַּעְלָהּ – לָא, וְלָאו הַבָּא מִכְּלַל עֲשֵׂה – עֲשֵׂה!

The Gemara refutes this argument: **Perhaps after her husband's death** it is **a mitzva** for her brother-in-law to marry her, whereas **during her husband's lifetime** their marriage is **optional. Alternatively,** perhaps **after her husband's death, yes,** she is permitted to him, while **during her husband's lifetime, no,** they are not permitted to marry, but there is no punishment of *karet* if they do. This is because the source of the prohibition is the mitzva for them to marry after the husband's death, **and a prohibition that stems from a positive mitzva** has the status of **a positive mitzva,** but nothing more.

אָמַר קְרָא: "וְאִישׁ אֲשֶׁר יִקַּח אֶת אֵשֶׁת אָחִיו נִדָּה הִיא", וְכִי אֵשֶׁת אָחִיו נִדָּה הִיא? אֶלָּא כְּנִדָּה, מַה נִּדָּה, אַף עַל פִּי שֶׁיֵּשׁ לָהּ הֶיתֵּר לְאַחַר מִכָּאן – בִּשְׁעַת אִיסּוּרָא בְּכָרֵת, אַף אֵשֶׁת אָח [נַמִּי], אַף עַל פִּי שֶׁיֵּשׁ לָהּ הֶיתֵּר לְאַחַר מִכָּאן – בְּחַיֵּי בַּעְלָהּ בְּכָרֵת.

Therefore, **the verse states: "And if a man shall take his brother's wife, it is impurity [*nidda*]"** (Leviticus 20:21). **Is his brother's wife** necessarily **a menstruating woman [*nidda*]? Rather,** she is **like a menstruating woman** in the following manner: **Just as** with regard to **a menstruating woman, although she has a permitted** stage **afterward, at the time** that she is **forbidden,** one who has intercourse with her is liable **to** receive the punishment of ***karet***,[H] **so too,** with regard to **a brother's wife, although she has a permitted** stage **afterward, during her husband's lifetime**[H] marriage to her brother-in-law is punishable **by *karet*.**

אֶלָּא הַעֲרָאָה דִּכְתִיבָא גַּבֵּי אֲחוֹת אָב וַאֲחוֹת אֵם לָמָּה לִי?

The Gemara asks: **But** if the source of the *halakha* that the initial stage of intercourse is considered sexual intercourse is as stated above, **why do I need** this *halakha* to be indicated by the word *he'era* (Leviticus 20:19) in the case of **a father's sister and a mother's sister?**

לִכְדִבְעָא מִינֵּיהּ רָבִינָא מֵרָבָא: הַמְעָרֶה בְּזָכוּר, מַהוּ? בְּזָכוּר – "מִשְׁכְּבֵי אִשָּׁה" כְּתִיבָא!

The Gemara answers that it is needed **for the dilemma that Ravina raised before Rava:** With regard to **one who performs the initial stage of intercourse with** another **male,**[H] **what is** the *halakha*? Is it considered to be a forbidden act of homosexual intercourse? The Gemara is puzzled by this dilemma: **With regard to a male, it is written** explicitly: "You shall not lie with a man **as with a woman"** (Leviticus 18:22), which indicates that anything considered an act of sexual intercourse with a woman is also considered an act of sexual intercourse with a man.

אֶלָּא: הַמְעָרֶה בִּבְהֵמָה מַהוּ? אֲמַר לֵיהּ: אִם אֵינוֹ עִנְיָן לְהַעֲרָאָה, דִּכְתִיבָא גַּבֵּי אֲחוֹת אָב וַאֲחוֹת אֵם, דְּאָתְיָא בְּהֶקֵּישָׁא מִדְּרַבִּי יוֹנָה – תְּנֵהוּ עִנְיָן לְהַעֲרָאָה דִּבְהֵמָה.

Rather, the word *he'era* in the case of a father's sister and a mother's sister is needed to resolve the following dilemma: With regard to **one** who **performs the initial stage of intercourse with an animal,**[H] **what is** the *halakha*? Rava **said to** Ravina: **If** the word *he'era* **does not** refer **to the matter of the initial stage of intercourse** in the context **where it is written,** i.e., the prohibition with regard to a **father's sister and a mother's sister, as** this *halakha* **is derived from a comparison based upon** the statement of **Rabbi Yona, refer it to the matter of the initial stage of intercourse** with **an animal.** The superfluous expression written in the case of a father's sister and a mother's sister teaches that the initial stage of intercourse is considered sexual intercourse even with an animal.

מִכְּדִי בְּהֵמָה חַיָּיבֵי מִיתוֹת בֵּית דִּין הִיא, מַאי טַעֲמָא כְּתִיב לְהַעֲרָאָה דִּידָהּ גַּבֵּי חַיָּיבֵי כָּרֵיתוֹת? לִכְתּוֹב גַּבֵּי מִיתַת בֵּית דִּין, וְנֵילַף מִיתַת בֵּית דִּין מִמִּיתַת בֵּית דִּין!

The Gemara asks: **Since** intercourse with **an animal is** a prohibition for which one is **liable to** receive **capital punishment from the court, what is the reason** that the *halakha* of **the initial stage of intercourse** that applies to **it is written with regard to** the prohibitions proscribing a father's sister and a mother's sister, for which one is **liable to** receive ***karet***? **Let** the word *he'era* **be written with regard to** prohibitions for which one is liable to receive **capital punishment from the court, and let us derive** the *halakha* with regard to a prohibition punishable by **capital punishment from the court,** i.e., the case of bestiality, **from** another prohibition punishable by **capital punishment from the court.**

אַיְּידֵי דְּכוּלֵּיהּ קְרָא לִדְרָשָׁא אָתֵי – כְּתִיב בֵּיהּ נַמִּי הָא מִילְּתָא לִדְרָשָׁא.

The Gemara answers: **Since the entire verse** of a father's sister and a mother's sister **comes for** the purpose of **an exposition,** as the Gemara is about to explain, **this matter,** i.e., that the initial stage of intercourse is considered intercourse, **is also written for** the purpose of **an exposition,** i.e., to indicate that this principle holds true in a different context, i.e., that of bestiality.

HALAKHA

One who has intercourse with a menstruating woman is liable to *karet* – נִדָּה בְּכָרֵת: One who intentionally had intercourse with a menstruating woman is liable to receive *karet*, as is similarly the case with any other forbidden relation, even if they merely perform the initial stage of intercourse (Rambam *Sefer Kedusha, Hilkhot Issurei Bia* 4:1).

A brother's wife…during her husband's lifetime – אֵשֶׁת אָח...בְּחַיֵּי בַּעְלָהּ: One who has intercourse with his brother's wife while his brother is alive is liable to receive *karet*, even if his brother has already divorced her (Rambam *Sefer Kedusha, Hilkhot Issurei Bia* 1:1, 2:1).

One who performs the initial stage of intercourse with another male – הַמְעָרֶה בְּזָכוּר: One who performs the initial stage of intercourse with another male is liable to receive the punishment of stoning (Rambam *Sefer Kedusha, Hilkhot Issurei Bia* 1:14).

One who performs the initial stage of intercourse with an animal – הַמְעָרֶה בִּבְהֵמָה: A man or woman who performs the initial stage of intercourse with an animal is liable to receive the punishment of stoning. The animal is likewise stoned (Rambam *Sefer Kedusha, Hilkhot Issurei Bia* 1:16).

מַאי דְּרָשָׁא – דְּתַנְיָא: ״עֶרְוַת אֲחוֹת אָבִיךָ לֹא תְגַלֵּה״ בֵּין מִן הָאָב בֵּין מִן הָאֵם. אַתָּה אוֹמֵר בֵּין מִן הָאָב בֵּין מִן הָאֵם, אוֹ אֵינוֹ אֶלָּא מִן הָאָב וְלֹא מִן הָאֵם?

The Gemara asks: **What is the exposition** that the rest of the verse introduces? **As it is taught in a** *baraita*, the verse **"You shall not uncover the nakedness of your father's sister"** (Leviticus 18:12) indicates that the prohibition applies **whether** she is your father's sister **from** his **father, or from** his **mother.**[H] **Do you say** that she is forbidden **whether** she is your father's sister **from** his **father or from** his **mother, or** perhaps **it is only** a sister **from** his **father** who is forbidden, **but not from** his **mother?**

וְדִין הוּא: חַיֵּיב כָּאן – וְחַיֵּיב בַּאֲחוֹתוֹ. מָה אֲחוֹתוֹ – בֵּין מִן הָאָב בֵּין מִן הָאֵם, אַף כָּאן – בֵּין מִן הָאָב בֵּין מִן הָאֵם.

It may be inferred **logically** from the fact that the Torah **rendered him liable here and rendered him liable with his sister: Just as** with regard to **his sister**[H] he is liable to receive punishment **whether** she is his sister **from** his **father or from** his **mother, so too here,** he is liable **whether** she is his father's sister **from** his **father or from** his **mother.**

אוֹ כְּלָךְ לְדֶרֶךְ זוֹ: חַיֵּיב כָּאן וְחַיֵּיב בְּדוֹדָתוֹ, מָה דּוֹדָתוֹ – מִן הָאָב וְלֹא מִן הָאֵם, אַף כָּאן – מִן הָאָב וְלֹא מִן הָאֵם.

Or perhaps **go this way** and compare a father's sister and a mother's sister to a different *halakha*: The Torah **rendered him liable here and rendered him liable with his aunt,**[H] i.e., the wife of his father's brother: **Just as** concerning **his aunt,** he is liable to receive punishment only with regard to the wife of his father's brother **from** his **father,** i.e., the wife of his father's paternal brother, **and not** for the wife of his father's brother **from** his **mother,** i.e., the wife of his father's maternal brother, **so too here,** he is liable only with regard to a father's sister or a mother's sister **from** their **father,** i.e., a paternal sister, **and not from** their **mother,** a maternal sister.

נִרְאֶה לְמִי דּוֹמֶה: דָּנִין אִיסּוּר הַבָּא מֵאֵלָיו מֵאִיסּוּר הַבָּא מֵאֵלָיו, וְאַל תּוֹכִיחַ דּוֹדָתוֹ – שֶׁאֵין אִיסּוּר הַבָּא מֵאֵלָיו.

The Gemara analyzes these two possibilities: **Let us see to which** case **it is** more **similar,** i.e., which is a better comparison. **We should derive** the *halakha* with regard to **a prohibition that comes on its own,** i.e., a father's sister and a mother's sister, **from a prohibition that** also **comes on its own,** i.e., a sister, **and** the *halakha* with regard to **his aunt cannot** be used to **prove** otherwise, **as** it is **not a prohibition that comes on its own,** but through marriage.

אוֹ כְּלָךְ לְדֶרֶךְ זֶה: דָּנִין קְרוֹבֵי הָאָב מִקְּרוֹבֵי הָאָב, וְאַל תּוֹכִיחַ אֲחוֹתוֹ שֶׁקְּרוֹבֵי עַצְמוֹ?

The Gemara counters this argument: **Or** perhaps **go this way** and claim that **we** should **derive the** *halakha* with regard to **the relatives of** his **father,** i.e., his father's sister, **from the** *halakha* with regard to **the relatives of** his **father,** i.e., his father's brother's wife, **and** the case of **his sister cannot** be used to **prove** otherwise, **as** she is **his own relative.** Consequently, there is no conclusive proof based on reasoning alone.

תַּלְמוּד לוֹמַר ״עֶרְוַת אֲחוֹת אָבִיךָ לֹא תְגַלֵּה״ בֵּין מִן הָאָב בֵּין מִן הָאֵם. ״עֶרְוַת אֲחוֹת אִמְּךָ לֹא תְגַלֵּה״ בֵּין מִן הָאָב בֵּין מִן הָאֵם.

Therefore **the verse states: "You shall not uncover the nakedness of your father's sister,"** which teaches that this prohibition applies **whether** she is your father's sister **from** his **father or from** his **mother.** Similarly, the verse **"You shall not uncover the nakedness of your mother's sister"** indicates that the prohibition applies **whether** she is your mother's sister **from** her **father or from** her **mother.** These prohibitions are stated twice (Leviticus 18:12–13 and 20:19), and the superfluous verse indicates that the prohibition applies even to the maternal sister of one's father or mother.

לָמָּה לִי לְמִכְתְּבָא בַּאֲחוֹת אָב, לָמָּה לִי לְמִכְתְּבָא בַּאֲחוֹת אֵם? אָמַר רַבִּי אַבָּהוּ: צְרִיכִי, דְּאִי כְּתַב רַחֲמָנָא בַּאֲחוֹת אָב – שֶׁכֵּן יֵשׁ לָהּ חַיִיס, אֲבָל אֲחוֹת אֵם – אֵימָא לָא.

The Gemara asks: **Why do I** need the Torah **to write** this *halakha* **with regard to a father's sister,** and **why do I** need the Torah **to write** it again **with regard to a mother's sister? Rabbi Abbahu said:** Both verses **are necessary. If the Merciful One had written** this *halakha* only **with regard to** one's **father's sister,** one might say that it is limited to that case, **as she has** common **lineage** with her nephew, since lineage goes through one's father. **However,** with regard to one's **mother's sister** you might **say** that she is **not** prohibited, as she is not considered to share common lineage with him.

וְאִי כְּתַב רַחֲמָנָא בַּאֲחוֹת אֵם – שֶׁכֵּן וַדָּאִית, אֲבָל אֲחוֹת אָב – אֵימָא לָא, צְרִיכָא.

And conversely, **if the Merciful One had written** this *halakha* only **with regard to** one's **mother's sister,** one might say that it is limited to that case, **as she is certainly** his relative, since one's biological relationship with his mother is absolutely certain. **However,** with regard to one's **father's sister,** one might **say no,** that she is not forbidden, as paternity can never be established beyond doubt. It is therefore **necessary** for this *halakha* to be stated in both cases.

HALAKHA

A father's sister – אֲחוֹת הָאָב: One's father's sister is a forbidden relative and he is liable to receive *karet* for having intercourse with her, regardless of whether she is his father's paternal sister or maternal sister (Rambam *Sefer Kedusha, Hilkhot Issurei Bia* 2:5; *Shulḥan Arukh, Even HaEzer* 15:16).

His sister – אֲחוֹתוֹ: One's sister is forbidden to him by Torah law, regardless of whether she is his paternal sister or maternal sister, or whether she was born in or out of wedlock. He is liable to receive punishment for engaging in intercourse with her even if she is a *mamzeret* (Rambam *Sefer Kedusha, Hilkhot Issurei Bia* 2:2; *Shulḥan Arukh, Even HaEzer* 15:10).

His aunt – דּוֹדָתוֹ: The wife of one's father's paternal brother is forbidden by Torah law. However, the wife of one's father's maternal brother is forbidden only by rabbinic law (Rambam *Sefer Kedusha, Hilkhot Issurei Bia* 2:2; *Shulḥan Arukh, Even HaEzer* 15:8).

וְדוֹדָתוֹ, דִּפְשִׁיטָא לֵיהּ לְתַנָּא דְּמִן הָאָב וְלֹא מִן הָאֵם, מְנָא לֵיהּ?

The Gemara asks: **And** with regard to **his aunt, where it is obvious to the *tanna*** that the prohibition includes only the wife of his father's brother **from** his **father and not from** his **mother, from where does he** derive this *halakha*?

אֲמַר רָבָא: אָתְיָא ״דּוֹדוֹ״ ״דּוֹדוֹ״, כְּתִיב הָכָא ״עֶרְוַת דֹּדוֹ גִּלָּה״ וּכְתִיב הָתָם ״אוֹ דֹדוֹ אוֹ בֶן דֹּדוֹ יִגְאָלֶנּוּ״ מַה לְהַלָּן מִן הָאָב וְלֹא מִן הָאֵם – אַף כָּאן מִן הָאָב וְלֹא מִן הָאֵם.

Rava said: It is **derived** through a verbal analogy between the terms **"his uncle"** and **"his uncle." It is written here: "He has uncovered his uncle's nakedness"** (Leviticus 20:20), **and it is written there,** with regard to the redemption of a Jew who has been sold to a gentile: **"Either his uncle or his uncle's son shall redeem him"** (Leviticus 25:49). **Just as there,** in the case of redemption, it must be a relative **from the** side of his **father and not from the** side of his **mother, so too here,** with regard to forbidden relations, the prohibition applies to the wife of his father's brother **from** his **father,** i.e., the wife of his father's paternal brother, **and not from** his **mother.**

וְהָתָם מְנָלַן? אָמַר קְרָא ״מִמִּשְׁפַּחְתּוֹ יִגְאָלֶנּוּ״, מִשְׁפַּחַת אָב – קְרוּיָה מִשְׁפָּחָה, מִשְׁפַּחַת אֵם – אֵינָהּ קְרוּיָה מִשְׁפָּחָה.

The Gemara asks: **And there,** with regard to the *halakhot* of redemption, **from where do we** derive that a maternal relative is not included? **The verse states:** "Or any that is near of kin to him **of his family shall redeem him"** (Leviticus 25:49), and it is an established principle that only **the family of** one's **father is called family,** while **the family of** one's **mother is not called family,**[H] as lineage is determined based upon one's father.

וְהִדְתְנַן: אָמְרוּ לוֹ: מֵתָה אִשְׁתְּךָ, וְנָשָׂא אֲחוֹתָהּ מֵאָבִיהָ. מֵתָה, וְנָשָׂא אֲחוֹתָהּ מֵאִמָּהּ. מֵתָה, וְנָשָׂא אֲחוֹתָהּ מֵאָבִיהָ. מֵתָה, וְנָשָׂא אֲחוֹתָהּ מֵאִמָּהּ –

And with regard to **that which we learned** in a mishna: If **they said to him: Your wife is dead, and he** then **married her sister from her father.** He was subsequently informed that his second wife **died, and he married her sister from her mother,** i.e., his second wife's maternal sister. He was then informed that his third wife **died, and he married her sister from her father,** i.e., his third wife's paternal sister. He was then informed that his fourth wife **died, and he married her sister from her mother,** i.e., his fourth wife's maternal sister. It later became apparent that all these rumors were unfounded and all the women were still alive. Consequently, since one cannot marry his wife's sister during his wife's lifetime, some of the marriages are void.

מוּתָּר בָּרִאשׁוֹנָה וּבַשְּׁלִישִׁית וּבַחֲמִישִׁית, וּפוֹטְרוֹת צָרוֹתֵיהֶן. וְאָסוּר בַּשְּׁנִיָּה וּבָרְבִיעִית, וְאֵין בִּיאַת אַחַת מֵהֶן פּוֹטֶרֶת צָרָתָהּ.

The *halakha* in this case is that it is **permitted** for him to marry his **first, third, and fifth** wives, as they are not related to each other. Consequently, these marriages are valid, **and** these women **exempt their rival wives** from levirate marriage if they all became subject to levirate marriage and one of them performed levirate marriage or *ḥalitza*. However, it is **prohibited** for him to marry his **second and fourth** wives, as they are both sisters of one of his previous wives, and their marriages are therefore void. Consequently, **sexual intercourse** between **one of them** and his brother, if he has died childless, **does not exempt her rival wife,** i.e., the real wives of the deceased, from levirate marriage.

וְאִם בָּא עַל הַשְּׁנִיָּה לְאַחַר מִיתַת הָרִאשׁוֹנָה – מוּתָּר בַּשְּׁנִיָּה וּבָרְבִיעִית, וּפוֹטְרוֹת צָרוֹתֵיהֶן, וְאָסוּר בַּשְּׁלִישִׁית וּבַחֲמִישִׁית.

And if the first wife indeed died, **and he had intercourse with the second** woman **after the death of the first** one, it is **permitted** for him to marry **the second and fourth** women, who are not related to each other, **and they exempt their rival wives** from levirate marriage if they perform levirate marriage or *ḥalitza*, **and** it is **prohibited** for him to marry **the third and fifth** women, as they are sisters of his previous wives, who are still alive, and consequently these marriages are void.

HALAKHA

The family of one's mother is not called family – מִשְׁפַּחַת אֵם אֵינָהּ קְרוּיָה מִשְׁפָּחָה: The family of one's mother is not considered family with regard to inheritance. Therefore, maternal brothers are not considered heirs; each one is an heir of his paternal relatives only. Even if the identity of one's father is unknown, his maternal relatives are still not considered his heirs (*Terumat HaDeshen*; Rambam *Sefer Mishpatim*, *Hilkhot Naḥalot* 1:6; *Shulḥan Arukh*, *Ḥoshen Mishpat* 276:4).

אַלְמָא אֲחוֹת אִשְׁתּוֹ בֵּין מִן הָאָב בֵּין מִן הָאֵם אֲסוּרוֹת. מְנָלַן? יָלֵיף מֵאֲחוֹתוֹ, מָה אֲחוֹתוֹ – בֵּין מִן הָאָב בֵּין מִן הָאֵם, אַף כָּאן בֵּין מִן הָאָב בֵּין מִן הָאֵם.

Apparently, this mishna indicates that **his wife's sister,**[NH] **whether from the father,** i.e., a paternal sister, **or from the mother,** i.e., a maternal sister, **is forbidden. From where do we** derive this *halakha* that the prohibition applies even to his wife's maternal sister? The Gemara responds: **It is derived from** the prohibition proscribing **his sister. Just as his sister** is forbidden **whether** she is his sister **from his father or from his mother, so too here, a wife's sister is forbidden whether from the father or from the mother.**

וְלֵילַף מִדּוֹדָתוֹ, מַה דּוֹדָתוֹ – מִן הָאָב וְלֹא מִן הָאֵם, אַף כָּאן – מִן הָאָב וְלֹא מִן הָאֵם! מִסְתַּבְּרָא, מֵאֲחוֹתוֹ הֲוָה לֵיהּ לְמֵילַף, שֶׁכֵּן קְרוֹבֵי עַצְמוֹ מִקְּרוֹבֵי עַצְמוֹ.

The Gemara challenges the validity of this source: **And let it be derived from** the *halakha* with regard to **his aunt: Just as** the prohibition with regard to **his aunt** applies only to the wife of his father's brother **from his father but not from his mother,** i.e., the wife of his father's paternal brother but not the wife of his father's maternal brother, **so too here,** the prohibition with regard to his wife's sister should apply only to her sister **from** her **father but not** to her sister **from** her **mother.** The Gemara answers: **It is reasonable** that **he should derive** the *halakha* in this case **from** the case of **his sister, as** the *tanna* thereby derives the *halakha* of **one's own relatives from** another case of **his own relatives,** whereas his aunt is forbidden as his father's relative.

אַדְּרַבָּה, מִדּוֹדָתוֹ הֲוָה לֵיהּ לְמֵילַף שֶׁכֵּן דָּבָר עַל יְדֵי קִדּוּשִׁין מִדָּבָר שֶׁעַל יְדֵי קִדּוּשִׁין! אֶלָּא: מֵאֵשֶׁת אָח יָלְפִינַן, דְּשֶׁכֵּן דָּבָר עַל יְדֵי קִדּוּשִׁין, וּקְרוֹבֵי עַצְמוֹ.

The Gemara counters: **On the contrary, he should derive** the *halakha* in this instance **from** the case of **his aunt, as** he thereby derives the *halakha* in **a matter** prohibited **through betrothal from** another **matter** prohibited **through betrothal.** The Gemara concludes: **Rather,** the *halakha* of a wife's sister **is derived from** that of **a brother's wife,**[NH] **as** they are both **something** forbidden **by means of betrothal and** they are **his own relatives.**

וְאֵשֶׁת אָח גּוּפָהּ מְנָא לָן? דְּתַנְיָא: "עֶרְוַת אֵשֶׁת אָחִיךָ לֹא תְגַלֵּה" בֵּין מִן הָאָב בֵּין מִן הָאֵם.

The Gemara asks: **And** in the case of **a brother's wife itself, from where do we** derive that the prohibition applies to the wife of both a paternal and a maternal brother? **As it is taught in a** *baraita*: **"You shall not uncover the nakedness of your brother's wife"** (Leviticus 18:16), which indicates: **Whether from the father or from the mother.**

אַתָּה אוֹמֵר בֵּין מִן הָאָב בֵּין מִן הָאֵם, אוֹ אֵינוֹ אֶלָּא מִן הָאָב וְלֹא מִן הָאֵם? וְדִין הוּא: חִיֵּיב כָּאן, וְחִיֵּיב בַּאֲחוֹתוֹ. מָה אֲחוֹתוֹ – בֵּין מִן הָאָב בֵּין מִן הָאֵם, אַף כָּאן – בֵּין מִן הָאָב בֵּין מִן הָאֵם.

The *baraita* elaborates: **Do you say** the prohibition applies **whether** she is the wife of one's brother **from** his **father or from** his **mother,** i.e., whether she is the wife of one's paternal brother or maternal brother? **Or** perhaps **it is only** the wife of one's brother **from** his **father and not from** his **mother? It** may be inferred **logically** from the fact that the Torah **rendered him liable here and rendered him liable with** regard to **his sister: Just as** with regard to **his sister** he is liable to receive punishment **whether** she is his sister **from** his **father or from** his **mother, so too here,** he is liable to receive punishment **whether** she is the wife of his brother **from** his **father or from** his **mother.**

אוֹ כְּלָךְ לְדֶרֶךְ זוֹ: חִיֵּיב כָּאן וְחִיֵּיב בְּדוֹדָתוֹ. מַה דּוֹדָתוֹ – מִן הָאָב וְלֹא מִן הָאֵם, אַף כָּאן – מִן הָאָב וְלֹא מִן הָאֵם?

Or perhaps **go this way** and compare this case to the case of an aunt. The Torah **rendered him liable here and rendered him liable with** regard to **his aunt,** i.e., the wife of his father's brother: **Just as** with regard to **his aunt,** he is liable to receive punishment only for the wife of his father's brother **from** his **father and not** for the wife of his father's brother **from** his **mother, so too here,** he is liable to receive punishment only for the wife of his brother **from** his **father and not from** his **mother.**

נִרְאֶה לְמִי דּוֹמֶה; דָּנִין קְרוֹבֵי עַצְמוֹ מִקְּרוֹבֵי עַצְמוֹ, וְאַל תּוֹכִיחַ דּוֹדָתוֹ שֶׁקְּרוֹבֵי הָאָב. אוֹ כְּלָךְ לְדֶרֶךְ זוֹ: דָּנִין דָּבָר שֶׁעַל יְדֵי קִדּוּשִׁין מִדָּבָר שֶׁעַל יְדֵי קִדּוּשִׁין, וְאַל תּוֹכִיחַ אֲחוֹתוֹ שֶׁאִיסּוּר הַבָּא מֵאֵלָיו?

The Gemara analyzes these two possibilities: **Let us see to which** case **it is** more **similar. We** should **derive** the *halakha* with regard to **his own relatives,** i.e., his brother's wife, **from** another case of **his own relatives,** i.e., his sister, **and** the *halakha* with regard to **his aunt cannot** be used to **prove** otherwise, **as** she is his **father's relative. Or** perhaps **go this way: We** should **derive** the *halakha* of **a matter** prohibited **through betrothal,** i.e., a brother's wife, **from** another **matter** prohibited **through betrothal,** i.e., his father's brother's wife, **and** the *halakha* with regard to **his sister cannot** be used to **prove** otherwise, **as** it is **a prohibition that comes on its own.**

NOTES

Apparently, his wife's sister, etc. – אַלְמָא אֲחוֹת אִשְׁתּוֹ וכו׳: The proof that his wife's maternal sister is forbidden is from the ruling that the third woman is permitted to him. The implication is that she is permitted only because the marriage of the second woman was void. However, if that marriage had been valid, the woman would be forbidden because she is the maternal sister of the second woman (Rashi; see *Tosefot HaRosh*).

The *halakha* of a wife's sister is derived from that of a brother's wife – מֵאֵשֶׁת אָח יָלְפִינַן: The Ramban, who perhaps had a slightly different version of the text, explains as follows: The definition of brotherhood can be derived from the case of a brother's wife, as it is clear from the verses that the relationship is the same whether they are paternal or maternal brothers (see *Tosafot*). By extension, a maternal sister is also considered a sister. Furthermore, although one cannot administer corporal punishment for prohibitions derived from logical analysis, in this case the prohibition itself is written explicitly in the Torah, and it is the definition of the term sister that is derived on the basis of the comparison to a brother's wife.

HALAKHA

The prohibition proscribing a wife's sister – אִיסּוּר אֲחוֹת אִשְׁתּוֹ: The sister of one's wife is forbidden to him as long as his wife is alive. This applies both to paternal and maternal sisters, including those born out of wedlock (Rambam *Sefer Kedusha, Hilkhot Issurei Bia* 2:9; *Shulḥan Arukh, Even HaEzer* 15:26).

A brother's wife – אֵשֶׁת אָח: The wife of one's brother is forbidden to him. This applies to both paternal and maternal brothers, including brothers born out of wedlock (Rambam *Sefer Kedusha, Hilkhot Issurei Bia* 2:2; *Shulḥan Arukh, Even HaEzer* 15:22).

תַּלְמוּד לוֹמַר ״עֶרְוַת אָחִיךָ הִיא״ בֵּין מִן הָאָב בֵּין מִן הָאֵם.

Since it is impossible to prove which *halakha* should serve as the model for the case of a brother's wife, **the verse states** a second time in the same verse: **"It is your brother's nakedness"** (Leviticus 18:16), in order to emphasize that she is forbidden **whether** she is the wife of his brother **from** his **father or from** his **mother.**

וְאֵימָא: אִידִי וְאִידִי בְּאֵשֶׁת אָח מִן הָאָב, חֲדָא – דְּיֵשׁ לָהּ בָּנִים בְּחַיֵּי בַּעֲלָהּ, וַחֲדָא – דְּאֵין לָהּ בָּנִים בְּחַיֵּי בַּעֲלָהּ. אֵין לָהּ בָּנִים בְּחַיֵּי בַּעֲלָהּ – מִדְּרַב הוּנָא נָפְקָא!

The Gemara challenges this interpretation of the extra phrase in the verse: **Say** that both **this** first part of the verse **and that** latter part refer **to the wife of a brother from the father,** i.e., the wife of one's paternal brother. As for the repetition, **one** part of the verse renders prohibited a woman **who has children,** who is prohibited from marrying her husband's brother **during her husband's lifetime** even after they are divorced, **and** the other **one** renders prohibited a woman **who does not have children,** who is also prohibited from marrying her husband's brother **during her husband's lifetime,** even after she is divorced. The Gemara responds: The prohibition proscribing a woman who **does not have children** for the duration of **her husband's lifetime is derived from** the statement of **Rav Huna** (54b), and it requires no further source.

וְאֵימָא: אִידִי וְאִידִי בְּאֵשֶׁת אָח מִן הָאָב, חֲדָא – דְּיֵשׁ לָהּ בָּנִים בְּחַיֵּי בַּעֲלָהּ, וַחֲדָא – דְּיֵשׁ לָהּ בָּנִים לְאַחַר מִיתַת בַּעֲלָהּ!

The Gemara presents another challenge: **Say** that both **this** first part of the verse **and that** latter part refer **to the wife of a brother from the father,** i.e., the wife of one's paternal brother. As for the repetition, **one** part of the verse renders a woman **who has children** prohibited from marrying her husband's brother for the duration of **her husband's lifetime,** even after she is divorced, **and** the other **one** renders prohibited a woman **who has children** and indicates that it is prohibited for her to marry her husband's brother even **after her husband's death.**

יֵשׁ לָהּ בָּנִים לְאַחַר מִיתַת בַּעֲלָהּ לָא צְרִיכָא קְרָא, מִדְּאָמַר רַחֲמָנָא שֶׁאֵין לָהּ בָּנִים מוּתֶּרֶת – הָא יֵשׁ לָהּ בָּנִים אֲסוּרָה.

The Gemara responds: The *halakha* that it is prohibited for a woman **who has children** to marry her husband's brother even **after her husband's death does not require a verse. From** the fact **that the Merciful One says that** one **who has no children is permitted** to marry the brother after her husband's death, it can be inferred **that** if **she has children,** it is **prohibited** for her to marry her husband's brother.

וְדִלְמָא: אֵין לָהּ בָּנִים – אֲסוּרָה לְעָלְמָא וְשַׁרְיָא לְיָבָם. יֵשׁ לָהּ בָּנִים – שַׁרְיָא לְעָלְמָא וְשַׁרְיָא לְיָבָם! אִי נַמִי: אֵין לָהּ בָּנִים – מִצְוָה, יֵשׁ לָהּ בָּנִים – רְשׁוּת,

The Gemara raises another challenge: **But perhaps** if **she does not have children** it is **prohibited** for her to marry **everyone** else **and permitted** for her to marry her *yavam*, as specified by the Torah. However, if **she does have children** it **is permitted** for her to marry **everyone and** it **is permitted** for her to marry her *yavam* as well. **Alternatively,** perhaps **if she does not have children** it is **a mitzva** for her husband's brother to marry her, and if **she does have children** it is **optional.** Consequently, the extra phrase in the verse should be necessary in order to indicate that the prohibition against marriage applies in all of these cases.

אִי נַמִי: אֵין לָהּ בָּנִים – אִין, יֵשׁ לָהּ בָּנִים – לָא, וְלָאו הַבָּא מִכְּלַל עֲשֵׂה – עֲשֵׂה!

Alternatively, if **she does not have children, yes,** she is permitted to her husband's brother, and if **she does have children, no,** she is not permitted to him, but the punishment of *karet* does not apply to this prohibition. This is because the source of the prohibition is the mitzva for them to marry after the husband's death, **and a prohibition that stems from a positive mitzva** has the status of **a positive mitzva,** but nothing more. Consequently, the extra phrase in the verse should be necessary in order to indicate that the punishment of *karet* is still applicable.

כְּתַב קְרָא אַחֲרִינָא: ״עֶרְוַת אָחִיו גִּלָּה״.

The Gemara responds: The Torah **wrote a different verse** to teach that the prohibition against marrying one's brother's wife is in full force, including the punishment of *karet*, in these cases: **"He has uncovered his brother's nakedness;** they shall be childless" (Leviticus 20:21). Therefore, the extra phrase mentioned in the *baraita* can indicate that the prohibition against marrying one's brother's wife applies both to the wife of a paternal brother and to the wife of a maternal brother.

וְאֵימָא אֵשֶׁת אָח מִן הָאֵם כְּאֵשֶׁת אָח מִן הָאָב: מָה אֵשֶׁת אָח מִן הָאָב – לְאַחַר מִיתַת בַּעְלָהּ שַׁרְיָא, אַף אֵשֶׁת אָח מִן הָאֵם – לְאַחַר מִיתַת בַּעְלָהּ שַׁרְיָא! אָמַר קְרָא "הִיא" בַּהֲוָיָיתָהּ תְּהֵא.

The Gemara suggests: **Say** that the *halakha* of **the wife of a brother from** one's **mother** should be just **like** that of **the wife of a brother from** his **father: Just as the wife of a brother from** one's **father is permitted,** i.e., one can marry her, **after her husband's death, so too, the wife of a brother from** his **mother should be permitted after her husband's death.** The Gemara responds: **The verse states: "She** is your brother's nakedness," thereby emphasizing that **she shall** remain after her husband's death **as she is** during his life.[H]

אֲחוֹתוֹ דִּכְתַב בָּהּ כָּרֵת לָמָּה לִי?

§ The Gemara above stated that all of the instances of forbidden intercourse are compared to one another. Therefore, since there is already a verse that states: "For whoever shall do any of these abominations, the souls that do them shall be cut off from among their people" (Leviticus 18:29), the Gemara asks: **Why do I need** the phrase **written with regard to one's sister** that states that intercourse is punishable by ***karet*?**

לְכִדְרַבִּי יוֹחָנָן. דְּאָמַר רַבִּי יוֹחָנָן: שֶׁאִם עֲשָׂאָן כּוּלָּם בְּהֶעְלֵם אַחַת – חַיָּיב עַל כָּל אַחַת וְאַחַת.

The Gemara answers that it is necessary **for that** which **Rabbi Yoḥanan** said, as **Rabbi Yoḥanan said that if he performed all of them,** i.e., he violated every prohibition against engaging in forbidden intercourse **in a single lapse of awareness, he is liable** to receive punishment **for each and every one.** One might have thought that there is one prohibition against engaging in forbidden intercourse, and many different ways to violate the prohibition. Therefore, if one violated the prohibition in different ways during one lapse of awareness, one is liable to bring only one sin-offering. This verse therefore indicates that each act of intercourse with a relative with whom intercourse is forbidden is a violation of an independent prohibition.

וּלְרַבִּי יִצְחָק, דְּאָמַר: כָּל חַיָּיבֵי כָּרֵיתוֹת בִּכְלָל הָיוּ, וְלָמָּה יָצְתָה כָּרֵת בַּאֲחוֹתוֹ – לְדוּנוֹ בְּכָרֵת וְלֹא בְּמַלְקוֹת, לְחַלֵּק מְנָלַן?

The Gemara asks: **And according to Rabbi Yitzḥak, who said** that **all** forbidden relations for which one is **liable to** receive ***karet* were included** in the verse: "The souls that do them shall be cut off from among their people," **why was** the punishment of ***karet* with regard to one's sister singled out?** In order **to sentence him to *karet* and not to flogging.** Although he has violated a prohibition, which generally carries a punishment of flogging, he is not flogged due to the fact that he is liable to receive the more severe punishment of *karet*. Since he has used the verse to teach this *halakha*, **from where do we** know **to divide** the prohibitions against engaging in forbidden intercourse and consider each an independent prohibition?

נָפְקָא לֵיהּ: מִ"וְאֶל אִשָּׁה בְּנִדַּת טוּמְאָתָהּ" לְחַיֵּיב עַל כָּל אִשָּׁה וְאִשָּׁה.

The Gemara answers: **He derives it from** the verse **"And** you shall not approach **a woman** to uncover her nakedness **as long as she is impure by her uncleanness"** (Leviticus 18:19), which serves **to render** him **liable** to receive punishment **for each and every woman.**

דּוֹדָתוֹ דִּכְתַב בָּהּ רַחֲמָנָא "עֲרִירִים יִהְיוּ" לָמָּה לִי? לְכִדְרַבָּה. דְּרַבָּה רָמֵי: כְּתִיב "עֲרִירִים יִהְיוּ" וּכְתִיב "עֲרִירִים יָמֻתוּ"! הָא כֵּיצַד? יֵשׁ לוֹ בָּנִים – קוֹבְרָן, אֵין לוֹ בָּנִים – הוֹלֵךְ עֲרִירִי.

The Gemara poses another question: **Why do I need** the phrase that **the Merciful One writes with regard to one's aunt,**[N] which states: **They shall be childless?**[N] The death of one's children is included in the punishment of *karet*, and it has already been established that all of the forbidden intercourse is punishable by *karet*. The Gemara answers that it is necessary **for that** which **Rabba** said, as **Rabba raised a contradiction: It is written** with regard to one who had intercourse with his brother's wife: **"They shall be childless"** (Leviticus 20:22), **and it** also **states** with regard to one who had intercourse with his aunt: **"They shall die childless"** (Leviticus 20:21). **How so? If he** already **has children, he will** eventually **bury them;** if **he does not have children, he will go childless.**

HALAKHA

She shall remain after her husband's death as she is during his life – **הִיא בַּהֲוָיָיתָהּ תְּהֵא**: The mitzva of levirate marriage applies only to the wife of one's paternal brother. The wife of a maternal brother remains forbidden forever (Rambam *Sefer Kedusha, Hilkhot Yibbum* 2:2; *Shulḥan Arukh, Even HaEzer* 157:1).

NOTES

The phrase the Merciful One writes with regard to one's aunt, etc. – **דּוֹדָתוֹ דִּכְתַב בָּהּ רַחֲמָנָא וכו׳**: Many commentaries have noted that the phrase "They shall be childless" (Leviticus 20:21) does not appear in the context of an aunt, but rather in the context of a brother's wife. In the context of an aunt, the Torah states: "They shall die childless" (Leviticus 20:20). In fact, there were medieval commentaries whose texts of the Gemara stated: Why do I need the phrase the Merciful One writes with regard to one's aunt that states: "They shall die childless."

Why do I need the phrase…They shall be childless – **עֲרִירִים יִהְיוּ לָמָּה לִי**: The commentaries note that this supports Rashi's opinion that being childless is included in the punishment of *karet*, whereas it is difficult to explain this according to the opinion of the Riva, who maintains that being childless is a special punishment in addition to *karet*, which simply consists of the offender's life being cut short (see *Tosafot* on 2a and *Yam shel Shlomo*).

וְאִיצְטְרִיךְ לְמִכְתַּב ״עֲרִירִים יִהְיוּ״ וְאִיצְטְרִיךְ לְמִכְתַּב ״עֲרִירִים יָמֻתוּ״. דְּאִי כָּתַב רַחֲמָנָא ״עֲרִירִים יִהְיוּ״ הֲוָה אָמִינָא: עַד חֶטְאֵיהּ, אֲבָל מֵחֶטְאֵיהּ וְאֵילָךְ – לָא, כָּתַב רַחֲמָנָא ״עֲרִירִים יָמֻתוּ״. וְאִי כָּתַב רַחֲמָנָא ״עֲרִירִים יָמֻתוּ״ הֲוָה אָמִינָא: מֵחֶטְאֵיהּ וְאֵילָךְ, אֲבָל מֵעִיקָּרָא – לָא, צְרִיכָא.

The Gemara comments: **And it is necessary to state: They shall be childless, and it is** also **necessary to state: They shall die childless. As, if the Merciful One had written** only: **They shall be childless, I would have said** that only those children he had **before his sin** will die, **but** those born to him **from** the time of **his sin and on, no,** they will not die. **The Torah** therefore **states: They shall die childless,** indicating that even if he has children afterward they will die and he will remain childless. **And** similarly, **if the Merciful One had written** only: **They shall die childless, I would have said** that this is referring to children born **from** the time of **his sin and on, but** those born **from the beginning,** before he sinned, **no,** they will not die. It is therefore **necessary** to mention both expressions.

הַעֲרָאָה דְּחַיָּיבֵי לָאוִין מְנָלַן?

§ The Gemara above (54a–54b) derived that the initial stage of intercourse is considered an act of sexual intercourse with regard to prohibitions that are punishable by capital punishment or *karet*. The Gemara asks: **From where do we** derive that **the initial stage of intercourse** is considered an act of sexual intercourse **with regard to those liable** to receive punishment **for** violating ordinary Torah **prohibitions?**

מִדְּגַלֵּי רַחֲמָנָא ״שִׁכְבַת זֶרַע״ גַּבֵּי שִׁפְחָה חֲרוּפָה – מִכְּלָל דְּחַיָּיבֵי לָאוִין בְּהַעֲרָאָה.

The Gemara answers: **From** the fact that **the Merciful One reveals with regard to a designated maidservant**[N] that the prohibition has been violated only through an act of **cohabitation with seed,** i.e., a complete act of sexual intercourse, in the verse "And whoever lies with a woman in cohabitation with seed, and she is a bondmaid designated to a man" (Leviticus 19:20), **by inference, those liable** to receive punishment **for** violating ordinary **prohibitions** are liable even **through the initial stage of intercourse.**

אַדְּרַבָּה, מִדְּגַלֵּי רַחֲמָנָא הַעֲרָאָה בְּחַיָּיבֵי כָּרֵיתוֹת – מִכְּלָל דְּחַיָּיבֵי לָאוִין בִּגְמַר בִּיאָה! אֲמַר רַב אַשִׁי: אִם כֵּן לִשְׁתּוֹק קְרָא מִשִּׁפְחָה חֲרוּפָה.

The Gemara responds: **On the contrary, from** the fact **that the Merciful One reveals** that **the initial stage of intercourse** is considered sexual intercourse **with regard to** forbidden relationships for which one is **liable to** receive *karet*, then, **by inference, those liable for** violating ordinary **prohibitions** are liable only **through the completion of** the act of **sexual intercourse** and not merely for the initial stage of intercourse. **Rav Ashi said: If so, let the verse remain silent** in the case of a **designated maidservant,** and it would be assumed that one is liable to receive punishment only for completing the act of sexual intercourse. The fact that the Torah specified that in this case one is liable to receive punishment only for completing the act of sexual intercourse indicates that with regard to other ordinary prohibitions one is liable even for the initial stage of intercourse.

הַעֲרָאָה דְּחַיָּיבֵי לָאוִין דִּכְהוּנָּה מְנָלַן? אָתְיָא ״קִיחָה״ ״קִיחָה״.

The Gemara asks: **From where do we** derive that **the initial stage of intercourse** is considered an act of sexual intercourse **with regard to those liable** to receive punishment **for** violating **prohibitions** specific to **the priesthood?** Since these prohibitions are unique in that they apply only to priests, their parameters cannot be derived from prohibitions that apply to the entire population. The Gemara answers: It **is derived** from a verbal analogy between the words **taking** and **taking.** This verb appears in prohibitions punishable by *karet*, e.g., "And if a man shall take his sister" (Leviticus 20:17), and in prohibitions of the priesthood, where it states: "They shall not take a woman that is a harlot" (Leviticus 21:7).

דְּחַיָּיבֵי עֲשֵׂה מְנָלַן?

The Gemara asks further: **From where do we** derive that the initial stage of intercourse is considered an act of sexual intercourse with regard to **those liable** to receive punishment for violating **a positive mitzva,**[H] e.g., one who has intercourse with an Egyptian or Edomite convert? The verse states: "The children that are born to them of the third generation may enter into the assembly of the Lord" (Deuteronomy 23:9). It is therefore a positive mitzva that only the grandchildren of these converts may have intercourse with a Jew.

NOTES

A designated maidservant – שִׁפְחָה חֲרוּפָה: Rashi explains that a designated maidservant is a Canaanite maidservant betrothed to a Hebrew servant. A Hebrew servant is permitted to marry such a woman, but she is forbidden to all other Jews.

HALAKHA

The initial stage of intercourse with regard to those liable for violating prohibitions and positive mitzvot – הַעֲרָאָה בְּחַיָּיבֵי לָאוִין וַעֲשִׂין: The initial stage of intercourse is considered sexual intercourse with regard to all forbidden relations, including those prohibited due to both negative and positive mitzvot. The one exception is the case of a designated maidservant (Rambam *Sefer Kedusha, Hilkhot Issurei Bia* 1:10).

אָתְיָא ״בִּיאָה״ ״בִּיאָה״.

It is derived from a verbal analogy between the terms **entering** and **entering.** The verse states in the context of a prohibition: "A *mamzer* shall not enter into the assembly of the Lord" (Deuteronomy 23:3), and in the context of a prohibition derived from a positive mitzva: "The children that are born to them of the third generation may enter into the assembly of the Lord" (Deuteronomy 23:9). Consequently, these types of prohibitions are equated.

יְבָמָה לַשּׁוּק מְנָלַן? אִי לְמַאן דְּאָמַר לָאו – לָאו, אִי לְמַאן דְּאָמַר עֲשֵׂה – עֲשֵׂה.

The Gemara poses another question: **From where do we** derive that the initial stage of intercourse is considered sexual intercourse with regard to the prohibition against a *yevama* having intercourse with a man from **the general public?** The Gemara answers that there is no need for an independent source in this case: **If** you are asking **according to the one who said** that this is an ordinary **prohibition,** it is **a prohibition** like any other. **If** you are asking **according to the one who said** that this is **a positive mitzva,**[N] it is **a positive mitzva** like any other.

אֶלָּא יְבָמָה לִיבָם מְנָלַן? אָתְיָא ״בִּיאָה״ ״בִּיאָה״.

Rather, the question is as follows: **From where do we** derive that a *yevama* is acquired by her *yavam* via the initial stage of intercourse? The Gemara answers: **It is derived** from a verbal analogy between the **words entering** and **entering.** This verb is used with regard to ordinary Torah prohibitions, as mentioned above, and also with regard to levirate marriage, in the verse "Her brother-in-law will have intercourse with her" (Deuteronomy 25:5).

אִשָּׁה לְבַעְלָהּ מְנָלַן? אָתְיָא ״קִיחָה״ ״קִיחָה״.

The Gemara asks further: **From where do we** derive that a **woman** is betrothed **to her husband** through the initial stage of intercourse?[N] The Gemara answers: **It is derived** from a verbal analogy between the words **taking** and **taking.** With regard to betrothal, the verse states: "When a man takes a wife and marries her" (Deuteronomy 24:1). This verb is also used with regard to forbidden intercourse, as in the verse: "And if a man shall take his sister" (Leviticus 20:17).

אָמַר רָבָא: לָמָּה לִי דִּכְתַב רַחֲמָנָא ״שִׁכְבַת זֶרַע״ בְּשִׁפְחָה חֲרוּפָה, ״שִׁכְבַת זֶרַע״ בְּאֵשֶׁת אִישׁ, ״שִׁכְבַת זֶרַע״ בְּסוֹטָה.

§ **Rava said:** Now that it has been established that the initial stage of intercourse is considered an act of sexual intercourse, **why do I** need the expression **"cohabitation with seed"** (Leviticus 19:20) **that the Merciful One writes with regard to a designated maidservant;** the expression **"cohabitation with seed"** (Leviticus 18:20) written **with regard to a married woman;** and the expression **"cohabitation with seed"** (Numbers 5:13) written with regard to **a** ***sota*****?**[B]

דְּשִׁפְחָה חֲרוּפָה – כְּדַאֲמָרַן. דְּאֵשֶׁת אִישׁ – פְּרָט לִמְשַׁמֵּשׁ מֵת.

The Gemara explains that the expression is necessary with regard to **a designated maidservant as we said** above (55a), because it indicates that one is liable to receive punishment only for a complete act of intercourse with a designated maidservant[H] but not for the initial stage of intercourse. With regard to **a married woman,** the word seed **excludes one who has intercourse** with a **dead** organ,[H] i.e., one that is not erect, as this cannot lead to childbirth.

הָנִיחָא לְמַאן דְּאָמַר מְשַׁמֵּשׁ מֵת בַּעֲרָיוֹת פָּטוּר, אֶלָּא לְמַאן דְּאָמַר חַיָּיב – מַאי אִיכָּא לְמֵימַר? אֶלָּא פְּרָט לִמְשַׁמֵּשׁ מֵתָה. דְּסָלְקָא דַּעְתָּךְ אָמֵינָא: [הוֹאִיל] לְאַחַר מִיתָה נַמִּי אִיקְּרִי שְׁאֵרוֹ, אֵימָא לִיחַיֵּיב עֲלַהּ בְּאֵשֶׁת אִישׁ – קָא מַשְׁמַע לַן.

The Gemara questions this resolution: **This works out well according to the one who said** that one who **has intercourse** while his organ is **dead** with **those with whom relations are forbidden, is exempt,** as this is not considered an act of intercourse. **However, according to the one who said** that **he is liable, what is there to say? Rather,** according to this opinion, the verse **excludes one who has intercourse with a dead** woman.[H] As it might **enter your mind to say: Since after death** she **is also called** her husband's **kin, say that** one who had intercourse with her **should be liable** to receive punishment for committing adultery **with a married woman.** It therefore **teaches us** that intercourse with a dead woman is not considered intercourse at all.

NOTES

If you are asking according to the one who said that this is a positive mitzva, etc. – אִי לְמַאן דְּאָמַר עֲשֵׂה וכו׳: *Tosafot* omit this sentence, as they maintain that everyone agrees that a *yevama* who has intercourse with another man has transgressed a prohibition. Rabbeinu Ḥananel and most medieval commentaries concur. See the Ramban for an attempt to explain Rashi's opinion, which maintains this sentence.

From where do we derive that a woman is betrothed to her husband through the initial stage of intercourse – אִשָּׁה לְבַעְלָהּ מְנָלַן: The commentaries point out an apparent contradiction between this passage and the Gemara in tractate *Kiddushin* (10a), which states that in the case of betrothal via intercourse, since the man is focused on the completion of the act, betrothal takes effect only at completion and not after the initial stage of intercourse (see Rif and *Tosafot*).

BACKGROUND

Sota – סוֹטָה: The Torah describes the procedure governing such a woman (Numbers 5:11–31). First, her husband warns her in the presence of witnesses against being alone together with a specific man about whom he is suspicious. If she disobeys this warning and is observed alone with that man, even though there is no concrete evidence that she actually committed adultery, she and her husband may no longer live together as man and wife until she has undergone the following ordeal to determine whether she has committed adultery. The woman, accompanied by her husband and two Torah scholars, is taken to the Temple in Jerusalem and forced by the priests to stand in a public place while holding the special meal-offering that she is required to bring. There she is again questioned about her behavior. If she continues to protest her fidelity and takes an oath to that effect, a scroll is brought and the curses of the *sota* mentioned in the Torah passage cited above are written on it. The scroll is submerged in a clay vessel filled with water taken from the Temple basin and some earth from the Temple floor, and the scroll's writing is dissolved in the water. She is then forced to drink that water. If she has committed adultery, in the words of the Torah, "her belly shall swell and her thigh shall fall away" (Numbers 5:27), until ultimately she dies from the water's curse. If she is innocent, the water will bring her blessing and she is permitted to resume normal marital relations with her husband.

HALAKHA

Intercourse with a designated maidservant – בִּיאָה בְּשִׁפְחָה חֲרוּפָה: The unique *halakha* of a designated maidservant is that one is liable to receive punishment only for a complete act of intercourse and only if it is performed in a typical manner (Rambam *Sefer Kedusha, Hilkhot Issurei Bia* 3:15; *Tur, Even HaEzer* 20).

One who has intercourse with a dead organ – מְשַׁמֵּשׁ מֵת: If one engages in a prohibited act of intercourse without an erection, but rather with a completely limp organ that he inserts manually, he is not liable to receive *karet* or lashes and he is certainly exempt from capital punishment. However, in accordance with the opinion of Rava in tractate *Shevuot* (18a), he is flogged by rabbinic decree (Rambam *Sefer Kedusha, Hilkhot Issurei Bia* 1:11; *Tur, Even HaEzer* 20).

One who has intercourse with a dead woman – מְשַׁמֵּשׁ מֵתָה: One who has intercourse with the corpse of a woman with whom relations are forbidden is exempt (Rambam *Sefer Kedusha, Hilkhot Issurei Bia* 1:12; *Tur, Even HaEzer* 20).

BACKGROUND

The initial stage of intercourse – הַעֲרָאָה: The definition of the term intercourse is problematic in virtually all legal systems. One of the missing features in this discussion with regard to the initial stage of intercourse, discussed by later halakhic commentaries, is the exact definition of the female sexual organ. Regardless, it seems that the halakhic conclusion concerning the first stage of sexual contact is, to a great extent, a minimal degree of penetration of the penis into the vagina.

NOTES

A kiss, i.e., external contact of the sexual organs – נְשִׁיקָה: It is noted in the Jerusalem Talmud that even according to Shmuel the contact must include a slight insertion of the organ.

דְּסוֹטָה לָמָּה לִי? לְכִדְתַנְיָא: ״שִׁכְבַת זֶרַע״ פְּרָט לְדָבָר אַחֵר. מַאי דָּבָר אַחֵר? אֲמַר רַב שֵׁשֶׁת: פְּרָט לְשֶׁקִּינֵּא לָהּ שֶׁלֹּא כְּדַרְכָּהּ. אֲמַר לֵיהּ רָבָא: ״מִשְׁכְּבֵי אִשָּׁה״ כְּתִיב!

The Gemara addresses the third case: **Why do I need** the expression cohabitation with seed in the context of **a *sota*?** It is needed **for that which is taught** in a *baraita*, that the expression **a cohabitation with seed excludes something else.** The Gemara asks: **What is this something else? Rav Sheshet said: It excludes** a case **where** the husband **was jealous with regard to her** and warned her not to seclude herself and have **atypical,** i.e., anal, sexual intercourse with another man. **Rava** objected to this explanation and **said to him: It is written: "The cohabitations of a woman"** (Leviticus 18:22), indicating that there are two types of intercourse with a woman, and the same *halakha* applies to both.

אֶלָּא אֲמַר רָבָא: פְּרָט לְשֶׁקִּינֵּא לָהּ דֶּרֶךְ אֵבָרִים. אֲמַר לֵיהּ אַבַּיֵי: פְּרִיצוּתָא אֲסַר רַחֲמָנָא?

Rather, Rava said: It **excludes** a situation **where** the husband **was jealous with regard to her** and warned her not to seclude herself with another man and engage in intimate contact **by way of** other **limbs.** The verse indicates that the wife does not become prohibited to her husband if she secludes herself with the man after this warning. **Abaye said to him:** Does **the Merciful One prohibit** a woman to her husband due merely to **licentious** behavior without sexual intercourse? Since this behavior would not render a woman prohibited to her husband, it is obvious that a warning that explicitly mentions this behavior is insufficient to cause the woman to become a *sota* if she then secludes herself with the man.

אֶלָּא אֲמַר אַבַּיֵי: פְּרָט לְשֶׁקִּינֵּא לָהּ בִּנְשִׁיקָה. הָנִיחָא לְמַאן דַּאֲמַר הַעֲרָאָה זוֹ הַכְנָסַת עֲטָרָה, אֶלָּא לְמַאן דַּאֲמַר זוֹ נְשִׁיקָה – מַאי אִיכָּא לְמֵימַר?

Rather, Abaye said: It excludes a case **where** he **was jealous with regard to her** and warned her not to seclude herself with another man and **kiss,** i.e., have external contact of the sexual organs. The Gemara asks: **This works out well according to the one who said** that the definition of **the initial stage of intercourse is the insertion of the corona;** therefore, mere external contact is not considered sexual intercourse. **However, according to the one who said** that the definition of the initial stage of intercourse is a **kiss, what is there to say?**

אֶלָּא, לְעוֹלָם לְשֶׁקִּינֵּא לָהּ דֶּרֶךְ אֵבָרִים, וְאִיצְטְרִיךְ: סָלְקָא דַּעְתָּךְ אָמִינָא: בִּקְפֵידָא דְּבַעַל תָּלָה רַחֲמָנָא, וְהָא קָא קָפֵיד, קָא מַשְׁמַע לַן.

Rather, the expression: Something else, in the *baraita*, is **actually** referring to a case **where** the husband **was jealous with regard to her** and warned her not to seclude herself with another man and engage in intimate contact **by way of** other **limbs. And it is necessary** to state that the woman does not become prohibited to her husband as a *sota* in this case, as **it might enter your mind to say that the Merciful One made** this *halakha* **dependent on the husband's objection,** as it is his decision to warn his wife, **and** since **he objects** to contact of this nature, she becomes a *sota* if she secludes herself after this warning. The Torah therefore **teaches us** that this is not considered a warning.

אֲמַר שְׁמוּאֵל: הַעֲרָאָה זוֹ נְשִׁיקָה, מָשָׁל לְאָדָם שֶׁמַּנִּיחַ אֶצְבָּעוֹ עַל פִּיו – אִי אֶפְשָׁר שֶׁלֹּא יִדְחוֹק הַבָּשָׂר.

§ The Gemara returns to the precise definition of the initial stage of intercourse. **Shmuel said:** The definition of **the initial stage of intercourse**[B] **is a kiss,** i.e., external contact of the sexual organs.[N] Shmuel explains: This is **comparable to a person who places his finger on his mouth;** it is **impossible that he not press the flesh** of his lips. Similarly, when there is contact of the sexual organs, there will certainly be at least a small amount of penetration, and this is considered an act of sexual intercourse.

כִּי אֲתָא רַבָּה בַּר בַּר חָנָה אֲמַר רַבִּי יוֹחָנָן: גְּמַר בִּיאָה בְּשִׁפְחָה חֲרוּפָה – זוֹ הַכְנָסַת עֲטָרָה. מְתִיב רַב שֵׁשֶׁת: ״שִׁכְבַת זֶרַע״ אֵינוֹ חַיָּיב אֶלָּא עַל בִּיאַת הַמֵּירוּק. מַאי לָאו – מֵירוּק גִּיד? לָא, מֵירוּק עֲטָרָה.

When Rabba bar bar Ḥana came from Eretz Yisrael, **he said** that **Rabbi Yoḥanan said: The completion of intercourse** stated **with regard to a designated maidservant is the insertion of the corona,** and no more. **Rav Sheshet raised an objection** based upon the following *baraita*: The phrase **cohabitation with seed** indicates that **one is liable** to receive punishment **only for a complete** act of **sexual intercourse. What, does** this **not** refer to the **complete** insertion of the **member?** The Gemara responds: **No,** it is possible that it is referring to the **complete** insertion of the **corona.**

כִּי אֲתָא רַב דִּימִי אָמַר רַבִּי יוֹחָנָן: הַעֲרָאָה – זוֹ הַכְנָסַת עֲטָרָה. אָמְרוּ לֵיהּ: וְהָא רַבָּה בַּר בַּר חָנָה לָא אָמַר הָכִי? אָמַר לְהוּ: אוֹ אִיהוּ שַׁקְרַאי אוֹ אֲנָא שָׁקְרִי.

When Rav Dimi came[B] from Eretz Yisrael **he said** that **Rabbi Yoḥanan** said: The definition of **the initial stage of intercourse is the insertion of the corona. They said to him: But Rabba bar bar Ḥana did not say so,** as he taught that Rabbi Yoḥanan said that the insertion of the corona constitutes a complete act of sexual intercourse and is not considered merely the initial stage of intercourse. **He said to them: Either he lied or I am lying.** There is clearly a contradiction, and one of us cited Rabbi Yoḥanan's opinion incorrectly.

כִּי אֲתָא רָבִין אָמַר רַבִּי יוֹחָנָן: הַעֲרָאָה זוֹ הַכְנָסַת עֲטָרָה. אַדְּרַבָּה בַּר בַּר חָנָה – וַדַּאי פָּלֵיג, אַדִּשְׁמוּאֵל מִי לֵימָא פָּלֵיג?!

When Ravin came from Eretz Yisrael **he said** that **Rabbi Yoḥanan** said: The definition of **the initial stage of intercourse is the insertion of the corona.** The Gemara comments: He **certainly disagrees with Rabba bar bar Ḥana,** who cited Rabbi Yoḥanan as stating that insertion of the corona constitutes a complete act of sexual intercourse. **Shall we say that he** also **disagrees with Shmuel,** who defined the initial stage of intercourse as external contact of the sexual organs?

לָא, מִנְּשִׁיקָה וְעַד הַכְנָסַת עֲטָרָה – הַעֲרָאָה קָרֵי לַהּ.

The Gemara responds: **No;** it is possible that there is no dispute between them, and Ravin said that Rabbi Yoḥanan **calls** the entire process **from a kiss until the insertion of the corona the initial stage of intercourse,** while anything beyond that point is a complete act of sexual intercourse.

כִּי אֲתָא רַב שְׁמוּאֵל בַּר יְהוּדָה אָמַר רַבִּי יוֹחָנָן הַעֲרָאָה – זוֹ הַכְנָסַת עֲטָרָה, גְּמַר בִּיאָה – גְּמַר בִּיאָה מַמָּשׁ.

When Rav Shmuel bar Yehuda came from Eretz Yisrael he reported that **Rabbi Yoḥanan said:** The definition of **the initial stage of intercourse is the insertion of the corona,**[H] whereas a **complete** act of **sexual intercourse is literally a complete** act of **sexual intercourse,** i.e., insertion of the male organ beyond the corona.

BACKGROUND

When Rav Dimi came – כִּי אֲתָא רַב דִּימִי: Rav Dimi was one of the Sages who would often travel from Eretz Yisrael to Babylonia, primarily to transmit the Torah of Eretz Yisrael to the Torah centers of the Diaspora, although occasionally he traveled on business as well. Consequently, many questions, particularly those concerning the Torah of Eretz Yisrael, remained unresolved until the messenger from Zion, Rav Dimi, would arrive and elucidate the *halakha*, the novel expression, or the unique circumstances pertaining to a particular statement that required clarification.

HALAKHA

What is the initial stage of intercourse – מַה הִיא הַעֲרָאָה: The initial stage of intercourse is the insertion of the corona. Anything less than this is called mere external contact, for which one is exempt. The *halakha* is in accordance with the opinion of Ravin and Rav Shmuel bar Yehuda in the name of Rabbi Yoḥanan (Rambam *Sefer Kedusha*, *Hilkhot Issurei Bia* 1:10; *Shulḥan Arukh*, *Even HaEzer* 20:1, and in the comment of Rema; see *Beit Shmuel*).

Perek **VI**
Daf **56** Amud **a**

מִכָּאן וְאֵילָךְ אֵינוֹ אֶלָּא נְשִׁיקָה, וּפָטוּר עָלֶיהָ. וּפָלֵיג אַדִּשְׁמוּאֵל.

From this point **forward,** insertion of anything less than the corona **is only** considered **a kiss, for which he is exempt. And** this statement **disagrees with** that of **Shmuel,** who maintains that one is liable to receive punishment for external contact of the sexual organs.

"אֶחָד הַמְעָרֶה וְאֶחָד הַגּוֹמֵר קָנָה". מַאי קָנָה? רַב אָמַר: קָנָה לַכֹּל. וּשְׁמוּאֵל אָמַר: לֹא קָנָה אֶלָּא לִדְבָרִים הָאֲמוּרִים בַּפָּרָשָׁה: לִירַשׁ בְּנִכְסֵי אָחִיו, וּלְפוֹטְרָהּ מִן הַיִּיבּוּם.

§ It was taught in the mishna that **both one who** merely **engages in the initial stage of intercourse and one who completes** the act of intercourse **have** thereby **acquired** the *yevama*. The Gemara asks: **What** does it mean that he has **acquired** his *yevama*?[NH] **Rav said:** He has **acquired** her **for everything.** In other words, she is considered his wife in all regards. Therefore, if he is a priest, she may partake of *teruma*. **And Shmuel said he has only acquired her with regard to the matters stated in the chapter** of levirate marriage, i.e., **to inherit his brother's property and to exempt her from levirate marriage** if he then dies and leaves behind children from another wife.

HALAKHA

What does it mean that he has acquired his *yevama* – מַאי קָנָה: If a priest performed a deficient act of intercourse with his *yevama*, meaning that he did not intend to thereby perform levirate marriage, and she had merely been betrothed to the deceased brother, she may not partake of *teruma* and they are not considered fully married. Some say that the same applies if he intended to perform levirate marriage, but performed only the initial stage of intercourse. However, if she had been not only betrothed but also married to the deceased brother, even a deficient act of intercourse effects levirate marriage, and she may partake of *teruma*, as she had in the past. The *halakha* is in accordance with the opinion of Rav as presented in the second interpretation of the dispute between Rav and Shmuel (Rambam *Sefer Zera'im*, *Hilkhot Terumot* 8:6; *Shulḥan Arukh*, *Even HaEzer* 166:9).

NOTES

What does it mean that he has acquired his *yevama* – מַאי קָנָה: The commentaries disagree over the meaning of this passage. According to *Tosafot*, the Ramban, and the Rashba, the discussion concerns a case in which his intercourse was deficient because he did not intend thereby to perform levirate marriage. However, if he intended to perform levirate marriage and engaged only in the initial stage of intercourse, all agree that they are fully married, as this is considered a complete act of intercourse.

Conversely, the Rif apparently understood that the discussion also applies to anyone who performs only the initial stage of intercourse. The Rambam explicitly endorses this opinion as well. According to this opinion, when the Gemara mentions unwitting and intentional intercourse, it is merely citing examples, but does not mean to exclude the case of one who performs only the initial stage of intercourse (Rabbi Avraham min HaHar). The *Arukh LaNer* claims that the Rif is consistent with his opinion above (see NOTES to 55b) that the initial stage of intercourse consummates a marriage only if the woman had previously been betrothed to the man. Consequently, the *amora'im* here dispute whether the levirate bond is sufficiently strong to allow the levirate marriage to be consummated via the initial stage of intercourse.

NOTES

Say as follows: If he did not have a chance, etc. – **אֵימָא הָכִי: וְלֹא הִסְפִּיק וכו׳:** Shmuel does not mean to say that the *baraita* is incomplete. Rather, he understands that when the *baraita* states that the woman may partake of *teruma* if her first husband died and the woman happens before her *yavam* for levirate marriage, it means that if she had already been married to her first husband before he died, she may partake of *teruma* after performing levirate marriage with her deaf-mute *yavam*. The case is not comparable to one where she had merely been betrothed to her first husband (Ritva).

מִן הַנְּשׂוּאִין לְדִבְרֵי הַכֹּל אָכְלָה, דְּהָא הֲוַת קָאָכְלָה מֵעִיקָּרָא. כִּי פְּלִיגִי – מִן הָאֵירוּסִין. רַב אָמַר: אוֹכֶלֶת, דְּהָא רַבֵּי רַחֲמָנָא בִּיאַת שׁוֹגֵג כְּמֵזִיד.

The Gemara adds: If she was a *yevama* **from marriage, everyone agrees** that she may **partake** of *teruma* after the initial stage of intercourse, **as she was** already **partaking at the outset,** when she was married to the deceased brother. Therefore, even a minimal act of intercourse is enough to allow her to continue to partake of *teruma*. **When they disagree** it is with regard to a *yevama* **from betrothal. Rav said:** She **may partake, as the Merciful One includes unwitting intercourse** and the other forms of intercourse listed in the mishna, and considers them **like intentional** intercourse.

וּשְׁמוּאֵל אָמַר: כִּי רַבֵּי רַחֲמָנָא – לְאוֹקְמֵיהּ בִּמְקוֹם בַּעַל, לְאַלּוֹמֵי מִבַּעַל – לָא.

And Shmuel said: When the Merciful One includes these forms of intercourse, He does so only **to establish** the *yavam* **in place of** the **husband,** but **to strengthen** him more **than the husband, no.** Since she was merely betrothed to the deceased brother, she was not permitted to partake of *teruma*, and therefore she may not partake of *teruma* at this point either.

וְאָזְדָא שְׁמוּאֵל לְטַעְמֵיהּ, דְּאָמַר רַב נַחְמָן אָמַר שְׁמוּאֵל: כׇּל שֶׁהַבַּעַל מַאֲכִיל – יָבָם מַאֲכִיל, וְכׇל שֶׁאֵין הַבַּעַל מַאֲכִיל – יָבָם אֵינוֹ מַאֲכִיל.

The Gemara comments: **And Shmuel follows his** regular line of **reasoning, as Rav Naḥman said** that **Shmuel said:** In **any** case **where the** woman's marriage to her original **husband entitles** her **to partake** of *teruma*, intercourse with the ***yavam*** in any of the manners described in the mishna also **entitles** her **to partake** of *teruma*, **and any** case **where** her relationship with her original **husband does not entitle** her **to partake** of *teruma*, i.e., if she had been betrothed but not married, intercourse with the ***yavam*** in the manners described in the mishna also **does not entitle** her **to partake** of *teruma*.

מֵיתִיבִי: בַּת יִשְׂרָאֵל פִּקַּחַת שֶׁנִּתְאָרְסָה לְכֹהֵן פִּקֵּחַ, וְלֹא הִסְפִּיק לְכוֹנְסָהּ עַד שֶׁנִּתְחָרֵשׁ – אֵינָהּ אוֹכֶלֶת. מֵת, וְנָפְלָה לִפְנֵי יָבָם חֵרֵשׁ – אוֹכֶלֶת. וּבְזוֹ יָפֶה כֹּחַ הַיָּבָם מִכֹּחַ הַבַּעַל.

The Gemara **raises an objection** from the following *baraita*: In the case of a mentally **competent daughter of an Israelite who was betrothed to a competent priest, and he did not have a chance to marry her before he became a deaf-mute** and was no longer mentally competent, **she may not partake** of *teruma*, as marriage to a deaf-mute does not enable a woman to partake of *teruma*. If the deaf-mute husband subsequently **died and** the *yevama* **happened before a deaf-mute** ***yavam*** for levirate marriage, **she** may **partake** of *teruma*. **And in this** regard **the strength of the** ***yavam*** **is greater than the strength of the husband.**

בִּשְׁלָמָא לְרַב – נִיחָא, אֶלָּא לִשְׁמוּאֵל – קַשְׁיָא!

Granted, according Rav, this **works out well,** as intercourse with the deaf-mute *yavam*, which is comparable to the unwitting intercourse mentioned in the mishna because the deaf-mute is not mentally competent, effects the levirate marriage and allows her to partake of *teruma* despite the fact that she could not do so during the lifetime of her first husband. **However, according to Shmuel,** this is **difficult,** as he maintains that a *yavam* cannot have more rights than the deceased husband due to intercourse undertaken without intent to perform levirate marriage.

אָמַר לָךְ שְׁמוּאֵל: אֵימָא הָכִי: וְלֹא הִסְפִּיק לְכוֹנְסָהּ עַד שֶׁנִּתְחָרֵשׁ – אֵינָהּ אוֹכֶלֶת בִּתְרוּמָה. כְּנָסָהּ וְאַחַר כָּךְ נִתְחָרֵשׁ – אוֹכֶלֶת, מֵת וְנָפְלָה לִפְנֵי יָבָם חֵרֵשׁ – אוֹכֶלֶת.

The Gemara answers: **Shmuel** could have **said to you:** Amend the *baraita* and **say as follows:** If **he did not have a chance**[N] **to marry her before he became a deaf-mute, she may not partake of** ***teruma***. If **he married her and afterward became a deaf-mute, she** may **partake** of *teruma*. If he then **died, and** she **happened before a deaf-mute** ***yavam*** for levirate marriage, **she** may **partake** of *teruma*.

וּמַאי "בְּזוֹ" דְּאִילּוּ בַּעַל חֵרֵשׁ מֵעִיקָּרָא – לֹא אוֹכֶלֶת, וְאִילּוּ יָבָם חֵרֵשׁ מֵעִיקָּרָא – אָכְלָה.

And what is the meaning of the phrase: **In this** regard the strength of the *yavam* is greater than the strength of the husband? It means to say **that if** the original **husband** was a **deaf-mute from the outset,** i.e., before consummating the marriage, **she would not** have been allowed to **partake** of *teruma*, **whereas if the** ***yavam*** was a **deaf-mute from the outset** she may **partake** of *teruma* once they perform levirate marriage, because she had been fully married to the deceased brother.

וְאִיכָּא דְּאָמְרִי: מִן הָאֵירוּסִין – דִּבְרֵי הַכֹּל לֹא אָכְלָה, דְּהָא לֹא אָכְלָה בְּחַיֵּי בַעַל.

And some say a different version of the dispute between Rav and Shmuel: If she was a *yevama* **from betrothal,** i.e., her marriage with the deceased brother had never been completed, and she and the brother-in-law engaged in an inferior form of intercourse as described in the mishna, **everyone agrees** that she may **not partake** of *teruma*, **as she did not partake** of *teruma* **in her husband's lifetime.**

כי פליגי – מן הנשואין. רב אמר: אוכלת, דהא הות אכלה מעיקרא. ושמואל אמר: אינה אוכלת, כי רבי רחמנא ביאת שוגג כמזיד – לדברים האמורים בפרשה, אבל לכל מילי – לא.

When they disagree, it is with regard to a *yevama* **from marriage. Rav says: She** may **partake** of *teruma* **as she was** permitted to partake of *teruma* **initially,** while married to the deceased brother. **And Shmuel says** she **may not partake** of *teruma,* because **when the Merciful One includes unwitting intercourse** and considers it **like intentional** intercourse, it was only with regard to **the matters stated in the chapter** of levirate marriage, **but for every** other **issue, no.**

והאמר רב נחמן אמר שמואל: כל שהבעל מאכיל – יבם מאכיל! אימא: כל ביאה שהבעל מאכיל בה – יבם מאכיל בה – וכל ביאה שאין הבעל מאכיל בה – אין היבם מאכיל בה.

The Gemara raises a difficulty: **Didn't Rav Naḥman say that Shmuel** himself **said:** In **any** case **where the** woman's marriage to her original **husband entitles** her to **partake** of *teruma,* intercourse with the *yavam* in one of the manners listed in the mishna also **entitles** her to **partake** of *teruma*? The Gemara answers: Emend the wording and **say** as follows: With regard to **any** act of **intercourse through which the husband entitles** her to **partake** of *teruma,* **a** *yavam* also **entitles** her to **partake** of *teruma;* **and** with regard to **any** act of **intercourse through which the husband does not entitle** her to **partake** of *teruma,* **a** *yavam* also **does not entitle** her to **partake** of *teruma.* Just as betrothal cannot be performed via an unwitting act of intercourse, this act does not entitle a *yevama* to partake of *teruma.*

מיתיבי בת ישראל פקחת שנתארסה לכהן פקח, ולא הספיק לכונסה עד שנתחרש – אינה אוכלת. מת ונפלה לפני יבם חרש – אוכלת, ובזו יפה כח יבם מכח בעל. בשלמא לרב מתרץ כדתריץ מעיקרא. אלא לשמואל קשיא! קשיא.

The Gemara **raises an objection** from the following *baraita*: In the case of a mentally **competent daughter of an Israelite who was betrothed to a competent priest, and he did not have a chance to marry her before he became a deaf-mute** and was no longer mentally competent, **she may not partake** of *teruma.* If the deaf-mute husband subsequently **died, and the** *yevama* **happened before a deaf-mute** *yavam* for levirate marriage, **she may partake** of *teruma.*[H] **And in this** regard **the strength of the** *yavam* **is greater than the strength of the husband. Granted, according to Rav,** he can **answer as** Shmuel **answered initially,** i.e., according to the first version of the dispute between Rav and Shmuel. **However, according to Shmuel,** it is **difficult.**[N] The Gemara concludes: Indeed, it is **difficult.**

תנו רבנן: בת ישראל פקחת שנתארסה לכהן פקח, ולא הספיק לכונסה עד שנתחרש – אינה אוכלת, נולד לה בן – אוכלת. מת הבן, רבי נתן אומר: אוכלת, וחכמים אומרים: אינה אוכלת.

§ **The Sages taught:** In the case of a mentally **competent daughter of an Israelite who was betrothed to** a mentally **competent priest, and he did not have a chance to marry her before he became a deaf-mute** and was no longer mentally competent, **she may not partake** of *teruma.* **If a son was born to her**[H] from this priest, **she** may **partake** of *teruma* on account of her son. If **the son died, Rabbi Natan says she may** continue to **partake** of *teruma,* **and the Rabbis say she may not** continue to **partake** of *teruma.*

מאי טעמא דרבי נתן? אמר רבה: הואיל שכבר אכלה. אמר ליה אביי: אלא מעתה בת ישראל שניסת לכהן ומית ליה – תיכול, שכבר אכלה! אלא, כיון דמית ליה פקע ליה קדושתיה מינה – הכא נמי, כיון דמית ליה פקע קדושתיה מינה!

The Gemara asks: **What is the reasoning of Rabbi Natan? Rabba said: Since she has** already **partaken of** *teruma* in a permitted manner, she may continue. **Abaye said to him: However, if** that is so, in the case of the **daughter of an Israelite who was married to a priest, and he died** childless, she **should** be allowed to **partake** of *teruma,* **as she has** already **partaken of** it in the past. **Rather,** it must be that **since he has passed away,** his priestly **sanctity has left her,** and she is considered a regular Israelite in all regards. **Here too, since** the son **has passed away, his** priestly **sanctity has left her,** and therefore she should not be entitled to partake of *teruma.* Rabba's explanation should consequently be rejected.

אלא אמר רב יוסף: קסבר רבי נתן נשואי חרש מאכילין בתרומה, ולא גזרינן נשואי חרש אטו קדושי חרש. אמר ליה אביי: אי הכי, נולד לה בן למה לי! משום רבנן.

Rather, Rav Yosef said: Rabbi Natan holds that **the marriage of a deaf-mute** who was competent when he betrothed his wife **entitles her to partake of** *teruma,* **and we do not** issue a **decree** against the wife partaking of *teruma* through **marriage** to **a deaf-mute due to** the case of **betrothal** to **a deaf-mute.** Although the betrothal of a deaf-mute does not take effect, his consummation of a marriage does take effect and entitles his wife to partake of *teruma.* **Abaye said to him: If so, why do I** need the *baraita* to specify that **a son was born to her?** She should be entitled to eat *teruma* even if she did not have a son. Rav Yosef responded: That case is mentioned **due to** the opinion of **the Rabbis,** who hold that she is entitled to partake of *teruma* only if she has a child.

HALAKHA

A mentally competent woman who married a priest and he became a deaf-mute, etc. – פקחת שנשאה לכהן ונתחרש וכו׳: If a woman from a non-priestly family was betrothed to a priest, and before they were fully married he became a deaf-mute and was no longer mentally competent, she may not partake of *teruma.* If he died and she performed levirate marriage with her deaf-mute *yavam,* she still may not partake of *teruma.* However, if her first husband married her and only then became a deaf-mute, she may partake of *teruma.* If he then died and she performed levirate marriage with her deaf-mute *yavam,* she may partake of *teruma* (Rambam *Sefer Zera'im, Hilkhot Terumot* 8:10).

If a son was born to her – נולד לה בן: If a priest was a deaf-mute when he married, his wife may not partake of *teruma.* Nevertheless, if she has a child, she may partake of *teruma* on his account (Rambam *Sefer Zera'im, Hilkhot Terumot* 8:10).

NOTES

However, according to Shmuel it is difficult – אלא לשמואל קשיא: Even so, Shmuel's opinion is not entirely refuted, as even according to Rav, the text of the *baraita* must be adjusted or interpreted in a manner that is not immediately obvious. Therefore, Shmuel's opinion cannot be rejected by dint of a *baraita* of questionable reliability (Ritva; see *Keren Ora*).

וְלִיפְלוֹג רַבִּי נָתָן עֲלַיְיהוּ בְּרֵישָׁא – שָׁבֵיק לְהוּ לְרַבָּנַן עַד דִּמְסַיְּימִי מִילְּתַיְיהוּ, וַהֲדַר פְּלֵיג עֲלַיְיהוּ. אִי הָכִי לִיתְנֵי: מֵת הַבֵּן אֵינָהּ אוֹכֶלֶת, רַבִּי נָתָן אוֹמֵר: אוֹכֶלֶת! קַשְׁיָא.

Abaye asks further: **And let Rabbi Natan disagree with them in the first clause** of the *baraita* as well. Rav Yosef responds: Rabbi Natan **left the Rabbis until they finished their statement, and then disagreed with them** with regard to their entire statement. The Gemara asks: **If so,** let the *baraita* first **teach** that if **the son died** she **may not partake** of *teruma*, and subsequently state: **Rabbi Natan said** she **may eat.** Why is Rabbi Natan's opinion mentioned before the Rabbis finished stating their opinion? The Gemara concludes: Indeed, this **is difficult** according to Rav Yosef.

״וְכֵן הַבָּא עַל אַחַת מִכׇּל הָעֲרָיוֹת״. אָמַר רַב עַמְרָם: הָא מִלְּתָא אֲמַר לַן רַב שֵׁשֶׁת,

§ It was taught in the mishna: **And so too, one who had intercourse with any one of those with whom relations are forbidden** by **the Torah** in any form is liable to receive punishment. **Rav Amram said: This matter was said** to us by **Rav Sheshet,**

Perek **VI**
Daf **56** Amud **b**

וְאַנְהֲרִינְהוּ לְעַיְינִין מִמַּתְנִיתִין: אֵשֶׁת יִשְׂרָאֵל שֶׁנֶּאֶנְסָה, אַף עַל פִּי שֶׁמּוּתֶּרֶת לְבַעְלָהּ – פְּסוּלָה לִכְהוּנָּה. וְתָנָא תּוּנָא: וְכֵן הַבָּא עַל אַחַת מִכׇּל הָעֲרָיוֹת הָאֲמוּרוֹת בַּתּוֹרָה, אוֹ פְּסוּלוֹת.

and he illuminated our eyes from the mishna, i.e., he demonstrated that the mishna serves as the basis for his opinion: With regard to **the wife of an Israelite who was raped,**[NH] **although she is permitted to her husband, she is disqualified for the priesthood.** Therefore, if her husband dies, she may not marry a priest. **And the *tanna*** of our mishna also **taught: And so too,** in the case of **one who had intercourse with any one of those with whom relations are forbidden** [*arayot*] **by the Torah or** with those who are **unfit** to marry **him** even though they are not in the category of *arayot*, the woman is disqualified from marrying a priest.

מַאי ״וְכֵן״? מַאי לָאו: לָא שְׁנָא בְּשׁוֹגֵג וְלָא שְׁנָא בְּמֵזִיד וְלָא שְׁנָא בְּאוֹנֶס וְלָא שְׁנָא בְּרָצוֹן. וְקָתָנֵי ״פְּסָלָהּ״.

What is the meaning of the phrase: **And so too? What, is it not** that **it is no different** whether they have intercourse **unwittingly or intentionally, and it is no different** whether they have intercourse **due to coercion or willingly? And it is taught** that **he has rendered her disqualified** from marrying a priest.

לָא, מַאי ״וְכֵן״ – אַהַעֲרָאָה. הַעֲרָאָה דְּמַאן? אִילֵּימָא דַּעֲרָיוֹת – לְמֵימְרָא דַּעֲרָיוֹת יָלְפִינַן מִיבָמָה? אַדְּרַבָּה, יְבָמָה יָלְפִינַן מֵעֲרָיוֹת, דְּעִיקַּר הַעֲרָאָה בַּעֲרָיוֹת כְּתִיב!

The Gemara refutes this proof: **No,** what is the meaning of the phrase: **And so too?** It is referring **to the initial stage of intercourse,** as this too invalidates her. The Gemara asks: **The initial stage of intercourse of whom? If we say** it is referring to **those with whom relations are prohibited** and carry a punishment of *karet* or death [*arayot*], **is this to say that** the *halakha* **with regard to those with whom relations are prohibited is derived from** the *halakha* with regard to a ***yevama***, as implied by the phrase: And so too? **On the contrary, we derive** the *halakha* of a ***yevama*** from the *halakha* **with regard to those with whom relations are prohibited, as the main** source that indicates that **the initial stage of intercourse** is considered intercourse **is stated in** the context of **those with whom relations are prohibited** and not in the context of a *yevama*.

אֶלָּא מַאי ״וְכֵן״ – אֶשֶׁלֹּא כְּדַרְכָּהּ דַּעֲרָיוֹת – אַדְּרַבָּה, עִיקַּר ״מִשְׁכְּבֵי אִשָּׁה״ בַּעֲרָיוֹת כְּתִיב?

Rather, what is the meaning of the phrase: **And so too?** It is referring **to atypical,** i.e., anal, **sexual intercourse with those with whom relations are prohibited** [*arayot*]. The Gemara rejects this suggestion: **On the contrary, the main** source that atypical intercourse is considered intercourse, which is based upon the verse **"The cohabitations of a woman"** (Leviticus 18:22) **is written with regard to those with whom relations are prohibited** [*arayot*].

אֶלָּא מַאי ״וְכֵן״ אֶשֶׁלֹּא כְּדַרְכָּהּ דְּחַיָּיבֵי לָאוִין.

Rather, what is the meaning of the phrase: **And so too?** It is referring **to atypical** intercourse **by those liable for** violating an ordinary **prohibition** not punishable by *karet*, with regard to whom the expression: The cohabitations of a woman, does not appear. In any event, Rav Sheshet's proof from the mishna is not conclusive.

NOTES

The wife of an Israelite who was raped – אֵשֶׁת יִשְׂרָאֵל שֶׁנֶּאֶנְסָה: Several of the dilemmas raised in this passage are related to defining who is considered a *zona* and is therefore forbidden to a priest. It was clear to the Sages that the halakhic category of *zona* does not refer to a prostitute, as it does in both biblical and modern Hebrew. It refers instead to a woman who had intercourse with a man whom it is prohibited for her to marry, and with whom an act of betrothal would be ineffective. There is room to suggest a difference in this regard between a married woman and other forbidden relationships. In the case of other forbidden relationships, the woman is prohibited to the man due to her personal status, either because she is his close relative or because she is Jewish and he is not. In the case of a married woman, the prohibition stems from the marital bond, which is itself initially dependent upon her consent. Furthermore, this tie can be broken through the death of the husband or their divorce. Consequently, adultery is an act of infidelity on the part of a woman toward her husband, and a married woman who was raped is not prohibited to her husband, as she was not unfaithful to him. One might therefore have assumed that just as the woman is permitted to her husband, she is not considered a *zona*, and it is permitted for her to marry a priest if she becomes a widow (see *Tosafot* and *Tosafot Yeshanim*).

HALAKHA

The wife of an Israelite who was raped – אֵשֶׁת יִשְׂרָאֵל שֶׁנֶּאֶנְסָה: If the wife of an Israelite was raped, she is permitted to her husband. However, if her husband dies, she is forbidden to a priest, in accordance with the ruling of Rav Sheshet (Rambam *Sefer Kedusha, Hilkhot Issurei Bia* 18:8; *Shulḥan Arukh, Even HaEzer* 6:11).

אָמַר רָבָא: אֵשֶׁת כֹּהֵן שֶׁנֶּאֶנְסָה – בַּעְלָהּ לוֹקֶה עָלֶיהָ מִשּׁוּם זוֹנָה. מִשּׁוּם זוֹנָה – אִין, מִשּׁוּם טוּמְאָה – לָא? אֵימָא: אַף מִשּׁוּם זוֹנָה.

§ **Rava said:**[N] With regard to **the wife of a priest who was raped,**[H] **her husband is flogged** if he later has intercourse with **her, due to** the fact that it is prohibited for a priest to have intercourse with a ***zona***.[B] The Gemara expresses surprise: **Due to** the prohibition proscribing a ***zona*, yes; due to ritual impurity,**[N] **no?** The Torah refers to a married woman who has had intercourse with another man as ritually impure, and she is forbidden to her husband. The Gemara emends Rava's statement: **Say** that he is **also** flogged **due to** the prohibition with regard to a ***zona***.

מְתִיב רַבִּי זֵירָא: ״וְהִיא לֹא נִתְפָּשָׂה״ – אֲסוּרָה, הָא נִתְפְּשָׂה – מוּתֶּרֶת. וְיֵשׁ לְךָ אַחֶרֶת שֶׁאַף עַל פִּי שֶׁנִּתְפְּשָׂה – אֲסוּרָה, וְאֵי זוֹ – זוֹ אֵשֶׁת כֹּהֵן,

Rabbi Zeira raised an objection based upon a verse with regard to a *sota*: **"And neither was she taken"** (Numbers 5:13) indicates that **she is forbidden** to her husband because she willingly committed adultery, **but** if **she was** forcibly **taken,** i.e., raped, **she is permitted** to her husband. The term "And… she" indicates that although these principles apply in this case, **you have another** case of a woman **who is prohibited even though she was** forcibly **taken. And which is this? This is the wife of a priest.**

וְלָאו הַבָּא מִכְּלַל עֲשֵׂה – עֲשֵׂה!

And a prohibition that stems from a positive mitzva, e.g., the prohibition proscribing a priest's wife to her husband if she has been raped, which is derived from the fact that the Torah indicates that the wife of an Israelite remains permitted, has the status of a **positive mitzva,** not a prohibition. Consequently, one should not be flogged for this offense, as one is flogged only for violating a prohibition.

אָמַר רַבָּה: הַכֹּל הָיוּ בִּכְלַל זוֹנָה, כְּשֶׁפָּרַט לְךָ הַכָּתוּב גַּבֵּי אֵשֶׁת יִשְׂרָאֵל ״וְהִיא לֹא נִתְפָּשָׂה״ אֲסוּרָה, הָא נִתְפְּשָׂה – מוּתֶּרֶת, מִכְּלָל דְּאֵשֶׁת כֹּהֵן – כִּדְקַיְימָא קַיְימָא.

Rabba said in response: **All** married women who engaged in extramarital intercourse **were included** in the category of ***zona***.[N] **When the verse specified with regard to the wife of an Israelite: "And neither was she taken,"** as it is only in that case that she is **forbidden,** it thereby indicates that if in fact **she was** forcibly **taken,** she is **permitted. By inference,** unlike the wife of an Israelite, **the wife of a priest remains as she was.** Since the Torah does not limit the category of *zona* with regard to the wife of a priest, she is considered a *zona* even if she was raped.

וְאִיכָּא דְּאָמְרִי, אָמַר רַבָּה: אֵשֶׁת כֹּהֵן שֶׁנֶּאֶנְסָה – בַּעְלָהּ לוֹקֶה עָלֶיהָ מִשּׁוּם טוּמְאָה. מִשּׁוּם טוּמְאָה – אִין, מִשּׁוּם זוֹנָה – לָא, אַלְמָא: בְּאוֹנֶס לָא קָרֵינָא בֵּיהּ זוֹנָה.

And some say a different version of this discussion. **Rabba said:** With regard to **the wife of a priest who was raped, her husband is flogged for** having intercourse with **her due to** her **ritual impurity.** The Gemara asks: **Due to ritual impurity, yes; due to** the prohibition proscribing a ***zona*, no? Apparently, in** a case of **rape,** the victim **is not called a *zona*.**

מְתִיב רַבִּי זֵירָא: ״וְהִיא לֹא נִתְפָּשָׂה״ – אֲסוּרָה, הָא נִתְפְּשָׂה – מוּתֶּרֶת, וְיֵשׁ לְךָ אַחֶרֶת שֶׁאַף עַל פִּי שֶׁנִּתְפְּשָׂה אֲסוּרָה, וְאֵיזוֹ זוֹ – אֵשֶׁת כֹּהֵן, וְלָאו הַבָּא מִכְּלַל עֲשֵׂה – עֲשֵׂה!

Rabbi Zeira raised an objection from the verse: **"And neither was she taken"** indicates that **she is forbidden** to her husband because she willingly committed adultery, **but if she was** forcibly **taken, she is permitted** to her husband. The term: "And… she," indicates that although these principles apply in this case, **you have another** case of a woman **who is forbidden even though she was** forcibly **taken. And which is this? This is the wife of a priest. And a prohibition that stems from a positive mitzva** has the status of a **positive mitzva,** not a prohibition. Consequently, one should not be flogged for this offense, as one is flogged only for violating a prohibition.

אָמַר רָבָא: הַכֹּל הָיוּ בִּכְלַל ״אַחֲרֵי אֲשֶׁר הֻטַּמָּאָה״, כְּשֶׁפָּרַט לְךָ הַכָּתוּב גַּבֵּי אֵשֶׁת יִשְׂרָאֵל ״וְהִיא לֹא נִתְפָּשָׂה״ אֲסוּרָה״ הָא נִתְפְּשָׂה – מוּתֶּרֶת, מִכְּלָל דְּאֵשֶׁת כֹּהֵן כִּדְקַיְימָא קַיְימָא.

Rava said: All were included in the verse "Her former husband, who sent her away, may not take her again to be his wife **after she was made ritually impure"** (Deuteronomy 24:4). **When the verse specified with regard to the wife of an Israelite: "And neither was she taken,"** as it is only in that case that she is **forbidden,** it thereby indicates that if **she was** forcibly **taken** she is **permitted. By inference, the wife of a priest remains as she was,** and she is forbidden.

NOTES

Rava said – אָמַר רָבָא: Other versions of the text attribute this statement to Rabba, which seems to be more consistent with the Gemara's ensuing discussion.

Due to ritual impurity – מִשּׁוּם טוּמְאָה: This prohibition is derived from two sources. The first is a verse with regard to a *sota*: "And she was made ritually impure" (Numbers 5:13). Second, the Torah states with regard to a divorced woman who was remarried and then divorced from her second husband: "Her former husband, who sent her away, may not return to take her to be his wife after she was made ritually impure" (Deuteronomy 24:4). The Sages explain (see *Nidda* 11b) that this verse also renders prohibited a married woman who had intercourse with another man (see *Tosefot HaRosh*).

All married women who engaged in extramarital intercourse were included in the category of *zona* – הַכֹּל הָיוּ בִּכְלַל זוֹנָה: The commentaries are puzzled by this statement. Since a *zona* is forbidden only to a priest, what does it mean that initially the wife of an Israelite who was raped would also have been considered a *zona*, implying that she would have been prohibited to her husband, had the verse not excluded her from this prohibition? The *Tosefot HaRosh* explains that initially the wife of an Israelite was considered a *zona*, and was also prohibited to her husband due to becoming ritually impure. The Torah indicates that she is not prohibited to him if she was raped, but she remains classified as a *zona* and is prohibited to a priest. Consequently, the wife of a priest is also classified as a *zona* if she was raped, and therefore she is forbidden to her husband (see Rashba).

HALAKHA

The wife of a priest who was raped – אֵשֶׁת כֹּהֵן שֶׁנֶּאֶנְסָה: The wife of a priest who was raped is forbidden to her husband. If he engages in intercourse with her, he is flogged for violating the prohibition against having intercourse with a *zona* (*Mishne LaMelekh*), in accordance with the first version of Rabba's statement (Rambam *Sefer Kedusha*, *Hilkhot Issurei Bia* 18:7; *Shulḥan Arukh*, *Even HaEzer* 6:10).

BACKGROUND

***Zona* – זוֹנָה:** In halakhic terms, the category of *zona* refers to a woman who has had sexual relations with a man forbidden to her by the Torah, with whom she cannot establish a marriage bond. Furthermore, it is prohibited for a woman who is categorized as a *zona* to thereafter marry a priest or remain married to one (Leviticus 21:7). There is no connection between the halakhic definition of this term and its everyday usage in modern Hebrew.

HALAKHA

A widow to a High Priest, etc. – **אַלְמָנָה לְכֹהֵן גָּדוֹל וכו׳**: If a widow is betrothed to a High Priest, or a divorcée is betrothed to a priest, even if they are daughters of priests, they may not partake of *teruma*. This is in accordance with the opinion of Rabbi Meir. If they were then widowed or divorced before completing the marriage, they may once again partake of *teruma*. However, if their marriage to the priest was consummated, they are *ḥalalot* and are permanently disqualified from partaking of *teruma* (Rambam *Sefer Zera'im*, *Hilkhot Terumot* 7:21).

A priest with crushed testicles who betrothed a valid woman – **פְּצוּעַ דַּכָּא כֹּהֵן שֶׁקִּדֵּשׁ כְּשֵׁרָה**: If a priest with crushed testicles betrothed a woman, even if she is the daughter of a priest, she may not partake of *teruma* (Rambam *Sefer Zera'im*, *Hilkhot Terumot* 7:14).

NOTES

Ḥalala – **חֲלָלָה**: If it is forbidden for a woman to marry a regular priest or a High Priest and she engages in sexual intercourse with him, she is rendered a *ḥalala*. A woman is also considered a *ḥalala* if she is born from the union of a priest and a woman who is forbidden from marrying a priest; or if she is the wife or daughter of a *ḥalal*, which is a son born from the union of a priest and a woman who is forbidden from marrying a priest. It is prohibited for a *ḥalala* to marry a priest or partake of *teruma*.

A priest with crushed testicles who betrothed the daughter of an Israelite – **פְּצוּעַ דַּכָּא כֹּהֵן שֶׁקִּדֵּשׁ בַּת יִשְׂרָאֵל**: Virtually all the commentaries prefer Rabbeinu Ḥananel's reading: A priest with crushed testicles who betrothed the daughter of a priest (see *Tosafot*).

מתני׳ אַלְמָנָה לְכֹהֵן גָּדוֹל, גְּרוּשָׁה וַחֲלוּצָה לְכֹהֵן הֶדְיוֹט מִן הָאֵירוּסִין – לֹא יֹאכְלוּ בִּתְרוּמָה, רַבִּי אֶלְעָזָר וְרַבִּי שִׁמְעוֹן מַכְשִׁירִין.

MISHNA **A widow to a High Priest,**[H] **a divorcée, or a *ḥalutza* to a common priest,** even if they had only engaged in **betrothal** and had not yet had intercourse, **may not partake of *teruma*.** Since they are forbidden to the men who betrothed them, the betrothal itself disqualifies them from the privileges of priesthood even if they are the daughters of priests. **Rabbi Elazar and Rabbi Shimon declare them fit** to partake of *teruma*. Since the prohibition is violated through the act of intercourse and not betrothal, the women are disqualified only once they have intercourse.

נִתְאַרְמְלוּ אוֹ נִתְגָּרְשׁוּ, מִן הַנִּשּׂוּאִין – פְּסוּלוֹת, מִן הָאֵירוּסִין – כְּשֵׁרוֹת.

In a case where these women **were widowed or divorced,** if it was **from marriage, they are disqualified** from the priesthood and may not partake of *teruma*. This is because a woman prohibited from marrying a priest who has intercourse with a priest becomes a *ḥalala*,[N] and is thereby disqualified from partaking of *teruma*. However, if they were widowed or divorced **from** their state of **betrothal,** they are once again **fit** to partake of *teruma* according to all opinions.

גמ׳ תַּנְיָא, אָמַר רַבִּי מֵאִיר: קַל וָחוֹמֶר, וּמָה קִדּוּשֵׁי רְשׁוּת – אֵין מַאֲכִילִין, קִדּוּשֵׁי עֲבֵירָה – לֹא כׇּל שֶׁכֵּן?!

GEMARA **It is taught in a *baraita*** that **Rabbi Meir said:** This is **an *a fortiori* inference: Just as optional betrothal,** e.g., in the case of an Israelite who betroths the daughter of a priest, **does not entitle her to partake** of *teruma*, as her betrothal to a non-priest disqualifies her from partaking of her father's *teruma*, **is it not all the more so** true in a case of **betrothal** that constitutes **a transgression,** as in the cases in the mishna?

אָמְרוּ לוֹ: לֹא, אִם אָמַרְתָּ בְּקִידּוּשֵׁי רְשׁוּת – שֶׁכֵּן אֵין לוֹ לְהַאֲכִיל בְּמָקוֹם אַחֵר, תֹּאמַר בְּקִדּוּשֵׁי עֲבֵירָה – שֶׁכֵּן יֵשׁ לוֹ לְהַאֲכִיל בְּמָקוֹם אַחֵר.

They said to him: No, if you say that this is true with regard to an Israelite, **whose** status **cannot entitle her to partake** of *teruma* **in another case,** as one betrothed to an Israelite may never partake of *teruma*, **shall you** also **say** that this is the case with regard to **betrothal** to a priest that constitutes **a transgression, where his** status **does entitle her to partake** of *teruma* **in a different case,** as marriage to a priest entitles a woman to partake of *teruma* in a case where it is permitted for them to marry?

אָמַר רַבִּי אֶלְעָזָר אָמַר רַבִּי אוֹשַׁעְיָא: פְּצוּעַ דַּכָּא כֹּהֵן שֶׁקִּדֵּשׁ בַּת יִשְׂרָאֵל – בָּאנוּ לְמַחְלוֹקֶת רַבִּי מֵאִיר וְרַבִּי אֶלְעָזָר וְרַבִּי שִׁמְעוֹן.

Rabbi Elazar said that **Rabbi Oshaya said:** In the case of **a priest with crushed testicles** or with other wounds to his genitals **who betrothed the daughter of an Israelite,**[HN] which is prohibited by the verse "He that is crushed or maimed shall not enter into the congregation of the Lord" (Deuteronomy 23:2), **we have arrived at the dispute** between **Rabbi Meir** on the one hand **and Rabbi Elazar and Rabbi Shimon** on the other.

לְרַבִּי מֵאִיר דְּאָמַר מִשְׁתַּמֶּרֶת לְבִיאָה פְּסוּלָה דְּאוֹרָיְיתָא לָא אָכְלָה – הָא נַמִי לָא אָכְלָה, לְרַבִּי אֶלְעָזָר וְרַבִּי שִׁמְעוֹן דְּאָמְרִי מִשְׁתַּמֶּרֶת לְבִיאָה פְּסוּלָה דְּאוֹרָיְיתָא אָכְלָה

According to Rabbi Meir, who said that a woman who is **reserved for intercourse that is invalid,** i.e., prohibited, **by Torah law may not partake** of *teruma*, **this one may also not partake** of *teruma*, as it is prohibited by Torah law for her to have intercourse with a man with crushed testicles. **According to Rabbi Elazar and Rabbi Shimon, who say** that a woman who is **reserved for intercourse that is invalid by Torah** law **may partake** of *teruma* until she actually engages in the prohibited act of intercourse,

Perek **VI**
Daf **57** Amud **a**

הָא נַמִי אָכְלָה. מִמַּאי? דִּלְמָא עַד כָּאן לָא קָאָמְרִי רַבִּי אֶלְעָזָר וְרַבִּי שִׁמְעוֹן הָתָם אֶלָּא דְּיֵשׁ לוֹ לְהַאֲכִיל בְּמָקוֹם אַחֵר, אֲבָל הָכָא, דְּאֵין לוֹ לְהַאֲכִיל בְּמָקוֹם אַחֵר – לָא.

this one may also partake of *teruma* until that time. The Gemara refutes this argument: **From where** do we know that this is correct? **Perhaps Rabbi Elazar and Rabbi Shimon stated** their opinion **there only** with regard to a priest **whose** status **can entitle her to partake** of *teruma* **in another case, but here,** in the case of a priest with crushed testicles, **whose** status **cannot entitle her to partake** of *teruma* **in another case,** as it is forbidden for him to marry a woman who was born Jewish, **no,** they did not state their opinion.

וכי תימא: הכא נמי יש לו להאכיל בבת גרים – והא מיבעיא בעי לה רבי יוחנן מרבי אושעיא, ולא פשיט ליה.

And if you say that here too, his status can at least entitle his wife **to partake of** *teruma* if he marries **the daughter of converts, wasn't it** already **raised as a dilemma by Rabbi Yoḥanan before Rabbi Oshaya**[P] whether the daughter of converts who married a priest with crushed testicles may partake of *teruma*, **and he was unable to resolve it for him?** Therefore, there is a difference between a priest with crushed testicles and other priests who betroth women who are disqualified by their intercourse.

איתמר, אביי אמר: הואיל ומאכילה בלא ידעה.

It was stated that **Abaye said:** Women betrothed to a priest with crushed testicles may eat *teruma* **since his** status **entitles** his wife **to partake** of *teruma* **in** a case where **he has not known her.** If a priest was properly married and then his testicles became crushed, as long as he has not known his wife, i.e., engaged in intercourse with her, after that point in time, she may continue partaking of *teruma* as his wife.

רבא אמר: הואיל ומאכילה בעבדיו ושפחותיו הכנענים.

Rava said she may continue to partake of *teruma* for a different reason: She may eat *teruma* **since** the status of this priest **entitles his Canaanite slaves and maidservants to partake** of *teruma*. Because he has the power to enable others to partake of *teruma*, the case of a woman betrothed to a priest with crushed testicles is comparable to the cases in the mishna, and Rabbi Elazar and Rabbi Shimon would permit the woman to partake of *teruma*.

אביי לא אמר כרבא, קנין דאישות מקנין דאישות – ילפינן, ולא ילפינן קנין דאישות מקנין דעבדים.

The Gemara clarifies the two opinions. **Abaye did not say in accordance with** the opinion of **Rava** because he claims that **we derive** the *halakhot* related to **the acquisition of marriage from the acquisition of marriage, and we do not derive** the *halakhot* related to **the acquisition of marriage from the acquisition of slaves.**

ורבא לא אמר כאביי – שאני התם שכבר אכלה. ואביי: שכבר אכלה לא אמרינן, דאי לא תימא הכי – בת ישראל שניסת לכהן ומית – תיכול, שכבר אכלה. ורבא: התם – פקע קניניה, הכא – לא פקע קניניה.

And Rava did not state his opinion **in accordance with** the opinion of **Abaye,** as he maintains that **it is different there, as she had already partaken of** *teruma*[N] before her husband's testicles were crushed and therefore she may continue to partake of it. **And Abaye** would respond that **we do not say** that the case is different because **she had already partaken of** *teruma*, **as, if you do not say so,** the **daughter of an Israelite who was married to a priest who died** childless **should** be allowed to **partake** of *teruma*, **as she had already partaken of** *teruma* while her husband was alive. **And Rava** replies that there is no comparison between the two cases: **There, his acquisition lapses** upon his death; **here, his acquisition does not lapse,** as she is still his wife.

גופא, בעא מיניה רבי יוחנן מרבי אושעיא: פצוע דכא כהן שנשא בת גרים, מהו שיאכילנה בתרומה? אישתיק ולא אמר ליה ולא מידי. לסוף אתא גברא רבה אחרינא, ובעא מיניה מילתא [אחריתא], ופשט ליה. ומנו – ריש לקיש. אמר ליה רבי יהודה נשיאה לרבי אושעיא: אטו רבי יוחנן לאו גברא רבה הוא? אמר ליה: דקבעי מינאי מילתא דלית לה פתרי.

§ The Gemara earlier mentioned a question that Rabbi Yoḥanan posed to Rabbi Oshaya, and it now turns its attention to that matter **itself. Rabbi Yoḥanan raised a dilemma before Rabbi Oshaya:** With regard to **a priest** with **crushed testicles** or with other wounds to his genitals **who married the daughter of converts, what is the** *halakha* concerning whether **his** status **entitles her to partake of** *teruma*? Rabbi Oshaya **was silent and said nothing to him. Eventually another great man came and raised a different dilemma before** Rabbi Oshaya, **and he resolved his** question. **And who was** this great man? **Reish Lakish. Rabbi Yehuda Nesia said to Rabbi Oshaya: Is Rabbi Yoḥanan not a great man?** Why didn't you address his dilemma? Rabbi Oshaya **said to him:** I did not respond **because he raised a dilemma before me that has no resolution.**

PERSONALITIES

Rabbi Oshaya – רבי אושעיא: Rabbi Oshaya was one of the greatest of the first generation of *amora'im* in Eretz Yisrael. Due to his prominence and influence, he was known as Rabbi Oshaya the Great, and was also given the honorific title Father of the Mishna.

His family came from the south, where he was apparently born and raised. At some point he moved to the Galilee and settled in Tzippori and Caesarea. The verse "A threefold cord is not quickly broken" (Ecclesiastes 4:12) was used to describe him, as his father, Rabbi Ḥama, and his grandfather, Rabbi Bisa, were also renowned Sages.

Rabbi Oshaya was originally a disciple of bar Kappara, and later, probably after his move to the Galilee, he became a disciple of Rabbi Ḥiyya. Like Rabbi Ḥiyya, Rabbi Oshaya authored a collection of *baraitot* that is considered highly authoritative and reliable, to the extent that the Sages stated a principle that any collection of *baraitot* other than that of Rabbi Ḥiyya and Rabbi Oshaya is of questionable validity.

It seems that as a young man Rabbi Oshaya was a member of the rabbinical court of Rabbi Yehuda HaNasi. However, his most active years came during the time of Rabbi Yehuda HaNasi's students, and especially during the time of Rabbi Yehuda HaNasi's grandson, Rabbi Yehuda Nesia, when Rabbi Oshaya was considered the outstanding scholar of the generation. Rabbi Oshaya's family maintained close ties with the house of the *Nasi*.

All the important *amora'im* in Eretz Yisrael viewed themselves as Rabbi Oshaya's students, including the illustrious Rabbi Yoḥanan. Together with his greatness in Torah, Rabbi Oshaya was also known for his exemplary behavior and for his consideration in tending to the physical and emotional needs of those in distress. It seems that he was also well versed in worldly wisdom, as his masters occasionally sent him to explain issues to various individuals from other nations.

It is not known what Rabbi Oshaya's occupation was, but it is clear that he barely made a living. He lived a long life, as his students' students were prominent scholars in Eretz Yisrael during his own lifetime. His son, Rabbi Marinos, is mentioned in the Jerusalem Talmud.

NOTES

It is different there, as she had already partaken of ***teruma*** **– שאני התם שכבר אכלה:** According to the text of Rabbeinu Ḥananel and many others, the case under discussion is about a priest with crushed testicles who betrothed the daughter of a priest. In that case, the woman has already partaken of *teruma* due to the fact that she is the daughter of a priest. Consequently, why should there be a distinction between that case and the case of the priest whose wife was entitled to partake of *teruma* before his testicles were crushed? The Ritva explains that by getting married she has left her father's household, and therefore her earlier consumption of *teruma* is no longer relevant.

לְמַאן? אִי לְרַבִּי יְהוּדָה – בֵּין בִּקְדוּשָּׁתֵיהּ קָאֵי בֵּין לָאו בִּקְדוּשָּׁתֵיהּ קָאֵי – לָא אָכְלָה. אִי בִּקְדוּשָּׁתֵיהּ קָאֵי לָא אָכְלָה, דְּהָא אֲמַר מָר: בַּת גֵּר זָכָר כְּבַת חָלָל זָכָר.

The Gemara explains: **According to whom** did he raise his dilemma? **If** it was **in accordance with** the opinion of **Rabbi Yehuda,** then, **whether** the priest with crushed testicles **retains his** priestly **sanctity or whether he does not retain his** priestly **sanctity** and may marry women forbidden to priests, she **may not partake** of *teruma.* The reasoning is as follows: **If he retains his** priestly **sanctity she may not partake** of *teruma,* **as the Master said:** The status of the **daughter of a male convert is like** that of the **daughter of a male *ḥalal*.** They are both prohibited from marrying a priest, and therefore even if they marry a priest, it is prohibited for them to eat *teruma.*

אִי לָאו בִּקְדוּשָּׁתֵיהּ קָאֵי – לָא אָכְלָה, דְּהָא אָמְרִינַן: קְהַל גֵּרִים אִיקְּרֵי קָהָל.

Even **if he does not retain his** priestly **sanctity she may not eat, as we say** that according to Rabbi Yehuda, **the congregation of converts is called** the **congregation** of the Lord. Therefore, when the Torah renders it prohibited for a man with crushed testicles to marry into the congregation of the Lord (see Deuteronomy 23:2), it renders it prohibited for him to marry converts.

וְאִי לְרַבִּי יוֹסֵי, בֵּין בִּקְדוּשָּׁתֵיהּ קָאֵי בֵּין לָאו בִּקְדוּשָּׁתֵיהּ קָאֵי – אָכְלָה. בִּקְדוּשָּׁתֵיהּ קָאֵי אָכְלָה – דְּהָא אֲמַר: אַף גֵּר שֶׁנָּשָׂא גִּיּוֹרֶת בִּתּוֹ כְּשֵׁרָה לִכְהוּנָּה. אִי לָאו בִּקְדוּשָּׁתֵיהּ קָאֵי אָכְלָה – דְּהָא אֲמַר: קְהַל גֵּרִים לָא אִיקְּרֵי קָהָל.

And if he raised his dilemma **in accordance with** the opinion of **Rabbi Yosei,** then, **whether he retains his** priestly **sanctity** or **whether he does not retain his** priestly **sanctity, she** may **partake** of *teruma.* If **he retains his sanctity** she **may partake,** as Rabbi Yosei **said: Even** if a **convert married a convert, his daughter is fit for** marrying into **the priesthood. If he does not retain his sanctity** she **may partake,** as Rabbi Yosei **said:** The **congregation of converts is not called** the **congregation** of the Lord,[H] and therefore even those forbidden from entering the congregation may marry converts. Consequently, it is certainly permitted for the priest with crushed testicles to marry the daughter of converts.

אֶלָּא אַלִּיבָּא דְּהַאי תַּנָּא. דִּתְנַן, רַבִּי אֱלִיעֶזֶר בֶּן יַעֲקֹב אוֹמֵר: אִשָּׁה בַּת גֵּרִים לֹא תִּנָּשֵׂא לִכְהוּנָּה עַד שֶׁתְּהֵא אִמָּהּ מִיִּשְׂרָאֵל.

Rather, Rabbi Yoḥanan raised his dilemma **in accordance with** the opinion of **this *tanna,* as we learned** in a mishna (*Bikkurim* 1:5) that **Rabbi Eliezer ben Ya'akov says: A woman** who is **the daughter of converts may not marry into the priesthood**[NH] **unless her mother was Jewish** from birth.

וְהָכִי קָמִיבַּעְיָא לֵיהּ: כַּשְׁרוּת מִיתּוֹסְפָא בַּהּ וְאָכְלָה, אוֹ דִּלְמָא קְדוּשָּׁה מִיתּוֹסְפָא בַּהּ וְלָא אָכְלָה?

And his dilemma was as follows: Is the reason she may marry a priest if her mother was Jewish from birth that **fitness** to marry a priest **has been added to her,** but she is not considered a member of the congregation of the Lord and may therefore marry a man with crushed testicles? If so, since she may marry a priest, **she** may **partake** of *teruma* once she does so. **Or perhaps sanctity has been added to her** and she is considered a member of the congregation of the Lord. Consequently, she may not marry a man with crushed testicles, and if she does, **she may not partake** of *teruma* even if he is a priest.

תָּא שְׁמַע: כִּי אֲתָא רַבִּי אַחָא בַּר חִינָּנָא מִדָּרוֹמָא, אֲתָא וְאַיְיתֵי מַתְנִיתָא בִּידֵיהּ: מִנַּיִן לִפְצוּעַ דַּכָּא כֹּהֵן שֶׁנָּשָׂא בַּת גֵּרִים שֶׁמַּאֲכִילָהּ בִּתְרוּמָה – שֶׁנֶּאֱמַר ״וְכֹהֵן כִּי יִקְנֶה נֶפֶשׁ קִנְיַן כַּסְפּוֹ וגו׳ יֹאכַל בּוֹ״,

The Gemara suggests an answer to this dilemma. **Come and hear: When Rabbi Aḥa bar Ḥinnana came from the south,**[B] **he came and brought** this ***baraita* in hand: From where** is it derived that **a priest with crushed testicles** or with other wounds to his genitals[H] **who married the daughter of converts entitles her to partake of *teruma*? As it is stated: "But if a priest buys any soul, the purchase of his money,** he **may eat of it"** (Leviticus 22:11). In this context, a wife is also considered his monetary acquisition, and therefore she may partake of *teruma.*

HALAKHA

The congregation of converts is not called the congregation of the Lord – קְהַל גֵּרִים לָא אִיקְּרֵי קָהָל: It is permitted for a convert to marry a *mamzeret*, and it is permitted for a female convert to marry a *mamzer* or a man with crushed testicles. The children of converts may also marry these individuals, even if they were conceived and born after their parents' conversion. This is true even after the passage of several generations, as long as they are still known as converts and neither of their parents is a natural-born Jew. The *halakha* is in accordance with the opinion of Rabbi Yosei (Rambam *Sefer Kedusha, Hilkhot Issurei Bia* 15:7–8; *Shulḥan Arukh, Even HaEzer* 4:22).

A woman who is the daughter of converts…into the priesthood – אִשָּׁה בַּת גֵּרִים...לִכְהוּנָּה: A woman who is the daughter of two converts may not marry a priest. If she nevertheless married a priest, they are not forced to divorce if she was conceived after her parents converted. This is based upon the conclusion of the Gemara in tractate *Kiddushin* (78b) that, after the fact, the *halakha* is in accordance with the opinion of Rabbi Yosei. If one of her parents was a natural-born Jew, she may marry a priest even *ab initio*, as stated by Rabbi Eliezer ben Ya'akov (Rambam *Sefer Kedusha, Hilkhot Issurei Bia* 19:12; *Shulḥan Arukh, Even HaEzer* 7:21).

A priest with crushed testicles or with other wounds to his genitals – פְּצוּעַ דַּכָּא כֹּהֵן: If a priest with crushed testicles married a daughter of converts she may partake of *teruma* on his account, in accordance with the opinions of Rabbi Yosei and Rabbi Eliezer ben Ya'akov (*Kesef Mishne*; Rambam *Sefer Zera'im, Hilkhot Terumot* 7:13).

NOTES

A woman who is the daughter of converts may not marry into the priesthood – בַּת גֵּרִים לֹא תִּנָּשֵׂא לִכְהוּנָּה: As explained in tractate *Kiddushin* (78a), this *halakha* is based on the verse "Neither shall they take for their wives a widow…but they shall take virgins from the seed of the house of Israel" (Ezekiel 44:22). See the Gemara there for other reasons that apply to a female convert herself.

BACKGROUND

From the south – מִדָּרוֹמָא: From the time of the bar Kokheva revolt, the center of Jewish life in Eretz Yisrael was in the Galilee. Judea was mostly desolate, as the majority of the population, and the Sanhedrin, were in the Galilee. However, some important centers of Jewish life in Judea remained, including Lod and other cities. There were some Sages who lived south of the Galilee and preserved ancient traditions. At times, these Sages would travel north to the Galilee and report halakhic traditions, *baraitot*, or statements of earlier Sages that were not known to the Sages in the Galilee.

לְמַאן? אִילֵימָא לְרַבִּי יְהוּדָה – הָאָמַר: בֵּין בִּקְדוּשָּׁתֵיהּ קָאֵי בֵּין לָאו בִּקְדוּשָּׁתֵיהּ קָאֵי – לָא אָכְלָה. וְאִי לְרַבִּי יוֹסֵי – לָמָּה לִי קְרָא? הָאָמַר: בֵּין בִּקְדוּשָּׁתֵיהּ קָאֵי, בֵּין לָאו בִּקְדוּשָּׁתֵיהּ קָאֵי – אָכְלָה. אֶלָּא לָאו – לְרַבִּי אֱלִיעֶזֶר בֶּן יַעֲקֹב, וּשְׁמַע מִינָּהּ: כַּשְׁרוּת אִיתּוֹסְפָא בָּהּ, וְאָכְלָה. שְׁמַע מִינָּהּ.

The Gemara analyzes this source: **According to whom** is this *baraita* stated? **If we say** it is **in accordance with** the opinion of **Rabbi Yehuda, didn't he say** that **whether** this priest **retains his sanctity** or **whether he does not retain his sanctity, she may not partake** of *teruma*? **And if** it is **in accordance with** the opinion of **Rabbi Yosei, why do I need** a special **verse** to teach this *halakha*? **Didn't he say** that **whether** he **retains his sanctity** or **whether he does not retain his sanctity, she** may **partake** of *teruma*? **Rather, is it not in accordance with** the opinion of **Rabbi Eliezer ben Ya'akov? And** you can **learn from this** *baraita* that **fitness was added to her, and** therefore **she** may **partake** of *teruma*. The Gemara concludes: Indeed, **learn from this** that it is so.

אִיתְּמַר, רַב אָמַר

§ The Gemara cites a dispute with regard to an issue related to the previous discussion. **It was stated** that the *amora'im* disagreed about the following question. **Rav said:**

Perek **VI**
Daf **57** Amud **b**

יֵשׁ חוּפָּה לִפְסוּלוֹת, וּשְׁמוּאֵל אָמַר: אֵין חוּפָּה לִפְסוּלוֹת.

There is significance to a priest entering **a wedding canopy**[NB] with women who are **unfit** to marry a priest.[NH] If a priest's daughter who is unfit to marry a priest enters the wedding canopy with a priest, she becomes disqualified from partaking of *teruma* from her father's household. This is the case even if the priest did not betroth her and they did not engage in sexual intercourse. **And Shmuel said: There is no** significance **to** a priest entering the **wedding canopy** with women who are **unfit** to marry a priest. Only sexual intercourse disqualifies her from the privileges of priesthood.

אָמַר שְׁמוּאֵל: וּמוֹדֶה לִי אַבָּא בְּתִינוֹקֶת פְּחוּתָה מִבַּת שָׁלֹשׁ שָׁנִים וְיוֹם אֶחָד, הוֹאִיל וְאֵין לָהּ בִּיאָה – אֵין לָהּ חוּפָּה.

Shmuel said: And Abba, i.e., Rav, whose first name was Abba, **concedes to me,**[N] **with regard to a girl less than three years and one day old,** that she is not disqualified by merely entering the wedding canopy. **Since there is no** legal significance to an act of **intercourse with her, there is no** legal significance to entering the **wedding canopy** with **her.**

BACKGROUND

Wedding canopy – חוּפָּה: In the talmudic era, the wedding canopy was a kind of small, decorated room, sometimes constructed from braided myrtle branches, where the bride and groom would be left alone together. It was a closed space that afforded enough privacy for the couple to engage in intimate relations. In later generations, when the wedding canopy took on a more symbolic function, the Sages debated whether entering the wedding canopy still fulfills the halakhic requirements of marriage, as mentioned in the Talmud.

HALAKHA

A wedding canopy with women who are unfit to marry a priest – חוּפָּה לִפְסוּלוֹת: If the widowed daughter of a priest enters the wedding canopy in order to marry a High Priest, or if a divorcée enters the wedding canopy in order to marry a common priest, she becomes disqualified from partaking of *teruma*. With regard to ritual *halakha*, the *halakha* is in accordance with Rav in his disputes with Shmuel (Rambam *Sefer Zera'im*, *Hilkhot Terumot* 7:21).

NOTES

Wedding canopy [*ḥuppa*] – חוּפָּה: There are differences of opinion as to what constitutes a wedding canopy. Some maintain that it refers to the ceremony where a shawl is spread over the heads of the bride and groom. Others say that *ḥuppa* requires them to be secluded for the amount of time necessary to engage in intercourse. Still others contend that *ḥuppa* occurs when the groom brings his bride into his home as his wife (see *Shulḥan Arukh*, *Even HaEzer* 55).

A wedding canopy with women who are unfit to marry a priest – חוּפָּה לִפְסוּלוֹת: Among the commentaries, there are many opinions with regard to the meaning of this passage. According to Rashi, the reference is to entering the wedding canopy without betrothal. Rav and Shmuel agree that the couple is not considered married. Nevertheless, Rav holds that the woman becomes disqualified from partaking of *teruma* because entering the wedding canopy is a preparatory stage for sexual intercourse.

Most medieval commentaries, however, maintain that this is a case where they entered the wedding canopy after betrothal. Rabbeinu Tam, cited in *Tosafot*, claims that Rav and Shmuel disagree about whether a priest and a woman unfit to marry him are considered married once they enter the wedding canopy, so that she would be disqualified from partaking of *teruma* from her father's house, or if they are not considered married in this regard until they engage in intercourse (see *Tosafot*; *Tosefot Ḥad MiKamma'ei*; Ramban; Ritva; *Yam shel Shlomo*).

Abba concedes to me – מוֹדֶה לִי אַבָּא: Rashi and Rabbi Avraham min HaHar explain that Abba was an honorific title. However, *Tosafot* provide proofs that it was Rav's first name. It is possible that both explanations are correct, and Rashi is explaining why it was not disrespectful to call Rav by his first name. Halakhic commentaries address the question of whether it is permitted to call one's father by his first name if that name is also an honorific title, such as *Abba*, which means father, or *Morenu*, which means our master.

אֲמַר רָבָא: אַף אֲנַן נַמִּי תָּנֵינָא, בַּת שָׁלֹשׁ שָׁנִים וְיוֹם אֶחָד מִתְקַדֶּשֶׁת בְּבִיאָה וְאִם בָּא עָלֶיהָ יָבָם קְנָאָהּ, וְחַיָּיבִין עָלֶיהָ מִשּׁוּם אֵשֶׁת אִישׁ, וּמְטַמְּאָה אֶת בּוֹעֲלָהּ לְטַמֵּא מִשְׁכָּב תַּחְתּוֹן כְּעֶלְיוֹן.

Rava said: We, too, learn in the following *baraita* that there is no legal significance to an act of intercourse with a girl less than three years old: **A girl three years and one day old can be betrothed via sexual intercourse;**[H] **and if** she was a *yevama* and her *yavam* **had intercourse with her, he has acquired her;**[H] **and** a man who has intercourse with her while she is married to someone else **is liable on her account because** of the prohibition of intercourse with **a married woman;**[H] **and** if she experiences a menstrual discharge **she renders ritually impure a man who has intercourse with her,**[H] **so that he renders impure the object upon which he lies like the upper one.**[N]

נְשֵׂאת לְכֹהֵן – אוֹכֶלֶת בִּתְרוּמָה, בָּא עָלֶיהָ אֶחָד מִכׇּל הַפְּסוּלִין – פְּסָלָהּ.

If she is married to a priest she may partake of ***teruma*****.**[H] **If one of** those who render women **unfit** for marrying a priest **had intercourse with her, he has disqualified her**[H] from being able to partake of *teruma*.

בַּת שָׁלֹשׁ שָׁנִים וְיוֹם אֶחָד הוּא דִּמְפַסְּלָה בְּבִיאָה – מְפַסְּלָה בְּחוּפָּה, הָא פְּחוּתָה מִבַּת שָׁלֹשׁ שָׁנִים וְיוֹם אֶחָד, דְּלָא מְפַסְּלָה בְּבִיאָה – לָא מְפַסְּלָה נַמִּי בְּחוּפָּה, שְׁמַע מִינָּהּ.

Rava infers from this *baraita* that **it is a girl three years and one day old who is disqualified via intercourse,** and consequently **she is** also **disqualified via the wedding canopy.** However, a girl who is **less than three years and one day old, who is not disqualified via intercourse, is also not disqualified via the wedding canopy.** The Gemara concludes: Indeed, **learn from this** that it is so.

אָמַר רָמִי בַּר חָמָא: יֵשׁ חוּפָּה לִפְסוּלוֹת – בָּאנוּ לְמַחֲלוֹקֶת רַבִּי מֵאִיר וְרַבִּי אֶלְעָזָר וְרַבִּי שִׁמְעוֹן,

Rami bar Ḥama said: With regard to the question of whether **there is** legal significance **to** a priest entering the **wedding canopy** with women who are **unfit** to marry a priest, **we have arrived at the dispute** cited in the mishna between **Rabbi Meir** on the one hand **and Rabbi Elazar and Rabbi Shimon** on the other.

NOTES

So that he renders impure the object upon which he lies like the upper one – לְטַמֵּא מִשְׁכָּב תַּחְתּוֹן כְּעֶלְיוֹן: The Torah states that if a man has intercourse with a menstruating woman, "her impurity shall be upon him" (Leviticus 15:24). This indicates that he is not merely impure with a first-degree level of impurity, as one who touches a menstruating woman; rather, he becomes a primary source of impurity, similar to the woman herself. Nevertheless, there is a difference between the impurity of a menstruating woman and that of a man who has intercourse with her. If a menstruating woman or a *zav* sits or lies upon objects that are designated for that purpose, even if she does not make direct contact with those objects because there is something else covering them, the objects are rendered a primary source of impurity.

A man who has intercourse with a menstruating woman also renders these items impure, but only at the level of first-degree impurity, similar to the upper cover, i.e., the blanket on top of him, which is impure due to contact. Consequently, these items can render only food and drink impure, but not people or vessels.

HALAKHA

A girl three years and one day old can be betrothed via sexual intercourse – בַּת שָׁלֹשׁ שָׁנִים וְיוֹם אֶחָד מִתְקַדֶּשֶׁת בְּבִיאָה: An act of intercourse with a girl younger than three years and one day is not considered an act of intercourse and therefore, even if it is performed with her father's consent, betrothal cannot be accomplished. However, technically, in the case of a girl who is three years and one day old, betrothal can be accomplished by means of intercourse (Rambam *Sefer Nashim, Hilkhot Ishut* 3:11; *Shulḥan Arukh, Even HaEzer* 37:1).

If her ***yavam*** **had intercourse with her he has acquired her** – בָּא עָלֶיהָ יָבָם קְנָאָהּ: Intercourse with a *yevama* aged less than three years and one day does not accomplish levirate marriage (*Shulḥan Arukh, Even HaEzer* 167:4).

Liable on her account because of the prohibition of intercourse with a married woman – חַיָּיבִין עָלֶיהָ מִשּׁוּם אֵשֶׁת אִישׁ: An adult male who engaged in intercourse with a married minor less than three years and one day old is exempt from punishment for adultery with a married woman (Rambam *Sefer Kedusha, Hilkhot Issurei Bia* 3:2).

She renders ritually impure a man who has intercourse with her – מְטַמְּאָה אֶת בּוֹעֲלָהּ: One who has intercourse with a menstruating woman attains the status of a primary source of impurity, even if she is a minor, provided she is at least three years and one day old. If he sits or lies on an object that is designated for this purpose, the object attains first-degree impurity, even if he did not touch it directly. Therefore, it can render food and drink impure, but not people or vessels (Rambam *Sefer Tahara, Hilkhot Metamei Mishkav UMoshav* 3:1–3).

She may partake of ***teruma*** – אוֹכֶלֶת בִּתְרוּמָה: If a girl at least three years and one day old is married to a priest, she is permitted to partake of *teruma* (Rambam *Sefer Zera'im, Hilkhot Terumot* 6:3).

If one of those who render women unfit had intercourse with her, he has disqualified her – בָּא עָלֶיהָ אֶחָד מִכׇּל הַפְּסוּלִין פְּסָלָהּ: If a man who renders a woman unfit for the priesthood, such as a *ḥalal*, a gentile, a Canaanite slave, or one of her relatives, has intercourse with her when she is at least three years and one day old, she is thereby disqualified from the priesthood (Rambam *Sefer Kedusha, Hilkhot Issurei Bia* 19:1–2; *Shulḥan Arukh, Even HaEzer* 6:9; 7:12).

לְרַבִּי מֵאִיר דְּאָמַר קִדּוּשִׁין פָּסְלִי – חוּפָּה נַמִי פָּסְלָה, לְרַבִּי אֶלְעָזָר וְרַבִּי שִׁמְעוֹן דְּאָמְרִי קִדּוּשִׁין לָא פָּסְלִי – חוּפָּה נַמִי לָא פָּסְלָה.

According to Rabbi Meir, who says that betrothal to a priest **disqualifies** a woman who is unfit to marry him from partaking of *teruma* even if she is the daughter of a priest, entering the **wedding canopy** with a priest **also disqualifies** her. Conversely, **according to Rabbi Elazar and Rabbi Shimon, who say** that **betrothal does not disqualify** her, entering the **wedding canopy also does not disqualify** her.

וּמִמַּאי? דִּלְמָא עַד כָּאן לָא קָאָמַר רַבִּי מֵאִיר הָתָם אֶלָּא בְּקִדּוּשִׁין דְּקָנֵי לָהּ. אֲבָל חוּפָּה דְּלָא קָנָה לָהּ – לָא.

The Gemara refutes this claim: **And from where** do we know that these *tanna'im* would apply their opinions with regard to betrothal to entering the wedding canopy? **Perhaps Rabbi Meir only stated** his opinion **there, with regard to betrothal, which acquires her. However,** in the case of **a wedding canopy, which does not acquire her, no,** she is not disqualified.

אִי נַמִי, עַד כָּאן לָא קָאָמְרִי רַבִּי אֶלְעָזָר וְרַבִּי שִׁמְעוֹן הָתָם – אֶלָּא בְּקִדּוּשִׁין, דְּלָא קְרִיבִי לְבִיאָה, אֲבָל חוּפָּה דִּקְרִיבָא לְבִיאָה – הָכִי נַמִי דְּפָסְלָה.

Alternatively, perhaps **Rabbi Elazar and Rabbi Shimon stated** their opinion **only there, with regard to betrothal, as it is not close to** an act of **sexual intercourse. However,** with regard to entering the **wedding canopy, which is close to** an act of **sexual intercourse,** as it is the place where the bride and groom are secluded together and symbolizes the woman's entrance into her husband's home, it is possible **that it also disqualifies** her from partaking of *teruma*.

אֶלָּא אִי אִיכָּא לְמֵימַר – בִּפְלוּגְתָּא דְּהָנֵי תַּנָּאֵי, דְּתַנְיָא: נִישְּׂאוּ זוֹ וָזוֹ, כְּשֵׁרוֹת וּפְסוּלוֹת, אוֹ שֶׁנִּכְנְסוּ לְחוּפָּה וְלֹא נִבְעֲלוּ – אוֹכְלוֹת מִשֶּׁלּוֹ וְאוֹכְלוֹת בִּתְרוּמָה.

Rather, if it can be said that this issue was already discussed by earlier Sages, it was **in the dispute** between **these** other *tanna'im*, **as it is taught in** a *baraita*: **If they married one another,** i.e., either a woman who is **fit or** a woman who is **unfit** married a priest, **or they entered the wedding canopy and did not** yet **have intercourse** with him, **they** are entitled to **eat of his food and** to **partake of** *teruma*.

נִכְנְסוּ, מִכְּלָל דְּנִישְּׂאוּ – נִישְּׂאוּ מַמָּשׁ?

The Gemara interrupts its presentation of the *baraita* to examine its wording. The fact that the *baraita* mentions a case where **they entered** the wedding canopy but did not yet have intercourse proves **by inference that** the earlier case, where **they married,** is referring to **actual marriage.** However, this is difficult because if they were actually married and had engaged in intercourse, the woman who was unfit to marry a priest is certainly disqualified from partaking of *teruma* due to the prohibited act of intercourse.

אֶלָּא לָאו – כְּגוֹן שֶׁנִּכְנְסוּ לְחוּפָּה וְלֹא נִבְעֲלוּ. וְקָתָנֵי: אוֹכְלוֹת מִשֶּׁלּוֹ וְאוֹכְלוֹת בִּתְרוּמָה.

Rather, is it not that the *baraita* is referring to a single case: **Where** they were married, and **they entered the canopy, and had not had intercourse? And it is taught** in the *baraita* that **they** are entitled to **partake of his** food **and** to **partake of** *teruma*. This indicates that entrance into the wedding canopy does not disqualify a woman who is unfit to marry a priest from eating *teruma*, although the act of intercourse does.

רַבִּי יִשְׁמָעֵאל בְּנוֹ שֶׁל רַבִּי יוֹחָנָן בֶּן בְּרוֹקָה אוֹמֵר: כׇּל שֶׁבִּיאָתָהּ מַאֲכִילָתָהּ – חוּפָּתָהּ מַאֲכִילָתָהּ, וְכׇל שֶׁאֵין בִּיאָתָהּ מַאֲכִילָתָהּ – אֵין חוּפָּתָהּ מַאֲכִילָתָהּ.

The *baraita* continues: Conversely, **Rabbi Yishmael, son of Rabbi Yoḥanan ben Beroka, says:** Any woman **whose** act of **intercourse entitles her to partake of** *teruma*, **her wedding canopy** also **entitles her to partake of** *teruma*; **and any** woman **whose** act of **intercourse does not entitle her to partake of** *teruma*, **her wedding canopy** also **does not entitle her to partake of** *teruma*. Consequently, it appears that the *tanna'im* cited in this *baraita* disagree over the very question of whether the entry of a priest and a woman unfit to marry him into the wedding canopy has legal significance.

מִמַּאי? דִּלְמָא רַבִּי יִשְׁמָעֵאל בְּנוֹ שֶׁל רַבִּי יוֹחָנָן בֶּן בְּרוֹקָה כְּרַבִּי מֵאִיר סְבִירָא לֵיהּ, דְּאָמַר: קִדּוּשִׁין לָא אָכְלָה.

The Gemara refutes this claim: **From where** do we know that this is correct? **Perhaps Rabbi Yishmael, son of Rabbi Yoḥanan ben Beroka, holds in accordance with** the opinion of **Rabbi Meir, who said** that in the case of the **betrothal** of a woman unfit for a priest **she may not partake of** *teruma*?

NOTES

Amen that I did not go astray while betrothed – אָמֵן שֶׁלֹּא שָׂטִיתִי אֲרוּסָה: These *halakhot* are apparently derived from the repetitive usage of the term amen in the phrase (Numbers 5:22): "And the woman shall say: Amen, amen" (see Rashi, Rivan, and *Tosafot*).

הַאי כָּל שֶׁאֵין בִּיאָתָהּ מַאֲכִילָתָהּ אֵין חוּפָּתָהּ מַאֲכִילָתָהּ? כָּל שֶׁאֵין בִּיאָתָהּ מַאֲכִילָתָהּ אֵין כַּסְפָּהּ מַאֲכִילָתָהּ מִיבָּעֵי לֵיהּ! דִּלְמָא, אַיְּידֵי דַּאֲמַר תַּנָּא קַמָּא חוּפָּה – אֲמַר אִיהוּ נַמִי חוּפָּה.

The Gemara expresses surprise: According to this suggestion, **this** expression in the *baraita* is difficult: **Any** woman **whose** act of **intercourse does not entitle her to partake** of *teruma*, **her wedding canopy** also **does not entitle her to partake** of *teruma*. **It should have said: Any** woman **whose** act of **intercourse does not entitle her to partake** of *teruma*, **her** betrothal **money** also **does not entitle her to partake** of *teruma*, as it was the betrothal that disqualified her. The Gemara counters this argument: **Perhaps** it can be suggested that **since** the **first** *tanna* **said** his ruling with regard to **a wedding canopy,** Rabbi Yishmael, son of Rabbi Yoḥanan ben Beroka, **also said** his ruling with regard to **a wedding canopy,** even though he holds that she was already disqualified from the time of her betrothal.

אֲמַר רַב עַמְרָם: הָא מִילְּתָא אֲמַר לָן רַב שֵׁשֶׁת, וְאַנְהֲרִינְהוּ לְעַיְינִין מִמַּתְנִיתִין: יֵשׁ חוּפָּה לִפְסוּלוֹת, וְתַנָּא תּוּנָא: ״אָמֵן שֶׁלֹּא שָׂטִיתִי אֲרוּסָה, וּנְשׂוּאָה, שׁוֹמֶרֶת יָבָם, וּכְנוּסָה״.

§ **Rav Amram said: This matter was said** to us by **Rav Sheshet, and he illuminated our eyes from the mishna,** i.e., he demonstrated that the mishna serves as the basis for his opinion. Rav Sheshet's statement was as follows: **There is** significance **to** a priest entering the **wedding canopy** with women who are **unfit** to marry a priest. **And the** *tanna* of the mishna also **taught** this *halakha* with regard to a *sota* (*Sota* 18a–b): When a *sota* is brought to the Temple to drink the bitter waters, she affirms the oath imposed on her by a priest that she has not committed adultery. The mishna explains that when she says **amen,** it is as though she herself states **that: I did not go astray** while **betrothed,**[NH] **or married,** or as **a widow waiting for her** ***yavam*****,** **or** as a fully **married** woman.

הַאי אֲרוּסָה הֵיכִי דָּמֵי? אִילֵימָא דְּקַנֵּי לָהּ כְּשֶׁהִיא אֲרוּסָה, וְקָא מַשְׁקֶה לָהּ כְּשֶׁהִיא אֲרוּסָה – אֲרוּסָה בַּת מִשְׁתְּיָא הִיא? וְהָא תְּנַן: אֲרוּסָה וְשׁוֹמֶרֶת יָבָם לֹא שׁוֹתוֹת וְלֹא נוֹטְלוֹת כְּתוּבָּה!

The Gemara inquires: **This** case of **a betrothed** woman, **what are the circumstances? If we say that he was jealous of her** and warned her not to seclude herself with a particular man **when she was betrothed, and he** also **causes her to drink** the waters **when she is betrothed,** is **a betrothed** woman **fit to drink** the waters of a *sota*? **Didn't we learn** in a mishna (*Sota* 23b): **A betrothed** woman **and a widow waiting for her** ***yavam*** **do not drink,**[H] as the *halakha* of the *sota* waters applies only to married women; **and they do not collect their marriage contract** if they secluded themselves after being warned, as they have acted in a licentious fashion?

אֶלָּא דְּקַנֵּי לָהּ כְּשֶׁהִיא אֲרוּסָה, וְאִיסְתַּתְּרָה, וְקָמַשְׁקֶה לָהּ כְּשֶׁהִיא נְשׂוּאָה – מִי בָּדְקִי לָהּ מַיָּא? וְהָתַנְיָא: ״וְנִקָּה הָאִישׁ מֵעָוֹן״ בִּזְמַן שֶׁהָאִישׁ מְנוּקֶּה מֵעָוֹן הַמַּיִם בּוֹדְקִין אֶת אִשְׁתּוֹ, אֵין הָאִישׁ מְנוּקֶּה מֵעָוֹן – אֵין הַמַּיִם בּוֹדְקִין אֶת אִשְׁתּוֹ!

Rather, the case in the first mishna cited above is **that he was jealous of her** and warned her not to seclude herself with a particular man **when she was betrothed, and she secluded herself** with that man, **and** her husband **causes her to drink when she is** already **married.** However, in that case **do the waters examine her? Isn't it taught** in a *baraita* with regard to the verse: **"And the man shall be clear from iniquity,** and that woman shall bear her iniquity" (Numbers 5:31), that **when the man is clear of iniquity**[H] **the waters examine his wife,** but if **the man is not clear of iniquity the waters do not examine his wife?** By secluding herself with the other man when she was betrothed, the woman rendered herself forbidden to her husband. If he then married her, he cannot be described as clear of iniquity, and therefore the *sota* waters are ineffective.

HALAKHA

Amen that I did not go astray while betrothed, etc. – אָמֵן שֶׁלֹּא שָׂטִיתִי אֲרוּסָה וכו׳: When a husband makes his wife drink the waters of a *sota*, he can extend her oath beyond the man he originally specified in his warning. Therefore, she must swear that she did not have intercourse with anyone other than her husband, including during the period of her betrothal. However, she may not be forced to swear that she was faithful while waiting for her *yavam* (Rambam *Sefer Nashim*, *Hilkhot Sota* 4:17).

A betrothed woman and a widow waiting for her ***yavam*** **do not drink, etc. – אֲרוּסָה וְשׁוֹמֶרֶת יָבָם לֹא שׁוֹתוֹת וכו׳:** A betrothed woman and a woman awaiting levirate marriage do not drink the bitter waters, even if they were warned about a particular man and they secluded themselves with him. Even if they want to drink the waters and their husbands also want them to, they may not do so. Rather, their husbands must divorce them, and they do not collect their marriage contract (Rambam *Sefer Nashim*, *Hilkhot Sota* 2:2).

When the man is clear of iniquity – בִּזְמַן שֶׁהָאִישׁ מְנוּקֶּה מֵעָוֹן: The waters examine the woman only if her husband is clear of iniquity. If he has engaged in relations prohibited by rabbinic law, the waters are ineffective (Rambam *Sefer Nashim*, *Hilkhot Sota* 2:8, 3:17).

אֶלָּא דְּקַנֵּי לָהּ כְּשֶׁהִיא אֲרוּסָה, וְאִיסְתַּתְּרָה וְנִכְנְסָה לְחוּפָּה וְלֹא נִבְעֲלָה, וּשְׁמַע מִינַּהּ: יֵשׁ חוּפָּה לִפְסוּלוֹת.

Rather, it must be **that he was jealous of her when she was betrothed, and she secluded herself** with the other man anyway, **and she had entered the wedding canopy but did not** yet **have intercourse** with her husband when he brought her to the priest. Consequently, she is made to drink the *sota* waters as a married woman, and her husband has not committed a transgression, as he has not had intercourse with her. **Learn from this** that **there is** significance **to** a priest entering the **wedding canopy** with women who are **unfit** to marry a priest, as demonstrated by the fact that the *sota* waters will examine her in these circumstances.

אֲמַר רָבָא: וְתִסְבְּרָא דְּהָא מְתָרַצְתָּא הִיא? וְהָא כִּי אֲתָא רַבִּי אַחָא בַּר חֲנִינָא מִדָּרוֹמָא, אֲתָא וְאַיְיתֵי מַתְנִיתָא בִּידֵיהּ: ״מִבַּלְעֲדֵי אִישֵׁךְ״ מִי שֶׁקָּדְמָה שְׁכִיבַת בַּעַל לְבוֹעֵל, וְלֹא שֶׁקָּדְמָה שְׁכִיבַת בּוֹעֵל לְבַעַל.

Rava said: Do you hold that this *baraita* **is** sufficiently **accurate** to rely upon? **But when Rabbi Aḥa bar Ḥanina came from the South, he came with** this ***baraita*** **in hand:** The verse states with regard to the oath of the *sota*: "And some man has lain with you **besides your husband"** (Numbers 5:20), which indicates that it applies only **when the cohabitation of the husband preceded that of the adulterer, but not when the cohabitation of the adulterer preceded**[H] **that of the husband.** Consequently, in the case under discussion, drinking the *sota* waters would not be effective.

אֲמַר רָמִי בַּר חָמָא: מַשְׁכַּחַתְּ לָהּ כְּגוֹן שֶׁבָּא עָלֶיהָ אֲרוּסָהּ בְּבֵית אָבִיהָ.

Rami bar Ḥama said: You find it in a case **such as** where **her betrothed had intercourse with her** licentiously when she was a betrothed woman **in her father's house.** Since the act of intercourse was committed licentiously rather than for the purpose of consummating the marriage, the woman is still considered betrothed. Subsequently, her betrothed warned her not to seclude herself with a particular man, and she disobeyed. Then, they entered the wedding canopy together, despite the fact that they are forbidden to one another. Once they entered the wedding canopy, the woman can be made to drink the bitter waters. This proves that there is significance to entering the wedding canopy with a woman that is unfit for one to marry.

דִּכְוָותָהּ גַּבֵּי שׁוֹמֶרֶת יָבָם – שֶׁבָּא עָלֶיהָ יָבָם בְּבֵית חָמִיהָ,

The Gemara asks: If so, in **the corresponding** case **with regard to a widow waiting for** her ***yavam***, in **which the** ***yavam*** **had** licentious **intercourse with her in her father-in-law's house,**

Perek **VI**
Daf **58** Amud **b**

שׁוֹמֶרֶת יָבָם קָרֵית לָהּ?! אִשְׁתּוֹ מַעַלְיָא הִיא! דְּהָא אָמַר רַב: קָנָה לַכֹּל. כִּשְׁמוּאֵל דְּאָמַר: לֹא קָנָה אֶלָּא לַדְּבָרִים הָאֲמוּרִים בַּפָּרָשָׁה.

do you call her a widow waiting for her ***yavam***? Once they have engaged in intercourse, **she is his proper wife, as Rav said** that one who has intercourse with his *yevama*, even without intending to thereby perform levirate marriage, **has acquired her for all** matters. The Gemara responds: This is in accordance **with the** opinion of **Shmuel, who said** that he **has acquired her only with regard to the matters stated in the chapter** of levirate marriage, but not with regard to other matters, and therefore she is not considered his wife with regard to the *halakhot* of *sota*.

מִידֵּי הוּא טַעְמָא – אֶלָּא לְרַב, הָא אֲמַר רַב קָנָה לַכֹּל! הָכָא בְּמַאי עָסְקִינַן, כְּגוֹן דַּעֲבַד בָּהּ מַאֲמָר, וּבֵית שַׁמַּאי הִיא, דְּאָמְרִי: מַאֲמָר קוֹנֶה קִנְיָן גָּמוּר.

The Gemara responds: **The only reason** this proof was presented is to support the opinion of **Rav,** who is the one who holds that there is legal significance to a priest entering the wedding canopy with a woman who is unfit to marry him. **Didn't Rav say he has acquired her for all** matters? The Gemara answers: **With what are we dealing here? For example,** a case where the *yavam* **performed levirate betrothal with her** and afterward had intercourse with her for the sake of promiscuity. **And this is** in accordance with the opinion of **Beit Shammai, who say: Levirate betrothal acquires** a *yevama* in **a full-fledged** manner and removes the levirate bond. Therefore, when they have intercourse, they do not become fully married.

HALAKHA

The cohabitation of the adulterer preceded – שֶׁקָּדְמָה שְׁכִיבַת בּוֹעֵל: If a woman who was warned by her husband secluded herself with the man in question before she had intercourse with her husband, she does not drink the *sota* waters. Her husband divorces her and she does not collect her marriage contract, as stated in the *baraita* cited by Rav Aḥa bar Ḥanina (Rambam *Sefer Nashim*, *Hilkhot Sota* 2:5).

אִי הָכִי, הַיְינוּ אֲרוּסָה! וּלְטַעֲמִיךְ, נְשׂוּאָה וּכְנוּסָה לָאו חֲדָא מִילְּתָא הִיא? אֶלָּא: נְשׂוּאָה – דִּידֵיהּ, וּכְנוּסָה – דְּחַבְרֵיהּ. הָכָא נַמִי: אֲרוּסָה – דִּידֵיהּ, וְשׁוֹמֶרֶת יָבָם – דְּחַבְרֵיהּ.

The Gemara raises a difficulty: **If so,** the case of the *yevama* who was betrothed **is the same as** the case of **a betrothed** woman. What is the difference between the two cases? The Gemara responds: **And according to your reasoning,** are the examples in the mishna of a **married** woman **and a fully married** woman **not a single matter? Rather,** the mishna must be referring to two very similar cases, with the following difference: **A married** woman means **his own** wife **and** a fully **married** woman is referring **to that of his fellow,** i.e., his brother's wife who became his wife through levirate marriage. **Here too,** the case of **a betrothed** woman is referring to **his own** wife **and** the case of **a widow waiting for her *yavam*** is **that of his fellow,** i.e., his *yevama*, who is now betrothed to him.

רַב פַּפָּא אָמַר: הַאי תַּנָּא הוּא, דְּתַנְיָא: אֵין מְקַנִּין לָהּ לַאֲרוּסָה לְהַשְׁקוֹתָהּ כְּשֶׁהִיא אֲרוּסָה, אֲבָל מְקַנִּין אוֹתָהּ לְהַשְׁקוֹתָהּ כְּשֶׁהִיא נְשׂוּאָה.

Rav Pappa said: Rava's question can be resolved in a manner unrelated to the question about a priest entering the wedding canopy with a woman unfit for him. The *baraita* he cited **is** in accordance with **this *tanna*,** who does not require the man to be clear of iniquity, **as it is taught in a *baraita*: One cannot be jealous over a betrothed** woman and warn her not to seclude herself with a particular man in order **to cause her to drink** the *sota* waters **when she is betrothed, but one can be jealous over her to cause her to drink** the *sota* waters **when she is married,** even if she secluded herself with the man when she was still betrothed.

רַב נַחְמָן בַּר יִצְחָק אָמַר: עַל יְדֵי גִלְגּוּל.

Rav Naḥman bar Yitzḥak said: The question never arises at all, as the oath is formulated **by means of extension.**[NH] The woman cannot be forced to drink the *sota* waters for events that took place while she was betrothed. However, if she is obligated to drink due to events that took place when she was married, the oath may be extended to include any possible acts of infidelity when she was betrothed.

שָׁלַח רַב חֲנִינָא מִשְּׁמֵיהּ דְּרַבִּי יוֹחָנָן: הָעוֹשֶׂה מַאֲמָר בִּיבִמְתּוֹ, [וְיֵשׁ לוֹ אָח], אֲפִילּוּ הוּא כֹּהֵן וְהִיא כֹּהֶנֶת – פְּסָלָהּ מִן הַתְּרוּמָה.

§ **Rav Ḥanina sent in the name of Rabbi Yoḥanan: One who performs levirate betrothal with his *yevama* and he has a brother, even if he is a priest and she is** the daughter of **a priest, he has disqualified her from** partaking of **teruma.** By Torah law, the other brother may still have intercourse with her and thereby perform levirate marriage, but by rabbinic law only the brother who betrothed her may perform levirate marriage. Due to the fact that she is considered to be waiting for levirate marriage even vis-à-vis the brother who is rabbinically prohibited from marrying her, she is classified as a woman who is waiting for an invalid act of intercourse. Consequently, she may not partake of *teruma* until the consummation of the levirate marriage.

לְמַאן? אִילֵימָא לְרַבִּי מֵאִיר, אֵימַר דְּאָמַר רַבִּי מֵאִיר מִשְׁתַּמֶּרֶת לְבִיאָה פְּסוּלָה לָא אָכְלָה – מִדְּאוֹרַיְיתָא, דְּרַבָּנַן מִי אָמַר? וְאֶלָּא לְרַבִּי אֶלְעָזָר וְרַבִּי שִׁמְעוֹן, הָשְׁתָּא מִשְׁתַּמֶּרֶת לְבִיאָה פְּסוּלָה דְּאוֹרַיְיתָא אָכְלָה, דְּרַבָּנַן מִיבַּעְיָא?

The Gemara asks: **According to whom** did Rabbi Yoḥanan make this statement? **If we say** it is **in accordance with** the opinion of **Rabbi Meir, say that Rabbi Meir said** that a woman who is **reserved for an invalid** act of **intercourse may not eat** *teruma* when the act of intercourse is prohibited **by Torah** law. However, if the act of intercourse is prohibited **by rabbinic** law, **did** Rabbi Meir actually **say** that the woman is disqualified from eating *teruma*? **Rather,** if we say it is **in accordance with** the opinions of **Rabbi Elazar and Rabbi Shimon, now** that they hold that even a woman who is **reserved for intercourse prohibited by Torah** law **may partake of** *teruma*, **is it necessary** to state that she may partake of *teruma* if she is reserved for intercourse prohibited **by rabbinic** law?

אֶלָּא כִּי אֲתָא רָבִין אֲמַר: עָשָׂה בָּהּ מַאֲמָר בִּיבִמְתּוֹ – דִּבְרֵי הַכֹּל אָכְלָה, יֵשׁ לוֹ אָח חָלָל – דִּבְרֵי הַכֹּל אֵינָהּ אוֹכֶלֶת. לֹא נֶחְלְקוּ אֶלָּא שֶׁנָּתַן לָהּ גֵּט, רַבִּי יוֹחָנָן אָמַר: אוֹכֶלֶת, רֵישׁ לָקִישׁ אָמַר: אֵינָהּ אוֹכֶלֶת.

Rather, when Ravin came from Eretz Yisrael **he said** an accurate version of Rabbi Yoḥanan's statement: If a *yavam* who **performed levirate betrothal with his *yevama*** has a brother, **all agree** that the *yevama* **may partake** of *teruma*. If **he has a brother** who is **a *ḥalal*,**[NH] e.g., his mother was a divorcée and therefore unfit to marry his father, who was a priest, **all agree** that the *yevama* **may not partake** of *teruma*, as she is considered reserved for an invalid act of intercourse. **They disagreed only** in a case when **he gave her a bill of divorce.**[NH] **Rabbi Yoḥanan said she may partake of** *teruma*, as she is considered to have returned to her father's house, while **Reish Lakish said** that **she may not partake of** *teruma*.

NOTES

By means of extension – עַל יְדֵי גִלְגּוּל: Rashi notes that this *halakha* is the source of the Torah law of the extension of oaths. This means that if an individual is required to take an oath in court due to a claim made by the opposing party, the latter can force him to extend his oath to include cases for which he would not otherwise have been liable to take an oath.

If he has a brother who is a *ḥalal* – יֵשׁ לוֹ אָח חָלָל וכו׳: The relationship between the woman and the *ḥalal* is not invalid in the normal sense of the term, as it is entirely permitted for them to marry. Nevertheless, since a *ḥalal* is considered like a regular Israelite, if she marries him she is disqualified from partaking of her father's *teruma* (Ritva).

He gave her a bill of divorce – שֶׁנָּתַן לָהּ גֵּט: Rashi explains that the *yavam* gave the *yevama* a bill of divorce, which makes her unfit to marry him by rabbinic law. Nevertheless, since by Torah law the levirate bond still exists, she is considered reserved for a prohibited act of intercourse. Rabbeinu Ḥananel explains differently, that he gave her a bill of divorce and subsequently performed levirate betrothal with her. In that case, he is prohibited from having intercourse with her, and yet she is considered to be reserved for him. This fits in well with the continuation of the discussion, as a priest who divorced his wife and betrothed her once again certainly does not entitle her to partake of *teruma* (see Rashba).

HALAKHA

By means of extension – עַל יְדֵי גִלְגּוּל: Although a betrothed woman who secluded herself with another man does not drink the *sota* waters or take an oath, if she becomes liable to do so for having secluded herself after marriage, she must extend her oath and confirm that she did not commit adultery while she was betrothed, as stated by Rav Naḥman bar Yitzḥak (Rambam *Sefer Nashim*, *Hilkhot Sota* 4:17).

One of the *yevamin* was a *ḥalal* – אֶחָד הַיְּבָמִים שֶׁהָיָה חָלָל: If the daughter of a priest was married to a priest who died without children, and one of his brothers was a *ḥalal*, she may not eat *teruma* due to the levirate bond she has with the *ḥalal*. Even if one of the other brothers performed levirate betrothal with her, she may not partake of *teruma* until after she is married to him (Rambam *Sefer Zera'im*, *Hilkhot Terumot* 7:22).

He gave her a bill of divorce – נָתַן לָהּ גֵּט: If a priest gave a bill of divorce to his *yevama* who is the daughter of a priest, although she is forbidden to him and yet bound to him by the levirate bond, as she has not undergone *ḥalitza*, she is nevertheless permitted to partake of *teruma*. This is because relations between them are prohibited by rabbinic law but not Torah law. The *halakha* is in accordance with the opinion of Rabbi Yoḥanan as opposed to that of Reish Lakish (Rambam *Sefer Zera'im*, *Hilkhot Terumot* 7:23).

רַבִּי יוֹחָנָן אָמַר: אוֹכֶלֶת, אֲפִילּוּ לְרַבִּי מֵאִיר דְּאָמַר אֵינָהּ אוֹכֶלֶת – הָנֵי מִילֵּי מִשְׁתַּמֶּרֶת לְבִיאָה פְּסוּלָה דְּאוֹרָיְיתָא, אֲבָל דְּרַבָּנַן – אָכְלָה.

The Gemara analyzes the two opinions: **Rabbi Yoḥanan said she may eat** *teruma* because **even according to Rabbi Meir, who said** in the mishna that **she may not partake of** *teruma*, **this applies only** when she is **waiting for intercourse** that is **invalid by Torah** law, **but** if the intercourse is prohibited **by rabbinic** law, **she may partake** of *teruma*. In this case, since they have not yet performed *ḥalitza*, the levirate bond still applies by Torah law, but they are prohibited by rabbinic law from consummating the levirate marriage.

וְרֵישׁ לָקִישׁ אָמַר: אֵינָהּ אוֹכֶלֶת, אֲפִילּוּ לְרַבִּי אֶלְעָזָר וְרַבִּי שִׁמְעוֹן דְּאָמְרִי אוֹכֶלֶת – הָנֵי מִילֵּי דְּיֵשׁ לוֹ לְהַאֲכִיל בְּמָקוֹם אַחֵר, אֲבָל הָכָא, כֵּיוָן דְּאֵין לוֹ לְהַאֲכִיל בְּמָקוֹם אַחֵר – לָא.

And Reish Lakish said: She may not partake of *teruma* **because even according to Rabbi Elazar and Rabbi Shimon, who say** in the mishna that **she may partake** of *teruma*, **this applies only** to a case of betrothal, as a priest **can entitle** a woman **to partake** of *teruma* **in another case** via betrothal. **But here,** where he gave her a bill of divorce, **since he cannot entitle** a woman **to partake** of *teruma* **in** any **other case** by giving her a bill of divorce, **no.**

וְכִי תֵּימָא: הָכָא נַמִי יֵשׁ לוֹ לְהַאֲכִילָהּ בְּחוֹזֶרֶת – חוֹזֶרֶת פְּסָקָה מִינֵּיהּ, וּקְרוֹבָה לְבֵי נָשָׁא, אֲבָל הָא אֲגִידָא בֵּיהּ.

And lest you say here too, in the case of a bill of divorce, **he can entitle her to partake of** *teruma* **when she returns** to her father's house, this case is different for the following reason: A woman **who returns** to her father's house **has been severed from** her husband **and she is close to her** father's **house** [***bei nasha***],[N] and therefore she may once again partake of *teruma* on her father's account. **However, this** *yevama* who has received a bill of divorce **is** still **bound to** her *yavam* until they perform *ḥalitza*, and she is therefore disqualified from eating *teruma*.

"נִתְאַרְמְלוּ אוֹ נִתְגָּרְשׁוּ" וכו׳. בְּעָא מִינֵּיהּ רַבִּי חִיָּיא בַּר יוֹסֵף מִשְּׁמוּאֵל: כֹּהֵן גָּדוֹל שֶׁקִּידֵּשׁ אֶת הַקְּטַנָּה וּבָגְרָה תַּחְתָּיו,

§ It was taught in the mishna that in the case of women who married priests despite the fact that they were unfit to do so, if **they were widowed or divorced** from that marriage, they are disqualified from eating *teruma*, but if they were widowed or divorced while they were only betrothed, they are fit to partake of *teruma*. **Rabbi Ḥiyya bar Yosef raised a dilemma before Shmuel:** In the case of **a High Priest who betrothed a minor and she matured under him,** i.e., while betrothed to him,

NOTES

Her father's house [*bei nasha*] – **בֵּי נָשָׁא**: Meaning literally a woman's house, this term is used in the general sense of a woman's family's house. Some explained, apparently in a homiletical sense, that the term comes from the from the root *n-sh-h*, meaning forget, as a woman forgets her father's house upon marriage.

מַהוּ? בָּתַר נִישּׂוּאִין אָזְלִינַן, אוֹ בָּתַר אֵירוּסִין אָזְלִינַן?

what is the *halakha*? The Gemara clarifies the dilemma: **Do we follow** the time of **marriage,**[N] at which point she was unfit for him according to most *tanna'im*, who hold that a High Priest may not marry a grown woman, as she is no longer called "a wife in her virginity" (Leviticus 21:13)? **Or do we follow** the time of **betrothal,**[B] at which point she was of suitable age?

אָמַר לֵיהּ: תְּנֵיתוּהָ, נִתְאַרְמְלוּ אוֹ נִתְגָּרְשׁוּ, מִן הַנִּשּׂוּאִין – פְּסוּלוֹת, מִן הָאֵירוּסִין – כְּשֵׁרוֹת.

Shmuel **said to him: You learned it** in the mishna: If **they were widowed or divorced from marriage, they are disqualified** from partaking of *teruma*, but if they were widowed or divorced **from betrothal, they are fit** to partake of *teruma*. This indicates that disqualifications from the privileges of priesthood are determined based upon marriage rather than betrothal.

NOTES

What is the ***halakha*****? Do we follow the time of marriage, etc.** – **מַהוּ? בָּתַר נִשּׂוּאִין וכו׳**: According to Rashi and others, Shmuel's initial understanding of Rabbi Ḥiyya bar Yosef's question was the same as the Gemara's final interpretation: Is a High Priest permitted to marry a young woman who matured while she was betrothed to him? Others question this opinion based upon the continuation of the discussion recorded in the Gemara (see *Tosafot*). They explain that Shmuel initially thought that the question was whether the woman is considered to be designated for an invalid act of relations, in which case she would be prohibited from partaking of her father's *teruma* if she is the daughter of a priest (Ritva). The Rashba explains that the question was whether she should be permanently disqualified from the priesthood as a *ḥalala* if this High Priest died (Rashba).

BACKGROUND

Betrothal and marriage – **אֵירוּסִין וְנִישּׂוּאִין**: A Jewish wedding is divided into two distinct parts. Betrothal is the first stage of the marriage process. The bond created by betrothal is so strong that, after betrothal, a woman requires a divorce before she can marry another man. Similarly, sexual relations with other men are considered adulterous and are punishable by death. At this stage, the betrothed couple may not yet live together as husband and wife, and most of the couple's mutual obligations do not yet apply.

The second stage of the marriage occurs when the bride and groom come under the bridal canopy, and it immediately confers both the privileges and the responsibilities associated with marriage upon the newlywed couple. After marriage, if one spouse dies, all the *halakhot* of mourning for a close blood relation apply to the surviving spouse. If the wife of a priest dies, he is permitted to make himself ritually impure to bury her. All the monetary rights and obligations applying to married couples take effect after marriage. Today, betrothal and marriage are both performed in a single ceremony, but in talmudic times there was usually a year-long gap between the two.

אָמַר לֵיהּ: לְשַׁוּוֹיַהּ חֲלָלָה – לָא קָמִיבַּעְיָא לִי דְּבִיאָה הִיא דִּמְשַׁוְּיָא חֲלָלָה. כִּי קָמִיבַּעְיָא לִי "וְהוּא אִשָּׁה בִבְתוּלֶיהָ יִקָּח" מַאי? קִיחָה דְּקִדּוּשִׁין בָּעֵינַן, אוֹ קִיחָה דְּנִישּׂוּאִין בָּעֵינַן?

Rabbi Ḥiyya bar Yosef **said to** Shmuel: With regard to **causing her** to become a ***ḥalala*** **I did not raise a dilemma,** as it is clear **that it is intercourse that causes her** to become a ***ḥalala***. **When I raised a dilemma,** it was with regard to the verse pertaining to a High Priest: **"And he shall take a wife in her virginity"** (Leviticus 21:13). **What** does "take" mean in this verse? **Do we require** that only **the taking of betrothal** must occur when she is in her virginity, i.e., when she is a minor or a young woman, **or** perhaps **we require** even **the taking of marriage** to be performed when she is a minor or young woman?

אָמַר לֵיהּ, הָא נַמִי תְּנֵיתוּהָ: אֵירַס אֶת הָאַלְמָנָה וְנִתְמַנָּה לִהְיוֹת כֹּהֵן גָּדוֹל – יִכְנוֹס. שָׁאנֵי הָתָם, דִּכְתִיב "יִקַּח אִשָּׁה".

Shmuel **said to him: This, too, you learned** in a mishna (61a): If **he betrothed a widow and was** subsequently **appointed to be High Priest,**[H] **he may marry** her, despite the fact that a High Priest is prohibited from marrying a widow. This indicates that her permissibility to him is determined according to the time of the betrothal rather than the time of marriage. The Gemara refutes this proof: **There it is different, as it is written: "He shall take for a wife"** (Leviticus 21:14). The superfluous expression "for a wife" indicates that he is permitted to marry the widow in this case.

הָכָא נַמִי כְּתִיב "אִשָּׁה". אַחַת וְלֹא שְׁתַּיִם.

The Gemara objects: **Here, too,** with regard to a woman who matured after betrothal, **it is written:** "And he shall take **a wife** in her virginity," and this should indicate that he may marry the grown woman in this case. The Gemara answers that the term "wife" allows for the inclusion of **one** case **but not two.**[N] Consequently, since a High Priest may marry a widow he had betrothed before he was appointed High Priest, it cannot also be derived that he may marry a grown woman that he had betrothed before she matured.

וּמָה רָאִיתָ? הָא אִישְׁתַּנֵּי גּוּפָהּ, וְהָא לָא אִישְׁתַּנֵּי גּוּפָהּ.

The Gemara asks: **And what did you see**[N] that led you to include the case of a widow and exclude that of a grown woman? The Gemara answers: In **this** case, of the grown woman, **her body has changed,**[NH] and therefore she is forbidden to him even though she was betrothed before she matured. In **that** case, of the widow, **her body has not changed.** It is the priest's personal status that has changed, and therefore she remains permitted.

מתני׳ כֹּהֵן גָּדוֹל לֹא יִשָּׂא אַלְמָנָה, בֵּין אַלְמָנָה מִן הָאֵירוּסִין בֵּין אַלְמָנָה מִן הַנִּישּׂוּאִין. וְלֹא יִשָּׂא אֶת הַבּוֹגֶרֶת, רַבִּי אֶלְעָזָר וְרַבִּי שִׁמְעוֹן מַכְשִׁירִין בְּבוֹגֶרֶת. [וְלֹא יִשָּׂא אֶת מוּכַּת עֵץ].

MISHNA **A High Priest may not marry a widow,**[H] **whether** she is **a widow from betrothal or a widow from marriage. And he may not marry a grown woman.**[H] He may marry only a minor or a young woman. **Rabbi Elazar and Rabbi Shimon declare a grown woman fit** to marry a High Priest. **And he may not marry a woman whose hymen was torn accidentally.**[H]

גמ׳ תָּנוּ רַבָּנַן: "אַלְמָנָה לֹא יִקָּח", בֵּין אַלְמָנָה מִן הָאֵירוּסִין, בֵּין אַלְמָנָה מִן הַנִּישּׂוּאִין. פְּשִׁיטָא! מַהוּ דְּתֵימָא: לֵילַף אַלְמָנָה אַלְמָנָה מִתָּמָר, מָה לְהַלָּן – מִן הַנִּישּׂוּאִין, אַף כָּאן – מִן הַנִּישּׂוּאִין, קָא מַשְׁמַע לַן.

GEMARA **The Sages taught:** The verse states with regard to a High Priest: **"A widow…he shall not take"** (Leviticus 21:14), which prohibits him from marrying any widow, **whether** she is **a widow from betrothal or a widow from marriage.** The Gemara is surprised by this statement: This is **obvious,** as the verse is referring to a widow without further specification. The Gemara answers: It is necessary; **lest you say that one should derive** a verbal analogy between the words **"widow"** and **"widow,"** based upon the usage of that term in a verse with regard to **Tamar,** Judah's daughter-in-law (Genesis 38:11), as follows: **Just as there,** Tamar was a widow **from marriage, so too here** the verse is referring only to a widow **from marriage.** The *tanna* therefore **teaches us** that this is not the case.

וְאֵימָא הָכִי נַמִי! דּוּמְיָא דִּגְרוּשָׁה, מָה גְּרוּשָׁה בֵּין מִן הַנִּישּׂוּאִין בֵּין מִן הָאֵירוּסִין, אַף אַלְמָנָה בֵּין מִן הָאֵירוּסִין בֵּין מִן הַנִּישּׂוּאִין.

The Gemara asks: **And say that it is indeed so,** that the suggested verbal analogy is correct. The Gemara answers: It is **similar to the** case of **a divorcée:**[N] **Just as a divorcée** is forbidden to a priest **whether** she was divorced **from marriage or from betrothal, so too a widow** is forbidden to a High Priest **whether** she is a widow **from marriage or from betrothal.**

HALAKHA

He betrothed a widow and was subsequently appointed to be High Priest – אֵירַס אֶת הָאַלְמָנָה וְנִתְמַנָּה לִהְיוֹת כֹּהֵן גָּדוֹל: If a priest was appointed High Priest after he had betrothed a widow he is permitted to marry her (Rambam *Sefer Kedusha, Hilkhot Issurei Bia* 17:12).

Her body has changed – אִישְׁתַּנֵּי גּוּפָהּ: If a High Priest betrothed a minor and she matured before their marriage he may not marry her *ab initio*. However, if he did marry her, he is not forced to divorce her. This is because a High Priest is not forced to divorce his wife even if she was a grown woman when he betrothed her (Rambam *Sefer Kedusha, Hilkhot Issurei Bia* 17:17 and *Maggid Mishne* there).

A High Priest may not marry a widow – כֹּהֵן גָּדוֹל לֹא יִשָּׂא אַלְמָנָה: A High Priest may not marry a widow, whether she was widowed from betrothal or marriage (Rambam *Sefer Kedusha, Hilkhot Issurei Bia* 17:1, 11).

He may not marry a grown woman – לֹא יִשָּׂא אֶת הַבּוֹגֶרֶת: It is a mitzva for a High Priest to marry a young woman who is a virgin. He is prohibited from marrying a grown woman (Rambam *Sefer Kedusha, Hilkhot Issurei Bia* 17:13).

He may not marry a woman whose hymen was torn accidentally – לֹא יִשָּׂא אֶת מוּכַּת עֵץ: A High Priest may not marry a woman whose hymen was torn accidentally (Rambam *Sefer Kedusha, Hilkhot Issurei Bia* 17:14).

NOTES

A wife in one case but not two – אִשָּׁה אַחַת וְלֹא שְׁתַּיִם: In context, the simple meaning of this statement, as explained by Rashi and other commentaries, is that since there is only one superfluous usage of the word "wife" only one case can be permitted on the basis of this derivation. The Rambam however, understands the Gemara's statement literally, as reading: One wife and not two, and consequently rules that it is prohibited for a High Priest to marry two women (see *Maggid Mishne* and *Yam shel Shlomo*). The Ra'avad disagrees and offers proofs to the contrary, including the fact that Jehoiada the High Priest was righteous and had two wives (see II Chronicles 24:3).

And what did you see – וּמָה רָאִיתָ: It would seem to have been equally possible to arrive at the opposite conclusion, that it is permitted for the High Priest to marry the woman who matured while betrothed and prohibited for him to marry a widow he had betrothed before being appointed High Priest. This is especially reasonable given that the prohibition for a High Priest to marry a widow is more severe than the prohibition for him to marry a grown woman (Ritva).

In this case of the grown woman her body has changed – הָאִי אִישְׁתַּנֵּי גּוּפָהּ: Apparently, since her body has changed, she is no longer viewed as the same person but as a different being, and therefore she is now forbidden to him (see *Keren Ora*).

Similar to the case of a divorcée – דּוּמְיָא דִּגְרוּשָׁה: *Tosafot* ask why the opposite cannot be stated: Just as the prohibition for a High Priest to marry a widow applies only to a woman who has been married, as indicated by the precedent of Tamar, so too a divorcée is prohibited only if she had been married. See the answers of *Tosafot*. *Tosefot HaRosh* and the Meiri explain that since a common priest is prohibited from marrying a divorcée but is permitted to marry a non-virgin, it must be the divorce itself that causes the prohibition regardless of whether her marriage had been consummated. The Ritva presents an alternative explanation, accepted by many later commentaries. He claims that although the case of Tamar is a biblical precedent, it is not a full-fledged verbal analogy and consequently cannot serve as a model for other *halakhot*.

״וְלֹא יִשָּׂא אֶת הַבּוֹגֶרֶת״. תָּנוּ רַבָּנַן: ״וְהוּא אִשָּׁה בִבְתוּלֶיהָ יִקָּח״, פְּרָט לְבוֹגֶרֶת שֶׁכָּלוּ לָהּ בְּתוּלֶיהָ, דִּבְרֵי רַבִּי מֵאִיר. רַבִּי אֶלְעָזָר וְרַבִּי שִׁמְעוֹן מַכְשִׁירִין בְּבוֹגֶרֶת.

§ It was taught in the mishna: And a High Priest may not marry a grown woman. The Sages taught that the verse: "And he shall take a wife in her virginity" (Leviticus 21:13) excludes a grown woman, whose hymen has worn away,[B] i.e., it is no longer as complete as that of a minor or a young woman; this is the statement of Rabbi Meir. Rabbi Elazar and Rabbi Shimon declare a grown woman fit to marry a High Priest.

בְּמַאי קָא מִיפַּלְגִי? רַבִּי מֵאִיר סָבַר: ״בְּתוּלָה״ אֲפִילּוּ מִקְצָת בְּתוּלִים מַשְׁמַע, ״בְּתוּלֶיהָ״ עַד דְּאִיכָּא כָּל הַבְּתוּלִים, ״בִּבְתוּלֶיהָ״ בִּכְדַרְכָּהּ אִין, שֶׁלֹּא כְּדַרְכָּהּ לָא.

The Gemara asks: With regard to what do they disagree? The Gemara explains: Rabbi Meir holds that were the verse referring simply to a virgin it would have indicated that even a woman with partial signs of virginity, i.e., a grown woman, is permitted. Since the verse states "her virginity," it means that she is fit to marry a High Priest only if all of the signs of her virginity are intact, which excludes a grown woman. The full expression "in her virginity"[N] indicates that if she has experienced sexual intercourse in a typical manner, which takes place in the area of her virginity, i.e., her hymen, yes, she is disqualified from marrying a High Priest; but if she has experienced sexual intercourse in an atypical manner i.e., anal intercourse, no, she is not disqualified.

וְרַבִּי אֶלְעָזָר וְרַבִּי שִׁמְעוֹן סָבְרִי: ״בְּתוּלָה״ בְּתוּלָה שְׁלֵימָה מַשְׁמַע, ״בְּתוּלֶיהָ״ וַאֲפִילּוּ מִקְצָת בְּתוּלִים, ״בִּבְתוּלֶיהָ״ עַד שֶׁיִּהְיוּ כׇּל בְּתוּלֶיהָ קַיָּימִין, בֵּין בִּכְדַרְכָּהּ בֵּין שֶׁלֹּא כְּדַרְכָּהּ.

And Rabbi Elazar and Rabbi Shimon hold that were the verse referring simply to a virgin, it would have indicated that only a complete virgin is fit to marry a High Priest, but not a grown woman. When it states "her virginity," it indicates that even a woman with partial signs of virginity, i.e., a grown woman, is fit to marry the High Priest. The full expression "in her virginity" indicates that she is not fit to marry to marry a High Priest unless all of her virginity is intact, i.e., she has not engaged in intercourse of any kind, whether typical sexual intercourse or atypical sexual intercourse.

אָמַר רַב יְהוּדָה אָמַר רַב: נִבְעֲלָה שֶׁלֹּא כְּדַרְכָּהּ – פְּסוּלָה לִכְהוּנָּה. מְתִיב רָבָא: ״וְלוֹ תִהְיֶה לְאִשָּׁה״ בְּאִשָּׁה הָרְאוּיָה לוֹ, פְּרָט לְאַלְמָנָה לְכֹהֵן גָּדוֹל, גְּרוּשָׁה וַחֲלוּצָה לְכֹהֵן הֶדְיוֹט.

Rav Yehuda said that Rav said: If she had atypical sexual intercourse,[H] she is disqualified from the High Priesthood, i.e., from marrying the High Priest. Rava raised an objection based upon a *baraita*: The verse states with regard to rape: "And she shall be his wife" (Deuteronomy 22:19), and the Sages explained that this is referring only to a woman suitable for him, excluding a widow for a High Priest[H] and a divorcée or a *ḥalutza* for a common priest. In these cases, the rapist is not permitted to marry his victim.

הֵיכִי דָּמֵי? אִילֵּימָא בִּכְדַרְכָּהּ – מַאי אִירְיָא מִשּׁוּם אַלְמָנָה? תֵּיפוֹק לֵיהּ מִשּׁוּם דַּהֲוָיא לַהּ בְּעוּלָה. אֶלָּא לָאו שֶׁלֹּא כְּדַרְכָּהּ. וּמִשּׁוּם אַלְמָנָה – אִין, מִשּׁוּם בְּעוּלָה – לָא.

The Gemara clarifies: What are the circumstances of this *halakha*? If we say that the High Priest raped her by engaging in typical intercourse, why does the *baraita* specifically state that she is forbidden to him because she is a widow? Let him derive this *halakha* from the fact that she is now a non-virgin.[N] Rather, is it not that he had atypical intercourse with her, and due to the fact that she is a widow, yes, that is the reason she is forbidden, but due to the fact that she is a non-virgin, no, that is not the reason she is forbidden? This indicates that a woman who had intercourse in an atypical manner is not considered a non-virgin and is not disqualified from marrying a High Priest.

Perek **VI**
Daf **59** Amud **b**

הָא מַנִּי – רַבִּי מֵאִיר הִיא, וְרַב דְּאָמַר כְּרַבִּי אֶלְעָזָר.

The Gemara refutes this proof: In accordance with whose opinion is this *baraita*? It is in accordance with the opinion of Rabbi Meir, who maintains that a woman who engaged in atypical intercourse is permitted to a High Priest, and when Rav said his statement, it was in accordance with the opinion of Rabbi Elazar, who holds that such a woman is disqualified from marrying a High Priest.

BACKGROUND

A grown woman, whose hymen has worn away – בּוֹגֶרֶת שֶׁכָּלוּ לָהּ בְּתוּלֶיהָ: As *Tosafot* point out, this does not mean that the hymen has worn away completely, as it usually remains intact as long as it has not been forcibly broken. However, before the onset of adolescence the hymen is more prominent and relatively larger. As a girl matures, the size of the hymen decreases in relation to the vagina.

NOTES

A virgin, her virginity, in her virginity – בְּתוּלָה, בְּתוּלֶיהָ, בִּבְתוּלֶיהָ: It appears that the dispute concerns the meanings of the terms virgin and virginity. Do these words refer to the physical sign of virginity, i.e., a fully intact hymen, or are they abstract terms that refer to the status of a woman who has never experienced any form of sexual intercourse? In *Arukh LaNer*, it is explained how these *halakhot* are derived based upon the hermeneutical principle that one restrictive expression after another amplifies the *halakha* in regard to which the verse employs these expressions.

Let him derive this *halakha* from the fact that she is now a non-virgin – תֵּיפוֹק לֵיהּ מִשּׁוּם דַּהֲוָיא בְּעוּלָה: One might argue that since mitzvot that are limited to specific individuals are generally considered less stringent than those that apply equally to all, the requirement that a rapist marry his victim should override the requirement that a High Priest marry a virgin. The Rashba explains, based upon tractate *Ketubot* (40a), that since the obligation for a rapist to marry his victim is not absolute, as the victim or her father have the right of refusal, it does not override the positive mitzva for a High Priest to marry a virgin.

HALAKHA

If she had atypical sexual intercourse – נִבְעֲלָה שֶׁלֹּא כְּדַרְכָּהּ: A High Priest may not marry a woman who has had atypical, i.e., anal, sexual intercourse (Rambam *Sefer Kedusha*, *Hilkhot Issurei Bia* 17:14).

Excluding a widow for a High Priest – פְּרָט לְאַלְמָנָה לְכֹהֵן גָּדוֹל וכו׳: One who raped a woman who is forbidden to him, even if she was forbidden to him by rabbinic decree, may not marry her despite the general requirement that a rapist marry his victim if she consents. Consequently, if a priest raped a divorcée or a *ḥalutza*, or if a High Priest raped a widow, he may not marry his victim (Rambam *Sefer Nashim*, *Hilkhot Na'ara Betula* 1:5; *Shulḥan Arukh*, *Even HaEzer* 177:4).

HALAKHA

One who refused – מְמָאֶנֶת: If a young girl was married off by her mother or brother and then refused to remain with her husband, she is permitted to a priest. This is the *halakha* even if he wrote her a bill of divorce, they subsequently married again, and she again refused to remain married to him (Rambam *Sefer Kedusha, Hilkhot Issurei Bia* 17:18).

A woman who had intercourse with an animal – נִבְעֲלָה לִבְהֵמָה: A woman who had intercourse with an animal is liable for capital punishment. However, she is not considered a *zona* and is not disqualified from marrying a priest. If she had only atypical intercourse with an animal, she is permitted even to a High Priest (Rambam *Sefer Kedusha, Hilkhot Issurei Bia* 18:1, 17:14; *Shulḥan Arukh, Even HaEzer* 6:8).

אִי כְּרַבִּי אֶלְעָזָר, מַאי אִירְיָא מִשּׁוּם בְּעוּלָה? תֵּיפוֹק לֵיהּ דְּהָוְיָא לָהּ זוֹנָה, דְּהָא אָמַר רַבִּי אֶלְעָזָר: פָּנוּי הַבָּא עַל הַפְּנוּיָה שֶׁלֹּא לְשֵׁם אִישׁוּת עֲשָׂאָהּ זוֹנָה!

The Gemara asks: **If** Rav's statement is **in accordance with** the opinion of **Rabbi Elazar,**[N] **why** did he **specifically** state that she is forbidden to him **because she is a non-virgin? Let him derive** it **from** the fact **that she is a** ***zona*****,**[N] **as Rabbi Elazar said:** Even in the case of **an unmarried man who had intercourse with an unmarried woman not for the purpose of marriage, he has** thereby **caused her to become a** ***zona*****.**

אֲמַר רַב יוֹסֵף: כְּגוֹן שֶׁנִּבְעֲלָה לִבְהֵמָה, דְּהָתָם, מִשּׁוּם בְּעוּלָה – אִיכָּא, מִשּׁוּם זוֹנָה – לֵיכָּא.

Rav Yosef said: When Rav said that a woman who had anal intercourse is disqualified from marrying a High Priest, he was referring **to** a woman **who had intercourse with an animal, as there** she **is** disqualified **because** she is **a non-virgin,**[N] but she **is not** disqualified **because** of the prohibition of **a** ***zona*****.**

אֲמַר לֵיהּ אַבַּיֵי: מִמָּה נַפְשָׁךְ, אִי בְּעוּלָה הָוְיָא – זוֹנָה נַמִי הָוְיָא, וְאִי זוֹנָה לָא הָוְיָא – בְּעוּלָה נַמִי לָא הָוְיָא. וְכִי תֵּימָא: מִידֵּי דְּהָוְיָא אַמּוּכַּת עֵץ שֶׁלֹּא כְּדַרְכָּהּ – אִם כֵּן אֵין לְךָ אִשָּׁה שֶׁכְּשֵׁרָה לִכְהוּנָּה שֶׁלֹּא נַעֲשֵׂית מוּכַּת עֵץ עַל יְדֵי צְרוֹר.

Abaye said to him: Whichever way you look at it, there is a difficulty with this answer: **If she is** considered **a non-virgin, she is also a** ***zona*****, and if she is not a** ***zona*** she **is also not a non-virgin. And lest you say** that it is **analogous to** a case of **a woman who lost her virginity via penetration by a foreign object atypically,** i.e., anally, whose hymen was therefore not damaged and she is not forbidden as a *zona*, yet she is no longer considered a virgin, that is not correct: **If so,** if such a woman is considered a non-virgin and forbidden to a High Priest, **you** would **have no woman who is fit for the** High **Priesthood, who has not lost her virginity via penetration by a foreign object** atypically, i.e., **by a pebble** used to clean herself in the lavatory.

אֶלָּא אֲמַר רַבִּי זֵירָא: בִּמְמָאֶנֶת.

Rather, Rabbi Zeira said that Rav was referring **to one who refused**[HN] her husband after having only atypical intercourse with him. Although the act of intercourse was not licentious, as she was married at the time, she is nevertheless disqualified from marrying into the priesthood because she is not a virgin.

אָמַר רַב שִׁימִי בַּר חִיָּיא: נִבְעֲלָה לִבְהֵמָה – כְּשֵׁרָה לִכְהוּנָּה. תַּנְיָא נַמִי הָכִי: נִבְעֲלָה לְמִי שֶׁאֵינוֹ אִישׁ, אַף עַל פִּי שֶׁבִּסְקִילָה – כְּשֵׁרָה לִכְהוּנָּה.

§ **Rabbi Shimi bar Ḥiyya said:** A woman who **had intercourse with an animal**[H] is like one whose hymen was torn accidentally. Consequently, she is not a *zona* and is **fit for the priesthood. This is also taught** in a *baraita*: If a woman **had intercourse with one who is not a man,**[N] i.e., an animal, **although** she is liable to **stoning** if she did so intentionally and in the presence of witnesses who forewarned her of her punishment, she is nevertheless **fit for the priesthood.**

NOTES

If Rav's statement is in accordance with the opinion of Rabbi Elazar, etc. – אִי כְּרַבִּי אֶלְעָזָר וכו׳: The commentaries raise the following difficulty with this question: Even if Rav agrees with Rabbi Elazar with regard to atypical intercourse, how does the Gemara know that Rav accepts his opinion with regard to the effect of intercourse between an unmarried man and an unmarried woman? In fact, there is a *tanna*, Rabbi Shimon, who agrees with Rabbi Elazar only with regard to atypical intercourse, and it is possible that Rav agrees with Rabbi Shimon. Some commentaries explain that the Gemara could have answered its question by making this point but chose instead to give a better answer (see Ramban and Rashba). Alternatively, as *Tosafot* explain, the Gemara's primary concern is not with the opinion of Rav himself but with the opinion of Rabbi Elazar (see Ritva).

Let him derive it from the fact that she is a *zona* – תֵּיפוֹק לֵיהּ דְּהָוְיָא לָהּ זוֹנָה: The commentaries wonder why the Gemara assumes that Rav does not hold that the woman is a *zona*. Perhaps Rav actually holds that she is prohibited for two reasons, because she is a non-virgin and also because she is a *zona*. The Rashba and Ritva answer that since there would be significant ramifications to such an opinion, as a *zona* is forbidden to all priests and not just the High Priest, Rav would have mentioned that she is considered a *zona*. The fact that he does not mention this point indicates clearly that he does not consider it to be correct.

The Maharsha explains that it was known that Rav made his statement with regard to the mishna, and therefore his *halakha* was stated only with regard to the High Priest, the subject of the mishna. Alternatively, if Rav were of the opinion that an unmarried man who had intercourse with an unmarried woman has caused her to become a *zona*, his *halakha* with regard to atypical intercourse would be obvious and unnecessary, as the mishna states at the beginning of the chapter that there is no difference between typical and atypical intercourse with regard to causing a woman to become disqualified from marrying into the priesthood (*Arukh LaNer*).

She is disqualified because she is a non-virgin – מִשּׁוּם בְּעוּלָה, אִיכָּא: The Rashba and others note that this issue appears to involve two separate factors: The prohibition against a High Priest marrying a non-virgin and his obligation to marry a woman "in her virginity." They explain that it is possible for a woman to have an intact hymen and yet not meet the criteria of a woman in her virginity.

One who refused – מְמָאֶנֶת: This refers to a girl under the age of twelve whose father is no longer alive. The Sages instituted that the girl's mother or brother may marry her off, but she may terminate the marriage by a process called refusal, whereby she announces that she is not interested in the marriage. The Ritva points out that, upon refusal, the girl is considered retroactively never to have been married. Therefore, this should be a case of intercourse between an unmarried man and woman, and according to Rabbi Elazar she should be considered a *zona*. He explains that Rabbi Elazar considers the woman to be a *zona* only if the act of intercourse was performed outside of the context of marriage, but in this case, at the time when the act was performed, they were considered married.

If a woman had intercourse with one who is not a man – נִבְעֲלָה לְמִי שֶׁאֵינוֹ אִישׁ: The *baraita* is precise in its wording, which includes any form of living being. Rashi notes that a woman who had intercourse with an animal is not any more fit to marry a High Priest than a woman who hymen was accidentally torn. Consequently, according to the opinions that hold that a woman whose hymen was accidentally torn in prohibited from marrying a High Priest, this statement about a woman who had intercourse with an animal must refer to one who had anal intercourse. Alternatively, if the woman had typical intercourse that broke her hymen, it means to say that she is permitted to an ordinary priest but not to a High Priest (see Meiri and *Yam shel Shlomo*).

כִּי אֲתָא רַב דִּימִי אֲמַר: מַעֲשֶׂה בְּרִיבָה אַחַת בְּהִיתְלוּ שֶׁהָיְתָה מְכַבֶּדֶת אֶת הַבַּיִת, וּרְבָעָהּ כֶּלֶב כּוּפְרִי מֵאַחֲרֶיהָ, וְהִכְשִׁירָהּ רַבִּי לִכְהוּנָּה. אֲמַר שְׁמוּאֵל: וּלְכֹהֵן גָּדוֹל. בִּימֵי רַבִּי כֹּהֵן גָּדוֹל מִי הֲוָה? אֶלָּא: רְאוּיָה לְכֹהֵן גָּדוֹל.

When Rav Dimi came from Eretz Yisrael **he said:** There was an **incident** involving **a certain girl** [*riva*][N] **in the village of Hitlu**[B] **who was sweeping the house, and a village** [*kufri*] **dog**[B] used for hunting **sodomized her from behind. And Rabbi** Yehuda HaNasi **permitted her to the priesthood,** as she was not considered a *zona*. **Shmuel said: And** Rabbi Yehuda HaNasi permitted her even **to a High Priest,** as she was still considered a virgin. The Gemara is puzzled by this comment: **Was there a High Priest in the days of Rabbi** Yehuda HaNasi?[N] **Rather,** Shmuel meant that **she is fit for a High Priest.**

אֲמַר לֵיהּ רָבָא מִפִּרְקִין לְרַב אַשִׁי: מְנָא הָא מִילְּתָא דַּאֲמוּר רַבָּנַן אֵין זְנוּת לִבְהֵמָה – דִּכְתִיב ״לֹא תָבִיא אֶתְנַן זוֹנָה וּמְחִיר כֶּלֶב״,

Rava of Pirkin said to Rav Ashi: From where is this matter derived **that the Sages stated** that **there is no harlotry with regard to an animal?** Rav Ashi responded that it is **as it is written: "You shall not bring the hire of a harlot or the price of a dog** into the House of the Lord your God for any vow; for both of them are an abomination to the Lord your God" (Deuteronomy 23:19). This verse prohibits one from sacrificing an animal as an offering if that animal was ever used to pay a harlot for her services, or if it was ever used as payment in the purchase of a dog.

וּתְנַן: אֶתְנַן כֶּלֶב וּמְחִיר זוֹנָה מוּתָּרִין, (מִשּׁוּם) שֶׁנֶּאֱמַר ״גַּם שְׁנֵיהֶם״ שְׁנַיִם וְלֹא אַרְבָּעָה.

And we learned in a mishna (*Temura* 30a): **The hire of a dog,**[N] i.e., a kosher animal that a man or woman gave as payment to the owner of a dog in order to have sexual intercourse with it, **and** similarly **the price of a prostitute,**[H] a kosher animal used to purchase a prostitute as a maidservant, **are permitted** to be sacrificed as offerings. This is **because it is stated** that **both of them,** the specific items listed in the verse, are abominations. Consequently, only **two** items are prohibited, i.e., the payment given to a prostitute for her services, and the payment used in the purchase of a dog, **and not four,** as the reverse cases are excluded from this *halakha*.

תָּנוּ רַבָּנַן: אֲנוּסַת עַצְמוֹ וּמְפוּתַּת עַצְמוֹ – לֹא יִשָּׂא, וְאִם נָשָׂא – נָשׂוּי. אֲנוּסַת חֲבֵירוֹ וּמְפוּתַּת חֲבֵירוֹ – לֹא יִשָּׂא, וְאִם נָשָׂא, רַבִּי אֱלִיעֶזֶר בֶּן יַעֲקֹב אוֹמֵר: הַוָּלָד חָלָל, וַחֲכָמִים אוֹמְרִים: הַוָּלָד כָּשֵׁר.

§ **The Sages taught:** A High Priest **may not marry** a woman that **he himself raped and** a woman that **he himself seduced,**[H] as he is commanded to marry a virgin. **And if he married** her, **he is married.** With regard to a woman who was **raped by another** man **and** a woman **seduced by another man,**[H] **he may not marry** her. **And if he married** her, **Rabbi Eliezer ben Ya'akov says** that **the child** born from this union **is a *ḥalal*,**[B] **and the Rabbis say** the lineage of **the offspring is unflawed.**

NOTES

Girl [*riva*] – רִיבָה: This word is usually understood as parallel to *roveh*, a child, young man. According to this interpretation, the word was influenced by or borrowed from the Aramaic word for child, *ravya*.

Others explain that *riva* is the diminutive of *rava*, in the sense of a lady, with *riva* meaning a young lady. Similar terms are found in other languages.

Was there a High Priest in the days of Rabbi Yehuda HaNasi – בִּימֵי רַבִּי כֹּהֵן גָּדוֹל מִי הֲוָה: The same question can be asked with regard to Rav, who stated that a woman who had intercourse with an animal is still fit to marry a High Priest. It is explained in *Arukh LaNer* that the Gemara does not refrain from discussing *halakhot* that do not apply in practice. However, Rabbi Yehuda HaNasi issued a halakhic ruling for an incident that actually occurred, and therefore there was no reason for him to say something of no relevance to the case at hand.

The hire of a dog – אֶתְנַן כֶּלֶב: Some commentaries point out that it is prohibited to sacrifice the kosher animal as an offering, even if the animal was used to pay for an act of intercourse that causes one to be liable to capital punishment. The principle that multiple punishments are not meted out for one transgression does not apply here. Nevertheless, some say that it is due to the aforementioned principle that Rashi interprets the case as one where a man said to a woman: Take this lamb and have intercourse with my dog.

In that case, the individual who gave the present did not personally violate a prohibition for which he is liable for capital punishment (Meiri).

HALAKHA

The hire of a dog and the price of a prostitute – אֶתְנַן כֶּלֶב וּמְחִיר זוֹנָה: Kosher animals given as payment for the services of a prostitute or as payment for the purchase of a dog are unfit to be sacrificed as offerings in the Temple. However, kosher animals given as payment for the purchase of a prostitute as a maidservant, or as payment to a dog's owner for permission to have intercourse with the dog remain fit for use as an offering (Rambam *Sefer Avoda*, *Hilkhot Issurei Mizbe'aḥ* 4:18).

A woman that he himself raped and a woman that he himself seduced – אֲנוּסַת עַצְמוֹ וּמְפוּתַּת עַצְמוֹ: A High Priest who raped or seduced a young woman who was a virgin is not permitted to marry her, even if the incident occurred before he was appointed High Priest. If he did marry her, he is forced to divorce her, in accordance with Rav Huna's explanation of the *baraita* (Rambam *Sefer Nashim*, *Hilkhot Na'ara Betula* 1:6 and *Sefer Kedusha*, *Hilkhot Issurei Bia* 17:16).

The child of a woman raped or seduced by another man – וְלַד אֲנוּסַת וּמְפוּתַּת חֲבֵרוֹ: If a High Priest had intercourse with a woman who had previously been raped or seduced by another man, he has rendered her a *ḥalala*. Furthermore, any child born from the relationship is a *ḥalal* (Rambam *Sefer Kedusha*, *Hilkhot Issurei Bia* 19:3).

BACKGROUND

Hitlu – הִיתְלוּ: According to versions found in manuscripts and different sources, it seems that Hitlu is Ayatlu, a village known from other sources as the home of a group of priests. Ayatlu was a town in the Galilee, which is referred to today as Illut. It is about 4 km west of Nazareth. The fact that most if not all of its inhabitants were priests explains the need to determine whether this girl was halakhically permitted to marry a priest.

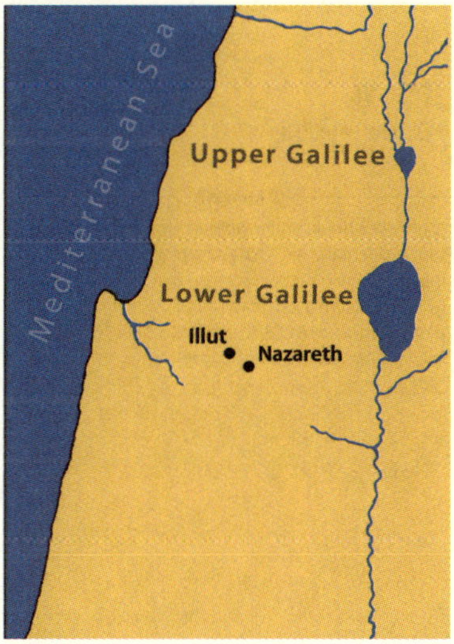

Location of Illut

Village [*kufri*] dog – כֶּלֶב כּוּפְרִי: The *kufri* is a special breed of dogs whose name is derived from the word *kefar*, village, that is to say, a dog raised in villages.

The mishna in tractate *Kilayim* (1:6) indicates that this kind of dog is similar to a fox, and it is therefore likely, in accordance with the explanation of the *Arukh* and others, that it was a small dog, similar in form to a jackal or a fox. These kinds of dogs were used to hunt mice, cats, and the like, and perhaps they also served as pets. The Rambam, in his commentary on that mishna, refers to a breed identified by some scholars today as the Saluki, a hound whose ancestors date back thousands of years. Some versions of the Talmud read monkey instead of dog.

Male Saluki

***Ḥalal* – חָלָל:** A *ḥalal* refers to one disqualified from priesthood, usually the offspring of a priest and a woman forbidden to the priest, e.g., a divorcée or a *zona*. Even though the priest is considered the father of the *ḥalal*, the son does not have the legal status of a priest but a status similar to that of an Israelite. A daughter born of such a forbidden relationship may not marry a priest.

"אִם נָשָׂא – נָשׂוּי". אָמַר רַב הוּנָא אָמַר רַב: וּמוֹצִיא בְּגֵט. וְאֶלָּא הָא דְּקָתָנֵי: "אִם נָשָׂא – נָשׂוּי"! אָמַר רַב אַחָא בַּר יַעֲקֹב: לוֹמַר

The Gemara analyzes this *baraita*. It states that **if he married** the woman that he himself raped or seduced, **he is married. Rav Huna said** that **Rav said: And he must divorce** her **with a bill of divorce.** The Gemara asks: **But** consider **that which** the *baraita* **teaches: If he married** her, **he is married.** Since it is obvious that the marriage is technically valid, it must be saying that they are permitted to remain married. **Rav Aḥa bar Ya'akov said:** No, it means **to say**

Perek **VI**
Daf **60** Amud **a**

HALAKHA

A grown woman and a woman whose hymen was torn accidentally, etc. – **בּוֹגֶרֶת וּמוּכַּת עֵץ וכו׳**: A High Priest may not marry a grown woman or a woman whose hymen was torn accidentally. Still, if he married one of these women, he is not forced to divorce her (Rambam *Sefer Kedusha*, *Hilkhot Issurei Bia* 17:13–15).

שֶׁאֵין מְשַׁלֵּם קְנָס בִּמְפוּתָּה.

that he does not pay the fine of a seduced woman.[N] One who seduced a woman and does not wish to marry her must pay a fine (see Exodus 22:14–15). Since in this case he did marry her, he is not liable to pay the fine even though he is required to divorce her.

אֲזַל רַב גְּבִיהָה מִבֵּי כְּתִיל, אֲמַרָהּ לִשְׁמַעְתָּא קַמֵּיהּ דְּרַב אַשִׁי. אֲמַר לֵיהּ: וְהָא רַב וְרַבִּי יוֹחָנָן דְּאָמְרִי תַּרְוַיְיהוּ: בּוֹגֶרֶת וּמוּכַּת עֵץ – לֹא יִשָּׂא, וְאִם נָשָׂא – נָשׂוּי.

The Gemara relates that when **Rav Geviha went from Bei Ketil he stated this *halakha* before Rav Ashi, who said to him: Isn't it Rav and Rabbi Yoḥanan who both say:** A High Priest **may not marry a grown woman and a woman whose hymen was torn accidentally,**[H] **but if he married** one of them **he is married?**[N]

אַלְמָא: סוֹפָהּ לִהְיוֹת בּוֹגֶרֶת תַּחְתָּיו, סוֹפָהּ לִהְיוֹת מוּכַּת עֵץ תַּחְתָּיו, הָכָא נַמִי – סוֹפָהּ לִהְיוֹת בְּעוּלָה תַּחְתָּיו! קַשְׁיָא.

Apparently, the reason for this *halakha* is that since **she will eventually be a grown woman under him,** i.e., while married to him, and **she will eventually be a woman whose hymen was torn under him,** as she will not remain a virgin, they are permitted to remain married after the fact. **Here too,** in the case of a High Priest who married a woman he raped or seduced, since **she will eventually be a non-virgin**[N] **under him,** the *baraita* should be understood as stating that they may remain married. The Gemara concludes: Indeed, this is **difficult** for Rav Huna.

"אֲנוּסַת חֲבֵירוֹ וּמְפוּתַּת חֲבֵירוֹ – לֹא יִשָּׂא, וְאִם נָשָׂא, רַבִּי אֱלִיעֶזֶר בֶּן יַעֲקֹב אוֹמֵר: הַוָּלָד חָלָל, וַחֲכָמִים אוֹמְרִים: הַוָּלָד כָּשֵׁר". אָמַר רַב הוּנָא אָמַר רַב: הֲלָכָה כְּרַבִּי אֱלִיעֶזֶר בֶּן יַעֲקֹב. וְכֵן אָמַר רַב גִּידֵּל אָמַר רַב: הֲלָכָה כְּרַבִּי אֱלִיעֶזֶר בֶּן יַעֲקֹב.

§ The *baraita* cited above taught: With regard to a woman who was **raped by another** man **and** a woman **seduced by another** man, the High Priest **may not marry** her. **And if he married** her, **Rabbi Eliezer ben Ya'akov says** that **the child** born from this union **is a *ḥalal*, and the Rabbis say** the lineage of **the offspring is unflawed. Rav Huna said** that **Rav said: The *halakha* is in accordance with** the opinion of **Rabbi Eliezer ben Ya'akov. And, so too, Rav Giddel said** that **Rav said: The *halakha* is in accordance with** the opinion of **Rabbi Eliezer ben Ya'akov.**

NOTES

That he does not pay the fine of a seduced woman – **שֶׁאֵין מְשַׁלֵּם קְנָס בִּמְפוּתָּה**: *Tosafot* ask: Since he is obligated to divorce her he must in any case pay her marriage contract. If so, what difference does it make whether he pays the sum as a fine or for the marriage contract? *Tosafot* offer several answers, one of which is that the Gemara is addressing Torah law, whereas the requirement that he divorce her and pay her marriage contract is by rabbinic law.

A grown woman and a woman whose hymen was torn accidentally, but if he married one of them he is married – **בּוֹגֶרֶת וּמוּכַּת עֵץ...וְאִם נָשָׂא, נָשׂוּי**: The Rashba asks what the source is for this ruling, as the mishna indicates simply that it is prohibited for a priest to be married to one of these women. He answers that Rav and Rabbi Yoḥanan rely on the *baraita* that states that a woman who had intercourse with an animal remains fit to marry a High Priest. This indicates that the definition of a virgin is one who has not had intercourse with a man. Consequently, a grown woman and a woman whose hymen was torn accidentally are also considered virgins.

It should also be noted that there is an alternate version of the mishna which is cited in the Jerusalem Talmud. According to that version, there are *tanna'im* who disagree with the ruling that a High Priest may not marry a woman whose hymen was accidentally torn.

Rav Huna explained the phrase: If he married one of them he is married, to mean that he is exempt from the fine but must divorce his wife. However, that interpretation is not applicable to the ruling of Rav and Rabbi Yoḥanan, as it does not address a case of rape or seduction, and therefore there is no fine involved. Consequently, the statement must be understood to mean that it is permitted for them to remain married (Rivan).

She will eventually be a non-virgin, etc. – **סוֹפָהּ לִהְיוֹת בְּעוּלָה וכו׳**: According to this reasoning, why should there be a distinction between a woman that he himself raped or seduced and a woman who was raped or seduced by another man? The argument that she would eventually have become a non-virgin while married to him is equally relevant to both cases. The Ritva answers that there is a difference between the cases due to the greater level of disgrace when the woman has been raped or seduced by another man. He adds that perhaps the reason that some halakhic authorities ruled in accordance with the statement of Rav Huna, despite Rav Ashi's question, is because they hold that there is disgrace even in the case of a woman that the priest himself raped or seduced.

אִיכָּא דְּאָמְרִי, אֲמַר רַב הוּנָא אֲמַר רַב: מַאי טַעֲמָא דְּרַבִּי אֱלִיעֶזֶר בֶּן יַעֲקֹב – סָבַר לַהּ כְּרַבִּי אֶלְעָזָר.

Some say a different version of this statement. **Rav Huna said that Rav said: What is the reason of Rabbi Eliezer ben Ya'akov? He holds in accordance with** the opinion of **Rabbi Elazar,** that an unmarried man who has intercourse with an unmarried woman has thereby caused her to become a *zona*. Consequently, since the other man had intercourse with this woman outside of the context of marriage, she is a *zona*.

וּמִי סָבַר לַהּ כְּוָתֵיהּ? וְהָא קַיְימָא לַן: מִשְׁנַת רַבִּי אֱלִיעֶזֶר בֶּן יַעֲקֹב קַב וְנָקִי, וְאִילּוּ בְּהָא אָמַר רַב עַמְרָם אָמַר רַב: אֵין הֲלָכָה כְּרַבִּי אֶלְעָזָר! קַשְׁיָא.

The Gemara asks: **Does** he really **hold in accordance with** the opinion of Rabbi Elazar? **Don't we maintain that the teaching of Rabbi Eliezer ben Ya'akov** measures **a *kav* but is clean,**[N] i.e., not many of his rulings have been recorded, but those that have been recorded are considered authoritative, and the *halakha* is always in accordance with his opinion? **However, with regard to this** ruling of Rabbi Elazar, **Rav Amram said that Rav said** that **the *halakha* is not in accordance with Rabbi Elazar.** The Gemara comments: This is indeed **difficult.**

רַב אַשִׁי אֲמַר: בְּיֵשׁ חָלָל מֵחַיָּיבֵי עֲשֵׂה קָמִיפַּלְגִי. רַבִּי אֱלִיעֶזֶר בֶּן יַעֲקֹב סָבַר: יֵשׁ חָלָל מֵחַיָּיבֵי עֲשֵׂה, וְרַבָּנַן סָבְרִי: אֵין חָלָל מֵחַיָּיבֵי עֲשֵׂה.

Rav Ashi said: This is not the reason for the dispute. Rather, they **disagree with regard to whether there is a *ḥalal* from** a relationship for which the man and woman are **liable for** transgressing **a positive mitzva.** The marriage of a High Priest to a non-virgin is a violation of the mitzva that a High Priest marry a virgin, but it is not expressed in the Torah as a prohibition against a High Priest marrying a non-virgin. **Rabbi Eliezer ben Ya'akov holds** that **there is a *ḥalal* from** a relationship for which the man and woman are **liable for** violating **a positive mitzva,**[N] **and the Rabbis hold** that **there is no *ḥalal* from** a relationship for which the man and woman are **liable for** violating **a positive mitzva.**

מַאי טַעֲמָא דְּרַבִּי אֱלִיעֶזֶר בֶּן יַעֲקֹב – דִּכְתִיב ״אַלְמָנָה וּגְרוּשָׁה וַחֲלָלָה זוֹנָה אֶת אֵלֶּה לֹא יִקָּח כִּי אִם בְּתוּלָה״ וגו׳, וּכְתִיב ״וְלֹא יְחַלֵּל זַרְעוֹ בְּעַמָּיו״ אַכּוּלְּהוּ.

What is the reason of Rabbi Eliezer ben Ya'akov? As it is written: "A widow, or one divorced, or a *ḥalala*, or a *zona*, these shall he not take; but a virgin of his own people shall he take for a wife" (Leviticus 21:14), **and it states** subsequently: **"And he shall not profane his seed among his people"** (Leviticus 21:15). Rabbi Eliezer ben Ya'akov maintains that this profanation is referring **to all of them,** i.e., he profanes his seed by marrying any woman unfit for him, including a non-virgin.

וְרַבָּנַן ״אֵלֶּה״ הִפְסִיק הָעִנְיָן. וְרַבִּי אֱלִיעֶזֶר בֶּן יַעֲקֹב – אָמַר ״אֵלֶּה״ לְמַעוּטֵי נִדָּה.

And what do **the Sages** hold? The word **"these" concluded** discussion of **that matter.** Consequently, only the prohibitions listed before the phrase "these shall he not take" result in the offspring being *ḥalal*. **And Rabbi Eliezer ben Ya'akov said:** The word **"these"** comes **to exclude a menstruating woman.** If a priest has relations with a menstruating woman, the offspring is not a *ḥalal*, as this is not a prohibition specific to priests.

כְּמַאן אָזְלָא הָא דְּתַנְיָא: מֵ״אֵלֶּה״ אַתָּה עוֹשֶׂה חָלָל, וְאִי אַתָּה עוֹשֶׂה חָלָל מִנִּדָּה, כְּמַאן – כְּרַבִּי אֱלִיעֶזֶר בֶּן יַעֲקֹב. וְרַבִּי אֱלִיעֶזֶר בֶּן יַעֲקֹב, נִכְתְּבֵיהּ לְ״אֵלֶּה״ לְבַסּוֹף! קַשְׁיָא.

The Gemara asks: **In accordance with whose** opinion **is that which is taught** in the following *baraita*: **From** the prohibitions preceding the phrase **"these** shall he not take" **you cause** your offspring to be **a *ḥalal*, but you do not cause** your offspring to be **a *ḥalal*** by having a child **with a menstruating woman.**[NH] **In accordance with whose** opinion is it? **It is in accordance with** the opinion of **Rabbi Eliezer ben Ya'akov.** The Gemara asks: **And** according to **Rabbi Eliezer ben Ya'akov, let** the verse **write** the word **these at the end,** after stating that a High Priest must marry a virgin, in order to make it clear that if he marries a non-virgin their child is a *ḥalal*. The Gemara responds: Indeed, this is **difficult.**

תָּנוּ רַבָּנַן: אֲחוֹתוֹ אֲרוּסָה, רַבִּי מֵאִיר וְרַבִּי יְהוּדָה אוֹמְרִים: מִטַּמֵּא לָהּ, רַבִּי יוֹסֵי וְרַבִּי שִׁמְעוֹן אוֹמְרִים: אֵין מִטַּמֵּא לָהּ. אֲנוּסָה וּמְפוּתָּה – דִּבְרֵי הַכֹּל אֵין מִטַּמֵּא לָהּ, וּמוּכַּת עֵץ – אֵין מִטַּמֵּא לָהּ, דִּבְרֵי רַבִּי שִׁמְעוֹן. שֶׁהָיָה רַבִּי שִׁמְעוֹן אוֹמֵר: רְאוּיָה לְכֹהֵן גָּדוֹל מִטַּמֵּא לָהּ, שֶׁאֵין רְאוּיָה לְכֹהֵן גָּדוֹל – אֵין מִטַּמֵּא לָהּ.

§ **The Sages taught:** With regard to a priest's **betrothed sister, Rabbi Meir and Rabbi Yehuda say: He** must **become impure for her** upon her death. **Rabbi Yosei and Rabbi Shimon say: He** may **not become impure for her.** With regard to his sister who has been **raped or seduced, all agree** that **he may not become impure for her** upon her death. With regard to his sister **whose hymen was torn accidentally, he may not become impure for her;** this is **the statement of Rabbi Shimon, as Rabbi Shimon would say** the following principle: If his sister was **fit for a High Priest, he** must **become impure for her,** but if she was **not fit for a High Priest, he may not become impure for her.**

NOTES

Measures a *kav*, but is clean – קַב וְנָקִי: This statement appears in several places in the Talmud. The commentaries discuss whether this principle is applied in every instance or if certain distinctions should be specified. Should one apply this principle only in the case of a mishna, or can it be applied to a *baraita* as well? Is Rabbi Eliezer ben Ya'akov's opinion accepted only in disputes with a single authority, or even when it is contrary to the majority opinion? The consensus is that the opinion of Rabbi Eliezer ben Ya'akov is accepted in all instances, even in a *baraita* and even contrary to the majority opinion, except where the Gemara explicitly rules otherwise. There is an ancient tradition that statements ascribed to Rabbi Eliezer ben Ya'akov are mentioned in 102 places, the numerical value of the word *kav*, and that his opinion is accepted in all of these cases. Consequently, the Sages have an aphorism that his teaching measures a *kav*, a common unit of measurement, but is clean (see *Yad Malakhi*; *Seder HaDorot*).

There is a *ḥalal* from a relationship for which the man and woman are liable for violating a positive mitzva – יֵשׁ חָלָל מֵחַיָּיבֵי עֲשֵׂה: Since there appears to be only one relationship included in this category, i.e., a High Priest who marries a non-virgin, why does the Gemara use the plural form: Those? One answer is that the woman herself becomes a *ḥalala* and her children also become *ḥalalim*. Furthermore, this ruling may impact other cases as well. If a woman has relations with a second-generation Egyptian convert, which constitutes the violation of a positive mitzva, she becomes a *zona*. If she then marries a priest, their children are *ḥalalim*, based upon the violation of that original positive mitzva (*Arukh LaNer*).

But you do not cause your offspring to be a *ḥalal* by having a child with a menstruating woman – וְאִי אַתָּה עוֹשֶׂה חָלָל מִנִּדָּה: The Ramban and Rashba point out that everyone agrees that the child of a menstruating woman is not a *ḥalal*, as only prohibitions specific to priests cause this status. They explain that the question here is merely related to the source of this *halakha*, as Rabbi Eliezer ben Ya'akov derives it from the word "these," while the Rabbis have a different source for the *halakha* (see *Tosafot*).

HALAKHA

But you do not cause a *ḥalal* by having a child with a menstruating woman – וְאִי אַתָּה עוֹשֶׂה חָלָל מִנִּדָּה: One who has intercourse with a menstruating woman does not thereby cause her to become a *zona*. A child conceived by this act is not considered a *ḥalal* (Rambam *Sefer Kedusha*, *Hilkhot Issurei Bia* 19:6; *Shulḥan Arukh*, *Even HaEzer* 6:8).

וּבוֹגֶרֶת מְטַמֵּא לָהּ – דִּבְרֵי כׇּל אָדָם.

And if his sister was **a grown woman, he** must **become impure for her according to everyone.** Even those who hold that a High Priest may not marry a grown woman because her hymen is no longer whole agree that with regard to a priest becoming impure, she is considered a virgin and he must therefore become impure for her upon her death.

מַאי טַעֲמָא דְּרַבִּי מֵאִיר וְרַבִּי יְהוּדָה? דְּדָרְשִׁי הָכִי: ״וְלַאֲחוֹתוֹ הַבְּתוּלָה״ פְּרָט לַאֲנוּסָה וּמְפוּתָּה.

The Gemara analyzes this *baraita*: **What is the reason of Rabbi Meir and Rabbi Yehuda? They expound** the verse **as follows:** "And for his virgin sister, who is near to him, who has had no man, for her must he defile himself" (Leviticus 21:3). **"And for his virgin sister" excludes** one who has been **raped or seduced,** as they are not virgins.

יָכוֹל שֶׁאֲנִי מוֹצִיא אַף מוּכַּת עֵץ – תַּלְמוּד לוֹמַר ״אֲשֶׁר לֹא הָיְתָה לְאִישׁ״, מִי שֶׁהֲוָיָיתָהּ עַל יְדֵי אִישׁ, יָצְאָה זוֹ שֶׁאֵין הֲוָיָיתָהּ עַל יְדֵי אִישׁ. ״הַקְּרוֹבָה״ לְרַבּוֹת הָאֲרוּסָה. ״אֵלָיו״ לְרַבּוֹת הַבּוֹגֶרֶת.

One **might** have thought **that I should exclude even a woman whose hymen was torn accidentally** via a foreign object. **The verse** therefore **states: "Who has had no man,"** to include only **one whose becoming** a non-virgin was caused **by a man,** i.e., through intercourse. **This** case of a woman **whose becoming** a non-virgin **was not** caused **by a man** but rather by an object is thereby **excluded** from the category of a non-virgin, and her brother does become impure for her. **"Who is near"**; this is **to include a betrothed** sister.[N] **"To him"**; this is **to include a grown woman.**[H]

הָא לָמָּה לִי קְרָא? וְהָאָמַר רַבִּי מֵאִיר: ״בְּתוּלָה״ אֲפִילּוּ מִקְצָת בְּתוּלָה מַשְׁמַע! אִיצְטְרִיךְ, סָלְקָא דַּעְתָּךְ אָמִינָא: נֵילַף ״בְּתוּלָה״ ״בְּתוּלָה״ מֵהָתָם, מַה לְהַלָּן נַעֲרָה – אַף כָּאן נַמִי נַעֲרָה, קָא מַשְׁמַע לַן.

The Gemara asks: **Why do I need a verse** to include a grown woman? **Didn't Rabbi Meir say** that the word **"virgin" indicates even** a woman who is **partly a virgin,** i.e., a grown woman, whose hymen is partially intact? Consequently, when the verse states that the priest becomes impure for his virgin sister, a grown woman is included. The Gemara answers: The derivation from the verse is **necessary,** as it might **enter your mind to say** that **we should derive** a verbal analogy from the word **"virgin"** in this context and the word **"virgin" from there,** the context of a High Priest: In the analogy, **just as there** the virgin referred to is **a young woman and not a grown woman, so too here** she must be **a young woman.** The verse therefore **teaches us** that a priest becomes impure for his sister even if she is a grown woman.

וְרַבִּי יוֹסֵי וְרַבִּי שִׁמְעוֹן, מַאי טַעֲמַיְיהוּ? דָּרְשִׁי הָכִי: ״וְלַאֲחוֹתוֹ הַבְּתוּלָה״ פְּרָט לַאֲנוּסָה וּמְפוּתָּה וּמוּכַּת עֵץ, ״אֲשֶׁר לֹא הָיְתָה״ פְּרָט לַאֲרוּסָה, ״הַקְּרוֹבָה״ לְרַבּוֹת אֲרוּסָה שֶׁנִּתְגָּרְשָׁה, ״אֵלָיו״ לְרַבּוֹת אֶת הַבּוֹגֶרֶת. ״הַקְּרוֹבָה״ לְרַבּוֹת אֲרוּסָה שֶׁנִּתְגָּרְשָׁה?

And Rabbi Yosei and Rabbi Shimon, what is their reason? They expound as follows: "And for his virgin sister" excludes a woman who was **raped or seduced**[H] **and a woman whose hymen was torn accidentally,** who is also not considered a virgin. **"Who has had no man" excludes a betrothed** sister,[H] although she is not yet fully married. **"Who is near"**; this is **to include a betrothed** woman **who was then divorced,**[N] as she is once again near to her brother. **"To him"**; this is **to include a grown woman.** The Gemara asks: Can the term **"who is near"** come **to include a betrothed** woman **who was divorced?**

NOTES

Who is near, this is to include a betrothed sister – **הַקְּרוֹבָה לְרַבּוֹת הָאֲרוּסָה**: Both the *tanna'im* who hold that a priest must become impure for his sister even if she was betrothed, and those who hold that he may not, agree that the phrase: Who has had no man, would naturally be understood to mean that a priest becomes impure only for a sister who was never even betrothed. The dispute is whether there is another part of the verse that specifically includes any woman who had been betrothed, because she remains near to her brother. It should be noted that there are Sages cited in the Jerusalem Talmud who held that a sister is presumed to remain a part of one's family unit until proven otherwise, whereas a betrothed woman is presumed not to be included in her husband's family unit until proven otherwise.

To include a betrothed woman who was then divorced – **לְרַבּוֹת אֲרוּסָה שֶׁנִּתְגָּרְשָׁה**: The commentaries disagree about the status of a woman who was married but had not yet had intercourse with her husband: Is her status comparable to that of a betrothed woman with regard to whether her brother becomes impure for her if he is a priest, or is her status comparable to that of a fully married woman? The Ramban rules that she has the status of a betrothed woman and that consequently, Rabbi Meir and Rabbi Yehuda hold that her brother must become impure for her. He explains further that if she is divorced without having intercourse, even Rabbi Yosei and Rabbi Shimon would agree that her brother must become impure. The Rashba holds that as long as she is married, all would agree that her brother does not become impure for her. However, if she is divorced without having intercourse, her brother must become impure for her (see Ritva and *Arukh LaNer*).

HALAKHA

A woman whose hymen was torn accidentally and a grown woman – **בּוֹגֶרֶת וּמוּכַּת עֵץ**: A priest becomes impure for his sister who never had intercourse with a man, whether she was a minor or an adult. Similarly, he becomes impure for his sister if her hymen was accidentally torn. The *halakha* is not in accordance with Rabbi Shimon, as his is a lone opinion opposed by the majority (Rambam *Sefer Shofetim*, *Hilkhot Evel* 2:10–11; *Shulḥan Arukh*, *Yoreh De'a* 373:4).

Raped or seduced – **אֲנוּסָה וּמְפוּתָּה**: If the sister of a priest was raped or seduced, he does not become impure for her upon her death (Rambam *Sefer Shofetim*, *Hilkhot Evel* 2:10–11; *Shulḥan Arukh*, *Yoreh De'a* 373:4).

Betrothed sister – **אָחוֹת אֲרוּסָה**: A priest may not become impure for his betrothed sister, even if she was betrothed to a priest. If she was betrothed and then divorced, he does become impure for her. The *halakha* is in accordance with the opinion of Rabbi Yosei and Rabbi Shimon, as the *halakha* generally follows the opinions of Rabbi Yosei over those of a colleague (Rambam *Sefer Shofetim*, *Hilkhot Evel* 2:10–11; *Shulḥan Arukh*, *Yoreh De'a* 373:4).

Perek **VI**
Daf **60** Amud **b**

וְהָא אָמַר רַבִּי שִׁמְעוֹן: רְאוּיָה לְכֹהֵן גָּדוֹל – מְטַמֵּא לָהּ, שֶׁאֵין רְאוּיָה לְכֹהֵן גָּדוֹל – אֵין מְטַמֵּא לָהּ! שָׁאנֵי הָתָם דְּרַבֵּי רַחֲמָנָא ״קְרוֹבָה״.

Didn't Rabbi Shimon say: If she was **fit for a High Priest,** her brother must **become impure for her,** and if she was **not fit for a High Priest,** her brother **may not become impure for her?** A divorced woman is not fit for a High Priest even if she had been only betrothed before her divorce. The Gemara answers: **It is different there, as the Merciful One includes** her by the term: Who is **near,** which includes any sister who is close to him, even if she is unfit for a High Priest.

אִי הָכִי מוּכַּת עֵץ נַמִּי [רַבֵּי]! ״קְרוֹבָה״ אַחַת וְלֹא שְׁתַּיִם. וּמָה רָאִיתָ? הָא אִתְעֲבִיד בָּהּ מַעֲשֶׂה, הָא לָא אִתְעֲבִיד בָּהּ מַעֲשֶׂה.

The Gemara asks: **If so, a woman whose hymen was torn accidentally** should **also** be **included.** The Gemara responds that the term: Who is **near,** which is written in the singular, includes only **one** additional case **and not two.** The Gemara asks: **And what did you see**[N] to render forbidden a woman whose hymen was accidentally torn and permit a divorcée who had previously been only betrothed, and not the opposite? The Gemara answers: In **this** case of the women whose hymen was torn, **an action has been performed** on her body, whereas in **that** case of the divorcée, **no action has been performed** on her body.

וְרַבִּי יוֹסֵי, מִדְּשָׁבְקֵיהּ לְבַר זוּגֵיהּ – מִכְּלָל דִּבְמוּכַּת עֵץ כְּרַבִּי מֵאִיר סְבִירָא לֵיהּ, מְנָא לֵיהּ? מִ״לֹּא הָיְתָה לְאִישׁ״.

The *baraita* cites Rabbi Yosei and Rabbi Shimon as holding that a priest may not become impure for his sister who was betrothed and then divorced, and it cites only Rabbi Shimon as holding that he may not become impure for his sister who was a grown woman. Based on this, the Gemara asks: **From** the fact **that Rabbi Yosei left his partner,** Rabbi Shimon, **it may be inferred that with regard to a woman whose hymen was torn accidentally he holds in accordance with** the opinion of **Rabbi Meir,** that a priest does become impure. **From where** does **he** derive this *halakha*? The Gemara explains that he derives it **from** the phrase: "Who **has had no man,**" as a woman whose hymen was torn accidentally has not been with a man.

וְהָא אַפִּיקְתֵּיהּ! חַד מִ״לֹּא הָיְתָה״ וְחַד מִ״לְּאִישׁ״.

The Gemara asks: **Haven't you** already **derived** the *halakha* of a betrothed woman from that phrase? The Gemara answers: Rabbi Yosei learns **one** *halakha* **from** the phrase **"has had no,"** which indicates that she has not even been betrothed, **and** he derives **one** *halakha* **from** the term **"man,"** which indicates that only a woman who was with a man is no longer considered a virgin with regard to this *halakha*, but not one whose hymen was torn accidentally.

״אֵלָיו״ לְרַבּוֹת הַבּוֹגֶרֶת. וְהָא אָמַר רַבִּי שִׁמְעוֹן: ״בְּתוּלָה״ בְּתוּלָה שְׁלֵימָה מַשְׁמַע! טַעֲמָא דִּידֵיהּ נַמִּי הָתָם מֵהָכָא, דְּדָרֵישׁ הָכִי: מִדְּ״אֵלָיו״ לְרַבּוֹת הַבּוֹגֶרֶת, מִכְּלָל דִּ״בְתוּלָה״ בְּתוּלָה שְׁלֵימָה מַשְׁמַע.

It was stated previously that according to Rabbi Shimon, the term **"to him,"** comes **to include a grown woman.** The Gemara asks: **Didn't Rabbi Shimon say** with regard to a High Priest that the term **virgin indicates a complete virgin,** which does not include a grown woman? The Gemara answers: **His reason there is also** derived **from here, as he expounds as follows: From** the fact **that** the expression **"to him"** is needed **to include a grown woman,** it may be **inferred that** the term **virgin** by itself **indicates a complete virgin.**

תַּנְיָא, רַבִּי שִׁמְעוֹן בֶּן יוֹחַי אוֹמֵר: גִּיּוֹרֶת פְּחוּתָה מִבַּת שָׁלֹשׁ שָׁנִים וְיוֹם אֶחָד כְּשֵׁירָה לִכְהוּנָּה, שֶׁנֶּאֱמַר ״וְכֹל הַטַּף בַּנָּשִׁים אֲשֶׁר לֹא יָדְעוּ מִשְׁכַּב זָכָר הַחֲיוּ לָכֶם״ וַהֲרֵי פִּנְחָס עִמָּהֶם.

§ The Gemara cites another ruling of Rabbi Shimon ben Yoḥai, also related to the discussion of defining who is considered a virgin. **It is taught** in a *baraita* that **Rabbi Shimon ben Yoḥai says: A female convert**[N] who converted when she was **less than three years and one day old**[H] **is permitted to** marry into **the priesthood,**[N] **as it is stated: "But all the women children that have not known man by lying with him, keep alive for yourselves"** (Numbers 31:18). This verse indicates that these women were fit for all of the warriors, **and** since **Pinehas** the priest **was with them** (see Numbers 31:6), it is clear that young converts are permitted to priests.

וְרַבָּנַן: לַעֲבָדִים וְלִשְׁפָחוֹת. אִי הָכִי – בַּת שָׁלֹשׁ שָׁנִים וְיוֹם אֶחָד נַמִּי!

The Gemara asks: And how do **the Rabbis,** who disagree with Rabbi Shimon, interpret this verse? The Gemara responds: They understand the phrase "keep alive for yourselves" to mean that they could keep them **as slaves and as maidservants,** but they could not necessarily marry them. The Gemara asks: **If so,** if the source for Rabbi Shimon's ruling is this verse, a girl who converted at the **age of three years and one day old** should **also** be permitted to a priest, as long as she has never had intercourse, as stated by the verse.

NOTES

And what did you see – וּמָה רָאִיתָ: Since the verses are not conclusive, it would seem logical that one who was betrothed and divorced is more distant from her brother and the rest of her father's household than a woman whose hymen was torn accidentally (Ritva).

Female convert – גִּיּוֹרֶת: The primary discussion of a female convert's eligibility to marry a priest is in the final chapter of tractate *Kiddushin*. Some commentaries maintain that female converts are forbidden to priests because they have the status of a *zona*, as implied later in the Gemara here. This appears to be the opinion of Rashi and the Rambam.

Others commentaries question this explanation: If the definition of a *zona* is one who has had forbidden intercourse, how can any *tanna* disagree with Rabbi Shimon and hold that one who converted when she was less than three years old is prohibited from marrying a priest? Even if someone would have had intercourse with her before she converted, intercourse with a girl less than three years old is not halakhically recognized as intercourse. Furthermore, even if she converted as an adult it is not clear that she would still be considered a *zona* afterward, as one who converts is considered to be starting a new life.

Consequently, these commentaries explain that the prohibition is based upon a command of the prophet Ezekiel: "Neither shall they take for their wives a widow… but they shall take virgins of the seed of the house of Israel" (Ezekiel 44:22), as explained in tractate *Kiddushin* (78a).

The dispute among the *tanna'im* is over which type of convert is included in this verse. According to this opinion, despite the fact that this mitzva does not appear in the Torah, it is not a mere injunction of a prophet. Rather, the prophet only indicated that a Torah law was in existence (Ra'avad; Rashba). The Ritva combines these opinions and explains that the verse in Ezekiel indicates that the category of *zona* includes not only one who has engaged in forbidden relations but also anyone who is not from the seed of the house of Israel (see *Tosafot Yam shel Shlomo* and *Beit Shmuel*). Later commentaries attempt to prove from here that the prohibition for a priest to marry a convert is from Torah law, even if she converted when she was less than three years old.

A female convert less than…is permitted to the priesthood – גִּיּוֹרֶת פְּחוּתָה...כְּשֵׁירָה לִכְהוּנָּה: The fact that this is cited here, in the context of a discussion of whom the High Priest may marry, indicates that according to Rabbi Shimon, this convert is permitted to marry even a High Priest. The Gemara's proof from the story of Pinehas is consistent with this conclusion, as he was the priest anointed for war, and this priest has the same *halakhot* as a High Priest with regard to the prohibition against marrying a non-virgin (*Keren Ora*).

HALAKHA

A female convert less than three years and one day old – גִּיּוֹרֶת פְּחוּתָה מִבַּת שָׁלֹשׁ שָׁנִים: A priest may not marry a convert, even if she converted when she was less than three years old, as the *halakha* does not follow the opinion of Rabbi Shimon ben Yoḥai. If he married her, he is forced to divorce her (Rambam *Sefer Kedusha*, *Hilkhot Issurei Bia* 18:3; *Shulḥan Arukh*, *Even HaEzer* 6:8).

LANGUAGE

Hidrokan – הִדְרוֹקָן: From the Greek ὑδρωπικός, *hydropikos*, meaning one who suffers from ascites.

BACKGROUND

Hidrokan – הִדְרוֹקָן: The illness *hidrokan*, identified as ascites, has several causes, the most common being a dysfunction of the liver or the heart. Its symptoms are caused by a large accumulation of water under the skin, which causes significant swelling. Due to this accretion of water, and, occasionally, due to the effects of the illness itself, the faces of individuals suffering from this disease turn a pale yellow.

כִּדְרַב הוּנָא. דְּרַב הוּנָא רָמֵי: כְּתִיב ״כׇּל אִשָּׁה יֹדַעַת אִישׁ לְמִשְׁכַּב זָכָר הֲרֹגוּ״. הָא אֵינָהּ יוֹדַעַת – קַיְּימוּ, מִכְּלָל דְּהַטַּף בֵּין יָדְעוּ בֵּין לֹא יָדְעוּ – קַיְּימוּ, וּכְתִיב ״וְכֹל הַטַּף בַּנָּשִׁים אֲשֶׁר לֹא יָדְעוּ מִשְׁכַּב זָכָר הַחֲיוּ לָכֶם״, הָא יָדְעִי – הֲרוֹגוּ.

The Gemara replies: His reasoning is **as** stated by **Rav Huna, as Rav Huna raised a contradiction: It is written** in one verse: **"Kill every woman that has known man by lying with him"** (Numbers 31:17), which indicates that a woman who **has not known** a man in this way **you may keep** alive. This proves **by inference that the** female **children,** who are not classified as women, **you may keep** alive regardless of **whether they knew** a man **or they did not know** a man. **And it is written** in a different verse: **"But all the women children that have not known man by lying with him, keep alive for yourselves"** (Numbers 31:18), which indicates that if **they have known** men, **you must kill** them. This is an apparent contradiction.

הֱוֵי אוֹמֵר: בִּרְאוּיָה לִיבָּעֵל הַכָּתוּב מְדַבֵּר.

Rav Huna explains: **You must say that the verse is speaking of** a woman who is **fit for intercourse.** The verse does not mean to distinguish between women who have actually engaged in sexual intercourse and those who have not. Rather, it distinguishes between a girl over the age of three, with whom an act of intercourse is recognized as such, and a girl below the age of three.

תַּנְיָא נַמִי הָכִי: ״וְכׇל אִשָּׁה יוֹדַעַת אִישׁ״ בִּרְאוּיָה לִיבָּעֵל הַכָּתוּב מְדַבֵּר. אַתָּה אוֹמֵר בִּרְאוּיָה לִיבָּעֵל, אוֹ אֵינוֹ אֶלָּא נִבְעֲלָה מַמָּשׁ? כְּשֶׁהוּא אוֹמֵר ״וְכֹל הַטַּף בַּנָּשִׁים אֲשֶׁר לֹא יָדְעוּ מִשְׁכַּב זָכָר״ הֱוֵי אוֹמֵר בִּרְאוּיָה לִיבָּעֵל הַכָּתוּב מְדַבֵּר.

This is also taught in a *baraita*: **"Every woman that has known man"; the verse is speaking of** a woman **who is fit for intercourse.** The *baraita* proceeds to discuss this *halakha*: Do **you say** it is referring **to** one who is **fit for intercourse,** or perhaps **it is** referring **only** to **one who has actually had intercourse? When** the verse **states: "But all the women children that have not known man by lying with him,** keep alive for yourselves," which indicates that grown women must be killed even if they have not had intercourse with a man, **you must say that the verse is speaking of** a woman **who is fit for intercourse.**

מְנָא יָדְעִי? אָמַר רַב הוּנָא בַּר בִּיזְנָא אָמַר רַבִּי שִׁמְעוֹן חֲסִידָא: הֶעֱבִירוּם לִפְנֵי הַצִּיץ, כׇּל שֶׁפָּנֶיהָ מוֹרִיקוֹת – בְּיָדוּעַ שֶׁהִיא רְאוּיָה לִיבָּעֵל, כׇּל שֶׁאֵין פָּנֶיהָ מוֹרִיקוֹת – בְּיָדוּעַ שֶׁאֵינָהּ רְאוּיָה לִיבָּעֵל. אָמַר רַב נַחְמָן: סִימָן לַעֲבֵירָה הִדְרוֹקָן.

The Gemara asks a practical question with regard to the events described by the Torah: **From where did they know** whether a particular girl was already three years old and fit for intercourse? **Rav Huna bar Bizna said that Rabbi Shimon Ḥasida said: They passed them before the frontplate** of the High Priest. **Any** girl **whose face** miraculously **turned sallow, it was known that she was fit for intercourse,** and any girl **whose face did not turn sallow,** it was thereby **known that she was not fit for intercourse.** Similarly, **Rav Naḥman said: A sign of transgression** in the area of sexual morality **is** the disease ***hidrokan***,[LB] which causes one's face to turn sallow.

כַּיּוֹצֵא בַּדָּבָר אַתָּה אוֹמֵר: ״וַיִּמְצְאוּ מִיּוֹשְׁבֵי יָבֵישׁ גִּלְעָד אַרְבַּע מֵאוֹת נַעֲרָה בְתוּלָה אֲשֶׁר לֹא יָדְעוּ אִישׁ לְמִשְׁכַּב זָכָר״. מְנָא יָדְעִי? אָמַר רַב כָּהֲנָא: הוֹשִׁיבוּם עַל פִּי חָבִית שֶׁל יַיִן, בְּעוּלָה – רֵיחָהּ נוֹדֵף, בְּתוּלָה – אֵין רֵיחָהּ נוֹדֵף.

Similarly, you can **say** with regard to the verse: **"And they found among the inhabitants of Jabesh-gilead four hundred young virgins that had not known man by lying with him"** (Judges 21:12). **From where did they know** that they were virgins? **Rav Kahana said: They sat them on the opening of a barrel of wine.** If she was **a non-virgin, her breath** would **smell** like wine; if she was **a virgin, her breath did not smell** like wine.

וְנַעַבְרִינְהוּ לִפְנֵי צִיץ! אָמַר רַב כָּהֲנָא בְּרֵיהּ דְּרַב נָתָן: ״לְרָצוֹן לָהֶם״ כְּתִיב, לְרָצוֹן וְלֹא לְפוּרְעָנוּת. אִי הָכִי בְּמִדְיָן נַמִי! אֲמַר רַב אַשִׁי: ״לָהֶם״ כְּתִיב, לָהֶם לְרָצוֹן וְלֹא לְפוּרְעָנוּת, וּלְגוֹיִם – אֲפִילּוּ לְפוּרְעָנוּת.

The Gemara suggests: **They should** have **passed them before the frontplate,** as described previously with regard to the daughters of Midian. **Rav Kahana, son of Rav Natan, said:** The verse states with regard to the frontplate: "And it shall be upon Aaron's forehead … **that they may be accepted** before the Lord" (Exodus 28:38), which indicates that the frontplate is worn **for acceptance but not for calamity.** The Gemara raises a difficulty: **If so,** the frontplate should **also** not have been used **with regard to** the women of **Midian. Rav Ashi said:** The word **"they" is written** in the verse, indicating that **for them,** the Jewish people, the frontplate is **for acceptance but not for calamity; but for gentiles** it can be used **even for calamity.**

אָמַר רַבִּי יַעֲקֹב בַּר אִידִי אָמַר רַבִּי יְהוֹשֻׁעַ בֶּן לֵוִי: הֲלָכָה כְּרַבִּי שִׁמְעוֹן בֶּן יוֹחַאי. אֲמַר לֵיהּ רַבִּי זֵירָא לְרַבִּי יַעֲקֹב בַּר אִידִי: בְּפֵירוּשׁ שְׁמִיעַ לָךְ, אוֹ מִכְּלָלָא שְׁמִיעַ לָךְ?

Rabbi Ya'akov bar Idi said that Rabbi Yehoshua ben Levi said: The *halakha* is in accordance with the opinion of **Rabbi Shimon ben Yoḥai. Rabbi Zeira said to Rabbi Ya'akov bar Idi:** Did you **hear** Rabbi Yehoshua ben Levi say this **explicitly or** did **you learn** it **by inference?**

מַאי כְּלָלָא? דְּאָמַר רַבִּי יְהוֹשֻׁעַ בֶּן לֵוִי: עִיר אַחַת הָיְתָה בְּאֶרֶץ יִשְׂרָאֵל שֶׁקָּרָא עָלֶיהָ עַרְעָר, וְשִׁגֵּר רַבִּי אֶת רַבִּי רוֹמָנוּס וּבְדָקָהּ, וּמָצָא בָּהּ בַּת גִּיּוֹרֶת פְּחוּתָה מִבַּת שָׁלֹשׁ שָׁנִים וְיוֹם אֶחָד – וְהִכְשִׁירָהּ רַבִּי לִכְהוּנָּה. אֲמַר לֵיהּ: בְּפֵירוּשׁ שְׁמִיעַ לִי.

The Gemara asks: **What inference** was Rabbi Zeira hinting at? The Gemara explains: **As Rabbi Yehoshua ben Levi said: There was a certain city in Eretz Yisrael where they contested** the lineage[N] of a particular family. **And Rabbi** Yehuda HaNasi **sent Rabbi Romanus, and he examined** the family's lineage **and found** that it included **the daughter** of **a convert** who had converted when she was **less than three years and one day old,** and she had married a priest. **And Rabbi** Yehuda HaNasi **permitted her to the priesthood.** This indicates that Rabbi Yehoshua ben Levi ruled in accordance with Rabbi Shimon. Rabbi Ya'akov bar Idi **said to him: I heard explicitly** that Rabbi Yehoshua ben Levi ruled in this manner.

וְאִי מִכְּלָלָא מַאי? דִּלְמָא שָׁאנֵי הָתָם, הוֹאִיל וְאִנְסִיב – אִנְסִיב. דְּהָא רַב וְרַבִּי יוֹחָנָן דְּאָמְרִי תַּרְוַיְיהוּ: בּוֹגֶרֶת וּמוּכַּת עֵץ – לֹא יִשָּׂא, וְאִם נָשָׂא – נָשׂוּי.

The Gemara asks: **And if** Rabbi Yehoshua ben Levi's opinion had been derived **by inference, what** of it? The Gemara answers: **Perhaps it was different there,** because **since she** had already **married** a priest, **she** could remain **married** after the fact, but it would not be permitted for her to marry a priest *ab initio*, **as it is Rav and Rabbi Yoḥanan who both say:** A High Priest **may not marry a grown woman and a woman whose hymen was torn accidentally, but if he married** one of them **he is married** and not required to divorce her.

הָכִי הַשְׁתָּא?! בִּשְׁלָמָא הָתָם – סוֹפָהּ לִהְיוֹת בּוֹגֶרֶת תַּחְתָּיו, סוֹפָהּ לִהְיוֹת בְּעוּלָה תַּחְתָּיו. הָכָא – סוֹפָהּ לִהְיוֹת זוֹנָה תַּחְתָּיו?!

The Gemara refutes this claim: **How can** these cases **be compared? Granted, there,** in the case of a grown woman, it is reasonable for her to be permitted after the fact, as a young woman **will eventually be a grown woman under him,** i.e., while married to him, and **she will eventually be a non-virgin under him.** However, **here,** in the case of a convert, **will she eventually be a *zona* under him?** If she is forbidden to a priest *ab initio* it is because she has the status of a *zona*, in which case she should be prohibited after the fact as well. Consequently, it can be proven from the incident cited previously that Rabbi Yehoshua ben Levi rules in accordance with the opinion of Rabbi Shimon.

רַב סָפְרָא מַתְנֵי לַהּ מִכְּלָלָא, וְקַשְׁיָא לֵיהּ, וּמְשַׁנֵּי לֵיהּ הָכִי.

The Gemara comments: **Rav Safra taught this** *halakha* after deriving Rabbi Yehoshua ben Levi's ruling **by inference,** although he had never heard this ruling explicitly. **And** the question mentioned above was **difficult for him, and he resolved it in this** same manner.

הַהוּא כָּהֲנָא דְּאִנְסִיב גִּיּוֹרֶת פְּחוּתָה מִבַּת שָׁלֹשׁ שָׁנִים וְיוֹם אֶחָד. אֲמַר לֵיהּ רַב נַחְמָן בַּר יִצְחָק: מַאי הַאי? אֲמַר לֵיהּ: דְּאָמַר רַבִּי יַעֲקֹב בַּר אִידִי אָמַר רַבִּי יְהוֹשֻׁעַ בֶּן לֵוִי: הֲלָכָה כְּרַבִּי שִׁמְעוֹן בֶּן יוֹחַאי. אֲמַר לֵיהּ: זִיל אַפֵּיק, וְאִי לָא – מַפֵּיקְנָא לָךְ רַבִּי יַעֲקֹב בַּר אִידִי מֵאוּנָךְ.

The Gemara relates another incident related to this *halakha*: **A certain priest married a convert,** who had converted when she was **less than three years and one day old. Rav Naḥman bar Yitzḥak said to him: What is this?** Why are you violating the *halakha*? **He said to him:** It is permitted for me to marry her, **as Rabbi Ya'akov bar Idi said that Rabbi Yehoshua ben Levi said** that **the *halakha* is in accordance with** the opinion of **Rabbi Shimon ben Yoḥai. He said to him: Go remove** her, i.e., divorce her. **And if not, I will remove Rabbi Ya'akov bar Idi from your ear [*me'unekh*]**[N] **for you.** In other words, I will take the necessary action to ensure that you obey and divorce her, so that you can no longer follow Rabbi Ya'akov bar Idi's opinion.

תַּנְיָא וְכֵן הָיָה רַבִּי שִׁמְעוֹן בֶּן יוֹחַאי אוֹמֵר

§ **It is taught** in a *baraita*: **And similarly, Rabbi Shimon ben Yoḥai would say:**[N]

NOTES

Where they contested the lineage, etc. – **שֶׁקָּרָא עָלֶיהָ עַרְעָר וכו׳**: The Gemara indicates that a priest from that town married a woman who had converted when she was less than three years old. The Jerusalem Talmud offers an alternative account, in which the ruling follows the opinion of the Rabbis as well as that of Rabbi Shimon. According to that account, it was a regular Israelite who married the convert, and Rabbi Yehuda HaNasi permitted their descendants to marry priests.

From your ear [*me'unekh*] – **מֵאוּנָךְ**: *Unekh* comes from the word *una*, a shortened form of *udna*, meaning ear. Some explain that he meant he would punish him until he removed the words of Rabbi Ya'akov bar Idi, so that his ears would no longer listen to him. Others maintain that he claimed he would make him forget Rabbi Ya'akov bar Idi until he would no longer mention his name (*Arukh*).

And similarly, Rabbi Shimon ben Yoḥai would say, etc. – **וְכֵן הָיָה רַבִּי שִׁמְעוֹן בֶּן יוֹחַאי אוֹמֵר וכו׳**: What is the connection between the following statement and the previous discussion? Rabbi Shimon must have taught many other *halakhot* that are not cited here. The Rivan explains that the *tanna* wanted to quote another case in which Rabbi Shimon ruled more leniently than the Rabbis. It is suggested in the *Yam shel Shlomo* that this statement is cited here in order to emphasize that just as the *halakha* does not follow the opinion of Rabbi Shimon with regard to the previous discussion, it does not follow his opinion with regard to the upcoming discussion, although this is subject to a dispute between the early commentaries. The *Keren Ora* and the *Arukh LaNer* explain simply that these two *halakhot* are cited together because Rabbi Shimon derived both of them from verses with regard to the war against Midian.

BACKGROUND

The tent of a corpse – אֹהֶל הַמֵּת: The *halakhot* of the impurity imparted by a corpse, including the *halakhot* of a tent covering a corpse, are cited in great detail in tractate *Oholot*. The essential *halakhot* of the tent over a corpse are detailed in the Torah (Numbers, chapter 19). The Sages derived that any structure that has a cavity that is at least one cubic handbreadth in volume and contains a corpse or part of a corpse, e.g., its flesh, bones, or limbs, becomes a tent over a corpse. Not only do all articles subject to ritual impurity contained within it become ritually impure themselves, but they also become a primary source of ritual impurity, capable of imparting ritual impurity to people and objects.

HALAKHA

The impurity of a corpse of gentiles – טוּמְאַת הַמֵּת שֶׁל נׇכְרִים: Some commentaries maintain that the corpses of gentiles do not convey impurity via a tent, in accordance with the opinion of Rabbi Shimon ben Yoḥai. Others disagree (*Tosafot*; Rosh). It is proper for a priest to act stringently in this regard. The corpse of a gentile certainly conveys impurity to one who touches or carries it (Rambam *Sefer Tahara, Hilkhot Tumat Met* 1:13 and *Sefer Shofetim, Hilkhot Evel* 3:3; *Shulḥan Arukh, Yoreh De'a* 372:2).

קִבְרֵי גוֹיִם אֵינָן מְטַמְּאִין בְּאֹהֶל, שֶׁנֶּאֱמַר ״וְאַתֵּן צֹאנִי צֹאן מַרְעִיתִי אָדָם אַתֶּם״ אַתֶּם קְרוּיִין ״אָדָם״, וְאֵין הַגּוֹיִם קְרוּיִין ״אָדָם״.

The graves of gentiles do not render items **impure though a tent,**[B] **as it is stated: "And you My sheep, the sheep of My pasture, are men [*adam*]"** (Ezekiel 34:31), from which it is derived that **you,** the Jewish people, **are called men [*adam*]**[N] **but gentiles are not called men [*adam*].** Since the Torah introduces the *halakha* of ritual impurity of a tent with the words: "When a man [*adam*] dies in a tent" (Numbers 19:14), this *halakha* applies only to corpses of Jews but not those of gentiles.[H]

מֵיתִיבֵי: ״וְנֶפֶשׁ אָדָם שִׁשָּׁה עָשָׂר אָלֶף״! מִשּׁוּם בְּהֵמָה.

The Gemara **raises an objection** based upon the verse with regard to captives taken during the war against Midian: **"And the persons [*nefesh adam*] were sixteen thousand"** (Numbers 31:40), which indicates that gentiles are also referred to as *adam*. The Gemara answers: They are given this title **due to** the need to distinguish the people taken captive from the **animals** that were taken as spoils of war.

״אֲשֶׁר יֶשׁ בָּהּ הַרְבֵּה מִשְׁתֵּים עֶשְׂרֵה רִבּוֹא אָדָם אֲשֶׁר לֹא יָדַע בֵּין יְמִינוֹ לִשְׂמֹאלוֹ (וּבְהֵמָה רַבָּה)״. מִשּׁוּם בְּהֵמָה.

The Gemara raises another difficulty based upon a verse with regard to the city of Nineveh: **"Wherein are more than one hundred and twenty thousand men [*adam*] that cannot discern between their right hand and their left hand, and also much cattle"** (Jonah 4:11). The Gemara answers: There, too, the gentiles are given this title **due to** the need to distinguish them from the **animals** mentioned in the verse.

״כׇּל הוֹרֵג נֶפֶשׁ וְכֹל נוֹגֵעַ בֶּחָלָל תִּתְחַטְּאוּ״! דִּלְמָא אִיקְּטִיל חַד מִיִּשְׂרָאֵל. וְרַבָּנַן: ״לֹא נִפְקַד מִמֶּנּוּ אִישׁ״. וְרַבִּי שִׁמְעוֹן בֶּן יוֹחַי: ״לֹא נִפְקַד מִמֶּנּוּ אִישׁ״ לַעֲבֵירָה.

The Gemara continues to question Rabbi Shimon's ruling based upon a verse pertaining to the war against Midian: **"Whoever has killed anyone, and whoever has touched any slain, purify yourselves"** (Numbers 31:19). This indicates that gentile corpses convey ritual impurity. The Gemara answers: **Perhaps a Jew was killed,** and the concern was for impurity caused by his corpse. **And the Rabbis** reply that the verse attests: **"Not one man of us is missing"** (Numbers 31:49). No Jewish soldiers fell in battle, and therefore the concern for impurity must have been due to the corpses of gentiles. **And Rabbi Shimon ben Yoḥai** responds: The intent of that verse is that **not one man of us is missing** due to **transgression,** i.e., none of them sinned.

רָבִינָא אָמַר: נְהִי דְּמַעֲטִינְהוּ קְרָא מֵאִטַּמּוֹיֵי בְּאֹהֶל, דִּכְתִיב ״אָדָם כִּי יָמוּת בְּאֹהֶל״, מִמַּגָּע וּמַשָּׂא מִי מַעֲטִינְהוּ קְרָא?

Ravina said that the explanation above is unnecessary: **Granted, the verse excluded** gentiles **from rendering** items **impure through a tent, as it is written: "When a man [*adam*] dies in a tent"** (Numbers 19:14); but **did the verse exclude them from** rendering items impure via **touching and carrying?**[N] Since gentile corpses convey impurity in these ways, they could have rendered impure the Jews involved in the war with Midian, even according to Rabbi Shimon ben Yoḥai.

NOTES

You are called men [*adam*] – אַתֶּם קְרוּיִים אָדָם: Since the Torah was given to the Jewish people, it is assumed that whenever it refers to men [*adam*], it is referring to its primary audience, the Jewish people. If a wider meaning is intended the verse so specifies (see Maharatz Ḥayyut).

The commentaries analyze many instances where the Torah uses the term *adam*. Their conclusion is that the word *adam* is sometimes stated with regard to gentiles, but only when the verse must use this word, e.g., a verse that distinguishes between man and animal or between a commoner and a man of social standing.

Tosafot cite the opinion of Rabbeinu Meshullam that the Torah uses the term *adam* instead of referring directly to the Jewish people in the context of punishment or tragedy, while it refers directly to the Jewish people in more positive contexts. Rabbeinu Tam contends that the term: Man [*adam*], always refers to the Jewish people, whereas the term: The man [*ha'adam*], refers to the entire human race. Some commentaries note that the numerical value of: The man [*ha'adam*], is the same as the numerical value of the word impure [*tamei*]. See Rabbi Avraham min HaHar's response to this exposition. Later commentaries suggest other homiletic explanations of this idea (see *Iyyun Ya'akov*).

Did the verse exclude them from rendering items impure via touching and carrying – מִמַּגָּע וּמַשָּׂא מִי מַעֲטִינְהוּ קְרָא: Ezekiel prophesies that in the future any place that contains the bones of the corpses of Gog and Magog will be marked off (Ezekiel 39:15), which seemingly indicates that gentile corpses also convey impurity through a tent. The Ramban offers two answers: First, it is always possible that any corpse found is that of a Jew. Moreover, purity will be so widespread in the future that any source of impurity will be marked, even if it does not convey impurity through a tent (see Meiri).

מתני׳ אֵירַס אֶת הָאַלְמָנָה וְנִתְמַנָּה לִהְיוֹת כֹּהֵן גָּדוֹל – יִכְנוֹס. וּמַעֲשֶׂה בִּיהוֹשֻׁעַ בֶּן גַּמְלָא שֶׁקִּדֵּשׁ אֶת מָרְתָא בַּת בַּיְתוֹס, וּמִנָּהוּ הַמֶּלֶךְ לִהְיוֹת כֹּהֵן גָּדוֹל, וּכְנָסָהּ. שׁוֹמֶרֶת יָבָם שֶׁנָּפְלָה לִפְנֵי כֹּהֵן הֶדְיוֹט, וְנִתְמַנָּה לִהְיוֹת כֹּהֵן גָּדוֹל, אַף עַל פִּי שֶׁעָשָׂה בָּהּ מַאֲמָר – הֲרֵי זֶה לֹא יִכְנוֹס.

MISHNA If a priest **betrothed a widow**[N] **and was** subsequently **appointed to be High Priest,**[H] **he may marry** her. **And there was an incident with Yehoshua ben Gamla,**[P] **who betrothed Marta bat Baitos,**[P] a widow, **and the king** subsequently **appointed him to be High Priest, and** he nevertheless **married her.** Conversely, in the case **of a widow waiting for her *yavam* who happened before a common priest,** i.e., the priest was her *yavam*, **and he was** subsequently **appointed to be High Priest,** then **even if he** had already **performed levirate betrothal with her, he may not marry her,** because she is a widow.

גמ׳ תָּנוּ רַבָּנַן: מִנַּיִן שֶׁאִם אֵירַס אֶת הָאַלְמָנָה וְנִתְמַנָּה לִהְיוֹת כֹּהֵן גָּדוֹל שֶׁיִּכְנוֹס – תַּלְמוּד לוֹמַר ״יִקַּח אִשָּׁה״. אִי הָכִי שׁוֹמֶרֶת יָבָם נַמִּי! ״אִשָּׁה״ וְלֹא יְבָמָה.

GEMARA **The Sages taught: From where is it** derived **that if** a priest **betrothed a widow and was** subsequently **appointed to be High Priest, that he may marry** her? **The verse states: "Shall he take for a wife"**[N] (Leviticus 21:14), an inclusive phrase that indicates that he may marry her in this situation despite the general prohibition for a High Priest to marry a widow. The Gemara asks: **If so, a widow waiting for her *yavam*** should **also** be permitted to a High Priest.[H] The Gemara answers: The word **"wife"** indicates that this does **not** include a ***yevama*,**[N] who was not initially his wife but his brother's.

״מַעֲשֶׂה בִּיהוֹשֻׁעַ״ וכו׳. מִנָּהוּ – אִין, נִתְמַנָּה – לָא. אֲמַר רַב יוֹסֵף: קְטִיר קְחָזֵינָא הָכָא. דַּאֲמַר רַב אַסִּי: תַּרְקַבָּא דְּדִינָרֵי עַיְּילָה לֵיהּ מָרְתָא בַּת בַּיְתוֹס לְיַנַּאי מַלְכָּא, עַד דְּמוֹקֵי לֵיהּ לִיהוֹשֻׁעַ בֶּן גַּמְלָא בְּכָהֲנֵי רַבְרְבֵי.

The mishna related **an incident with Yehoshua** ben Gamla. The Gemara notes that the mishna states that the king **appointed him,** **yes,** but **not** that he was worthy of being **appointed. Rav Yosef said: I see a conspiracy here,**[N] as this was clearly not a proper appointment by the priests and the Sanhedrin but rather a political appointment, **as Rav Asi said: Marta bat Baitos brought** a vessel the size of a **half-*se'a* [*tarkav*]** full **of dinars to King Yannai**[P] **until he appointed Yehoshua ben Gamla High Priest.**

מתני׳ כֹּהֵן גָּדוֹל שֶׁמֵּת אָחִיו – חוֹלֵץ וְלֹא מְיַיבֵּם.

MISHNA **A High Priest whose brother died** without children **performs *ḥalitza* and he does not perform levirate marriage,** as he may not marry a widow.

גמ׳ קָא פָּסֵיק וְתָנֵי, לָא שְׁנָא מִן הָאֵירוּסִין וְלָא שְׁנָא מִן הַנִּשּׂוּאִין. בִּשְׁלָמָא מִן הַנִּשּׂוּאִין – עֲשֵׂה וְלֹא תַעֲשֶׂה הוּא, וְאֵין עֲשֵׂה דּוֹחֶה לֹא תַעֲשֶׂה וַעֲשֵׂה. אֶלָּא מִן הָאֵירוּסִין, יָבֹא עֲשֵׂה וְיִדְחֶה אֶת לֹא תַעֲשֶׂה!

GEMARA The Gemara comments: The mishna **teaches this *halakha* categorically,** indicating that **it is no different** if she is his brother's widow **from betrothal, and it is no different** if she is his widow **from marriage.**[H] The Gemara analyzes this *halakha*: **Granted,** she is forbidden to him if she was widowed **from marriage, as,** if he were to marry her, **it** would be a violation of both the **positive mitzva** that the High Priest marry a virgin **and the prohibition** for him to marry a widow. **And a positive mitzva,** i.e., levirate marriage, **does not override a prohibition and a positive** mitzva together. **However,** if she was a widow **from betrothal** and is therefore still a virgin, **the positive mitzva** of levirate marriage **should come and override the prohibition** for a High Priest to marry a widow.

NOTES

If a priest betrothed a widow, etc. – אֵירַס אֶת הָאַלְמָנָה וכו׳: This policy does not extend to a case where a man betrothed a woman and then his testicles became crushed. The reason for the distinction is that the Torah expresses the prohibition to marry a man with crushed testicles by stating that he "shall not enter into the congregation of the Lord" (Deuteronomy 23:2). Conversely, with regard to a High Priest, the verse states that "he shall not take" a widow (Leviticus 21:14), which indicates that it is only the taking, i.e., the betrothal, that is prohibited (*Yosef Lekaḥ*).

Shall he take for a wife – יִקַּח אִשָּׁה: Since the word wife is entirely superfluous in this verse, the Sages derived that despite the requirement that the High Priest marry a virgin, there are instances where he may take even a woman who is not a virgin as a wife (Rivan).

The word wife indicates that this does not include a *yevama* – אִשָּׁה וְלֹא יְבָמָה: The Gemara does not employ the exposition cited earlier, that "wife" is written in singular and includes only one case but not two, because there is no legal difference between a woman waiting for her *yavam* and any other widow (Ritva).

I see a conspiracy here – קְטִיר קְחָזֵינָא הָכָא: In tractate *Bava Batra* (21a), the Gemara praises Yehoshua ben Gamla for strengthening Torah observance among the Jewish people; how does that fit in with the account here? In the *Tosafot Yeshanim*, it is suggested that the two passages are actually referring to two different individuals who had the same name. However, *Tosafot* on *Bava Batra* 21a and the *Tosefot HaRosh* explain that he was indeed great, but there were others who were more righteous and worthy of being appointed High Priest. Furthermore, he should not have accepted a royal appointment without the approval of the Sanhedrin. In the Jerusalem Talmud, it is stated that Yehoshua ben Gamla craftily spread a rumor that he had betrothed Marta bat Baitos. Once the rumor took hold, no one else would have agreed to marry her unless she obtained a bill of divorce from him. She therefore agreed to marry him and used her influence to have him appointed High Priest, as befitting her honor.

HALAKHA

Betrothed a widow and was appointed to be High Priest – אֵירַס אֶת הָאַלְמָנָה וְנִתְמַנָּה לִהְיוֹת כֹּהֵן גָּדוֹל: If a priest is appointed High Priest after betrothing a widow, he is permitted to marry her (Rambam *Sefer Kedusha*, *Hilkhot Issurei Bia* 19:12).

A widow waiting for her *yavam* should also be permitted to a High Priest – שׁוֹמֶרֶת יָבָם נַמִּי: A High Priest must perform *ḥalitza* and not enter into levirate marriage. This applies even if the obligation to perform *ḥalitza* or levirate marriage took effect before he was appointed High Priest (Rambam *Sefer Kedusha*, *Hilkhot Issurei Bia* 19:12 and *Sefer Avoda*, *Hilkhot Kelei HaMikdash* 5:10).

A widow from marriage – אַלְמָנָה מִן הַנִּשּׂוּאִין: If a *yevama* was widowed from marriage and her *yavam*, the High Priest, had intercourse with her, they have not fulfilled the mitzva of levirate marriage because a positive mitzva does not override both a positive mitzva and a prohibition. Therefore, the rival wives of a *yevama* are not permitted to marry anyone else until they have performed *ḥalitza* (Rambam *Sefer Nashim*, *Hilkhot Yibbum* 6:11).

PERSONALITIES

Yehoshua ben Gamla – יְהוֹשֻׁעַ בֶּן גַּמְלָא: Yehoshua ben Gamla, referred to by Josephus as Yehoshua ben Gamliel, was apparently one of the last High Priests in the Second Temple. He was appointed by King Agrippa II and was killed during the destruction of the Second Temple. Although the Sages criticized the way he became High Priest, they also noted his good deeds. He was praised for donating golden lots for the Yom Kippur service and was especially commended for expanding the circle of Jewish education by establishing an extensive network of schools in every town in Eretz Yisrael. It is even said that were it not for him, the Torah would have been forgotten from the Jewish people. However, some claim that there were two men with the same name, and the Yehoshua ben Gamla mentioned here is not the one who established the network of schools (see *Tosafot Yeshanim*).

Marta bat Baitos – מָרְתָא בַּת בַּיְתוֹס: Marta bat Baitos is mentioned in several places in the Talmud. Due to her great wealth, she has served throughout the ages as the archetype of a very wealthy woman. The house of Baitos was one of the most powerful and wealthy families of priests in Jerusalem, and many members of this household served as High Priest or in other important positions in the Temple. According to the Jerusalem Talmud, Marta married Yehoshua ben Gamla as a result of trickery on his part, yet after becoming betrothed to him, she sought to secure him the most elevated position possible.

The Talmud relates that during the siege of Jerusalem all her wealth was to no avail and she died of starvation.

King Yannai – יַנַּאי מַלְכָּא: As *Tosafot* note, it is inconceivable that this could have been Yannai the Hasmonean king, as he himself was High Priest and would not have given up the position to someone else. The Sages referred to several kings from the second Temple era as Yannai, to indicate their disapproval of these kings' actions.

גְּזֵירָה בִּיאָה רִאשׁוֹנָה אַטּוּ בִּיאָה שְׁנִיָּה.

The Gemara answers: By Torah law, levirate marriage is permitted in this case. However, there is a rabbinic **decree** prohibiting their **first** act of **intercourse due to** their **second** act of **intercourse.**[H] After they have engaged in intercourse once, they have fulfilled the mitzva of levirate marriage, and any subsequent act of intercourse would constitute a violation of the prohibition without the fulfillment of a mitzva.

מתני׳ כֹּהֵן הֶדְיוֹט לֹא יִשָּׂא אַיְלוֹנִית, אֶלָּא אִם כֵּן יֵשׁ לוֹ אִשָּׁה וּבָנִים. רַבִּי יְהוּדָה אוֹמֵר: אַף עַל פִּי שֶׁיֵּשׁ לוֹ אִשָּׁה וּבָנִים – לֹא יִשָּׂא אַיְלוֹנִית, שֶׁהִיא זוֹנָה הָאֲמוּרָה בַּתּוֹרָה. וַחֲכָמִים אוֹמְרִים: אֵין זוֹנָה אֶלָּא גִּיּוֹרֶת, וּמְשׁוּחְרֶרֶת, וְשֶׁנִּבְעֲלָה בְּעִילַת זְנוּת.

MISHNA **A common priest may not marry a sexually underdeveloped woman** [*aylonit*],[H] who is incapable of bearing children, **unless he** already **has a wife and children. Rabbi Yehuda says: Even if he has a wife and children, he may not marry a sexually underdeveloped woman, as she is the *zona*** about whom it is **stated in the Torah** that a priest may not marry her. Intercourse with her is considered a licentious act because she is incapable of bearing children. **And the Rabbis say: The only** women in the category of ***zona***,[H] who are therefore forbidden to a priest, are **a female convert, a freed** maidservant, **and** any woman **who engaged in licentious sexual intercourse** with a man she is prohibited from marrying.

גמ׳ אֲמַר לֵיהּ רֵישׁ גָּלוּתָא לְרַב הוּנָא: מַאי טַעֲמָא – מִשּׁוּם פְּרִיָּה וּרְבִיָּה, אַפְּרִיָּה וּרְבִיָּה כֹּהֲנִים הוּא דְּמִפַּקְדִי, וְיִשְׂרָאֵל לָא מִפַּקְדִי?! אֲמַר לֵיהּ: מִשּׁוּם דְּקָא בָּעֵי לְמִיתְנֵי סֵיפָא, רַבִּי יְהוּדָה אוֹמֵר: אַף עַל פִּי שֶׁיֵּשׁ לוֹ אִשָּׁה

GEMARA **The Exilarch said to Rav Huna: What is the reason** for the *halakha* that a priest may not marry a sexually underdeveloped woman? It is **because** he is obligated to fulfill the mitzva to **be fruitful and multiply.**[N] **Is it** only **priests who were commanded to be fruitful and multiply, but Israelites were not commanded?** Why does the mishna specify that a priest may not marry a sexually underdeveloped woman? Rav Huna **said to him:** This *halakha* does in fact apply even to Israelites, and the *tanna* mentions priests **because he wants to teach** it in a way that would parallel **the latter clause** of the mishna, which states that **Rabbi Yehuda says: Even if he has a wife**

NOTES

It is because he is obligated to fulfill the mitzva to be fruitful and multiply, etc. – מִשּׁוּם פְּרִיָּה וּרְבִיָּה וכו׳: The Gemara could also have pointed out that if the reason was due to the mitzva to have children, the mishna should also have mentioned that it is prohibited for him to marry any barren or elderly woman. In any case, Rav Huna's answer resolves these difficulties as well (*Arukh LaNer*).

HALAKHA

There is a rabbinic decree prohibiting their first act of intercourse due to their second act of intercourse – גְּזֵירָה בִּיאָה רִאשׁוֹנָה אַטּוּ בִּיאָה שְׁנִיָּה: If a *yevama* was forbidden to her *yavam* due to an ordinary Torah prohibition, i.e., one that does not carry with it a punishment of *karet* or the death penalty; due to a positive mitzva; or due to a rabbinic decree, they must perform *ḥalitza* and not enter into levirate marriage. Although the mitzva of levirate marriage should override the prohibition, the Sages prohibited the first act of intercourse due to the possibility that they would engage in a further act of intercourse, in which case they would violate the prohibition without fulfilling the mitzva. If they entered into levirate marriage nevertheless, they are considered fully married, and the woman's rival wives are exempt from *ḥalitza*. However, the *yavam* is required to divorce her (Rambam *Sefer Nashim, Hilkhot Yibbum* 6:10).

He may not marry a sexually underdeveloped woman [*aylonit*] – לֹא יִשָּׂא אַיְלוֹנִית: A man may not marry a sexually underdeveloped woman or any other woman incapable of bearing children, unless he has already fulfilled the mitzva of procreation or unless he has another wife who can bear children (Rambam *Sefer Nashim, Hilkhot Ishut* 15:7; *Shulḥan Arukh, Even HaEzer* 1:8).

Who is considered a *zona* – אֵיזוֹהִי זוֹנָה: A woman who had intercourse with a man she is prohibited from marrying, a gentile, or a slave is classified as a *zona* and is forbidden to a priest. However, if she was prohibited from marrying only a priest but permitted to marry other Jewish men, and she had intercourse with a priest, she is not classified as a *zona*. The category of *zona* also includes a female convert and a freed maidservant (Rambam *Sefer Kedusha, Hilkhot Issurei Bia* 18:2; *Shulḥan Arukh, Even HaEzer* 6:8).

וְיֵשׁ לוֹ בָּנִים לֹא יִשָּׂא אַיְלוֹנִית, שֶׁהִיא זוֹנָה הָאֲמוּרָה בַּתּוֹרָה. דְּאַזּוֹנָה כֹּהֲנִים הוּא דְּמִפַּקְּדִי, וְיִשְׂרָאֵל לָא מִפַּקְּדִי, מִשּׁוּם הָכִי קָתָנֵי כֹּהֵן.

and he has children, he may not marry a sexually underdeveloped woman, as she is the ***zona*** about whom it is **stated in the Torah** that a priest may not marry her. **It is priests who were commanded** not to marry a ***zona*****, but Israelites were not commanded** this. It is **due to that** reason that **he taught** the first clause of the mishna about **a priest**, even though that *halakha* applies equally to Israelites.

אָמַר רַב הוּנָא: מַאי טַעְמָא דְּרַבִּי יְהוּדָה – דִּכְתִיב ״אָכְלוּ וְלֹא יִשְׂבָּעוּ הִזְנוּ וְלֹא יִפְרֹצוּ״, כׇּל בִּיאָה שֶׁאֵין בָּהּ פִּירְצָה – אֵינָהּ אֶלָּא בְּעִילַת זְנוּת.

Rav Huna said: What is the reason for the opinion of **Rabbi Yehuda? As it is written: "And they shall eat, and not have enough, they shall commit harlotry, and shall not increase"** (Hosea 4:10). He expounds the verse as follows: **Any intercourse that does not** have the possibility to **increase** the population because the woman is incapable of having children, **is nothing other** than **licentious sexual intercourse.**

תַּנְיָא, רַבִּי אֱלִיעֶזֶר אוֹמֵר: כֹּהֵן לֹא יִשָּׂא אֶת הַקְּטַנָּה. אֲמַר לֵיהּ רַב חִסְדָּא לְרַבָּה: פּוּק עַיֵּין בַּהּ, דְּלָאוּרְתָּא בָּעֵי לָהּ רַב הוּנָא מִינָּךְ. נְפַק עַיֵּין בַּהּ: רַבִּי אֱלִיעֶזֶר סָבַר לָהּ כְּרַבִּי מֵאִיר, וְסָבַר לָהּ כְּרַבִּי יְהוּדָה.

§ **It is taught** in a *baraita* that **Rabbi Eliezer says: A priest may not marry a minor. Rav Ḥisda said to Rabba: Go and investigate** this *halakha*, **as in the evening Rav Huna** will **ask you** the reason for Rabbi Eliezer's ruling. **He went** and **investigated it,** and arrived at the following conclusion: **Rabbi Eliezer holds in accordance** with the opinion **of Rabbi Meir, and he** also **holds in accordance** with the opinion **of Rabbi Yehuda.**

סָבַר לָהּ כְּרַבִּי מֵאִיר – דְּחָיֵישׁ לְמִיעוּטָא, וְסָבַר לָהּ כְּרַבִּי יְהוּדָה – דְּאָמַר: אַיְלוֹנִית זוֹנָה הֲוְיָא.

Rabba explains: **He holds in accordance with** the opinion of **Rabbi Meir, who** says that **one must be concerned for the minority.** Rabbi Meir does not allow one to assume that an unknown case is similar to the majority of cases. Consequently, one must take into account the possibility that a minor will turn out to be sexually underdeveloped, although this will not be true of most individuals. **And he** also **holds in accordance with** the opinion of **Rabbi Yehuda, who said** that **a sexually underdeveloped woman is a** ***zona*** and therefore forbidden to a priest.

וּכְרַבִּי מֵאִיר מִי סָבַר לַהּ? וְהָתַנְיָא: קָטָן וּקְטַנָּה – לֹא חוֹלְצִין וְלֹא מְיַבְּמִין, דִּבְרֵי רַבִּי מֵאִיר. אָמְרוּ לוֹ לְרַבִּי מֵאִיר: יָפֶה אָמַרְתָּ שֶׁאֵין חוֹלְצִין ״אִישׁ״ כְּתִיב בְּפָרָשָׁה, וּמַקְשִׁינַן אִשָּׁה לְאִישׁ. אֶלָּא מַאי טַעְמָא אֵין מְיַבְּמִין?

The Gemara challenges Rabba's explanation: **And does** Rabbi Eliezer **hold in accordance with** the opinion of **Rabbi Meir? Isn't it taught** in a *baraita*: **A boy minor and a girl minor may not perform** ***ḥalitza***[H] **or levirate marriage;** this is **the statement of Rabbi Meir. The Rabbis said to Rabbi Meir: You spoke well** when you said **that they may not perform** ***ḥalitza*****,** as the term **"man" is written in the passage** of *ḥalitza* (Deuteronomy 25:7–10), which limits the *halakha* to an adult male, **and we compare a woman to a man**[N] and therefore limit *ḥalitza* to an adult woman. **However, what is the reason** that **they may not perform levirate marriage?**

HALAKHA

The ***ḥalitza*** **of a minor** – **חֲלִיצַת קָטָן**: A minor boy cannot perform *ḥalitza*. If he was nine years and one day old and had intercourse with his *yevama*, he has partially acquired her and she must wait until he matures, at which point he must either marry her fully or perform *ḥalitza* and also write her a bill of divorce. Similarly, a girl may not perform *ḥalitza* until she is twelve years old and develops two pubic hairs, at which point she is considered an adult (Rambam *Sefer Nashim*, *Hilkhot Yibbum* 1:16–18; *Shulḥan Arukh*, *Even HaEzer* 167:3–4).

NOTES

And we compare a woman to a man – **וּמַקְשִׁינַן אִשָּׁה לְאִישׁ**: Rashi explains that the reason a minor girl may not perform *ḥalitza* is because the actions of a minor have no legal standing. Later commentaries question the need for Rashi to mention this: Since this has been derived from a verse, why would further explanation be necessary? It seems that according to the opinion of Rashi, this *halakha* is derived from the verse only according to Rabbi Meir. However, the Rabbis, who hold that a minor may perform levirate marriage, do not exclude minors based upon the verse, and therefore they must have another reason to exclude them from *ḥalitza* (see *Arukh LaNer*).

[אָמַר לָהֶם]: קָטָן – שֶׁמָּא יִמָּצֵא סָרִיס, קְטַנָּה – שֶׁמָּא תִּמָּצֵא אַיְלוֹנִית, וְנִמְצְאוּ פּוֹגְעִין בְּעֶרְוָה, וְתַנְיָא: קְטַנָּה – מִתְיַיבֶּמֶת וְאֵינָהּ חוֹלֶצֶת, דִּבְרֵי רַבִּי אֱלִיעֶזֶר.

Rabbi Meir **said to them: A boy minor** may not perform levirate marriage **lest he be found** to be **a eunuch,** i.e., one who is incapable of fathering children for his late brother. Similarly, **a girl minor** may not perform levirate marriage **lest she be found** to be **sexually underdeveloped** when she grows up. In either case, the mitzva of levirate marriage does not apply, **and they turn out** to have **encountered a forbidden relative. And it was taught** in a different *baraita*: **A girl minor enters into levirate marriage but does not perform *ḥalitza*;** this is **the statement of Rabbi Eliezer.** This proves that Rabbi Eliezer disagrees with Rabbi Meir and is not concerned that a girl may turn out to be sexually underdeveloped.

וּכְרַבִּי יְהוּדָה מִי סָבַר לַהּ? וְהָתַנְיָא: ״זוֹנָה״ זוֹנָה כִּשְׁמָהּ, דִּבְרֵי רַבִּי אֱלִיעֶזֶר. רַבִּי עֲקִיבָא אוֹמֵר: ״זוֹנָה״ זוֹ מוּפְקֶרֶת. רַבִּי מַתְיָא בֶּן חָרָשׁ אוֹמֵר: אֲפִילּוּ הָלַךְ בַּעְלָהּ לְהַשְׁקוֹתָהּ, וּבָא עָלֶיהָ בַּדֶּרֶךְ – עֲשָׂאָהּ זוֹנָה.

The Gemara continues to challenge Rabba's explanation of Rabbi Eliezer's ruling. **And does** Rabbi Eliezer **hold in accordance with** the opinion of **Rabbi Yehuda? Wasn't it is taught in a** *baraita*: The ***zona***[N] forbidden to a priest is as **the name *zona* implies,**[N] i.e., a married woman who committed adultery; this is **the statement of Rabbi Eliezer. Rabbi Akiva says: A *zona* is** a woman, even an unmarried woman, **who is available** to all, i.e., she has intercourse with whoever is interested. **Rabbi Matya ben Ḥarash says: Even** if **her husband went to make her drink**[N] the bitter waters after she disregarded his warning not to seclude herself with a certain man, and **he had intercourse with her on the way, he has** thereby **caused her** to become **a *zona*** because she was forbidden to him at the time, despite the fact that she is his wife.

רַבִּי יְהוּדָה אוֹמֵר: ״זוֹנָה״ זוֹ אַיְלוֹנִית. וַחֲכָמִים אוֹמְרִים: אֵין זוֹנָה אֶלָּא גִּיּוֹרֶת וּמְשׁוּחְרֶרֶת וְשֶׁנִּבְעֲלָה בְּעִילַת זְנוּת. רַבִּי אֶלְעָזָר אוֹמֵר: פָּנוּי הַבָּא עַל הַפְּנוּיָה שֶׁלֹּא לְשֵׁם אִישׁוּת – עֲשָׂאָהּ זוֹנָה.

Rabbi Yehuda says: A *zona* is a sexually underdeveloped woman. And the Rabbis say: The term ***zona*** applies **only to a female convert, a freed** maidservant, **and one who engaged in licentious sexual intercourse. Rabbi Elazar says:** Even in the case of **an unmarried man who had intercourse with an unmarried woman**[H] **not for the purpose of marriage, he has** thereby **caused her** to become **a *zona*.** This *baraita* proves that Rabbi Eliezer does not agree with Rabbi Yehuda.

אֶלָּא אָמַר רַב אַדָּא בַּר אַהֲבָה: הָכָא בְּכֹהֵן גָּדוֹל עָסְקִינַן, לְאֵימַת קָנֵי לַהּ – לְכִי גָּדְלָה, בְּעוּלָה הִיא.

Rather, Rav Adda bar Ahava said that Rabbi Eliezer's ruling that a priest may not marry a minor must be explained differently: **Here we are dealing with a High Priest,** and the problem is as follows: **When can he acquire her** as his wife? Only **when she is grown up.** However, if they had started living together as husband and wife when she was a minor, then when she is grown up and the marriage can legally take effect, **she is** already **a non-virgin,** and a High Priest is commanded to marry a virgin.

אֲמַר רָבָא: מִכַּלֵּי לֵב! אִי דְּקִדְּשָׁהּ אֲבוּהָ – מֵהַהִיא שַׁעְתָּא הוּא דְּקָנֵי לַהּ, וְאִי דְּקִדְּשָׁה נַפְשָׁהּ – הָא רַבִּי אֱלִיעֶזֶר הִיא וְלָא רַבָּנַן!

Rava said: This explanation is **without reason.**[N] **If her father betrothed her** to her husband, her husband **acquired her from that time,** as betrothal that a father carries out on his daughter's behalf when she is a minor is effective by Torah law. **And if** the minor **betrothed herself, is this Rabbi Eliezer's** opinion **and not** that of **the Rabbis?**[N] The Rabbis would certainly agree that a High Priest may not marry a minor under these circumstances.

אֶלָּא אֲמַר רָבָא: לְעוֹלָם בְּכֹהֵן הֶדְיוֹט, וְחָיְישִׁינַן שֶׁמָּא תִּתְפַּתֶּה עָלָיו. אִי הָכִי יִשְׂרָאֵל נַמִי! פִּתּוּיֵי קְטַנָּה אוֹנֶס הוּא, וְאוֹנֶס בְּיִשְׂרָאֵל מִישְׁרָא שָׁרֵי.

Rather, Rava said: Actually, Rabbi Eliezer's ruling includes **a common priest,** and the reason he cannot marry a minor is that **we are concerned lest she be seduced** by another man, due to her tender age and naïveté, while married **to him.** The Gemara asks: **If so,** the same concern should apply to **an Israelite also.** The Gemara answers: **The seduction of a minor is** considered **rape, and a rape** victim remains **permitted** to her husband **in** a case where she is married to **an Israelite,** but not if she is married to a priest.

NOTES

Who is considered a *zona* – אֵיזוֹהִי זוֹנָה: This dispute between the *tanna'im* relates to the meaning of this term with regard to the prohibition for a priest to marry a *zona* and with regard to the prohibition against sacrificing as an offering an animal used as payment for a *zona*. The word *zona* appears many times in the Bible, usually in reference to a prostitute. However, since these verses do not refer to halakhic topics, they cannot serve as proof of the halakhic meaning of the term, as it is possible that the term is borrowed from its precise legal meaning and used in other contexts. Therefore, it was necessary to clarify the precise legal definition of this term.

As the name *zona* implies – זוֹנָה כִּשְׁמָהּ: The commentaries explain that according to Rabbi Eliezer a *zona* is a married woman who committed adultery. The Meiri states that the word is understood as in the verse: "And they shall go astray [*vezanu*] after foreign gods" (Deuteronomy 31:16). In other words, she strays from her husband to another man.

Even if her husband went to make her drink, etc. – אֲפִילּוּ הָלַךְ בַּעְלָהּ לְהַשְׁקוֹתָהּ וכו׳: Her status as a *zona* would be significant only if her husband died and she then wanted to marry a priest. However, even if she did not engage in intercourse with her husband once she became a *sota*, if he died before she drank the waters, she no longer drinks the waters and therefore has no way to prove her innocence. Consequently, she would be forbidden to a priest in any event, due to the possibility that she is a *zona* because she committed adultery. Rabbi Akiva Eiger explains that intercourse between the husband and wife on her way to drink the *sota* waters is still significant, as it would cause the woman to be a definite *zona*, not merely an uncertain one. Consequently, if a priest marries her he is liable by Torah law to receive lashes.

Without reason [*mekhalei lev*] – מִכַּלֵּי לֵב: According to the versions of the Gemara text recorded by the *ge'onim* and many of the early commentaries, this expression should read *mibeli lev*, i.e., something said without understanding or knowledge. The version of the text printed in the Vilna edition of the Talmud, which was also Rashi's version, is difficult to understand, but is interpreted in the same manner, in accordance with one of the connotations of the root *k-l-a*.

Is this Rabbi Eliezer's opinion and not that of the Rabbis – רַבִּי אֱלִיעֶזֶר הִיא וְלָא רַבָּנַן: The Rashba asks how Rava can be certain that the Rabbis would agree with Rabbi Eliezer. Perhaps, according to the Rabbis, if the High Priest marries her he is not required to divorce her, in accordance with the reasoning mentioned earlier in the Gemara, that she would have become a non-virgin while married to him anyway. Rabbi Eliezer, on the other hand, holds that he would have to divorce her. The Rashba answers that since all agree that the High Priest may not marry her *ab initio*, the ruling prohibiting their marriage would not have been stated in the name of Rabbi Eliezer alone.

HALAKHA

An unmarried man who had intercourse with an unmarried woman – פָּנוּי הַבָּא עַל הַפְּנוּיָה: If an unmarried man had intercourse with an unmarried woman not for the purpose of marriage, she does not thereby become a *zona*, even if she has made herself available to all for licentious purposes. The *halakha* is in accordance with the opinion of the Rabbis, that only the following women have the status of a *zona*: A female convert, a freed maidservant, and a woman who has had intercourse with a man she is not permitted to marry (Rambam *Sefer Kedusha*, *Hilkhot Issurei Bia* 18:2).

רַב פַּפָּא אֲמַר: בְּכֹהֵן גָּדוֹל, וְהַאי תַּנָּא הוּא, דְּתַנְיָא: ״בְּתוּלָה״ יָכוֹל קְטַנָּה – תַּלְמוּד לוֹמַר ״אִשָּׁה״. אִי ״אִשָּׁה״ יָכוֹל בּוֹגֶרֶת – תַּלְמוּד לוֹמַר ״בְּתוּלָה״. הָא כֵּיצַד? יָצְתָה מִכְּלַל קַטְנוּת, וְלִכְלַל בַּגְרוּת לֹא בָּאתָה.

Rav Pappa said: Rabbi Eliezer's ruling applies specifically **to a High Priest, and it is** the opinion of **this *tanna*, as it is taught** in a *baraita* that when the verse states: **"A virgin** of his own people shall he take for a wife [*isha*]" (Leviticus 21:14), one **might** have thought a High Priest may marry **a minor; the verse** therefore **states** that he must marry **a woman** [*isha*], i.e., an adult. **If** he must marry a **woman,** one **might** have thought it means **a grown woman. The verse** therefore **states** that he must marry **a virgin,** which excludes a grown woman, who is considered only a partial virgin because her hymen is not fully intact. **How so?** He must marry a woman who **has left the class of minority but** who **has not** yet **reached the class of grown womanhood,** i.e., he must marry a maiden.[H]

רַב נַחְמָן בַּר יִצְחָק אֲמַר: הַאי תַּנָּא הוּא, דְּתַנְיָא ״בְּתוּלָה״ אֵין בְּתוּלָה אֶלָּא נַעֲרָה, וְכֵן הוּא אוֹמֵר ״וְהַנַּעֲרָה טוֹבַת מַרְאֶה מְאֹד בְּתוּלָה״.

Rav Naḥman bar Yitzḥak said: It is the opinion of **this *tanna*, as it is taught** in a *baraita*: The High Priest must marry **a virgin,** and the term **virgin** refers **only** to **a maiden. And a verse similarly states: "And the maiden was very fair to look upon, a virgin,** and no man had known her" (Genesis 24:16).

רַבִּי אֶלְעָזָר אוֹמֵר: פָּנוּי הַבָּא עַל הַפְּנוּיָה שֶׁלֹּא לְשֵׁם אִישׁוּת – עֲשָׂאָהּ זוֹנָה. אֲמַר רַב עַמְרָם: אֵין הֲלָכָה כְּרַבִּי אֶלְעָזָר.

The *baraita* cited above mentioned that **Rabbi Elazar says:** In the case of **an unmarried man who had intercourse with an unmarried woman not for the purpose of marriage, he has caused her** to become **a *zona*. Rav Amram said: The *halakha* is not in accordance with** the opinion of **Rabbi Elazar.**

מתני׳ לֹא יִבָּטֵל אָדָם מִפְּרִיָּה וּרְבִיָּה אֶלָּא אִם כֵּן יֵשׁ לוֹ בָּנִים. בֵּית שַׁמַּאי אוֹמְרִים: שְׁנֵי זְכָרִים, וּבֵית הִלֵּל אוֹמְרִים: זָכָר וּנְקֵבָה, שֶׁנֶּאֱמַר ״זָכָר וּנְקֵבָה בְּרָאָם״.

MISHNA A man may not neglect the mitzva **to be fruitful and multiply**[H] **unless he** already **has children.**[N] **Beit Shammai say:**[N] One fulfills this mitzva with **two males, and Beit Hillel say: A male and a female,**[H] **as it is stated: "Male and female He created them"** (Genesis 5:2).

גמ׳ הָא יֵשׁ לוֹ בָּנִים, מִפְּרִיָּה וּרְבִיָּה – בָּטֵיל, מֵאִשָּׁה – לָא בָּטֵיל. מְסַיְּיעָא לֵיהּ לְרַב נַחְמָן אָמַר שְׁמוּאֵל, דְּאָמַר: אַף עַל פִּי שֶׁיֵּשׁ לוֹ לְאָדָם כַּמָּה בָּנִים – אָסוּר לַעֲמוֹד בְּלֹא אִשָּׁה, שֶׁנֶּאֱמַר ״לֹא טוֹב הֱיוֹת הָאָדָם לְבַדּוֹ״.

GEMARA The Gemara infers from the mishna's wording that if **he** already **has children** he **may neglect** the mitzva **to be fruitful and multiply,** but he **may not neglect** the mitzva to have **a wife.** This **supports** what **Rav Naḥman said** in the name of **Shmuel, who said: Even if a man has several children, it is prohibited to remain without a wife,**[HN] **as it is stated: "It is not good that the man should be alone"** (Genesis 2:18).

וְאִיכָּא דְּאָמְרִי: הָא יֵשׁ לוֹ בָּנִים – בָּטֵיל מִפְּרִיָּה וּרְבִיָּה, וּבָטֵיל נַמִי מֵאִשָּׁה. נֵימָא תֶּיהֱוֵי תְּיוּבְתָּא דְּרַב נַחְמָן אָמַר שְׁמוּאֵל! לָא, אֵין לוֹ בָּנִים – נוֹשֵׂא אִשָּׁה בַּת בָּנִים, יֵשׁ לוֹ בָּנִים – נוֹשֵׂא אִשָּׁה דְּלָאו בַּת בָּנִים. נָפְקָא מִינָּהּ – לִמְכּוֹר סֵפֶר תּוֹרָה בִּשְׁבִיל בָּנִים.

And some say a different version of the inference from the mishna: If **he** already **has children, he may neglect** the mitzva **to be fruitful and multiply and** he **may also neglect** the mitzva to have **a wife. Shall we say** this **is a conclusive refutation of** what **Rav Naḥman said** that **Shmuel** said? The Gemara responds: **No,** it means that **if he does not have children he must marry a woman** capable of bearing **children,** whereas if **he has children he may marry a woman who is not** capable of bearing **children. A practical difference** between a man who has children and one who does not is whether he is permitted **to sell a Torah scroll in order to** marry a woman capable of having **children.** This is permitted only for one who does not yet have children.

״בֵּית שַׁמַּאי אוֹמְרִים שְׁנֵי זְכָרִים״. מַאי טַעֲמַיְיהוּ דְּבֵית שַׁמַּאי – יָלְפִינַן מִמֹּשֶׁה, דִּכְתִיב ״בְּנֵי מֹשֶׁה גֵּרְשׁוֹם וֶאֱלִיעֶזֶר״, וּבֵית הִלֵּל – יָלְפִינַן מִבְּרִיָּיתוֹ שֶׁל עוֹלָם. וּבֵית שַׁמַּאי, לֵילְפֵי מִבְּרִיָּיתוֹ שֶׁל עוֹלָם! אֵין דָּנִין אֶפְשָׁר

§ The mishna states that **Beit Shammai say** that one fulfills the mitzva to be fruitful and multiply when he has **two males.** The Gemara asks: **What is the reason of Beit Shammai?** The Gemara answers: **We learn** this **from Moses as it is written: "The sons of Moses, Gershom and Eliezer"** (I Chronicles 23:15). Since Moses did not have any other children, two sons must be sufficient to fulfill the mitzva. **And** the reason of **Beit Hillel** is that **we learn from the creation of the world,** as mankind was created male and female. The Gemara asks: **And Beit Shammai, let them learn from the creation of the world** as well. The Gemara answers that Beit Shammai could say to you: **We do not derive** a case where it is **possible**

HALAKHA

A High Priest must marry a maiden – נַעֲרָה לְכֹהֵן גָּדוֹל: A High Priest may not marry a minor or a grown woman. He must marry a maiden, i.e., a young woman in the first six months of adulthood (Rambam *Sefer Kedusha, Hilkhot Issurei Bia* 17:13).

A man may not neglect the mitzva to be fruitful and multiply – לֹא יִבָּטֵל אָדָם מִפְּרִיָּה וּרְבִיָּה: A man may not neglect the mitzva to be fruitful and multiply. Rather, he must marry and have children. Even if his wife foregoes her conjugal rights, he may desist from fulfilling them only if he has already fathered children (Rambam *Sefer Nashim, Hilkhot Ishut* 15:1; *Shulḥan Arukh, Even HaEzer* 1:1).

And Beit Hillel say, a male and a female – וּבֵית הִלֵּל אוֹמְרִים, זָכָר וּנְקֵבָה: A man who has a daughter and son who are capable of bearing children has fulfilled the mitzva to be fruitful and multiply, in accordance with the opinion of Beit Hillel (Rambam *Sefer Nashim, Hilkhot Ishut* 15:4; *Shulḥan Arukh, Even HaEzer* 1:5).

It is prohibited to remain without a wife – אָסוּר לַעֲמוֹד בְּלֹא אִשָּׁה: Even if a man has fulfilled the mitzva to be fruitful and multiply, the Sages nevertheless said that he should not remain without a wife. If he can, he should marry a woman who can bear children. If he has not fathered children and is in need of money in order to marry a wife, he may even sell a Torah scroll for this purpose. If he already has children he may not sell a Torah scroll in order to marry, although some authorities permit him to do so even in this case (Rambam *Sefer Nashim, Hilkhot Ishut* 15:16; *Shulḥan Arukh, Even HaEzer* 1:8).

NOTES

Unless he has children – אֶלָּא אִם כֵּן יֵשׁ לוֹ בָּנִים: *Tosafot* ask: why is it necessary to state this point if it was already made clear in the previous mishna? The *Arukh LaNer* contends that the precise formulation of this mishna adds a new element to what was stated earlier. The previous mishna said that one may not marry a sexually underdeveloped woman unless he has a wife and children. In this mishna, it states that one may not neglect the mitzva to procreate unless he has children. This emphasizes that unless one already has children, it is not sufficient to be married; one must actively try to have children.

Beit Shammai say, etc. – בֵּית שַׁמַּאי אוֹמְרִים וכו׳: The commentaries dispute whether Beit Shammai and Beit Hillel insist on these combinations of children. Many early commentaries cite Rashi as holding that Beit Shammai agree that one fulfills the mitzva if he has a son and daughter, and merely add that one can also fulfill the mitzva by fathering two sons. Conversely, some hold that it is Beit Hillel who are lenient and hold that one fulfills the mitzva with a son and daughter or with two sons (Rid; *Tosefot Ḥad MiKamma'ei*). This latter view is stated explicitly in the Jerusalem Talmud. However, most commentaries assume that according to Beit Hillel one must father a son and a daughter in order to fulfill the mitzva, and according to Beit Shammai one must father two sons.

It is prohibited to remain without a wife – אָסוּר לַעֲמוֹד בְּלֹא אִשָּׁה: On a basic level, the reason for this is so that one will not fall prey to sinful thoughts (*Nimmukei Yosef*). Alternatively, the verse indicates that mankind is complete only through marriage (see Maharsha).

מִשֶּׁאִי אֶפְשָׁר. וּבֵית הִלֵּל נַמִּי, לֵילְפוּ מִמֹּשֶׁה! אָמְרִי לָךְ: מֹשֶׁה מִדַּעְתֵּיהּ הוּא דַּעֲבַד. דְּתַנְיָא: שְׁלֹשָׁה דְּבָרִים עָשָׂה מֹשֶׁה מִדַּעְתּוֹ, וְהִסְכִּימָה דַּעְתּוֹ לְדַעַת הַמָּקוֹם: פֵּירַשׁ מִן הָאִשָּׁה, וְשִׁיבֵּר הַלּוּחוֹת, וְהוֹסִיף יוֹם אֶחָד.

from one that is **not possible.** Mankind was initially created with a male and female because otherwise reproduction would not have been possible. However, this fact cannot serve as a source that the mitzva to be fruitful and multiply is fulfilled only once one has a son and a daughter. The Gemara asks: **And Beit Hillel, let them also learn from Moses.** Beit Hillel could **say to you: Moses acted** based **on his own perception**[N] when he separated from his wife, but this does not mean that a man is permitted to neglect the mitzva to be fruitful and multiply after fathering two males, **as it is taught in a** *baraita*: **Moses did three things** based **on his own perception, and his perception agreed with the perception of the Omnipresent: He separated from** his **wife,**[N] **he broke the tablets, and he added one day** to the days of separation before the revelation at Sinai.

פֵּירַשׁ מִן הָאִשָּׁה, מַאי דְּרַשׁ? אָמַר: וּמָה יִשְׂרָאֵל שֶׁלֹּא דִּבְּרָה עִמָּהֶם שְׁכִינָה אֶלָּא לְפִי שָׁעָה, וְקָבַע לָהֶם זְמַן – אָמְרָה תּוֹרָה ״אַל תִּגְּשׁוּ אֶל אִשָּׁה״, אֲנִי שֶׁמְּיוּחָד לְדִבּוּר בְּכָל שָׁעָה וְשָׁעָה, וְלֹא קָבַע לִי זְמַן – עַל אַחַת כַּמָּה וְכַמָּה. וְהִסְכִּימָה דַּעְתּוֹ לְדַעַת הַמָּקוֹם, שֶׁנֶּאֱמַר ״לֵךְ אֱמוֹר לָהֶם שׁוּבוּ לָכֶם לְאׇהֳלֵיכֶם וְאַתָּה פֹּה עֲמוֹד עִמָּדִי״.

The Gemara clarifies: When Moses **separated from** his **wife** after the revelation at Sinai, **what did he interpret** that led him to do so? **He said:** If in the case of **Israel, with whom the Divine Presence spoke only temporarily and for whom** God **set** a specific **time** for revelation, **the Torah stated: "Do not approach a woman"** (Exodus 19:15), **I,** Moses, **who am set aside for** divine **speech all the time and for whom** God **did not set** a specific **time, all the more so** I must separate from my wife. **And his perception agreed with the perception of the Omnipresent,** as **it is stated** after the revelation at Sinai: **"Go say to them: Return to your tents; and you, stand here with Me"** (Deuteronomy 5:26–27). This indicates that whereas others could return to their homes and normal married life after the revelation at Sinai, Moses was to stay with God and not return to his wife.

שִׁיבֵּר אֶת הַלּוּחוֹת, מַאי דְּרַשׁ? אָמַר: וּמָה פֶּסַח, שֶׁהוּא אֶחָד מִשֵּׁשׁ מֵאוֹת וּשְׁלֹשׁ עֶשְׂרֵה מִצְוֹת, אָמְרָה תּוֹרָה ״כׇּל בֶּן נֵכָר לֹא יֹאכַל בּוֹ״, הַתּוֹרָה כּוּלָּהּ וְיִשְׂרָאֵל מְשׁוּמָּדִים – עַל אַחַת כַּמָּה וְכַמָּה.

Moses **broke the tablets** following the sin of the Golden Calf. **What did he interpret** that led him to do so? Moses **said:** If in the case of the **Paschal lamb, which is** only **one of 613 mitzvot, the Torah states: "No alien shall eat of it"** (Exodus 12:43), excluding not only gentiles but apostate Jews as well, then here, in the case of the Golden Calf, where the tablets represent **the entire Torah** and where **the Jewish people** are **apostates,** as they are worshipping the calf, **all the more so** must they be excluded from receiving them.

וְהִסְכִּימָה דַּעְתּוֹ לְדַעַת הַמָּקוֹם, דִּכְתִיב ״אֲשֶׁר שִׁבַּרְתָּ״, וְאָמַר רֵישׁ לָקִישׁ: אֲמַר לֵיהּ הַקָּדוֹשׁ בָּרוּךְ הוּא לְמֹשֶׁה: יִישַׁר כֹּחֲךָ שֶׁשִּׁבַּרְתָּ.

And his perception agreed with the perception of the Omnipresent, as it is written: "The first tablets **that you broke** [*asher shibbarta*]**"**[N] (Exodus 34:1), **and Reish Lakish said:** The word *asher* is an allusion to the fact that **the Holy One, Blessed be He, said to Moses: May your strength be true** [*yishar koḥakha*] **that you broke** the tablets.

הוֹסִיף יוֹם אֶחָד מִדַּעְתּוֹ, מַאי דְּרַשׁ? דִּכְתִיב ״וְקִדַּשְׁתָּם הַיּוֹם וּמָחָר״ הַיּוֹם כְּמָחָר, מַה מָּחָר לֵילוֹ עִמּוֹ – אַף הַיּוֹם לֵילוֹ עִמּוֹ. וְלֵילְיָא דְּהָאִידָּנָא נָפַק לֵיהּ. שְׁמַע מִינָּהּ: תְּרֵי יוֹמֵי, לְבַר מֵהָאִידָּנָא. וְהִסְכִּימָה דַּעְתּוֹ לְדַעַת הַמָּקוֹם – דְּלָא שַׁרְיָא שְׁכִינָה עַד שַׁבְּתָא.

When Moses **added one day** to the days of separation before the revelation at Sinai based **on his own perception, what did he interpret** that led him to do so? He reasoned **that** since **it is written: "And sanctify them today and tomorrow"** (Exodus 19:10), the juxtaposition of the words "today" and "tomorrow" teaches that **today is like tomorrow: Just as tomorrow** the men and women will separate for that day **and the night** preceding **it, so too, today** requires separation for the day **and the night** preceding **it.** Since God spoke to him in the morning, **and the night of that day** already **passed,** Moses said: **Conclude from** this that separation must be in effect for **two days aside from now,** i.e., not including the day of the command. Therefore, he extended the mitzva of separation by one day. **And his perception agreed with the perception of the Omnipresent,** as the **Divine Presence did not rest** upon Mount Sinai **until Shabbat** morning, as Moses had determined.

NOTES

Moses acted based on his own perception – מֹשֶׁה מִדַּעְתֵּיהּ הוּא דַּעֲבַד: *Tosafot*, *Tosefot HaRosh*, and other commentaries attempt to prove that Moses' *a fortiori* inference with regard to separating from his wife is not irrefutable. Had it been a perfectly valid argument, the Gemara would not have said that he acted based on his own perception, as *a fortiori* inferences are a valid method of deriving *halakha*, and *halakhot* derived in this manner have the same status as those written explicitly in the Torah itself. The Gemara's point here is that the reason it was permitted for Moses to separate from his wife was not because he had already fulfilled the mitzva to be fruitful and multiply. His case was exceptional, and therefore it cannot serve as halakhic precedent with regard to the definition of the mitzva to be fruitful and multiply (Meiri; Rabbi Avraham min HaHar).

He separated from his wife – פֵּירַשׁ מִן הָאִשָּׁה: *Tosafot* ask how the Sages knew that Moses separated from his wife on his own accord; perhaps he did so only once God commanded him: "And you, stand here with Me" (Deuteronomy 5:27). The Ramban (*Shabbat* 87a) explains that this verse is stated after the revelation at Sinai. If God had wanted Moses to separate from his wife but Moses did not do so on his own, God would not have waited until after the revelation at Sinai to issue His command; He would have issued the command when He began to communicate regularly with Moses.

As it is written, The first tablets that you broke [*asher shibbarta*] – דִּכְתִיב, אֲשֶׁר שִׁבַּרְתָּ: The commentaries are puzzled by this proof, as the word *asher* appears many times in the Torah, and it is not generally understood to indicate approval of an action that a particular individual performed. The Maharsha explains that the phrase "that you broke" is entirely superfluous, as it had already been stated that Moses broke the tablets. Therefore, it must be taken to mean that God affirmed Moses' decision. The Ramban and the Ritva maintain (*Shabbat* 87a) that the proof that God approved of Moses' actions is from the verse in Deuteronomy (10:2) that states *asher shibbarta*, and continues: "And you shall place them in the Ark," which is understood to mean that the broken tablets were placed in the Ark together with the second, whole tablets. The fact that God commanded Moses to preserve the broken tablets demonstrates that He approved of his actions.

תניא, רבי נתן אומר, בית שמאי אומרים: שני זכרים ושתי נקבות, ובית הלל אומרים: זכר ונקבה.

§ **It is taught in a** *baraita* that **Rabbi Natan says** that **Beit Shammai say:** The mitzva to be fruitful and multiply is fulfilled with **two males and two females. And Beit Hillel say: A male and a female.**

אמר רב הונא: מאי טעמא דרבי נתן אליבא דבית שמאי – דכתיב "ותוסף ללדת את אחיו את הבל" הבל ואחותו, קין ואחותו. וכתיב "כי שת לי אלהים זרע אחר תחת הבל כי הרגו קין". ורבנן אודויי הוא דקא מודית.

Rav Huna said: What is the reason of Rabbi Natan, in accordance with the opinion of **Beit Shammai? It is as it is written: "And again she bore his brother [*et aḥiv*] Abel [*et Hevel*]"** (Genesis 4:2). The use of the superfluous word "et" indicates that she gave birth to **Abel and his sister,** in addition to **Cain and his sister. And it states: "For God has appointed me another seed**[N] **instead of Abel; for Cain slew him"** (Genesis 4:25). This indicates that one must have at least four children. **And the Rabbis,** how do they understand this verse? In their opinion, Eve was **thanking God** for granting her another child, but one is not obligated to have four children.

תניא אידך, רבי נתן אומר: בית שמאי אומרים: זכר ונקבה, ובית הלל אומרים: או זכר או נקבה. אמר רבא מאי טעמא דרבי נתן אליבא דבית הלל – שנאמר "לא תהו בראה לשבת יצרה" והא עבד לה שבת.

It is taught in another *baraita* that **Rabbi Natan says** that **Beit Shammai say:** The mitzva to be fruitful and multiply is fulfilled with **a male and a female. And Beit Hillel say: Either a male or a female. Rava said: What is the reason of Rabbi Natan in accordance with the opinion of Beit Hillel?** It is **as it is stated: "He did not create it a waste; He formed it to be inhabited"** (Isaiah 45:18), **and one has made** the earth **inhabited** to a greater degree by adding even one child to the world.

איתמר, היו לו בנים בגויותו ונתגייר, רבי יוחנן אמר: קיים פריה ורביה, וריש לקיש אמר: לא קיים פריה ורביה. רבי יוחנן אמר: קיים פריה ורביה, דהא הוו ליה. וריש לקיש אמר: לא קיים פריה ורביה – גר שנתגייר כקטן שנולד דמי.

§ **It was stated** that *amora'im* disagreed over the following issue: If a man **had children when he** was **a gentile**[NH] **and** he subsequently **converted, Rabbi Yoḥanan said:** He **has** already **fulfilled** the mitzva **to be fruitful and multiply, and Reish Lakish said:** He **has not fulfilled** the mitzva to **be fruitful and multiply. Rabbi Yoḥanan said he has fulfilled** the mitzva **to be fruitful and multiply,** as he already **had** children. **And Reish Lakish said he has not fulfilled** the mitzva to **be fruitful and multiply,** as the legal status of **a convert who** just **converted is like** that of **a child** just **born,** and it is considered as though he did not have children.

ואזדו לטעמייהו, דאיתמר, היו לו בנים בגויותו ונתגייר, רבי יוחנן אמר: אין לו בכור לנחלה, דהא הוה ליה "ראשית אונו". וריש לקיש אמר: יש לו בכור לנחלה, גר שנתגייר כקטן שנולד דמי.

The Gemara comments: **And they follow their** regular line of **reasoning, as it was stated: If one had children when** he was **a gentile and he** subsequently **converted, Rabbi Yoḥanan said: He does not have a firstborn with regard to inheritance,**[HB] i.e., the first son born to him after his conversion does not inherit a double portion, **as** this man already **had "the first of his strength"** (Deuteronomy 21:17), the Torah's description of the firstborn in this context, before he converted. **And Reish Lakish said: He does have a firstborn with regard to inheritance,** as the legal status of **a convert who** just **converted is like** that of **a child** just **born.**

וצריכא, דאי אשמעינן בההיא קמייתא – בההיא קאמר רבי יוחנן, משום דמעיקרא נמי בני פריה ורביה נינהו, אבל לענין נחלה, דלאו בני נחלה נינהו, אימא מודי ליה לריש לקיש.

The Gemara adds: **And** it is **necessary** to state their opinions in both cases. **As, had it** only been **taught to us with regard to that first** case of the mitzva to be fruitful and multiply, one might have said that it is only **in that** case that **Rabbi Yoḥanan said** his opinion, **because from the outset,** gentiles **are also subject to** the mitzva to be **fruitful and multiply.**[N] **However, with regard to inheritance,** since **they are not subject** to the *halakhot* of **inheritance,** one might **say** that Rabbi Yoḥanan **concedes to Reish Lakish.**

ואי איתמר בהא – בהא קאמר ריש לקיש, אבל בההיא – אימא מודה ליה לרבי יוחנן, צריכא.

And conversely, **if** their dispute **was stated** only **with regard to this** issue of inheritance, I would have said that **it is** only **in this** case that **Reish Lakish said** his opinion, as the *halakhot* of inheritance do not apply to gentiles. **But with regard to that** case, the mitzva to be fruitful and multiply, one might **say** that **he concedes to Rabbi Yoḥanan.** Consequently, **it is necessary** for both disputes to be recorded.

NOTES

For God has appointed me another seed – כי שת לי אלהים זרע אחר: In order to prove that one must have two sons and two daughters this verse is also necessary. If only the first verse had been written, one might have thought that the Torah was merely relating how many children Adam and Eve had. This verse, however, indicates that it was necessary for them to have Seth as a replacement for Abel. Furthermore, one might have thought that one must father two daughters but that one son is sufficient, as a single male can father children through multiple females. The Gemara therefore cites a verse indicating that Adam required an additional son (*Ḥokhmat Shlomo*; see Maharsha).

If a man had children when he was a gentile – היו לו בנים בגויותו: According to the Rambam and other commentaries, Rabbi Yoḥanan stated his opinion only in a case where the children also converted, so that the father has Jewish offspring. Others, however, maintain that he has fulfilled the mitzva even if his children do not convert (Maharil; see *Tosafot*). This dispute depends upon the meaning of the Gemara's statement that gentiles are subject to the mitzva to be fruitful and multiply.

Gentiles are also subject to the mitzva to be fruitful and multiply – בני פריה ורביה נינהו: Some commentaries cite this statement as proof that gentiles are commanded to be fruitful and multiply. This is indicated by the Torah as well, as the command to be fruitful and multiply was issued to Adam (Genesis 1:28) and Noah (Genesis 9:1). Others disagree, pointing to the fact that the mitzva to be fruitful and multiply is not listed as one of the seven Noahide mitzvot. This is consistent with the general principle that any mitzva mentioned in the Torah that is not repeated in Deuteronomy was given only to the Jewish people. They interpret the Gemara here as stating that gentiles fulfill the will of God by having children, although they do not fulfill an actual mitzva, as God created the world for it to be inhabited, and therefore it is praiseworthy for them to have children (see Meiri).

HALAKHA

If a man had children when he was a gentile – היו לו בנים בגויותו: If a gentile had children and subsequently converted to Judaism, he has fulfilled the mitzva to be fruitful and multiply through them if his children converted as well, in accordance with the opinion of Rabbi Yoḥanan. According to many authorities, he has fulfilled the mitzva even if his children did not convert (Rambam *Sefer Nashim, Hilkhot Ishut* 15:6; *Shulḥan Arukh, Even HaEzer* 1:7; Vilna Gaon).

A firstborn with regard to inheritance – בכור לנחלה: If a gentile who already had children converted and then fathered another son, the latter is not considered a firstborn with regard to the *halakhot* of inheritance, in accordance with the opinion of Rabbi Yoḥanan (Rambam *Sefer Mishpatim, Hilkhot Naḥalot* 2:12; *Shulḥan Arukh, Ḥoshen Mishpat* 277:9).

BACKGROUND

A firstborn with regard to inheritance – בכור לנחלה: A father's firstborn son receives an extra share in the inheritance (Deuteronomy 21:17). This privilege is granted even if he is not the mother's firstborn son and even if he is illegitimate. The firstborn son receives a share twice as great as that received by each of the other sons. This double share is, however, given only from property actually possessed by the estate at the time of the father's death, not from property accruing to the estate later. The latter property is divided equally among the heirs.

HALAKHA

A Canaanite slave, that he does not have family lineage – עֶבֶד שֶׁאֵין לוֹ חַיִיס: If a Canaanite slave and his children were freed and thereby become Jewish, the father has not fulfilled the mitzva to be fruitful and multiply because his children are not halakhically recognized as his offspring. Similarly, if a Jew fathers a son from a Canaanite maidservant, the boy is not considered his son, and therefore the first son born to him from a Jewish mother is considered his firstborn with regard to inheritance (Rambam *Sefer Nashim, Hilkhot Ishut* 15:6 and *Sefer Mishpatim, Hilkhot Naḥalot* 2:12; *Shulḥan Arukh, Even HaEzer* 1:7 and *Ḥoshen Mishpat* 277:9).

If a man had children and they died – הָיוּ לוֹ בָּנִים וּמֵתוּ: If a man's children died without leaving descendants, he has not fulfilled the mitzva to be fruitful and multiply, in accordance with the opinion of Rabbi Yoḥanan (Rambam *Sefer Nashim, Hilkhot Ishut* 15:5; *Shulḥan Arukh, Even HaEzer* 1:6).

אֵיתִיבֵיהּ רַבִּי יוֹחָנָן לְרֵישׁ לָקִישׁ: ״בָּעֵת הַהִיא שָׁלַח בְּרֹאדַךְ בַּלְאֲדָן בֶּן בַּלְאֲדָן מֶלֶךְ בָּבֶל״ וגו׳! אָמַר לֵיהּ: בְּגוֹיוּתָן – אִית לְהוּ חַיִיס, נִתְגַּיְּירוּ – לֵית לְהוּ חַיִיס.

Rabbi Yoḥanan raises an objection to Reish Lakish based upon the verse: **"At that time Berodach-baladan, son of Baladan, king of Babylon, sent** a letter" (II Kings 20:12), which indicates that gentiles are considered to be the children of their parents. Therefore, when they convert, they should already have fulfilled the mitzva to be fruitful and multiply. Reish Lakish **said to** Rabbi Yoḥanan: **When they are gentiles they do have** family **lineage,** but when **they convert they do not have lineage,** as they now belong to the family of the Jewish people and their previous lineage is disregarded.

אָמַר רַב: הַכֹּל מוֹדִין בְּעֶבֶד שֶׁאֵין לוֹ חַיִיס, דִּכְתִיב ״שְׁבוּ לָכֶם פֹּה עִם הַחֲמוֹר״, עַם הַדּוֹמֶה לַחֲמוֹר. מֵיתִיבֵי: ״וּלְצִיבָא חֲמִשָּׁה עָשָׂר בָּנִים וְעֶשְׂרִים עֲבָדִים״! אָמַר רַב אַחָא בַּר יַעֲקֹב: כְּ״פַר בֶּן בָּקָר״.

Rav said: Everyone agrees with regard to a Canaanite **slave, that he does not have lineage,**[H] **as it is written** that Abraham said to his slaves: **"Remain here with the donkey"** (Genesis 22:5). This verse is interpreted to mean that they are **a nation comparable to a donkey,**[N] which has no lineage. The Gemara **raises an objection** based upon a verse pertaining to Jonathan's Canaanite slave: **"And Ziba had fifteen sons and twenty servants"** (II Samuel 9:10), which indicates that a slave's sons are in fact considered his sons. **Rav Aḥa bar Ya'akov said:** This is **like** the expression: **A bullock, son of a bull.** The word son in this context merely denotes progeny, not lineage.

אִי הָכִי, הָכָא נַמִי! שָׁאנֵי הָתָם דְּיַחֲסִינְהוּ בִּשְׁמַיְיהוּ וּבִשְׁמָא דַּאֲבוּהוֹן, וְהָכָא לָא מְפָרֵשׁ. וְאִיבָּעֵית אֵימָא: יַחֲסִינְהוּ בְּדוּכְתָּא אַחֲרִיתֵי בַּאֲבוּהוֹן וּבְאַבָּא דַּאֲבוּהוֹן, דִּכְתִיב ״וַיִּשְׁלָחֵם הַמֶּלֶךְ אָסָא אֶל בֶּן הֲדַד בֶּן טַבְרִימוֹן בֶּן חֶזְיוֹן מֶלֶךְ אֲרָם הַיּוֹשֵׁב בְּדַמֶּשֶׂק לֵאמֹר״.

The Gemara asks: **If so, here too,** with regard to gentiles, there is no proof from the verse about Berodach-baladan that they have family lineage. The Gemara answers: **There it is different,** as the Bible **identified him by his name and by his father's name,**[N] thereby emphasizing the family connection. **But here,** it does **not specify** the names of Ziba's children. **And if you wish, say** instead that the Bible **identified** gentiles **elsewhere by their father and their father's father, as it is written: "And King Asa sent them to Ben-hadad, son of Tabrimmon, son of Hezion, king of Aram, who dwelled in Damascus, saying"** (I Kings 15:18). This indicates that there is lineage for gentiles.

אִיתְּמַר, הָיוּ לוֹ בָּנִים וּמֵתוּ, רַב הוּנָא אָמַר: קִיֵּים פְּרִיָּה וּרְבִיָּה, רַבִּי יוֹחָנָן אָמַר: לֹא קִיֵּים.

§ **It was stated** that *amora'im* disagreed over the following issue: If a man **had children and they died,**[H] **Rav Huna said:** He has **fulfilled** the mitzva to be **fruitful and multiply** through these children. **Rabbi Yoḥanan said:** He has **not fulfilled** the mitzva.

רַב הוּנָא אָמַר: קִיֵּים – מִשּׁוּם דְּרַב אַסִּי, דְּאָמַר רַב אַסִּי: אֵין בֶּן דָּוִד בָּא עַד שֶׁיִּכְלוּ כׇּל נְשָׁמוֹת שֶׁבַּגּוּף, שֶׁנֶּאֱמַר ״כִּי רוּחַ מִלְּפָנַי יַעֲטוֹף״ וגו׳. וְרַבִּי יוֹחָנָן אָמַר: לֹא קִיֵּים פְּרִיָּה וּרְבִיָּה, ״לָשֶׁבֶת יְצָרָהּ״ בָּעֵינַן – וְהָא לֵיכָּא.

The Gemara clarifies the reasons for their opinions: **Rav Huna said** he has **fulfilled** the mitzva **due to** a statement **of Rav Asi, as Rav Asi said** that the reason for this mitzva is that the Messiah, **son of David, will not come until all the souls of the body**[N] **have been finished,** i.e., until all souls that are destined to inhabit physical bodies will do so, **as it is stated: "For the spirit that enwraps itself is from Me,** and the souls that I have made" (Isaiah 57:16). Consequently, once a child has been born and his soul has entered a body the mitzva has been fulfilled, even if the child subsequently dies. **And Rabbi Yoḥanan said** he has **not fulfilled** the mitzva, as **we require "He formed it to be inhabited"** (Isaiah 45:18), **and this is not** fulfilled when the children have passed away and no longer inhabit the earth.

מֵיתִיבֵי

The Gemara **raises an objection** with regard to the opinion of Rav Huna based upon the following *baraita*:

NOTES

A nation [*am*] comparable to a donkey – עַם הַדּוֹמֶה לַחֲמוֹר: This interpretation is based on reading the word "with [*im*]" as though it were vocalized *am*, meaning nation. Furthermore, the Sages often interpret the word *im* in the Bible as indicating that a comparison can be drawn between two items (*Gilyonei HaShas*; see *Kiddushin* 76b).

By his name and by his father's name – בִּשְׁמַיְיהוּ וּבִשְׁמָא דַּאֲבוּהוֹן: The *Keren Ora* asks: Why does the Gemara choose the particular example of Berodach-baladan when there are many other instances where the Torah mentions the name of a gentile and his father, e.g., the list of Edomite kings in Genesis, chapter 37? The Ritva notes that this verse does not merely mention the name of Berodach-baladan's father, it demonstrates that his father's name was incorporated into his own name. It may be explained that this fact emphasizes the significance of the father-son relationship.

The souls of the body – נְשָׁמוֹת שֶׁבַּגּוּף: See NOTES on 63b for an explanation of this term.

בְּנֵי בָנִים הֲרֵי הֵן כְּבָנִים! כִּי תַּנְיָא הַהִיא – לְהַשְׁלִים.

Grandchildren are considered **like children.**[H] This indicates that if one's children have passed away, he has fulfilled the mitzva to be fruitful and multiply only if they had children of their own, as they are considered like his own children. The Gemara responds: **When that** *baraita* **is taught** it is with regard **to completing** the required number of children, e.g., if he had only a son, but his son had a daughter, he has fulfilled the mitzva to be fruitful and multiply.

מֵיתִיבֵי: בְּנֵי בָנִים הֲרֵי הֵם כְּבָנִים, מֵת אֶחָד מֵהֶם, אוֹ שֶׁנִּמְצָא סָרִיס, לֹא קִיֵּים פְּרִיָּה וּרְבִיָּה. תְּיוּבְתָּא דְּרַב הוּנָא! תְּיוּבְתָּא.

The Gemara **raises an objection** to the opinion of Rav Huna from another *baraita*: **Grandchildren are** considered **like children. If one** of a man's children **died or was discovered** to be **a eunuch,**[H] the father has **not fulfilled** the mitzva to be **fruitful and multiply.** This directly contradicts Rav Huna's statement that one fulfills the mitzva even if his children die. The Gemara concludes: **The refutation** of the opinion **of Rav Huna is** indeed **a conclusive refutation.**

״בְּנֵי בָנִים הֲרֵי הֵם כְּבָנִים״. סָבַר אַבָּיֵי לְמֵימַר: בְּרָא לִבְרָא וּבְרַתָּא לִבְרַתָּא, וְכָל שֶׁכֵּן בְּרָא לִבְרַתָּא, אֲבָל בְּרַתָּא לִבְרָא – לָא. אָמַר לֵיהּ רָבָא: ״לָשֶׁבֶת יְצָרָהּ״ בָּעֵינָא, וְהָא אִיכָּא.

§ It was taught in the *baraita* that **grandchildren are** considered **like children. Abaye thought to say**[N] that if one's children die, he fulfills the mitzva to be fruitful and multiply through grandchildren, provided **a son** was born **to** his **son and a daughter to** his **daughter, and all the more so** if **a son** was born **to** his **daughter,** as his grandchildren take the place of his children in these cases. **However,** if **a daughter** was born **to** his **son, no,** she cannot take the place of her father. **Rava said to him:** We **require** merely fulfillment of the verse: **"He formed it to be inhabited," and there is** fulfillment in this case, as the earth is inhabited by his descendants.

דְּכוּלֵּי עָלְמָא מִיהַת תְּרֵי מֵחַד לָא. וְלָא?! וְהָא אָמְרִי לֵיהּ רַבָּנַן לְרַב שֵׁשֶׁת: נְסֵיב אִיתְּתָא וְאוֹלֵיד בְּנֵי! וַאֲמַר לְהוּ: בְּנֵי בְּרַתִּי בָּנַי נִינְהוּ.

The Gemara comments: **In any event, everyone** agrees that if one has **two** grandchildren **from one** child, **no,** he has not fulfilled the mitzva to be fruitful and multiply, even if he has both a grandson and a granddaughter. The Gemara asks: **And** has he **not? Didn't the Rabbis say to Rav Sheshet:**[P] **Marry a woman**[N] **and have sons,** as you have not yet fathered any sons, **and** Rav Sheshet **said to them: The sons of my daughter are my sons?** This indicates that one can fulfill the mitzva through grandchildren even if he did not have a son and daughter of his own.

הָתָם דַּחוּיֵי קָמַדְחֵי לְהוּ, דְּרַב שֵׁשֶׁת אִיעַקַר מִפִּירְקֵיהּ דְּרַב הוּנָא.

The Gemara answers: **There,** Rav Sheshet **was** merely **putting them off.** The real reason he did not want to get remarried was **because Rav Sheshet became impotent from Rav Huna's**[P] **discourse.** Rav Huna's discourses were so lengthy that Rav Sheshet became impotent after waiting for so long without relieving himself.

אֲמַר לֵיהּ רַבָּה לְרָבָא בַּר מָארִי: מְנָא הָא מִילְּתָא דַּאֲמוּר רַבָּנַן בְּנֵי בָנִים הֲרֵי הֵן כְּבָנִים? אִילֵימָא מִדִּכְתִיב ״הַבָּנוֹת בְּנוֹתַי וְהַבָּנִים בָּנַי״ אֶלָּא מֵעַתָּה, ״וְהַצֹּאן צֹאנִי״ הָכִי נַמִי? אֶלָּא – דְּקָנֵית מִינַּאי, הָכָא נַמִי – דְּקָנֵית מִינַּאי!

Rabba said to Rava bar Mari: From where is this matter that the Sages stated derived, that **grandchildren are** considered **like children? If we say** it is derived **from** the fact **that it is written** in Laban's speech to Jacob: **"The daughters are my daughters and the children are my children"** (Genesis 31:43), which indicates that Jacob's children were also considered to be the children of their grandfather Laban, **if** that is **so,** does the continuation of Laban's statement: **"And the flocks are my flocks"** (Genesis 31:43), indicate that **so too,** Jacob's flocks were considered as belonging to Laban? **Rather,** Laban was saying **that you,** Jacob, **acquired** them **from me. Here too,** with regard to the children, Laban was saying: **You acquired** them **from me,** i.e., it is only due to me that you have children.

HALAKHA

Grandchildren are considered like children – בְּנֵי בָנִים הֲרֵי הֵן כְּבָנִים: If a man had a son and a daughter and both died, but one of them had a son and one of them had a daughter, since his surviving descendants include a male and a female, he has fulfilled the mitzva to be fruitful and multiply. However, if they were both the offspring of only one of his children, he has not fulfilled the mitzva (Rambam *Sefer Nashim*, *Hilkhot Ishut* 15:5; *Shulḥan Arukh*, *Even HaEzer* 1:6).

Or was discovered to be a eunuch – אוֹ שֶׁנִּמְצָא סָרִיס: If a man had a son who turned out to be a eunuch, or a daughter who grew up to be a sexually underdeveloped woman, he has not fulfilled the mitzva to be fruitful and multiply through them (Rambam *Sefer Nashim*, *Hilkhot Ishut* 15:4; *Shulḥan Arukh*, *Even HaEzer* 1:5).

PERSONALITIES

Rav Sheshet – רַב שֵׁשֶׁת: A prominent third-generation Babylonian *amora*, Rav Sheshet was the primary student of Rav Huna, even though he also served and studied under the rest of the Sages of Rav Huna's generation. Rav Sheshet was famous for his unsurpassed expertise in Mishna and *baraita*. Many of the Sages of his generation came to study under him, as they knew that his teachings were always based on early sources. In his later years Rav Sheshet became blind, but remained involved in all aspects of life and was a frequent visitor to the house of the Exilarch. He was characteristically extremely forceful, hard as steel, and did not defer even to eminent political leaders. Apparently, He supported himself as a garment merchant and earned enough to live comfortably.

Rav Huna – רַב הוּנָא: One of the great second-generation Babylonian *amora'im*, Rav Huna was most closely associated with his teacher, Rav. Rav Huna was of aristocratic descent, from the house of the Exilarchs, but despite that lineage, he lived in abject poverty for many years. Later in life he became wealthy and lived comfortably, and distributed his resources for the public good. Rav Huna was the greatest of Rav's students, to the extent that Shmuel, Rav's colleague, used to treat him deferentially and direct questions to him. After Rav's death Rav Huna became the head of the yeshiva of Sura and filled that position for forty years. His prominence in Torah and his loftiness of character helped make the yeshiva of Sura the preeminent center of Torah for many centuries. Because of Rav Huna's extensive Torah knowledge, the *halakha* is almost invariably ruled in accordance with his opinion in disputes with his colleagues and contemporaries. The only exception is in civil *halakha*, where the rulings are in accordance with the opinion of Rav Naḥman.

Rav Huna had many students, some of whom studied exclusively with him. Moreover, Rav's younger students remained to study with Rav Huna, his disciple, after Rav's death. Rav Huna's son, Rabba bar Rav Huna, was one of the greatest Sages of the following generation.

NOTES

Abaye thought to say, etc. – סָבַר אַבָּיֵי לְמֵימַר וכו׳: An opinion is cited in the Jerusalem Talmud that limits the possibility of fulfilling the mitzva to be fruitful and multiply through grandchildren to an even greater degree than Abaye had thought to say. According to this opinion, only the daughter of a daughter and the son of a son are counted as one's own children, but not a son of a daughter or a daughter of a son.

Marry a woman, etc. – נְסֵיב אִיתְּתָא וכו׳: Rav Sheshet's response does not appear to be sufficient, as Rabbi Yehoshua, cited below, holds that even if one has fulfilled the mitzva to be fruitful and multiply he should still have more children. Even according to the Gemara's statement that Rav Sheshet became impotent, he still should have gotten married, in accordance with the opinion of Shmuel that it is always preferable for a man to be married. It is possible that since he was constantly involved in Torah study it was permissible for him to remain unmarried, similar to the case of ben Azzai (see 63b; Ramban).

BACKGROUND

The students of Rabbi Akiva – תַּלְמִידֵי רַבִּי עֲקִיבָא: It appears from the Gemara that most of Rabbi Akiva's disciples died in a plague. However, Rav Sherira Gaon explains in his letter that this was a *shemada*, meaning their death was due either to governmental persecution or to war. If so, this would appear to be related to the bar Kokheva revolt, of which Rabbi Akiva was an ardent supporter. It is reasonable to surmise that Rabbi Akiva's students served as soldiers under bar Kokheva and when the Romans suppressed the revolt with great brutality, these students were killed.

The image depicts an engraving that was prepared by the Roman senate in honor of Hadrian after he succeeded in suppressing the bar Kokheva revolt. It is currently at the Israel Museum in Jerusalem.

Engraving in honor of Hadrian after he suppressed the bar Kokheva revolt

From Gevat to Antipatris – מִגְּבַת עַד אַנְטִיפְּרַס: The location of Gevat is not entirely clear. Some identify it with a hill just north of Beersheba. According to some sources, Gevat is located on the border of the desert. Antipatris is the city of Ἀντιπατρίς, built by Herod in northern Judea. The city was located close to the source of the Yarkon River and near modern-day Rosh HaAyin. It served as a landmark, as it was the northernmost point in Judea, with Samaria continuing to the north.

The expression from Gevat to Antipatris means that the area stretched along the entire length of the land of Judea, from its southernmost edge to its northernmost edge.

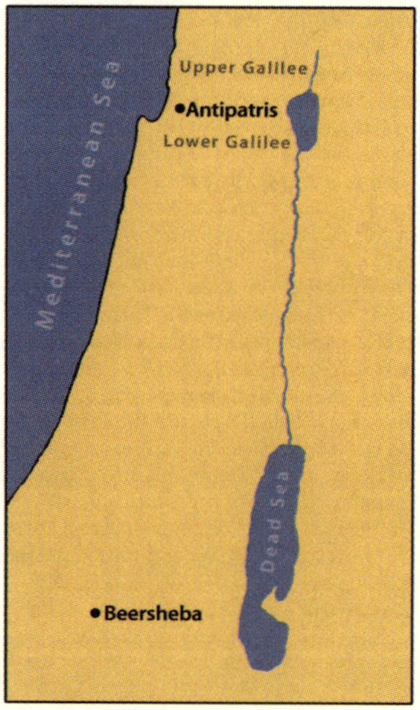

Location of Antipatris

Antipatris

אֶלָּא מֵהָכָא: ״וְאַחַר בָּא חֶצְרוֹן אֶל בַּת מָכִיר אֲבִי גִלְעָד...וַתֵּלֶד לוֹ אֶת שְׂגוּב״, וּכְתִיב: ״מִנִּי מָכִיר יָרְדוּ מְחוֹקְקִים״ וּכְתִיב ״יְהוּדָה מְחוֹקְקִי״.

Rather, the proof is **from here: "And afterward Hezron went in to the daughter of Machir, the father of Gilead…and she bore him Segub"** (I Chronicles 2:21), **and it is written: "Out of Machir came down governors"** (Judges 5:14), **and it is written: "Judah is my governor"** (Psalms 60:9). Consequently, the governors, who were from the tribe of Judah, were also called the sons of Machir, who was from the tribe of Manasseh. This must be because they were the children of Machir's daughter and Hezron, indicating that grandchildren are considered like children.

מַתְנִיתִין דְּלָאו כְּרַבִּי יְהוֹשֻׁעַ. דְּתַנְיָא, רַבִּי יְהוֹשֻׁעַ אוֹמֵר: נָשָׂא אָדָם אִשָּׁה בְּיַלְדוּתוֹ – יִשָּׂא אִשָּׁה בְּזִקְנוּתוֹ, הָיוּ לוֹ בָּנִים בְּיַלְדוּתוֹ – יִהְיוּ לוֹ בָּנִים בְּזִקְנוּתוֹ, שֶׁנֶּאֱמַר ״בַּבֹּקֶר זְרַע אֶת זַרְעֶךָ וְלָעֶרֶב אַל תַּנַּח יָדֶךָ כִּי אֵינְךָ יוֹדֵעַ אֵי זֶה יִכְשַׁר הֲזֶה אוֹ זֶה וְאִם שְׁנֵיהֶם כְּאֶחָד טוֹבִים״.

§ The Gemara comments: **The mishna is not in accordance with** the opinion of **Rabbi Yehoshua. As it is taught in a** *baraita* that **Rabbi Yehoshua says: If a man married a woman in his youth,** and she passed away, **he should marry** another **woman in his old age. If he had children in his youth, he should have** more **children in his old age, as it is stated: "In the morning sow your seed, and in the evening do not withhold your hand; for you do not know which shall prosper, whether this or that, or whether they both alike shall be good"** (Ecclesiastes 11:6). This verse indicates that a man should continue having children even after he has fulfilled the mitzva to be fruitful and multiply.

רַבִּי עֲקִיבָא אוֹמֵר: לָמַד תּוֹרָה בְּיַלְדוּתוֹ – יִלְמוֹד תּוֹרָה בְּזִקְנוּתוֹ, הָיוּ לוֹ תַּלְמִידִים בְּיַלְדוּתוֹ – יִהְיוּ לוֹ תַּלְמִידִים בְּזִקְנוּתוֹ, שֶׁנֶּאֱמַר ״בַּבֹּקֶר זְרַע אֶת זַרְעֶךָ״ וגו׳. אָמְרוּ: שְׁנֵים עָשָׂר אֶלֶף זוּגִים תַּלְמִידִים הָיוּ לוֹ לְרַבִּי עֲקִיבָא מִגְּבַת עַד אַנְטִיפְּרַס, וְכוּלָּן מֵתוּ בְּפֶרֶק אֶחָד, מִפְּנֵי שֶׁלֹּא נָהֲגוּ כָּבוֹד זֶה לָזֶה.

Rabbi Akiva says that the verse should be understood as follows: If one **studied Torah in his youth**[N] **he should study** more **Torah in his old age;** if **he had students in his youth he should have** additional **students in his old age, as it is stated: "In the morning sow your seed, etc." They said** by way of example that **Rabbi Akiva had twelve thousand pairs**[N] **of students**[B] in an area of land that stretched **from Gevat to Antipatris**[B] in Judea, **and they all died in one period** of time, **because they did not treat each other with respect.**

וְהָיָה הָעוֹלָם שָׁמֵם, עַד שֶׁבָּא רַבִּי עֲקִיבָא אֵצֶל רַבּוֹתֵינוּ שֶׁבַּדָּרוֹם וּשְׁנָאָהּ לָהֶם: רַבִּי מֵאִיר, וְרַבִּי יְהוּדָה, וְרַבִּי יוֹסֵי, וְרַבִּי שִׁמְעוֹן, וְרַבִּי אֶלְעָזָר בֶּן שַׁמּוּעַ. וְהֵם הֵם הֶעֱמִידוּ תּוֹרָה אוֹתָהּ שָׁעָה.

And the world was desolate of Torah **until Rabbi Akiva came to our Rabbis in the South and taught** his Torah **to them.** This second group of disciples consisted of **Rabbi Meir, Rabbi Yehuda, Rabbi Yosei, Rabbi Shimon, and Rabbi Elazar ben Shamua. And these are the very ones** who **upheld** the study of **Torah at that time.** Although Rabbi Akiva's earlier students did not survive, his later disciples were able to transmit the Torah to future generations.

תָּנָא: כּוּלָּם מֵתוּ מִפֶּסַח וְעַד עֲצֶרֶת. אָמַר רַב חָמָא בַּר אַבָּא וְאִיתֵּימָא רַבִּי חִיָּיא בַּר אָבִין: כּוּלָּם מֵתוּ מִיתָה רָעָה. מַאי הִיא? אָמַר רַב נַחְמָן: אַסְכָּרָה.

With regard to the twelve thousand pairs of Rabbi Akiva's students, the Gemara adds: It is **taught** that **all of them died** in the period **from Passover until** ***Shavuot*. Rav Ḥama bar Abba said, and some say** it was **Rabbi Ḥiyya bar Avin: They all died a bad death.** The Gemara inquires: **What is it** that is called a bad death? **Rav Naḥman said: Diphtheria.**

אָמַר רַב מַתָּנָא: הֲלָכָה כְּרַבִּי יְהוֹשֻׁעַ.

Rav Mattana said: The ***halakha*** **is in accordance with** the opinion of **Rabbi Yehoshua,** who said that one must attempt to have more children even if he has already fulfilled the mitzva to be fruitful and multiply.

NOTES

Studied Torah in his youth, etc. – לָמַד תּוֹרָה בְּיַלְדוּתוֹ וכו׳: The commentaries questioned the necessity of this exposition. Since Torah study is a mitzva that applies at all times, why is it necessary to derive from this verse that even if one studied in his youth he should study more in his old age? The *Keren Ora* suggests that this is referring to the additional toil in Torah that one must undertake in order to weaken his sinful inclinations. It might have been thought that since the evil inclination is not as strong in old age, he does not have to follow such a regimen. The *Iyyun Ya'akov* explains that even if one studied and fully clarified a particular issue in depth when he was young, he should not rely on this but should review the matter when the matter arises in his later years. He might change his mind or add new insights in his maturity.

Twelve thousand pairs, etc. – שְׁנֵים עָשָׂר אֶלֶף זוּגִים וכו׳: Most commentaries read this passage in a straightforward manner, offering various reasons for the fate that befell Rabbi Akiva's students. Rav Sherira Gaon, however, writes in a letter that the disciples perished in a time of persecution by the government. According to this opinion, the events are connected to the contemporaneous bar Kokheva rebellion. The Meiri writes that it is customary to observe certain customs of mourning during the period between Passover and *Shavuot* due to the fact that Rabbi Akiva's students died during this time. Following the tradition of the *ge'onim* that the students ceased dying on *Lag BaOmer*, the thirty-third day of that time period, mourning customs are not observed on that day.

אָמַר רַבִּי תַּנְחוּם אָמַר רַבִּי חֲנִילָאִי: כׇּל אָדָם שֶׁאֵין לוֹ אִשָּׁה שָׁרוּי בְּלֹא שִׂמְחָה, בְּלֹא בְרָכָה, בְּלֹא טוֹבָה. בְּלֹא שִׂמְחָה – דִּכְתִיב "וְשָׂמַחְתָּ אַתָּה וּבֵיתֶךָ", בְּלֹא בְרָכָה – דִּכְתִיב "לְהָנִיחַ בְּרָכָה אֶל בֵּיתֶךָ", בְּלֹא טוֹבָה – דִּכְתִיב "לֹא טוֹב הֱיוֹת הָאָדָם לְבַדּוֹ".

§ Apropos the discussion with regard to the mitzva to have children, the Gemara cites statements about marriage in general. **Rabbi Tanḥum said** that **Rabbi Ḥanilai said: Any man who does not have a wife is left without joy, without blessing,**[N] **without goodness.** He proceeds to quote verses to support each part of his statement. He is **without joy, as it is written: "And you shall rejoice, you and your household"** (Deuteronomy 14:26), which indicates that the a man is in a joyful state only when he is with his household, i.e., his wife. He is **without blessing, as it is written: "To cause a blessing to rest in your house"** (Ezekiel 44:30), which indicates that blessing comes through one's house, i.e., one's wife. He is **without goodness, as it is written: "It is not good that man should be alone"** (Genesis 2:18), i.e., without a wife.

בְּמַעַרְבָא אָמְרִי: בְּלֹא תוֹרָה, בְּלֹא חוֹמָה. בְּלֹא תוֹרָה – דִּכְתִיב "הַאִם אֵין עֶזְרָתִי בִי וְתֻשִׁיָּה נִדְּחָה מִמֶּנִּי", בְּלֹא חוֹמָה – דִּכְתִיב "נְקֵבָה תְּסוֹבֵב גָּבֶר".

In the West, Eretz Yisrael, they **say:** One who lives without a wife is left **without Torah,** and **without a wall** of protection. He is **without Torah, as it is written: "Is it that I have no help in me, and that sound wisdom is driven from me?"** (Job 6:13), indicating that one who does not have a wife lacks sound wisdom, i.e., Torah. He is **without a wall, as it is written: "A woman shall go round a man"** (Jeremiah 31:21), similar to a protective wall.

רָבָא בַּר עוּלָּא אָמַר: בְּלֹא שָׁלוֹם, דִּכְתִיב "וְיָדַעְתָּ כִּי שָׁלוֹם אׇהֳלֶךָ וּפָקַדְתָּ נָוְךָ וְלֹא תֶחֱטָא".

Rava bar Ulla said: One who does not have a wife is left **without peace, as it is written: "And you shall know that your tent is in peace; and you shall visit your habitation and shall miss nothing"** (Job 5:24). This indicates that a man has peace only when he has a tent, i.e., a wife.

אָמַר רַבִּי יְהוֹשֻׁעַ בֶּן לֵוִי: כׇּל הַיּוֹדֵעַ בְּאִשְׁתּוֹ שֶׁהִיא יְרֵאַת שָׁמַיִם, וְאֵינוֹ פּוֹקְדָהּ – נִקְרָא חוֹטֵא, שֶׁנֶּאֱמַר "וְיָדַעְתָּ כִּי שָׁלוֹם אׇהֳלֶךָ" וגו׳. וְאָמַר רַבִּי יְהוֹשֻׁעַ בֶּן לֵוִי: חַיָּיב אָדָם לִפְקוֹד אֶת אִשְׁתּוֹ בְּשָׁעָה שֶׁהוּא יוֹצֵא לַדֶּרֶךְ, שֶׁנֶּאֱמַר "וְיָדַעְתָּ כִּי שָׁלוֹם אׇהֳלֶךָ" וגו׳.

On the same verse, **Rabbi Yehoshua ben Levi said: Whoever knows that his wife fears Heaven**[N] and she desires him, **and he does not visit her,** i.e., have intercourse with her, is **called a sinner, as it is stated: And you shall know that your tent is in peace;** and you shall visit your habitation. **And Rabbi Yehoshua ben Levi said: A man is obligated to visit his wife** for the purpose of having intercourse **when he** is about to **depart on a journey,**[H] **as it is stated: "And you shall know that your tent is in peace, etc."**

הָא מֵהָכָא נָפְקָא? מֵהָתָם נָפְקָא: "וְאֶל אִישֵׁךְ תְּשׁוּקָתֵךְ" מְלַמֵּד שֶׁהָאִשָּׁה מִשְׁתּוֹקֶקֶת עַל בַּעְלָהּ בְּשָׁעָה שֶׁהוּא יוֹצֵא לַדֶּרֶךְ! אָמַר רַב יוֹסֵף: לֹא נִצְרְכָה אֶלָּא סָמוּךְ לְוִוסְתָּהּ.

The Gemara asks: Is **this** last statement **derived from here?**[N] It is **derived from there: "And your desire shall be to your husband"** (Genesis 3:16), which **teaches that a wife desires her husband when he is about to depart on a journey. Rav Yosef said:** The additional derivation cited by Rabbi Yehoshua ben Levi **is necessary only near** the time of **her set pattern,**[N] i.e., when she expects to begin experiencing menstrual bleeding. Although the Sages generally prohibited intercourse at this time due to a concern that the couple might have intercourse after she begins bleeding, if he is about to depart on a journey he must have intercourse with her.

HALAKHA

A man is obligated to visit his wife when he is about to depart on a journey – חַיָּיב אָדָם לִפְקוֹד אֶת אִשְׁתּוֹ בְּשָׁעָה שֶׁהוּא יוֹצֵא: One who is about to depart on a journey that does not involve a mitzva must have intercourse with his wife, if she so desires, before he departs. This is permitted even if it is the time when she expects the onset of menstrual bleeding. However, some say that if he can accommodate her in some other manner instead, he is praiseworthy. Some say that if his wife is forbidden to him but will become permitted if he postpones his journey by a day or night, he must delay his departure (*Shulḥan Arukh, Oraḥ Ḥayyim* 240:1 and *Yoreh De'a* 184:10, and in the comment of Rema).

NOTES

Without blessing – בְּלֹא בְרָכָה: The *Beit Yosef* cites this statement as a source for the custom that an unmarried priest does not recite the Priestly Benediction, as one who is without a blessing cannot bless others. The *Zohar* states a similar opinion. Nevertheless, the common practice is that unmarried priests do recite the Priestly Benediction.

Whoever knows that his wife fears Heaven – כׇּל הַיּוֹדֵעַ בְּאִשְׁתּוֹ שֶׁהִיא יְרֵאַת שָׁמַיִם: The meaning here is that since she is God-fearing she is reluctant to express her desire openly. If he realizes from her behavior that she desires him, it is a mitzva for him to have intercourse with her.

Is this derived from here – הָא מֵהָכָא נָפְקָא: Although the verse "And your desire shall be to your husband" does not refer specifically to a woman whose husband is about to depart on a journey, once it has been established that a woman desires her husband, and it is well known that this desire increases before a departure, no additional verse is necessary to teach that a man must satisfy his wife when she desires him (see *Tosafot*).

Near the time of her set pattern – סָמוּךְ לְוִוסְתָּהּ: According to Rashi and others, this Gemara indicates that although it is generally forbidden to have intercourse at a time when a woman expects the onset of menstrual bleeding, in this case it is permitted. This is based upon the assumption that the general prohibition is by rabbinic decree, and the Sages did not apply this decree in cases where it would cause the woman suffering. However, other commentaries assert that intercourse at this time is forbidden even under these circumstances. *Tosafot* explain that the term visit referred to in the Gemara does not refer to intercourse, but to spending time together.

A different explanation is cited by the Ritva and the *Nimmukei Yosef*. They claim that this passage does not address the case of a woman who expects the onset of menstrual bleeding. Rather, the case is where the woman has already experienced menstrual bleeding, and the time for her to immerse herself in the ritual bath, and thereby become permitted to her husband, has almost arrived. In this case, the traveler must wait to leave home until it is permitted for him to have intercourse with his wife. It is with regard to this *halakha* that the Gemara states that the period of waiting is a night or a day, meaning that he must delay his trip if all he will have to wait is this amount of time. The next statement of the Gemara would then be understood as saying that if he is departing to fulfill a mitzva he should not delay his journey.

וְכַמָּה? אָמַר רָבָא: עוֹנָה. וְהָנֵי מִילֵּי – לִדְבַר הָרְשׁוּת, אֲבָל לִדְבַר מִצְוָה – מִיטְרִידֵי.

The Gemara asks: **And how much** before the expected onset of menstrual bleeding is considered near the time of her set pattern? **Rava said: An interval** of time,[H] i.e., half a daily cycle, either a day or a night. The Gemara comments: **And this** statement that a man must have intercourse with his wife before he departs on a journey **applies** only if he is traveling **for an optional matter, but** if he is traveling in order to attend **to a matter** pertaining to a **mitzva,** he is not required to have intercourse with his wife so that he not become **preoccupied** and neglect the mitzva.

תָּנוּ רַבָּנַן: הָאוֹהֵב אֶת אִשְׁתּוֹ כְּגוּפוֹ, וְהַמְכַבְּדָהּ יוֹתֵר מִגּוּפוֹ, וְהַמַּדְרִיךְ בָּנָיו וּבְנוֹתָיו בְּדֶרֶךְ יְשָׁרָה, וְהַמַּשִּׂיאָן סָמוּךְ לְפִירְקָן – עָלָיו הַכָּתוּב אוֹמֵר ״וְיָדַעְתָּ כִּי שָׁלוֹם אָהֳלֶךָ״. הָאוֹהֵב אֶת שְׁכֵנָיו, וְהַמְקָרֵב אֶת קְרוֹבָיו, וְהַנּוֹשֵׂא אֶת בַּת אֲחוֹתוֹ,

§ **The Sages taught:** One **who loves his wife** as he loves **himself,**[H] **and who honors her more than himself,**[N] **and who instructs his sons and daughters in an upright path, and who marries them off near the time** when **they** reach maturity,[HN] **about him the verse states: And you shall know that your tent is in peace.** As a result of his actions, there will be peace in his home, as it will be devoid of quarrel and sin. One **who loves his neighbors, and who draws his relatives close, and who marries the daughter of his sister,**[NH] a woman he knows and is fond of as a family relative and not only as a wife,

HALAKHA

Separating from one's wife for an interval of time – פְּרִישַׁת עוֹנָה: It is prohibited for a husband and wife to have intercourse at the time when the onset of menstrual bleeding is expected to occur. If this is expected to occur during the night they are forbidden to each other from the beginning of the night, and if it is expected to occur during the day they are forbidden to each other from the beginning of the day (Rambam *Sefer Kedusha, Hilkhot Issurei Bia* 4:12; *Shulḥan Arukh, Yoreh De'a* 184:2).

One who loves his wife as he loves himself – הָאוֹהֵב אֶת אִשְׁתּוֹ כְּגוּפוֹ: The Sages said that a man should love his wife as he loves himself and honor her more than himself. If he is a wealthy man, he should provide for her in accordance with his means (Rambam *Sefer Nashim, Hilkhot Ishut* 15:19).

Marries them off near the time when they reach maturity – מַשִּׂיאָן סָמוּךְ לְפִירְקָן: The Sages advised a man to marry off his sons and daughters near the time when they reach maturity so that they not be tempted by sinful thoughts (Rambam *Sefer Kedusha, Hilkhot Issurei Bia* 21:25; *Tur, Even HaEzer* 1).

The daughter of his sister – בַּת אֲחוֹתוֹ: The Sages counseled that a man should marry his sister's or his brother's daughter (Rambam *Sefer Kedusha, Hilkhot Issurei Bia* 2:14; see *Mishne LaMelekh*).

NOTES

And who honors her more than himself – וְהַמְכַבְּדָהּ יוֹתֵר מִגּוּפוֹ: With regard to all matters of honor a man must put his wife before himself. An example is with regard to clothing; a husband must make sure that his wife is dressed in a more respectable manner than himself (*Nimmukei Yosef*). Rabbi Yehuda al-Madari explains that the shame felt by a woman when her dignity is not upheld is greater than that of a man, and therefore upholding her dignity takes precedence.

Who marries them off near the time when they reach maturity – הַמַּשִּׂיאָן סָמוּךְ לְפִירְקָן: Most commentaries explain that this means that he marries them off before they reach adulthood. See *Tosafot*, who discuss how it is possible for a boy to get married at this age. Some say that the *baraita* is referring to a father who makes sure his son gets married as soon as he reaches the age of thirteen (see *Yam shel Shlomo*). The Meiri cites a different interpretation according to which the *baraita* is referring to a father who ensures that his son gets married near the usual age of marriage, eighteen.

And who marries the daughter of his sister – וְהַנּוֹשֵׂא אֶת בַּת אֲחוֹתוֹ: Some commentaries claim that this does not refer only to his sister's daughter but includes a brother's daughter as well (Rambam; *Tosafot*, citing Rashbam). The *Mishne LaMelekh* explains that family affection is a more natural feeling than the contingent, albeit stronger, love for a woman, and therefore a combination of these two emotions will ensure the success of the marriage.

Rabbeinu Tam and the Meiri maintain that this statement applies only to the daughter of a sister, because she is likely to be more compatible with him than the daughter of his brother. Rashi states that a man has stronger feelings for a sister than for a brother, and therefore he is closer to her daughter. Others contend that he should not marry his brother's daughter, as she would be unable to fulfill the mitzva of levirate marriage (*Tosafot Yeshanim*; Rivan). Yet others suggest that this is referring to a case of a sister's daughter who is fatherless, and it is a particular mitzva to marry her as an act of kindness, in order to provide for her (Rid). The *Yad Rama* explains in a similar fashion.

וְהַמַּלְוֶה סֶלַע לְעָנִי בִּשְׁעַת דׇּחְקוֹ – עָלָיו הַכָּתוּב אוֹמֵר "אָז תִּקְרָא וַה׳ יַעֲנֶה תְּשַׁוַּע וְיֹאמַר הִנֵּנִי".

and who lends a *sela* to a pauper[N] **at his time of need, about him the verse states:**[N] **"Then shall you call, and the Lord will answer; you shall cry, and He will say: Here I am"** (Isaiah 58:9).

סִימָן אִשָּׁ"ה וְקַרְקַ"ע עֵזֶ"ר זֹא"ת שְׁתֵּ"י הַבְּרָכוֹ"ת תַּגָּרֵ"י פָּחֵתֵ"י. אָמַר רַבִּי אֶלְעָזָר: כׇּל אָדָם שֶׁאֵין לוֹ אִשָּׁה – אֵינוֹ אָדָם, שֶׁנֶּאֱמַר "זָכָר וּנְקֵבָה בְּרָאָם וַיִּקְרָא אֶת שְׁמָם אָדָם". וְאָמַר רַבִּי אֶלְעָזָר: כׇּל אָדָם שֶׁאֵין לוֹ קַרְקַע – אֵינוֹ אָדָם, שֶׁנֶּאֱמַר "הַשָּׁמַיִם שָׁמַיִם לַה׳ וְהָאָרֶץ נָתַן לִבְנֵי אָדָם".

§ The Gemara provides **a mnemonic** device[B] for a series of statements cited in the name of Rabbi Elazar: **Woman; and land; helper; this; two; the blessings; merchants; lowly.** The Gemara presents these statements: **Rabbi Elazar said: Any man who does not have a wife is not a man,**[H] **as it is stated: "Male and female He created them…and called their name Adam"** (Genesis 5:2). **And Rabbi Elazar said: Any man who does not have** his own **land is not a man,**[N] **as it is stated: "The heavens are the heavens of the Lord; but the earth He has given to the children of men"** (Psalms 115:16).

וְאָמַר רַבִּי אֶלְעָזָר: מַאי דִּכְתִיב "אֶעֱשֶׂה לּוֹ עֵזֶר כְּנֶגְדּוֹ", זָכָה – עוֹזַרְתּוֹ, לֹא זָכָה – כְּנֶגְדּוֹ. וְאִיכָּא דְּאָמְרִי: רַבִּי אֶלְעָזָר רָמֵי, כְּתִיב "כְּנַגְדּוֹ" וְקָרֵינַן "כְּנֶגְדּוֹ", זָכָה – כְּנֶגְדּוֹ, לֹא זָכָה – מְנַגַּדְתּוֹ.

And Rabbi Elazar said: What is the meaning of **that** which **is written: "I will make him a helpmate for him [*kenegdo*]"** (Genesis 2:18)? If one is **worthy** his wife **helps him;** if he is **not worthy** she is **against him.**[N] **And some say** a slightly different version: **Rabbi Elazar raised a contradiction: It is written** in the Torah with a spelling that allows it to be read: **Striking him [*kenagdo*], and we read** it as though it said: **For him [*kenegdo*].** If he is **worthy** she is **for him** as his helpmate; if he is **not worthy** she **strikes him.**

אַשְׁכְּחֵיהּ רַבִּי יוֹסֵי לְאֵלִיָּהוּ, אֲמַר לֵיהּ: כְּתִיב "אֶעֱשֶׂה לּוֹ עֵזֶר", בַּמֶּה אִשָּׁה עוֹזַרְתּוֹ לְאָדָם? אֲמַר לֵיהּ: אָדָם מֵבִיא חִיטִּין – חִיטִּין כּוֹסֵס? פִּשְׁתָּן – פִּשְׁתָּן לוֹבֵשׁ? לֹא נִמְצֵאת מְאִירָה עֵינָיו וּמַעֲמִידָתוֹ עַל רַגְלָיו?!

The Gemara relates that **Rabbi Yosei encountered Elijah** the prophet and **said to him: It is written: I will make him a helpmate. In what** manner **does a woman help a man?**[N] Elijah **said to him:** When **a man brings wheat** from the field, does he **chew** raw **wheat?** When he brings home **flax,** does he **wear** unprocessed **flax?** His wife turns the raw products into bread and clothing. Is his wife **not found** to be the one who **lights up his eyes and stands him on his feet?**

NOTES

Who lends a *sela* to a pauper, etc. – הַמַּלְוֶה סֶלַע לְעָנִי וכו׳: *Tosafot* raise an apparent contradiction between this statement and the statement in tractate *Ḥagiga* (5a) that providing money to a pauper at his time of need brings trouble for the pauper. The Ritva explains that he is praised if he lends the pauper money for food. However, if the pauper's creditors force him to sell his belongings in order to pay his debt, which is not to his benefit, it is improper to provide the pauper with money by purchasing those belongings at reduced rates. Others explain that one is criticized if he covets the pauper's property and lends him money with the aim of taking something for himself when the loan is due. The *Iyyun Ya'akov* explains homiletically that the expression: His time of need, is referring to the lender. A lender who himself has fallen on troubled times and yet does not refrain from giving the pauper a loan is praiseworthy.

About him the verse states – עָלָיו הַכָּתוּב אוֹמֵר: According to many commentaries, an earlier verse: "When you see the naked and you cover him, and you do not hide yourself from your own flesh" (Isaiah 58:7), is an important part of this proof, as it demonstrates that the context of the verse cited in the Gemara is helping the poor and taking responsibility to help one's relatives and neighbors (see *Yad Rama* and Maharsha).

Is not a man, etc. – אֵינוֹ אָדָם וכו׳: The Maharsha explains that in order to be complete, a man must participate in creation, either by raising children or by growing crops from the land.

Against him – כְּנֶגְדּוֹ: This is derived from the fact that the term *kenegdo* is superfluous, as the verse could simply have said: I will make him a helpmate. Alternatively, the Meiri explains that the word *kenegdo* itself can be interpreted to mean: Against him, i.e., opposed to him.

In what manner does a woman help a man – בַּמֶּה אִשָּׁה עוֹזַרְתּוֹ לְאָדָם: The commentaries express surprise at both this question and its answer. Was Rabbi Yosei unaware of the assistance a wife provides her husband? And what is the point of such a simple response? The Riaf explains that the question was based upon the fact that although the main purpose of marriage is in order to have children, a woman is not merely man's helpmate in this regard, and therefore the verse does not refer to this aspect of their relationship. The Meiri explains that the main thrust of the answer is that the help a man receives from his wife provides him with his basic needs so that he has time for Torah study. Consequently, her assistance is not merely practical but enables him to achieve the ultimate goal of a Jewish man.

BACKGROUND

Mnemonic device – סִימָן: Because the Talmud was studied orally for many generations, mnemonic devices were necessary to remember a series of *halakhot* and the order in which they were taught.

HALAKHA

Is not a man – אֵינוֹ אָדָם: The Rema cites this teaching in the name of the *Tur*, in order to emphasize the importance of marriage (*Shulḥan Arukh, Even HaEzer* 1:1).

BACKGROUND

From Galia to Hispania – מִגַּלְיָא לְאַסְפַּמְיָא: Galia, or Gaul, is essentially modern-day France, while Hispania is Spain. Ships sailed back and forth frequently between the ports of France and Spain, especially when these two lands were Roman colonies. Commerce in the western Mediterranean serves here as an example of a matter that would seem to have no direct relevance to the Jewish people.

Conducting business – הַפּוּכֵי בְּעִיסְקָא: In the talmudic era most Jews still worked in agriculture, although this occupation was becoming harder, as farmers were laden with heavy tax burdens. In addition, the potential profit margin of commercial transactions was higher than anything that could be garnered from farming land in which one had invested a comparable sum of money.

וְאָמַר רַבִּי אֶלְעָזָר: מַאי דִּכְתִיב ״זֹאת הַפַּעַם עֶצֶם מֵעֲצָמַי וּבָשָׂר מִבְּשָׂרִי״ מְלַמֵּד שֶׁבָּא אָדָם עַל כָּל בְּהֵמָה וְחַיָּה וְלֹא נִתְקָרְרָה דַּעְתּוֹ עַד שֶׁבָּא עַל חַוָּה.

And Rabbi Elazar said: What is the meaning of **that which is written: "This is now bone of my bones and flesh of my flesh"** (Genesis 2:23)? This **teaches that Adam had intercourse**[N] **with each animal and beast** in his search for his mate, **and his mind was not at ease,** in accordance with the verse: "And for Adam, there was not found a helpmate for him" (Genesis 2:20), **until he had intercourse with Eve.**

וְאָמַר רַבִּי אֶלְעָזָר: מַאי דִּכְתִיב ״וְנִבְרְכוּ בְךָ כֹּל מִשְׁפְּחֹת הָאֲדָמָה״ אֲמַר לֵיהּ הַקָּדוֹשׁ בָּרוּךְ הוּא לְאַבְרָהָם: שְׁתֵּי בְּרֵכוֹת טוֹבוֹת יֵשׁ לִי לְהַבְרִיךְ בְּךָ: רוּת הַמּוֹאֲבִיָּה וְנַעֲמָה הָעַמּוֹנִית. ״כֹּל מִשְׁפְּחוֹת הָאֲדָמָה״ אֲפִילּוּ מִשְׁפָּחוֹת הַדָּרוֹת בָּאֲדָמָה אֵין מִתְבָּרְכוֹת אֶלָּא בִּשְׁבִיל יִשְׂרָאֵל. ״כָּל גּוֹיֵי הָאָרֶץ״ – אֲפִילּוּ סְפִינוֹת הַבָּאוֹת מִגַּלְיָא לְאַסְפַּמְיָא אֵינָן מִתְבָּרְכוֹת אֶלָּא בִּשְׁבִיל יִשְׂרָאֵל.

And Rabbi Elazar said: What is the meaning of **that which is written: "And in you shall all the families of the earth be blessed** [*nivrekhu*]**"** (Genesis 12:3)? **The Holy One, Blessed be He, said to Abraham: I have two good shoots**[N] **to graft** [*lehavrikh*] **onto you: Ruth the Moabite,** the ancestress of the house of David, **and Naamah the Ammonite,** whose marriage with Solomon led to the ensuing dynasty of the kings of Judea. **"All the families of the earth"** means: **Even families that live in the earth,** i.e., who have land of their own, **are blessed only due to the Jewish people.** Similarly, when the verse states: **"All the nations of the earth** shall be blessed in him" (Genesis 18:18), it indicates that **even ships that come from Galia to Hispania**[B] **are blessed only due to the Jewish people.**

וְאָמַר רַבִּי אֶלְעָזָר: עֲתִידִים כָּל בַּעֲלֵי אוּמָנִיּוֹת שֶׁיַּעַמְדוּ עַל הַקַּרְקַע, שֶׁנֶּאֱמַר ״וְיָרְדוּ מֵאֳנִיּוֹתֵיהֶם כֹּל תֹּפְשֵׂי מָשׁוֹט מַלָּחִים כֹּל חֹבְלֵי הַיָּם עַל הָאָרֶץ יַעֲמֹדוּ״. וְאָמַר רַבִּי אֶלְעָזָר: אֵין לְךָ אוּמָנוּת פְּחוּתָה מִן הַקַּרְקַע, שֶׁנֶּאֱמַר ״וְיָרְדוּ״. רַבִּי אֶלְעָזָר חֲזָיָא לְהַהִיא אַרְעָא דִּשְׁדִי בֵּיהּ כְּרָבָא לְפוּתְיָא, אָמַר לֵיהּ: אִי תִּשְׁדְּיֵיהּ לְאוּרְכֵּיךְ – הַפּוּכֵי בְּעִיסְקָא טַב מִינָּךְ.

And Rabbi Elazar said: All craftsmen are destined[N] **to stand upon** and work **the land, as it is stated: "And all that handle the oar, the mariners, and all the pilots of the sea, shall come down from their ships, they shall stand upon the land"** (Ezekiel 27:29). **And Rabbi Elazar said: There is no occupation lowlier**[N] **than** working **the land, as it is stated: "And they shall come down,"** implying that one who works the land is of lower stature than even a sailor. The Gemara similarly relates: **Rabbi Elazar saw land that was plowed** across **its width.**[N] **He said to it:** Even **if they plow you** once more **lengthwise,** for further improvement, **conducting business**[B] **is better than** farming with **you,** as the potential profits gained by selling merchandise are far greater than those from working the land.

רַב עָל לְבֵינֵי שִׁיבְּלֵי, חֲזַנְהוּ דְּקָא נָיְיפָן. אֲמַר לְהוּ: אִי נָיְיפַת אִיתְנוּפִי, הַפּוּכֵי בְּעִיסְקָא טַב מִינָּךְ. אֲמַר רָבָא: מֵאָה זוּזֵי בְּעִיסְקָא – כָּל יוֹמָא בִּשְׂרָא וְחַמְרָא, מֵאָה זוּזֵי בְּאַרְעָא – מִילְחָא וַחֲפוּרָה. וְלֹא עוֹד אֶלָּא מַגְנְיָא לֵיהּ אַאַרְעָא וּמַרְמְיָא לֵיהּ תִּיגְרֵי.

The Gemara relates a similar incident: **Rav entered between the sheaves** in a field and **saw them waving** in the wind. **He said to them: If you** want to **wave** go ahead and **wave,** but **conducting business is better than** farming with **you. Rava** similarly **said:** One who has **a hundred dinars** that are invested **in a business** is able to eat **meat and wine every day,** whereas he who has a **hundred dinars** worth **of land** eats only **salt and vegetables. And what is more,** working the land **causes him to lie on the ground**[N] at night in order to guard it, **and it draws quarrels upon him** with other people.

NOTES

This teaches that Adam had intercourse, etc. – מְלַמֵּד שֶׁבָּא אָדָם וכו׳: According to an interpretation cited by the Maharsha, this does not mean that he literally engaged in sexual intercourse with the animals but rather that he conducted an investigation in order to find a suitable creature to be his mate, without success. *Akedat Yitzḥak* explains this statement along the same lines, in greater detail.

Two good shoots, etc. – שְׁתֵּי בְּרֵכוֹת טוֹבוֹת וכו׳: This exposition is based on the fact that the Torah uses the unusual expression *venivrekhu* to mean: They shall be blessed, as opposed to the more proper term *vehitbarkhu*. The Sages associated the word used in the Gemara with grafting [*havrakha*], as these women were grafted onto Abraham's family, i.e., they joined the Jewish people (Riaf; see Maharsha).

All craftsmen are destined, etc. – עֲתִידִים כָּל בַּעֲלֵי אוּמָנִיּוֹת וכו׳: Rabbi Elazar's opinion toward working the land appears to be contradictory; previously he stated that one who does not own land is not a man, whereas here he stated that working the land is a lowly occupation. *Tosafot* explain that according to Rabbi Elazar, everyone should own land in order to grow food and build a house, but this does not mean that farming is a profitable occupation. The Maharsha interprets his comments about the future in this vein: Nowadays people seek a profession through which they can make money, but in the future they will be satisfied with little and will return to the land.

There is no occupation lowlier, etc. – אֵין לְךָ אוּמָנוּת פְּחוּתָה וכו׳: The proof is from the phrase "They shall come down," as it is more common to describe those who go to sea as descending to the sea. Consequently, it is clear that the unusual use of descent in this verse to refer to returning to land is referring not a physical descent on the part of the sailors but rather to their social status (*Arukh LaNer*).

Land that was plowed across its width – אַרְעָא דִּשְׁדִי בֵּיהּ כְּרָבָא לְפוּתְיָא: The Meiri cites a different version of the text, according to which a large pile of produce covered the entire width of the field. In this version Rabbi Eliezer said that even if the pile were large enough to cover the entire field lengthwise as well, farming the field would still not be a profitable enterprise.

Causes him to lie on the ground, etc. – מַגְנְיָא לֵיהּ אַאַרְעָא וכו׳: The Meiri explains that these are descriptions of poverty, as he lies on the ground because he cannot afford a bed, a sorry financial state that then causes constant arguments in his home (see Rashi).

אֲמַר רַב פַּפָּא: זְרַע וְלָא תִּזְבֵּין. אַף עַל גַּב דְּכִי הֲדָדֵי נִינְהוּ – הָנֵי מְבָרְכָן. זַבֵּין וְלָא תֵּיזוּל, הָנֵי מִילֵּי – בִּיסְתַּרְקֵי. אֲבָל גְּלִימָא – לָא מִיתְרַמְיָא לֵיהּ.

Rav Pappa[P] **said: Sow** your own produce **and do not buy** it. **Even though they are equal to each other** in value, **these** that you sow **will be blessed.** Conversely, **buy** your clothes **rather than weave** [*teizul*][L] them yourself. The Gemara comments: **This applies** only to **mats** [*bistarkei*],[L] **but** with regard to the **cloak** one wears, perhaps **he will not find it** precisely to his liking, and therefore he should make his own cloak, which fits his measurements.

טוּם וְלָא תְּשַׁפֵּיץ, שַׁפּוֹץ וְלָא תִּיבְנֵי, שֶׁכָּל הָעוֹסֵק בְּבִנְיָן מִתְמַסְכֵּן. קְפוֹץ זַבֵּין אַרְעָא, מְתוּן נְסֵיב אִיתְּתָא, נְחֵית דַּרְגָּא נְסֵיב אִיתְּתָא, סַק דַּרְגָּא בְּחַר שׁוּשְׁבִינָא.

Rav Pappa further advised: If there is a hole in your house, **close** it **up and do not** enlarge it and then **plaster it,**[N] or at least **plaster** it **and do not** knock it down and **build** it again. **As, whoever engages in construction becomes poor. Hurry to buy land** so that you do not lose the opportunity. Be **patient and marry a woman** who is suitable for you. **Descend a level** to **marry a woman** of lower social status, and **ascend a level** to **choose a friend** [*shushevina*].[L]

אָמַר רַבִּי אֶלְעָזָר בַּר אֲבִינָא: אֵין פּוּרְעָנוּת בָּאָה לָעוֹלָם אֶלָּא בִּשְׁבִיל יִשְׂרָאֵל, שֶׁנֶּאֱמַר ״הִכְרַתִּי גוֹיִם נָשַׁמּוּ פִּנּוֹתָם הֶחֱרַבְתִּי חוּצוֹתָם״ וּכְתִיב ״אָמַרְתִּי אַךְ תִּירְאִי אוֹתִי תִּקְחִי מוּסָר״.

Rabbi Elazar bar Avina said: Calamity befalls the world only[N] **due to** the sins of **the Jewish people, as it is stated: "I have cut off nations, their corners are desolate; I have made their streets waste"** (Zephaniah 3:6), **and it is written: "I said: Surely you will fear Me, you will receive correction"** (Zephaniah 3:7). This indicates that other nations were punished so that the Jewish people would mend their ways.

רַב הֲוָה מִיפַּטַר מֵרַבִּי חִיָּיא, אֲמַר לֵיהּ: רַחֲמָנָא לִיצְּלָךְ מִמִּידֵּי דְּקָשֶׁה מִמּוֹתָא. וּמִי אִיכָּא מִידֵּי דְּקָשֶׁה מִמּוֹתָא? נְפַק, דַּק וְאַשְׁכַּח ״וּמוֹצֶא אֲנִי מַר מִמָּוֶת אֶת הָאִשָּׁה״ וגו׳. רַב הֲוָה קָא מְצַעֲרָא לֵיהּ דְּבֵיתְהוּ, כִּי אֲמַר לָהּ ״עֲבִידִי לִי טְלוֹפְחֵי״ עָבְדָא לֵיהּ חִימְצֵי, ״חִימְצֵי״ – עָבְדָא לֵיהּ טְלוֹפְחֵי.

The Gemara cites more statements with regard to wives. When **Rav**[P] **was taking leave of** his uncle and teacher, **Rabbi Ḥiyya,** upon his return from Eretz Yisrael to Babylonia, Rabbi Ḥiyya **said to him: May the Merciful One save you from something that is worse than death.** Rav was perplexed: **Is there anything that is worse than death?**[N] **He went, examined** the sources, **and found** the following verse: **"And I find more bitter than death the woman, etc."** (Ecclesiastes 7:26). Rabbi Ḥiyya was hinting at this verse, and indeed, **Rav's wife would** constantly **aggravate him. When he would say to her: Prepare me lentils, she would prepare him peas;** if he asked her for **peas, she would prepare him lentils.**

כִּי גְּדַל חִיָּיא בְּרֵיהּ, אַפֵּיךְ לָהּ. אֲמַר לֵיהּ: אִיעַלְיָא לָךְ אִמָּךְ! אֲמַר לֵיהּ: אֲנָא הוּא דְּקָא אַפֵּיכְנָא לָהּ. אֲמַר לֵיהּ: הַיְינוּ דְּקָא אָמְרִי אֱינָשֵׁי: דְּנָפֵיק מִינָּךְ – טַעֲמָא מַלְּפָךְ. אַתְּ לָא תַּעֲבֵיד הָכִי, שֶׁנֶּאֱמַר ״לִמְּדוּ לְשׁוֹנָם דַּבֵּר שֶׁקֶר הַעֲוֵה״ וגו׳.

When Ḥiyya, his son, grew up, he would reverse the requests Rav asked him to convey **to her,** so that Rav would get what he wanted. Rav **said to** his son Ḥiyya: **Your mother has improved** now that **you** convey my requests. **He said to** Rav: **It is I who reverse** your request **to her.** Rav **said to him: This is** an example of the well-known adage **that people say:** He **who comes from you** shall teach you **wisdom;** I should have thought of that idea myself. **You,** however, **should not do so,**[N] i.e., reverse my request, **as it is stated: "They have taught their tongue to speak lies, they** weary themselves to **commit iniquity, etc."** (Jeremiah 9:4). If you attribute such a request to me, you will have uttered a falsehood.

LANGUAGE

Weave [*teizul*] – **תֵּיזוּל**: The versions of Gemara cited by the *ge'onim* and Rabbeinu Ḥananel read *teidul* or *teidvil*. In Syriac this word means weaving, which ties in well with the idea that one should buy an item ready-made.

Mats [*bistarkei*] – **בִּיסְתַּרְקֵי**: Apparently a loanword from the Middle Iranian bistarak, meaning bedding, mattress, or cover.

Friend [*shushevina*] – **שׁוּשְׁבִינָא**: This word is originally Akkadian, from where it was adapted into both Aramaic and Hebrew. Its primary meaning is the one who accompanies the groom to the wedding canopy and helps with some of the technical arrangements of the wedding, and so forth. Its meaning was broadened to a general term for a close friend.

NOTES

Close it up and do not enlarge it and plaster it – טוּם וְלָא תְּשַׁפֵּיץ: According to the Meiri this is an injunction to fix things quickly before they get worse, as it is easier to close up a hole than to plaster an entire wall. Similarly, he should replaster the wall in order to ensure that he will not have to build it again from scratch.

Calamity befalls…only, etc. – אֵין פּוּרְעָנוּת בָּאָה...אֶלָּא וכו׳: This complements the previous teaching: Just as the fate of the world depends on the Jewish people with regard to blessing, the same applies with regard to misfortune. Consequently, the Jewish people should know that their own fate as well as that of other nations lies in their hands (see Meiri and *Iyyun Ya'akov*).

Is there anything that is worse than death – וּמִי אִיכָּא מִידֵּי דְּקָשֶׁה מִמּוֹתָא: Elsewhere the Sages list numerous problems that are worse than death, including captivity and famine. The *Iyyun Ya'akov* explains that it was due to these different possibilities that Rav sought to discover the precise nature of his mentor's blessing. Since he realized that Rabbi Ḥiyya had presumably also been giving him advice along with his blessing, he concluded that Rabbi Ḥiyya was referring to a bad wife. Furthermore, knowing that Rabbi Ḥiyya's own wife caused him to suffer, Rav realized that this must have been what he meant.

You should not do so – אַתְּ לָא תַּעֲבֵיד הָכִי: Admittedly, it is permitted to depart from the truth for the sake of peace, but since in this case there is another way of achieving the same result, it is better not to grow accustomed to telling lies (Meiri; Rabbi Avraham min HaHar).

PERSONALITIES

Rav Pappa – רַב פַּפָּא: Rav Pappa, from the fifth generation of Babylonian *amora'im*, was a student of both Abaye and Rava in Pumbedita. After Rava's death Rav Pappa established an academy in Neresh, where he was joined by his close friend, Rav Huna, son of Rav Yehoshua, who was appointed chief lecturer. Many of Rava's students came to study under Rav Pappa, who had more than two hundred students attending his lectures.

Rav Pappa's father was a wealthy merchant and supported him throughout many years of Talmud study. Rav Pappa became a wealthy businessman in his own right and a successful brewer of date beer. He also prospered in other business ventures. The Talmud records that he engaged in trade with both Jews and gentiles and had a reputation for fairness and generosity in his business dealings. Rav Huna became his partner in many such undertakings and became wealthy as well.

Rav Pappa had great respect for the Sages, and upon entering a city he would immediately call upon the rabbinic head of the community. Once, Rav Pappa felt that he had spoken inappropriately about one of the Sages, and he took upon himself a personal fast as penance for his act. He was reluctant to offer final rulings in various areas of *halakha*, and he often chose to be stringent in accordance with both opinions in the Talmud rather than rule in accordance with a single opinion.

Rav Pappa was blessed with ten sons, all of whom were Torah scholars. Traditionally, the names of the ten sons of Rav Pappa are recited as part of the ceremony at the completion of the study of a tractate. While the source of this tradition is unclear and the identities of the sons are uncertain as well, the Rema suggests that it commemorates the celebrations made by Rav Pappa with his sons upon completing a course of study.

Rav – רַב: Rav, whose full name was Rabbi Abba ben Ayvu, was the first, and perhaps the greatest, of the Babylonian *amora'im*. Known as Abba Arikha because of his great height, Rav established the academy in Sura which lasted eight hundred years, through the period of the *ge'onim*. In addition to the visiting students who attended the academy only during the *kalla* months of Adar and Elul, the Gemara reports that twelve hundred full-time students studied in the academy throughout the year.

In his youth, Rav traveled to Eretz Yisrael with his uncle, Rabbi Ḥiyya, where he studied under Rabbi Yehuda HaNasi, the editor of the Mishna. He traveled back and forth between Israel and Babylonia until he settled in Babylonia in the year 219 CE. Rav's greatness is apparent not only in the large number of *amora'im* who were his students and who quote him throughout the Talmud, but also by the fact that in addition to his status as the first *amora*, he is recognized as the last of the *tanna'im* and consequently was permitted to disagree with tannaitic rulings.

Rav's teachings are found throughout both the Jerusalem and the Babylonian Talmuds. Among his many rulings are several that concern issues of marriage, such as his ruling that a man should not marry a woman without first meeting her, and that underage girls should not be married until they are old enough to state whom they want to marry. His rulings in the area of ritual *halakha* were invariably accepted, although the rulings of his colleague Shmuel were accepted in criminal and financial matters. Rav's son, Rabbi Ḥiyya, followed in his father's footsteps and became a great scholar; his other son, Ayvu, was a merchant.

רַבִּי חִיָּיא הֲוָה קָא מְצַעֲרָא לֵיהּ דְּבֵיתְהוּ. כִּי הֲוָה מַשְׁכַּח מִידֵּי – צָיֵיר לֵיהּ בְּסוּדָרֵיהּ, וּמַיְיתֵי נִיהֲלַהּ. אֲמַר לֵיהּ רַב: וְהָא קָא מְצַעֲרָא לֵיהּ לְמָר! אֲמַר לֵיהּ: דַּיֵּינוּ שֶׁמְּגַדְּלוֹת בָּנֵינוּ, וּמַצִּילוֹת אוֹתָנוּ

The Gemara relates a similar story. **Rabbi Ḥiyya's wife would** constantly **aggravate him.** Nevertheless, **when he would find something** she would appreciate, **he would wrap it in his shawl and bring it to her. Rav said to him: Doesn't she** constantly **aggravate you?** Why do you bring her things? Rabbi Ḥiyya **said to him: It is enough for us** that our wives **raise our children and save us**

Perek **VI**
Daf **63** Amud **b**

NOTES

His iniquities crumble [*mitpakekin*] – עֲוֹנוֹתָיו מִתְפַּקְּקִין: According to Rashi, *mitpakekin* means sealed. Riaf explains that Rashi means not that his sins are entirely forgiven, but that they are sealed up, pending his behavior after marriage. The *Arukh*, however, understands *mitpakekin* as meaning to become loosened.

***Matza* or *motze* – מָצָא אוֹ מוֹצֵא:** Some commentaries explain that in addition to alluding to the two verses this phrase is a question on its own: *Matza* means a good find, while *motze* refers not to someone who finds an item, but to the author of the book of Ecclesiastes, King Solomon, who found, i.e., realized and publicized, that a bad wife is more bitter than death. The *Arukh LaNer* explains the fact that the word *matza* is in past tense indicates an unusual occurrence, whereas *motze* is the more common usage.

Her rival is at her side – צָרָתָהּ בְּצִדָּהּ: The Meiri explains that he should threaten to marry another woman.

A day of heavy rain – יוֹם סַגְרִיר: Just as one cannot escape the continual dripping in a leaky house by escaping outside on a rainy day, this husband suffers from a continuous downpour of abuse from which he cannot escape (Maharsha).

מִן הַחֵטְא. מַקְרֵי לֵיהּ רַב יְהוּדָה לְרַב יִצְחָק בְּרֵיהּ: "וּמוֹצֶא אֲנִי מַר מִמָּוֶת אֶת הָאִשָּׁה". אֲמַר לֵיהּ: כְּגוֹן מַאן? כְּגוֹן אִמָּךְ.

from sin. We should therefore show our gratitude to them. The Gemara cites a related incident: **Rav Yehuda** was **teaching** Torah **to Rav Yitzḥak, his son,** and they encountered the verse: **"And I find more bitter than death the woman"** (Ecclesiastes 7:26). His son **said to him: For example, whom?** His father replied: **For example, your mother.**

וְהָא מַתְנֵי לֵיהּ רַב יְהוּדָה לְרַב יִצְחָק בְּרֵיהּ: אֵין אָדָם מוֹצֵא קוֹרַת רוּחַ אֶלָּא מֵאִשְׁתּוֹ רִאשׁוֹנָה, שֶׁנֶּאֱמַר "יְהִי מְקוֹרְךָ בָרוּךְ וּשְׂמַח מֵאֵשֶׁת נְעוּרֶךָ". וְאָמַר לֵיהּ: כְּגוֹן מַאן? כְּגוֹן אִמָּךְ. מַתְקִיף תְּקִיפָא, וַעֲבוּרֵי מִיעַבְרָא בְּמִלָּה.

The Gemara asks: **Didn't Rav Yehuda teach Rav Yitzḥak, his son,** the following *baraita*: **A man finds peace of mind only with his first wife, as it is stated: "Let your fountain be blessed, and have joy from the wife of your youth"** (Proverbs 5:18), **and his son said to him: For example, whom,** and his father responded in this case as well: **For example, your mother.** This indicates that Rav Yehuda did find peace of mind with his wife. The Gemara answers: She was aggressive and **forceful, but** she was **easily appeased.**

הֵיכִי דָּמֵי אִשָּׁה רָעָה? אָמַר אַבָּיֵי: מְקַשְּׁטָא לֵיהּ תַּכָּא, וּמְקַשְּׁטָא לֵיהּ פּוּמָא. רָבָא אָמַר: מְקַשְּׁטָא לֵיהּ תַּכָּא, וּמְהַדְרָא לֵיהּ גַּבָּא.

The Gemara asks: **What are the circumstances** when a woman is considered **a bad wife? Abaye said: She arranges a table for him and arranges** her **mouth for him** at the same time. In other words, although she prepares food for him, she verbally abuses him while he eats. **Rava said: She arranges a table for him and then turns** her **back to him,** displaying her lack of interest in his company.

אָמַר רַבִּי חָמָא בַּר חֲנִינָא: כֵּיוָן שֶׁנָּשָׂא אָדָם אִשָּׁה – עֲוֹנוֹתָיו מִתְפַּקְּקִין, שֶׁנֶּאֱמַר "מָצָא אִשָּׁה מָצָא טוֹב וַיָּפֶק רָצוֹן מֵה'". בְּמַעְרְבָא, כִּי נְסֵיב אֱינָשׁ אִיתְּתָא אָמְרִי לֵיהּ הָכִי: מָצָא אוֹ מוֹצֵא? מָצָא – דִּכְתִיב "מָצָא אִשָּׁה מָצָא טוֹב", "מוֹצֵא" – דִּכְתִיב "וּמוֹצֶא אֲנִי מַר מִמָּוֶת אֶת הָאִשָּׁה".

Rabbi Ḥama bar Ḥanina said: Once a man marries a woman his iniquities crumble [*mitpakekin*],[N] **as it is stated: "Whoever finds a wife finds good, and obtains [*veyafek*] favor of the Lord"** (Proverbs 18:22). **In the West,** i.e., Eretz Yisrael, **when a man married a woman they would say to him as follows: *Matza* or *motze*?**[N] In other words, they would ask the groom if the appropriate passage for his wife is that verse, which begins with the word *matza*, **as it is written: Whoever finds [*matza*] a wife finds good,** or whether the more appropriate verse is the one beginning with the word *motze*, **as it is written: "And I find [*motze*] more bitter than death the woman"** (Ecclesiastes 7:26).

אָמַר רָבָא: אִשָּׁה רָעָה מִצְוָה לְגָרְשָׁהּ, דִּכְתִיב "גָּרֵשׁ לֵץ וְיֵצֵא מָדוֹן וְיִשְׁבֹּת דִּין וְקָלוֹן". וְאָמַר רָבָא: אִשָּׁה רָעָה וּכְתוּבָּתָהּ מְרוּבָּה – צָרָתָהּ בְּצִדָּהּ, דְּאָמְרִי אֱינָשֵׁי: בְּחַבְרְתָהּ וְלָא בְּסִילְתָא. וְאָמַר רָבָא: קָשָׁה אִשָּׁה רָעָה כְּיוֹם סַגְרִיר, שֶׁנֶּאֱמַר "דֶּלֶף טוֹרֵד בְּיוֹם סַגְרִיר וְאֵשֶׁת מִדְיָנִים נִשְׁתָּוָה".

Rava said: It is a mitzva to divorce a bad wife, as it is written: "Cast out the scorner and contention will depart; strife and shame will cease" (Proverbs 22:10). **And Rava said: A bad wife whose marriage contract** settlement **is too large** for her husband to pay in the event of a divorce, **her rival wife is at her side.**[N] In other words, the only way for him to improve matters is to take another wife. **As people say** in the well-known adage: The way to trouble a woman is **with her peer and not with a thorn. And Rava said: A bad wife is as troublesome as a day of heavy rain,**[N] **as it is stated: "A continual dropping on a very rainy day and a contentious woman are alike"** (Proverbs 27:15).

וְאָמַר רָבָא: בֹּא וּרְאֵה כַּמָּה טוֹבָה אִשָּׁה טוֹבָה – וְכַמָּה רָעָה אִשָּׁה רָעָה. כַּמָּה טוֹבָה אִשָּׁה טוֹבָה – דִּכְתִיב ״מָצָא אִשָּׁה מָצָא טוֹב״. אִי בְּגַוָּהּ מִשְׁתָּעֵי קְרָא – כַּמָּה טוֹבָה אִשָּׁה טוֹבָה שֶׁהַכָּתוּב מְשַׁבְּחָהּ, אִי בַּתּוֹרָה מִשְׁתָּעֵי קְרָא – כַּמָּה טוֹבָה אִשָּׁה טוֹבָה שֶׁהַתּוֹרָה נִמְשְׁלָה בָּהּ. כַּמָּה רָעָה אִשָּׁה רָעָה – דִּכְתִיב ״וּמוֹצֶא אֲנִי מַר מִמָּוֶת אֶת הָאִשָּׁה״. אִי בְּגַוָּהּ מִשְׁתָּעֵי קְרָא – כַּמָּה רָעָה אִשָּׁה רָעָה שֶׁהַכָּתוּב מְגַנָּהּ, אִי בְּגֵיהִנָּם מִשְׁתָּעֵי קְרָא – כַּמָּה רָעָה אִשָּׁה רָעָה, שֶׁגֵּיהִנָּם נִמְשְׁלָה בָּהּ.

And Rava said: Come and see how good a good wife is and how bad a bad wife is. How good is a good wife? As it is written: Whoever finds a wife finds good. If the verse speaks of her, a wife, this demonstrates **how good a good wife is, as the Bible praises her. If the verse speaks** metaphorically **of the Torah,** it nevertheless indicates **how good a good wife is, as the Torah is compared to her.** Conversely, **how bad is a bad wife? As it is written: "And I find more bitter than death the woman." If the verse speaks of her,** this demonstrates **how bad a bad wife is, as the Bible condemns her. If the verse speaks** metaphorically **of Gehenna,** it still demonstrates **how bad a bad wife is, as Gehenna is compared to her.**

״הִנְנִי מֵבִיא רָעָה אֲשֶׁר לֹא יוּכְלוּ לָצֵאת מִמֶּנָּה״. אָמַר רַב נַחְמָן אָמַר רַבָּה בַּר אֲבוּהּ: זוֹ אִשָּׁה רָעָה וּכְתוּבָּתָהּ מְרוּבָּה. ״נְתָנַנִי ה׳ בִּידֵי לֹא אוּכַל קוּם״ אָמַר רַב חִסְדָּא אָמַר מַר עוּקְבָא בַּר חִיָּיא: זוֹ אִשָּׁה רָעָה וּכְתוּבָּתָהּ מְרוּבָּה. בְּמַעַרְבָא אָמְרוּ: זֶה שֶׁמְּזוֹנוֹתָיו תְּלוּיִן בְּכַסְפּוֹ.

The Gemara cites further statements on the same issue. The verse states: **"Behold, I will bring evil upon them, which they shall not be able to escape"** (Jeremiah 11:11). **Rav Naḥman said that Rabba bar Avuh said: This is a bad wife whose marriage contract is large.** Similarly, with regard to the verse: **"The Lord has given me into the hands of those against whom I cannot stand"** (Lamentations 1:14), **Rav Ḥisda said** that **Mar Ukva bar Ḥiyya said: This is a bad wife whose marriage contract is large. In the West,** Eretz Yisrael, **they said this** verse is referring to one **whose food is dependent on his money.**[N] He is forced to purchase his food with cash, as he does not possess land of his own.

״בָּנֶיךָ וּבְנוֹתֶיךָ נְתוּנִים לְעַם אַחֵר״ אָמַר רַב חָנָן בַּר רָבָא אָמַר רַב: זוֹ אֵשֶׁת הָאָב. ״בְּגוֹי נָבָל אַכְעִיסֵם״ אָמַר רַב חָנָן בַּר רָבָא אָמַר רַב: זוֹ אִשָּׁה רָעָה וּכְתוּבָּתָהּ מְרוּבָּה. רַבִּי אֱלִיעֶזֶר אוֹמֵר: אֵלּוּ הַמִּינִים. וְכֵן הוּא אוֹמֵר ״אָמַר נָבָל בְּלִבּוֹ אֵין אֱלֹהִים״ וגו׳.

With regard to the verse: **"Your sons and your daughters shall be given to another people"** (Deuteronomy 28:32), **Rav Ḥanan bar Rava said** that **Rav said: This is** a reference to the children's **father's wife,** their stepmother. With regard to the verse: **"I will provoke them with a vile nation"** (Deuteronomy 32:21), **Rav Ḥanan bar Rava said** that **Rav said: This is a bad wife whose marriage contract is large. Rabbi Eliezer says** that **these are apostates, and so too the verse states: "The vile man has said in his heart: There is no God,** they have dealt corruptly" (Psalms 14:1), which proves that an apostate is called vile.

בְּמַתְנִיתָא תָּנָא: אֵלּוּ אַנְשֵׁי בַּרְבַּרְיָא וְאַנְשֵׁי מָרְטְנַאי, שֶׁמְּהַלְּכִין עֲרוּמִים בַּשּׁוּק. שֶׁאֵין לְךָ מְשׁוּקָּץ וּמְתוֹעָב לִפְנֵי הַמָּקוֹם יוֹתֵר מִמִּי שֶׁמְּהַלֵּךְ בַּשּׁוּק עָרוֹם. רַבִּי יוֹחָנָן אָמַר: אֵלּוּ חַבָּרִים. אָמְרוּ לֵיהּ לְרַ׳ יוֹחָנָן: אָתוּ חַבָּרֵי לְבָבֶל, שְׁגָא נָפַל. אָמְרוּ לֵיהּ: מְקַבְּלֵי שׁוּחֲדָא. תְּרֵיץ יָתֵיב.

It was taught in a ***baraita*** with regard to the verse: "I will provoke them with a vile nation," that **these are the inhabitants of Barbarya and the inhabitants of Martenai,**[B] **who walk naked in the marketplace, as none is more despised and abominable before the Omnipresent than one who walks naked in the marketplace. Rabbi Yoḥanan said: These are the** ***Ḥabbarim*****,**[L] a sect of Persian priests. The Gemara relates: When **they said to Rabbi Yoḥanan:** The ***Ḥabbarim*** **have come to Babylonia,**[B] **he shuddered and fell** of his chair, out of concern for the Jews living there. **They said to him:** There is a way to deal with their persecution, as **they accept bribes.** Upon hearing that not all was lost, **he straightened himself** and **sat** in his place once again.

NOTES

Whose food is dependent on his money [*kaspo*] – שֶׁמְּזוֹנוֹתָיו תְּלוּיִן בְּכַסְפּוֹ: The version of the text cited by the Meiri reads: Whose food is dependent on his palm [*kappo*]. In other words, although manual labor is laudable, if it is one's only source of income, he will not earn a comfortable living.

LANGUAGE

Ḥabbarim **– חַבָּרִים:** This designation for Zoroastrian priests comes from the term *"ḥover ḥaver"* (Deuteronomy 18:11), referring to acts of sorcery. It implies that these priests were seen as involved in various magic rituals.

BACKGROUND

Barbarya and Martenai – בַּרְבַּרְיָא וּמָרְטְנַאי: Barbarya is a land in northern Africa, called **Βαρβαρία** in Greek, meaning foreign place. Their language sounded to the Greeks as though they were saying *barbarbar*, and consequently, the Greeks considered them to be uncivilized and primitive. The term has been used in various forms through the generations and in different languages, and it is still used today as the name for the local tribe, the Berbers as well as in the term barbarian, referring to uncivilized people.

Martenai is a version of the Roman province Mauritania, also in northern Africa, roughly corresponding to modern-day Morocco.

The Gemara is apparently referring to members of tribes from those two areas who were unaccustomed to wearing clothing, or who wore merely loincloths.

The *Ḥabbarim* have come to Babylonia – אָתוּ חַבָּרֵי לְבָבֶל: The *Ḥabbarim*, also called the *Amgoshim* in the Talmud, were priests of the Persian religion, Zoroastrianism. While the Parthians controlled Persia and Babylonia the *Ḥabbarim* did not enjoy important status, but at the beginning of the period of the *amora'im* the Sassanid dynasty rose to power, and as devout adherents to their religion they gave the *Ḥabbarim* great control. Apparently, it was the *Ḥabbarim* who initiated harsh decrees against the Jews. Rabbi Yoḥanan was therefore shocked and dismayed when he heard that they had reached Babylonia, then the largest Jewish center in the Persian Empire, with the new rulers. Nevertheless, it seems that this tribe of priests was corrupt and foolish, and through bribery and negotiations the Jews were able to withstand their decrees.

NOTES

Issue decrees against the Jewish people with regard to three matters – גזרו על שלשה: Some commentaries maintain that information about the decrees was included in the report delivered to Rabbi Yoḥanan, who proceeded to explain the reason for each decree. The Maharsha asks how it was possible that Babylonian Jews committed these transgressions. He explains that in the case of the priestly gifts, they would take on a gentile partner in order to be exempt, as one is exempt from giving the gifts to a priest if the animal was owned jointly by a Jew and a gentile. Furthermore, they actually performed ritual immersion, just not in precise accordance with halakhic requirements. Finally, they rejoiced on the gentiles' holidays on the pretext that the gentiles in their vicinity were not really idol worshippers.

Because the Jews rejoice on the holidays of the gentiles – מפני ששמחים ביום אידם: The Maharsha, the Maharshal, and other commentaries attempt to explain how this punishment fits the crime. The Meiri explains that idols are considered dead, and therefore the Jews were punished for celebrating a festival of the dead by having their own deceased relatives mistreated.

A plague to her husband – צרעת לבעלה: The Maharsha explains that as a man's wife is considered like his own flesh, a bad wife is like a plague on his own body. The *Arukh LaNer* suggests that this is a hint that just as a plague is a personal affliction that distances one from others, the same is true of a bad wife.

גזרו על שלשה מפני שלשה; גזרו על הבשר – מפני המתנות, גזרו על המרחצאות – מפני הטבילה,

Apropos the *Ḥabbarim*, the Gemara cites the following statement of the Sages: The *Ḥabbarim* were able to **issue decrees against** the Jewish people with regard to **three** matters,[NB] **due to three** transgressions on the part of the Jewish people. **They decreed against meat,** i.e., they banned ritual slaughter, **due to** the failure of the Jewish people to give the priests **the gifts** of the foreleg, the jaw, and the maw. **They decreed against** Jews bathing in **bathhouses, due to** their neglect of ritual **immersion.**

קא מחטטי שכבי – מפני ששמחים ביום אידם, שנאמר "והיתה יד ה' בכם ובאבותיכם", אמר רבה בר שמואל: זו חטוטי שכבי, דאמר מר: בעון חיים – מתים מתחטטין.

Third, **they exhumed the dead** from their graves **because** the Jews **rejoice on the holidays** of the gentiles,[N] **as it is stated: "Then shall the hand of the Lord be against you and against your fathers"** (I Samuel 12:15). **Rabba bar Shmuel said: This** verse is referring to **exhuming the dead,** which upsets both the living and the dead, **as the Master said:** Due **to the iniquity of the living, the dead are exhumed.**

אמר ליה רבא לרבה בר מארי: כתיב "לא יאספו ולא יקברו לדומן על פני האדמה יהיו" וכתיב "ונבחר מות מחיים". אמר ליה: נבחר מות לרשעים, שלא יחיו בעולם הזה ויחטאו ויפלו בגיהנם.

Rava said to Rabba bar Mari: It is written: "They shall not be gathered nor buried; they shall be for dung upon the face of the earth" (Jeremiah 8:2), **and it is written: "And death shall be chosen rather than life"** (Jeremiah 8:3). If death will be so indecent that their bodies will not even be buried, why would people choose death over life? Rabba bar Mari **said to him:** The latter verse does not refer to the previously described state of affairs, but rather it means: **Death is preferable for the wicked,** as it is better **that they not live in this world and sin** and consequently **descend into Gehenna.**

כתוב בספר בן סירא: "אשה טובה – מתנה טובה לבעלה". וכתיב "טובה בחיק ירא אלהים תנתן. אשה רעה – צרעת לבעלה". מאי תקנתיה – יגרשנה ויתרפא מצרעתו. "אשה יפה אשרי בעלה, מספר ימיו כפלים".

The Gemara cites more statements concerning women. **It is written in the book of Ben Sira:**[B] **A good wife is a good gift for her husband. And it is written: A good one will be placed in the bosom of a God-fearing man; a bad wife is a plague to her husband.**[N] **What is his remedy? He should divorce her and he will be cured of his plague. A beautiful wife, happy is her husband; the number of his days are doubled.** His pleasure in her beauty makes him feel as though he has lived twice as long.

"העלם עיניך מאשת חן פן תלכד במצודתה. אל תט אצל בעלה למסוך עמו יין ושכר, כי בתואר אשה יפה רבים הושחתו, ועצומים כל הרוגיה". "רבים היו פצעי רוכל המרגילים לדבר ערוה, כניצוץ מבעיר גחלת, ככלוב מלא עוף כן בתיהם מלאים מרמה",

Turn your eyes from a graceful woman who is married to another man, **lest you be caught in her trap. Do not turn to her husband to mix wine and strong drink with him,** which can lead to temptation. **For on** account of **the countenance of a beautiful woman many have been destroyed, and her slain is a mighty host.** Furthermore, **many have been the wounded peddlers.** This is referring to men who travel from place to place to sell women's jewelry. Their frequent dealings with women lead their husbands to harm the peddlers. **Those who accustom** themselves **to licentious matters are like a spark that ignites a coal. As a cage is full of birds, so are their houses full of deceit.**

BACKGROUND

Issue decrees against the Jewish people with regard to three matters – גזרו על שלשה: It is possible that the decrees mentioned here are linked to the beliefs of the *Ḥabbarim*, which included a complex set of laws concerning ritual purity. According to this cult, land possesses special sanctity; therefore, in addition to not burying their dead, they made every effort to remove corpses from their places of burial. Perhaps the decree barring Jews from bathhouses was due to the fact that the *Ḥabbarim* considered the Jews impure. Furthermore, it is reasonable to suggest that the ban against ritual slaughter was also related to these laws.

However, it is also possible that these decrees were promulgated in Eretz Yisrael as well, which would indicate that they were not promulgated by the *Ḥabbarim*, but were rather part of a general campaign to suppress Judaism.

The book of Ben Sira – ספר בן סירא: The book of *Ben Sira*, also called the Wisdom of Sira and Ecclesiasticus, was one of the first works composed after the closing of the biblical canon. It was written before the Hasmonean period by Shimon ben Yehoshua ben Sira, a resident of Jerusalem and a younger contemporary of Shimon HaTzaddik. The book was widely available and very popular. The author's grandson, who lived in Alexandria, translated it into Greek in 132 BCE, making it available to those who could not read the original Hebrew.

In the Septuagint, and consequently in many other translations, Ecclesiasticus is one of the books of the Bible. The Sages considered it apocryphal and even criticized those who read it, both because its council is uneven in value and due to the fact that people confused it with the *Alphabet of Sira*, a book of folk wisdom of dubious worth. In any case, the Sages quotes the book of Ben Sira on many occasions, and sometimes even treated it as one of the sacred writings. They certainly did not refrain from citing its good advice in their sermons, or from making use of its wisdom.

For centuries, the book was known only through translations, but recent discoveries on Masada, among other places, have unearthed large portions of the work in Hebrew. As it was not a sacred book, copyists apparently allowed themselves certain liberties, which accounts for the different versions of the text. Moreover, it seems that the Sages of the Talmud were able to cite it from memory.

"אל תצר צרת מחר כי לא תדע מה ילד יום, שמא מחר בא ואיננו, נמצא מצטער על העולם שאין שלו". "מנע רבים מתוך ביתך, ולא הכל תביא ביתך. רבים יהיו דורשי שלומך, גלה סוד לאחד מאלף".

The Gemara quotes additional statements from the book of Ben Sira: **Do not suffer from tomorrow's trouble,** that is, do not worry about problems that might arise in the future, **as you do not know what a day will bring. Perhaps** when **tomorrow comes,** the individual who was so worried will **not** be among the living, and **he was consequently upset over a world that is not his. Prevent a crowd from inside your house,** do not let many people enter, **and do not** even **bring all** your friends into **your house.** Make sure, however, that a **crowd seeks your welfare,** and that you have many allies. **Reveal a secret to** only **one in a thousand,** since most people are unable to keep a secret.

אמר רבי אסי: אין בן דוד בא עד שיכלו כל הנשמות שבגוף שנאמר "כי רוח מלפני יעטוף ונשמות אני עשיתי". תניא, רבי אליעזר אומר: כל מי שאין עוסק בפריה ורביה – כאילו שופך דמים שנאמר "שופך דם האדם באדם דמו ישפך" וכתיב בתריה "ואתם פרו ורבו".

Rabbi Asi said: The Messiah, son of David, will not come until all the souls of the body[N] **have been finished,** i.e., until all souls that are destined to inhabit physical bodies will do so. **As it is stated: "For the spirit that enwraps itself is from Me, and the souls that I have made"** (Isaiah 57:16). **It is taught** in a *baraita* that **Rabbi Eliezer says: Anyone who does not engage in** the mitzva to be **fruitful and multiply** is considered **as though he sheds blood, as it is stated: "Whoever sheds the blood of man, by man shall his blood be shed"** (Genesis 9:6), **and it is written** immediately **afterward: "And you, be fruitful and multiply"** (Genesis 9:7).

רבי יעקב אומר: כאילו ממעט הדמות, שנאמר "כי בצלם אלהים עשה את האדם" וכתיב בתריה "ואתם פרו" וגו'. בן עזאי אומר: כאילו שופך דמים, וממעט הדמות, שנאמר "ואתם פרו ורבו".

Rabbi Ya'akov says: It is as though he diminishes the Divine **Image, as it is stated: "For in the image of God He made man"** (Genesis 9:6), **and it is written** immediately **afterward: "And you, be fruitful** and multiply" (Genesis 9:7). **Ben Azzai says:** It is as **though he sheds blood and** also **diminishes the** Divine **Image,**[H] **as it is stated: "And you, be fruitful and multiply,"** after the verse that alludes to both shedding blood and the Divine Image.

אמרו לו לבן עזאי: יש נאה דורש ונאה מקיים, נאה מקיים ואין נאה דורש. ואתה – נאה דורש ואין נאה מקיים! אמר להן בן עזאי: ומה אעשה שנפשי חשקה בתורה, אפשר לעולם שיתקיים על ידי אחרים.

They said to ben Azzai: There is a type of scholar who **expounds well and fulfills** his own teachings **well,** and another who **fulfills well and does not expound well. But you,** who have never married, **expound well** on the importance of procreation, **and yet you do not fulfill well** your own teachings. **Ben Azzai**[P] **said to them: What shall I do, as my soul yearns for Torah,**[NH] and I do not wish to deal with anything else. **It is possible for the world to be maintained by others,** who are engaged in the mitzva to be fruitful and multiply.

תניא אידך, רבי אליעזר אומר: כל מי שאין עוסק בפריה ורביה – כאילו שופך דמים, שנאמר "שופך דם האדם" וסמיך ליה "ואתם פרו" וגו'. רבי אלעזר בן עזריה אומר: כאילו ממעט הדמות, בן עזאי אומר: וכו'. אמרו לו לבן עזאי יש נאה דורש וכו'.

It is similarly **taught** in **another** *baraita* that **Rabbi Eliezer says: Anyone who does not engage in** the mitzva to be **fruitful and multiply** is considered **as though he sheds blood, as it is stated: "Whoever sheds the blood of man,"** and it is stated **near it: "And you, be fruitful** and multiply." **Rabbi Elazar ben Azarya says:** It is **as though he diminishes the** Divine **Image. Ben Azzai says:** It is as though he both sheds blood and diminishes the Divine Image. **They said to ben Azzai: There is** a type of scholar who **expounds well, etc.**

תנו רבנן: "ובנחה יאמר שובה ה' רבבות אלפי ישראל".

The Sages taught with regard to the mitzva to be fruitful and multiply: **"And when it rested, he would say: Return, Lord, to the ten thousands of the thousands of Israel"** (Numbers 10:36).

NOTES

The souls of the body – הנשמות שבגוף: Many early commentaries explain that the body is referring to the place where the souls are kept. The *Arukh* states that it is a curtain before the Divine Presence with the images of all people destined to be born. Rabbi Avraham min HaHar cites a homiletic explanation that the final redemption will not arrive until all mankind's physical powers are worn out, and he is ready to become a receptacle for the spiritual.

As my soul yearns for Torah – שנפשי חשקה בתורה: Rabbi Avraham min HaHar explains that ben Azzai claimed he had such desire and fervor for Torah that he had no room left for other passions. He adds that this is why the Rambam says that this claim can be made only by one who is not troubled by his evil inclination.

HALAKHA

The mitzva of marriage – מצות נשואין: A man who does not marry is considered like one who sheds blood, diminishes the Divine Image, and causes the Divine Presence to depart from the Jewish people. Upon his marriage, his transgressions vanish, as per the Gemara (*Shulḥan Arukh, Even HaEzer* 1:1).

My soul yearns for Torah – נפשי חשקה בתורה: One whose soul yearns for Torah like ben Azzai, to the extent that his constant attachment to Torah study prevents him from getting married, is not considered a sinner, provided that he is not tempted by his evil inclination. Even so, he should not proceed in this manner *ab initio* (*Taz*; Rambam *Sefer Nashim*, *Hilkhot Ishut* 15:3; *Shulḥan Arukh, Even HaEzer* 1:4).

PERSONALITIES

Ben Azzai – בן עזאי: This is Shimon ben Azzai, one of the *tanna'im* of Yavne. Despite the fact that he was never ordained, which is why he is known by name alone, and usually simply as ben Azzai, he was considered among the greatest of the Sages and was renowned for his wisdom.

It appears that he did not study Torah in his youth, but only after he met Rabbi Akiva's daughter, who promised to marry him if he would become a scholar. Ben Azzai indeed went and studied under Rabbi Yehoshua, Rabbi Yishmael, and principally Rabbi Akiva. He was one of Rabbi Akiva's outstanding students and was eventually considered a disciple-colleague of Rabbi Akiva's, whom he considered to be the foremost scholar of his generation.

It is unclear whether he married Rabbi Akiva's daughter at all, or whether he married and separated from her a short while later. Due to his great passion for Torah he dedicated himself entirely to its study. It is therefore said about him that when ben Azzai died diligence in Torah study ceased (*Sota* 49a). His teachings of *halakha* and *aggada* are cited in the Mishna, in *baraitot*, and in the Talmud. It seems that he even established a body of students of his own in his hometown of Tiberias.

Ben Azzai also studied esoteric wisdom, and is listed as one of the four Sages who entered the orchard, i.e., the deepest secrets of Torah knowledge. He is said to have: Glimpsed at the Divine Presence and died (*Hagiga* 14b), and the verse "Precious in the eyes of the Lord is the death of His pious ones" (Psalms 116:15) is applied to him.

HALAKHA

If he divorced her she is permitted to marry another man – **גֵּירְשָׁהּ, מוּתֶּרֶת לִינָּשֵׂא לְאַחֵר:** If a woman was divorced because she failed to bear a child, she is permitted to marry another man. This second husband may stay with her ten years, but if she has not had children at this point he too must divorce her or marry an additional wife (Rambam *Sefer Nashim*, *Hilkhot Ishut* 15:14; *Shulḥan Arukh*, *Even HaEzer* 154:16).

A wife who did not give birth – **אִשָּׁה שֶׁלֹּא יָלְדָה:** If a man remained with his wife for ten years without having children, he must divorce her and pay her marriage contract in order to marry another woman who can bear children. Even if he does not want to divorce her, he is compelled to do so. Some commentaries say that if the man has already fathered a viable child, he is not compelled to divorce his wife even if he has not fulfilled the mitzva to be fruitful and multiply (Rema, citing Rivash). The Rema adds that nowadays the custom is not to force the couple to divorce in any situation (Rambam *Sefer Nashim*, *Hilkhot Ishut* 15:7; *Shulḥan Arukh*, *Even HaEzer* 154:10 and in the comment of Rema).

BACKGROUND

He did not merit to be built from her – **לֹא זָכָה לְהִבָּנוֹת מִמֶּנָּה:** From a medical standpoint it is possible for both a man and a woman to be fertile and yet be unable to have children together. Certain antibodies in the woman might destroy the sperm of a particular man and prevent pregnancy, or the genetic combination of the two could create a situation in which the fetus dies before it has a chance to develop.

מְלַמֵּד שֶׁאֵין הַשְּׁכִינָה שׁוֹרָה עַל פָּחוֹת מִשְּׁנֵי אֲלָפִים וּשְׁנֵי רְבָבוֹת מִיִּשְׂרָאֵל. הֲרֵי שֶׁהָיוּ יִשְׂרָאֵל שְׁנֵי אֲלָפִים וּשְׁנֵי רְבָבוֹת חָסֵר אֶחָד, וְזֶה לֹא עָסַק בִּפְרִיָּה וּרְבִיָּה – לֹא נִמְצָא זֶה גּוֹרֵם לַשְּׁכִינָה שֶׁתִּסְתַּלֵּק מִיִּשְׂרָאֵל?!

This teaches that the Divine Presence does not rest upon less than two thousands and two ten-thousands[N] **of the Jewish people,** as the terms thousands and ten-thousands are both in the plural. Consequently, if **there were two thousands and two ten-thousands of the Jewish people, less one, and this** man **did not engage in** the mitzva to be **fruitful and multiply, is he not found** to have **caused the Divine Presence to be depart from the Jewish people?**

אַבָּא חָנָן אָמַר מִשּׁוּם רַבִּי אֱלִיעֶזֶר: חַיָּיב מִיתָה, שֶׁנֶּאֱמַר ״וּבָנִים לֹא הָיוּ לָהֶם״ הָא הָיוּ לָהֶם בָּנִים – לֹא מֵתוּ. אֲחֵרִים אוֹמְרִים: גּוֹרֵם לַשְּׁכִינָה שֶׁתִּסְתַּלֵּק מִיִּשְׂרָאֵל, שֶׁנֶּאֱמַר ״לִהְיוֹת לְךָ לֵאלֹהִים וּלְזַרְעֲךָ אַחֲרֶיךָ״, בִּזְמַן שֶׁזַּרְעֲךָ אַחֲרֶיךָ – שְׁכִינָה שׁוֹרָה, אֵין זַרְעֲךָ אַחֲרֶיךָ – עַל מִי שׁוֹרָה, עַל הָעֵצִים וְעַל הָאֲבָנִים?!

Abba Ḥanan said in the name of Rabbi Eliezer: A man who does not engage in procreation is **liable to death,**[N] **as it is stated** with regard to the sons of Aaron: "And Nadav and Avihu died… **and they had no children**" (Numbers 3:4). This indicates that if they would have **had children they would not have died. Others say:** He **causes the Divine Presence to depart from the Jewish people, as it is stated: "To be a God to you and to your seed after you"** (Genesis 17:7). **When your seed is after you,** i.e., when you have children, **the Divine Presence rests** upon the Jewish people, but if **your seed is not after you, upon whom** can the Divine Presence **rest? Upon wood and stones?**

מתני׳ נָשָׂא אִשָּׁה וְשָׁהָה עִמָּהּ עֶשֶׂר שָׁנִים וְלֹא יָלְדָה – אֵינוֹ רַשַּׁאי לִבָּטֵל. גֵּירְשָׁהּ – מוּתֶּרֶת לִינָּשֵׂא לְאַחֵר, וְרַשַּׁאי הַשֵּׁנִי לִשְׁהוֹת עִמָּהּ עֶשֶׂר שָׁנִים. וְאִם הִפִּילָה – מוֹנֶה מִשָּׁעָה שֶׁהִפִּילָה.

MISHNA If a man **married a woman and stayed with her** for **ten years and she did not give birth,**[N] **he is** no longer **permitted to neglect** the mitzva to be fruitful and multiply. Consequently, he must either divorce her and marry someone else, or take another wife while still married to her. If **he divorced her she is permitted to marry another** man,[H] as it is not necessarily on her account that she and her first husband did not have children, **and the second** husband **is permitted to stay with her** for **ten years. And if she had a miscarriage, he counts** the ten years **from the time of the miscarriage.**

גמ׳ תָּנוּ רַבָּנַן: נָשָׂא אִשָּׁה וְשָׁהָה עִמָּהּ עֶשֶׂר שָׁנִים וְלֹא יָלְדָה – יוֹצִיא וְיִתֵּן כְּתוּבָּה, שֶׁמָּא לֹא זָכָה לְהִבָּנוֹת מִמֶּנָּה.

GEMARA **The Sages taught:** If a man **married a woman and stayed with her** for **ten years and she did not give birth,**[H] **he should divorce** her **and pay** her **marriage contract,** because **perhaps he did not merit to be built,**[N] i.e., to have children, **from her.**[B] It is not certain that their failure to have children is due to her, as it is possible that they are not a suitable match for bearing children.

NOTES

Two thousands and two ten-thousands – **שְׁנֵי אֲלָפִים וּשְׁנֵי רְבָבוֹת:** The Maharsha notes that the verse states: "The chariots of God are ten-thousands, thousands" (Psalms 68:18), and the Jewish people are worthy of serving as a chariot for the Divine Presence by this same number. Similarly, there were twenty-two thousand Levites in the wilderness who did not participate in the sin of the Golden Calf, and in whose merit the Divine Presence rested upon the Jewish people.

Liable to death – **חַיָּיב מִיתָה:** This is similar to the statement cited earlier that one who is not occupied with the mitzva to be fruitful and multiply is considered a bloodshedder, and is therefore liable to death (see *Iyyun Ya'akov*).

Married a woman…and she did not give birth – **נָשָׂא אִשָּׁה...וְלֹא יָלְדָה:** The commentaries debate whether this means that she has not given birth to any children at all, or perhaps, as explained in the Jerusalem Talmud, it even includes a case where she had a child and the child died, and then she did not have another child for ten years. A third possibility is that this applies even to a woman who had only one child, even if that child lived, and ten years have passed since then (see Ramban and Rashba). The *Nimmukei Yosef* summarizes these opinions.

Perhaps he did not merit to be built – **שֶׁמָּא לֹא זָכָה לְהִבָּנוֹת:** Even if he had children from a former wife, and therefore it is clear that he is capable of having children, perhaps his present wife is also capable of having children but the two simply did not merit to have children together (Ritva). The commentaries note that this consideration is strong enough to serve as the basis for a monetary claim, and he cannot withhold the payment of her marriage contract by claiming that there is at least a doubt as to whether she is fertile (*Gilyonei HaShas*).

אַף עַל פִּי שֶׁאֵין רְאָיָה לַדָּבָר – זֵכֶר לַדָּבָר: ״מִקֵּץ עֶשֶׂר שָׁנִים לְשֶׁבֶת אַבְרָם בְּאֶרֶץ כְּנָעַן״ לְלַמֶּדְךָ שֶׁאֵין יְשִׁיבַת חוּץ לָאָרֶץ עוֹלָה לוֹ מִן הַמִּנְיָן. לְפִיכָךְ, חָלָה הוּא אוֹ שֶׁחָלְתָה הִיא, אוֹ שְׁנֵיהֶם חֲבוּשִׁים בְּבֵית הָאֲסוּרִים – אֵין עוֹלִין לוֹ מִן הַמִּנְיָן.

Although there is no explicit proof[N] **for the matter** that one must take another wife if he has not had children after ten years of marriage, there is **an allusion to the matter,** as the verse states: "And Sarai, Abram's wife, took Hagar… **after Abram had dwelled ten years in the land of Canaan,** and gave her to Abram her husband to be his wife" (Genesis 16:3). Incidentally, this verse also comes **to teach you that** the years spent **dwelling outside of Eretz Yisrael do not count** as part of **his tally.**[N] **Consequently,** if **he was sick**[NH] during this period **or she was sick,** or if one **of the two of them** was **imprisoned in jail,** it **does not count** as part of **his tally.**

אָמַר לֵיהּ רָבָא לְרַב נַחְמָן: וְלֵילַף מִיִּצְחָק, דִּכְתִיב ״וַיְהִי יִצְחָק בֶּן אַרְבָּעִים שָׁנָה בְּקַחְתּוֹ אֶת רִבְקָה״ וגו׳ וּכְתִיב ״וְיִצְחָק בֶּן שִׁשִּׁים שָׁנָה בְּלֶדֶת אוֹתָם״! אָמַר לֵיהּ: יִצְחָק עָקוּר הָיָה.

Rava said to Rav Naḥman: Let us derive from Isaac that one may wait a longer period of time, **as it is written: "And Isaac was forty years old when he took Rebekah…** to be his wife" (Genesis 25:20), **and it is written** with regard to the birth of Jacob and Esau: **"And Isaac was sixty years old when she bore them"** (Genesis 25:26). This indicates that one may wait twenty years. Rav Naḥman **said to him: Isaac** knew that he **was infertile,** and therefore there was no reason for him to marry another woman, as Rebekah was not the cause of their infertility.

אִי הָכִי, אַבְרָהָם נַמִי עָקוּר הָיָה! הַהוּא מִיבָּעֵי לֵיהּ לְכִדְרַבִּי חִיָּיא בַּר אַבָּא. דְּאָמַר רַבִּי חִיָּיא בַּר אַבָּא אָמַר רַבִּי יוֹחָנָן: לָמָּה נִמְנוּ שְׁנוֹתָיו שֶׁל יִשְׁמָעֵאל – כְּדֵי לְיַיחֵס בָּהֶן שְׁנוֹתָיו שֶׁל יַעֲקֹב.

The Gemara responds: **If so, Abraham** also should not have married another woman, as he **was also infertile.** Rather, the *tanna* **requires that** verse that states when Jacob and Esau were born **for** that which **Rabbi Ḥiyya bar Abba** taught. This is **because Rabbi Ḥiyya bar Abba said** that **Rabbi Yoḥanan said: Why were Ishmael's years counted** in the Torah, as they do not appear to be relevant to its narrative? **In order to determine through them the years of Jacob,** i.e., Jacob's age at the time that various events took place, as explained in tractate *Megilla* (17a). The verse concerning Jacob's birth was not meant to allude to a *halakha* about remaining married before having children, but to make it possible to determine Jacob's age by relating it to the age of Ishmael.

HALAKHA

If he was sick, etc. – **חָלָה הוּא וכו׳**: The ten years that one may remain married before divorcing his wife if she has not borne him children do not include periods of time when one of them was sick, even if they engaged in intercourse during this period, or time when they were imprisoned, or when one of them was out of the country, as mentioned in the Jerusalem Talmud (Rambam *Sefer Nashim, Hilkhot Ishut* 15:11; *Shulḥan Arukh, Even HaEzer* 154:11).

NOTES

Although there is no explicit proof – **אַף עַל פִּי שֶׁאֵין רְאָיָה**: See the explanations of *Tosafot* and the *Tosefot HaRosh* as to why this source is considered to merely be an allusion and not an explicit proof. Rabbi Yehuda al-Madari states that the verse does not prove he is obligated to divorce her or marry another woman, because in the case of Avraham it was Sarah who freely chose to give Hagar to her husband.

Years spent dwelling outside of Eretz Yisrael do not count as part of his tally – **אֵין יְשִׁיבַת חוּץ לָאָרֶץ עוֹלָה לוֹ מִן הַמִּנְיָן**: The commentaries discuss this issue at length. Rashi's comments that the sin of living outside Eretz Yisrael may have prevented them from having children implies that the *halakha* that one must take another wife after ten years applies only in Eretz Yisrael. Some commentaries indeed write that a husband is not compelled to divorce his barren wife outside Eretz Yisrael, due to the possibility that the reason they have no children is because they are living outside the land (*Or Zarua*). Most commentaries, however, reject this opinion, arguing that there is no reason why the mitzva to be fruitful and multiply, which is not connected to the land, cannot be fulfilled properly outside of it.

One alternative explanation is that if a man whose permanent residence is in Eretz Yisrael leaves the country, the sin of his departure might prevent him from having children (Ramban, citing Rabbi Avraham *Av Beit Din*). The majority of the commentaries explain that one who did not have children outside Eretz Yisrael and subsequently immigrated to Eretz Yisrael must wait an additional ten years, as the merit of living in Eretz Yisrael might help him bear children (see Ritva). Rabbi Avraham min HaHar states that the expression: Count as part of his tally, is referring specifically to Abraham. He lived in sorrow over the fact that he was not in Eretz Yisrael, which might have led to his failure to have children.

Consequently if he was sick – **לְפִיכָךְ חָלָה הוּא**: Rashi explains the use of the word consequently in this context: The fact that the time Abraham and Sarah spent outside of Eretz Yisrael did not count toward the ten years indicates that whenever there is an external factor that may have been responsible for the couple's childlessness, the time when that factor applied is not taken into account. Consequently, if one of them was sick or incarcerated for a period of time, that time is not included in the ten years. The Rosh explains that the Gemara's statement is not limited to situations where the couple was unable to engage in intercourse, in which case there would have been no need to state that the time does not count toward the tally. Rather, the sin for which they were punished with their illness or incarceration may also be responsible for the fact that they have not conceived, and therefore the time does not count even if they were able to engage in intercourse.

NOTES

Concerning [*lenokhaḥ*] his wife – לְנֹכַח אִשְׁתּוֹ: Rashi explains that the term *lenokhaḥ* indicates that Isaac and Rebekah stood opposite each other and prayed. The Maharsha states that *lenokhaḥ* can mean corresponding to. Consequently, just as Rebekah required this prayer, so did Isaac, as his status was similar to hers.

Because the prayer…is not similar, etc. – לְפִי שֶׁאֵינוֹ דּוֹמֶה תְּפִלַּת וכו׳: This means not that the prayer of a righteous individual who is the son of a righteous individual is always answered, but that it is more likely to be answered. See the *Iyyun Ya'akov*.

Abraham and Sarah were originally *tumtumin* – אַבְרָהָם וְשָׂרָה טוּמְטְמִין הָיוּ: The Meiri writes that this informs us of the power of prayer, which can change even one's physical nature.

אָמַר רַבִּי יִצְחָק: יִצְחָק אָבִינוּ עָקוּר הָיָה, שֶׁנֶּאֱמַר ״וַיֶּעְתַּר יִצְחָק לַה׳ לְנֹכַח אִשְׁתּוֹ״, ״עַל אִשְׁתּוֹ״ לֹא נֶאֱמַר, אֶלָּא ״לְנוֹכַח״ מְלַמֵּד שֶׁשְּׁנֵיהֶם עֲקוּרִים הָיוּ. אִי הָכִי ״וַיֵּעָתֶר לוֹ״ ״וַיֵּעָתֶר לָהֶם״ מִיבָּעֵי לֵיהּ! לְפִי שֶׁאֵינוֹ דּוֹמֶה תְּפִלַּת צַדִּיק בֶּן צַדִּיק לִתְפִלַּת צַדִּיק בֶּן רָשָׁע.

Rabbi Yitzḥak said: Isaac our father was infertile, as it is **stated: "And Isaac entreated the Lord concerning [*lenokhaḥ*] his wife**[N] because she was barren" (Genesis 25:21). **It is not stated** that he entreated the Lord **for [*al*] his wife, but *lenokhaḥ*,** which can mean opposite, against, or corresponding to; this **teaches that they were both infertile.** The Gemara asks: **If so,** why does the verse continue: **"And the Lord let Himself be entreated of him"?** The verse **should say: And the Lord let Himself be entreated of them.** The Gemara answers that their prayers were answered due to Isaac, **because the prayer of a righteous individual** who is **the son of a righteous individual is not similar**[N] **to the prayer of a righteous individual** who is **the son of a wicked individual,** and Rebekah's father was the wicked Laban.

אָמַר רַבִּי יִצְחָק: מִפְּנֵי מָה הָיוּ אֲבוֹתֵינוּ עֲקוּרִים – מִפְּנֵי הַקָּדוֹשׁ בָּרוּךְ הוּא מִתְאַוֶּה לִתְפִלָּתָן שֶׁל צַדִּיקִים. אָמַר רַבִּי יִצְחָק: לָמָּה נִמְשְׁלָה תְּפִלָּתָן שֶׁל צַדִּיקִים כְּעֶתֶר – מָה עֶתֶר זֶה מְהַפֵּךְ הַתְּבוּאָה מִמָּקוֹם לְמָקוֹם, כָּךְ תְּפִלָּתָן שֶׁל צַדִּיקִים מְהַפֶּכֶת מִדּוֹתָיו שֶׁל הַקָּדוֹשׁ בָּרוּךְ הוּא מִמִּדַּת רַגְזָנוּת לְמִדַּת רַחְמָנוּת. אָמַר רַבִּי אַמִּי: אַבְרָהָם וְשָׂרָה טוּמְטְמִין הָיוּ, שֶׁנֶּאֱמַר ״הַבִּיטוּ אֶל צוּר

Rabbi Yitzḥak said: For what reason were our forefathers initially **infertile? Because the Holy One, Blessed be He, desires the prayers of the righteous,** and He therefore wanted them to pray for children. Similarly, **Rabbi Yitzḥak said: Why are the prayers of the righteous compared to a pitchfork [*eter*],**[B] as in the verse: "And He let Himself be entreated [*vaye'ater*]"? This indicates that **just as this pitchfork turns over produce from one place to another, so the prayer of the righteous turns over the attributes of the Holy One, Blessed be He, from** the **attribute of rage to** the **attribute of mercy. Rabbi Ami said: Abraham and Sarah were** originally ***tumtumin*,**[NB] people whose sexual organs are concealed and not functional, **as it is stated: "Look to the rock**

BACKGROUND

Pitchfork [*eter*] – עֶתֶר: Rashi explains here that *eter* means a shovel, but *Tosafot* (*Sukka* 14a) prove from various sources that an *eter* is a pitchfork used to dig the earth or turn over produce in the process of winnowing, which is the way Rashi explains the word in tractate *Sukka* (14a).

Farmer winnowing with a pitchfork

***Tumtum* – טוּמְטוּם:** A *tumtum* is one whose external sexual organs are concealed or otherwise indeterminate, and it is therefore unclear whether this person is male or female. In certain cases, the gender of the *tumtum* is later established, which is described in the language of the *halakha* as: A *tumtum* who was torn, revealing his or her gender, at which point this person is considered a full-fledged member of that gender.

חֲצַבְתֶּם וְאֶל מַקֶּבֶת בּוֹר נֻקַּרְתֶּם" וּכְתִיב "הַבִּיטוּ אֶל אַבְרָהָם אֲבִיכֶם וְאֶל שָׂרָה תְּחוֹלֶלְכֶם".

from where you were hewn, and to the hole of the pit from where you were dug" (Isaiah 51:1), **and it is written** in the next verse: **"Look to Abraham your father and to Sarah who bore you"** (Isaiah 51:2), which indicates that sexual organs were fashioned for them, signified by the words hewn and dug, over the course of time.

אָמַר רַב נַחְמָן אָמַר רַבָּה בַּר אֲבוּהּ: שָׂרָה אִמֵּנוּ אַיְלוֹנִית הָיְתָה, שֶׁנֶּאֱמַר "וַתְּהִי שָׂרַי עֲקָרָה אֵין לָהּ וָלָד" אֲפִילּוּ בֵּית וָלָד אֵין לָהּ.

Rav Naḥman said that **Rabba bar Avuh said: Our mother Sarah was** initially a **sexually underdeveloped woman** [*aylonit*], **as it is stated: "And Sarah was barren; she had no child"** (Genesis 11:30). The superfluous words: "She had no child," indicate that **she did not have even a place,** i.e., a womb, **for a child.**

אָמַר רַב יְהוּדָה בְּרֵיהּ דְּרַב שְׁמוּאֵל בַּר שֵׁילַת מִשְּׁמֵיהּ דְּרַב: לֹא שָׁנוּ אֶלָּא בַּדּוֹרוֹת הָרִאשׁוֹנִים, שֶׁשְּׁנוֹתֵיהֶן מְרוּבּוֹת. אֲבָל בַּדּוֹרוֹת הָאַחֲרוֹנִים שֶׁשְּׁנוֹתֵיהֶן מוּעָטוֹת – שְׁתֵּי שָׁנִים וּמֶחֱצָה, כְּנֶגֶד שְׁלֹשָׁה עִיבּוּרִים. רַבָּה אָמַר רַב נַחְמָן: שָׁלֹשׁ שָׁנִים, כְּנֶגֶד שָׁלֹשׁ פְּקִידוֹת. דְּאָמַר מָר: בְּרֹאשׁ הַשָּׁנָה נִפְקְדוּ שָׂרָה רָחֵל וְחַנָּה.

Rav Yehuda, son of Rav Shmuel bar Sheilat, said in the name of Rav: They taught that he waits ten years **only** with regard to the people who lived **in former generations, whose years** were **numerous,** i.e., they lived longer. **However,** with regard to the people who live **in later generations, whose years are few,** he waits only **two and half years**[N] before divorcing her, **corresponding to** the time period of **three pregnancies.**[B] **Rabba said** in the name of **Rav Naḥman:** He waits **three years, corresponding to** the **three remembrances** of barren women by God, **as the Master said: On Rosh HaShana Sarah, Rachel, and Hannah were remembered,** i.e., God gave them children. Since God determines on Rosh HaShana whether barren women will conceive that year, one may remain married until three such opportunities have passed.

אָמַר רַבָּה: לֵיתְנְהוּ לְהָנֵי כְּלָלֵי. מִכְּדִי מַתְנִיתִין מַאן תַּקֵּין – רַבִּי, וְהָא בִּימֵי דָּוִד אִימְּעוּט שְׁנֵי, דִּכְתִיב "יְמֵי שְׁנוֹתֵינוּ בָהֶם שִׁבְעִים שָׁנָה".

However, **Rabba** himself **said: These principles are not** accepted as *halakha*. Why not? **Now consider, who established** the content of the **mishna? Rabbi** Yehuda HaNasi. **Yet, in the days of** King **David,** many years before the time of Rabbi Yehuda HaNasi, **the years** of an average lifespan **were** already **diminished, as it is written: "The days of our years**[N] **are seventy years,** and if with strength eighty years" (Psalms 90:10). Consequently, if Rabbi Yehuda HaNasi included in the mishna the statement that one remains married for ten years, that must apply even nowadays.

וְהַאי "שֶׁמָּא לֹא זָכָה לְהִבָּנוֹת הֵימֶנָּה" וְדִלְמָא אִיהִי דְּלָא זַכְיָא! אִיהִי, כֵּיוָן דְּלָא מִפַּקְדָא אַפְּרִיָּה וּרְבִיָּה – לָא מִיעַנְשָׁה.

The Gemara asks about the language of the *baraita*. **And what about this** expression: **Perhaps he did not merit to be built from her; perhaps** it was **she who did not merit**[N] to build a family. The Gemara answers: **She, since she is not commanded** to be **fruitful and multiply, is not punished.** Their worthiness therefore depends on him, not her.

BACKGROUND

Three pregnancies – שְׁלֹשָׁה עִיבּוּרִים: It is possible for a woman to become pregnant and give birth three times in a period of two and a half years, and this phenomenon occasionally takes place.

NOTES

Two and a half years – שְׁתֵּי שָׁנִים וּמֶחֱצָה: Since the duration of three pregnancies is twenty-seven months, why does Rav say that one remains married for two and a half years, which is thirty months? One suggestion is that the thirty months include one month for the woman to become ritually pure and permitted to her husband between each of the three time periods corresponding to a pregnancy (Rabbi Avraham min HaHar). Alternatively, Rav was not particular about the exact duration, and allowed extra time (Rabbi Yehuda al-Madari).

The days of our years – יְמֵי שְׁנוֹתֵינוּ: *Tosafot* note that even though this psalm is entitled "A prayer of Moses," it was in fact composed by David. The phrase "A prayer of Moses," means a prayer for Moses (*HaKotev* in *Ein Ya'akov*).

Perhaps it was she who did not merit, etc. – וְדִלְמָא אִיהִי דְּלָא זַכְיָא וכו׳: Rashi explains that the point of this question is that therefore she should not be entitled to the payment of her marriage contract (see Rid). Rabbi Avraham min HaHar explains similarly that since she is not obligated to have children, their inability to have children is considered a punishment for the husband, not the wife. Consequently, although it is not known whether she is fertile, she nevertheless receives payment for her marriage contract.

However, some commentaries (Ramban; Rashba; *Tosefot Ḥad MiKamma'ei*) question the connection between not being obligated to have children and receiving payment of the marriage contract. The Ramban suggests that the Gemara's initial statement that he did not merit to have children through her is meant to explain that since they are not presumed to necessarily be infertile, he must divorce her in order to marry someone else. The Gemara's question here is simply linguistic; it asks why this statement was phrased from the perspective of the husband rather than the wife (see Rashba).

אֵינִי? וְהָא אָמְרוּ לֵיהּ רַבָּנַן לְרַבִּי אַבָּא בַּר זַבְדָּא: נְסֵיב אִיתְּתָא וְאוֹלֵיד בְּנֵי! וַאֲמַר לְהוּ: אִי זְכַאי – הָווּ לִי מִקַּמַּיְיתָא. הָתָם דַּחוּי קָא מַדְחֵי לְהוּ לְרַבָּנַן. דְּרַבִּי אַבָּא בַּר זַבְדָּא אִיעֲקַר מִפִּרְקֵיהּ דְּרַב הוּנָא,

The Gemara challenges the mishna's statement that if one did not have children after ten years he should marry a different woman. **Is that so? Didn't the Sages say to Rabbi Abba bar Zavda: Marry a woman and have children, and he said to them: If I had merited, I would** already **have children from my first** wife? This indicates that there is no obligation to remarry if one did not have children with his first wife. The Gemara answers: **There,** Rabbi Abba bar Zavda **was** merely **putting the Rabbis off** with an excuse, as the real reason why he would not marry was because **Rabbi Abba bar Zavda became impotent from Rav Huna's discourse.** Rav Huna's students would hold back from relieving themselves until his lengthy sermons were finished, which caused them to become sterile.

רַב גִּידֵּל אִיעֲקַר מִפִּרְקֵיהּ דְּרַב הוּנָא, רַבִּי חֶלְבּוֹ אִיעֲקַר מִפִּרְקֵיהּ דְּרַב הוּנָא, רַב שֵׁשֶׁת אִיעֲקַר מִפִּרְקֵיהּ דְּרַב הוּנָא. רַב אַחָא בַּר יַעֲקֹב אַחַדְתֵּיהּ סוּסְכִינְתָּא, תַּלְיוּהּ בְּאַרְזָא דְּבֵי רַב וּנְפַק מִינֵּיהּ כְּהוּצָא יָרְקָא. אֲמַר רַב אַחָא בַּר יַעֲקֹב: שִׁיתִּין סָבֵי הֲוֵינָא, וְכוּלְּהוּ אִיעֲקוּר מִפִּרְקֵיהּ דְּרַב הוּנָא, לְבַר מֵאֲנָא דְּקַיְּימֵי בְּנַפְשַׁאי ״הַחָכְמָה תְּחַיֶּה בְעָלֶיהָ״.

The Gemara similarly relates that **Rav Giddel became impotent from Rav Huna's discourse, Rav Ḥelbo became impotent from Rav Huna's discourse,** and **Rav Sheshet became impotent from Rav Huna's discourse.** The Gemara relates: **Rav Aḥa bar Ya'akov was afflicted by** ***suskhinta***, a disease caused by holding back from urinating. **They suspended him from the cedar** column that supported **the study hall, and** a substance that was as **green** as a palm **leaf emerged from him,** and he was healed. **Rav Aḥa bar Ya'akov said: We were sixty elders** present at the time, **and they all became impotent from Rav Huna's discourse, aside from me, as I fulfilled with regard to myself** the verse: **"Wisdom preserves the life of he who has it"** (Ecclesiastes 7:12). I used the above cure to avoid becoming impotent.

גֵּירְשָׁהּ מוּתֶּרֶת וכו׳. שֵׁנִי – אִין, שְׁלִישִׁי – לָא.

§ It was taught in the mishna that if a man **divorced** his wife after ten years without children, **she is permitted** to marry a second man, who may remain married to her for ten years. The Gemara comments: **A second** husband, **yes,** but **a third** one, **no.**[H] Once she has been married to two men without children for ten years each, it is presumed that she is unable to have children.

מַתְנִיתִין מַנִּי – רַבִּי הִיא. דְּתַנְיָא: מָלָה הָרִאשׁוֹן וּמֵת, שֵׁנִי וּמֵת, שְׁלִישִׁי – לֹא תָּמוּל, דִּבְרֵי רַבִּי. רַבָּן שִׁמְעוֹן בֶּן גַּמְלִיאֵל אוֹמֵר: שְׁלִישִׁי – תָּמוּל, רְבִיעִי – לֹא תָּמוּל.

The Gemara comments: **Who is the** ***tanna*** **of the mishna? It is Rabbi** Yehuda HaNasi, who holds that a legal presumption [*ḥazaka*] is established after two occurrences. **As it is taught** in a *baraita*: If a woman **circumcised** her **first** son **and he died**[H] as a result of the circumcision, and she circumcised her **second** son **and he** also **died, she should not circumcise** her **third** son, as the deaths of the first two produce a presumption that this woman's sons die as a result of circumcision. This is **the statement of Rabbi** Yehuda HaNasi. **Rabban Shimon ben Gamliel says: She should circumcise** her **third** son, as there is not considered to be a legal presumption that her sons die from circumcision, but **she should not circumcise** her **fourth** son if her first three sons died from circumcision.

וְהָתַנְיָא אִיפְּכָא, הֵי מִינַּיְיהוּ אַחֲרִינִיתָא?

The Gemara asks: **Isn't the reverse taught** in a *baraita*, that Rabbi Yehuda HaNasi holds that the woman's third son must be circumcised and Rabban Shimon ben Gamliel holds that he is not circumcised? **Which of them** was composed **later** and is therefore presumed to be more reliable?

תָּא שְׁמַע, דְּאָמַר רַבִּי חִיָּיא בַּר אַבָּא אָמַר רַבִּי יוֹחָנָן: מַעֲשֶׂה בְּאַרְבַּע אֲחָיוֹת בְּצִפּוֹרִי, שֶׁמָּלָה רִאשׁוֹנָה וּמֵת, שְׁנִיָּה וּמֵת, שְׁלִישִׁית וּמֵת, רְבִיעִית בָּאת לִפְנֵי רַבָּן שִׁמְעוֹן בֶּן גַּמְלִיאֵל, אָמַר לָהּ: אַל תָּמוּלִי.

The Gemara suggests: **Come** and **hear, as Rabbi Ḥiyya bar Abba said** that **Rabbi Yoḥanan said: An incident** occurred **involving four sisters in Tzippori, that** the **first** sister **circumcised** her son **and he died,**[B] and the **second** sister circumcised her son **and he died,** and the **third** one circumcised her son **and he** too **died.** The **fourth** sister **came before Rabban Shimon ben Gamliel,** who **said to her: Do not circumcise** him. This indicates that according to Rabban Shimon ben Gamliel a presumption is established only after three occurrences.

וְדִלְמָא אִי אָתְיָא שְׁלִישִׁית – נַמִי הֲוָה אֲמַר לָהּ? אִם כֵּן מַאי אַסְהֲדוּתֵיהּ דְּרַבִּי חִיָּיא בַּר אַבָּא. וְדִלְמָא הָא קָא מַשְׁמַע לַן דַּאֲחָיוֹת מַחְזִקוֹת!

The Gemara refutes this proof: **Perhaps if** the **third** sister had **come** before him **he would also have said to her** the same ruling. The Gemara asks: **If so, what is** the purpose **of Rabbi Ḥiyya bar Abba's testimony?** Why would he have related this incident if it does not teach us anything? The Gemara answers: **Perhaps** he comes to **teach us that sisters establish a presumption**[H] in a case like this even though the children who died were not from the same mother.

HALAKHA

A second husband yes, but a third one no – שֵׁנִי אִין, שְׁלִישִׁי לָא: If a woman had been married twice for ten years each without bearing a child by either husband, she may not marry a third time. If she does, her husband must divorce her unless he has another wife or has already fulfilled the mitzva to be fruitful and multiply. If he divorces her, he is required to pay her marriage contract only if he was aware of her background before he married her, in which case he must pay it even if he does not have another wife and has not fulfilled the mitzva to be fruitful and multiply (Rambam *Sefer Nashim, Hilkhot Ishut* 15:14; *Shulḥan Arukh, Even HaEzer* 154:17; *Beit Shmuel*).

Circumcised her first son and he died, etc. – מָלָה הָרִאשׁוֹן וּמֵת וכו׳: If a woman circumcised her first son and he died as a result of the circumcision, and she circumcised her second son and he too died, her third son is not circumcised at the usual time; rather, he is given time to grow and to become stronger. This applies regardless of whether the sons shared the same father. The same principle applies also to the sons of one father from different mothers. Some authorities disagree, but the *halakha* is in accordance with the lenient opinion in cases of potential danger (Rambam *Sefer Ahava, Hilkhot Mila* 1:18; *Shulḥan Arukh, Yoreh De'a* 263:2 and in the comment of Rema).

Sisters establish a presumption – אֲחָיוֹת מַחְזִיקוֹת: If a woman circumcised her son and he died as a result, and her sister also circumcised her son and he too died, their other sisters do not circumcise their sons at the proper time (*Shulḥan Arukh, Yoreh De'a* 263:3).

BACKGROUND

The first sister circumcised her son and he died, etc. – מָלָה רִאשׁוֹנָה וּמֵת וכו׳: Apparently, this is referring to a hereditary disease that prevents the blood from clotting, e.g., hemophilia. It is transmitted through the female, who carries the offending gene, although it affects primarily males. In this case it is certain that sisters establish a presumption, as they are all likely to pass on the disease.

אָמַר רָבָא: הָשְׁתָּא דְּאָמְרַתְּ אֲחָיוֹת מַחְזִיקוֹת – לֹא יִשָּׂא אָדָם אִשָּׁה לֹא מִמִּשְׁפַּחַת נִכְפִּין, וְלֹא מִמִּשְׁפַּחַת מְצוֹרָעִים, וְהוּא דְּאִתַּחְזַק תְּלָתָא זִימְנֵי.

Rava said: Now that you have said that sisters establish a presumption,[N] **a man should not marry a woman from a family of epileptics**[HB] **or from a family of lepers,** as these diseases might be hereditary. The Gemara adds: **And this** applies only if it **was established three times,** i.e., three members of the family are afflicted with the disease.

מַאי הֲוָה עֲלַהּ? כִּי אֲתָא רַב יִצְחָק בַּר יוֹסֵף אָמַר: עוּבְדָּא הֲוָה קַמֵּיהּ דְּרַבִּי יוֹחָנָן בִּכְנִישְׁתָּא דְּמָעוֹן בְּיוֹם הַכִּפּוּרִים שֶׁחָל לִהְיוֹת בְּשַׁבָּת, וּמָלָה רִאשׁוֹנָה וּמֵת, שְׁנִיָּה וּמֵת, שְׁלִישִׁית בָּאָה לְפָנָיו. אָמַר לָהּ: לְכִי וּמוּלִי.

The Gemara asks: **Which** halakhic conclusion **was about this** matter? Is a presumption established after two occurrences or only after three? **When Rav Yitzḥak bar Yosef came** from Eretz Yisrael, **he said: An incident occurred before Rabbi Yoḥanan in the synagogue of** the town of **Maon on a Yom Kippur that occurred on Shabbat.** The **first** sister had **circumcised** her son **and he died;** the **second** sister circumcised her son **and he** also **died.** The **third** sister **came before him,** and he **said to her: Go and circumcise** your son, as a presumption is not established after only two occurrences.

אָמַר לֵיהּ אַבָּיֵי: חֲזִי דְּקָשָׁרֵית אִיסּוּרָא וְסַכַּנְתָּא!

Abaye said to Rav Yitzḥak: **See** to it that your report is accurate, as **you are permitting** an action that would otherwise constitute a **prohibition and a danger.** If the third baby should not be circumcised, doing so would be a prohibited labor and would endanger the life of the child.

סָמַךְ עֲלַהּ אַבָּיֵי, וַאֲזַל נְסַבָהּ לְחוּמָה בְּרַתָּא דְּאִיסִי בְּרֵיהּ דְּרַב יִצְחָק בְּרֵיהּ דְּרַב יְהוּדָה. דִּנְסַבָהּ רַחֲבָא דְּפוּמְבְּדִיתָא וּשְׁכֵיב, רַב יִצְחָק בְּרֵיהּ דְּרַבָּה בַּר בַּר חָנָה וּשְׁכֵיב, וּנְסָבָהּ הוּא וּשְׁכֵיב.

The Gemara comments: **Abaye relied on this** report **and went** and **married Ḥuma, the daughter of Isi, son of Rav Yitzḥak, son of Rav Yehuda.** Ḥuma **had** previously **married Raḥava of Pumbedita, and he died,** and then she married **Rav Yitzḥak, son of Rabba bar bar Ḥana, and he died; and he,** Abaye, **married her** nevertheless, without concern that she had been established to be a woman whose husbands die; **and he died** as well while married to her.

אָמַר רָבָא: וּמִי אִיכָּא דְּעָבֵיד עוּבְדָּא בְּנַפְשֵׁיהּ כִּי הַאי, וְהָא אִיהוּ דְּאָמַר: אָבִין – דְּסָמְכָא, יִצְחָק סוּמָקָא – לָאו בַּר סָמְכָא. אָבִין – יֶשְׁנוֹ בַּחֲזָרָה, יִצְחָק סוּמָקָא – אֵינוֹ בַּחֲזָרָה. וְעוֹד: אֵימַר דִּפְלִיגִי לְעִנְיַן מִילָה, בְּנִישּׂוּאִין מִי פְּלִיגִי?

Rava said: Is there anyone **who performs an action like this** and endangers **himself** by marrying such a woman? **Wasn't it he,** Abaye, **who said** that **Avin is reliable** but **Yitzḥak the Red,** i.e., Rav Yitzḥak bar Yosef, **is not reliable?** He proceeds to explain the difference between them: **Avin returns** to Eretz Yisrael and hears whether the Sages there rescind their previous rulings, whereas **Yitzḥak the Red does not return** to Eretz Yisrael and never finds out if the Sages there rescind their rulings. **And furthermore, say that they disagree with regard to** whether a presumption is established by two or by three deaths due to **circumcision,**[N] but **do** they necessarily **argue with regard to marriage?**

אִין, וְהָתַנְיָא: נִיסֵּת לָרִאשׁוֹן וּמֵת, לַשֵּׁנִי וּמֵת, לַשְּׁלִישִׁי – לֹא תִּנָּשֵׂא, דִּבְרֵי רַבִּי. רַבָּן שִׁמְעוֹן בֶּן גַּמְלִיאֵל אוֹמֵר: לַשְּׁלִישִׁי תִּנָּשֵׂא, לָרְבִיעִי לֹא תִּנָּשֵׂא.

The Gemara responds: **Yes, and it is taught** in a *baraita*: If a woman **was married to** her **first** husband **and he died, to a second** one **and** he also **died, she may not get married to a third** husband.[N] This is **the statement of Rabbi** Yehuda HaNasi. **Rabban Shimon ben Gamliel says: She may get married to a third** husband, but if he also dies, **she may not get married to a fourth** husband.

בִּשְׁלָמָא גַּבֵּי מִילָה – אִיכָּא מִשְׁפָּחָה דְּרָפֵי דָּמָא וְאִיכָּא מִשְׁפָּחָה דְּקָמֵיט דָּמָא. אֶלָּא נִישּׂוּאִין מַאי טַעְמָא? אָמַר לֵיהּ רַב מָרְדְּכַי לְרַב אָשֵׁי, הָכִי אָמַר אֲבִימִי מֵהַגְרוֹנְיָא מִשְּׁמֵיהּ דְּרַב הוּנָא: מַעְיָן גּוֹרֵם. וְרַב אָשֵׁי אָמַר: מַזָּל גּוֹרֵם.

The Gemara asks: **Granted with regard to circumcision** a presumption of death due to circumcision can be established because **there are families whose blood is thin** and does not clot well, **and there are families whose blood clots. However,** in the case of **marriage, what is the reason** for concern that a subsequent husband will die? **Rav Mordekhai said to Rav Ashi: Avimi of Hagronya said in the name of Rav Huna as follows:** Her **spring** is the **cause.**[B] In other words, the woman has some sort of condition that causes those who have intercourse with her to die. **And Rav Ashi said** that her **constellation** is the **cause** of her husbands' deaths.[H]

NOTES

Sisters establish a presumption – **אֲחָיוֹת מַחְזִיקוֹת**: Although Rava himself maintains later in the discussion that one must be concerned that a presumption has been established after only two occurrences in the case of marriage to a woman whose previous husbands died, in this case of the sisters he admits that three occurrences are required in order to establish a presumption. The reason for the difference is that in the case of a woman whose husbands died, the presumption relates to the woman herself. Conversely, in this case the presumption is based on the experiences of other family members, and therefore more evidence is required in order to establish a legal presumption (Rashba).

Say that they disagree with regard to circumcision, etc. – **אֵימַר דִּפְלִיגִי לְעִנְיַן מִילָה וכו׳**: The difference between the cases is twofold. First, the presumption in the case of circumcision does not pertain to the same child, but to his brother. Secondly, the merit of the mitzva may prevent the tragedy. Therefore, even if three occurrences are required in order to establish a presumption in the case of circumcision, all should agree that if two husbands of a particular woman have died, one should not marry her (Rabbi Avraham min HaHar).

She may not get married to a third husband – **לַשְּׁלִישִׁי לֹא תִּנָּשֵׂא**: The Rambam rules that if she did get married, or even betrothed, her husband is not forced to divorce her. Other commentaries struggle to find a rationale for this opinion and support for it in the Gemara. The Rambam himself, in a responsum, explains that marrying a woman whose two previous husbands have died is not actually dangerous; however, if her husband thinks he is at risk, his own worry will in fact cause him to suffer a greater likelihood of harm. Therefore, if he is not concerned, he is not in danger and has committed no transgression by marrying this woman.

HALAKHA

A man should not marry a woman from a family of epileptics – **לֹא יִשָּׂא אָדָם אִשָּׁה לֹא מִמִּשְׁפַּחַת נִכְפִּין**: A man should not marry a woman from a family of epileptics, lepers, or the like. This applies only if three cases from the same family have been documented (Rambam *Sefer Kedusha, Hilkhot Issurei Bia* 21:30; *Shulḥan Arukh, Even HaEzer* 2:7).

Her constellation is the cause of her husbands' deaths – **מַזָּל גּוֹרֵם**: If a woman was married or betrothed twice and her husbands died she may not marry a third time, as there is a presumption that she was the cause of her husbands' deaths. However, if a third man married her he is not required to divorce her. Even if he has only betrothed her, he may marry her. If he was not aware of her previous history and wants to divorce her due to the fact that her previous husbands died, he is not required to pay her marriage contract.

The Rema writes that some authorities rule in accordance with the opinion that her spring is the cause, and therefore the presumption that she is the cause of her husbands' deaths is established only when they died on their own; however, if they died in accidents or due to an epidemic, no presumption is established. Therefore, many are lenient in regard to this *halakha*, and no objection to their practice is raised (Rambam *Sefer Kedusha, Hilkhot Issurei Bia* 21:31; *Shulḥan Arukh, Even HaEzer* 9:1 and in the comment of Rema).

BACKGROUND

A man should not marry a woman from a family of epileptics – **לֹא יִשָּׂא אָדָם אִשָּׁה לֹא מִמִּשְׁפַּחַת נִכְפִּין**: This is one of the earliest mentions in the history of medicine of the recognition that certain hereditary diseases are transmitted through a carrier. Consequently, although the woman displays no signs of the disease, the very occurrence of the hereditary disease in the family raises the possibility that she could pass it on to her children. Contemporary medicine knows of numerous such diseases, of which epilepsy is a prime example.

Her spring is the cause – **מַעְיָן גּוֹרֵם**: It is possible for bodily fluids to transmit infectious diseases. This applies especially to sexually transmitted illnesses, but it is true of other infectious diseases as well. It is also possible for a woman to carry a disease that does not threaten her but is deadly for a man.

מַאי בֵּינַיְיהוּ? אִיכָּא בֵּינַיְיהוּ דְּאֵירְסָהּ וּמֵית, אִי נַמִּי דְּנָפַל מִדִּיקְלָא וּמֵית.

The Gemara asks: **What is** the practical difference **between them?** The Gemara answers: **There is** a difference **between them** in a case **where** a man **betrothed her and died** before the wedding; **alternatively,** in a case **where he fell off a palm tree and died.** If the concern is due to intercourse, then in these cases the husband's death cannot be attributed to his wife. Conversely, if the concern is due to her bad fortune, the husband's death can be attributed to his wife even in these cases.

אֲמַר לֵיהּ רַב יוֹסֵף בְּרֵיהּ דְּרָבָא לְרָבָא: בְּעַי מִינֵּיהּ מֵרַב יוֹסֵף, הֲלָכָה כְּרַבִּי? וַאֲמַר לִי: אִין. הֲלָכָה כְּרַבָּן שִׁמְעוֹן בֶּן גַּמְלִיאֵל? וַאֲמַר לִי: אִין. אַחוּכֵי אַחֵיךְ בִּי?

Rav Yosef, son of Rava, said to Rava: I inquired of Rav Yosef[N] whether the ***halakha* is in accordance with** the opinion of **Rabbi** Yehuda HaNasi, **and he said to me: Yes.** I subsequently asked him if the ***halakha* is in accordance with** the opinion of **Rabban Shimon ben Gamliel, and he said to me: Yes. Was he mocking me** by issuing contradictory rulings?

אֲמַר לֵיהּ: לָא, סְתָמֵי הִיא, וּפְשֵׁיט לָךְ: נִישּׂוּאִין וּמַלְקִיּוֹת – כְּרַבִּי, וְסֻתּוֹת וְשׁוֹר הַמּוּעָד כְּרַבָּן שִׁמְעוֹן בֶּן גַּמְלִיאֵל.

Rava **said to him: No, there are unattributed** *mishnayot* in accordance with each opinion, **and he resolved for you** that the *halakha* is in accordance with each opinion in particular cases. With regard to **marriage and lashings**[N] the *halakha* is **in accordance with** the opinion of **Rabbi** Yehuda HaNasi that two occurrences are sufficient for a presumption. Concerning **set patterns** of menstrual bleeding **and a forewarned ox,** the *halakha* is **in accordance with** the opinion of **Rabban Shimon ben Gamliel** that a presumption is established after three occurrences.

נִישּׂוּאִין – הָא דַּאֲמַרַן, מַלְקִיּוֹת – דִּתְנַן: מִי שֶׁלָּקָה וְשָׁנָה – בֵּית דִּין כּוֹנְסִין אוֹתוֹ לְכִיפָּה, וּמַאֲכִילִין אוֹתוֹ שְׂעוֹרִים עַד שֶׁתְּהֵא כְּרֵיסוֹ נִבְקַעַת. וְסֻתּוֹת – דִּתְנַן: אֵין הָאִשָּׁה

The Gemara identifies the aforementioned *halakhot*. **Marriage** is referring to **that which we said** with regard to a woman whose husbands have died. The case of **lashings** is **as we learned** in a mishna (*Nidda* 63b): **One who was flogged** for transgressing a Torah law, **and repeated** the same transgression[H] and was flogged again, if he then repeats the sin a third time, the **court places him in a** narrow, **vaulted chamber and they feed him barley until his stomach bursts.** Once he has sinned and been flogged twice he has established a presumption of wickedness, and when he sins again he is caused to die so that he will not continue to sin. The case of **set patterns** of menstrual bleeding is **as we learned** in a mishna (*Nidda* 63b): **A woman does not**

NOTES

Rav Yosef – רַב יוֹסֵף: When the Gemara refers to Rav Yosef without further identification, it is referring to Rav Yosef bar Ḥiyya.

Marriage and lashings, etc. – נִישּׂוּאִין וּמַלְקִיּוֹת וכו׳: The commentaries discuss why the *halakha* distinguishes between different cases. They explain that with regard to marrying a woman whose previous husbands have died, since there is a concern of danger, the *halakha* is in accordance with the more cautious opinion of Rabbi Yehuda HaNasi. Although it is not mentioned in the Gemara, the same is true in a case of circumcision; if two brothers have already died as a result of circumcision, the third is not circumcised. In the case of lashings, the *halakha* is in accordance with the opinion of Rabbi Yehuda HaNasi due to the court's responsibility to protect society from evildoers.

Conversely, the *halakhot* of set patterns of menstrual bleeding are rabbinic, and therefore the *halakha* is in accordance with the lenient opinion of Rabban Shimon ben Gamliel. In the case of a forewarned ox, which involves monetary payment, the burden of proof rests upon the claimant and therefore he is not awarded the extra payment unless he can prove that a presumption has been established. Since he cannot prove that the *halakha* is in accordance with the opinion of Rabbi Yehuda HaNasi, he is awarded the extra payment of a forewarned ox only if its owner had been warned on three separate occasions.

HALAKHA

One who was flogged and repeated the same transgression – מִי שֶׁלָּקָה וְשָׁנָה: If one was flogged for committing a transgression that carries a punishment of *karet* and repeated the sin and was flogged again, if he repeats the sin a third time he is not flogged. Rather, he is placed in a narrow, vaulted chamber until he dies (Rambam *Sefer Shofetim*, *Hilkhot Sanhedrin* 18:4).

Perek **VI**
Daf **65** Amud **a**

קוֹבַעַת לָהּ וֶסֶת עַד שֶׁתִּקְבְּעֶנָּה שָׁלֹשׁ פְּעָמִים, וְאֵין מִטַּהֶרֶת מִן הַוֶּסֶת עַד שֶׁתֵּעָקֵר מִמֶּנָּה שָׁלֹשׁ פְּעָמִים. וְשׁוֹר הַמּוּעָד – דִּתְנַן: אֵין הַשּׁוֹר נַעֲשֶׂה מוּעָד עַד שֶׁיָּעִידוּ בּוֹ שְׁלֹשָׁה פְּעָמִים.

establish a set pattern of menstrual bleeding **for herself,** so that it can be assumed that she will start bleeding at a particular time, **until she has established it three times.**[H] Similarly, **she is not purified from her set pattern until it is uprooted from her three times,** i.e., until she did not experience menstrual bleeding at the expected time according to her pattern on three occasions. **And** the case of a **forewarned ox**[HN] is **as we learned** in a mishna (*Bava Kamma* 23b): **An ox does not become forewarned until** witnesses **testify** that it has gored **three times.** Consequently, in the cases of set patterns and a forewarned ox, a legal presumption is created only after three occurrences, in accordance with the opinion of Rabban Shimon ben Gamliel.

HALAKHA

A set pattern of menstrual bleeding is established after three occurrences – וֶסֶת בְּשָׁלֹשׁ פְּעָמִים: A woman establishes a set pattern if she experiences menstrual bleeding at a particular interval of days, or on a particular day of the month, or after a particular physiological phenomenon, on three consecutive occasions. She must assume that she will continue to experience menstrual bleeding according to her set pattern unless it is uprooted, which occurs if she does not experience menstrual bleeding according to her pattern on three consecutive occasions (Rambam *Sefer Kedusha*, *Hilkhot Issurei Bia* 8:5; *Shulḥan Arukh*, *Yoreh De'a* 189:2).

A forewarned ox – שׁוֹר הַמּוּעָד: An ox becomes forewarned only if witnesses testify that it caused damage by goring or biting on three consecutive days. If witnesses testified about three separate incidents on the same day, it is questionable whether the ox becomes a forewarned ox. However, if fewer than three incidents occurred during a three-day period, the ox certainly maintains its status as an innocuous ox, whose owner is liable to pay only half the value of damage that it caused intentionally (Rambam *Sefer Nezikin*, *Hilkhot Nizkei Mammon* 6:1).

NOTES

A forewarned ox – שׁוֹר הַמּוּעָד: *Tosafot* contend that Rabbi Yehuda HaNasi did not disagree with regard to a forewarned ox, as this *halakha* is explicitly stated in the Torah. Rather, the Gemara is saying that in certain cases a legal presumption is established only after three occurrences, which is consistent with the general principle stated by Rabban Shimon ben Gamliel. The Ramban, however, claims that Rabbi Yehuda HaNasi disagrees in the case of a forewarned ox as well, and holds that the third time the ox gores its owner must pay for the full value of the damages caused, because after the first two occurrences it is already considered a forewarned ox.

תָּנוּ רַבָּנַן: נִיסֵּת לָרִאשׁוֹן וְלֹא הָיוּ לָהּ בָּנִים, לַשֵּׁנִי וְלֹא הָיוּ לָהּ בָּנִים, לַשְּׁלִישִׁי – לֹא תִּנָּשֵׂא אֶלָּא לְמִי שֶׁיֵּשׁ לוֹ בָּנִים. נִישֵּׂאת לְמִי שֶׁאֵין לוֹ בָּנִים – תֵּצֵא בְּלֹא כְּתוּבָּה.

The Sages taught: If a woman **was married to** her **first** husband[N] **and she did not have children,** and then she was married **to** her **second** husband **and she did not have children, she may not get married to a third** husband **unless** it is **to one who** already **has children** and has fulfilled the mitzva to be fruitful and multiply, as it is presumed that she is unable to have children. **If she got married to one who does not have children** and he had been unaware of her presumptive status, **she is divorced without** receiving payment for her **marriage contract,**[N] as he married her erroneously.

אִיבַּעְיָא לְהוּ: נִישֵּׂאת לַשְּׁלִישִׁי וְלֹא הָיוּ לָהּ בָּנִים, מַהוּ דְּלִיתְבְּעוּהָ הָנָךְ קַמָּאֵי? מִי מָצוּ אָמְרִי לַהּ: אִיגַּלַּאי מִילְּתָא דְּאַתְּ הוּא דִּגְרַמְתְּ, אוֹ דִּלְמָא מָצֵית אָמְרָה לְהוּ: הַשְׁתָּא הוּא דְּכָחַשִׁי? מִסְתַּבְּרָא מָצֵית אָמְרָה לְהוּ: הַשְׁתָּא הוּא דְּכָחַשִׁי.

A dilemma was raised before the Sages: If she was married to a third husband **and she did not have children**[H] for ten years, **what is** the *halakha* with regard to whether **those first** husbands **can demand** the return of the money they paid for **her** marriage contracts? **Can they say to her: It has been revealed** retroactively **that it was you who caused** our inability to have children, and therefore we entered our marriages erroneously, **or perhaps** she **can say to them: It is now that** I am older that **I have become weak,** but in my youth I could have had children with a different husband. The Sages answer: It is **reasonable** that **she can say to them: It is now that I have become weak.**[BN]

אִיבַּעְיָא לְהוּ: נִישֵּׂאת לָרְבִיעִי וְהָיוּ לָהּ בָּנִים, מַהוּ דְּתִיתְבְּעֵיהּ לַשְּׁלִישִׁי? אָמְרִינַן לַהּ: שְׁתִיקוּתִיךְ יָפָה מִדִּיבּוּרִיךְ, דְּמָצֵי אָמַר לַהּ: אֲנָא אַדַּעְתָּא דְּהָכִי לָא גָּרַשְׁתִּיךְ.

Another **dilemma was raised before** the Sages: If **she was married to a fourth** husband **and she had children**[H] with him, **what is** the *halakha* with regard to whether **she can demand** the payment of her marriage contract from her **third** husband by claiming that it is now evident that she was capable of having children? The Gemara answers: **We say to her: Your silence is preferable to your speech,** i.e., you are better off not making this claim, **as he can say to her: I did not divorce you with this understanding,** and now that I know you are capable of having children, I regret divorcing you. This would invalidate her divorce and, consequently, her marriage to her fourth husband, and would render her child a *mamzer*.

מַתְקִיף לַהּ רַב פַּפָּא: אִי אִיהִי שָׁתְקָא אֲנַן מִי שָׁתְקִינַן? נִמְצָא גֵּט בָּטֵל וּבָנֶיהָ מַמְזֵרִין! אֶלָּא אָמְרִינַן: הַשְׁתָּא הוּא דִּבְרִיָּיתָא.

Rav Pappa strongly objects to this: If she was silent[N] **do we remain silent?** If there is room for concern that the divorce might be invalid, the concern exists regardless of her claim, and therefore the **bill of divorce** should be **found invalid and her children** from her fourth husband should be rendered ***mamzerin*****. Rather, we say** that **it is now that she has become healthy.** In other words, she was previously incapable of bearing children, but she has since recovered from that disability.

HALAKHA

If she was married to a third husband and she did not have children – נִישֵּׂאת לַשְּׁלִישִׁי וְלֹא הָיוּ לָהּ בָּנִים: If a woman was married to two husbands for ten years each without children, and then marries a third husband for ten years without children, she does not have to return the money that her first two husbands paid for her marriage contract. However, if she had not yet collected the money she is no longer entitled to it. Her claim that she was fertile in her younger years is not strong enough to enable her to claim money from others (*Shulḥan Arukh, Even HaEzer* 154:18).

If she was married to a fourth husband and she had children – נִישֵּׂאת לָרְבִיעִי וְהָיוּ לָהּ בָּנִים: If a woman's third husband divorced her without paying her marriage contract because she did not have children after ten years of marriage, and she married a fourth husband and did bear children, she cannot claim her marriage contract from the third, as it is possible that she became fertile only after they were divorced (*Shulḥan Arukh, Even HaEzer* 154:19).

BACKGROUND

It is now that I have become weak – הַשְׁתָּא הוּא דְּכָחַשִׁי: This statement is easily understandable, as the woman has already been married three times, for ten years each. Even if she married the first time at a very young age, she is likely to be approaching menopause. Furthermore, there is a significant drop in fertility for women in their thirties, and this weakening, as it is called here, is an expected occurrence.

NOTES

If a woman was married to her first husband, etc. – נִיסֵּת לָרִאשׁוֹן וכו׳: The commentaries point out that this *baraita* is in accordance with the opinion of Rabbi Yehuda HaNasi. A different opinion is cited in the Jerusalem Talmud which maintains that she is permitted to marry a third husband and forbidden to marry only a fourth husband.

She is divorced without receiving payment for her marriage contract – תֵּצֵא בְּלֹא כְּתוּבָּה: The reason for this *halakha* is that the husband entered the marriage erroneously, as stated in the *Tosefta*. However, the Ramban writes that the marriage is not considered to have been entirely erroneous, because if it were, the woman would not even require a bill of divorce. He explains that with regard to this issue it is considered uncertain whether the woman is fertile, and if she is fertile, her current marriage is not erroneous, and entering a new marriage would constitute adultery. Consequently, she requires a bill of divorce before marrying someone else. However, since there is a presumption that she is infertile, he does not have to pay her marriage contract, in accordance with the general principle that in monetary law, the burden of proof is upon the claimant.

It is now that I have become weak – הַשְׁתָּא הוּא דְּכָחַשִׁי: The commentaries ask: If this is a valid claim, why doesn't she receive payment for her marriage contract from her third husband as well, as she can claim that she was capable of having children at the time they got married? The *Tosefot HaRosh* and *Tosafot Yeshanim* explain that this claim is effective only to prevent her from having to pay back her previous husbands, but is not convincing enough to bolster claims on her part for additional money. Consequently, if for some reason her previous husbands have not yet fulfilled their obligation to pay her marriage contract, she is no longer able to force them to do so. Conversely, the Ritva explains that she cannot collect payment for her marriage contract from her third husband due to a rabbinically imposed penalty for marrying a man unsuitable for her.

If she was silent, etc. – אִי אִיהִי שָׁתְקָא וכו׳: The commentaries ask why this is a reason to deprive the woman of her marriage contract; it would seem that the husband can make this claim only if he explicitly stated at the time of the divorce that he was divorcing her because she was infertile. It is explained in the *Tosefot HaRosh* that in fact the case under discussion concerns only a situation when he made such a statement at the time of the divorce. The Ramban explains that since at the time of the divorce it was not known with absolute certainty that she was infertile, as she had no external signs of infertility, he divorced her with the understanding that she might actually be fertile. Therefore, the divorce cannot be retroactively nullified.

BACKGROUND

Shoots like an arrow – **יוֹרֶה כְּחֵץ**: As far as fertilization is concerned, it does not matter how the sperm enters the womb. Nevertheless, if his semen does not shoot like an arrow, which is an unusual predicament, there are grounds to suspect that it is a symptom of some other problem that prevents pregnancy, even if a small chance of conception still remains.

הוּא אָמַר: מִינַּהּ, וְהִיא אָמְרָה: מִינֵּיהּ – אָמַר רַבִּי אַמִי: דְּבָרִים שֶׁבֵּינוֹ לְבֵינָהּ נֶאֱמֶנֶת. וְטַעְמָא מַאי? הִיא – קַיְימָא לַהּ בְּיוֹרֶה כְּחֵץ, הוּא – לָא קִים לֵיהּ בְּיוֹרֶה כְּחֵץ.

§ The Gemara addresses a related case. If **he said** that the cause for their failure to have children is **from her,**[NH] i.e., it is she who is infertile, **and she said** it is **from him, Rabbi Ami said:** With regard to such **matters between him and her, she is believed.** The Gemara inquires: **What is the reason** for this ruling? **She is certain** whether his semen **shoots like an arrow,**[B] whereas **he is not certain** whether his semen **shoots like an arrow.**

אֲמַר אִיהוּ: אֵיזִיל אִינְסִיב אִיתְּתָא וְאִיבְדּוֹק נַפְשַׁאי. אָמַר רַבִּי אַמִי: אַף בְּזוֹ יוֹצִיא וְיִתֵּן כְּתוּבָּה, שֶׁאֲנִי אוֹמֵר: כָּל הַנּוֹשֵׂא אִשָּׁה עַל אִשְׁתּוֹ – יוֹצִיא וְיִתֵּן כְּתוּבָּה. רָבָא אָמַר: נוֹשֵׂא אָדָם כַּמָּה נָשִׁים עַל אִשְׁתּוֹ, וְהוּא דְּאִית לֵיהּ לְמֵיזַיְינִינְהִי.

If **he says: I will go and marry a** different **woman and examine myself**[N] to see if I am indeed the cause, **Rabbi Ami said: Even in this** case he **must divorce** his first wife **and give** her the payment for her **marriage contract, as I say** that **whoever marries a woman in addition to his** first **wife must divorce** his first wife **and give** her the payment for her **marriage contract.** Conversely, **Rava said** that **a man may marry several women**[H] **in addition to his** first **wife, and** there is nothing wrong with this practice **as long as he has** enough **to support them** all.

NOTES

He said it is from her – **הוּא אָמַר מִינַּהּ**: The commentaries offer many conflicting interpretations of this passage in light of the fact that it seems to contradict the Gemara in tractate *Nedarim* (91a), in which the Sages declared that a wife who claims that her husband's semen does not shoot like an arrow is not believed, due to the possibility that she is merely trying to force him to divorce her because she has set her eyes upon another man. Some *ge'onim* claim that the Gemara here is referring to the time before the rabbinic decree mentioned in tractate *Nedarim*, and the statement of the Gemara here is not accepted as *halakha*. The Rid writes that the Gemara in tractate *Nedarim* means that the court requests of the woman to withdraw her demand for a divorce and to try again, whereas the Gemara here states that if she insists on a divorce, her claim is accepted.

The Ra'avad explains that there is no contradiction because the Gemara in tractate *Nedarim* is referring to a case where she claims that her husband is completely unable to engage in intercourse, whereas here she claims that he does not ejaculate forcefully. Others explain that she is believed in the case here because there is circumstantial support to her claim, from the fact that they have been married for ten years without children. The Rif adds that in this situation it is the court that initiates the divorce process rather than the woman, and therefore there is no concern that she has set her eyes upon another man. See the Meiri, who cites several of these explanations and explains the differences between them.

An entirely different opinion is suggested by the Razah: The wife in the Gemara here does not want to be divorced from her husband, and her claim is that since he is the cause for their failure to have children there is no point in forcing him to divorce her, as he cannot father children in any case.

I will go and marry a different woman and examine myself – **אֵיזִיל אִינְסִיב אִיתְּתָא וְאִיבְדּוֹק נַפְשַׁאי**: According to most commentaries, this is a continuation of the previous case: Hearing his wife's claim that he is infertile, the husband suggests that he might try and have children with another woman. However, *Tosefot Ḥad MiKamma'ei* cites an alternative explanation, according to which this is a different case: The couple has not had children, and neither side is interested in a divorce. The husband claims that he wants to delay divorcing his wife until he determines that she is in fact the cause of their inability to have children. Rabbi Ami states that even in this case he must divorce her, and Rava disagrees.

HALAKHA

He said it is from her, etc. – **הוּא אָמַר מִינַּהּ וכו׳**: With regard to a woman who sues for divorce with the claim that she is unable to conceive because her husband does not ejaculate forcefully, if they have already been married for ten years without children and she has no other reason for demanding a divorce, then she is believed. Even if he had children from a previous marriage, it is possible that he has since become dysfunctional, and he is obligated to divorce her; however, he is required to pay only the main part of her marriage contract. This is two hundred dinars for a woman who was a virgin at the time of her marriage or one hundred dinars for a woman who was not a virgin when she married, which the Sages required a husband to include in the marriage contract. He is not required to pay any additional sum that he voluntarily included in the marriage contract. He may declare a ban on one who makes unsubstantiated claims of this kind.

If he wants to marry an additional woman in order to determine the veracity of his wife's claim before divorcing her he is permitted to do so, and if his second wife bears children he may divorce the first one without paying her marriage contract. Some commentaries state that if the second wife confirms the claim of the first wife, he must divorce them both and pay them their marriage contracts.

If the husband knows that he is infertile and his wife demands a divorce on these grounds, he must grant it at once. This is the opinion of the Rambam and the *Shulḥan Arukh*. However, the Rema rules in accordance with the opinion of the Ra'avad and the *Tur*, who contend that this *halakha* applies only to a third husband or in a case where the husband has children from a previous marriage. In other cases, the woman receives payment for her marriage contract even if she does not claim that they have been unable to have children due to her husband's dysfunction. See the *Beit Shmuel*, who cites the various opinions of the earlier halakhic commentaries on this matter (Rambam *Sefer Nashim*, *Hilkhot Ishut* 15:8–9; *Shulḥan Arukh*, *Even HaEzer* 154:6 and in the comment of Rema).

A man may marry several women – **נוֹשֵׂא אָדָם כַּמָּה נָשִׁים**: A man is permitted to be married to several women at once, on condition that he can provide for their sustenance, clothing, and conjugal rights. However, in a place where the custom is not to marry more than one wife he may not do so. The ban on polygamy of Rabbeinu Gershom Meor HaGola is generally accepted, and this is the binding custom of Ashkenazic Jews to this day (Rambam *Sefer Nashim*, *Hilkhot Ishut* 14:3; *Shulḥan Arukh*, *Even HaEzer* 1:9, 76:7).

הוא אָמַר: אִפַּלְתְּ בְּגוֹ עֶשֶׂר, וְהִיא אָמְרָה: לֹא אִפַּלְתִּי. אָמַר רַבִּי אַמִי: אַף בְּזוֹ הִיא נֶאֱמֶנֶת, דְּאִם אִיתָא דְּהִפִּילָה – נַפְשָׁהּ בְּעַקְרְתָה לָא מַחְזְקָה.

The Gemara addresses another case in which the court forces a man to divorce his wife who has not had children after ten years. If **he said: You miscarried**[NH] **within the ten** years of our marriage, and since less than ten years have elapsed since that time he should not have to divorce her, **and she said: I did not miscarry, Rabbi Ami said: Even in this case she is believed, because if it is so that she miscarried she** would **not establish herself as barren** through denying his claim.

הִפִּילָה, וְחָזְרָה וְהִפִּילָה, וְחָזְרָה וְהִפִּילָה – הוּחְזְקָה לִנְפָלִים. הוּא אָמַר: אִפִּילָה תְּרֵי, וְהִיא אָמְרָה: תְּלָת. אָמַר רַבִּי יִצְחָק בֶּן אֶלְעָזָר: עוּבְדָּא הֲוָה בֵּי מִדְרְשָׁא, וְאָמְרוּ: הִיא מְהֵימְנָא, דְּאִם אִיתָא דְּלָא אַפְּלָה – נַפְשָׁהּ בְּנִיפְלֵי לָא מַחְזְקָה.

If **she miscarried, and** then **miscarried again,**[N] **and miscarried again, she has been established to** be a woman who is prone to **miscarriages,**[NB] and her husband must divorce her so that he can have children with another woman. If **he said she miscarried twice,**[H] **and she said** it occurred **three** times, **Rabbi Yitzḥak ben Elazar said: There was an incident** of this kind that was adjudicated in **the study hall and they said** that **she is believed, because if it is so that** she had **not miscarried** a third time **she would not establish herself** as one who is prone to **miscarriages.**

מתני׳ הָאִישׁ מְצוּוֶּה עַל פְּרִיָּה וּרְבִיָּה, אֲבָל לֹא הָאִשָּׁה. רַבִּי יוֹחָנָן בֶּן בְּרוֹקָה אוֹמֵר: עַל שְׁנֵיהֶם הוּא אוֹמֵר ״וַיְבָרֶךְ אוֹתָם אֱלֹהִים וַיֹּאמֶר לָהֶם [אֱלֹהִים] פְּרוּ וּרְבוּ״.

MISHNA **A man is commanded with regard to the** mitzva to be **fruitful and multiply,**[H] **but not a woman.**[H] **Rabbi Yoḥanan ben Beroka says** that a woman is also commanded, as the verse **states with regard to both of them: "And God blessed them, and God said to them: Be fruitful and multiply"** (Genesis 1:28).

גמ׳ מְנָא הָנֵי מִילֵּי? אָמַר רַבִּי אִילְעָא מִשּׁוּם רַבִּי אֶלְעָזָר בְּרַבִּי שִׁמְעוֹן: אָמַר קְרָא ״וּמִלְאוּ אֶת הָאָרֶץ וְכִבְשׁוּהָ״ אִישׁ דַּרְכּוֹ לִכְבּוֹשׁ, וְאֵין אִשָּׁה דַּרְכָּהּ לִכְבּוֹשׁ.

GEMARA **From where are these matters** derived, that a woman is not obligated in the mitzva to be fruitful and multiply? **Rabbi Ile'a said in the name of Rabbi Elazar, son of Rabbi Shimon: The verse states:** "Be fruitful and multiply, **and fill the land and conquer it**" (Genesis 1:28). **It is the manner of a man to conquer and it is not the manner of a woman to conquer.** Consequently, it is evident that the entire command, including the mitzva to be fruitful and multiply, was given only to men and not to women.

אַדְּרַבָּה, ״וְכִבְשׁוּהָ״ תַּרְתֵּי מַשְׁמַע! אָמַר רַב נַחְמָן בַּר יִצְחָק: ״וְכִבְשָׁהּ״ כְּתִיב. רַב יוֹסֵף אָמַר: מֵהָכָא, ״אֲנִי אֵל שַׁדַּי פְּרֵה וּרְבֵה״ וְלֹא קָאָמַר ״פְּרוּ וּרְבוּ״.

The Gemara raises a difficulty. **On the contrary,** the plural term: **"And conquer it [*vekhivshuha*]," indicates** that the **two** of them are included. **Rav Naḥman bar Yitzḥak said: It is written** in the Torah without the letter *vav*, so that it can be read: **And conquer it [*vekhivsha*],**[N] in the singular. **Rav Yosef said:** The proof is **from here:** "And God said to him: **I am God Almighty, be fruitful and multiply [*perei urvei*]**" (Genesis 35:11), which is in singular, **and it does not state: Be fruitful and multiply [*peru urvu*]** in the plural.

NOTES

He said, you miscarried, etc. – הוּא אָמַר אִפַּלְתְּ וכו׳: The commentaries disagree over the context of this *halakha*. According to the *She'iltot deRav Aḥai Gaon* and other *ge'onim* it includes even a case where she is demanding a divorce. There is no concern that she is making this statement because she has set her eyes on another man, as she would presumably not publicize negative information about herself for this purpose. Others, however, claim that this *halakha* applies only if the wife did not ask for a divorce; rather, the court wanted to force the husband to divorce her and she informed them of her version of events (see Ramban; Rashba; Meiri).

If she miscarried and then miscarried again, etc. – הִפִּילָה וְחָזְרָה וְהִפִּילָה וכו׳: In this case the *halakha* is not in accordance with the opinion of Rabbi Yehuda HaNasi, and the presumption is established only after three miscarriages. Although it was stated above (64b) that the *halakha* is in accordance with the opinion of Rabbi Yehuda HaNasi with regard to marriage, since in this case it was permitted for them to marry, he is not obligated to divorce her after only two miscarriages. Furthermore, it is possible that Rabbi Yehuda HaNasi himself agrees that in this case he is obligated to divorce her only after three miscarriages (Ramban; Rashba).

She has been established to be a woman who is prone to miscarriages – הוּחְזְקָה לִנְפָלִים: In this case there is no need to wait ten years, and he must divorce her immediately (*ge'onim*; see Rid). However, just as in the case of a woman who was married for ten years without children, the woman may marry another man. This is because it has been established only that she miscarries after conceiving from her first husband; it is possible that she is capable of bearing children, but is incompatible with that man (see Meiri).

It is written, and conquer it [*vekhivshah*] – וְכִבְשָׁהּ כְּתִיב: There is a general dispute among the *tanna'im* whether the written form of the Torah's text is considered authoritative or whether it is the manner in which it is vocalized that is authoritative. Nevertheless, in this case all would agree that the written form is authoritative, because the verse implies that the purpose of procreation is for humankind to conquer the earth, and it is men who engage in conquest (Ritva).

BACKGROUND

She has been established to be a woman who is prone to miscarriages – הוּחְזְקָה לִנְפָלִים: Nowadays as well, the phenomenon of recurring miscarriages exists. While there are different reasons for this, it is clear that some women are prone to miscarry.

HALAKHA

He said, you miscarried, etc. – הוּא אָמַר אִפַּלְתְּ וכו׳: If a husband claims that his wife had a miscarriage during their ten years of marriage without children, and she denies it, she is believed (Rambam *Sefer Nashim, Hilkhot Ishut* 15:13; *Shulḥan Arukh, Even HaEzer* 154:13).

He said she miscarried twice, etc. – הוּא אָמַר אִפִּילָה תְּרֵי וכו׳: If a husband claims that his wife miscarried only twice and she says she miscarried three times, she is believed (Rambam *Sefer Nashim, Hilkhot Ishut* 15:13; *Shulḥan Arukh, Even HaEzer* 154:14).

A man is commanded…to be fruitful and multiply – הָאִישׁ מְצוּוֶּה עַל פְּרִיָּה וּרְבִיָּה: Every man is obligated to marry in order to fulfill the mitzva to be fruitful and multiply (Rambam *Sefer Nashim, Hilkhot Ishut* 15:2; *Shulḥan Arukh, Even HaEzer* 1:1).

But not a woman – אֲבָל לֹא הָאִשָּׁה: Women are not obligated to be fruitful and multiply, and therefore they do not have to marry. Some say that a woman should not remain unmarried, in order to avoid suspicions of indecent behavior (Rambam *Sefer Nashim, Hilkhot Ishut* 15:2; *Shulḥan Arukh, Even HaEzer* 1:13 and in the comment of Rema).

וְאָמַר רַבִּי אִילְעָא מִשּׁוּם רַבִּי אֶלְעָזָר בְּרַבִּי שִׁמְעוֹן: כְּשֵׁם שֶׁמִּצְוָה עַל אָדָם לוֹמַר דָּבָר הַנִּשְׁמָע – כָּךְ מִצְוָה עַל אָדָם שֶׁלֹּא לוֹמַר דָּבָר שֶׁאֵינוֹ נִשְׁמָע. רַבִּי אַבָּא אוֹמֵר: חוֹבָה, שֶׁנֶּאֱמַר ״אַל תּוֹכַח לֵץ פֶּן יִשְׂנָאֶךָּ הוֹכַח לְחָכָם וְיֶאֱהָבֶךָּ״.

The Gemara cites other statements made by Rabbi Ile'a in the name of Rabbi Elazar, son of Rabbi Shimon. **And Rabbi Ile'a said in the name of Rabbi Elazar, son of Rabbi Shimon: Just as it is a mitzva for a person to say that which will be heeded, so is it a mitzva for a person not to say**[N] **that which will not be heeded.** One should not rebuke those who will be unreceptive to his message. **Rabbi Abba says:** It is **obligatory** for him to refrain from speaking, **as it is stated: "Do not reprove a scorner lest he hate you; reprove a wise man and he will love you"** (Proverbs 9:8).

וְאָמַר רַבִּי אִילְעָא מִשּׁוּם רַבִּי אֶלְעָזָר בְּרַבִּי שִׁמְעוֹן: מוּתָּר לוֹ לְאָדָם לְשַׁנּוֹת בִּדְבַר הַשָּׁלוֹם, שֶׁנֶּאֱמַר ״אָבִיךָ צִוָּה״ וגו׳ ״כֹּה תֹאמְרוּ לְיוֹסֵף אָנָּא שָׂא נָא״ וגו׳.

And Rabbi Ile'a further **said in the name of Rabbi Elazar, son of Rabbi Shimon: It is permitted for a person to depart** from the truth[N] **in a matter** that will bring **peace, as it is stated: "Your father commanded** before he died, saying: **So you shall say to Joseph: Please pardon** your brothers' crime, etc." (Genesis 50:16–17). Jacob never issued this command, but his sons falsely attributed this statement to him in order to preserve peace between them and Joseph.

רַבִּי נָתָן אוֹמֵר: מִצְוָה, שֶׁנֶּאֱמַר ״וַיֹּאמֶר שְׁמוּאֵל אֵיךְ אֵלֵךְ וְשָׁמַע שָׁאוּל וַהֲרָגָנִי״ וגו׳.

Rabbi Natan says: It is **a mitzva** to depart from the truth in order to preserve peace, **as it is stated: "And Samuel said: How can I go, and Saul will hear and kill me"** (I Samuel 16:2). God responded in the next verse that Samuel should say he went to sacrifice an offering, indicating that God commands one to lie in order to preserve peace.

דְּבֵי רַבִּי יִשְׁמָעֵאל תָּנָא: גָּדוֹל הַשָּׁלוֹם שֶׁאַף הַקָּדוֹשׁ בָּרוּךְ הוּא שִׁינָּה בּוֹ. דְּמֵעִיקָּרָא כְּתִיב ״וַאֲדוֹנִי זָקֵן״ וּלְבַסּוֹף כְּתִיב ״וַאֲנִי זָקַנְתִּי״.

It was **taught** in **the school of Rabbi Yishmael: Great is peace,**[N] **as even the Holy One, Blessed be He, departed** from the truth for **it. As, initially it is written** that Sarah said of Abraham: **"And my lord is old"** (Genesis 18:12), **and in the end it is written** that God told Abraham that Sarah said: **"And I am old"** (Genesis 18:13). God adjusted Sarah's words in order to spare Abraham hurt feelings that might lead Abraham and Sarah to quarrel.

״רַבִּי יוֹחָנָן בֶּן בְּרוֹקָה אוֹמֵר״. אִתְּמַר, רַבִּי יוֹחָנָן וְרַבִּי יְהוֹשֻׁעַ בֶּן לֵוִי, חַד אָמַר: הֲלָכָה כְּרַבִּי יוֹחָנָן בֶּן בְּרוֹקָה, וְחַד אָמַר: אֵין הֲלָכָה כְּרַבִּי יוֹחָנָן בֶּן בְּרוֹקָה.

§ It is taught in the mishna that **Rabbi Yoḥanan ben Beroka says** that women are also included in the mitzva to be fruitful and multiply. **It was stated** that two *amora'im*, **Rabbi Yoḥanan and Rabbi Yehoshua ben Levi,** disagreed concerning this matter. **One said** that the ***halakha* is in accordance with** the opinion of **Rabbi Yoḥanan ben Beroka, and one said** that the ***halakha* is not in accordance with** the opinion of **Rabbi Yoḥanan ben Beroka.**

תִּסְתַּיֵּים דְּרַבִּי יוֹחָנָן הוּא דַּאֲמַר אֵין הֲלָכָה דְּיָתֵיב רַבִּי אַבָּהוּ וְקָאָמַר מִשְּׁמֵיהּ דְּרַבִּי יוֹחָנָן הֲלָכָה, וְאַהַדְרִינְהוּ רַבִּי אַמִּי וְרַבִּי אַסִּי לְאַפַּיְיהוּ.

The Gemara comments: **Conclude that it was Rabbi Yoḥanan**[N] **who said** that the ***halakha* is not** in accordance with the opinion of Rabbi Yoḥanan ben Beroka, **as Rabbi Abbahu sat and said in the name of Rabbi Yoḥanan** that the ***halakha*** is in accordance with the opinion of Rabbi Yoḥanan ben Beroka, **and Rabbi Ami and Rabbi Asi,** who were sitting across from him, **turned their faces** as an indication that they disagreed with this report of Rabbi Yoḥanan's opinion, but did not want to explicitly contradict Rabbi Abbahu's statement out of respect for him.

NOTES

So is it a mitzva for a person not to say – כָּךְ מִצְוָה עַל אָדָם שֶׁלֹּא לוֹמַר: The commentaries question why it is permissible to remain silent when there is a mitzva to rebuke wrongdoers (see Leviticus 19:17). The Ritva answers that the Gemara is referring to addressing a group of people, whereas one is always obligated to rebuke an individual. The *Shela* explains that if the offender knows that he is acting improperly it is proper to rebuke him, but if he does not think he has transgressed the criticism is better left unsaid. Alternatively, if one rebukes another who does not accept reproof, this will only cause the latter to act willfully in the future, and it is preferable for him to remain an unwitting sinner (*Iyyun Ya'akov*).

It is permitted for a person to depart from the truth – מוּתָּר לוֹ לְאָדָם לְשַׁנּוֹת: The Gemara does not cite Sarah's reaction: "And Sarah denied, saying I did not laugh" (Genesis 18:15), as proof that one may depart from the truth, as she did so only when faced with an accusation, whereas the other verses prove that one may take the initiative in stating falsehoods for the sake of peace (*Arukh LaNer*).

It is a mitzva to depart from the truth…great is peace – מִצְוָה...גָּדוֹל הַשָּׁלוֹם: The commentaries point out that God did not command Samuel to tell an outright lie, but rather to take an animal with him and sacrifice it. In this way he would not be lying if he said that he was traveling to sacrifice an offering, even though he would be omitting the main purpose of his journey, which was to anoint David as the next king of the Jewish people. A similar claim can be made with regard to God's report to Abraham that Sarah said: And I am old; as she herself did say: "After my withering shall I have youth" (Genesis 18:12). God simply left out her additional comment: "And my lord is old" (Meiri; see *Tosafot Yeshanim*).

Conclude that it was Rabbi Yoḥanan, etc. – תִּסְתַּיֵּים דְּרַבִּי יוֹחָנָן הוּא וכו׳: It would appear that the Gemara does not prove what Rabbi Yoḥanan's opinion is, as it merely cites a dispute among his students about the matter. Perhaps that is why the Gemara continues by citing Rabbi Abbahu in the name of Rabbi Asi with regard to the incident in Caesarea; it is an attempt to prove that they actually both agree that Rabbi Yoḥanan held in accordance with the opinion of Rabbi Yoḥanan ben Beroka (*Arukh LaNer*).

וְאִיכָּא דְּאָמְרִי: רַבִּי חִיָּיא בַּר אַבָּא אֲמַר, וְאַהַדְרִינְהוּ רַבִּי אַמִי וְרַבִּי אַסִי לְאַפַּיְיהוּ. אֲמַר רַב פַּפָּא: בִּשְׁלָמָא לְמַאן דַּאֲמַר רַבִּי אַבָּהוּ אֲמָרָהּ – מִשּׁוּם כְּבוֹד בֵּי קֵיסָר לָא אָמְרוּ לֵיהּ וְלָא מִידֵּי, אֶלָּא לְמַאן דְּאָמַר רַבִּי חִיָּיא בַּר אַבָּא אֲמָרָהּ – לֵימְרוּ לֵיהּ: לָא אֲמַר רַבִּי יוֹחָנָן הָכִי!

And some say a different version of the incident, that it was **Rabbi Ḥiyya bar Abba** who **said** this statement, **and Rabbi Ami and Rabbi Asi turned their faces. Rav Pappa said: Granted, according to the one who said** that **Rabbi Abbahu said it,** it makes sense that **due to the honor of Caesar's court,** where Rabbi Abbahu maintained close ties, Rabbi Ami and Rabbi Asi **did not say anything to him** and merely hinted at their disagreement. **However, according to the one who said** that **Rabbi Ḥiyya bar Abba said it, let them say to him explicitly: Rabbi Yoḥanan did not say this.** In any event, it is clear that according to Rabbi Ami and Rabbi Asi, Rabbi Yohanan disagreed with the opinion of Rabbi Yoḥanan ben Beroka.

מַאי הֲוָה עֲלַהּ? תָּא שְׁמַע, דַּאֲמַר רַבִּי אַחָא בַּר חֲנִינָא אֲמַר רַבִּי אַבָּהוּ אֲמַר רַבִּי אַסִי: עוּבְדָא הֲוָה קַמֵּיהּ דְּרַבִּי יוֹחָנָן בִּכְנִישְׁתָּא דְּקֵיסָרִי, וַאֲמַר: "יוֹצִיא וְיִתֵּן כְּתוּבָּה". וְאִי סָלְקָא דַּעְתָּךְ לָא מִפַּקְדָה – כְּתוּבָּה מַאי עֲבִידְתֵּיהּ?

The Gemara asks: **What** conclusion **was** reached **about** this issue? The Gemara suggests: **Come and hear, as Rabbi Aḥa bar Ḥanina said** that **Rabbi Abbahu said** that **Rabbi Asi said: There was an incident** that came **before Rabbi Yoḥanan in the synagogue of Caesarea** involving a woman who wanted a divorce from her husband after ten years of childless marriage, **and he said** that the husband **must divorce** her **and give** her the payment for her **marriage contract. If it enters your mind** to say **that she is not commanded** to be fruitful and multiply, **what is** payment for **a marriage contract doing** here? Why does she have a right to demand to be divorced and to receive the payment for her marriage contract?

דִּלְמָא בְּבָאָה מֵחֲמַת טַעֲנָה.

The Gemara responds: **Perhaps** that was **in** a case when **she came** to demand a divorce **due to another claim,** i.e., she wanted children for a reason other than the fulfillment of the mitzva to be fruitful and multiply. Since this claim has merit, her husband must divorce her and pay her marriage contract.

כִּי הַהִיא דַּאֲתַאי לְקַמֵּיהּ דְּרַבִּי אַמִי, אָמְרָה לֵיהּ: הַב לִי כְּתוּבָּה. אֲמַר לָהּ: זִיל, לָא מִיפַּקְדַתְּ. אָמְרָה לֵיהּ: מִסִּיבוּ דִּילָהּ מַאי תֶּיהֱוֵי עֲלַהּ דְּהָךְ אִתְּתָא? אֲמַר: כִּי הָא – וַדַּאי כָּפֵינַן.

This is **like** the case of **a certain** woman **who came before Rabbi Ami** and requested a divorce due to her husband's inability to father children. **She said to** her husband: **Give me** the payment for my **marriage contract. He said to her:** Go away, as **you are not commanded** to be fruitful and multiply and have no right to demand a divorce. **She said to him: In her old age, what will be with this woman,** i.e., if I have no children, who will take care of me when I grow old? Rabbi Ami **said:** In a situation **such as this, we certainly force** the husband to divorce and her and pay her marriage contract.

הַהִיא דַּאֲתַאי לְקַמֵּיהּ דְּרַב נַחְמָן, אֲמַר לָהּ: לָא מִיפַּקְדַתְּ. אָמְרָה לֵיהּ: לָא בָּעֲיָא הַךְ אִתְּתָא חוּטְרָא לְיָדַהּ וּמָרָה לִקְבוּרָה? אֲמַר: כִּי הָא – וַדַּאי כָּפֵינַן.

The Gemara relates a similar incident: **A certain** woman **came before Rav Naḥman** and requested a divorce due to her husband's inability to father children. **He said to her: You are not commanded** to be fruitful and multiply. **She said to him: Does this woman not require a staff for her hand and a hoe for** her **burial?** In other words, the woman said that she wanted children so that they could care for her in her old age and bury her when she would die. Rav Naḥman **said:** In a case **such as this, we certainly force** the husband to divorce her.

יְהוּדָה וְחִזְקִיָּה תְּאוֹמִים הָיוּ, אֶחָד נִגְמְרָה צוּרָתוֹ לְסוֹף תִּשְׁעָה וְאֶחָד נִגְמְרָה צוּרָתוֹ לִתְחִלַּת שִׁבְעָה. יְהוּדִית, דְּבֵיתְהוּ דְּרַבִּי חִיָּיא, הֲוָה לָהּ צַעַר לֵידָה, שַׁנַּאי מָנָא וְאַתְיָא לְקַמֵּיהּ דְּרַבִּי חִיָּיא, אָמְרָה: אִתְּתָא מִפַּקְדָא אַפְּרִיָּה וּרְבִיָּה? אֲמַר לָהּ: לָא. אָזְלָא אִשְׁתְּיָא סַמָּא דְּעַקַּרְתָּא.

The Gemara relates that Rabbi Ḥiyya's sons, **Yehuda and Ḥizkiyya, were twins,** but **one** of them **was fully developed after nine** months of pregnancy **and one was fully developed at the beginning of the seventh** month, and they were born two months apart.[B] **Yehudit, the wife of Rabbi Ḥiyya,**[P] **had** acute **birthing pain** from these unusual deliveries. She **changed her clothes** to prevent Rabbi Ḥiyya from recognizing her **and came before Rabbi Ḥiyya** to ask him a halakhic question. **She said: Is a woman commanded** to be **fruitful and multiply? He said to her: No. She went and drank an infertility potion.**

לְסוֹף אִיגַּלַּאי מִילְּתָא. אֲמַר לָהּ: אִיכּוּ יָלַדְתְּ לִי חֲדָא כְּרֵסָא אַחֲרִיתָא! דַּאֲמַר מָר: יְהוּדָה וְחִזְקִיָּה – אַחֵי, פַּזִּי וְטַוִּי

Eventually the matter was revealed, and Rabbi Ḥiyya found out about what Yehudit had done. **He said to her: If only you had given birth to one more belly**[B] **for me,** i.e., another set of twins. **As the Master said: Yehuda and Ḥizkiyya** were twin **brothers** and became prominent Torah scholars, and **Pazi and Tavi,** Rabbi Ḥiyya's daughters,

BACKGROUND

Twins born at different times – תְּאוֹמִים שֶׁנּוֹלְדוּ בְּהֶפְרֵשׁ זְמַן: Although rare, it is possible for twins to be born at different times, occasionally with a significant interval between the births. There have been documented cases of the birth of twins separated by a gap of over fifty days, and even up to eighty-five days.

One more belly – חֲדָא כְּרֵסָא אַחֲרִיתָא: There is a hereditary tendency among certain women to give birth to twins, and therefore a woman who gave birth to two sets of twins has a considerable likelihood of having an additional set of twins. The birth of twins, and in particular the unusual occurrence of a lengthy interval between their births, explains why Rabbi Ḥiyya's wife was worried about significant labor pains.

PERSONALITIES

Rabbi Ḥiyya and his family – רַבִּי חִיָּיא וּמִשְׁפַּחְתּוֹ: Rabbi Ḥiyya ben Abba, who was from the city of Kafri, Babylonia, was among the last of the *tanna'im* and was a disciple-colleague of Rabbi Yehuda HaNasi. Rabbi Ḥiyya descended from a family of distinguished lineage that traced its ancestry back to King David and produced many Sages. While he was still in Babylonia, Rabbi Ḥiyya was considered a Torah luminary. When he ascended with his family from Babylonia to Eretz Yisrael, some, engaging in hyperbole, said that the Torah was about to be forgotten in Eretz Yisrael until he came from Babylonia and reestablished it. When he came to Eretz Yisrael, he became a disciple and a colleague of Rabbi Yehuda HaNasi, with whom he had a very close relationship. He was especially close with Rabbi Yehuda HaNasi's son Shimon, who was also his business partner.

All of the students of Rabbi Yehuda HaNasi were Rabbi Ḥiyya's colleagues, and he was close with the *tanna* Rabbi Shimon ben Ḥalafta. The younger disciples of Rabbi Yehuda HaNasi, e.g., Rabbi Ḥanina, Rabbi Oshaya, Rabbi Yannai, and others, studied Torah from Rabbi Ḥiyya and were, to a certain degree, his disciples as well. His brothers' sons, Rabba bar bar Ḥana, and above all, the great *amora*, Rav, were his primary disciples. In addition to his prominence as a Torah scholar, Rabbi Ḥiyya was outstanding in his piety, as reflected in several anecdotes throughout the Talmud. Rabbi Ḥiyya also appears as a central figure in the *Zohar*. He was buried in Tiberias and his two sons were later buried alongside him.

Rabbi Ḥiyya's sons, Yehuda, son-in-law of Rabbi Yannai, and Ḥizkiyya, were both among the leading Torah scholars in the transitional generation between the *tanna'im* and the *amora'im*. They apparently succeeded Rabbi Ḥiyya at the head of his private yeshiva in the city of his residence, Tiberias.

The *ge'onim* had a tradition, also cited in *Tosafot* (*Bava Batra* 149a), that Rabbi Ḥiyya's daughter Pazi was the mother of a large family that included several important Sages such as Rabbi Shimon ben Pazi and his son, Rabbi Yehuda. Out of respect for Rabbi Ḥiyya, they were referred to by Pazi's name rather than that of her husband. It is possible that the family of Ḥiyya's other daughter Tavi was also renowned, and for this reason the two sisters, Pazi and Tavi, are mentioned alongside their brothers, Yehuda and Ḥizkiyya, to explain why Rabbi Ḥiyya was so upset that his wife did not give birth to another set of twins.

אַחֲווֹתָא.

were twin **sisters,** and became the matriarchs of families of distinguished Torah scholars.

וְלָא מִיפַּקְדָי? וְהָאָמַר רַב אַחָא בַּר רַב קְטִינָא אָמַר רַבִּי יִצְחָק: מַעֲשֶׂה בְּאִשָּׁה אַחַת שֶׁחֶצְיָהּ שִׁפְחָה וְחֶצְיָהּ בַּת חוֹרִין, וְכָפוּ אֶת רַבָּהּ וַעֲשָׂאָהּ בַּת חוֹרִין! אָמַר רַב נַחְמָן בַּר יִצְחָק: מִנְהַג הֶפְקֵר נָהֲגוּ בָּהּ.

The Gemara asks: **Are** women **not commanded** to be fruitful and multiply? **Didn't Rav Aḥa bar Rav Ketina say** that **Rabbi Yitzḥak said:** There was **an incident with a certain woman who** was **half-slave**[N] **and half-free woman** and therefore could marry neither a Canaanite slave nor a Jew, **and they forced her master**[N] **and he made her a free** woman. Presumably, the reason the court forced her master to free her was so that she could fulfill the mitzva to be fruitful and multiply. **Rav Naḥman bar Yitzḥak said:** The reason they forced her master to free her was because others **treated her in a loose manner.**[H] Since she knew that she could not marry she engaged in promiscuous activity, and the court forced her master to free her in order to save her and others from sin.

הדרן עלך הבא על יבמתו

NOTES

Who was half-slave, etc. – **שֶׁחֶצְיָהּ שִׁפְחָה וכו׳:** This case can occur when a Canaanite maidservant is jointly owned by two people and one them releaser her from bondage. With regard to the case discussed here, some commentaries hold that the master is forced to free only a half-slave who acts in a promiscuous fashion, because her actions are due to the fact that she cannot marry (see *Tur*; *Shakh*). Others hold that the same would be true with regard to a full maidservant who acts promiscuously. They argue that the fact that the incident cited in the Gemara involved a half-slave does not indicate that the *halakha* is limited to this case (Rabbeinu Yeruḥam; Rambam).

A similar *halakha* applies in a case of a man who is half-Canaanite slave and half-free, and therefore cannot marry. His master is therefore forced to free him. However, in this case the reason given is so that he can fulfill the mitzva expressed in the verse: "He did not create it a waste; He formed it to be inhabited" (Isaiah 45:18).

And they forced her master – **וְכָפוּ אֶת רַבָּהּ:** The novelty here is twofold: First, the Sages required the master to forfeit his slave, who is considered his property. Additionally, it is generally prohibited to free a Canaanite slave unless one is doing so for the sake of a mitzva. Therefore, the Gemara assumed that they must have forced her master to release her so that she could fulfill a mitzva by marrying and having children. The Gemara answers that the mitzva involved was preventing people from sinning, not the mitzva to be fruitful and multiply.

HALAKHA

They treated her in a loose manner – **מִנְהַג הֶפְקֵר נָהֲגוּ בָּהּ:** If a maidservant is involved in widespread promiscuous activity, her master is forced to release her so that she can marry, thereby removing the stumbling block from the community (Rambam *Sefer Kinyan*, *Hilkhot Avadim* 9:6; *Shulḥan Arukh*, *Yoreh De'a* 267:79).

Summary of **Perek VI**

The Torah decrees that a woman is acquired by her *yavam* in levirate marriage through sexual intercourse. This chapter clarified that as long as they intended to engage in an act of intercourse it makes no difference whether they did so willingly or whether they intended only to fulfill the mitzva of levirate marriage; the very act itself serves to consummate and validate the levirate bond. With regard to the definition of the sexual act, even the first stage of sexual intercourse is considered an act of intercourse and consummates the levirate marriage.

With regard to other forbidden sexual relations, the intention of the parties involved is relevant with regard to punishment, as one is not punished unless he intentionally violates a prohibition. However, other ramifications of forbidden relations apply regardless of intent. This includes the disqualification of a *zona*, i.e., a woman who had relations with a man whom she is forbidden to marry, from marrying a priest.

With regard to women disqualified from the priesthood, the Gemara clarified that even if a woman is considered reserved for an invalid act of intercourse, she is, at least temporarily, disqualified from partaking of *teruma*. A common priest may not marry a *zona*, a divorcée, a woman who underwent *ḥalitza*, or a convert. The High Priest may marry only a minor or a maiden, i.e., a woman within the first twelve months of adulthood, who is a virgin and has never been betrothed. However, if a priest betrothed a widow and was then appointed to be High Priest, he may marry her.

All Jewish men are obligated by Torah law to marry and have children in order to fulfill the mitzva to be fruitful and multiply. One has fulfilled this mitzva if he has both a son and a daughter. If his children die after bearing children of their own, he may still be in fulfillment of the mitzva through his grandchildren. One is even required to divorce his wife in order to marry another woman and fulfill the mitzva to be fruitful and multiply, if his wife is unable to bear children. This chapter further clarified when this obligation applies, when a woman is presumed to be unable to bear children, and what the rights of a woman who cannot bear children are when she is divorced from her husband. Also included were aggadic statements pertaining to marriage in general, and the mitzva to be fruitful and multiply in particular.

Introduction to **Perek VII**

They [the priests] shall not take a woman who is a harlot, or profaned; neither shall they take a woman divorced from her husband, for he is holy to his God.

(Leviticus 21:7)

A widow, or one divorced, or a profaned woman, or a harlot, these he shall not take; but a virgin of his own people he shall take as a wife.

(Leviticus 21:14)

But if a priest buys any soul, the purchase of his money, he may eat of it; and such as are born in his house, they may eat of his bread. And if a priest's daughter be married to a common man, she shall not eat of that which is set apart from the sacred. But if a priest's daughter be a widow, or divorced, and have no child, and is returned to her father's house, as in her youth, she may eat of her father's bread; but there shall no common man eat of it.

(Leviticus 22:11–13)

One of the topics discussed in the previous chapter is the *halakha* that a woman who has intercourse with a man who is unfit for her is rendered disqualified from marrying a priest. If she is the daughter of a priest, she may no longer partake of *teruma*. This chapter discusses the matter at length, although it is connected only tangentially to the main subject of the tractate.

The Torah states that all the members of a priest's household, i.e., his wife, his sons and daughters, and their slaves, may partake of *teruma*. If the priest dies or divorces his wife, she may continue to partake of *teruma* only if she has children from him. Conversely, a priest's daughter who is married to a non-priest may not partake of *teruma*. If she is widowed or divorced from him, and has no children from him, she resumes partaking of *teruma*.

These principles raise questions with regard to different types of unions between a priest and an Israelite woman or between the daughter of a priest and an Israelite man: If a priest betroths a woman who is unfit for him but whose betrothal to him is nevertheless valid, are she and her slaves entitled to partake of *teruma*? If not, are the slaves that she brings into the marriage considered his or hers? Also, what is the ruling with regard to a levirate bond between a priest and an Israelite woman?

Precisely what constitutes the definition of a woman's having children from her husband is also discussed. Is a pregnant woman considered one who already has children from her husband, or is she still considered childless? Does the term children here refer specifically to their children, or does it apply to all of their descendants? Do children who are unfit to marry into the assembly of Israel qualify, or do only unflawed children count?

This chapter discusses these issues both in principle and in detail.

מתני׳ אַלְמָנָה לְכֹהֵן גָּדוֹל, גְּרוּשָׁה וַחֲלוּצָה לְכֹהֵן הֶדְיוֹט, הִכְנִיסָה לוֹ עַבְדֵי מְלוֹג וְעַבְדֵי צֹאן בַּרְזֶל, עַבְדֵי מְלוֹג – לֹא יֹאכְלוּ בִּתְרוּמָה, עַבְדֵי צֹאן בַּרְזֶל – יֹאכְלוּ.

MISHNA A widow married **to a High Priest,** and a **divorcée or a** *yevama* **who performed** ***ḥalitza*** [*ḥalutza*] married **to a common priest** are all unions prohibited by Torah law. If one of these women **brought** with her **into the** marriage **slaves of usufruct** [*melog*][L] property **or slaves of guaranteed investment,**[N] then the **slaves of usufruct** property **do not partake of** ***teruma*** but the **slaves of guaranteed investment do partake** of *teruma*.[H]

וְאֵלּוּ הֵן עַבְדֵי מְלוֹג: אִם מֵתוּ – מֵתוּ לָהּ, וְאִם הוֹתִירוּ – הוֹתִירוּ לָהּ, אַף עַל פִּי שֶׁהוּא חַיָּיב בִּמְזוֹנוֹתָן הֲרֵי אֵלּוּ לֹא יֹאכְלוּ בִּתְרוּמָה. וְאֵלּוּ הֵן עַבְדֵי צֹאן בַּרְזֶל: אִם מֵתוּ – מֵתוּ לוֹ, וְאִם הוֹתִירוּ – הוֹתִירוּ לוֹ, הוֹאִיל וְהוּא חַיָּיב בְּאַחֲרָיוּתָן הֲרֵי אֵלּוּ יֹאכְלוּ בִּתְרוּמָה.

And these are slaves of usufruct property: They are those with regard to whom the couple stipulated that **if** the slaves **die, their death is her** loss, **and if they increase** in value, **their increase is her** gain. **Although** the husband **is obligated in their sustenance,**[H] **they do not partake of** ***teruma***, as they belong to her, not to him. He owns only the right of their use while he is married to her. **And these are slaves of guaranteed investment:**[H] They are those with regard to whom the couple stipulated that **if they die, their death is his loss,**[N] **and if they increase** in value, **their increase is his gain. Since he bears financial responsibility** for compensating her in the event of **their** loss, **they partake of** ***teruma***, as they are considered his property.

בַּת יִשְׂרָאֵל שֶׁנִּיסֵּת לְכֹהֵן וְהִכְנִיסָה לוֹ עֲבָדִים, בֵּין עַבְדֵי מְלוֹג בֵּין עַבְדֵי צֹאן בַּרְזֶל, הֲרֵי אֵלּוּ יֹאכְלוּ בִּתְרוּמָה. וּבַת כֹּהֵן שֶׁנִּיסֵּת לְיִשְׂרָאֵל וְהִכְנִיסָה לוֹ עֲבָדִים, בֵּין עַבְדֵי מְלוֹג בֵּין עַבְדֵי צֹאן בַּרְזֶל, הֲרֵי אֵלּוּ לֹא יֹאכְלוּ בִּתְרוּמָה.

In the case of **an Israelite woman who married a priest** in a halakhic marriage **and** who **brought slaves with her into the marriage, whether** they are **slaves of usufruct** property **or slaves of guaranteed investment, they partake of** ***teruma***.[H] **And** in the case of **the daughter of a priest who married an Israelite**[H] **and** who **brought slaves with her into** the marriage, **whether** they are **slaves of usufruct** property **or slaves of guaranteed investment, they do not partake of** ***teruma***, although, as she is the daughter of a priest, it is permitted for her and her slaves to partake of *teruma* beforehand.

גמ׳ וְעַבְדֵי מְלוֹג לֹא יֹאכְלוּ בִּתְרוּמָה, אַמַּאי? לֶהֱוֵי כְּקִנְיָנוֹ שֶׁקָּנָה קִנְיָן! דְּתַנְיָא: מִנַּיִן לְכֹהֵן שֶׁנָּשָׂא אִשָּׁה וְקָנָה עֲבָדִים שֶׁיֹּאכְלוּ בִּתְרוּמָה – שֶׁנֶּאֱמַר ״וְכֹהֵן כִּי יִקְנֶה נֶפֶשׁ קִנְיַן כַּסְפּוֹ הוּא יֹאכַל בּוֹ״.

GEMARA The mishna states that if a priest married a woman forbidden to him, his wife's **slaves of usufruct** property **do not partake of** ***teruma***. The Gemara asks: **Why** is this so? **Let** this case **be like** that of **his acquisition who acquired an acquisition, as it is taught** in a *baraita*: **From where** is it derived with regard **to a priest who married a woman**[H] **and acquired slaves**[H] **that they partake of** ***teruma***? **As it is stated: "But if a priest buys any soul, the purchase of his money, he may eat of it"** (Leviticus 22:11).

LANGUAGE

Usufruct [*melog*] – מְלוֹג: The search after the origin of this word dates back to the early commentaries. Some claim that it stems from the root *m-l-g*, which means to scald the skin of an animal in order to remove its hair. Here too, the husband removes, so to speak, the profits from his wife's assets. Others suggest that it is derived from the Greek **λόγος**, *logos*, which means word or speech, indicating that the husband receives rights to these properties as the result of verbal stipulation. However, it is apparently an original Akkadian term that means assets that a woman brings with her into the marriage.

NOTES

Guaranteed investment [*tzon barzel*] – צֹאן בַּרְזֶל: This idiom existed in Roman law as well. It literally means iron sheep. The proprietorship of guaranteed property is like that of something that never dies or gets damaged, as another individual has taken upon himself responsibility for its value. This metaphor is also appropriate in the sense that these assets bring no profit to their owners; rather, they remain at a fixed value.

If they die their death is his loss – אִם מֵתוּ, מֵתוּ לוֹ: The question was raised: What is the husband's responsibility for guaranteed property in a case where a slave does not die but merely decreases in value? Most early commentaries rule that the husband does not need to reimburse his wife unless the slave dies or is incapacitated. As long as the slaves are able to work, the husband returns them to his wife without compensation for their loss in value. This *halakha* is inferred from the use of the expression: If they die, their death is his loss, i.e., he must compensate her only in cases where the guaranteed property no longer exists in its original form. This *halakha* applies not only to slaves but to any sort of guaranteed property (Rabbeinu Ḥananel; Rif).

HALAKHA

The slaves of usufruct property do not partake of *teruma* but the slaves of guaranteed investment do partake of *teruma* – עַבְדֵי מְלוֹג לֹא יֹאכְלוּ בִּתְרוּמָה, עַבְדֵי צֹאן בַּרְזֶל יֹאכְלוּ: If a widow married to a High Priest or a *ḥalutza* married to a common priest brought slaves with her into the marriage, her slaves of usufruct property do not partake of *teruma*. However, her slaves of guaranteed investment partake of *teruma* (Rambam *Sefer Zera'im*, *Hilkhot Terumot* 7:20).

The husband is obligated in their sustenance – חַיָּיב בִּמְזוֹנוֹתָן: The husband is obligated to sustain his slaves of usufruct property, and he must fulfill all of their needs. They must work for him, and the profits earned through their work are his (Rambam *Sefer Nashim*, *Hilkhot Ishut* 22:25; *Shulḥan Arukh*, *Even HaEzer* 85:16).

And these are slaves of usufruct property…And these are slaves of guaranteed investment – וְאֵלּוּ הֵן עַבְדֵי מְלוֹג...וְאֵלּוּ הֵן עַבְדֵי צֹאן בַּרְזֶל: If a husband does not accept financial responsibility for property a woman brings with her into a marriage, that property remains hers. As a result, if its value has increased or decreased at the conclusion of the marriage, the loss or gain is hers. On the other hand, if the husband accepts financial responsibility for this dowry, it is entirely in his possession. He must pay her the original value of the property upon the dissolution of the marriage (Rambam *Sefer Nashim*, *Hilkhot Ishut* 16:1; *Shulḥan Arukh*, *Even HaEzer* 85:2).

The slaves of a priest's wife – עַבְדֵי אֵשֶׁת כֹּהֵן: If an Israelite or Levite woman is halakhically married to a priest and brought slaves with her into the marriage, whether they are usufruct or guaranteed property they partake of *teruma* (Rambam *Sefer Zera'im*, *Hilkhot Terumot* 7:18).

The daughter of a priest who married an Israelite – בַּת כֹּהֵן שֶׁנִּיסֵּת לְיִשְׂרָאֵל: If the daughter of a priest married an Israelite and brought slaves with her into the marriage, they may no longer partake of *teruma*, whether they are slaves of usufruct property or slaves of guaranteed investment (Rambam *Sefer Zera'im*, *Hilkhot Terumot* 7:19).

The wife of a priest partakes of *teruma* – אֵשֶׁת כֹּהֵן אוֹכֶלֶת בִּתְרוּמָה: An Israelite woman who married a priest partakes of *teruma* as well as the breast and right hind leg of animal offerings that belong to the priests. By Torah law, she partakes of these from the time of betrothal, but the Sages decreed that she not partake of them until her marriage (Rambam *Sefer Zera'im*, *Hilkhot Terumot* 6:3).

The slaves of a priest partake of *teruma* – עַבְדֵי כֹּהֵן אוֹכְלִים בִּתְרוּמָה: The slaves and animals of a priest partake of *teruma* and the *teruma* of the tithe (Rambam *Sefer Zera'im*, *Hilkhot Terumot* 6:1).

וּמִנַּיִן לְאִשָּׁה שֶׁקָּנְתָה עֲבָדִים, וַעֲבָדָיו שֶׁקָּנוּ עֲבָדִים, שֶׁיֹּאכְלוּ בִּתְרוּמָה – שֶׁנֶּאֱמַר ״וְכֹהֵן כִּי יִקְנֶה נֶפֶשׁ קִנְיַן כַּסְפּוֹ הוּא יֹאכַל בּוֹ״. קִנְיָנוֹ שֶׁקָּנָה קִנְיָן – אוֹכֵל!

And from where is it derived with regard **to** both the **wife** of a priest **who acquired slaves and** a priest's **slaves who acquired slaves,**[N] **that** the acquired slaves **may** also **partake of *teruma*?**[H] **As it is stated: "But if a priest buys any soul, the purchase of his money, he may eat of it,"** which is interpreted to mean: If **his acquisition acquired an acquisition,** the latter **partakes** of *teruma*. Here too, since the **slaves of usufruct** property belong to his wife, it should be permitted for them to partake of *teruma*.

כָּל הָאוֹכֵל – מַאֲכִיל, כָּל שֶׁאֵין אוֹכֵל – אֵינוֹ מַאֲכִיל.

The Gemara answers: The principle is that **anyone who** is fit to **partake** of *teruma* **can enable** others **to partake** of *teruma*, and **anyone who does not partake** of *teruma* **cannot enable** others **to partake.** Since the priest's wife in this case does not partake of *teruma*, as her marriage is forbidden, her slaves do not partake of *teruma* either.

וְלָא? וַהֲרֵי עָרֵל וְכָל הַטְּמֵאִים, שֶׁאֵינָן אוֹכְלִין וּמַאֲכִילִין! הָתָם פּוּמַיְיהוּ כָּאֵיב לְהוּ.

The Gemara asks: **And** is it so that one who does not partake of *teruma* **cannot enable** others **to partake? But aren't** there the cases of a priest who is **uncircumcised** because it was considered too dangerous for him **and all impure** priests, **who do not partake** of *teruma*, **and** yet **they enable** their wives and slaves **to partake** of *teruma*? The Gemara answers: The difference is that **there,** in those cases, there is no inherent disqualification rendering them unfit to partake of *teruma*. The hindrance to their partaking of *teruma* is tantamount to a situation where **their mouths hurt,**[N] and that is why they refrain from eating *teruma*. They retain, however, the fundamental right to partake of *teruma*, and therefore they can enable others to partake as well.

וַהֲרֵי מַמְזֵר, שֶׁאֵין אוֹכֵל – וּמַאֲכִיל!

The Gemara asks: **But isn't** there the case of **a son born from an incestuous or adulterous relationship** [*mamzer*],[N] **who does not partake** of *teruma* yet **enables** others to partake? If an Israelite woman was married to a priest and was subsequently widowed or divorced, and a child from that union married a *mamzer* and then had a child, in that case, even if the woman's child is dead, she partakes of *teruma* due to her grandchild, as she has a living descendant from a priest, although that descendant is a *mamzer*. Although this child does not partake of *teruma*, he enables his grandmother to partake of it.

אֲמַר רָבִינָא: קִנְיַן אוֹכֵל קָאָמַר, קִנְיַן אוֹכֵל – מַאֲכִיל, שֶׁאֵינוֹ אוֹכֵל – אֵינוֹ מַאֲכִיל.

Ravina said that the above principle **is referring** to the case of **an acquisition who partakes** of *teruma*.[N] If the **acquisition** of a priest **partakes** of *teruma*, **he enables** others **to partake,**[H] whereas an acquisition **who does not partake,** e.g., his forbidden wife, **cannot enable** others **to partake.**

וְרָבָא אֲמַר: מִדְּאוֹרַיְיתָא מֵיכַל אָכְלֵי, וְרַבָּנַן הוּא דִּגְזַרוּ בְּהוּ, כְּדֵי שֶׁתֹּאמַר: אֲנִי אֵינִי אוֹכֶלֶת, עֲבָדַי אֵינָן אוֹכְלִין, זוֹנָה הִיא אֶצְלוֹ! הִלְכָּךְ אָתֵי לְאַפּוּקָהּ.

And Rava said a different solution. **By Torah** law, the forbidden wife's slaves indeed **partake** of *teruma*, as they are included in the category of: His acquisition who acquired an acquisition. **And it was the Sages who issued a decree**[N] prohibiting **them** from partaking of *teruma*, **so that** the woman unlawfully married to a priest **would say: I do not partake** of his *teruma* and **my slaves do not partake** of it either, so that she will realize that she is not a valid wife, but rather **she is** like **a prostitute to him.** Her husband will **therefore come to divorce her,**[N] which is the desired outcome.

רַב אָשֵׁי אָמַר: גְּזֵירָה שֶׁמָּא תַּאֲכִיל לְאַחַר מִיתָה.

Rav Ashi said a different reason for the prohibition: It is a rabbinic **decree lest she have** those slaves **partake** of *teruma* even **after** the **death** of her husband the priest. As long as he is alive, they are permitted to partake of *teruma*, as she is considered his acquisition and they belong to her. Once he dies, she is no longer his acquisition.

NOTES

And a priest's slaves who acquired slaves – וַעֲבָדָיו שֶׁקָּנוּ עֲבָדִים: If whatever a slave acquires is acquired by his owner, how can a slave buy a slave for himself? This question was raised by Rashi and many other early commentaries, and it is also addressed in the Jerusalem Talmud. Rashi explains that a slave may acquire a slave when he buys him with money that was given to him under the stipulation that his master will have no access to it. *Tosefot HaRosh* adds that according to the opinion that such a stipulation is ineffective, and whatever a slave acquires always belongs to his owner, the verse from which this *halakha* is derived must be understood as referring only to wives who buy slaves. The *halakha* that whatever a wife acquires is acquired by her husband is a rabbinic ordinance, and by Torah law it is possible for a wife to acquire slaves independently. The verse teaches that such slaves would be permitted to partake of *teruma*.

Their mouths hurt – פּוּמַיְיהוּ כָּאֵיב לְהוּ: Rashi offers an explanation different from the commentary here: Although in those cases the priests are disqualified, their disqualifications are only temporary, as they can potentially be rectified, whereas the woman is disqualified permanently.

But isn't there the case of a son born from an incestuous or adulterous relationship [*mamzer*] – וַהֲרֵי מַמְזֵר: The *halakha* is that the widow of a priest with any living descendant from the priest is permitted to partake of *teruma*. The Gemara's question is therefore not related to the fact that the descendant is specifically a *mamzer* but uses the *mamzer* as an example of a descendant who is not a priest. Rabbi Avraham min HaHar adds that the Gemara uses *mamzer* to allude to the mishna later on (69b) that elaborates on this *halakha* using the example of a *mamzer*.

Is referring to the case of an acquisition who partakes of *teruma* – קִנְיַן אוֹכֵל קָאָמַר: It appears that Ravina derived his interpretation of the principle directly from the verse that is its source: "The purchase of his money, he may eat of it." The verse is referring to an acquisition who may himself partake of *teruma*, and only if that is so does he enable his own acquisition to do so.

And it was the Sages who issued a decree – וְרַבָּנַן הוּא דִּגְזַרוּ בְּהוּ: The Rambam rules in accordance with Ravina's assertion that it is Torah law that slaves of usufruct property belonging to a priest's forbidden wife do not partake of *teruma*. Other commentaries follow the other opinions in the Gemara and maintain that it is a rabbinic decree.

In the Jerusalem Talmud, both possibilities are cited, and then it is pointed out that whether or not it is a Torah law has a practical difference: If by Torah law, one who cannot partake of *teruma* cannot enable his property to do so, then slaves belonging to the uncircumcised slave of a priest will not be allowed to partake of *teruma*. If the property of property that traces back to a priest may partake of *teruma*, and the Sages restricted the slaves of an unlawful wife from doing so as a penalty, then the slaves of this slave should be allowed to partake of *teruma*. Their master did nothing wrong.

Her husband will therefore come to divorce her – הִלְכָּךְ אָתֵי לְאַפּוּקָהּ: The woman's realization will lead to a quarrel between her and her husband, which will presumably result in divorce (Meiri).

HALAKHA

The slaves of a priest's acquisition – עַבְדֵי קִנְיַן כֹּהֵן: The slaves of a priest and the slaves of the wife of a priest who themselves acquired slaves partake of *teruma* (Rambam *Sefer Zera'im*, *Hilkhot Terumot* 7:18).

Anyone who is fit to partake of *teruma* can enable others to partake of *teruma* – כָּל הָאוֹכֵל מַאֲכִיל: A priest's acquisition can enable others to partake of *teruma* only if he partakes of *teruma* himself (Rambam *Sefer Zera'im*, *Hilkhot Terumot* 7:18).

אֶלָּא מֵעַתָּה, בַּת יִשְׂרָאֵל שֶׁנִּשֵּׂאת לְכֹהֵן לֹא תַּאֲכִיל גְּזֵירָה שֶׁמָּא תַּאֲכִיל לְאַחַר מִיתָה!

The Gemara asks: **However, if** that is **so,** that the decree is lest she have those slaves partake of *teruma* after her husband's death, any **Israelite woman who marries a priest should not enable** her slaves of usufruct property **to partake**[N] of *teruma* either, due to the same rabbinic **decree, lest she have them partake** of *teruma* **after** her husband's **death.**

אֶלָּא אָמַר רַב אָשֵׁי: בְּאַלְמָנָה כֹּהֶנֶת, דְּאָתְיָא לְאוֹרוּיֵי: מֵעִיקָּרָא אָכְלִי בִּתְרוּמָה דְּבֵי נָשָׁא, אִינְסְבִי לֵיהּ לְהַאי – אָכְלִי בִּתְרוּמָה דְּגַבְרָאי, וְהָשְׁתָּא הֲדַרִי לִי לְמִילְּתֵיהּ קַמַּיְיתָא, וְלָא יָדְעָה דְּמֵעִיקָּרָא לָא שַׁוְּיתָהּ לְנַפְשָׁהּ חֲלָלָה, הָשְׁתָּא שַׁוְּיתָהּ לְנַפְשָׁהּ חֲלָלָה.

Rather, Rav Ashi said that the decree is dealing **with a widowed priestess,** the daughter of a priest, who then married the High Priest, **as she is likely to rationalize** enabling her slaves to partake of *teruma* after the death of the High Priest as follows: **Initially,** my slaves **partook of the *teruma* of my father's house. I** then **married this man, and they partook of the *teruma* of my husband. And now** that my husband died, **I have returned to the original circumstance,** and therefore they may once again partake of my father's *teruma*. **And she does not realize that** this is not so, as **initially she did not render herself a woman disqualified from marrying a priest [*ḥalala*],** but **now,** by marrying a High Priest unlawfully, **she rendered herself a *ḥalala*,** and both she and her slaves do not partake of *teruma* even upon returning to her father's house.

תֵּינַח אַלְמָנָה כֹּהֶנֶת, אַלְמָנָה בַּת יִשְׂרָאֵל מַאי אִיכָּא לְמֵימַר – בְּאַלְמְנוּתָה לָא פְּלִיגִי רַבָּנַן.

The Gemara asks: This **works out well** as an explanation of the mishna, with regard to **a widowed priestess.** However, if that **widow** who married a High Priest was **an Israelite woman, what can be said?** There is no reason for the decree in that case. The Gemara answers: **With regard to widowhood, the Sages did not distinguish** between one type of widow and another. Once they issued a decree due to one widow, they applied it to all widows.

אִיתְּמַר: הַמַּכְנֶסֶת שׁוּם לְבַעְלָהּ, הִיא אוֹמֶרֶת: כֵּלַי אֲנִי נוֹטֶלֶת, וְהוּא אוֹמֵר: דָּמִים אֲנִי נוֹתֵן, הַדִּין עִם מִי? רַב יְהוּדָה אָמַר:

It was stated: With regard to a woman **who brings appraised,** guaranteed **property into her** marital contract with her **husband,** he is obligated to return it at the conclusion of the marriage. Upon collection of her marriage contract, e.g., following divorce, if **she says: I am taking my belongings,**[H] **and he says: I am** willing to **give you** only their **monetary** value, **the *halakha* favors whom?**[N] **Rav Yehuda said:**

NOTES

Any Israelite woman who marries a priest should not enable her slaves of usufruct property to partake [*ta'akhil*] – **בַּת יִשְׂרָאֵל שֶׁנִּשֵּׂאת לְכֹהֵן לֹא תַּאֲכִיל**: A textual variant mentioned by the early commentaries reads: Should also not partake [*tokhal*], lest she partake after her husband's death. While Rashi reads *ta'akhil*, and *Tosafot* defend Rashi's reading, the Ramban and the Rashba contend that the alternative reading is preferable, as it renders the difficulty raised by the Gemara more sensible and more pronounced.

The *halakha* favors whom – **הַדִּין עִם מִי**: The early commentaries addressed the opposite case: What if the husband wants to return the guaranteed assets while the wife demands their value in money? Some say that the property is in his possession and therefore she can refuse to accept it; it is her right to have the property returned to her but not her obligation (*Tosefot Ḥad MiKamma'ei*). Rivash claims that the husband may return the assets against her will, as they are not entirely in his possession, but are like a deposit. The Meiri maintains that he can compel her to accept them only if he lacks the funds to pay his debt.

HALAKHA

A wife who wants to receive her belongings – **אִשָּׁה הָרוֹצָה לְקַבֵּל כֵּלֶיהָ**: If a wife brought guaranteed property with her into the marriage, and upon divorce she demands to receive the actual assets she brought with her, her demand is accepted, as they are the assets of her paternal family (*Shulḥan Arukh, Even HaEzer* 88:3).

Perek **VII**
Daf **66** Amud **b**

הַדִּין עִמָּהּ, וְרַב אַמִי אָמַר: הַדִּין עִמּוֹ.

The *halakha* favors her; she may take the belongings. **And Rav Ami said: The *halakha* favors him;** he may retain the items and return their value.

רַב יְהוּדָה אָמַר: הַדִּין עִמָּהּ, מִשּׁוּם שֶׁבַח בֵּית אָבִיהָ – דִּידַהּ הָוֵי. רַבִּי אַמִי אָמַר: הַדִּין עִמּוֹ, כֵּיוָן דַּאֲמַר מָר: אִם מֵתוּ – מֵתוּ לוֹ, וְאִם הוֹתִירוּ – הוֹתִירוּ לוֹ, הוֹאִיל וְחַיָּיב בְּאַחֲרָיוּתָן – יֹאכְלוּ. אָמַר רַב סָפְרָא: מִי קָתָנֵי ״וְהֵן שֶׁלּוֹ״? ״הוֹאִיל וְחַיָּיב בְּאַחֲרָיוּתָן״ קָתָנֵי, וּלְעוֹלָם לָאו דִּידֵיהּ נִינְהוּ.

The Gemara explains that **Rav Yehuda said** that **the *halakha* favors her because** they are **the assets of her paternal family,**[N] whose prestige will suffer if they aren't returned. Therefore, **they are hers. Rabbi Ami said that the *halakha* favors him, since the Master said** in the mishna, with regard to guaranteed property: **If they die, their death** is **his** loss, **and if they increase** in value, **their increase is his** gain. **Since he bears** financial **responsibility for their** loss, **they partake** of *teruma*. Apparently, the slaves belong to the husband. Therefore, he is obligated to return only their monetary value. **Rav Safra said** in rejection of Rabbi Ami's reasoning: **Does** the mishna **teach** that **they are his?** It **teaches** only that **he bears** financial **responsibility for their** loss, **but actually they are not his.**

NOTES

The assets of her paternal family – **שֶׁבַח בֵּית אָבִיהָ**: The Rid explains that her family gave her these belongings for her own use, not for the use of others after her divorce.

וְכׇל הֵיכָא דְּחַיָּיב בְּאַחְרָיוּתָן אָכְלֵי בִּתְרוּמָה? וְהָתְנַן: יִשְׂרָאֵל שֶׁשָּׂכַר פָּרָה מִכֹּהֵן – הֲרֵי זֶה יַאֲכִילֶנָּה כַּרְשִׁינֵי תְּרוּמָה. כֹּהֵן שֶׁשָּׂכַר פָּרָה מִיִּשְׂרָאֵל, אַף עַל פִּי שֶׁמְּזוֹנוֹתֶיהָ עָלָיו – לֹא יַאֲכִילֶנָּה כַּרְשִׁינֵי תְּרוּמָה!

The Gemara asks: **And do they partake of *teruma* wherever he bears** financial **responsibility for their** loss, even if they are not his actual possession? **But didn't we learn** in a mishna (*Terumot* 11:9): **An Israelite who rented a cow from a priest may feed it vetches** [*karshinin*][B] **of *teruma*,** since the animal belongs to a priest? With regard to **a priest who rented a cow from an Israelite, although** its feed **is** incumbent **upon him, he may not feed it vetches of *teruma*,** as it does not belong to him.[H] This indicates that the requirement for enabling an acquisition to eat *teruma* is possession, not responsibility.

וְתִסְבְּרָא? נְהִי נַמִּי דְּמִחַיַּיב בִּגְנֵבָה וַאֲבֵדָה – בְּאוֹנָסֶיהָ, בְּכַחֲשָׁהּ, וּבְנִפְחַת דָּמֶיהָ מִי מִיחַיַּיב? הָא לָא דָּמְיָא אֶלָּא לְסֵיפָא: יִשְׂרָאֵל שֶׁשָּׁם פָּרָה מִכֹּהֵן – לֹא יַאֲכִילֶנָּה כַּרְשִׁינֵי תְּרוּמָה, אֲבָל כֹּהֵן שֶׁשָּׁם פָּרָה מִיִּשְׂרָאֵל – יַאֲכִילֶנָּה כַּרְשִׁינֵי תְּרוּמָה.

The Gemara rejects this proof: **And** how can **you understand** that the case of the rented cow is parallel to the case of guaranteed property? **Though** the renter **is indeed liable for theft and loss, is he liable for unavoidable accidents, for emaciation,** i.e., the cow became thinner or weaker for any reason, **or for** any other **decrease in its value?** Certainly he is not. In fact, the case of guaranteed property **is similar only to the latter clause** of that mishna: In the case of **an Israelite who appraised a cow** upon renting it **from a priest**[N] under an arrangement where he guaranteed its value to the owner, he **may not feed it vetches of *teruma*,** as it is considered his own. **However, a priest who appraised a cow** upon renting it **from an Israelite may feed it vetches of *teruma*.**[H] This indicates that guaranteed property is considered the acquisition of its recipient with regard to enabling it to eat *teruma*.

יָתֵיב רַבָּה וְרַב יוֹסֵף בְּשִׁילְהֵי פִּרְקֵיהּ דְּרַב נַחְמָן, וְיָתְבֵי וְקָאָמְרִי: תַּנְיָא כְּוָותֵיהּ דְּרַב יְהוּדָה, וְתַנְיָא כְּוָותֵיהּ דְּרַבִּי אַמִּי. תַּנְיָא כְּוָותֵיהּ דְּרַבִּי אַמִּי: עַבְדֵי צֹאן בַּרְזֶל יוֹצְאִין בְּשֵׁן וָעַיִן לְאִישׁ, אֲבָל לֹא לְאִשָּׁה.

Rabba and Rav Yosef sat at the conclusion of Rav Naḥman's sermon, and they sat and said: It is taught in a *baraita* **in accordance with** the opinion of **Rav Yehuda, and it is taught** in another *baraita* **in accordance with** the opinion of **Rabbi Ami. It is taught in accordance with** the opinion of **Rabbi Ami** in the following *baraita*: If a slave's owner strikes him and knocks out his tooth or blinds him in an eye, he is set free. **Slaves of guaranteed investment go free at the loss of a tooth or an eye**[NH] caused **by the husband, but not** at such loss caused **by the wife.** This indicates that they belong to the husband.

תַּנְיָא כְּוָותֵיהּ דְּרַב יְהוּדָה: הַמַּכְנֶסֶת שׁוּם לְבַעְלָהּ, אִם רָצָה הַבַּעַל לִמְכּוֹר – לֹא יִמְכּוֹר, וְלֹא עוֹד אֶלָּא אֲפִילּוּ הִכְנִיס לָהּ שׁוּם מִשֶּׁלּוֹ, אִם רָצָה הַבַּעַל לִמְכּוֹר – לֹא יִמְכּוֹר. מָכְרוּ שְׁנֵיהֶם לְפַרְנָסָה, זֶה הָיָה מַעֲשֶׂה לִפְנֵי רַבָּן שִׁמְעוֹן בֶּן גַּמְלִיאֵל, וְאָמַר: הַבַּעַל מוֹצִיא מִיַּד הַלָּקוֹחוֹת.

Conversely, **it is taught** in a *baraita* **in accordance with** the opinion of **Rav Yehuda:** When a woman **brings appraised,** guaranteed **property** into her marriage **to her husband, if the husband wishes to sell** it, **he may not sell** it, as it belongs to her. **And not only** that, but **even** when her husband **brought** property **into** the marriage and added it to **her** dowry as **an appraised,** guaranteed gift **of his own,**[H] even **if the husband wishes to sell** that gift **he may not sell** it. With regard to a case in which **either** the husband or wife unlawfully **sold** this property **for subsistence,** there **was an incident** like **this** that came **before Rabban Shimon ben Gamliel, and he said:** Although **the husband** executed the sale, **he may repossess** the property **from the purchasers,** as the sale is void.[H]

BACKGROUND

Vetches [*karshinin*] – כַּרְשִׁינִין: The vetch, *Vicia*, is an annual of the legume family. It grows to 10–50 cm in height. Its seeds are brown, round, or oblong, and 0.25–0.5 cm in diameter. Like other legumes, vetches are high in nutritional value and are easily digested by animals.

Vetches are a winter crop in the spring fields of Mediterranean lands and are still grown nowadays in Arab villages.

The plant and its seeds are usually used as animal fodder. In order to soften the seeds, they are sometimes soaked overnight in water. Although the vetch is consumed mostly by animals, its seeds are edible for humans as well. They were eaten during years of famine and other times of need. As it is edible for humans, the vetch must be tithed, although its *teruma* was usually fed to the animals of priests.

Vetch

NOTES

Who appraised a cow upon renting it from a priest – שֶׁשָּׁם פָּרָה מִכֹּהֵן: Rashi explains that the Israelite rented a cow from the priest and appraised it due to his guarantee to return the full value of the cow. *Tosafot*, however, contend that a rental agreement of this sort is prohibited as a form of interest. Since the renter has obligated himself to give the owner its present value no matter what, his receiving the cow is viewed as a loan, and the rental fee is considered interest (see *Bava Metzia* 70a). *Tosafot* therefore contend that the case of appraisal is one where the cow is merely borrowed from the owner, and there is no rental fee.

Go free at the loss of a tooth or an eye – יוֹצְאִין בְּשֵׁן וָעַיִן: A gentile slave is set free if his owner strikes him causing his tooth to fall out; his eye to be blinded; or other extremities, e.g., his fingers and toes, to be destroyed (Exodus 21:26–27).

HALAKHA

Feeding *teruma* to a rented cow – הַאֲכָלַת תְּרוּמָה לְפָרָה שְׂכוּרָה: An Israelite who rented a cow from a priest may feed it *teruma*. On the other hand, a priest who rented a cow from an Israelite may not because it does not belong to him, even though he is responsible for its sustenance (Rambam *Sefer Zera'im*, *Hilkhot Terumot* 9:7).

Feeding *teruma* to an appraised cow – הַאֲכָלַת תְּרוּמָה לְפָרָה שֶׁנִּשׁוּמָה: If an Israelite received a cow from a priest and appraised it, guaranteeing its value to the original owner, in order to fatten it and share the profits, he may not feed it *teruma*, although the priest has a share in the profits. If a priest received a cow from an Israelite under the same stipulation, he may feed it *teruma* (Rambam *Sefer Zera'im*, *Hilkhot Terumot* 9:8).

Slaves of guaranteed investment go free at the loss of a tooth or an eye – עַבְדֵי צֹאן בַּרְזֶל יוֹצְאִין בְּשֵׁן וָעַיִן: Slaves of guaranteed investment brought into a marriage by the wife are set free at the loss of a tooth or an eye, if the injury was caused by the husband, not by the wife (Rambam *Sefer Kinyan*, *Hilkhot Avadim* 5:16).

Even brought property into the marriage…as an appraised, guaranteed gift of his own – אֲפִילּוּ הִכְנִיס לָהּ שׁוּם מִשֶּׁלּוֹ: In addition to her own possessions, a wife's guaranteed property includes the gifts she received from her husband (Rambam *Sefer Kinyan*, *Hilkhot Mekhira* 30:5; *Shulḥan Arukh*, *Even HaEzer* 90:15).

Selling guaranteed property – מְכִירַת נִכְסֵי צֹאן בַּרְזֶל: If a woman brought movable property into her marriage as guaranteed property, the husband does not have the right to sell it. However, if he violates this *halakha* and sells it, the sale is valid (Rav Hai Gaon). Some commentaries disagree, maintaining that the sale is void (Ramban; Rashba; Rosh; Rambam *Sefer Kinyan*, *Hilkhot Mekhira* 30:5 and *Sefer Nashim*, *Hilkhot Ishut* 22:15; *Shulḥan Arukh*, *Even HaEzer* 90:14).

אָמַר רָבָא אָמַר רַב נַחְמָן: הֲלָכָה כְּרַב יְהוּדָה. אֲמַר לֵיהּ רָבָא לְרַב נַחְמָן: וְהָתַנְיָא כְּוָתֵיהּ דְּרַבִּי אַמִי! אַף עַל גַּב דְּתַנְיָא כְּוָתֵיהּ דְּרַבִּי אַמִי, מִסְתַּבְּרָא טַעְמָא דְּרַב יְהוּדָה, מִשּׁוּם שֶׁבַח בֵּית אָבִיהָ.

Rava said that **Rav Naḥman said: The *halakha* is in accordance with** the opinion of **Rav Yehuda. Rava said to Rav Naḥman: But isn't it taught** in a *baraita* **in accordance with** the opinion of **Rabbi Ami?** He replied: **Although it is taught in accordance with** the opinion of **Rabbi Ami, Rav Yehuda's rationale,** that the wife may take the objects in question **because** they are **assets of her paternal family** and their complete removal from her domain would hurt the family's prestige, **is more reasonable.**

הַהִיא אִיתְּתָא דְּעַיְּילָה לֵיהּ לְגַבְרָא אִיצְטְלָא דְּמֵילְתָא בִּכְתוּבְּתָהּ, שְׁכֵיב, שְׁקַלוּהָ יַתְמֵי וּפַרְסוּהָ אַמִּיתָנָא.

The Gemara relates an incident: **A certain woman brought into** her marriage to her **husband a robe** [*itztela*][L] **of fine wool** [*meileta*],[L] which was deemed guaranteed property **by her marriage contract.** Her husband subsequently **died,** and **the orphans took** that robe **and spread it over the corpse** as a shroud.[N] The woman demanded that the robe be returned to her.

אָמַר רָבָא: קָנְיֵיהּ מִיתְנָא. אֲמַר לֵיהּ נָנַאי, בְּרֵיהּ דְּרַב יוֹסֵף, בְּרֵיהּ דְּרָבָא, לְרַב כָּהֲנָא: וְהָאָמַר רָבָא אָמַר רַב נַחְמָן: הֲלָכָה כְּרַב יְהוּדָה! אֲמַר לֵיהּ: מִי לָא מוֹדֶה רַב יְהוּדָה דִּמְחוּסַּר גּוּבַיְינָא? וְכֵיוָן דִּמְחוּסַּר גּוּבַיְינָא – בִּרְשׁוּתֵיהּ קָאֵי.

Rava said: The dead has acquired it,[NH] as deriving benefit from anything consecrated for the dead is prohibited. **Nanai, son of Rav Yosef, son of Rava, said to Rav Kahana: But didn't Rava say** that **Rav Naḥman said** that **the *halakha* is in accordance with** the opinion of **Rav Yehuda?** Accordingly, the woman's robe must be returned. **He said to him: Doesn't Rav Yehuda admit that** the robe **has not yet been collected? And since it has not yet been collected, it remains in his possession,** and his inheritors can render its use as a burial shroud prohibited.

רָבָא לְטַעְמֵיהּ, דְּאָמַר רָבָא: הֶקְדֵּשׁ, חָמֵץ,

The Gemara adds that in this regard **Rava** conforms **to his** standard line of **reasoning, as Rava said: Consecration** of property, the prohibition against benefiting from **leavened bread** on Passover,[N]

HALAKHA

Guaranteed property that was consecrated to the Temple or used for the dead – נִכְסֵי צֹאן בַּרְזֶל שֶׁהוּקְדְּשׁוּ אוֹ נִתְּנוּ לְמֵת: If a dead man's inheritors consecrate his widow's guaranteed property or place an object of that property on the corpse, rendering it prohibited to derive benefit from the property or item, the woman's lien is released and she receives only its value (*Shulḥan Arukh, Even HaEzer* 88:5).

LANGUAGE

Robe [*itztela*] – **אִיצְטְלָא:** From the Greek στολή, *stolè*, meaning garment or robe.

Fine wool [*meileta*] – **מֵילְתָא:** Some assert that this means fine wool, named after the city Μίλητος, Milètos, where it was manufactured (Rabbi Ovadya MiBartenura). Others explain that the source of the word is the Greek μηλωτή, *mēlotē*, meaning wool.

NOTES

And spread it over the corpse as a shroud – וּפַרְסוּהָ אַמִּיתָנָא: The Gemara relates that at first taking the dead out for burial was more difficult for the relatives than the actual death, because it was customary to bury the dead in expensive shrouds, which the poor could not afford (*Moed Katan* 27b). The problem grew to the point that relatives would sometimes abandon the corpse. This lasted until Rabban Gamliel left instructions that he be taken out for burial in simple linen garments, waiving his honor. Afterward, the entire Jewish people adopted this practice and had themselves taken out for burial in linen garments.

The dead has acquired it – קָנְיֵיהּ מִיתְנָא: It is prohibited to derive benefit from a human corpse or from any object that serves its burial. Therefore, it is prohibited to use any object designated for a corpse or its burial that has been used to that end, e.g., a robe spread over the corpse as a shroud. However, one cannot render prohibited an object that belongs to someone else, even by using it for a human corpse.

Consecration of property, the prohibition against benefiting from leavened bread on Passover, etc. – הֶקְדֵּשׁ, חָמֵץ וכו׳: The Meiri explains that the *halakha* that these cannot release the property from a lien applies not only to items consecrated for the Temple, but to items consecrated for a corpse as well. The Ritva maintains that this *halakha* is a principle that applies to all items from which it is prohibited to derive benefit. In his opinion, consecrated property, leavened bread, and manumission (see 67a) are merely examples.

Perek **VII**
Daf **67** Amud **a**

וְשִׁחְרוּר – מַפְקִיעִין מִידֵי שִׁעְבּוּד.

and the manumission of a slave[N] **release** the property **from a lien.** If someone placed an asset under a lien for his debt and subsequently consecrated it; or if the asset under lien is leavened bread and the festival of Passover arrived; or if the asset is a slave and he freed him, the lien is released, and the creditor must claim his debt from the debtor's other property. In the case of the robe as well, because it was placed over the corpse, it was consecrated for the dead. Consequently, it is prohibited to derive benefit from it. Therefore, it is released to the woman from under the lien.

אָמַר רַב יְהוּדָה: הִכְנִיסָה לוֹ שְׁנֵי כֵּלִים בְּאֶלֶף זוּז, וְשָׁבְחוּ וְעָמְדוּ עַל שְׁנֵי אֲלָפִים – אֶחָד נוֹטַלְתּוֹ בִּכְתוּבָּתָהּ, וְאֶחָד נוֹתֶנֶת דָּמִים וְנוֹטַלְתּוֹ, מִפְּנֵי שֶׁבַח בֵּית אָבִיהָ.

Rav Yehuda said: If the wife **brought** with her **into** the marriage **two belongings**[NH] of guaranteed investment worth **one thousand dinars, and they appreciated** until **they stood at two thousand, one** of them **she collects** as payment of **her marriage contract,** as it is now worth her dowry of one thousand dinars. **And** as for the other **one, she pays its monetary** value **and takes it** from her husband **because** it is **an asset of her paternal family.**

HALAKHA

If the wife brought with her into the marriage two belongings, etc. – הִכְנִיסָה לוֹ שְׁנֵי כֵּלִים וכו׳: If the wife brought with her into her marriage two belongings or two maidservants of guaranteed investment, and they were appraised at one thousand dinars, and over the course of the marriage their value increased to two thousand dinars, upon her divorce she takes one of them for her one thousand dinars. If she wishes, she has the right to receive the other at its price at the time of her divorce, in accordance with Rav Yehuda's ruling (Rambam *Sefer Nashim, Hilkhot Ishut* 22:26; *Shulḥan Arukh, Even HaEzer* 88:3).

NOTES

And the manumission of a slave – וְשִׁחְרוּר: The Ramban points out that according to this ruling, the *baraita* cited by the Gemara in support of Rabbi Ami's opinion does not in fact lend his opinion any support. The *halakha* that slaves of guaranteed investment go free at the loss of a tooth or an eye by the husband can be explained by the fact that the wife's possession of them is nullified through their manumission, and therefore it cannot prove that the slaves belong to the husband.

If the wife brought with her into the marriage two belongings, etc. – הִכְנִיסָה לוֹ שְׁנֵי כֵּלִים וכו׳: A controversy between Babylonian *amora'im* is cited in the Jerusalem Talmud with regard to this issue. However, the conclusion is the same as in this Gemara.

מַאי קָא מַשְׁמַע לָן, שֶׁבַח בֵּית אָבִיהָ דִּידָהּ הָוֵי – הָא אֲמָרָהּ רַב יְהוּדָה חֲדָא זִימְנָא! מַהוּ דְּתֵימָא: הָנֵי מִילֵּי – הֵיכָא דְּמָטְיָא לְמִשְׁקַל בִּכְתוּבָּתָהּ, אֲבָל מֵיתַן דָּמֵי וּמִישְׁקַל לָא – קָא מַשְׁמַע לָן.

The Gemara asks: **What is he teaching us?** Is it that **assets of her paternal family are hers? Rav Yehuda** already **said this once,** in his previous statement. The Gemara answers: The latter statement was necessary as well, **lest you say** that **this applies** only **where she comes to collect her marriage contract,** which is rightfully hers, **but to give money and take** assets that are worth beyond what her husband owes her, you might say that she may **not** do so, although the property in question is an asset of her paternal family. Rav Yehuda therefore **teaches us** that she may take all of the assets of her paternal family and pay for what they are worth beyond her husband's debt to her.

מתני׳ בַּת יִשְׂרָאֵל שֶׁנִּיסֵּת לְכֹהֵן וָמֵת, וְהִנִּיחָהּ מְעוּבֶּרֶת, לֹא יֹאכְלוּ עֲבָדֶיהָ בִּתְרוּמָה, מִפְּנֵי חֶלְקוֹ שֶׁל עוּבָּר. שֶׁהָעוּבָּר פּוֹסֵל, וְאֵינוֹ מַאֲכִיל, דִּבְרֵי רַבִּי יוֹסֵי.

MISHNA With regard to **an Israelite woman who married a priest and he died and left her pregnant, her slaves** of guaranteed investment **may not partake of** ***teruma***[N] during her pregnancy, **due to the share of the fetus,** as an inheritor of his father, in the ownership of the slaves. In the opposite case, **where** the Israelite husband of a priest's daughter died and left her pregnant, **the fetus disqualifies** her from partaking of *teruma*. However, in the current case, the fetus **does not enable** its mother or the slaves **to partake**[N] of *teruma,*[H] despite the fact that it is the child of a priest. This is **the statement of Rabbi Yosei.**

אָמְרוּ לוֹ: מֵאַחַר שֶׁהֵעַדְתָּ לָנוּ עַל בַּת יִשְׂרָאֵל לְכֹהֵן – אַף בַּת כֹּהֵן לְכֹהֵן וָמֵת, וְהִנִּיחָהּ מְעוּבֶּרֶת – לֹא יֹאכְלוּ עֲבָדֶיהָ בִּתְרוּמָה, מִפְּנֵי חֶלְקוֹ שֶׁל עוּבָּר.

The Rabbis **said to him: Since you testified before us about** the case of **an Israelite woman** who was married **to a priest,** in the case of **the daughter of a priest** who was married **to a priest and he died and left her pregnant, her slaves should not partake of** ***teruma*** **either, due to the fetus's share.** The same *halakha* should apply whether the woman is an Israelite or the daughter of a priest.

גמ׳ אִיבַּעְיָא לְהוּ: טַעְמָא דְּרַבִּי יוֹסֵי מִשּׁוּם דְּקָסָבַר עוּבָּר בִּמְעֵי זָרָה זָר הוּא, אוֹ דִּלְמָא: יָלוּד – מַאֲכִיל, שֶׁאֵינוֹ יָלוּד – אֵינוֹ מַאֲכִיל?

GEMARA **A dilemma was raised before** the scholars: Is **the reason for** the ruling of **Rabbi Yosei because he holds that a fetus in the womb of a non-priest is a non-priest,** as it is considered part of its mother's body and it becomes a priest only upon birth, and therefore the slaves in which it owns a share will be allowed to eat *teruma* only at that stage? **Or,** is Rabbi Yosei **perhaps** of the opinion that only **one who was born enables** others **to partake** of *teruma,* whereas **one who is not** yet **born does not enable** others **to partake,** although it is considered a priest?

לְמַאי נָפְקָא מִינָּהּ – לְעוּבָּר בִּמְעֵי כֹּהֶנֶת, מַאי? אָמַר רַבָּה: הַיְינוּ טַעְמָא דְּרַבִּי יוֹסֵי: דְּקָסָבַר עוּבָּר בִּמְעֵי זָרָה – זָר הוּא. רַב יוֹסֵף אָמַר: יָלוּד – מַאֲכִיל, שֶׁאֵין יָלוּד – אֵינוֹ מַאֲכִיל.

What is the **practical difference** between the two possible reasons? It is the case of a **fetus in the womb of the priestess,** the daughter of a priest. If Rabbi Yosei's rationale is that the fetus in the womb of a non-priest is a non-priest, that is not the case here, and therefore the slaves should partake of *teruma.* **What** is the *halakha* in this case? **Rabba said** that **this is Rabbi Yosei's reasoning: He holds** that **a fetus in the womb of a non-priest is a non-priest. Rav Yosef said:** His rationale is that only **one who was born enables** others **to partake** of *teruma,* whereas **one who is not** yet **born does not enable** others **to partake.**[N]

מֵיתִיבֵי, אָמְרוּ לוֹ לְרַבִּי יוֹסֵי: מֵאַחַר שֶׁהֵעַדְתָּ לָנוּ עַל בַּת יִשְׂרָאֵל לְכֹהֵן – בַּת כֹּהֵן לְכֹהֵן מַהוּ? אָמַר לָהֶם: זוֹ שָׁמַעְתִּי, וְזוֹ לֹא שָׁמַעְתִּי.

The Gemara **raises an objection** to Rav Yosef's opinion from a *baraita* that continues the last clause of the mishna: The Rabbis **said to Rabbi Yosei: Since you testified before us about** the case of **an Israelite woman** married **to a priest,** in the case of **the daughter of a priest** married **to a priest, what is** the *halakha*? **He said to them:** With regard to the former case, **I heard** from my teachers that the slaves do not partake of *teruma,* **but** with regard to **this one, I did not hear** such a thing.[N]

אִי אָמְרַתְּ בִּשְׁלָמָא עוּבָּר בִּמְעֵי זָרָה זָר הוּא – הַיְינוּ דְּקָאָמַר לְהוּ: ״זוֹ שָׁמַעְתִּי, וְזוֹ לֹא שָׁמַעְתִּי״. אֶלָּא, אִי אָמְרַתְּ יָלוּד – מַאֲכִיל, שֶׁאֵין יָלוּד – אֵין מַאֲכִיל, מַאי ״זוֹ שָׁמַעְתִּי וְזוֹ לֹא שָׁמַעְתִּי״ אִיהִי הִיא! קַשְׁיָא.

Granted, if you say that Rabbi Yosei's reasoning is that **a fetus in the womb of a non-priest is a non-priest, this is** the reason **that he said to them: This** case **I heard but this** case **I did not hear.** There is a logical distinction between the two cases, as in the latter case the fetus is not in the womb of a non-priest. **However, if you say** that his rationale is that only **one who was born enables** others **to partake** of *teruma,* whereas **one who is not** yet **born does not enable** others **to partake, what** does he mean by saying: **This** case **I heard but this** case **I did not hear? It is the same** case with regard to this principle. The Gemara concludes: This is a **difficult** objection.

NOTES

Her slaves may not partake of *teruma* – לֹא יֹאכְלוּ עֲבָדֶיהָ בִּתְרוּמָה: An emendation to the text is suggested in the Jerusalem Talmud, so that it reads: His slaves may not partake of *teruma*. This is because the slaves under discussion must be slaves of guaranteed investment, which belonged to the husband, and therefore belong to the fetus after his death. On the other hand, slaves of usufruct property, who belong to the woman, partake of *teruma* if she does, i.e., in a case where the woman has other children from the husband besides the fetus. A different opinion cited there suggests that according to Rabbi Yosei, the woman does not partake of *teruma* even if they had other children, due to her pregnancy, and neither do her slaves of usufruct property. Therefore, the emendation is unnecessary.

Where the Israelite husband died the fetus disqualifies her from partaking, however in the current case the fetus does not enable them to partake – שֶׁהָעוּבָּר פּוֹסֵל וְאֵינוֹ מַאֲכִיל: Rashi explains that a fetus disqualifies its mother in the opposite case, i.e., the daughter of a priest married to an Israelite man, but does not enable her to partake of *teruma* in the case of the mishna. *Tosafot*, however, explain that in the case mentioned in the mishna, the fetus disqualifies the slaves of guaranteed investment from partaking of *teruma* but does not enable its mother or her slaves of usufruct property to partake. This explanation is supported by the fact that the principle that a fetus can disqualify its mother but cannot enable her to partake is stated in the next mishna (67b), so its mention in both *mishnayot* is superfluous unless here it carries a slightly different meaning.

Only one who was born enables others to partake of *teruma*, whereas one who is not yet born does not enable others to partake – יָלוּד מַאֲכִיל, שֶׁאֵין יָלוּד אֵינוֹ מַאֲכִיל: This principle is derived by the Gemara (*Nidda* 44b) from the verse "And such as are born in his house, they may eat [*yokhlu*] of his bread" (Leviticus 22:11). One who was not born may not, so to speak, feed [*ya'akhilu*] others either (Rashi).

The former case I heard, but with regard to this one I did not hear such a thing – זוֹ שָׁמַעְתִּי וְזוֹ לֹא שָׁמַעְתִּי: According to Rashi, Rabbi Yosei means that he heard from his teachers that in this case the slaves do partake of *teruma*. However, the Ritva raises several problems with this explanation and prefers a simpler understanding of Rabbi Yosei's statement: He did not hear what the *halakha* is in the latter case, and therefore he has nothing to say on the matter.

HALAKHA

A fetus does not enable others to partake of *teruma* – עוּבָּר אֵינוֹ מַאֲכִיל: If an Israelite woman married a priest, and he subsequently died and left her pregnant, her slaves may not partake of *teruma*, as only one who was born enables others to partake of *teruma*, but a fetus does not. Conversely, a fetus does not disqualify its mother from partaking of *teruma*. Therefore, if the fetus is categorized as a priest disqualified due to flawed lineage [*ḥalal*], and it has non-*ḥalal* brothers, the mother partakes of *teruma* until it is born. This ruling apparently follows the Rabbis' opinion (Rambam *Sefer Zera'im, Hilkhot Terumot* 8:4; *Tur, Yoreh De'a* 331).

אָמַר רַב יְהוּדָה אָמַר שְׁמוּאֵל: זוֹ דִּבְרֵי רַבִּי יוֹסֵי, אֲבָל חֲכָמִים אוֹמְרִים: יֵשׁ לוֹ בָּנִים – אוֹכְלִים מִשּׁוּם בָּנִים, אֵין לוֹ בָּנִים – אוֹכְלִים מִשּׁוּם אַחִים. אֵין לוֹ אַחִים – אוֹכְלִים מִשּׁוּם מִשְׁפָּחָה כּוּלָּהּ.

Rav Yehuda said that **Shmuel said: This is the statement of Rabbi Yosei. However, the Rabbis say** that if the dead husband **has children,** the slaves **partake** of *teruma* **due to the children,** as they inherit the slaves. If **he does not have children, they partake** of *teruma* **due to** his **brothers,** who inherit his property. If **he does not have brothers** either, **they partake due to** the **entire family,** which inherits his property. The fetus does not disqualify them, as it does not yet own its share of the inheritance.

״זוֹ״ וְלָא סְבִירָא לֵיהּ?! הָא אָמַר לֵיהּ שְׁמוּאֵל לְרַב חָנָא בַּגְדָּתָאָה: פּוֹק אַיְיתִי לִי בֵּי עֲשָׂרָה, דְּאֵימָא לָךְ בְּאַנְפַּיְיהוּ: הַמְזַכֶּה לְעוּבָּר – קָנָה! אֶלָּא: ״זוֹ״ וּסְבִירָא לֵיהּ. מַאי קָא מַשְׁמַע לָן, דִּפְלִיגִי רַבָּנַן עֲלֵיהּ דְּרַבִּי יוֹסֵי.

The Gemara asks: By saying that **this** is only Rabbi Yosei's stance, Shmuel seemingly indicates that **he** himself **does not maintain** that opinion. However, **Shmuel said to Rav Ḥana of Baghdad:**[P] **Go and bring me an assembly of ten men**[N] **and I will say to you before them** a *halakha* that I seek to disseminate: **One who transfers ownership** of an object **to a fetus,** the fetus **acquires** it.[N] Consequently, according to Shmuel, a fetus can own property, which is the premise of Rabbi Yosei's stance that a fetus shares the inheritance even before he is born. The Gemara answers: **Rather,** although Shmuel said that **this** is only Rabbi Yosei's stance, **he holds** likewise. **What is** Shmuel **teaching us** by saying so? He is teaching us **that the Rabbis disagree with Rabbi Yosei.**

וּמִי פְּלִיגִי? מְתִיב רַבִּי זַכַּאי: זוֹ עֵדוּת הֵעִיד רַבִּי יוֹסֵי מִפִּי שְׁמַעְיָה וְאַבְטַלְיוֹן, וְהוֹדוּ לוֹ. אָמַר רַב אַשִׁי: מִי קָתָנֵי ״וְקִבְּלוּ״? ״וְהוֹדוּ לוֹ״ קָתָנֵי, דְּמִסְתַּבֵּר טַעְמֵיהּ.

The Gemara asks: **But do they** really **disagree? Rabbi Zakkai raised an objection** to this statement from a *baraita*: **This** was **a testimony** that **Rabbi Yosei testified** that he heard **from the mouths of Shemaya and Avtalyon, and** the Rabbis **acknowledged** his testimony. Apparently, they accepted his opinion. **Rav Ashi said: Does** that *baraita* **state: And** the Rabbis **accepted** his testimony?[N] **It states: And they acknowledged** his testimony, which indicates **that his opinion is reasonable.** However, they did not accept his ruling.

תָּנוּ רַבָּנַן: הִנִּיחַ בָּנִים – אֵלּוּ וָאֵלּוּ אוֹכְלִים. הִנִּיחָהּ מְעוּבֶּרֶת – אֵלּוּ וָאֵלּוּ אֵין אוֹכְלִים. הִנִּיחַ בָּנִים וְהִנִּיחָהּ מְעוּבֶּרֶת, עַבְדֵי מְלוֹג אוֹכְלִים, כְּדֶרֶךְ שֶׁהִיא אוֹכֶלֶת. עַבְדֵי צֹאן בַּרְזֶל לֹא יֹאכְלוּ, מִפְּנֵי חֶלְקוֹ שֶׁל עוּבָּר, שֶׁהָעוּבָּר פּוֹסֵל וְאֵינוֹ מַאֲכִיל, דִּבְרֵי רַבִּי יוֹסֵי.

The Sages taught in a *baraita*: If the priest who was married to an Israelite woman and died **left children,**[H] both the slaves of usufruct property **and** the slaves of guaranteed investment **may partake** of *teruma*. The slaves of guaranteed investment are owned by the children, who are priests, and the slaves of usufruct property are owned by the woman, who partakes of *teruma* due to her children. If **he left** his wife **pregnant** and did not leave children, both **these** slaves **and those** slaves **may not partake** of *teruma*. If **he left children and left her pregnant,**[H] the **slaves of usufruct** property who belong to her **partake** of *teruma* **just as she partakes** due to her children. However, the **slaves of guaranteed investment,** who are inherited by the children, **may not partake, due to the fetus's share,** as it too inherits them, **as a fetus can disqualify** one from partaking of *teruma* **but it cannot not enable** one **to partake.** This **is the statement of Rabbi Yosei.**

רַבִּי יִשְׁמָעֵאל בְּרַבִּי יוֹסֵי אוֹמֵר מִשּׁוּם אָבִיו: הַבַּת – מַאֲכֶלֶת, הַבֵּן – אֵינוֹ מַאֲכִיל. רַבִּי שִׁמְעוֹן בֶּן יוֹחַי אוֹמֵר: זְכָרִים – יֹאכְלוּ, כּוּלָּן נְקֵבוֹת – לֹא יֹאכְלוּ, שֶׁמָּא יִמָּצֵא עוּבָּר זָכָר, וְאֵין לְבָנוֹת בִּמְקוֹם הַבֵּן כְּלוּם.

Rabbi Yishmael, son of Rabbi Yosei, says in the name of his father: If the priest left behind **a daughter,** she **enables** the slaves **to partake** of *teruma*; however, **a son does not enable** them **to partake. Rabbi Shimon ben Yoḥai says:** If among the priest's children there are **males,** the slaves **partake** of *teruma*. But if they are **all females, they do not partake, lest the fetus be found** to be **a male, and daughters do not** receive **any** of the inheritance **where** there is **a son.** The male fetus would be the sole inheritor, and it does not enable slaves to partake of *teruma*.

מַאי אִירְיָא שֶׁמָּא יִמָּצֵא עוּבָּר זָכָר? תֵּיפוֹק לֵיהּ דִּנְקֵבָה נַמִּי פָּסְלָה! חֲדָא וְעוֹד קָאָמַר; חֲדָא – דִּנְקֵבָה נַמִּי פָּסְלָה, וְעוֹד: שֶׁמָּא יִמָּצֵא עוּבָּר זָכָר, וְאֵין לְבָנוֹת בִּמְקוֹם הַבֵּן כְּלוּם.

The Gemara asks: **Why** does Rabbi Shimon ben Yoḥai **specifically** explain that if the children are females, the slaves may not partake of *teruma*, **lest the fetus be found** to be **a male? Derive** the ruling that the slaves do not partake of *teruma* from the *halakha* **that a female** fetus **also disqualifies** its slaves from partaking of *teruma*. Since the priest has only daughters, they inherit from him, and the female fetus receives a share in the inheritance too. The Gemara answers: Rabbi Shimon ben Yoḥai **stated one** reason **and another. One** reason is **that a female also disqualifies** its slaves from partaking of *teruma*, **and another** reason is **lest the fetus be found** to be **a male, and daughters have no** share in the inheritance **at all in a place** where there is **a son.**

PERSONALITIES

Rav Ḥana of Baghdad [*Bagdata'a*] – רַב חָנָא בַּגְדָּתָאָה: Rav Ḥana of Baghdad was a second-generation Babylonian *amora*. He was Shmuel's preeminent disciple and transmitted several *halakhot* in his teacher's name. He was also a colleague of Rav Yehuda, another disciple of Shmuel.

Rav Ḥana was apparently from the city of Baghdad, called in those days Bagdat, which was on the border of the Jewish settlement in Babylonia, and a small city at the time.

NOTES

Bring me an assembly of ten men – אַיְיתִי לִי בֵּי עֲשָׂרָה: Although it is a legal principle that anything said in the presence of three is considered publicized, making a statement in front of a gathering of ten constitutes a special declaration before a bona fide assembly, which serves to emphasize the importance of the announcement.

One who transfers ownership of an object to a fetus, it acquires it – הַמְזַכֶּה לְעוּבָּר קָנָה: The Gemara in several places reaches the conclusion that a fetus cannot acquire or own anything. The early commentaries discuss the apparent contradiction between that ruling and the *halakha* that one may grant property to his child while the latter is still a fetus. One opinion is that a parent's grant carries more weight than an ordinary acquisition or inheritance, due to the emotional closeness of a parent to his child. The Ramban, on the other hand, claims that the *halakha* that a parent may grant property to a fetus is not Torah law but a rabbinical ordinance that applies only to someone on his deathbed, as it is designed to calm the mind of such an individual.

Does that *baraita* state: And the Rabbis accepted his testimony, etc. – מִי קָתָנֵי, וְקִבְּלוּ וכו׳: If the Rabbis acknowledged Rabbi Yosei's testimony, why didn't they accept his ruling? The Ritva explains that while the Rabbis conceded that Rabbi Yosei's opinion is both reasonable and an accepted tradition, they had their own conflicting tradition, which they were unwilling to disregard in favor of his. Others explain that although they accepted his opinion, the wording indicates that they had initially disagreed with him (Rabbi Avraham min HaHar). Another explanation is that while they acknowledged Rabbi Yosei's tradition, they interpreted it differently than he did (*Tosafot*).

HALAKHA

If the priest who died left children – הִנִּיחַ בָּנִים: If a priest married an Israelite woman and subsequently died, and she has descendants from him and is not pregnant, she and her slaves, both slaves of usufruct property and of slaves of guaranteed investment, partake of *teruma* (*Tur, Yoreh De'a* 331).

If he left children and left her pregnant – הִנִּיחַ בָּנִים וְהִנִּיחָהּ מְעוּבֶּרֶת: The Rambam rules that if a priest married an Israelite woman and died, leaving her pregnant, if she has other children from him she and her slaves of usufruct property may partake of *teruma*. However, her slaves of guaranteed investment may not, due to the fetus's share in their ownership. Alternatively, the Rosh follows Rabbi Shimon's ruling that if they had sons, both types of slaves may partake of *teruma*. However, if they had only daughters, the slaves of guaranteed investment may not partake of *teruma* due to the fetus's share. The *Tur* concurs with this ruling (Rambam *Sefer Zera'im, Hilkhot Terumot* 8:4; *Yoreh De'a* 331).

זְכָרִים יֹאכְלוּ. וְהָאִיכָּא עוּבָּר! קָסָבַר:

The Gemara asks with regard to the first clause of Rabbi Shimon's statement, that if among the priest's children there are **males,** the slaves **may partake** of *teruma*: **But** even though sons inherit from their father, **isn't there a fetus** to be accounted for, as perhaps he too is a male, and therefore has a share in the inheritance? The Gemara answers: Rabbi Shimon **holds**

Perek **VII**
Daf **67** Amud **b**

HALAKHA

Minor orphans who came to court to divide up their father's property, etc. – יְתוֹמִים שֶׁבָּאוּ לַחֲלוֹק בְּנִכְסֵי אֲבִיהֶם וכו׳: With regard to sons, some of whom are adults and others of whom are minors, whose father dies and who want to divide up their father's property so that the adults can receive their share, the court appoints a steward for the minors, who selects for them a suitable share. The minors cannot object, even when they come of age, as the division was performed under the auspices of the court. This ruling follows Rav Naḥman's own opinion. However, the Ritva rules in accordance with Shmuel (*Shakh*; Rambam *Sefer Mishpatim, Hilkhot Naḥalot* 10:4; *Shulḥan Arukh, Ḥoshen Mishpat* 289:1).

LANGUAGE

Steward [*apotropos*] – אַפּוֹטְרוֹפּוֹס: From the Greek ἐπίτροπος, *epitropos*, meaning one with the power of attorney, a trustee. It generally refers to anyone who has the right to run the properties or affairs of another.

אֵין חוֹשְׁשִׁין לְמִיעוּטָא. וְאִיבָּעֵית אֵימָא: לְעוֹלָם קָסָבַר חוֹשְׁשִׁין לְמִיעוּטָא, דְּעָבְדִינַן לֵיהּ תַּקַּנְתָּא כְּרַב נַחְמָן אָמַר שְׁמוּאֵל.

that **we are not concerned about the minority**[N] of cases. Only a minority of fetuses are male inheritors, as roughly half are female, and some are stillborn. Therefore, the majority of fetuses will not become male children. **And if you wish, say** that **actually he holds** that **we are concerned about the minority.** However, **we make an arrangement for** the slaves, **in accordance with** what **Rav Naḥman** said that **Shmuel said.**

דְּאָמַר רַב נַחְמָן אָמַר שְׁמוּאֵל: יְתוֹמִים שֶׁבָּאוּ לַחֲלוֹק בְּנִכְסֵי אֲבִיהֶם, בֵּית דִּין מַעֲמִידִין לָהֶם אַפּוֹטְרוֹפּוֹס וּבוֹרֵר לָהֶם חֵלֶק יָפֶה. הִגְדִּילוּ – יְכוֹלִין לִמְחוֹת. וְרַב נַחְמָן דִּידֵיהּ אָמַר: הִגְדִּילוּ – אֵין יְכוֹלִין לִמְחוֹת. דְּאִם כֵּן – מָה כֹּחַ בֵּית דִּין יָפֶה?

This is as **Rav Naḥman said** that **Shmuel said:** With regard to minor **orphans who came to** court to **divide up their father's property,**[H] the **court appoints for** each of **them a steward [*apotropos*],**[LN] **and he selects for them a fine share.** When the orphans **have grown up, they may object** to the manner in which the property was divided and redistribute it. **And Rav Naḥman himself said** that when **they have grown up they may not object, as,** if they may object, **what good is the power of the court?** Here too, an appointed steward selects a share of the inheritance on behalf of the fetus, and this share does not include any of the slaves. Therefore, the slaves may partake of *teruma*. However, if all of the children are females, this arrangement is impossible because if the fetus is a son all the property belongs to him.

לֵימָא, דְּרַב נַחְמָן תַּנָּאֵי הִיא! לָא, דְּכוּלֵּי עָלְמָא אִית לְהוּ דְּרַב נַחְמָן, וְהָכָא בְּחוֹשְׁשִׁין לְמִיעוּטָא קָמִיפַּלְגִי.

Based on the use of Rav Naḥman's ruling to explain Rabbi Shimon's opinion, the Gemara suggests: **Let us say** that **Rav Naḥman's** opinion **is** corresponding to one side of a dispute between ***tanna'im***, as the Rabbis disagree with Rabbi Shimon. The Gemara rejects this suggestion: **No;** it is possible **that everyone** in the dispute **accepts Rav Naḥman's** ruling, **and here they disagree** only **with regard** to whether **we are concerned about the minority,** as previously suggested, in a case where the arrangement was not made.

רַבִּי יִשְׁמָעֵאל בְּרַבִּי יוֹסֵי אוֹמֵר מִשּׁוּם אָבִיו: הַבַּת – מַאֲכִיל, הַבֵּן – אֵינוֹ מַאֲכִיל. מַאי שְׁנָא בֵּן דְּלָא מַאֲכִיל – מִשּׁוּם חֶלְקוֹ שֶׁל עוּבָּר, בַּת נָמֵי לֹא תַּאֲכִיל – מִפְּנֵי חֶלְקוֹ שֶׁל עוּבָּר!

It was taught in the previous clause of the *baraita* that **Rabbi Yishmael, son of Rabbi Yosei, says in the name of his father:** If the priest left behind **a daughter,** she **enables** the slaves **to partake** of *teruma*; however, **a son does not enable** them **to partake** of it. The Gemara asks: **What is different** about **a son, who does not enable** them **to partake, due to the fetus's share,** as it owns a share of the property if it is a male? **A daughter should not enable** them **to partake either, due to the fetus's share.**

NOTES

We are not concerned about the minority – אֵין חוֹשְׁשִׁין לְמִיעוּטָא: With regard to Rabbi Yosei's opinion toward less probable possibilities, the early commentaries raise a contradiction between the Gemara here, which indicates that Rabbi Yosei is not concerned about the minority of cases, and other statements of his that indicate that he does take such possibilities into account.

Some commentaries claim that what is indicated here should be seen as a local ruling and not a principle (Meiri). Others differentiate between uncertainties with regard to the present reality, as is the case here, and uncertainties with regard to the future (see Ramban; *Tosefot HaRosh*). A third opinion distinguishes between ritual and monetary matters, as the former field often demands stringency, whereas with regard to monetary matters there is no such thing as stringency, since a stringent ruling for one party is a lenient one for the other.

The court appoints for them a steward – בֵּית דִּין מַעֲמִידִין לָהֶם אַפּוֹטְרוֹפּוֹס: According to Rashi, the court appoints a private steward for each orphan to select his share. The Ritva argues that there is no need to divide up the property between the minor orphans at this stage. Rather, a steward is appointed only if there are both minor and adult orphans, and the adults demand to receive their share. In that case, the court appoints one steward for all the minors. He selects a fine share for all of them, and when they come of age they can divide it up among themselves.

There is also a dispute as to whether a steward has the authority to select property according to its monetary value, or whether he may participate only in the distribution of identical items. The Gemara here apparently supports the opinion that lends him the authority to select property according to its monetary value, as the steward here selects land for the fetus in exchange for slaves. Those who hold otherwise explain that a steward should prefer land for the orphan that he is representing, as the value of slaves is likely to depreciate over time. Therefore, this is an exchange that he may perform (*Nimmukei Yosef*).

אֲמַר אַבַּיֵי: הָכָא בִּנְכָסִים מוּעָטִים עָסְקִינַן, וּכְגוֹן דְּאִיכָּא בֵּן בַּהֲדֵי בַּת,

Abaye said: Here we are dealing with a case of an inheritance of **insufficient property** that is enough only to sustain the daughters until they come of age. With regard to this case, the Sages instituted that the daughters receive their sustenance while the sons get nothing.[NH] This is **also** a case **where there is** a surviving **son together with** the **daughter.**

מַה נַּפְשָׁךְ: אִי הַאי דִּמְעַבְּרָא בֵּן הוּא – לָא עֲדִיף מֵהַאי דְּקָאֵי, אִי בַּת הִיא – אַמַּאי אָכְלָה, בְּתַקַּנְתָּא דְּרַבָּנַן – כַּמָּה דְּלָא נָפַק לַאֲוִיר הָעוֹלָם לָא תַּקִּינוּ רַבָּנַן.

Therefore, **no matter what,** the slaves do not partake of *teruma*. **If this** fetus, **with which she is pregnant, is a son, it is no better than this** son **who** already **exists.**[N] Just as the existing son does not inherit the insufficient property, the same applies to the male fetus. **If it is a daughter,** it does not yet receive a share of the inheritance. This can be explained: **Why does** the daughter **partake** of the inheritance? It is **by** virtue of **a rabbinic ordinance.** Therefore, **as long as** the fetus **has not emerged into the atmosphere of the world, the Sages did not establish** that it should receive the inheritance. Consequently, the slaves partake of *teruma* by virtue of the existing daughter, as only she inherits them.

בְּמַאי אוֹקִימְתָּא – בִּנְכָסִים מוּעָטִים, אֵימָא סֵיפָא: שֶׁמָּא יִמָּצֵא הָעוּבָּר זָכָר, וְאֵין לְבָנוֹת בִּמְקוֹם בֵּן כְּלוּם, אַדְּרַבָּה, נְכָסִים מוּעָטִים דְּבָנוֹת נִינְהוּ! סֵיפָא אֲתָאן לִנְכָסִים מְרוּבִּין.

The Gemara asks: **In what** manner **did you establish** the *baraita*? You established it as referring **to insufficient property.** However, **say the latter clause** of the *baraita*: **Lest the fetus be found** to be **a male, and daughters do not** receive **any** of the inheritance **where** there is **a son.** Yet according to Abaye's explanation, **on the contrary,** the **insufficient property is the daughters',** whether or not there are any sons. The Gemara answers: In **the latter clause we have come to** a different case, in which there is **sufficient property.**

וּנְכָסִים מוּעָטִים דְּבָנוֹת נִינְהוּ? וְהָאָמַר רַבִּי אַסִּי אָמַר רַבִּי יוֹחָנָן: יְתוֹמִין שֶׁקָּדְמוּ וּמָכְרוּ בִּנְכָסִים מוּעָטִים, מַה שֶּׁמָּכְרוּ מָכְרוּ!

The Gemara raises another objection to Abaye's explanation: Does an inheritance of **insufficient property** belong **to the daughters? Didn't Rabbi Asi say** that **Rabbi Yoḥanan said:** If the male **orphans proceeded to sell** the **insufficient property,**[H] although by rabbinic ordinance it is designated for the daughters' sustenance, **what they sold was sold.** Apparently, the Sages did not expropriate the properties from the male inheritors, but merely designated them for the daughters' sustenance. How, then, can the sons' ownership be disregarded with regard to the slaves' partaking of *teruma*?

וְאֶלָּא מַאי בַּת דְּקָתָנֵי – אֵם – אִי הָכִי, הַיְינוּ רַבִּי יוֹסֵי! כּוּלָּהּ רַבִּי יִשְׁמָעֵאל בְּרַבִּי יוֹסֵי קָתָנֵי לָהּ.

Rather, what is the meaning of the word **daughter** in the context of the ruling **that is taught** by Rabbi Yishmael? It means female and is referring to the **mother** of the fetus. She enables her slaves of usufruct property to partake of *teruma*, as her husband's heirs have no share in them, whereas the son does not enable the slaves guaranteed investment to partake, due to the fetus's share. The Gemara asks: **If so, this is** the same as **Rabbi Yosei's** statement in the first clause. What was added by Rabbi Yishmael? The Gemara answers: Indeed, the **entire** *baraita* **is taught by Rabbi Yishmael, son of Rabbi Yosei.** There are not conflicting versions of Rabbi Yosei's opinion. Rather, Rabbi Yishmael is clarifying that he is the author of that *baraita*.

מתני׳ הָעוּבָּר, וְהַיָּבָם, וְהָאֵירוּסִין, וְהַחֵרֵשׁ, וּבֶן תֵּשַׁע שָׁנִים וְיוֹם אֶחָד – פּוֹסְלִין וְלֹא מַאֲכִילִין.

MISHNA With regard to **the fetus**[H] of a divorcée or a widow whose husband left her pregnant; **and a man whose married brother died childless** [*yavam*];[H] **and betrothal; and a married deaf-mute;**[N] **and a nine-year-and-one-day-old** boy[B] who engaged in intercourse with a woman; if any of these men are Israelites and the woman is the daughter of a priest, they **disqualify** her from partaking of *teruma*. **But** if she is an Israelite and they are priests, they **do not enable**[N] her **to partake** of *teruma*.

NOTES

The distribution of an inheritance – חֲלוּקַת יְרוּשָּׁה: According to Torah law, if a man passes away, leaving sons and daughters, only the males inherit from him. Daughters inherit from him only if there are no sons. However, the Sages instituted as one of the stipulations of a marriage contract that the daughters of the married couple receive their sustenance from their father's property until they come of age or marry. As a marriage contract is essentially a promissory note, this stipulation places a lien on the inheritance. Consequently, the daughters' right to the property takes precedence over the sons', to the extent that if the property is meager and is sufficient only for the daughters' sustenance, the sons get nothing, not even their own sustenance. Nevertheless, since the sons are the inheritors, if they unlawfully sell the property, the sale is valid.

It is no better than this son who already exists – לָא עֲדִיף מֵהַאי דְּקָאֵי: The Rashba asks how it is possible that a rabbinical ordinance overrules the Torah law that the slaves do not partake of *teruma*. He leaves this difficulty unresolved. In the Jerusalem Talmud, it is answered that according to Rabbi Yosei, by Torah law there is no obligation to separate *teruma* and tithes after the destruction of the First Temple; rather, the obligation is by rabbinic law.

Deaf-mute [*ḥeresh*] – חֵרֵשׁ: When the unmodified term *ḥeresh* is employed, the reference is to one who can neither hear nor speak. In earlier times, these deaf-mutes were considered uneducable and were often placed in the same category as imbeciles and minors, who are exempt from all of the mitzvot in the Torah. In contemporary times, great strides have been made in the education of the deaf. Consequently, many rabbinic commentaries rule that those who can communicate intelligently are considered obligated in mitzvot like any Jew.

Disqualify but do not enable to partake – פּוֹסְלִין וְלֹא מַאֲכִילִין: Rabbi Shimon is cited in the Jerusalem Talmud as claiming that this principle is unjust, as any sexual relationship that disqualifies the daughter of priest from partaking of *teruma* should enable the wife of a priest to partake of *teruma*, and vice versa.

HALAKHA

An inheritance of insufficient property goes to the daughters – נְכָסִים מוּעָטִים לַבָּנוֹת: If a person died and left property, his daughters receive their sustenance from the estate until they come of age, and the rest is divided up among the sons. If the inheritance is sufficient only for the daughters' sustenance, they receive their sustenance from the property until they come of age or get betrothed, even if the sons are forced to beg for their livelihood (Rambam *Sefer Nashim*, *Hilkhot Ishut* 19:19; *Shulḥan Arukh*, *Even HaEzer* 112:14).

If the male orphans proceeded to sell the insufficient property, etc. – יְתוֹמִין שֶׁקָּדְמוּ וּמָכְרוּ בִּנְכָסִים מוּעָטִים וכו׳: If the father left only a meager inheritance and the sons proceeded to sell it, their sale is valid (Rambam *Sefer Nashim*, *Hilkhot Ishut* 19:17; *Shulḥan Arukh*, *Even HaEzer* 112:14).

A fetus disqualifies but does not enable to partake – עוּבָּר פּוֹסֵל וְאֵינוֹ מַאֲכִיל: An Israelite woman who is pregnant from a priest may not eat *teruma* due to the fetus, and the daughter of a priest who is pregnant from an Israelite does not partake of *teruma* either, even if she has no other child from him (Rambam *Sefer Zera'im*, *Hilkhot Terumot* 8:2).

The fetus and a…*yavam*, etc. – הָעוּבָּר וְהַיָּבָם וכו׳: With regard to a fetus, a *yavam*, betrothal, a married deaf-mute, and a nine-year-and-one-day-old boy who engaged in intercourse with a woman, if any of these are Israelites and the woman is the daughter of a priest, they disqualify her from partaking of *teruma*. If they are priests and she is an Israelite, they do not enable her to partake of *teruma* (Rambam *Sefer Zera'im*, *Hilkhot Terumot* 8:1).

BACKGROUND

A nine-year-and-one-day-old boy – בֶּן תֵּשַׁע שָׁנִים וְיוֹם אֶחָד: Although most boys do not experience a significant bodily change at the age of nine, the development of the testicles begins to accelerate at around this time, with the attending increase in the capacity for intercourse. Though it roughly corresponds to the average age of this development, this specification, like other specific ages the Sages established for different levels of maturity, is somewhat arbitrary.

ספק שהוא בן תשע שנים ויום אחד ספק שאינו, ספק הביא שתי שערות וספק שלא הביא.

Likewise, in the case of a boy with regard to whom there is **uncertainty** as to **whether he is nine years and one day old**[NH] and **uncertainty** whether **he is not,** who engaged in intercourse with a woman; and in the case of a boy who betrothed a woman, with regard to whom there is **uncertainty** as to **whether he has grown two** pubic **hairs** and is considered an adult **and uncertainty whether he has not grown,** they too can disqualify the woman from partaking of *teruma* and cannot enable her to partake, as in the previous cases.

נָפַל הַבַּיִת עָלָיו וְעַל בַּת אָחִיו וְאֵין יָדוּעַ אֵי זֶה מֵת רִאשׁוֹן – צָרָתָהּ חוֹלֶצֶת וְלֹא מִתְיַיבֶּמֶת.

If **the house fell**[N] **upon** a man **and upon his brother's daughter,**[H] to whom he was married, **and it is unknown which** of them **died first, her rival wife performs *ḥalitza* and does not enter into levirate marriage.** Entering into levirate marriage is not possible, as, if the wife died after her husband, the surviving wife would be rendered the rival wife of a forbidden relative, since the *yavam* is the father of the wife who died. This status prevents the creation of a levirate bond between him and the surviving wife as well. On the other hand, *ḥalitza* is necessary in case the wife died before her husband, thereby allowing the creation of a levirate bond between her rival wife and her father, the *yavam*.

גמ׳ ״הָעוּבָּר״. אִי בַּת כֹּהֵן לְיִשְׂרָאֵל הִיא פָּסֵיל לָהּ, ״כִּנְעוּרֶיהָ״ – פְּרָט לִמְעוּבֶּרֶת. אִי בַּת יִשְׂרָאֵל לְכֹהֵן הִיא לֹא מַאֲכִיל לָהּ, יָלוּד מַאֲכִיל, שֶׁאֵינוֹ יָלוּד אֵינוֹ מַאֲכִיל.

GEMARA It is taught in the mishna that **the fetus** disqualifies its mother from partaking of *teruma* and does not enable her to do so. The Gemara explains: **If she is the daughter of a priest** married **to an Israelite,** and her husband died and left her pregnant, the fetus **disqualifies her** from partaking of *teruma*, as it is stated: "But if a priest's daughter be a widow, or divorced, and have no child, and is returned to her father's house, as in her youth, she may eat of her father's bread" (Leviticus 22:13). The phrase **"as in her youth" excludes a pregnant woman,** whose body has changed from her youth. **If she is an Israelite woman** married **to a priest,** the fetus **does not enable her to partake,** as **one who was born enables** others **to partake** of *teruma*, whereas **one who is not** yet **born does not enable** others **to partake.**

״הַיָּבָם״. אִי בַּת כֹּהֵן לְיִשְׂרָאֵל הִיא פָּסֵיל לָהּ, ״וְשָׁבָה אֶל בֵּית אָבִיהָ״ פְּרָט לְשׁוֹמֶרֶת יָבָם, אִי בַּת יִשְׂרָאֵל לְכֹהֵן הִיא לֹא מַאֲכִיל לָהּ, ״קִנְיַן כַּסְפּוֹ״ אָמַר רַחֲמָנָא, וְהָא קִנְיַן דְּאָחִיו הוּא.

It is taught in the mishna that the same principle applies to **a *yavam*.** The Gemara explains: **If she is the daughter of a priest** who has a levirate bond **to an Israelite, he disqualifies her,** as it is stated in the verse cited above: **"And is returned to her father's house,"** which **excludes a widow waiting for her *yavam*,** who has not returned to her father's house, as a levirate bond was created with her *yavam*. **If she is an Israelite woman** with a levirate bond **to a priest, he does not enable her to partake** of *teruma*, as **the Merciful One states** in the Torah: **"The purchase of his money,** he may eat of it" (Leviticus 22:11), **and this woman is his brother's acquisition.**[N] The bond with her *yavam* ensued from his late brother's marriage to her, not through any action of his own.[H]

״וְהָאֵירוּסִין״. אִי בַּת כֹּהֵן לְיִשְׂרָאֵל הִיא, פָּסֵיל לָהּ,

The mishna teaches that the same principle **also** applies to **betrothal.** The Gemara explains: **If she is the daughter of a priest** betrothed **to an Israelite, he disqualifies her,**

NOTES

There is uncertainty as to whether he is nine years and one day old, etc. – **ספק שהוא בן תשע שנים ויום אחד וכו׳**: The commentaries point out that this cannot be referring to a case where it is currently uncertain whether or not the boy is nine years old, as in such a case the court would have had to follow his presumptive physical status, i.e., that of a minor under the age of nine. Rather, the reference is apparently to a case where he is currently at least nine years old, and the court must determine in retrospect what his age was at the time of the incident. Since he no longer has the presumptive status of a minor under the age of nine, his status at the time of the incident is deemed uncertain (see Maharshal, Rabbi Ovadya MiBartenura, and *Tosefot Yom Tov*).

If the house fell, etc. – **נפל הבית וכו׳**: This clause appears unrelated to the rest of the mishna. One suggestion is that since the mishna includes cases of uncertainty in which the ruling is stringent, it adds this similar case as well (Rid; Rabbi Avraham min HaHar). In the Jerusalem Talmud, it is explained that the previous case of uncertainty, i.e., a boy whose adulthood is in doubt, is taught with regard to both the matter discussed in the first clause of the mishna, i.e., the partaking of *teruma*, and the rival wife's issue of her levirate bond, which is discussed in the latter clause. If there is uncertainty as to whether the first wife was betrothed before or after the husband reached adulthood, then after the husband's death the rival wife performs *ḥalitza* and does not enter into levirate marriage. Therefore, the mishna cites this clause as well.

And this woman is his brother's acquisition – **וְהָא קִנְיַן דְּאָחִיו הוּא**: The early commentaries disagree whether the *halakha* that the *yevama* of a priest may not partake of *teruma* is Torah law (*Tosafot Yeshanim*) or rabbinic law (*Tosafot*, citing Rabbeinu Tam). According to the latter opinion, the verse that is cited is not a proper derivation from the Torah, but rather a support of the rabbinic law.

HALAKHA

Uncertainty as to whether he is nine years and one day old, etc. – **ספק שהוא בן תשע שנים ויום אחד וכו׳**: In the case of a boy with regard to whom there is uncertainty as to whether or not he is nine years old who engaged in intercourse with a woman, and similarly in the case of one who married a woman and with regard to whom there is uncertainty as to whether or not he has grown two pubic hairs, they disqualify the woman from partaking of *teruma* and cannot enable her to partake of it (Rambam *Sefer Zera'im*, *Hilkhot Terumot* 8:11).

If a house fell upon a man and upon his brother's daughter – **נפל הבית עליו ועל בת אחיו**: If a man had two wives, one who was related to the *yavam* and the other who was not, and the man and the wife related to the *yavam* both died and it is unknown which of them died first, the rival wife performs *ḥalitza* and not levirate marriage (*Shulḥan Arukh*, *Even HaEzer* 173:8).

A *yavam* disqualifies and does not enable to partake of *teruma* – **יבם פוסל ואינו מאכיל**: An Israelite widow waiting for her *yavam*, who is a priest, does not partake of *teruma*, despite their bond. The daughter of a priest waiting for an Israelite *yavam* does not partake of *teruma* either, due to their bond (Rambam *Sefer Zera'im*, *Hilkhot Terumot* 8:5).

דְּהָא קָנְיָה בַּהֲוָיָה, וְאִי בַּת יִשְׂרָאֵל לְכֹהֵן הִיא – לָא מַאֲכִיל לַהּ מִשּׁוּם דְּעוּלָּא.

as he acquired her by means of betrothal.[N] **And if she is an Israelite woman** betrothed **to a priest, he does not enable her to partake** of *teruma* **due to** the reason given by **Ulla:**[N] Although by Torah law a priest's betrothed partakes of *teruma*, the Sages rendered it prohibited for her to do so, lest she allow other members of her family to eat it.[H]

״וְהַחֵרֵשׁ״. אִי בַּת כֹּהֵן לְיִשְׂרָאֵל הִיא – פָּסֵיל לַהּ, דְּהָא קָנְיָה בְּתַקַּנְתָּא דְּרַבָּנַן, וְאִי בַּת יִשְׂרָאֵל לְכֹהֵן הִיא – לָא מַאֲכִיל, ״קִנְיַן כַּסְפּוֹ״ אָמַר רַחֲמָנָא, וְהַאי לָאו בַּר קִנְיָן הוּא.

It is **also** taught in the mishna that a **deaf-mute**[N] disqualifies a woman from partaking of *teruma* and does not enable her to do so.[H] The Gemara elaborates: **If she is the daughter of a priest** married to a deaf-mute **Israelite, he disqualifies her, as he acquired her through** marriage sanctioned by **an ordinance of the Sages.** Although the marriage of a deaf-mute is invalid by Torah law, the Sages instituted an ordinance validating this type of marriage. **And if she is an Israelite woman** married **to a** deaf-mute **priest, he does not enable** her **to partake** of *teruma*, as **the Merciful One states** in the Torah: **"The purchase of his money,** he may eat of it" (Leviticus 22:11), **and this** deaf-mute **is not capable of acquisition** by Torah law, as he is not legally competent.

״וּבֶן תֵּשַׁע שָׁנִים״ וכו׳. קָא סָלְקָא דַּעְתָּן בְּשׁוֹמֶרֶת יָבָם לְבֶן תֵּשַׁע וְיוֹם אֶחָד. לְמַאי? אִי לְמִיפְסַל – קָטָן נַמִי מִיפְסַל פָּסֵיל, אִי לְאַכּוֹלֵי – גָּדוֹל נַמִי לָא מַאֲכִיל!

§ It is **also** taught in the mishna that **a nine-year old** boy disqualifies a woman from partaking of *teruma* and does not enable her to partake. **It enters our mind** that the mishna is referring **to a widow waiting for her *yavam*,** who is **nine** years **and one day old.** The Gemara therefore inquires: With regard **to what** is this taught? **If** it is with regard **to disqualifying** her from partaking of *teruma*, **a younger *yavam* also disqualifies** her, as a levirate bond was created and she cannot return to her father's house. And **if** it was with regard **to enabling** her **to partake** of *teruma*, **an older *yavam* does not enable** her **to partake either,** as discussed above.

אָמַר אַבָּיֵי: הָכָא בְּיָבָם בֶּן תֵּשַׁע שָׁנִים וְיוֹם אֶחָד הַבָּא עַל יְבִמְתּוֹ עָסְקִינַן, דְּמִדְּאוֹרָיְיתָא קָנְיָא לֵיהּ. סָלְקָא דַּעְתָּךְ אָמֵינָא: הוֹאִיל וּמִדְּאוֹרָיְיתָא קָנְיָא לֵיהּ, וּבִיאָתוֹ בִּיאָה, אֵימָא לוֹכִיל – קָא מַשְׁמַע לַן: עָשׂוּ בִּיאַת בֶּן תֵּשַׁע שָׁנִים וְיוֹם אֶחָד כְּמַאֲמָר בְּגָדוֹל.

Abaye said: Here we are dealing with a nine-year-and-one-day-old *yavam* who already **engaged in intercourse with his *yevama*,**[N] **as** she was thereby **acquired by him by Torah** law.[N] It might **enter your mind to say that since by Torah** law **she was acquired by him,** as the legal status of **his** act of **intercourse is** that of **intercourse,** perhaps **he enables** her **to partake** of *teruma*. The mishna therefore **teaches us** that the Sages **rendered the** legal status of the **intercourse of a nine-year-and-one-day-old** boy **like** that of **levirate betrothal** by means of money or a document performed **by an adult man,**[H] which is not sufficient for her to partake of *teruma*. Since levirate betrothal is effective only by rabbinic law, the *yevama* is not considered the acquisition of his money by Torah law and may not partake of *teruma*.

NOTES

As he acquired her by means of betrothal [*havaya*] – דְּהָא קָנְיָה בַּהֲוָיָה: *Tosafot* note that the use of the word *havaya* indicates that this *halakha* is derived from the verse "And if a priest's daughter be [*tihye*] married to a common man" (Leviticus 22:12). However, it appears from the Gemara later on that it is derived from a different verse. *Tosafot* conclude that the Gemara hints to this verse because it is a clearer source. The Gemara is not particular about referring to the accurate source because it is inconsequential here. The Ramban discusses the Gemara's tendency to cite inaccurate sources from the Torah for incidentally mentioned *halakhot* when the quoted source is clearer than the actual one.

Due to the reason given by Ulla – מִשּׁוּם דְּעוּלָּא: Ulla's rationale is that the woman is not yet accustomed to the priesthood, as she is still living in her father's house, and she is likely to forget that she may not allow members of her Israelite family to partake of the *teruma*. It should be noted that another *amora* suggests a different rationale for this ordinance (see *Ketubot* 57b): The priest might discover a blemish in the woman following their marriage, which would render the betrothal mistaken and annul it retroactively. However, Ulla's rationale is the one usually quoted.

And a deaf-mute – וְהַחֵרֵשׁ: The Jerusalem Talmud explains this case differently. It says that the mishna is referring to a woman who engaged in intercourse with a deaf-mute who is either her *yavam* or who is unfit to enter the assembly. Accordingly, he disqualifies her by Torah law, and not by rabbinic law as is explained by the Gemara.

The difference between the explanations in the Babylonian Talmud and the Jerusalem Talmud with regard to the case of a deaf-mute corresponds to the dispute between Abaye and Rava with regard to the case of a nine-year-old boy.

A nine-year-and-one-day-old *yavam* who engaged in intercourse with his *yevama* – יָבָם בֶּן תֵּשַׁע שָׁנִים וְיוֹם אֶחָד הַבָּא עַל יְבִמְתּוֹ: By Torah law, an act of intercourse performed by a boy is recognized from the age of nine. Any adult who engaged in forbidden intercourse with him is liable, but he is exempt from punishment, as he is a minor. He is also unable to acquire property or betroth a woman, as he is not legally competent. The complexity of a minor's levirate marriage stems from the fact that levirate marriage is an acquisition created exclusively through intercourse.

As she was thereby acquired by him by Torah law – דְּמִדְּאוֹרָיְיתָא קָנְיָא לֵיהּ: Most commentaries maintain that the levirate marriage of a minor *yavam* is invalid by Torah law and is no more effective than betrothal of a *yevama*, which is a rabbinic institution (see *Tosafot*). Therefore, they claim that this phrase is inaccurate and refers not to acquisition but to the preexisting levirate bond between them (Ritva). Accordingly, the rationale that the mishna rejects is that the combination of the levirate bond, which exists by Torah law, and the levirate betrothal might enable the woman to partake of *teruma*.

Rashi (*Kiddushin* 19a) and Rabbi Avraham min HaHar, however, hold that a *yavam* who is a minor can perform levirate marriage by Torah law, and it was the Sages who instituted that it should be equivalent only to levirate betrothal.

HALAKHA

Betrothal disqualifies and does not enable her to partake – הָאֵירוּסִין פּוֹסְלִין וְלֹא מַאֲכִילִין: The daughter of a priest who is betrothed to an Israelite is disqualified from partaking of *teruma*, as she is considered like his wife. Although an Israelite woman betrothed to a priest may partake of *teruma* by Torah law, the Sages decreed that she not do so, lest she allow other members of her family to partake of *teruma*, as stated by Ulla (Rambam *Sefer Zera'im*, *Hilkhot Terumot* 8:7).

A deaf-mute disqualifies and does not enable her to partake – חֵרֵשׁ פּוֹסֵל וְאֵינוֹ מַאֲכִיל: The daughter of a priest who married a deaf-mute Israelite is disqualified from partaking of *teruma* due to this marriage, as it is valid by rabbinic ordinance. An Israelite woman married to a deaf-mute priest does not partake of *teruma*, as he has not acquired her by Torah law (Rambam *Sefer Zera'im*, *Hilkhot Terumot* 8:9).

The intercourse of a nine-year-old *yavam* – בִּיאַת יָבָם בֶּן תֵּשַׁע: If a minor *yavam* aged nine years and one day engaged in intercourse with his *yevama*, the intercourse does not fully consummate the levirate marriage. Rather, it is equivalent to an adult's betrothal to his *yevama* (Rambam *Sefer Nashim*, *Hilkhot Yibbum* 5:18; *Shulḥan Arukh*, *Even HaEzer* 167:1).

אָמַר לֵיהּ רָבָא: אִי הָכִי, סֵיפָא דְּקָתָנֵי: סָפֵק בֶּן תֵּשַׁע שָׁנִים וְיוֹם אֶחָד סָפֵק שֶׁאֵינוֹ, הָשְׁתָּא וַדַּאי בֶּן תֵּשַׁע לָא מַאֲכִיל – סָפֵק מִיבַּעְיָא?!

Rava said to him: If so, consider **the latter clause** of the mishna, **which teaches** that a boy with regard to whom there is **uncertainty** whether **he is nine years and one day old** and **uncertainty** whether **he is not,** disqualifies a woman from partaking of *teruma*, and he does not enable her to partake. **Now** that, according to your explanation, one who is **definitely nine** years **old does not enable** her **to partake** of *teruma*, **is it necessary** to teach the same concerning a boy with regard to whom there is **uncertainty** as to whether or not he reached that age?

אֶלָּא אֲמַר רָבָא: בְּבֶן תֵּשַׁע שָׁנִים וְיוֹם אֶחָד דְּהָנָךְ פְּסוּלִים קָתָנֵי, דְּפָסְלֵי בְּבִיאָתָן. וְכִדְתַנְיָא: בֶּן תֵּשַׁע שָׁנִים וְיוֹם אֶחָד גֵּר עַמּוֹנִי וּמוֹאָבִי, מִצְרִי וַאֲדוֹמִי, כּוּתִי, נָתִין, חָלָל וּמַמְזֵר, שֶׁבָּאוּ עַל כֹּהֶנֶת לְוִיָּה וְיִשְׂרְאֵלִית – פְּסָלוּהָ.

Rather, Rava said that the mishna **is teaching** this *halakha* **with regard to a nine-year-and-one-day-old** boy who is one **of those unfit** males listed in a *baraita*,[H] **who disqualify** a woman from marrying a priest **by their intercourse,** as they are unfit to enter the assembly of Israel through marriage, **as it is taught** in a *baraita*: **A nine-year-and-one-day-old** boy who is **an Ammonite or a Moabite convert;** or who is **an Egyptian or an Edomite** convert; or who is either **a Samaritan** [*kuti*], **a Gibeonite,** a ***ḥalal***, **or a** ***mamzer***, when he **engaged in intercourse with a priestess,** i.e., the daughter of a priest, **a Levite, or an Israelite,** he thereby **disqualified her** from marrying a priest,[H] and, in the case of the daughter of a priest, from partaking of *teruma*.

וְהָא מִדְּקָתָנֵי סֵיפָא: אִם אֵינָן רְאוּיִן לָבֹא בְּיִשְׂרָאֵל הֲרֵי אֵלּוּ פּוֹסְלִים, מִכְּלָל דְּרֵישָׁא לָאו בִּפְסוּלִים עָסְקִינַן! רֵישָׁא פְּסוּלֵי קָהָל, סֵיפָא פְּסוּלֵי כְּהוּנָּה.

The Gemara raises a difficulty **from** the fact **that the latter clause,** the next mishna (69a), **teaches** that **if** men who **are unfit to enter** the assembly of **Israel** by marriage engage in extramarital intercourse with women, **they disqualify** them from marrying into the priesthood: **It may be inferred that** in **the first clause,** the mishna above, **we are dealing not with unfit** individuals but with men fit to marry Jews of unflawed lineage. The Gemara answers: That inference is incorrect. **The first clause** of the mishna is dealing with those **unfit to** enter **the assembly**[N] of Israel by marriage, while **the latter clause** is dealing with those who are merely **unfit for** the **priesthood.** That is why the mishna is referring to them separately. Accordingly, Rava's explanation that the mishna is referring to an unfit nine-year-old boy is viable.

גּוּפָא, בֶּן תֵּשַׁע שָׁנִים וְיוֹם אֶחָד גֵּר עַמּוֹנִי וּמוֹאָבִי מִצְרִי וַאֲדוֹמִי כּוּתִי נָתִין חָלָל וּמַמְזֵר שֶׁבָּאוּ עַל כֹּהֶנֶת לְוִיָּה וְיִשְׂרְאֵלִית – פְּסָלָן.

§ The Gemara addresses the matter **itself** and cites the complete *baraita*. **A nine-year-and-one-day-old** boy who is **an Ammonite or a Moabite convert;**[N] or who is **an Egyptian or an Edomite** convert;[N] or who is either **a Samaritan,**[N] **a Gibeonite,**[N] **a** ***ḥalal***, **or a** ***mamzer***, when he **engaged in intercourse with a priestess,** or **a Levite, or an Israelite,** he thereby **disqualified her** from marrying into the priesthood.

רַבִּי יוֹסֵי אוֹמֵר: כׇּל שֶׁזַּרְעוֹ פָּסוּל – פּוֹסֵל, כׇּל שֶׁאֵין זַרְעוֹ פָּסוּל – אֵינוֹ פּוֹסֵל. רַבָּן שִׁמְעוֹן בֶּן גַּמְלִיאֵל אוֹמֵר: כׇּל שֶׁאַתָּה נוֹשֵׂא בִּתּוֹ – אַתָּה נוֹשֵׂא אַלְמְנָתוֹ, וְכׇל שֶׁאֵין אַתָּה נוֹשֵׂא בִּתּוֹ – אִי אַתָּה נוֹשֵׂא אַלְמְנָתוֹ.

Rabbi Yosei says: Of the individuals mentioned above, **anyone whose offspring is unfit** to enter the assembly of Israel, **disqualifies** a woman with whom he engaged in intercourse from marrying into the priesthood. However, **anyone whose offspring is not unfit does not disqualify** a woman through intercourse. **Rabban Shimon ben Gamliel says: Anyone whose daughter you may marry, you may marry his widow,** even if you are a priest. Anyone whose daughter may marry a Jew of unflawed lineage does not disqualify a woman with whom he engaged in intercourse from marrying into the priesthood. **And anyone whose daughter you may not marry, you may not marry his widow** if you are a priest.

NOTES

The first clause is dealing with those unfit to enter the assembly, etc. – **רֵישָׁא פְּסוּלֵי קָהָל וכו׳**: According to Rabbeinu Ḥananel's version of the text, which is accepted by most early commentaries, the Gemara states the opposite: The first clause is dealing with those unfit for the priesthood, and the latter clause is referring to those who are unfit to enter the assembly.

Most commentaries agree with Rashi's interpretation that the expression: Those unfit for the priesthood, is referring only to a *ḥalal*, whereas the expression: Those unfit to enter the assembly, is referring to all those who are unfit.

An Ammonite or a Moabite convert – **גֵּר עַמּוֹנִי וּמוֹאָבִי**: Torah law prohibits a male convert from these nations and his male descendants to ever marry freely among the Jewish people (see Deuteronomy 23:4).

An Egyptian or an Edomite convert – **גֵּר מִצְרִי וַאֲדוֹמִי**: A convert of Egyptian or Edomite descent, whether male or female, may not marry a Jew by birth. This restriction applies for two generations (see Deuteronomy 23:8–9).

Samaritan – **כּוּתִי**: The Samaritans are the descendants of the nations displaced by Sennacherib, King of Assyria, and brought to settle in Eretz Yisrael. Eventually, they accepted upon themselves several mitzvot (II Kings, chapter 17). At the beginning of the Second Temple period, during the times of Ezra and Nehemiah, relations between the Samaritans and the Jews deteriorated. Later, the Samaritans established a center of worship on Mount Gerizim, as they claimed that the sanctity of that mountain was established by one of the Ten Commandments. Some generations of Sages recognized Samaritans as half-Jewish. They went so far as to say that the Samaritans are extremely exacting in the fulfillment of the mitzvot they adopted, even more so than Jews. Ultimately, as the Samaritans continued to distance themselves from the Jewish people in virtually every regard, they were accorded the legal status of gentiles.

Gibeonite – **נָתִין**: A Gibeonite is a descendant of the nation that tricked the Jewish people into making a covenant with them in the time of Joshua. According to most commentaries, by Torah law, the Gibeonites could have been treated as ordinary converts, but first Joshua and then King David decreed that they be treated as *mamzerim*, and therefore it became prohibited for Jews to marry them.

HALAKHA

The intercourse of an unfit nine-year-old boy – **בִּיאַת פָּסוּל בֶּן תֵּשַׁע**: If the intercourse of a male disqualifies a woman from marrying into the priesthood, it does so from the time the male is nine years and one day old. The woman with whom he engaged in intercourse is thereby disqualified from marrying a priest, and if she is the daughter of a priest she may no longer partake of *teruma* (Rambam *Sefer Zera'im*, *Hilkhot Terumot* 8:11).

Individuals who disqualify women from marrying into the priesthood – **הַפּוֹסְלִים לִכְהוּנָּה**: If a woman engaged in intercourse with a gentile; a Gibeonite, a *mamzer*, an Ammonite or a Moabite convert, an Egyptian or an Edomite convert of the first or second generation, or a *ḥalal*, she is disqualified from marrying into the priesthood, and if she is the daughter of a priest she may no longer partake of *teruma*. Some commentaries claim that she is disqualified from marrying into the priesthood only if she engaged in forbidden intercourse that renders her liable to receive *karet* (*Tosafot*; Rosh; Rambam *Sefer Kedusha*, *Hilkhot Issurei Bia* 18:3; *Shulḥan Arukh*, *Even HaEzer* 6:8).

מנא הני מילי? אמר רב יהודה אמר רב: אמר קרא "ובת כהן כי תהיה לאיש זר", כיון שנבעלה לפסול לה – פסלה.

The Gemara asks: **From where are these matters** derived, that intercourse with an unfit man renders a woman unfit to partake of *teruma* and marry a priest? **Rav Yehuda said** that **Rav said: The verse states: "And if a priest's daughter be married to a common man** [*ish zar*], she shall not eat of that which is set apart from the sacred" (Leviticus 22:12). It may be derived that **since she engaged in intercourse with one who is unfit for her, he disqualified her**[N] from marrying into the priesthood, as the literal meaning of the expression *ish zar* is a man who is excluded.

האי מיבעי ליה דקאמר רחמנא: בת כהן דמינסבא לזר לא תיכול!

The Gemara asks: **That** verse **is necessary** to teach the *halakha* **that the Merciful One says: The daughter of a priest who marries a non-priest,** even one that she is permitted to marry, **may not partake** of *teruma*. Therefore, it cannot be the source for the *halakha* that intercourse with an unfit man renders a woman unfit to partake of *teruma* and marry a priest.

ההיא מ"ושבה אל בית אביה כנעוריה מלחם אביה תאכל" נפקא, מדקאמר רחמנא: "ושבה אל בית אביה תאכל" מכלל דמעיקרא לא אכלה!

The Gemara answers: **That** prohibition **is derived from** the verse "But if a priest's daughter be a widow, or divorced, and have no child, **and is returned to her father's house, as in her youth, she may eat of her father's bread"** (Leviticus 22:13). **From the fact that the Merciful One says: "And is returned to her father's house…she may eat," it may be inferred that initially,** while married to a non-priest, **she** was **not** permitted to **eat.** Therefore, the prohibition against a woman who engaged in intercourse with an unfit man partaking of *teruma* may be derived from the former verse, as it is not necessary for this *halakha*.

אי מההיא הוה אמינא לאו הבא מכלל עשה – עשה, כתב רחמנא האי ללאו. [לאו] מ"וכל זר לא יאכל קדש" נפקא.

The Gemara rejects this answer: **If** the prohibition against the daughter of a priest who married a non-priest partaking of *teruma* had been derived only **from that** latter verse, **I would have said** that it is a prohibition that stems from a positive mitzva, as it is stated in positive form, and according to the principle that **a prohibition that stems from a positive mitzva is a positive mitzva,** she would not be liable to receive a court-imposed punishment. **The Merciful One** therefore **writes that** former verse, **to** establish an explicit **prohibition.** The Gemara counters: The **prohibition** against the wife of a non-priest partaking of *teruma* **is derived from** a different verse: **"No common man may eat of the sacred"** (Leviticus 22:10).

Perek **VII**
Daf **68** Amud **b**

ההוא מיבעי ליה לגופיה! תרי "וכל זר" כתיבי.

The Gemara rejects this assertion: **That** verse **is necessary to** teach **its own** basic *halakha*, that a non-priest is prohibited from partaking of *teruma*. The Gemara responds: **Two** prohibitions with regard to **a "common man" are written,** one in the verse previously cited and the other in Leviticus 22:13: "But there shall no common man eat of it." One of them prohibits a non-priest from partaking of *teruma*, while the other is referring to the daughter of a priest married to a non-priest.

ואכתי מיבעי ליה לכדרבי יוסי ברבי חנינא. דאמר רבי יוסי ברבי חנינא: "וכל זר" – זרות אמרתי לך, ולא אנינות! דרבי יוסי ברבי חנינא מן "זר" "וכל זר" נפקא,

The Gemara asks: One of these verses **is still necessary to** teach another *halakha* **that** is taught **by Rabbi Yosei, son of Rabbi Ḥanina, as Rabbi Yosei, son of Rabbi Ḥanina, said** that the phrase **"no common man"** indicates that **I,** God, **said to you** that **commonness,** i.e., non-priesthood, renders one unfit to partake of *teruma*, **but acute mourning,** i.e., mourning on the day when one's close relative died, does **not** render one unfit to eat *teruma*. The Gemara answers: This teaching **of Rabbi Yosei, son of Rabbi Ḥanina, is derived from** a superfluous word in the verse, as it could have stated: **A common man** may not eat of the holy thing, and it actually states: **"No common man."**

NOTES

Since she engaged in intercourse with one who is unfit for her, he disqualified her – כיון שנבעלה לפסול לה, פסלה: Most commentaries maintain that any man unfit to enter the assembly of Israel who engaged in intercourse with a woman rendered her a *zona*, and it is prohibited for a priest to marry her, as the verse states: "They shall not take a woman who is a harlot [*zona*]" (Leviticus 21:7). The commentaries therefore ask why the Gemara derives this *halakha* from Leviticus 22:12. The Rashba answers that the *halakha* under discussion relates to a woman who was raped and therefore cannot be deemed a harlot. He adds that the derivation is clearly necessary according to an opinion mentioned previously, that only a woman who engaged in forbidden intercourse that renders her liable to receive *karet* has the status of a *zona* (61a).

וְאַכַּתִּי מִיבָּעֵי לֵיהּ לְכִדְתַנְיָא: כְּשֶׁהִיא חוֹזֶרֶת – חוֹזֶרֶת לִתְרוּמָה, וְאֵינָהּ חוֹזֶרֶת לְחָזֶה וָשׁוֹק, וַאֲמַר רַב חִסְדָּא אֲמַר רָבִינָא בַּר רַב שֵׁילָא: מַאי קְרָא? דִּכְתִיב: ״וּבַת כֹּהֵן כִּי תִהְיֶה לְאִישׁ זָר הִיא בִּתְרוּמַת הַקֳּדָשִׁים לֹא תֹאכֵל״ – לֹא תֹאכַל בַּמּוּרָם מִן הַקֳּדָשִׁים.

The Gemara asks: The verse "And if a priest's daughter be married to a common man" (Leviticus 22:12), from which Rav derived the *halakha* being discussed, that intercourse with an unfit man renders a woman unfit to partake of *teruma* and marry a priest, **is still necessary for that which is taught** in a *baraita*: **When a** priest's daughter **returns** to her father's house after the death of her Israelite husband, **she resumes** partaking of ***teruma*, but she does not resume** partaking of the **breast and** the right **hind leg**[H] of sacrificial offerings. **And Rav Ḥisda said** that **Ravina, son of Rav Sheila, said: What is the verse** from which this is derived? **As it is written: "And if a priest's daughter be married to a common man, she may not eat of that which is set apart from the sacred"** (Leviticus 22:12). This implies that even after her husband's death, **she may not partake of the** portion **separated from consecrated** offerings. Therefore, the verse cannot be the source for the above *halakha*.

אִם כֵּן לִכְתּוֹב קְרָא ״הִיא בַּקֳּדָשִׁים לֹא תֹאכֵל״, מַאי ״בִּתְרוּמַת הַקֳּדָשִׁים״ – שָׁמְעַתְּ מִינָּהּ תַּרְתֵּי.

The Gemara answers: **If so,** if this is the only *halakha* derived from this verse, **let the verse** merely **write:**[N] **She may not eat of the sacred. What is** the significance of the seemingly superfluous expression **"that which is set apart from the sacred"? Conclude from this** that the prohibition is referring to **two** deeds:[H] The daughter of a priest who engaged in intercourse with an unfit man may not partake of *teruma*, and if she weds a non-priest she may not partake of the priestly portion of offerings, the breast and right hind leg.

אַשְׁכְּחַן כֹּהֶנֶת, לְוִיָּה וְיִשְׂרְאֵלִית מְנָלַן? כִּדְאָמַר רַבִּי אַבָּא אֲמַר רַב: ״בַּת״ ״וּבַת״, הָכָא נַמִי ״בַּת״ ״וּבַת״.

The Gemara asks: **We found** a source for **a priestess; from where do we** derive the same *halakha* with regard to **a Levite or an Israelite** woman[H] who engaged in intercourse with an unfit man, i.e., that they do not partake of *teruma* even if they marry a priest? The Gemara answers that it is **as Rabbi Abba** said that **Rav said:** The verse states: **"But** if a priest's **daughter** be a widow, or divorced" (Leviticus 22:13). It could have begun: If a priest's **daughter.** The word "but," the prefix *vav*, is seemingly superfluous, and therefore it may indicate the expansion of the prohibition to include additional women. **Here too,** it may be derived from the distinction between the phrase: If a priest's **daughter,** and the phrase: **"And** if a priest's **daughter,"** which utilizes the prefix *vav*, that Levite and Israelite women are subject to the prohibition as well.

כְּמַאן – כְּרַבִּי עֲקִיבָא, דְּדָרֵישׁ וָוִין! אֲפִילּוּ תֵּימָא רַבָּנַן, כּוּלֵּיהּ ״וּבַת״ קְרָא יְתֵירָא הוּא.

The Gemara asks: **In accordance with whose** opinion is this exposition possible? It is **in accordance** only **with** the opinion of **Rabbi Akiva, as** he **derives** *halakhot* from the prefix ***vav***, which means "and" or "but." The Gemara responds: **Even if you say** it is in accordance with **the Rabbis,** who do not derive *halakhot* from the prefix *vav*,[N] **the entire** phrase: **"And** if a priest's **daughter," is superfluous** in **the verse,** as the previous verse already mentioned the priest's daughter. Therefore, the inclusion of Levite and Israelite women in the prohibition may be derived from the entire expression.

NOTES

If so, let the verse merely write, etc. – **אִם כֵּן לִכְתּוֹב קְרָא וכו׳**: *Tosafot* explain this statement as follows: If the verse intended to disqualify the woman only from partaking of *teruma*, it should have simply referred to the sacred, and it would have been clear that this expression is referring to *teruma*, as that is the topic under discussion. Therefore, the expression "that which is set apart from the sacred" indicates that the prohibition pertains to other consecrated foods as well.

Derivation of *halakhot* from the prefix *vav* – **דְּרִישַׁת וָוִין**: Apparently, all the Sages derived *halakhot* from the prefix *vav* in various contexts. The Rabbis that the Gemara is referring to must therefore be Rabbis who interpret the prefix *vav* as only connecting between a phrase and the statement previous to it, whereas Rabbi Akiva maintains that it also implies the inclusion of additional cases relevant to the subject at hand (see *Tosafot*).

HALAKHA

But she does not resume partaking of the breast and the right hind leg – **וְאֵינָהּ חוֹזֶרֶת לְחָזֶה וָשׁוֹק**: If the daughter of a priest married a non-priest and was widowed or divorced without any surviving children from her husband, she may resume partaking of *teruma*. However, she may not partake of the breast and the right hind leg of offerings (Rambam *Sefer Zera'im*, *Hilkhot Terumot* 6:8–9).

Conclude from this that the prohibition is referring to two deeds – **שָׁמְעַתְּ מִינָּהּ תַּרְתֵּי**: Two prohibitions are derived from the verse "And if a priest's daughter be married to a common man, she may not eat of that which is set apart from the sacred" (Leviticus 22:12). The first is that a woman who engaged in sexual intercourse with a man forbidden to her is rendered a *zona* or a *ḥalala*, and she is permanently prohibited from partaking of *teruma*. The second is that the daughter of a priest who was married to a priest and subsequently widowed or divorced may resume partaking of *teruma*, but she may not eat the breast and the right hind leg of offerings (Rambam *Sefer Zera'im*, *Hilkhot Terumot* 6:7).

From where do we derive the same *halakha* with regard to a Levite or an Israelite woman – **לְוִיָּה וְיִשְׂרְאֵלִית מְנָלַן**: Not only is the daughter of a priest prohibited from partaking of *teruma* if she engaged in intercourse with a man unfit for her, but even a Levite or an Israelite woman who has a child from a priest is prohibited from eating *teruma* if she engaged in intercourse with a man forbidden to her (Rambam *Sefer Zera'im*, *Hilkhot Terumot* 6:10).

אַשְׁכְּחַן לִתְרוּמָה, לִכְהוּנָּה מְנָלַן? אַטּוּ לְוִיָּה וְיִשְׂרְאֵלִית לָא לִכְהוּנָּה מְרַבִּינַן לְהוּ? דְּאִי לִתְרוּמָה – בְּנוֹת מֵיכַל תְּרוּמָה נִינְהוּ?

The Gemara asks: **We found** a source for the woman's disqualification from partaking of ***teruma*; from where do we** derive that she is disqualified **from** marrying into the **priesthood?** The Gemara counters: **Is that to say that we did not include a Levite and an Israelite woman** in the verse "But if a priest's daughter be a widow, or divorced, etc." (Leviticus 22:13), with regard to their marriage **to** a member of **the priesthood?** The derivation that a Levite and an Israelite woman are included in this verse was clearly with regard to their marriage to a priest; **as if** the inclusion was with regard **to *teruma*, are** these women **fit to partake of *teruma*** at all, regardless of their having engaged in intercourse with an unfit man? Clearly, their inclusion pertains to their marriage to a priest and their partaking of *teruma* as his wife.

אַלְמָה לָא? מַשְׁכַּחַתְּ לָהּ דְּקָאָכְלָה בִּשְׁבִיל בְּנָהּ!

The Gemara rejects this assertion: **Why not?** Why can't the inclusion be referring to the partaking of *teruma* exclusively? **You find that** possibility **when she partakes** of *teruma* **due to her son.** If an Israelite woman has a son from a priest, she may partake of *teruma*. Therefore, it is necessary to include a Levite or Israelite woman in the prohibition against partaking of *teruma* if she engaged in intercourse with an unfit man.

בִּשְׁבִיל בְּנָהּ – קַל וָחוֹמֶר: וּמַה כֹּהֶנֶת, דִּבִקְדוּשָּׁה דְּנַפְשָׁהּ אָכְלָה, פָּסֵיל לָהּ, לְוִיָּה וְיִשְׂרְאֵלִית דְּלָא אָכְלָה אֶלָּא בִּשְׁבִיל בְּנָהּ – לֹא כׇּל שֶׁכֵּן?!

The Gemara responds: The *halakha* that this woman does not partake of *teruma* **due to her son is** deduced through **an *a fortiori*** inference: **If a priestess, who partakes** of *teruma* **by** virtue of **her own sanctity, is disqualified** from partaking of *teruma* by an unfit man who engaged in intercourse with her, then with regard to a **Levite or Israelite woman, who partakes** of *teruma* **only due to her son,** is it **not all the more so** that it should be prohibited for her to partake of *teruma* after this act?

וְהִיא הַנּוֹתֶנֶת: כֹּהֶנֶת דְּקָדֵישׁ גּוּפָהּ – פָּסֵיל לָהּ, הָא דְּלָא קָדֵישׁ גּוּפָהּ – לָא פָּסֵיל לָהּ. אֶלָּא לִכְהוּנָּה, קַל וָחוֹמֶר מִגְּרוּשָׁה! וּמַה גְּרוּשָׁה שֶׁמּוּתֶּרֶת בִּתְרוּמָה – אֲסוּרָה לִכְהוּנָּה, זוֹ שֶׁאֲסוּרָה בִּתְרוּמָה – אֵינוֹ דִּין שֶׁפְּסוּלָה לִכְהוּנָּה?

The Gemara rejects that response: **But that provides** support for the contrary reasoning. It is logical that **a priestess, who is herself sacred, is disqualified** by intercourse with an unfit man. However, with regard to **this woman, who is not sacred herself,** and who eats *teruma* only due to her son, intercourse with an unfit man should **not disqualify her. Rather,** the prohibition against these women marrying **into the priesthood** is derived by **an *a fortiori*** inference **from** the case of **a divorcée:**[N] **If a divorcée** who is the daughter of a priest, **who is permitted to** partake of ***teruma*,**[H] **is** nevertheless **prohibited** from marrying **into the priesthood,** as is written in the Torah (Leviticus 21:7), then with regard to **this** woman, for **whom** it **is prohibited to** partake of ***teruma*, is it not right that** she should be **disqualified** from marrying **into the priesthood?**

וְכִי מַזְהִירִין מִן הַדִּין? גִּלּוּי מִילְּתָא בְּעָלְמָא הוּא.

The Gemara raises an objection to that inference: **But do we warn,** i.e., do we deduce a prohibition through **logical derivation?** The Gemara answers: This is not a new prohibition; rather, **it is merely a revelation**[N] of the above prohibition's scope. In other words, the prohibition against marrying a priest is subsumed under the prohibition against partaking of *teruma*.

וְאֵימָא: נִבְעֲלָה לְפָסוּל לָהּ – חַיָּיבֵי כְּרֵיתוֹת! ״כִּי תִהְיֶה״ אָמַר רַחֲמָנָא, הָנָךְ דְּאִית בְּהוּ הֲוָיָה, חַיָּיבֵי כְּרֵיתוֹת – לָאו בְּנֵי הֲוָיָה.

Now that the source has been established, the Gemara asks: **And** perhaps you should **say** that this *halakha* pertaining to a woman who **engaged in intercourse with** a man **unfit for her** applies only to **those liable to receive *karet***[N] for their act of intercourse, but not to intercourse with a man who is unfit to marry into the assembly of Israel. The Gemara answers that **the Merciful One states** in the Torah: **"If a priest's daughter be married"** (Leviticus 22:12), indicating that this *halakha* is referring to **those who** can **have** a valid **marriage,** while **those liable to receive *karet*** for their act of intercourse **are not fit for marriage.**[N]

NOTES

An *a fortiori* inference from a divorcée – קַל וָחוֹמֶר מִגְּרוּשָׁה: The *Tosefot HaRosh* argues that the case of an Israelite or a Levite woman should serve as a rebuttal of this inference, as she does not partake of *teruma* but she may marry a priest. He answers that the latter woman's unfitness to partake of *teruma* is inherent, and it is therefore irrelevant to the discussion. The case under discussion is a woman who was disqualified from marrying into the priesthood by an action. He continues to argue that the inference can be rebutted with the case of a daughter of a priest who was widowed by a non-priest and has children from him, as she does not partake of *teruma* but she may marry a priest. He answers that the prohibition against her partaking of *teruma* is only circumstantial; if her Israelite descendants die, she may resume partaking of *teruma*.

It is merely a revelation – גִּלּוּי מִילְּתָא בְּעָלְמָא הוּא: The commentaries offer various interpretations of this answer. The *Ḥazon Ish* explains that the prohibition against this woman partaking of *teruma* shows that she is rendered a *zona*. Once that has been established, all *halakhot* pertaining to a *zona* apply to her as well, e.g., her unfitness to marry a priest.

And perhaps you should say that it…applies only to those liable to receive *karet* – וְאֵימָא...חַיָּיבֵי כְּרֵיתוֹת: The Ritva explains that since the verse does not identify this "common man," perhaps it is referring to the type of man least suitable for her. Although those liable to receive the death penalty for their acts of intercourse are presumably less suitable than those liable to receive *karet*, they are not considered a separate legal category from those liable to receive *karet*.

Those liable to receive *karet* are not fit for marriage – חַיָּיבֵי כְּרֵיתוֹת לָאו בְּנֵי הֲוָיָה: If so, what is the source of the *halakha* that those liable to receive *karet* also disqualify the woman from marrying a priest? *Tosafot* answer that the primary meaning of the phrase *ish zar*, translated as common man, refers to a man who renders a woman liable to receive to *karet* through intercourse. The Gemara merely proves from the wording of the verse that the verse is referring to less severe acts of intercourse as well. Rashi, on the other hand, maintains that the source is Rabbi Yishmael's teaching that any man who cannot render a woman a widow or a divorcée, i.e., his marriage to her is invalid, also disqualifies her from marrying into the priesthood.

HALAKHA

A divorcée who is permitted to partake of *teruma* – גְּרוּשָׁה שֶׁמּוּתֶּרֶת בִּתְרוּמָה: The daughter of a priest who got divorced from a non-priest and does not have children with him is permitted to partake of *teruma* (Rambam *Sefer Zera'im*, *Hilkhot Terumot* 8:8).

אי הכי, גוי ועבד לא ליפסלו! הנך פסלי מדרבי ישמעאל. דאמר רבי יוחנן משום רבי ישמעאל: מנין לגוי ועבד שבא על בת ישראל, ועל כהנת ולויה, שפסלוה – שנאמר "ובת כהן כי תהיה אלמנה וגרושה" וגו׳.

The Gemara asks: **If so, a gentile or a slave** who engaged in intercourse with a Jewish woman **should not have disqualified** her from marrying into the priesthood, as they cannot marry her. The Gemara answers: **These disqualify** her, as derived **by Rabbi Yishmael, as Rabbi Yoḥanan said in the name of Rabbi Yishmael: From where** is it derived with regard **to a gentile or a slave who engaged in intercourse with an Israelite woman, or with a priestess, or a Levite woman, that they have disqualified her? As it is stated: "But if a priest's daughter be a widow, or divorced,** and have no child, and is returned to her father's house, as in her youth, she may eat of her father's bread" (Leviticus 22:13).

Perek **VII**
Daf **69** Amud **a**

NOTES

But perhaps you should say, one who has, etc. – ואימא מי שיש לו וכו׳: *Tosafot* ask why the Gemara suggests a lenient interpretation, contrary to the principle that whenever a Torah juxtaposition can be interpreted in either a stringent or a lenient manner, the stringent interpretation is accepted. *Tosefot HaRosh* writes that since a Jewish woman's marriage to a gentile or a slave is invalid, and any child of theirs is considered the child of his mother only, it makes sense that the child should not cause her to be disqualified.

מי שיש לו אלמנות וגירושין בה, יצאו גוי ועבד שאין לו אלמנות וגירושין.

This verse is referring to a man **who has** potential **widowhood and divorce with her, excluding a gentile and a slave, who do not have widowhood and divorce** with her, as they cannot marry Jews at all. Therefore, they disqualify a woman from marrying into the priesthood through sexual intercourse, even if she does not have a child with them.

אשכחן כהנת, לויה וישראלית מנא לן? כדאמר רבי אבא אמר רב: "בת" "ובת" הכא נמי "בת" "ובת".

The Gemara asks: **We have found** a source for the *halakha* that a gentile and a slave disqualify **a priestess. From where do we** derive this with regard to **a Levite and an Israelite woman?** The Gemara answers: It is **as Rabbi Abba** said that **Rav said:** The verse **"But** if a priest's **daughter** be a widow, or divorced" (Leviticus 22:13) could have begun with the words: If a priest's **daughter.** The word "but," the prefix *vav*, expands the prohibition to include additional women. **Here too,** it may be derived from the distinction between the phrase: If a priest's **daughter,** and the phrase as it actually appears in the verse: **"But** if a priest's **daughter,"** that Levite and Israelite women are subject to the prohibition as well.

כמאן, כרבי עקיבא, דדריש ווי? אפילו תימא רבנן, כולה "ובת" קרא יתירא הוא.

The Gemara asks: **In accordance with whose** opinion is this exposition possible? It is **in accordance** only **with** the opinion of **Rabbi Akiva, as he derives** *halakhot* from the prefix *vav***.** The Gemara responds: **Even** if **you say** it is accordance with **the Rabbis, the entire** phrase: **"But** if a priest's **daughter,"** is **superfluous** in the **verse,** as the previous verses had already mentioned the priest's daughter. Therefore, the inclusion of Levite and Israelite women in the prohibition may be derived from the entire expression.

ואימא: מי שיש לו אלמנות וגירושין בה, כי לית ליה זרע – קאכלה, כי אית ליה זרע – לא אכלה, מי שאין לו אלמנות וגירושין בה, אף על גב דאית ליה זרע – נמי תיכול!

The Gemara suggests: **But** perhaps you should **say** a different interpretation of the mention of widowhood and divorce in the verse: In the case of **one who has**[N] potential **widowhood and divorce with her, if he does not have offspring** from her **she may partake** of *teruma* upon her widowhood or divorce, whereas **if he does have offspring** from her **she does not partake.** However, in the case of **one who does not have widowhood and divorce with her, even if she has offspring** from him, **she should** be allowed to **partake** of *teruma*, as the offspring is not considered his.

אם כן רבויי לויה וישראלית למה לי?

The Gemara answers: **If so, why do I** need to **include a Levite and an Israelite woman?** If the daughter of a priest is not disqualified from *teruma* due to intercourse with a gentile or slave, certainly a Levite or Israelite woman is not. The fact that the verse indicates inclusion of Levite and Israelite women proves that the *halakha* that is derived from it is a stringency and not a leniency.

וּלְרַבִּי עֲקִיבָא, דְּאָמַר: אֵין קִדּוּשִׁין תּוֹפְסִין בְּחַיָּיבֵי לָאוִין, וּמַאי ״כִּי תִהְיֶה לְאִישׁ זָר״ כִּי תִּיבָּעֵל, ״אַלְמָנָה וּגְרוּשָׁה״ לָמָּה לִי?

The Gemara asks: **And according to Rabbi Akiva, who said** that **betrothal of those** who may not engage in intercourse, as they are **liable for** violating **a prohibition, does not take effect, and** therefore the meaning of the phrase **"And if** a priest's daughter **be** [*tihye*] **to a common man"** (Leviticus 22:12) is not: If she marries him, but rather: **If she engages in intercourse** with him,[N] **why do I** need the Torah to mention the phrase **"a widow, or divorced"** in the verse: "But if a priest's daughter be a widow, or divorced… she may eat of her father's bread" (Leviticus 22:13)? It is not necessary for this phrase to teach that a gentile and a slave disqualify a woman from marrying into the priesthood through sexual intercourse, as suggested by Rabbi Yishmael, as they are included in the prohibition proscribing a woman who engaged in intercourse with a man who is unfit for her.

אַלְמָנָה לְהַחְמִיר עָלֶיהָ, וּגְרוּשָׁה לְהָקֵל עָלֶיהָ. וּצְרִיכָא, דְּאִי אַשְׁמְעִינַן אַלְמָנָה – אַלְמָנָה הוּא דְּכִי לֵית לַהּ זֶרַע אָכְלָה, מִשּׁוּם דַּחֲזְיָא לִכְהוּנָּה, אֲבָל גְּרוּשָׁה דְּלָא חַזְיָא לִכְהוּנָּה – אֵימָא אַף עַל גַּב דְּלֵית לַהּ זֶרַע לָא אָכְלָה. וְאִי אַשְׁמְעִינַן גְּרוּשָׁה – גְּרוּשָׁה הוּא דְּכִי אִית לַהּ זֶרַע לָא אָכְלָה, מִשּׁוּם דְּלָא חַזְיָא לִכְהוּנָּה, אֲבָל אַלְמָנָה, דַּחֲזְיָא לִכְהוּנָּה, אֵימָא: אַף עַל גַּב דְּאִית לַהּ זֶרַע נָמֵי תֵּיכוּל – צְרִיכָא.

The Gemara answers: **A widow** is mentioned **to be stringent with her, and a divorcée to be lenient with her, and** both are **necessary. As,** had the Torah **taught us** only the case of **a widow,** you might have assumed that **specifically** if this daughter of a priest is **a widow** she **partakes** of *teruma* **when she does not have offspring because she is fit for the priesthood,** as she may marry a common priest, **but** with regard to **a divorcée, who is not fit for the priesthood** at all, you might **say** that **even if she does not have offspring she does not partake** of *teruma*. **And had it taught us** only the case of **a divorcée,** you might have assumed that only **a divorcée does not partake** of *teruma* **when she has offspring** from a non-priest **because she is not fit for the priesthood, but** with regard to **a widow, who is fit for the priesthood,** you might **say** that **even if she has offspring she should also partake** of *teruma*. It is therefore **necessary** for both cases to be stated.

וְאֵימָא: נִבְעֲלָה לְפָסוּל לָהּ – אַף מַחֲזִיר גְּרוּשָׁתוֹ! ״לְאִישׁ זָר״ אָמַר רַחֲמָנָא, מִי שֶׁזָּר אֶצְלָהּ מֵעִיקָּרָא, לְאַפּוֹקֵי הַאי דְּלָא זָר אֶצְלָהּ מֵעִיקָּרָא הוּא.

The Gemara asks: **And** perhaps you should **say** that the category of a woman **who engaged in intercourse with** a man who is **unfit for her** and is therefore disqualified from the priesthood applies **even** to the case of a man **remarrying his divorcée** after she had been married to another man in the meantime, which is prohibited. The Gemara answers: **The Merciful One states** in the Torah: **"To a common man** [*ish zar*]**,"** literally, a man who is a stranger, "she shall not eat of that which is set apart from the sacred." The Gemara understands the notion of a stranger to be one whom she was forbidden to marry and interprets homiletically: Only marriage to one **who was a stranger,** i.e., forbidden, **to her from the outset** precludes her from partaking of *teruma*, **to the exclusion of one who was not a stranger to her from the outset,** such as her ex-husband.

אִי הָכִי, חָלָל דְּלָאו זָר הוּא מֵעִיקָּרָא, לָא לִפְסוֹל! אָמַר קְרָא: ״לֹא יְחַלֵּל זַרְעוֹ בְּעַמָּיו״, מַקִּישׁ זַרְעוֹ לוֹ: מָה הוּא פּוֹסֵל, אַף זַרְעוֹ נָמֵי פּוֹסֵל.

The Gemara asks: **If so, a *ḥalal*, who was not excluded at the outset,** as he may marry even the daughter of a priest, **should not disqualify** a woman from marrying into the priesthood. The Gemara answers that **the verse states,** with regard to a priest who marries a woman unfit for the priesthood: **"He shall not profane his seed among his people"** (Leviticus 21:15), thereby **juxtaposing his seed to him.**[N] **Just as he,** a priest who married a woman forbidden to him, **disqualifies** her from the priesthood, **so too, his seed,** the *ḥalal*, **also disqualifies** a woman with whom he engaged in intercourse.[H]

וְאֵימָא: מִשְּׁעַת הֲוָיָה? דּוּמְיָא דְּכֹהֵן גָּדוֹל בְּאַלְמָנָה, מָה כֹּהֵן גָּדוֹל בְּאַלְמָנָה – בְּבִיאָה, אַף הַאי נָמֵי – בְּבִיאָה.

The Gemara asks: **And** perhaps you should **say** that a woman who engaged in intercourse with a man unfit for her is disqualified **from the time of** their **betrothal,** even before they engaged in intercourse. The Gemara answers that this is **similar to a High Priest** who engaged in intercourse **with a widow: Just as a High Priest** who engaged in intercourse **with a widow**[H] has disqualified her **through intercourse,** not betrothal, **so too, this** unfit man has **also** disqualified her **through intercourse.**

NOTES

And the meaning of, If a priest's daughter be [*tihye*] to a common man is: If she engages in intercourse with him – וּמַאי ״כִּי תִהְיֶה לְאִישׁ זָר״, כִּי תִּיבָּעֵל: Some commentaries ask why the verse must be interpreted according to Rabbi Akiva as referring to intercourse alone, as there is an amoraic opinion that even according to Rabbi Akiva's opinion, there are several forbidden unions with regard to which betrothal does take effect, such as those that do not involve close relatives and those prohibited only due to positive mitzvot. The Rashba and the Ritva answer that the Gemara's question applies only to the amoraic opinion that, according to Rabbi Akiva, betrothal never takes effect in any forbidden union.

Juxtaposing his seed to him – מַקִּישׁ זַרְעוֹ לוֹ: The *Shela* explains that in the case discussed by the verse, the priest has not yet fathered a child. Therefore, the phrase "his seed" is superfluous.

HALAKHA

A *ḥalal* disqualifies – חָלָל פּוֹסֵל: Although it is permitted for any Jewish woman, even the daughter of a priest, to marry a *ḥalal*, their intercourse permanently disqualifies her from marrying into the priesthood and from partaking of *teruma* (Rambam *Sefer Kedusha, Hilkhot Issurei Bia* 18:1; *Shulḥan Arukh, Even HaEzer* 6:8).

A High Priest who engaged in intercourse with a widow – כֹּהֵן גָּדוֹל בְּאַלְמָנָה: A High Priest who engages in intercourse with a widow is liable to receive lashes even if he did not betroth her beforehand. As for her, she becomes a *ḥalula* and is disqualified from marrying into the priesthood (Rambam *Sefer Kedusha, Hilkhot Issurei Bia* 17:3).

HALAKHA

A second-generation Egyptian and a second-generation Edomite – **מִצְרִי שֵׁנִי וַאֲדוֹמִי שֵׁנִי**: It is prohibited for an Egyptian or Edomite convert and his son to enter the assembly of Israel by marriage, however, his grandson may marry an Israelite (Rambam *Sefer Kedusha, Hilkhot Issurei Bia* 12:19).

וְאֵימָא: עַד דְּאִיכָּא הֲוָיָה וּבִיאָה! דּוּמְיָא דְּכֹהֵן גָּדוֹל בְּאַלְמָנָה, מַה כֹּהֵן גָּדוֹל בְּאַלְמָנָה – בְּבִיאָה לְחוּדָהּ, אַף הַאי נַמִּי בְּבִיאָה לְחוּדָהּ.

The Gemara asks: **And** perhaps you should **say** that he does not disqualify her **until there is** both **betrothal and intercourse.** The Gemara again answers that this is **similar to a High Priest** who engaged in intercourse **with a widow: Just as a High Priest** who engaged in intercourse **with a widow** disqualifies her **through intercourse alone,**[N] **so too, this** man **also** disqualified her **through intercourse alone.**

״וְרַבִּי יוֹסֵי אוֹמֵר: כָּל שֶׁזַּרְעוֹ פָּסוּל – פּוֹסֵל, וְכָל שֶׁאֵין זַרְעוֹ פָּסוּל – אֵינוֹ פּוֹסֵל״. מַאי אִיכָּא בֵּין תַּנָּא קַמָּא לְרַבִּי יוֹסֵי?

§ It was taught in the *baraita* under discussion (68a) that **Rabbi Yosei says:** Of the men unfit to enter the assembly of Israel, **anyone whose offspring are** also **unfit disqualifies** a woman with whom he engaged in intercourse from the priesthood. However, **anyone whose offspring are not unfit does not disqualify** her. The Gemara asks: **What** difference **is there between the first *tanna*** of the *baraita* **and Rabbi Yosei?**

אֲמַר רַבִּי יוֹחָנָן: מִצְרִי שֵׁנִי וַאֲדוֹמִי שֵׁנִי אִיכָּא בֵּינַיְיהוּ.

Rabbi Yoḥanan said: The practical difference **between them** pertains to **a second**-generation **Egyptian and a second**-generation **Edomite.**[H] The children of these men, i.e., the third generation, may marry Jews of unflawed lineage. Therefore, according to Rabbi Yosei, they too do not disqualify a woman from the priesthood through intercourse with them. The first *tanna*, however, holds that they have the same status as a first-generation Egyptian or Edomite convert, in that they disqualify a woman from the priesthood through intercourse.

וּשְׁנֵיהֶם לֹא לְמָדוּהָ אֶלָּא מִכֹּהֵן גָּדוֹל בְּאַלְמָנָה. תַּנָּא קַמָּא סָבַר: מַה כֹּהֵן גָּדוֹל בְּאַלְמָנָה, שֶׁבִּיאָתוֹ בַּעֲבֵירָה – וּפוֹסֵל, אַף הַאי נַמִּי פּוֹסֵל.

And both *tanna'im* **derived** their respective opinions **only from** the case of **a High Priest** who engaged in intercourse **with a widow,** although they reached different conclusions. **The first *tanna* reasoned: Just as** with regard to **a High Priest** who engaged in intercourse **with a widow, his** act of **intercourse** with her **is a transgression, and** therefore **he disqualifies** her from the priesthood, **so too, this** man, a second-generation Egyptian or Edomite, **also disqualifies** her.

וְרַבִּי יוֹסֵי סָבַר: כְּכֹהֵן גָּדוֹל, מַה כֹּהֵן גָּדוֹל – שֶׁזַּרְעוֹ פָּסוּל וּפוֹסֵל, אַף כָּל שֶׁזַּרְעוֹ פָּסוּל פּוֹסֵל, לְאַפּוּקֵי מִצְרִי שֵׁנִי דְּאֵין זַרְעוֹ פָּסוּל, דִּכְתִיב: ״בָּנִים אֲשֶׁר יִוָּלְדוּ לָהֶם דּוֹר שְׁלִישִׁי יָבֹא לָהֶם בִּקְהַל ה׳״.

And Rabbi Yosei also **reasoned:** This is **like a High Priest** who engaged in intercourse with a widow. **Just as** the **High Priest's children are unfit** for the priesthood, **and he** himself **disqualifies** the widow from marrying into the priesthood, **so too, any** man **whose children are unfit** to marry Jews of unflawed lineage **disqualifies** a woman with whom he engaged in intercourse from marrying into the priesthood. This inference comes **to exclude a second**-generation **Egyptian, whose children are not unfit, as it is written: "The children of the third generation that are born to them may enter into the assembly of the Lord"** (Deuteronomy 23:9).

״רַבָּן שִׁמְעוֹן בֶּן גַּמְלִיאֵל אוֹמֵר: כָּל שֶׁאַתָּה נוֹשֵׂא בִּתּוֹ אַתָּה נוֹשֵׂא אַלְמָנָתוֹ״ וכו׳. מַאי אִיכָּא בֵּין רַבִּי יוֹסֵי לְרַבָּן שִׁמְעוֹן בֶּן גַּמְלִיאֵל?

It is taught in the *baraita* under discussion that **Rabban Shimon ben Gamliel says: Anyone whose daughter you may marry, you may marry his widow;** anyone whose daughter you may not marry, you may not marry his widow. The Gemara asks: **What difference is there between Rabbi Yosei and Rabban Shimon ben Gamliel?** They appear to be stating the same principle, that a man disqualifies a woman from the priesthood only if his children are unfit to marry Jews of unflawed lineage as well.

אֲמַר עוּלָּא: גֵּר עַמּוֹנִי וּמוֹאָבִי אִיכָּא בֵּינַיְיהוּ. וּשְׁנֵיהֶם לֹא לְמָדוּהָ אֶלָּא מִכֹּהֵן גָּדוֹל בְּאַלְמָנָה. רַבִּי יוֹסֵי סָבַר: מַה כֹּהֵן גָּדוֹל בְּאַלְמָנָה – שֶׁזַּרְעוֹ פָּסוּל וּפוֹסֵל, אַף כָּל שֶׁזַּרְעוֹ פָּסוּל – פּוֹסֵל.

Ulla said: The practical difference **between them** is in the case of **an Ammonite and a Moabite convert. And both of them derived** their respective opinions **from none other than** the case of **a High Priest with a widow. Rabbi Yosei reasoned: Just as** with regard to **a High Priest** who engaged in intercourse **with a widow, his children are unfit** for the priesthood **and he** himself **disqualifies** the widow, **so too, any** man **whose children are unfit disqualifies** a woman with whom he engaged in intercourse.

NOTES

Just as a High Priest who engaged in intercourse with a widow disqualifies her through intercourse alone – **מַה כֹּהֵן גָּדוֹל בְּאַלְמָנָה בְּבִיאָה לְחוּדָהּ**: *Tosefot HaRosh* asks why the Gemara assumes that a High Priest disqualifies a widow through intercourse, even if he did not betroth her. It is answered that from the juxtaposition in the verse (Leviticus 21:14–15) between the prohibition against a High Priest marrying a widow and the disqualification of his child from the priesthood as a result, it is derived that just as the child is disqualified whether or not his parents were betrothed, so too, the High Priest transgresses the prohibition and disqualifies the widow through intercourse alone, even without betrothal.

רַבָּן שִׁמְעוֹן בֶּן גַּמְלִיאֵל סָבַר: מָה כֹּהֵן גָּדוֹל בְּאַלְמָנָה – שֶׁכָּל זַרְעוֹ פָּסוּל וּפוֹסֵל, אַף שֶׁכָּל זַרְעוֹ פָּסוּל וּפוֹסֵל, לְאַפּוּקֵי עַמּוֹנִי וּמוֹאָבִי דְּאֵין כָּל זַרְעוֹ פָּסוּל, דְּאָמַר מָר: עַמּוֹנִי וְלֹא עַמּוֹנִית, מוֹאָבִי וְלֹא מוֹאָבִית.

Rabban Shimon ben Gamliel reasoned: Just as in the case of **a High Priest** who engaged in intercourse **with a widow, where all of his children** from her **are unfit** for the priesthood **and he disqualifies** her as well, **so too,** in the case of a man **all of whose children are unfit, he disqualifies** a woman with whom he engaged in intercourse. This is **to the exclusion of an Ammonite or a Moabite** convert, **as not all of his children are unfit** to marry Jews of unflawed lineage, **as the Master said: An Ammonite man** is unfit to enter the assembly **but not an Ammonite woman; a Moabite man** is unfit **but not a Moabite woman.**[NH] Since only the sons of an Ammonite or Moabite convert are unfit, they do not disqualify a woman with whom they engaged in intercourse from marrying into the priesthood.

מתני׳ הָאוֹנֵס וְהַמְפַתֶּה וְהַשּׁוֹטֶה – לֹא פּוֹסְלִין וְלֹא מַאֲכִילִין. וְאִם אֵינָן רְאוּיִין לָבֹא בְּיִשְׂרָאֵל – הֲרֵי אֵלּוּ פּוֹסְלִין. כֵּיצַד? (הָיָה) יִשְׂרָאֵל שֶׁבָּא עַל בַּת כֹּהֵן – תֹּאכַל בִּתְרוּמָה.

MISHNA In the case of **one who rapes** a woman without marrying her; **or one who seduces** a woman[H] without marrying her; **or an imbecile**[N] who engages in intercourse with a woman, even if he did marry her, if they are non-priests **they do not disqualify** the daughter of a priest from partaking of *teruma*, **and** if they are priests **they do not enable** an Israelite woman **to partake** of *teruma*. **And if they are not fit to enter** the assembly of **Israel** through marriage, **they disqualify** the daughter of a priest from partaking of *teruma*. **How so? If it was an Israelite who engaged in** extramarital **intercourse with the daughter of a priest, she may partake of** *teruma*, as this act of intercourse does not disqualify her.

NOTES

An Ammonite man but not an Ammonite woman, a Moabite man but not a Moabite woman – עַמּוֹנִי וְלֹא עַמּוֹנִית, מוֹאָבִי וְלֹא מוֹאָבִית: This ruling was introduced upon Ruth the Moabite's arrival in Bethlehem. It was not well known and was a cause of her rejection by her relatives before Boaz, the head of the Sanhedrin, married her (*Yalkut Shimoni*).

One who rapes, or one who seduces, or an imbecile, etc. – הָאוֹנֵס וְהַמְפַתֶּה וְהַשּׁוֹטֶה וכו׳: *Tosafot* ask why the mishna does not list a minor as well, as he too does not disqualify a woman from partaking of *teruma* through intercourse, nor can he enable her to partake of *teruma* if he is a priest. They answer that since the mishna subsequently discusses the case of a pregnant woman, it cannot list a minor, as he is incapable of impregnating a woman.

HALAKHA

An Ammonite man but not an Ammonite woman, a Moabite man but not a Moabite woman – עַמּוֹנִי וְלֹא עַמּוֹנִית, מוֹאָבִי וְלֹא מוֹאָבִית: Ammonite and Moabite men are permanently prohibited from entering the assembly of Israel by marriage. This includes their sons and their sons' sons until the end of time. However, an Ammonite or Moabite female convert is permitted to marry into the assembly immediately, just like converts from other nations (Rambam *Sefer Kedusha, Hilkhot Issurei Bia* 12:18; *Shulḥan Arukh, Even HaEzer* 4:2).

One who rapes or one who seduces a woman, etc. – הָאוֹנֵס וְהַמְפַתֶּה וכו׳: If the daughter of a priest was raped or seduced by an Israelite man, or if she engaged in intercourse with an imbecile Israelite, she is not disqualified from partaking of *teruma*, unless the intercourse was prohibited. If an Israelite woman had one of those experiences with a priest, the priest does not enable her to partake of *teruma* (Rambam *Sefer Zera'im, Hilkhot Terumot* 8:13).

Perek **VII**
Daf **69** Amud **b**

עִיבְּרָה – לֹא תֹּאכַל בִּתְרוּמָה, נֶחְתַּךְ הָעוּבָּר בְּמֵעֶיהָ – תֹּאכַל. הָיָה כֹּהֵן שֶׁבָּא עַל בַּת יִשְׂרָאֵל – לֹא תֹּאכַל בִּתְרוּמָה, עִיבְּרָה – לֹא תֹּאכַל, יָלְדָה – תֹּאכַל. נִמְצָא כֹּחוֹ שֶׁל בֵּן גָּדוֹל מִשֶּׁל אָב.

If he impregnated her, she may not partake of ***teruma*****,**[N] as she is carrying an Israelite fetus. **If the fetus was cut in her womb,**[H] i.e., she miscarried, **she may partake** of *teruma*. If the man **was a priest who engaged in** intercourse **with an Israelite woman, she may not partake of** ***teruma*****. If he impregnated her, she** still **may not partake** of *teruma*, as a fetus does not enable its mother to partake. **If she gave birth she may partake** due to her child, a priest.[H] It is therefore **found** in this case that **the power of the son is greater than** that **of the father,** as the father of this child does not enable the woman to partake of *teruma*, but the son does.

NOTES

If he impregnated her she may not partake of ***teruma*** – עִיבְּרָה לֹא תֹּאכַל בִּתְרוּמָה: This is not because the fetus is a non-priest, but because she partakes of *teruma* only as long as her body doesn't change due to pregnancy, as derived by the Gemara (67b) from the verse "As in her youth, she may eat of her father's bread" (Leviticus 22:13). Her body cannot be described as being "as in her youth" if she is pregnant (see Ritva).

HALAKHA

If the fetus was cut in her womb – נֶחְתַּךְ הָעוּבָּר בְּמֵעֶיהָ: If the daughter of a priest married an imbecile Israelite, or if she was raped or seduced by an Israelite, and she was impregnated, she may not partake of *teruma* due to the fetus. If she miscarried, she may partake of *teruma* (Rambam *Sefer Zera'im, Hilkhot Terumot* 8:14).

An Israelite woman impregnated by a priest – יִשְׂרְאֵלִית מְעוּבֶּרֶת מִכֹּהֵן: If an Israelite woman married an imbecile priest, or if she was raped or seduced by a priest, she may not partake of *teruma*, even if she is impregnated by him. However, once she has borne him a child, she may partake of *teruma* due to her child (Rambam *Sefer Zera'im, Hilkhot Terumot* 8:14).

NOTES

A slave disqualifies, etc. – הָעֶבֶד פּוֹסֵל וכו׳: A slave disqualifies a woman with whom he engaged in intercourse from partaking of *teruma*, but he does not disqualify his Jewish mother. This principle applies to a gentile as well. In addition, both a slave and a gentile whose paternal grandparents are a priest and an Israelite woman do not enable their grandmother to partake of *teruma*. Why, then, is this principle stated specifically with regard to a slave? The novel element of this case is explained in *Arukh LaNer*: Even the slave of a priest, who partakes of *teruma* himself, does not enable his Israelite grandmother to partake of *teruma*.

A *mamzer* disqualifies and enables a woman to partake of *teruma* – מַמְזֵר פּוֹסֵל וּמַאֲכִיל: The commentaries disagree as to whether a *mamzer* who is the son of a priest partakes of *teruma* himself. The Rambam holds that he is a *mamzer* priest. Others maintain that his mother became a *ḥalala* due to the forbidden intercourse through which he was conceived, and he is therefore rendered a *ḥalal*, who is unfit for the priesthood (Rosh; Ritva).

This son is a *mamzer* – הֲרֵי זֶה מַמְזֵר: This mishna is of the opinion that the child of an Israelite woman and a slave or a gentile man is a *mamzer*. The commentaries do not follow this opinion. However, the principle that a *mamzer* whose maternal grandfather is a priest enables his maternal grandmother to partake of *teruma* is accepted unanimously (Rambam's Commentary on the Mishna).

הָעֶבֶד פּוֹסֵל מִשּׁוּם בִּיאָה, וְאֵינוֹ פּוֹסֵל מִשּׁוּם זֶרַע. כֵּיצַד? בַּת יִשְׂרָאֵל לְכֹהֵן, בַּת כֹּהֵן לְיִשְׂרָאֵל, וְיָלְדָה הֵימֶנּוּ בֵּן, וְהָלַךְ הַבֵּן וְנִכְבַּשׁ עַל הַשִּׁפְחָה, וְיָלְדָה הֵימֶנּוּ בֵּן – הֲרֵי זֶה עֶבֶד. הָיְתָה אֵם אָבִיו בַּת יִשְׂרָאֵל לְכֹהֵן – לֹא תֹאכַל בִּתְרוּמָה, בַּת כֹּהֵן לְיִשְׂרָאֵל – תֹּאכַל בִּתְרוּמָה.

A slave disqualifies[N] a woman from partaking of *teruma* **due to** his engaging in **intercourse** with her, **and he does not disqualify** a woman **because** he is her **offspring. How so?** In what case would a slave theoretically disqualify a woman because he is her offspring? If an **Israelite woman** was married **to a priest,** or **the daughter of a priest** was married **to an Israelite; and she a bore him a son; and the son went and pressed himself onto a maidservant,** an epithet for intercourse used in this context due to the shame involved in having intercourse with a maidservant; **and she bore him a son,** then **this son is a slave.** If the latter's **father's mother was an Israelite** who was married **to a priest,** and her husband died, **she may not partake of *teruma*** due to her grandson, as he is not a priest but a slave. On the other hand, if **she was the daughter of a priest** married **to an Israelite,** and he died, leaving only this grandson, **she may partake of *teruma*,** as the grandson is not considered his father's offspring.[H]

מַמְזֵר פּוֹסֵל וּמַאֲכִיל. כֵּיצַד? בַּת יִשְׂרָאֵל לְכֹהֵן, וּבַת כֹּהֵן לְיִשְׂרָאֵל, וְיָלְדָה הֵימֶנּוּ בַּת, וְהָלְכָה הַבַּת וְנִישֵּׂאת לְעֶבֶד אוֹ לְגוֹי וְיָלְדָה הֵימֶנּוּ בֵּן – הֲרֵי זֶה מַמְזֵר. הָיְתָה אֵם אִמּוֹ בַּת יִשְׂרָאֵל לְכֹהֵן – תֹּאכַל בִּתְרוּמָה. בַּת כֹּהֵן לְיִשְׂרָאֵל – לֹא תֹאכַל בִּתְרוּמָה.

A *mamzer* disqualifies a woman from partaking of *teruma*, **and** he also **enables** a woman **to partake** of *teruma*.[NH] **How so?** If an **Israelite woman** was married **to a priest, or the daughter of a priest** was married **to an Israelite, and she bore him a daughter, and the daughter went and married a slave or a gentile and bore him a son, this son is a *mamzer*.**[N] If **his mother's mother was an Israelite woman** married **to a priest,** even if her husband died, **she may partake of *teruma*,** as she has surviving offspring from a priest. Conversely, if she is **the daughter of a priest** married **to an Israelite, she may not partake of *teruma*,** even after her Israelite husband's death, as she has offspring from him.

כֹּהֵן גָּדוֹל, פְּעָמִים שֶׁהוּא פּוֹסֵל, כֵּיצַד? בַּת כֹּהֵן לְיִשְׂרָאֵל וְיָלְדָה הֵימֶנּוּ בַּת, וְהָלְכָה הַבַּת וְנִיסֵּת לְכֹהֵן וְיָלְדָה הֵימֶנּוּ בֵּן – הֲרֵי זֶה רָאוּי לִהְיוֹת כֹּהֵן גָּדוֹל עוֹמֵד וּמְשַׁמֵּשׁ עַל גַּבֵּי הַמִּזְבֵּחַ, מַאֲכִיל אֶת אִמּוֹ, וּפוֹסֵל אֵם אִמּוֹ. זֹאת אוֹמֶרֶת: לֹא כִּבְנִי כֹּהֵן גָּדוֹל שֶׁהוּא פּוֹסְלֵנִי מִן הַתְּרוּמָה.

Even with regard to a **High Priest, sometimes he disqualifies**[H] his grandmother from partaking of *teruma*. **How so?** If **the daughter of a priest** was married **to an Israelite, and she bore him a daughter, and the daughter went and married a priest and bore him a son, this son is fit to be a High Priest,** who **stands and serves on the altar.** This son **enables his mother to partake** of *teruma*, as he is a priest. **And** yet, **he disqualifies his mother's mother** from partaking of *teruma*, as he is her offspring from her Israelite husband. **This** grandmother **can say** in disapproval: Let there **not** be many **like my** daughter's **son,** the **High Priest, as he disqualifies me from** partaking of ***teruma*.**

גמ׳ תָּנֵינָא לְהָא דְּתָנוּ רַבָּנַן: שׁוֹטֶה וְקָטָן שֶׁנָּשְׂאוּ נָשִׁים וָמֵתוּ – נְשׁוֹתֵיהֶן פְּטוּרוֹת מִן הַחֲלִיצָה וּמִן הַיִּיבּוּם.

GEMARA We already **learned that** the marriage of an imbecile is invalid, **as the Sages taught** in a *baraita*: With regard to **an imbecile and a minor boy who married women and died, their wives are exempt from *ḥalitza* and from levirate marriage.**[H]

HALAKHA

The son of a slave is not considered his offspring – בֶּן הָעֶבֶד אֵינוֹ נֶחְשָׁב לְזֶרַע: If an Israelite woman was married to a priest, or the daughter of a priest was married to an Israelite, and she bore a son, and that son engaged in intercourse with a maidservant and fathered a son, the son is rendered a slave. If the woman's son died and her grandson, the slave, is still alive, he is not considered his father's offspring. Therefore, if the woman is an Israelite who was married to a priest, she may not partake of *teruma* due to this grandson; if she is the daughter of a priest who was married to an Israelite, she is not disqualified from partaking of *teruma* because of him (Rambam *Sefer Zera'im*, *Hilkhot Terumot* 6:16).

A *mamzer* disqualifies and enables a woman to partake of *teruma* – מַמְזֵר פּוֹסֵל וּמַאֲכִיל: If the daughter of a priest was married to an Israelite, or an Israelite woman was married to a priest, and she bore him a daughter, and that daughter engaged in forbidden intercourse that renders her child a *mamzer*, the child is still considered the offspring of his grandparents. Therefore, if she is an Israelite woman married to a priest, she may partake of *teruma*; if she is the daughter of a priest married to an Israelite, she may not partake of *teruma* (Rambam *Sefer Zera'im*, *Hilkhot Terumot* 6:13–14).

A High Priest, sometimes he disqualifies – כֹּהֵן גָּדוֹל פְּעָמִים שֶׁהוּא פּוֹסֵל: If the daughter of a priest married an Israelite and bore him a daughter, and the daughter later married a priest and bore him a son, even if the daughter dies, her mother may not partake of *teruma* due to her grandson, who is her offspring from an Israelite. This is so even if the grandson becomes the High Priest (Rambam *Sefer Zera'im*, *Hilkhot Terumot* 6:15).

The wife of an imbecile or a minor – אֵשֶׁת שׁוֹטֶה וְקָטָן: The wife of an imbecile or a minor whose husband died is exempt from *ḥalitza* and levirate marriage, as their marriage was invalid (Rambam *Sefer Nashim*, *Hilkhot Yibbum* 6:8; *Shulḥan Arukh*, *Even HaEzer* 172:16).

§ It is stated in the mishna: **How so? If an Israelite engaged** in extramarital **intercourse with the daughter of a priest, she may partake of *teruma*. If he impregnated her, she may not partake** of *teruma*. The Gemara asks: **Since if he impregnated her she may not partake, let us be concerned** in any case of intercourse between an Israelite and the daughter of a priest **lest he impregnated her,**[N] thereby rendering it prohibited for her to partake of *teruma*. **Didn't we learn** in a mishna that if two men betrothed two women, and then at the time that they entered the wedding canopy, they accidently switched wives, and engaged in relations with each other's wives that night, in this case, after the accident is discovered, the court **removes** the wives from their husbands **for three months, lest they are pregnant** from the men they presumed to be their husbands and the fetus is therefore a *mamzer*, although they engaged in intercourse only once (33b)?

כֵּיצַד? הָיָה יִשְׂרָאֵל שֶׁבָּא עַל בַּת כֹּהֵן – תֹּאכַל בִּתְרוּמָה. עִיבְּרָהּ – לֹא תֹּאכַל. כֵּיוָן דְּעִיבְּרָהּ לֹא תֹּאכַל – לֵיחוּשׁ שֶׁמָּא עִיבְּרָהּ! מִי לָא תְּנַן: מַפְרִישִׁין אוֹתָן שְׁלֹשָׁה חֳדָשִׁים שֶׁמָּא מְעוּבָּרוֹת הֵן!

The Gemara answers that **Rabba, son of Rav Huna, said: About lineage** the Sages **were concerned,** and they therefore decreed a three-month separation of the husbands and wives, to prevent the possibility of a child being of uncertain lineage. However, **about** the prohibition against a non-priest eating ***teruma* they were not concerned.**[N] The Gemara asks: **And for *teruma* were they not concerned? Isn't it taught** in a *baraita* that if a husband says to his wife: **This is your bill of divorce**[H] **one hour before my death,** if she is an Israelite woman married to a priest **it is prohibited for her to partake of *teruma* immediately,** as the Sages were concerned that her husband might die within the hour?

אָמַר רַבָּה בַּר רַב הוּנָא: לְיוּחֲסִין חָשְׁשׁוּ, לִתְרוּמָה לֹא חָשְׁשׁוּ. וְלִתְרוּמָה לֹא חָשְׁשׁוּ? וְהָתַנְיָא: ״הֲרֵי זֶה גִּיטֵּיךְ שָׁעָה אַחַת קוֹדֶם לְמִיתָתִי״ – אֲסוּרָה לֶאֱכוֹל בִּתְרוּמָה מִיָּד!

Rather, Rabba, son of Rav Huna, said: About impregnation through an act of **marriage they were concerned,** but **about** impregnation through **licentious intercourse they were not concerned,**[N] as the woman generally takes precautions to ensure that she will not become pregnant.

אֶלָּא אֲמַר רַבָּה בַּר רַב הוּנָא: בְּנִישּׂוּאִין – חָשְׁשׁוּ, בִּזְנוּת – לֹא חָשְׁשׁוּ.

The Gemara asks: **And about marriage were they concerned? Isn't it taught** in a *baraita*: In the case of **the daughter of a priest who married an Israelite and** her husband **died** on that same day, **she immerses** to purify herself, as she is ritually impure due to their intercourse, **and she may partake of *teruma*** that same **evening?** Evidently, the Sages were not concerned that she became pregnant from the initial act of intercourse, even that of marriage.

וּבְנִישּׂוּאִין מִי חָשְׁשׁוּ? וְהָתַנְיָא: בַּת כֹּהֵן שֶׁנִּישֵּׂאת לְיִשְׂרָאֵל וָמֵת – טוֹבֶלֶת וְאוֹכֶלֶת בִּתְרוּמָה לָעֶרֶב!

Rav Ḥisda said: She immerses and partakes of *teruma* only **until forty** days after her husband's death, when there is still no reason for concern, **as if she is not pregnant** then **she is not pregnant. And if she is pregnant, until forty** days[B] from conception the fetus **is merely water.** It is not yet considered a living being, and therefore it does not disqualify its mother from partaking of *teruma*.

אֲמַר רַב חִסְדָּא: טוֹבֶלֶת וְאוֹכֶלֶת עַד אַרְבָּעִים, דְּאִי לָא מִיעַבְּרָא – הָא לָא מִיעַבְּרָא, וְאִי מִיעַבְּרָא – עַד אַרְבָּעִים מַיָּא בְּעָלְמָא הִיא.

HALAKHA

This is your bill of divorce, etc. – **הֲרֵי זֶה גִּיטֵּיךְ וכו׳**: If a priest said to his Israelite wife: This is your bill of divorce one hour before my death, it is prohibited for her to partake of *teruma* immediately, lest he die within the hour (Rambam *Sefer Zera'im, Hilkhot Terumot* 9:ו).

BACKGROUND

Until forty days – **עַד אַרְבָּעִים**: The Sages established this date as the definitive point in time from when a fetus is considered a human being, not only a growth of tissue. From the fortieth day onward, the human fetus no longer resembles that of animals, as the tail disappears, and the head, arms, and legs have a human shape to them. Although it is still very small and undeveloped, it can be visually recognized as human, and it can therefore be considered a human being. At one month, the human embryo has no visible, distinctly human characteristics.

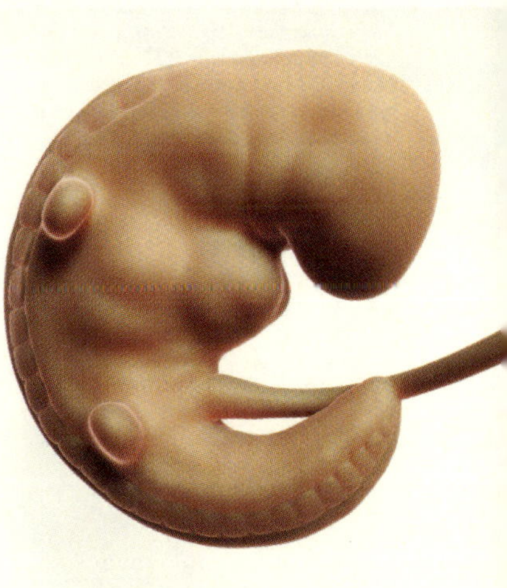

Digital rendering of a human embryo at one month

NOTES

Let us be concerned lest he impregnated her – **לֵיחוּשׁ שֶׁמָּא עִיבְּרָהּ**: The Ritva asks why the Gemara raises this question with regard to this clause of the mishna and not with regard to the first clause, which states that a man who rapes or seduces a woman does not disqualify her from partaking of *teruma*. He answers that the first clause can be interpreted as referring to a virgin, as that is the case of rape and seduction that is discussed in the Torah, and the Sages did not factor into their ruling the possibility of a virgin becoming pregnant from her first experience of intercourse.

About lineage the Sages were concerned, about *teruma* they were not concerned – **לְיוּחֲסִין חָשְׁשׁוּ, לִתְרוּמָה לֹא חָשְׁשׁוּ**: Apparently, temporary problems relating to *teruma* were less of a concern than the lasting stain of defective lineage. A principle is indicated in the Jerusalem Talmud that the Sages were not concerned about possible occurrences that would disqualify a woman from partaking of *teruma*. For example, an Israelite woman married to a priest whose husband went overseas may continue to partake of *teruma* in his absence, without worrying that he might have passed away.

About impregnation through licentious intercourse they were not concerned – **בִּזְנוּת לֹא חָשְׁשׁוּ**: Why does the mishna permit the wife of an imbecile to partake of *teruma*? *Tosafot* maintain that she also takes precautions to avoid pregnancy, and therefore the Sages were not concerned that she might be pregnant. The Maharsha infers from Rashi that perhaps there is concern that she is pregnant, and therefore she should partake of *teruma* only if she knows that she is not. However, it is stated in the Jerusalem Talmud that since the marriage of an imbecile is invalid, she is considered unmarried for all intents and purposes.

אמר ליה אביי: אי הכי, אימא סיפא: הוכר עוברה במעיה – תהא מקולקלת למפרע! מאי מקולקלת: עד ארבעים.

Abaye said to him: If so, say the latter clause of the *baraita*: Once **her fetus in her womb is noticeable,** she **is ruined retroactively.**[N] Her prior consumption of *teruma* is retroactively prohibited. Evidently, pregnancy immediately disqualifies her from partaking of *teruma*. Therefore, the reason that she may partake of *teruma* immediately after her husband's death is that the Sages were not concerned that she became pregnant. Rav Ḥisda responded: **What is** the period in which she is retroactively **ruined?** It is from the moment the fetus is noticeable and back in time **until forty** days from the beginning of her pregnancy. During the first forty days of the pregnancy, she is not retroactively ruined, as the fetus is not yet considered a living being.[H]

איתמר, הבא על ארוסתו בבית חמיו. רב אמר: הולד ממזר, ושמואל אמר: הולד שתוקי. אמר רבא: מסתברא מילתיה דרב – דדיימא מעלמא, אבל לא דיימא מעלמא – בתרא דידיה שדינן ליה.

It was stated: With regard to a man **who engaged in intercourse with his betrothed in his father-in-law's house,**[H] i.e., before they got married, **Rav said** that **the offspring is a** *mamzer*,[N] as the future husband is not considered his father. **And Shmuel said** that **the offspring is a** *shetuki*,[N] a child of unknown paternity. **Rava said: Rav's statement stands to reason** in a case **where she is rumored** to have engaged in intercourse **with others. However,** if **she is not rumored** to have engaged in intercourse **with others, we cast** the child **after him,** i.e., we assume that the child is the betrothed's son.

אמר רבא: מנא אמינא לה – דקתני: ילדה תאכל. היכי דמי? אילימא דדיימא מעלמא – ילדה אמאי תאכל? אלא לאו – מיניה דיימא ולא דיימא מעלמא.

Rava said: From where do I say that? What is the source for my assertion? The source is the mishna, which **teaches** that if a priest engaged in extramarital intercourse with an Israelite woman and she **gave birth, she may partake** of *teruma* due to her child, who is a priest. **What are the circumstances? If we say that she is rumored** to have engaged in intercourse **with others,** even if **she gave birth, why may she partake** of *teruma*? Shouldn't there be concern that the child's father is not the priest? **Rather, is it not** a case where **she is rumored** to have engaged in intercourse **with him and is not rumored** to have engaged in intercourse **with others?**

ומה התם, דלהאי איסורא ולהאי איסורא – בתרא דידיה שדינן ליה, הכא, דלהאי איסורא ולהאי היתירא – לא כל שכן?!

And if there, in the case of the mishna, **where** for her **to** engage in intercourse with **this** priest is **a prohibition, and to** engage in intercourse with **that** non-priest, with whom she is not rumored to have engaged in intercourse, is **a prohibition** of the same degree, nevertheless, **we cast** the child **after** the priest, then **here, where** for her **to** engage in intercourse with **that** man who is not her betrothed is a Torah **prohibition, and to** engage in intercourse with **this** man, her betrothed, **is permitted** by Torah law, is it **not all the more so** that her betrothed should be considered the father? Therefore, Rav's statement stands to reason only if the woman is rumored to have engaged in intercourse with others as well.

HALAKHA

The daughter of a priest who might be pregnant – בת כהן ספק מעוברת: If the daughter of a priest engaged in intercourse with an Israelite, there is no concern that she might have been impregnated, and she may immerse herself and eat *teruma* that evening, as stated by Rabba, son of Rav Huna. However, if she was married to an Israelite and her husband died, she may immerse and partake of *teruma* only for forty days. If she continues to partake of *teruma* after the forty days and it becomes noticeable that she is pregnant, she is retroactively considered to have sinned from after the forty days. However, during those forty days the fetus is considered merely water and does not disqualify her from partaking of *teruma* (Rambam *Sefer Zera'im*, *Hilkhot Terumot* 8:3).

A man who engaged in intercourse with his betrothed in his father-in-law's house – הבא על ארוסתו בבית חמיו: If a betrothed woman became pregnant while still living with her parents, and the couple agrees that the betrothed is the father, or if the woman claims that he is the father and he is unavailable for comment or says that he does not remember, the child is unflawed (Rema). This ruling follows the second version of the dispute between Rav and Shmuel, according to which Rav agrees with Shmuel in this case (Rambam *Sefer Kedusha*, *Hilkhot Issurei Bia* 15:17; *Shulḥan Arukh*, *Even HaEzer* 4:27).

NOTES

Ruined retroactively – מקולקלת למפרע: In what way is she ruined? Rashi explains that she must pay for the *teruma* she consumed and add a fifth. Rabbi Avraham min HaHar and other commentaries argue that the daughter of a priest is never obligated to pay for consumption of *teruma*, even *teruma* that she consumed unlawfully, as stated in *Torat Kohanim*. Accordingly, her ruin must be her transgression of a Torah prohibition.

The offspring is a ***mamzer*** **– הולד ממזר:** According to Rashi, the child is rendered a definite *mamzer*. However, the Rashba cites the Gemara in *Kiddushin* (75b), which indicates that Rav meant that the child is rendered a *mamzer* of uncertain status, who may not marry a Jew of unflawed lineage or a *mamzeret*.

A child whose father's identity is unknown [*shetuki*] – שתוקי: A child whose father's identity is not known is referred to as a *shetuki*, from the Hebrew root *sh-t-k*, which means to silence. The Gemara explains that when a *shetuki* calls his father, his mother silences him (*Kiddushin* 70a).

אָמַר לֵיהּ אַבַּיֵי: לְעוֹלָם אֵימָא לָךְ: כָּל הֵיכָא דְּדַיְימָא מִינֵּיהּ אַף עַל גַּב דְּלָא דַּיְימָא מֵעָלְמָא – אָמַר רַב הַוָּלָד מַמְזֵר, מַאי טַעֲמָא? דְּאָמְרִינַן: מִדְּאַפְקְרָא נַפְשָׁהּ לְגַבֵּי אָרוּס – אַפְקְרָא נַפְשָׁהּ לְעָלְמָא. וּמַתְנִיתִין – שֶׁהָיוּ שְׁנֵיהֶם חֲבוּשִׁים בְּבֵית הָאֲסוּרִין.

Abaye said to him in rejection of his proof: **Actually, I could say to you** that **anywhere that she is rumored** to have engaged in intercourse **with him,** her betrothed, **even if she is not rumored** to have engaged in intercourse **with others, Rav said** that **the offspring is a *mamzer*. What is the reason?** It is that **we say** that **since she exposed herself to her betrothed,**[N] although they were not married yet, **she** apparently **exposed herself to others** as well. **And the mishna** that you cited as support for your assertion is referring to a situation **where they were both incarcerated** alone together **in prison.** Therefore, there is no concern that she engaged in intercourse with another man. This is one version of the dispute between Rav and Shmuel.

איכָּא דְּאָמְרִי: בְּבָא עָלֶיהָ – כּוּלֵּי עָלְמָא לָא פְּלִיגִי דְּבַתְרֵיהּ דִּידֵיהּ שָׁדֵינַן לֵיהּ, וְהָכִי אִיתְּמַר: אֲרוּסָה שֶׁעִיבְּרָה, רַב אָמַר: הַוָּלָד מַמְזֵר, וּשְׁמוּאֵל אָמַר: הַוָּלָד שְׁתוּקִי. אֲמַר רָבָא: מִסְתַּבְּרָא מִילְּתֵיהּ דְּרַב – דְּלָא דַּיְימָא מִינֵּיהּ וְדַיְימָא מֵעָלְמָא,

Some say that **when** the betrothed admits that **he engaged in intercourse with her, everyone agrees that we cast** the child **after him.** Rather, their dispute **was stated as follows:** In the case of **a betrothed woman who became pregnant,**[H] if her betrothed denies that he engaged in intercourse with her, **Rav said** that **the offspring is a *mamzer*, and Shmuel said** that **the offspring is a child whose father's identity is not known. Rava said: Rav's statement stands to reason** in a case **where** the woman **is not rumored** to have engaged in intercourse **with him and she is rumored** to have engaged in intercourse **with others.** Therefore, it is assumed that the child is a *mamzer*.

NOTES

Since she exposed herself to her betrothed – מִדְּאַפְקְרָא נַפְשָׁהּ לְגַבֵּי אָרוּס: Sexual intercourse between a betrothed couple is prohibited only by rabbinic law. Accordingly, the blessing over betrothal: Blessed are You…Who prohibited us from incest, and forbade the betrothed to us, and permitted those married to us through a canopy and betrothal, is referring both to Torah and rabbinic prohibitions.

Early commentaries question Abaye's rationale, as intercourse between a betrothed couple is prohibited but the lineage of the child conceived through this act is completely untainted. This leads some commentaries to accept Rava's distinction and others to accept Shmuel's opinion.

HALAKHA

A betrothed woman who became pregnant – אֲרוּסָה שֶׁעִיבְּרָה: If a betrothed woman became pregnant while still living with her parents, and her betrothed denies having engaged in intercourse with her, the child is rendered a definite *mamzer*. If she is unavailable for questioning, or if she says that she does not know the father's identity, the child is rendered a *mamzer* of uncertain status.

If there are rumors that a betrothed woman engaged in licentious intercourse with her betrothed and with others, the child is rendered a *mamzer* of uncertain status, even if her betrothed admits that he engaged in intercourse with her. If she is questioned and says that she engaged in intercourse only with her betrothed, the child is rendered unflawed. It goes without saying that the child is unflawed if it is known that she engaged in intercourse with her betrothed and there are no rumors with regard to others. This ruling follows Shmuel's opinion as cited in the second version of the dispute. Some commentaries (Rosh; Rashba; *Beit Shmuel*) add that even if there were rumors that she engaged in intercourse with others, if it is known that she engaged in intercourse with her betrothed, or if he acknowledges the same, the child is unflawed, as stated by Rava (Rambam *Sefer Kedusha, Hilkhot Issurei Bia* 15:17–18; *Shulḥan Arukh, Even HaEzer* 4:27–28).

Perek **VII**
Daf **70** Amud **a**

אֲבָל דַּיְימָא מִנֵּיהּ, אַף עַל גַּב דְּדַיְימָא מֵעָלְמָא, בַּתְרֵיהּ דִּידֵיהּ שָׁדֵינַן לֵיהּ,

However, if **she is rumored** to have engaged in intercourse **with him,**[N] **even if she is** also **rumored** to have engaged in intercourse **with others, we cast** the child **after him.**

אֲמַר רָבָא: מְנָא אָמִינָא לָהּ, דְּקָתָנֵי: יָלְדָה – תֹּאכַל. הֵיכִי דָּמֵי? אִילֵימָא דְּדַיְימָא מִנֵּיהּ וְלָא דַּיְימָא מֵעָלְמָא – צְרִיכָא לְמֵימַר דְּתֵיכוּל?! אֶלָּא לָאו – דְּדַיְימָא נַמִי מֵעָלְמָא,

Rava said: From where do I say that? My source is the mishna that **teaches** that if a priest engaged in extramarital intercourse with an Israelite woman and she **gave birth, she may partake** of *teruma* due to her child. **What are the circumstances? If we say that she is rumored** to have engaged in intercourse **with him** and **she is not rumored** to have engaged in intercourse **with others, need it be said that she may partake** of *teruma*? It can easily be assumed that the priest is the father. **Rather, is it not** a case **where she is rumored** to have engaged in intercourse **with others as well?**

וּמָה הָתָם, דִּלְהַאי אִיסּוּרָא וּלְהַאי אִיסּוּרָא, בַּתְרֵיהּ דִּידֵיהּ שָׁדֵינַן לֵיהּ, הָכָא דִּלְהַאי אִיסּוּרָא וּלְהַאי הֶיתֵּירָא – לֹא כָּל שֶׁכֵּן?!

And if there, where for her **to** engage in intercourse with **this** priest is in violation of **a prohibition and to** engage in intercourse with **that** non-priest is in violation of **a prohibition** of the same degree, and she is rumored to have engaged in intercourse with both, nevertheless, **we cast** the child **after** the priest, then **here, where** for her **to** engage in intercourse with **that** man who is not her betrothed is in violation of a Torah **prohibition and to** engage in intercourse with **this** man, her betrothed, **is permitted** by Torah law, is it **not all the more so** that he should be considered the father?

NOTES

Rumored to have engaged in intercourse with him – דַּיְימָא מִינֵּיהּ: *Tosafot* explain that she is known to have engaged in intercourse with him. Otherwise, Rava's proof from the mishna, which discusses a case of definite sexual intercourse with an Israelite, is problematic. However, the wording of Rava's statement is difficult according to this opinion. Rabbi Avraham min HaHar explains that she is rumored to have had an extensive affair with him, which raises the probability that the child is his in the mishna's case.

אָמַר לֵיהּ אַבַּיֵי: לְעוֹלָם אֵימָא לָךְ, כָּל הֵיכָא דִּדַיְימָא מֵעָלְמָא, אַף עַל גַּב דְּדַיְימָא מִנֵּיהּ אֲמַר רַב הַוָּלָד מַמְזֵר, וּמַתְנִיתִין בִּדְלָא דַּיְימָא כְּלָל.

Abaye said to him: Actually, I could **say to you** that **anywhere that she is rumored** to have engaged in intercourse **with others, even if she is** also **rumored** to have engaged in intercourse **with him, Rav said** that **the offspring is a *mamzer*. And the mishna,** which you cited as support for your claim, is referring to a situation **where she is not rumored** to have engaged in intercourse with anyone **at all.** Therefore, if they both concur that he is the father, the child is considered his.

״הָעֶבֶד פּוֹסֵל מִשּׁוּם בִּיאָה״ כו׳. מַאי טַעְמָא? אָמַר קְרָא ״הָאִשָּׁה וִילָדֶיהָ תִּהְיֶה״ וגו׳.

§ It is stated in the mishna that **a slave disqualifies** a woman from partaking of *teruma* **due to** his engaging in **intercourse** with her, but not due to his being her offspring. The Gemara asks: **What is the reason** that he does not disqualify a woman whose offspring he is? **The verse states** with regard to a maidservant married to a Hebrew slave, that when he is released, **"the wife and her children shall be** her master's" (Exodus 21:4). This indicates that the maidservant's children are considered her own and are not considered their father's offspring at all. Therefore, a maidservant's child does not disqualify his paternal grandmother from partaking of *teruma*.

״מַמְזֵר פּוֹסֵל וּמַאֲכִיל״. תָּנוּ רַבָּנַן: ״וְזֶרַע אֵין לָהּ״, אֵין לִי אֶלָּא זַרְעָהּ, זֶרַע זַרְעָהּ מִנַּיִן? תַּלְמוּד לוֹמַר ״וְזֶרַע אֵין לָהּ״, מִכָּל מָקוֹם.

§ It is stated in the mishna that **a *mamzer* disqualifies** a woman from partaking of *teruma*, **and he** also **enables** a woman **to partake** of *teruma*. **The Sages taught:** The Torah states, "But if a priest's daughter be a widow, or divorced, **and have no child**… she may eat of her father's bread" (Leviticus 22:13). **I have** derived **only** that **her** own **child** disqualifies her from partaking of *teruma*; **from where** do I derive that **her child's child** disqualifies her as well? **The verse states: "And she has no child [*zera*]"** at all, indicating that even her grandchild disqualifies her, as *zera* means offspring.[H]

אֵין לִי אֶלָּא זֶרַע כָּשֵׁר, זֶרַע פָּסוּל מִנַּיִן? תַּלְמוּד לוֹמַר ״וְזֶרַע אֵין לָהּ״ – עַיֵּין עָלֶיהָ.

I have derived **only** that **an unflawed child** disqualifies her; **from where** do I derive that **an unfit child** disqualifies her[N] as well? **The verse states: "And she has no [*ein la*] child,"** which can be homiletically interpreted as **examine her [*ayyein ala*]** to check if she has any offspring, fit or unfit.

וְהָא אַפִּיקְתֵּיהּ לְזֶרַע זַרְעָהּ! זֶרַע זַרְעָהּ לָא אִיצְטְרִיךְ קְרָא, בְּנֵי בָנִים הֲרֵי הֵן כְּבָנִים, כִּי אִיצְטְרִיךְ קְרָא – לְזֶרַע פָּסוּל.

The Gemara asks: **But didn't you** already **derive** from that phrase **that her child's child** disqualifies her? The Gemara answers: To derive the *halakha* with regard to **her child's child, no verse was necessary,** as **the children of children are** considered **like children. The verse was** therefore **necessary for** deriving the *halakha* of **an unfit child.**

אָמַר לֵיהּ רֵישׁ לָקִישׁ לְרַבִּי יוֹחָנָן: כְּמַאן, כְּרַבִּי עֲקִיבָא, דְּאָמַר: יֵשׁ מַמְזֵר מֵחַיָּיבֵי לָאוִין? אֲפִילּוּ תֵּימָא רַבָּנַן, בְּעוֹבֵד כּוֹכָבִים וְעֶבֶד מוֹדוּ. דְּכִי אֲתָא רַב דִּימִי אָמַר רַבִּי יִצְחָק בַּר אַבְדִּימִי מִשּׁוּם רַבֵּינוּ: גּוֹי וְעֶבֶד הַבָּא עַל בַּת יִשְׂרָאֵל – הַוָּלָד מַמְזֵר.

Reish Lakish said to Rabbi Yoḥanan: In accordance with whose opinion is the assumption of the mishna that the child of a Jewess and a slave or a gentile is a *mamzer*? Is it **in accordance** only **with** the opinion of **Rabbi Akiva, who said** that the offspring of relations **for which** one **is liable** for violating **a prohibition is a *mamzer*?** The Gemara answers: **You** can **even say** that it is in accordance with **the Rabbis,** who hold that the offspring is a *mamzer* only if the parents are liable to receive *karet*. This is because **they concede with regard to a slave and a gentile, as when Rav Dimi came** from Eretz Yisrael to Babylonia, he said that **Rabbi Yitzḥak bar Avdimi said in the name of Rabbi** Yehuda HaNasi: With regard to **a gentile or a slave who engaged in intercourse with a Jewish woman, the offspring is a *mamzer*.**

״כֹּהֵן גָּדוֹל פְּעָמִים שֶׁפּוֹסֵל״. תָּנוּ רַבָּנַן: הֲרֵינִי כַּפָּרַת בֶּן בִּתִּי כּוּזָא – שֶׁמַּאֲכִילַנִי בִּתְרוּמָה, וְאֵינִי כַּפָּרַת בֶּן בִּתִּי כַּדָּא – שֶׁפּוֹסְלַנִי מִן הַתְּרוּמָה.

§ It was taught in the mishna that even **a High Priest sometimes disqualifies** his grandmother from partaking of *teruma*. **The Sages taught** that she can say in disapproval: **I am hereby atonement**[N] **for my daughter's son, the small jug [*kuza*],**[L] i.e., the *mamzer*. He is dear to me and I am willing to suffer to atone for him, **as he** is my offspring from a priest and therefore **enables me to partake of *teruma*. However, I am not** willing to be **atonement for my daughter's son, the large jug [*kada*],** the High Priest, **as he** is my offspring from an Israelite and therefore **disqualifies me from** partaking of *teruma*.

הדרן עלך אלמנה

HALAKHA

Her child and her child's child – זַרְעָהּ וְזֶרַע זַרְעָהּ: If an Israelite woman has a child from a priest she may partake of *teruma*, whether the child is male or female, or even if the child is a *tumtum*, one whose sexual organs are concealed, or a hermaphrodite. She may likewise partake of *teruma* due to her child's child, even if he is not a priest, or even if he is unfit to marry into the assembly of Israel (Rambam *Sefer Zera'im*, *Hilkhot Terumot* 6:12–13).

NOTES

From where do I derive that an unfit child disqualifies her – זֶרַע פָּסוּל מִנַּיִן: The commentaries ask how the mother of one who is unfit to marry into the assembly of Israel could possibly be allowed to partake of *teruma* as the daughter of a priest; the intercourse through which she conceived of him was prohibited, and it therefore rendered her a *zona*. In *Tosefot HaRosh*, it is answered that the *baraita* is referring to a grandchild. In *Tosafot Yeshanim*, it is suggested that the reference is to a woman who engaged in intercourse with an Egyptian or Edomite convert, which does not render her a *zona*.

I am hereby atonement, etc. – הֲרֵינִי כַּפָּרַת וכו׳: The *ge'onim* explain that this is an expression of affection. Rabbi Avraham min HaHar associates it with the expression one uses in relation to the deceased that he is mourning: I am hereby atonement for his resting-place. He therefore interprets the woman's statement to mean that she will mourn only her grandson the *mamzer* after his death and not the High Priest.

In *Arukh LaNer*, it is explained how a woman can partake of *teruma* due to one grandson and then be disqualified from partaking of *teruma* due to another grandson: She marries a priest and they have a son, and the son engages in forbidden intercourse, rendering his son a *mamzer*. After the woman is widowed, she marries an Israelite, and they have a daughter who marries a priest, and the couple's son is appointed as the High Priest. Before her daughter is born, she partakes of *teruma* due to her *mamzer* grandson. Afterward, even if her daughter dies, she does not partake of *teruma* due to her grandson the High Priest.

LANGUAGE

Small jug [*kuza*] – כּוּזָא: Apparently from the Middle Persian kūz, jug. In Hebrew and Arabic, it is called a كوز, *kūz*.

The sources that mention this term indicate that it is referring to a small jug, as opposed to a *kada*, which is a barrel, used mainly for storing drinks. A *kuza* was occasionally made out of metal but was usually ceramic, and it was used for drinking wine or water.

Summary of **Perek VII**

There is a principle, discussed in this chapter, that in a forbidden marriage between a priest and an Israelite woman, the wife may not partake of *teruma*, even if the marriage is valid. Therefore, her slaves may not partake of *teruma* either. However, her slaves of guaranteed investment may partake of *teruma*, as they are considered to be in the husband's possession.

This chapter also dealt with the principle that the daughter of a priest can be disqualified from partaking of *teruma* more easily than an Israelite woman can be entitled to partake of it. The daughter of a priest is disqualified from partaking of *teruma* by having a levirate bond with an Israelite, being impregnated by an Israelite, or engaging in intercourse with a man who is unfit for her, even if he is only nine years old. Only actual marriage to an adult priest or bearing his child entitle her to partake of *teruma*.

With regard to the definition of a woman who has children from a priest or a non-priest, any living Jewish offspring counts. This includes descendants and those who are unfit to marry into the assembly of Israel. However, descendants from gentile women or maidservants are excluded.

Image **Credits**

All images are copyright © Koren Publishers Jerusalem Ltd., except:

p399 2nd image © foaloce, www.shutterstock.com; **p416** 1st image © Or P; **p416** 3rd image © Offengenden; **p428** © Ryan Kilpatrick; **p446** © Erga Aloni, courtesy of Tzemaḥ HaSadeh, www.wildflowers.co.il; **p463** © Sebastian Kaulitzki, www.shutterstock.com

My Notes

תלמוד בבלי

— מהדורת נאה —

יבמות חלק ד

Steinsaltz
Center

ירושלים

KOREN

Please note that the number ranges that appear at the bottom of each daf of the Vilna pages indicate the corresponding pages of the Koren Talmud Bavli translation and commentary.

תלמוד בבלי

הוצאת קורן ירושלים

— מהדורת נאה —

מסכת יבמות
דף נג: עד דף ע.

COMMENTARY BY

Rabbi Adin Even-Israel
Steinsaltz

EDITOR-IN-CHIEF

Rabbi Dr Tzvi Hersh Weinreb

EXECUTIVE EDITOR

Rabbi Joshua Schreier

•

STEINSALTZ CENTER
KOREN PUBLISHERS JERUSALEM

"חָלַץ וְעָשָׂה מַאֲמָר וְנָתַן וכו'".§ בִּשְׁלָמָא חָלַץ וְעָשָׂה מַאֲמָר אִיצְטְרִיךְ, סד"א: נִגְזוֹר מַאֲמָר דְּבָתַר חֲלִיצָה אַטּוּ מַאֲמָר דְּקַמֵּי חֲלִיצָה — קמ"ל דְּלָא גָּזְרִינַן. אֶלָּא חָלַץ וְנָתַן גֵּט לָמָּה לִי? וּלְטַעְמֵיךְ אֵימָא סֵיפָא: בָּעַל וְעָשָׂה מַאֲמָר, בָּעַל וְנָתַן גֵּט — בִּשְׁלָמָא בָּעַל וְנָתַן גֵּט אִיצְטְרִיךְ, סד"א: נִגְזוֹר גֵּט דְּבָתַר בְּעִילָה אַטּוּ גֵּט דְּקַמֵּי בְּעִילָה, קמ"ל דְּלָא גָּזְרִינַן. אֲבָל בָּעַל וְעָשָׂה מַאֲמָר לָמָּה לִי? אֶלָּא: אַיְּידֵי דְּתָנָא חָלַץ וְעָשָׂה מַאֲמָר — תָּנָא נַמִּי בָּעַל וְעָשָׂה מַאֲמָר, וְאַיְּידֵי דְּבָעֵי לְמִיתְנֵי בָּעַל וְנָתַן גֵּט — תָּנָא נַמִּי חָלַץ וְנָתַן גֵּט.§ "בֵּין שֶׁהִיא וכו'".§ מַתְנִיתִין דְּלָא כִּי הַאי תַּנָּא, דְּתַנְיָא, אַבָּא יוֹסֵי בֶּן יוֹחָנָן אִישׁ יְרוּשָׁלַיִם אוֹמֵר מִשּׁוּם רַבִּי מֵאִיר: אַחַת בְּעִילָה וְאַחַת חֲלִיצָה, בַּתְּחִלָּה — אֵין אַחֲרֶיהָ כְּלוּם, בָּאֶמְצַע וּבַסּוֹף — יֵשׁ אַחֲרֶיהָ כְּלוּם. וְשָׁלֹשׁ מַחְלוֹקוֹת בַּדָּבָר, תַּנָּא קַמָּא סָבַר: בִּיאָה דְּאִיתָא לְמִיגְזַר — גָּזְרִינַן, חֲלִיצָה דְּלֵיתָא לְמִיגְזַר — לָא גָּזְרִינַן. וְר' נְחֶמְיָה סָבַר: בִּיאָה נַמִּי לֵיתָא לְמִיגְזַר. וְקָאָמְרַתְּ: לִיגְזוֹר בִּיאָה אַחַר הַגֵּט מִשּׁוּם בִּיאָה אַחַר חֲלִיצָה — כֵּיוָן דַּחֲלִיצָה דְּאוֹרָיְיתָא, מֵידָע יָדְעִי. וְקָאָמְרַתְּ לִיגְזוֹר בִּיאָה אַחַר מַאֲמָר מִשּׁוּם בִּיאָה אַחַר בִּיאָה — כֵּיוָן דְּבִיאָה דְּאוֹרָיְיתָא, הָא מֵידָע יָדְעִי. וְאַבָּא יוֹסֵי בֶּן חָנָן סָבַר לָהּ כְּרַבָּנַן דְּגָזְרִי בְּבִיאָה, וְגָזַר חֲלִיצָה מִשּׁוּם בִּיאָה.§

הדרן עלך רבן גמליאל

הַבָּא [א]עַל יְבִמְתּוֹ, בֵּין בְּשׁוֹגֵג בֵּין בְּמֵזִיד בֵּין בְּאוֹנֶס בֵּין בְּרָצוֹן, אֲפִי' הוּא שׁוֹגֵג וְהִיא מְזִידָה, הוּא מֵזִיד וְהִיא שׁוֹגֶגֶת, הוּא אָנוּס וְהִיא לֹא אֲנוּסָה, הִיא אֲנוּסָה וְהוּא לֹא אָנוּס. אֶחָד הַמְעָרֶה וְאֶחָד הַגּוֹמֵר — קָנָה, וְלֹא חִילֵּק בֵּין בִּיאָה לְבִיאָה. [ב]וְכֵן הַבָּא עַל אַחַת מִכָּל הָעֲרָיוֹת שֶׁבַּתּוֹרָה, אוֹ פְּסוּלוֹת, כְּגוֹן: אַלְמָנָה לְכ"ג, גְּרוּשָׁה וַחֲלוּצָה לְכֹהֵן הֶדְיוֹט, מַמְזֶרֶת וּנְתִינָה לְיִשְׂרָאֵל, בַּת יִשְׂרָאֵל לְמַמְזֵר וּלְנָתִין — פְּסָלָהּ, וְלֹא חִילֵּק בֵּין בִּיאָה לְבִיאָה.§

גמ' מַאי אֲפִי'? לָא מִיבַּעְיָא קָאָמַר: לָא מִיבַּעְיָא הוּא שׁוֹגֵג וְהִיא קָמְכַוְּונָה לְמִצְוָה, אִי נַמִּי הוּא מֵזִיד וְהִיא קָמְכַוְּונָה לְמִצְוָה, אֶלָּא אֲפִי' הוּא שׁוֹגֵג וְהִיא מְזִידָה(א), דְּתַרְוַיְיהוּ לָא קָמְכַוְּונֵי לְשֵׁם מִצְוָה — אֲפִילּוּ הָכִי קָנָה. תָּנֵי ר' חִיָּיא: אֲפִי' *שְׁנֵיהֶם שׁוֹגְגִים, שְׁנֵיהֶם מְזִידִים, שְׁנֵיהֶם אֲנוּסִים. אָנוּס דְּמַתְנִיתִין הֵיכִי דָּמֵי? אִילֵימָא כְּשֶׁאֲנָסוּהוּ גּוֹיִם וּבָא עָלֶיהָ — וְהָאָמַר רָבָא: [ג]אֵין אוֹנֶס לְעֶרְוָה, לְפִי שֶׁאֵין קִישּׁוּי אֶלָּא לְדַעַת. אֶלָּא בְּיָשֵׁן — וְהָאָמַר רַב יְהוּדָה: יָשֵׁן

רש"י

חָלַץ וְעָשָׂה מַאֲמָר. לְיַבֵּם אֶחָד וְיִבֵּם אֶת הַשְּׁנִיָּה, דְּאוֹקְמֵיהּ דִּצְרִיךְ לְמִתְנְיֵיהּ. בִּשְׁלָמָא חָלַץ וְעָשָׂה מַאֲמָר אִיצְטְרִיךְ. לְמִיתְנֵי דְּלֵיתוֹ כְּלוּם. סד"א. אֲפִי' לְר' עֲקִיבָא. לִיגְזוֹר מַאֲמָר דְּבָתַר חֲלִיצָה, דְּלִיבְעֵי גֵּט אַטּוּ מַאֲמָר דְּמִקַּמֵּי חֲלִיצָה, קמ"ל דְּלָא גָּזְרִינַן. אֶלָּא חָלַץ וְנָתַן גֵּט. לְיַבֵּם אֶחָד וְיִבֵּם אֶת הַשְּׁנִיָּה, לָמָּה לִי כו'? לְמַאי לִיתְנֵי הַאי גֵּט? אִי לְמִיקְנְיֵהּ — הָא אִיתְּפְקַע לֵיהּ זִקּוּקוֹתֶיהָ עָלָיו. וּלְטַעְמֵיךְ בָּעַל וְעָשָׂה מַאֲמָר. יִבֵּם וְיִבֵּם אֶת הַשְּׁנִיָּה לָמָּה לִי? בִּשְׁלָמָא בָּעַל וְנָתַן גֵּט — אִיצְטְרִיךְ לְמִתְנֵי אֵין אַחַר בִּיאָה כְּלוּם, דְּנִפְקָא מִינָּהּ גִּיטָּא וְלָא בָּעְיָא חֲלִיצָה, דְּבִיאָה קַנְיָיא מִשֶּׁקַּעְתָּהּ לְזִיקָה. סד"א לִגְזוֹר גֵּט דְּבָתַר בִּיאָה. דְּלָא תִּיסְגֵּי לֵיהּ בְּגֵט בְּלָא חֲלִיצָה — אַטּוּ גֵּט דְּמִקַּמֵּי בִּיאָה, דְּלָא לֵימְרוּ גֵּט סַגֵּי בִּיבָמָה דְּזִיקוּקָה חֲלִיצָה. אֶלָּא בָּעַל וְעָשָׂה מַאֲמָר לְמַאי קָבָעֵי אִיתְנוּיֵי? הָלֹא אִשְׁתּוֹ הִיא. אֶלָּא. אַיְּידֵי דִּתְנָא חָלַץ וְעָשָׂה מַאֲמָר דְּאִיצְטְרִיךְ לֵיהּ, כִּדְאָמְרַן, תְּנָא נַמִּי כו'. וְשָׁלֹשׁ מַחְלוֹקוֹת בַּדָּבָר. תַּנָּא קַמָּא. דְּמַתְנִיתִין, דְּקָאָמַר חֲלִיצָה פְּסוּלָה אֵין אַחֲרֶיהָ כְּלוּם, אֲבָל בִּיאָה פְּסוּלָה יֵשׁ אַחֲרֶיהָ כְּלוּם. וְר' נְחֶמְיָה. דְּאָמַר: אַחַת זוֹ וְאַחַת זוֹ אֵין אַחֲרֶיהָ כְּלוּם. וְאַבָּא יוֹסֵי בֶּן חָנָן. דְּאָמַר: אַחַת זוֹ וְאַחַת זוֹ יֵשׁ אַחֲרֶיהָ כְּלוּם בָּאֶמְצַע וּבַסּוֹף. כִּדְפָרֵישְׁנָא לֵיהּ בְּמַתְנִיתִין. בִּיאָה — דְּאִיכָּא לְמִיגְזַר כִּדְאָמְרַן בְּרֵישׁ פִּירְקִין (לעיל נ:), אִי בִּיאָה אַחַר הַגֵּט הִיא — גָּזְרִינַן בִּיאָה אַחַר הַגֵּט מִשּׁוּם בִּיאָה אַחַר חֲלִיצָה, דְּלָא לֵיתֵי לְמִיבְעַל אַחַר חֲלִיצָה. וְאִי בִּיאָה אַחַר מַאֲמָר כו'. חֲלִיצָה לֵיכָּא לְמִיגְזַר, כִּדְאָמַר בְּרֵישׁ פִּירְקִין (שם).

הדרן עלך רבן גמליאל

הַבָּא עַל יְבִמְתּוֹ שׁוֹגֵג. כְּסָבוּר שֶׁהִיא אִשְׁתּוֹ, אוֹ אִשָּׁה אַחֶרֶת. מֵזִיד. לְשֵׁם זְנוּת, וְלֹא לְשׁוּם מִצְוָה. אֲפִי'. מְפָרֵשׁ בַּגְּמָרָא. הַמְעָרֶה. שֶׁלֹּא גָּמַר בִּיאָתוֹ. קָנָה. וְזָכָה בַּנַּחֲלָה, וְיוֹצִיאָהּ בְּגֵט אִם בָּא לְהוֹצִיאָהּ. בֵּין בִּיאָה לְבִיאָה. [בֵּין בִּיאָה כְּדַרְכָּהּ לְשֶׁלֹּא כְּדַרְכָּהּ, וּבֵין הַעֲרָאָה לִגְמַר בִּיאָה]. וְכֵן הַבָּא עַל אַחַת מִכָּל הָעֲרָיוֹת. בְּאַחַת מִכָּל הַבִּיאוֹת הַלָּלוּ. אוֹ פְּסוּלוֹת. לִכְהוּנָּה, כְּגוֹן אַלְמָנָה כו'. פְּסָלָהּ לִכְהוּנָּה. מִשּׁוּם זוֹנָה. [וּגְרוּשָׁה מִיפַּסְלָא (ב) מִתְּרוּמָה דְּבֵי נָשָׁא אִם הִיא בַּת כֹּהֵן, דְּשַׁוְּיָהּ חֲלָלָה]. וְדַוְקָא עֲרָיוֹת אוֹ פְּסוּלוֹת, אֲבָל בִּיאַת זְנוּת דִּפְנוּיָה — לָא מְשַׁוְּיָא לָהּ זוֹנָה, וְלֹא פְּסָלָהּ מִן הַכְּהוּנָּה. דְּלָא אַשְׁכְּחָנָא תַּנָּא דְּפָסֵל אֶלָּא רַבִּי אֶלְעָזָר, דְּאָמַר: פָּנוּי הַבָּא עַל הַפְּנוּיָה שֶׁלֹּא לְשֵׁם אִישׁוּת עֲשָׂאָהּ זוֹנָה, לְקַמָּן בְּפִירְקִין*. מַמְזֶרֶת וּנְתִינָה. לָאו אַפְּסוּלָה לִכְהוּנָּה קָאֵי — דְּהָא פְּסוּלָה וְקַיְּימָא. וּלְעִנְיַן תְּרוּמָה דְּבֵי נָשָׁא נַמִּי לֵיכָּא לְמֵימַר. וְעוֹד, בִּיאַת כָּשֵׁר מַאי מִגְרְעָא לָהּ? אֶלָּא לְעִנְיַן הַעֲרָאָה נְקָטָהּ, וּלְמִילְקֵי עֲלֶיהָ הַאי יִשְׂרָאֵל בְּהַעֲרָאָה כִּגְמַר בִּיאָה.

גמ' אֶלָּא אֲפִילּוּ הוּא שׁוֹגֵג. כְּסָבוּר אִשָּׁה אַחֶרֶת הִיא. וְהִיא מְזִידָה. לְבִיאַת זְנוּת מְכַוֶּונֶת. דְּתַרְוַיְיהוּ לָא מִיכַּוְּונֵי לְמִצְוָה. אֲפִילּוּ הָכִי קָנֵי. אֶלָּא בְּיָשֵׁן. שֶׁנִּתְקַשָּׁה כְּשֶׁהוּא יָשֵׁן.

תוספות

הבא על יבמתו בין בשוגג בין במזיד. איכא למימר דמזיד ורצון תרי גווני ניניהו. דרצון היינו דמכוין למצוה, אע"ג דפשיטא הוא – קתני ליה, דהכי אורחיה בכל דוכתא. אבל בפ"ב דב"ק (דף כו: *ושם) גבי אדם מועד לעולם קשה: מה בין מזיד לרצון? וי"מ דה"ק: בין שיהא אותו שוגג ומזיד באונס, שאנסו לעשות כן, בין שיהא ברצון*.

הוא אנוס והיא לא אנוסה. תימה: דהוה ליה למינקט שניהם אנוסים, דהוי רבותא טפי! וי"ל: דאגב דנקט ברישא הוא שוגג והיא מזידה – נקט נמי הכא הוא אנוס והיא לא אנוסה. א"נ: לא קאמר והיא לא אנוסה אלא ברצון, אלא היא לא אנוסה אבל מזידה או שוגגת, דהשתא תרוייהו לא מיכווני לשם מצוה. **ולא** חילק בין ביאה לביאה. פי' הקונטרס: בין הערא לגמר ביאה. ובבבא שניה פירש: ולא חילק בין ביאה לביאה – בין כדרכה לשלא כדרכה. ואין נראה לר"י: דכיון דתנא סבר אחד המערה ואחד הגומר – למה ליה תו למיתני ולא חילק בין הערא לגמר ביאה? ועוד: דבגמ' (לקמן דף נו:) מפרש "מאי וכן" אשלא כדרכה בחייבי לאוין, מכלל דלא חילק דרישא איירי בשלא כדרכה! ונראה לר"י שהסופרים טעו וכתבו איפכא. ומיהו, ההיא דבבא שניה אפשר לפרשו כמו הראשון בין כדרכה לשלא כדרכה, ולפרושי "וכן" קאתי.

שאנסוהו גוים ובא עליה. אין לפרש שאנסוהו – היינו שאיימו עליו להרגו אם לא יבא עליה – דא"כ מאי פריך מרבא דאמר: אין קישוי אלא לדעת? פירוש: דאין זה אונס, שקישוי עושה מדעת, ואין דוחקין אותו לבעול בקישוי, ולוקמא כגון שמאיימין עליו לבעול בקישוי! ועוד: דמילתא דרבא אי אפשר לפרש במאיימין עליו להורגו אם לא שיבעול הערוה מעצמו, כמו שאפרש. אלא כל דבר שעושה מעצמו, אפילו ע"י אונס פחד מיתה לדעת חשיב. והאי שאנסוהו גוים ובא עליה דקאמר – היינו שהביאוהו עליה והדביקוהו ביבמתו, ולא שבא עליה מעצמו, כמו תקפתו יבמתו ובא עליה דבסמוך. והשתא פריך שפיר דאין אונס, דקישוי לא הוי אלא לדעת. ואר"י: דיש לדקדק מכאן דאין יבמה נקנית אלא בבא עליה בקישוי, מדלא מוקמי שהדביקוהו בלא קישוי. ואיכא למימר דאתי הך סוגיא כמ"ד: *משמש מת בעריות פטור, וילפינן קיאה מעריות דאינה נקנית אלא בקישוי. ועוד אר"י: דאתיא שפיר אפילו למאן דאמר משמש מת בעריות חייב, ולענין יבום – בעינן ביאה דרך הקמת שם.

אין אונס לערוה שאין קישוי אלא לדעת. אין לפרש במאיימין עליו להורגו אם לא יבא בעצמו על הערוה – דאם כן אפילו יש קישוי שלא לדעת תיפוק ליה דאגילוי עריות יהרג ואל יעבור, כדאמר בפרק "בן סורר" (סנהדרין דף עד. ושם), – אלא איירי כשגוים מדביקים אותו על הערוה, וא"א לו להשמט אם לא ע"י שיהרג. וקאמר רבא דיש לו למסור עצמו ליהרג אם יודע שאי אפשר לו אם לא יתקשה, דאין קישוי אלא לדעת(א), וחשיב כעושה מעשה. אבל אם יש קישוי שלא לדעת, או שהיה כבר מקושה, או שיודע שלא יתקשה – אין חייב למסור עצמו, כיון שהוא אינו עושה שום מעשה, והוי כקרקע עולם, כדאמר ב"בן סורר" (ג"ז שם) גבי אסתר, דקרקע עולם היתה. וטעמא, משום דנערה המאורסה ילפינן התם מרוצח

עין משפט נר מצוה

א א מיי' פ"ב מהלכות יבום הלכה ג סמג עשין נא טוש"ע אה"ע סי' קסו סעי' ז:

[עמ"ש שם על הגליון]

[ועי' פרש"י במס' ע"ז נג. ד"ה מזיד כו' ובפרש"י פסחים עז: ד"ה בין ביחיד וברש"י מנחות כה: ד"ה שוגג]

ב ב מיי' פ"א מהלכות איסורי ביאה הלכה יז ופי"ח הלכה ו סמג לאוין קכו טוש"ע שם סימן ו סעי' ט וסימן כ סעיף א:

ג ג מיי' פ"א מהלכות איסורי ביאה הל' ט:

תוספות ישנים

א) וא"ת ולמה ליה קישוי הלא אמרי' משמש מת בעריות חייב וי"ל דס"ל פטור. א"נ א) אפי' למ"ד חייב היינו משום שהיה לו לפרוש בהנאה מועטת ופירש בהנאה מרובה אבל הכא שהדביקו גוים כבר לא מתחייב עד שיקשה שהרי נאנס הוא ולא יכול לפרוש.

א) לכאורה אינו מובן דמה ענין בכאן שהיה לו לפרוש בהנאה מועטת ולא שייך זה רק גבי משמש עם הטהורה ואמרה לו נטמאתי ופירש מיד ועי' בשבועות י"ח.

תוספות חד מקמאי

פרק הבא על יבמתו. הא דתנן הבא על יבמתו פרישנא בגמ' ה"ק ל"מ הוא שוגג והיא מכוונה למצוה. א"נ הוא מזיד והיא מכוונה למצוה. [אלא] אפילו הוא שוגג והיא מזידה פירוש לזנות דתרווייהו לא מכווני למצוה קנה. תני רבי חייא אפילו שניהם מזידין שניהם אנוסים. אנוס דמתני' ה"ד אילימא שאנסוהו גוים ובא עליה. והא אמר [רבא] אין אונס בערוה שאין קישוי אלא לדעת אלא בישן והאמר רב יהודה ישן לא קנה ביבמתו

מסורת הש"ס

[שבועות עב. וש"נ]

שבועות יח. לקמן נה:

רש"ל

רש"ל

[עי' תוס' מעילה ב. ד"ה שחטן]

[דף נט:]

[א]ישן לא קנה ביבמתו! אלא — בנתקע? והא אמר *רבה: [ב]נפל מן הגג ונתקע — חייב בארבעה דברים, [ג]וביבמתו לא קנה! אלא: כגון שנתכוון לאשתו, ותקפתו יבמתו, ובא עליה, שניהם אנוסים דבי רבי חייא היכי דמי? כגון שנתכוון לאשתו, ותקפוהו גוים ודבקום זה בזה, ובא עליה. מנא הני מילי? דתנו רבנן: "°יבמה יבא עליה" מצוה. דבר אחר: "יבמה יבא עליה" בין בשוגג בין *במזיד, בין באונס בין ברצון. והא אפיקתיה למצוה! למצוה °מ"ואם לא יחפוץ האיש" נפקא, הא חפץ — יבם, וכי אתא קרא — בין בשוגג בין במזיד בין באונס בין ברצון. תניא אידך: *"יבמה יבא עליה" כדרכה, "ולקחה" שלא כדרכה. *"ויבם" [ד]ביאה גומרת בה [ה]ואין כסף ושטר גומרין בה. "ויבמה" בעל כרחה.(א) ד"א: "יבמה יבא עליה" בין בשוגג כו'. והא אפיקתי' לכדרכה! ההוא °מ"להקים לאחיו שם" נפקא, במקום שמקים שם. וכי אתא קרא — בין בשוגג בין במזיד בין באונס בין ברצון. גופא, אמר רב יהודה: ישן לא קנה ביבמתו, דאמר קרא "יבמה יבא עליה" עד דמכוין לה לשם ביאה. והתניא: בין ער [בין ישן! אימא: בין ערה בין ישנה. והתניא: בין ער] הוא בין ישן הוא. [ו]בין ערה היא בין ישנה היא! הכא במאי עסקינן — במתנמנם. *ה"ד מתנמנם? אמר רב אשי: נים ולא נים, תיר ולא תיר, כגון דקרו ליה ועני, ולא ידע לאהדורי סברא, וכי מדכרו ליה מדכר. גופא, אמר רבה: נפל מן הגג ונתקע חייב בארבעה דברים, וביבמתו לא קנה: בנזק, בצער, בשבת, ברפוי, אבל בושת לא מיחייב, *דאמר מר: [ז]אין חייב על הבושת עד שיתכוון. אמר רבא: [ח]נתכוון להטיח בכותל והטיח ביבמתו — לא קנה. להטיח בבהמה והטיח ביבמה — קנה, דהא קמכוין לשם ביאה בעולם. § "אחד המערה". §

אמר עולא: מנין להעראה מן התורה? שנאמר °"ואיש אשר ישכב את אשה דוה וגלה את ערותה את מקורה הערה" מכאן להעראה מן התורה. אשכחן נדה, שאר עריות מנין? וכ"ת: נילף מנדה — [ט]מה לנדה שכן מטמאה את בועלה! אלא: אתיא מאשת אח, דכתיב °"ואיש אשר יקח את אשת אחיו נדה היא", וכי אשת אחיו [לעולם] נדה היא? אלא: כנדה, מה נדה בהעראה — אף אשת אח בהעראה. מה לאשת אח שכן בידו לרבות, דאי בעי מקדש ואזיל כי אלפא! אלא אתיא מאחות אב ואחות אם, דכתיב °"וערות אחות אמך ואחות אביך לא תגלה כי את שארו הערה" איכא למיפרך: מה לאחות אב ואחות אם — שכן איסור הבא מאליו! מחדא לא אתיא, תיתי [חדא] מתרתי. מהי תיתי? תיתי מאשת אח ואחות אב ואחות אם — מה להנך, שכן אסורין משום שאר! אלא תיתי מנדה ואחות אב ואחות אם — מה להנך, שכן איסור הבא מאליו! אלא תיתי מנדה ואשת אח, דמאי פרכת? מתקיף לה רב אחא בריה דרב איקא: מה לנדה ואשת אח — שכן אין להם היתר בחיי אוסרן, תאמר באשת איש שכן יש לה היתר בחיי אוסרה! אמר ליה רב אחא מדפתי לרבינא: אטו נדה ואשת אח בחיי אוסרן הוא דאין להם היתר, אבל לאחר מכאן יש להם היתר? נדה

ביומי

רש"י

ישן לא קנה. דישן לאו בר דעת, ולאו הוה קנינו קנין. בנתקע. שנתקשה לאשתו, ונפל מן הגג ונתקע ביבמתו. חייב בד' דברים. בנזק וצער ורפוי ושבת, כדאמר ב"החובל" (ב"ק דף פה:) "פצע תחת פצע" — לרבות השוגג כמזיד, ואונס כרצון. אבל בושת — לא, כדמפרש לקמן. וביבמתו לא קנה. דלא אכוין לביאה. שנתכוון לאשתו. ונתקשה לה. מצוה. כלומר, בביאה יותר מבחליצה. הא חפץ. מצוה ליבומי. ולקחה שלא כדרכה. לרבות שאם בא עליה שלא כדרכה — קנה: במקום שמקים שם גרסינן. עד דמכוין לה. לשם ביאה בעולם. נזק. שמין אותה כאילו היא שפחה נמכרת:(ב) כמה היתה יפה וכמה היא יפה. להטיח בכותל. לאו לשום ביאה מיכוין. שכן מטמאה את בועלה. להיות כמותה טמא ז', דכתיב "ותהי נדתה עליו וטמא שבעת ימים" (ויקרא טו). וכי אשת אחיו לעולם נדה היא. ואינה פוסקת. שכן בידו. של אדם לרבות נשים הרבה על אחיו באיסור אשת אח. דאי בעי מקדש ואזיל כי אלפא. ותפשוט מינה כל עריות הנאסרות עליו מחמת אישות, כגון אשת אב וכלתו וחמותו ואחות אשתו. אבל אמו ואחותו ובתו וכיוצא בהן, דאין בידו לרבות — מנלן? שכן איסור הבא מאליו. ופשוט מינה אמו ואחותו ובתו וכיוצא בהן, ולא תפשוט מינה עריות הנאסרות לו מחמת קידושין. מאשת אח ואחות אב ואם. דכי פרכת: מה לאחות אב ואם שכן איסור הבא מאליו — אשת אח תוכיח. מה לאשת אח שכן בידו לרבות — אחות אב ואם תוכיח. וחזר הדין. הצד השוה שבהן, שהן אסורות עליו משום ערוה, ועשה בהן הערה כגמר ביאה — אף אני אביא כל העריות בדין הזה. שכן איסורן משום שאר. ותפשוט כל האסורות משום שאר. אבל אשת איש דלאו משום שאר — מנא תיתי? בחיי אוסרן. כל זמן* שאדם חי והיא שופעת. וכן אשת אח אין היתר בחיי אחיו, שאפילו הוא מגרשה אסורה לזה. אשת איש יש לה היתר בחייו על ידי גט.

ביומי

תוספות

מרולא ורולא גופיה קאמר התם דסברא הוא, דמאי חזית דדמא דידך סומקא טפי כו'. וזה לא שייך אלא במאנסין אותו להרוג בידים, אבל אם רוצים לזורקו על התינוק ויתמעך — בזה אדרבה, איכא למימר איפכא: מאי חזית דדמא דחבריה סומקא טפי כו', כיון שאין הורג בידים, ולא הוי אלא קרקע עולם בעלמא, ואין מצווה להציל חברו בגופו, לאדרבה: חייו קודמין, והיקש דקרא — בהורג בידים כתיב "כי כאשר יקום איש על רעהו וגו'". והשתא גרסינן בכל דוכתא: מה רוצח יהרג ואל יעבור. אף נערה המאורסה יהרג ואל יעבור. פירוש: יהרג הבועל, ולא גרסינן תיהרג, דקרקע עולם היא. אי נמי אר"י, דאפי' גרסינן תיהרג יש לפרש דהכי קאמר: תיהרג קודם שתעשה מעשה ותביא עליה את הערוה. וא"ת: במסכת ע"ז בפרק "רבי ישמעאל" (דף נד. ושם) דנעבד באונס אסור, ומפרש: כגון דאנסוהו גוים והשתחוה לבהמה דידיה. ופריך עלה רבי זירא: אונס רחמנא פטריה, דכתיב "ולנערה לא תעשה דבר" (דברים כב), ומאי קושיא? הא האי קרא דוקא בקרקע עולם איירי, אבל עשה מעשה חייב למסור עצמו, כדפרישי', ומשתחוה לעבודה זרה עושה מעשה הוא, דליכא לאוקמה כשכפוהו גוים לעבודה זרה, דאין זה משתחוה! ואר"י: דהכי פריך: אונס רחמנא פטריה ממיתה — אפי' בעושה מעשה, דנהי דחייב למסור עצמו, מ"מ אם לא מסר עצמו לא מיחייב מיתה. ד"ולנערה לא תעשה דבר" — אפילו בעשתה מעשה קאמר קרא דפטורה ממיתה, דבעשיית מעשה איירי היקישא דקרא. ועוד: דכיון דאפילו ברצון מיחייב מיתה, אע"ג דלא עביד מעשה, דהא אשה חייבת ברצון אע"ג דהויא קרקע עולם — ה"נ כשפטר הכתוב אונס במיתת בית דין. כדכתיב "ולנערה לא תעשה דבר" — פטר בכל ענין, לא שנא עביד לא שנא לא עביד. ולהכי פריך: כיון דפטור ממיתה לא חשיב נעבד ליאסר בהן עבודה. ומהדר ליה התם דחשיב שפיר נעבד באונס, אע"ג דפטור' ממית' בדיעבד, כיון דחייב למסור עצמו [וע"ע תוס' יומא פב. האריכו טובא].

ישן לא קנה. פי' בקונטרס: משום דלא הוי בר דעת. וקשיא: דהא קטן, אע"ג דלא הוי בר דעת הוה קונה אי לאו דמיעטיה קרא! אלא טעמא משום דלא איכוין לביאה כלל, והוי כ"מתכוין להטיח בכותל" דבסמוך.

וכי איצטריך קרא בין בשוגג כו'. וא"ת: והא איצטריך לאשמועינן ביאה ביבמה, דלא כתיב אלא הכא! וי"ל: דמ"להקים לאחיו שם" נפקא. וא"ת: והא אכתי איצטריך לג"ש דלקמן: יבמה מנין — אתיא ביאה ביאה! וי"ל: דביאה דסייבי לאוין מופנה, וה"ל מופנה מצד אחד.

דמכוין לה. לאו דוקא נקט דמכוין לה, דהא בסמוך אמר דנתכוון להטיח בבהמה והטיח ביבמתו — קנה.

שכן בידו לרבות. וא"ת: דבקדושין פרק "האומר" (דף סז:) בעי למילף כל העריות דלא תפסי בהו קידושין מאחות אשתו, וקאמר התם: בשלמא כולהו אתיין. והיכי אתיין? הא איכא למיפרך: מה לאחות אשה — שכן בידו לרבות! וי"ל: דבלאו הכי פריך שפיר. א"נ: דדוקא באשת אח חשיב יש בידו לרבות לחומרא, שכן יש בידו לרבות איסור על אחרים. אבל מה שבידו לרבות על עצמו — לא חשיב פירכא. **מה** לאחות אב ואחות אם שכן איסור הבא מאליו. הקשה ריב"ן: דמאחות אב ואם נילף איסור הבא מאליו, ומאשת אח נילף היכא דעל ידי קידושין! וי"ל: דאשת איש לא אתי, כדפריך בסמוך: מה להנך שכן שאר.

אלא

עין משפט נר מצוה

ד א מיי' פ"ב מהל' יבום הלכה ג ד סמג עשין נא טוש"ע אה"ע סימן קסו סעיף ח:

ה ב מיי' פ"א מהל' חובל ומזיק הלכה יב סמג עשין ע טוש"ע ח"מ סימן תכא סעיף יא:

ו ג מיי' פ"ב מהל' יבום הלכה ג סמג עשין נא טוש"ע אה"ע סימן קסו סעי' ח:

ז ד מיי' פ"ב שם ה"א ופ"ה שם הלכה ט טוש"ע שם סימן קע סעיף יב:

ח ה מיי' שם וטוש"ע שם סעיף ב וסימן קסו סעיף ב:

ט ו מיי' שם פ"ב הל' ג טוש"ע שם סימן קסו סעיף ז:

י ז מיי' פ"א מהל' חובל ומזיק הלכה י סמג עשין ע טוש"ע ח"מ סימן תכא סעיף א:

יא ח מיי' פ"ב מהלכות יבום הלכה ד סמג עשין נא טוש"ע אה"ע סימן קסו סעיף ח:

יב ט מיי' פ"ג מהל' מטמא משכב ומושב הל' א סמג עשין רמג:

תוספות ישנים

ישן לא קנה ביבמתו פ"ה משום דלא הוי בן דעת. ולא נהירא דאפילו חרש דלא הוי בר דעת אמרי' לקמן קנה. ונראה טעמא משום דבעינן כוונה וניחא דחרש יש לו כל הכוונה שיכול. אבל בישן אין לו כוונה שיש לו כמו שהוא ער. וכן נמי משמע לקמיה דמפיק ליה מיבא עליה עד דמכוין לה: **מה** לאשת אח שכן יש בידו לרבות. ותימה בקדושין (ס"ז) דיליף כל העריות [דאין קדושין תופסין] מאחות אשה נפרוך מה לאחות אשה שכן יש בידו לרבות שיקדש הרבה נשים וירבה עליו איסור אחות אשה וי"ל דהא לא קרי בידו לרבות אלא כשהוא מרבה איסור על אחרים כמו באשת אח דאי מקדש אלף כולן אסורות על אחיו משום אשת אח אבל אין זה חשיבות אם יכול להרבות איסור על עצמו: **מה** לאחות אב שכן איסור הבא מאליו והקשה ה"ר יהודה בר נתן אמאי לא שמעינן כל שאיסורו בא מאליו ולא ע"י קדושין מאחות אב והני דעל ידי קדושין שבידו לרבות ניליף מאשת אח. וי"ל כיון דמ"מ אצטריכו תרווייהו למילף עדיפא לן לאתויי מבינייא ועוי"ל דהא אי קאמר הכי הוה פרכינן אשת איש מנ"ל דמאשת אח לא מצינן למילף אשת איש שיש לה היתר בחיי בעלה משא"כ באשת אח אבל לקמן בסמוך בעי למילף מבינייא דנדה ואשת אח דנדה יש לה היתר בחיי בעלה ומ"מ פריך שפיר תלמודא מה לנדה ואשת

תוספות חד מקמאי

אלא בנתקע והאמר רבה נפל מן הגג פירוש ברוח מצויה ונתקע חייב בד' דברים [וביבמתו] לא קנה. אלא כגון שנתכוון לאשתו ותקפתו יבמתו ובא עליה שניהם אנוסים ה"ד כגון שנתכוון לאשתו ותקפוהו גוים ודבקום זו לזו. והא דאמר ישן לא קנה דוקא ישן אבל מתנמנם קנה בין היא ערה בין היא ישנה קנה: אמר רבה נתכוון להטיח (באשתו) [בכותל] והטיח ביבמתו לא קנה להטיח בבהמה והטיח ביבמתו קנה דהא קא מכוין לשום ביאה בעלמא

מסורת הש"ס

ב"ק כז.

[עי' תוספות לעיל לט: ד"ה ולשום]

קדושין יז.

נ"ל ויבמה. יעב"ץ

פסחים קכ: תענית יב. מגילה יח: חגיגה יח: נדה סג.

[נ"ל שהוא]

ב"ק פו.

תורה אור

דברים כה — שם — שם — ויקרא כ — שם — שם

הגהות הב"ח

(א) גמ' בעל כרחה אמר מר ד"א יבמה יבא עליה: (ב) רש"י ד"ה נזק וכו' נמכרת בשוק כמה:

גליון הש"ס

גמ' ויבם ביאה גומרת. עיין לעיל דף ח ע"ב תד"ה ויבמה ובקדושין יד ע"א רש"י ד"ה א"כ:

אלא רמז ליבמה שאסורה בחיי בעלה מנין. דכיון דשריא רחמנא אחר מיתה – אין סברא לומר דאסירא בחיי בעלה, דלא מיסתבר שהיה בא הכתוב לומר דאתי עשה ודחי לא תעשה שיש בו כרת, אי לאו דמוכח קרא בהדיא.

בזכור מהו. הא דלא יליף זכור ובהמה מהקישא דרבי יונה משום ד"את מקורה הערה" כתיב, והנהו לא שייך בהו מקור. ועוד, דאפסקינהו בקרא דמולך. אי נמי משום דזכור ובהמה לא חשיב ביאה, ואין לנו ללמוד מהן. ולהכי בפרק "ארבע מיתות" (סנהדרין נד:) צריך אזהרה ועונש לשוכב ונשכב בזכור, אע"ג דבעלמא לא בעי קרא לחייב האשה הנשכבת. **אמרו** לו מתה אשתך כו'. בתלתא הוה סגי, אלא קמ"ל דאף על פי שיש ערבוב, שכל חמשתן שלשלת אחוה, וצריך להוציא האסורות – לא גזרינן הנך דשרינן אטו הנך דאסירן.

צרותיהן איצטריך, אע"ג דס"ד דמוטב שיחלוץ הצרות – גזירה שלא יחלוץ לשניה או רביעית.

מאשת

ביומי תליא מילתא. אפי' אם מת האוסרה, שפסקה דם בראייה ראשונה – אסורה כל שבעה. בבנים תליא. אם יש לה בנים אפילו מת אחיו. אין אוסרן מתירן. אין כח באוסר להתיר, אלא דבר אחר מתירה: ימים מתירין את הנדה, ואשת אח – כשהוא ערירי. הוקשו כל העריות לנדה. שהרי כאן הוקשו כולן זו לזו, ונדה כתובה בפרשת עריות, הלכך בהעראה ילפינן כולהו מנדה. נדה דכתיב גבי אשת אח. דילפינן מיניה לעיל העראה לאשת אח מנדה. בחיי בעלה. אם גירשה אחיו. ולאו הבא מכלל עשה עשה. אבל כרת ליכא. משכבי אשה. וכיון דבאשה הוי העראה משכב, ממילא איתפרשא בזכור, דהא בזכור כתיב "משכבי אשה". המערה בבהמה. שלא גמר ביאתו ואחות אב ואחות אם. לאו מחייבי מיתות הן, דלא כתיבא בהו מיתה. ליכתבה במיתת בית דין. כגון בחמו וחמותו, וליתא נמי: אם אינו ענין להו, דאתיא בהיקישא דר' יונה, תנהו ענין לבהמה. איידי דכוליה קרא. דכתיב באחות אב ואחות אם בפרשת "קדושים תהיו" לדרשא אתא, כדתניא לקמן כתיב ביה נמי העראה, בלא צורך, לדרשא דבהמה. ערות אחות אביך. קרא ד"אחרי מות" קמא נקט. בין שהיא אחות אביך. מן האב בין מן האם. מה אחותו בין מן האב בין מן האם. דכתיב "בת אביך או בת אמך". מה דודתו מן האב ולא מן האם. שאם היה דודו אחי אביו מן האם ולא מן האב – אין אשתו עליו ערוה, ולקמן בעי מנלן. דודתו אין איסורה בא עליו מאליו. אלא על ידי קדושי דודו, ולא תוכיח אחותו. וכיון דלא נפקא לן מדינא, תלמוד לומר מקרא שני בפרשת "קדושים תהיו": "ערות אחות אביך ואחות אמך לא תגלה". ואין צריך להזהיר – שכבר הזהיר, ולא הוה ליה לאשמועינן אלא עונש, כדעבד באשת אח ובאחותו: "איש כי יקח אחות אביו ואחות אמו עונש ישאו", וקרא יתירא הוא, לרבות אחות אביו מן האם ואחות אמו מן האם. למה לי למכתב. האי קרא יתירא בתרוייהו? לכתוב בחדא, ואיתי אידך מיניה. יש לה חיים. דמשפחת אב קרויה משפחה, דכתיב "ויתילדו על משפחותם לבית אבותם" (במדבר א). אחות אם ודאי. קרובתו. אבל אחות אב, שמא ח"ו אין זה אביו? מה להלן מן האב. אם אחי אביו מן האב הוא – הוי קרוב לענין גאולה יותר, ומצות גאולה מוטל עליו יותר מקרובי האם, אף כאן – מן האב ולא מן האם: ה"ג. ממשפחתו יגאלנו משפחת אב קרויה משפחה כו'. והא דתנן אמרו לו מתה אשתך כו'. כגון דינה בת לאה מיעקב, ויוכבד בת לאה מחצרון, ושרה בת חצרון מקטורה, ורבקה בת קטורה מבתואל, ומלכה בת בתואל מחנה. וראובן נשא את מלכה, והלך למדינת הים. אמרו לו מתה אשתך, ונשא את רבקה, שהיא אחותה מאביה. חזרו ואמרו לו מתה רבקה, ונשא את שרה אחותה מאמה. אמרו לו מתה שרה, ונשא את יוכבד אחותה מאביה. אמרו לו מתה יוכבד, ונשא את דינה אחותה מאמה. חזרו ואמרו לו: כולן קיימות. מותר בראשונה. במלכה אשתו. ובשלישית. שרה, לפי שרבקה לא היו קידושיה קידושין, ודיאתה באונס הוא. ומותר בשרה אחותה, דתנן (לקמן דף נז.): נושאין על האנוסה. ובחמישית. דינה, ואע"פ שהיא אחות יוכבד הרביעית. לפי שביאת יוכבד פיתוי היא, ואינה קידושין, מפני שהשלישית היו קידושיה קידושין. ופוטרות צרותיהן. אם מת וחלצו האחין לאחת מהן – פוטרות צרותיהן. ואסור בשניה. מפני הראשונה, וברביעית מפני השלישית.

אלמא

תורה אור

ביומי תליא מילתא. אשת אח – בבנים תליא רחמנא. אלא פריך הכי: מה לנדה ואשת אח – שכן אין אוסרן מתירן, תאמר באשת איש – שאוסרה! מתירה! אלא *אמר ר' יונה ואיתימא רב הונא בריה דרב יהושע: אמר קרא °"כי כל אשר יעשה מכל התועבת האלה ונכרתו הנפשות העשת" הוקשו כל העריות כולן לנדה, מה נדה בהעראה – אף כל בהעראה. ואלא נדה דכתיבא גבי אשת אח למה לי? לכדרב הונא. דאמר רב הונא: רמז ליבמה מן התורה מנין? מנין?! הא כתיב "יבמה יבא עליה"! אלא: רמז ליבמה שאסורה בחיי בעלה מנין? האי – סברא היא, מדאמר רחמנא: לאחר מיתת בעלה שריא – מכלל דבחיי בעלה אסורה! ודלמא: לאחר מיתת בעלה – מצוה, בחיי בעלה – רשות? אי נמי: לאחר מיתת בעלה – אין, בחיי בעלה – לא, *ולאו הבא מכלל עשה – עשה! אמר קרא: °"ואיש אשר יקח את אשת אחיו נדה היא", וכי אשת אחיו נדה היא? אלא כנדה, מה נדה, אף על פי שיש לה היתר לאחר מכאן – [א]בשעת איסורא בכרת, אף אשת אח [נמי], אף על פי שיש לה היתר לאחר מכאן – [ב]בחיי בעלה בכרת. אלא העראה דכתיבא גבי אחות אב ואחות אם למה לי? לכדבעא מיניה רבינא מרבא: [ג]המערה *בזכור, מהו? בזכור – "משכבי אשה" כתיבא! אלא: המערה בבהמה מהו? אמר ליה: אם אינו ענין להעראה, דכתיבא גבי אחות אב ואחות אם, דאתיא בהקישא מדרבי יונה – [ד]תנהו ענין להעראה דבהמה. מכדי בהמה חייבי מיתות בית דין היא, מאי טעמא כתיב להעראה דידה גבי חייבי כריתות? לכתוב גבי מיתת בית דין, ונילף מיתת ב"ד ממיתת ב"ד! *איידי דכוליה קרא לדרשא אתי – כתיב ביה נמי הא מילתא לדרשא. מאי דרשא – דתניא: °"ערות אחות אביך לא תגלה" [ה]בין מן האב בין מן האם. אתה אומר בין מן האב בין מן האם, או אינו אלא מן האב ולא מן האם? ודין הוא: חייב כאן – וחייב באחותו. מה אחותו – [ו]בין מן האב בין מן האם, אף כאן – בין מן האב בין מן האם. או כלך לדרך זו: חייב כאן וחייב בדודתו, מה דודתו – [ז]מן האב ולא מן האם, אף כאן – מן האב ולא מן האם. נראה למי דומה: דנין איסור הבא מאליו מאיסור הבא מאליו, ואל תוכיח דודתו – שאין איסור הבא מאליו. או כלך לדרך זה: דנין קרובי האב מקרובי האב, ואל תוכיח אחותו שקרובי עצמו? תלמוד לומר "ערות אחות אביך לא תגלה" בין מן האב בין מן האם. "ערות אחות אמך לא תגלה" בין מן האב בין מן האם. למה לי למכתבא באחות אב, למה לי למכתבא באחות אם? אמר רבי אבהו: צריכי, דאי כתב רחמנא באחות אב – שכן יש לה חיים, אבל אחות אם – אימא לא. ואי כתב רחמנא באחות אם – שכן ודאית, אבל אחות אב – אימא לא, צריכא. ודודתו, דפשיטא ליה לתנא דמן האב ולא מן האם, מנא ליה? אמר רבא: אתיא "דודו" "דודו", כתיב הכא °"ערות דדו גלה" וכתיב התם °"או דדו או בן דדו יגאלנו" מה להלן מן האב ולא מן האם – אף כאן מן האב ולא מן האם. והתם מנלן? אמר קרא "ממשפחתו יגאלנו", *משפחת אב – קרויה משפחה, [ח]משפחת אם – אינה קרויה משפחה. והדתנן: *אמרו לו: מתה אשתך, ונשא אחותה מאביה. מתה, ונשא אחותה מאמה. מתה, ונשא אחותה מאביה. מתה, ונשא אחותה מאמה – מותר בראשונה ובשלישית ובחמישית, ופוטרות צרותיהן. ואסור בשניה וברביעית, ואין ביאת אחת מהן פוטרת צרתה. ואם בא על השניה לאחר מיתת הראשונה – מותר בשניה וברביעית, ופוטרות צרותיהן, ואסור בשלישית ובחמישית.

אלמא

יג א מיי' פ"ד מהל' איסורי ביאה הלכה א סמג לאוין קיד ועשין רמג:
יד ב מיי' פ"א שם הל' א ופ"ב הל' א:
טו ג מיי' פ"א שם הל' יד:
טז ד מיי' שם הל' טז:
יז ה מיי' פ"ב שם הל' ה סמג לאוין קד טוש"ע אה"ע סימן טו סעי' טז:
יח ו מיי' שם הל' ב טוש"ע שם סעי' י:
יט ז מיי' שם טוש"ע שם סעיף ח:
כ ח מיי' פ"א מהלכות נחלות הלכה ו סמג עשין צו טוש"ע ח"מ סימן רעו סעיף ד:

תוספות ישנים

את שאין להם היתר בחיי אוסרן. נדה בשעת הדם ואשת אח בחיי בעלה: **מותר** בראשונה ובשלישית ואינו אסור בה מטעם דנשואין [דשניה] לא הוו כלום מטעם הראשונה וביאתה הוי כמו אנוסה ואמרי' נושאין על האנוסה דאם אנס אשה אינו אסור בקרובותיה והשתא מייתי מהכא דאף מן האם אסורה מדקאמר אסור בשניה דוקא ובשלישית שרי משום דאין קדושי שניה כלום. הא אי הוה שרי בשניה הוי אסור בשלישית מפני שהיא אחותה אע"ג דשלישית הוי אחות שניה מן האם לבד. וה"ה דה"מ לאתויי ולאוכוחי בהדיא בלא דוחק מסיפא דמשמע דאף מן האם אסורה. דקאמר מתה הראשונה מותר בשניה וברביעית ואסור בשלישית

תוספות חד מקמאי

בעלמא: **תניא** ערות אחות אמך לא תגלה בין מן האב בין מן האם. (ומן האם). אשה אל אחותה לא תקח בין מן האב בין מן האם ערות אחי אביך לא תגלה אל אשתו לא תקרב דודתך היא מן האב ולא מן האם דאתייא דודו [דודו] כתיב הכא דודתך היא וכתיב התם או דודו או בן דודו יגאלנו מה להלן מן האב ולא מן האם דכתיב ממשפחתו יגאלנו ומשפחת אב קרויה משפחה ומשפחת אם אינה קרויה משפחה ומה שכתב הרב אלפס בענין העראת אשה לבעלה כבר כתבתי בקדושין סברת האחרים תוספת על סברת הרב ז"ל ולפי סברת הרב ז"ל משמע דביאה בלא חופה קונה ליורשה וליטמא לה ובפ' נערה שנתפתתה (מ"ח:) תניא נמי או שהיתה לה חצר בדרך ונכנסה עמו לשם נשואין אע"פ שכתובתה בבית אביה ומתה בעלה יורשה. בר"א לירושתה אבל

[ויקרא יח] [שם כ] [שם יח] [שם כ] [שם כה]

לעיל ח. קידושין סז: כריתות ב:
ולקמן נו: סח. עג: פסחים מח: זבחים לד: חולין פה.]
סנהדרין נה
[פסחים סז: לקמן עג. סוטה ג. ב"ק נא. ס. פד. פח. וע"ש שבועות ז. יח. סנהדרין עג:]
[ב"ב קטו: קי:]
לקמן נו.

תורה אור

אַלְמָא אֲחוֹת אִשְׁתּוֹ. בֵּין מִן הָאָב בֵּין מִן הָאֵם אֲסוּרוֹת. מְנָלַן? יָלֵיף מֵאֲחוֹתוֹ, מָה אֲחוֹתוֹ — בֵּין מִן הָאָב בֵּין מִן הָאֵם, אַף כָּאן בֵּין מִן הָאָב בֵּין מִן הָאֵם. וְלֵילַף מִדּוֹדָתוֹ, מַה דּוֹדָתוֹ — מִן הָאָב וְלֹא מִן הָאֵם, אַף כָּאן — מִן הָאָב וְלֹא מִן הָאֵם! מִסְתַּבְּרָא, מֵאֲחוֹתוֹ הֲוָה לֵיהּ לְמֵילַף, שֶׁכֵּן קְרוֹבֵי עַצְמוֹ מִקְּרוֹבֵי עַצְמוֹ. אַדְּרַבָּה, מִדּוֹדָתוֹ הֲוָה לֵיהּ לְמֵילַף שֶׁכֵּן דָּבָר עַל יְדֵי קִדּוּשִׁין מִדָּבָר שֶׁעַל יְדֵי קִדּוּשִׁין! אֶלָּא: מֵאֵשֶׁת אָח יָלְפִינַן, דְּשֶׁכֵּן דָּבָר עַל יְדֵי קִדּוּשִׁין, וּקְרוֹבֵי עַצְמוֹ. וְאֵשֶׁת אָח גּוּפָהּ מנ"ל? דְּתַנְיָא: (ויקרא יח) "עֶרְוַת אֵשֶׁת אָחִיךָ לֹא תְגַלֵּה" בֵּין מִן הָאָב בֵּין מִן הָאֵם. אַתָּה אוֹמֵר בֵּין מִן הָאָב בֵּין מִן הָאֵם, אוֹ אֵינוֹ אֶלָּא מִן הָאָב וְלֹא מִן הָאֵם? וְדִין הוּא: חַיָּיב כָּאן, וְחַיָּיב בַּאֲחוֹתוֹ. מָה אֲחוֹתוֹ — בֵּין מִן הָאָב בֵּין מִן הָאֵם, אַף כָּאן — בֵּין מִן הָאָב בֵּין מִן הָאֵם. אוֹ כְּלָךְ לְדֶרֶךְ זוֹ: חַיָּיב כָּאן וְחַיָּיב בְּדוֹדָתוֹ. מַה דּוֹדָתוֹ — מִן הָאָב וְלֹא מִן הָאֵם, אַף כָּאן — מִן הָאָב וְלֹא מִן הָאֵם? נִרְאֶה לְמִי דּוֹמֶה; דָּנִין קְרוֹבֵי עַצְמוֹ מִקְּרוֹבֵי עַצְמוֹ, וְאַל תּוֹכִיחַ דּוֹדָתוֹ שֶׁקְּרוֹבֵי הָאָב. אוֹ כְּלָךְ לְדֶרֶךְ זוֹ: דָּנִין דָּבָר שֶׁעַל יְדֵי קִדּוּשִׁין מִדָּבָר שֶׁעַל יְדֵי קִדּוּשִׁין, וְאַל תּוֹכִיחַ אֲחוֹתוֹ שֶׁאִיסּוּר הַבָּא מֵאֵלָיו? ת"ל "עֶרְוַת אָחִיךָ הִיא" בֵּין מִן הָאָב בֵּין מִן הָאֵם. וְאֵימָא: אִידִי וְאִידִי בְּאֵשֶׁת אָח מִן הָאָב, חֲדָא — דְּיֵשׁ לָהּ בָּנִים בְּחַיֵּי בַּעְלָהּ, וַחֲדָא — דְּאֵין לָהּ בָּנִים בְּחַיֵּי בַּעְלָהּ. אֵין לָהּ בָּנִים בְּחַיֵּי בַּעְלָהּ — מִדְּרַב הוּנָא נָפְקָא! וְאֵימָא: אִידִי וְאִידִי בְּאֵשֶׁת אָח מִן הָאָב, חֲדָא — דְּיֵשׁ לָהּ בָּנִים בְּחַיֵּי בַּעְלָהּ, וַחֲדָא — דְּיֵשׁ לָהּ בָּנִים לְאַחַר מִיתַת בַּעְלָהּ! יֵשׁ לָהּ בָּנִים לְאַחַר מִיתַת בַּעְלָהּ לָא צְרִיכָא קְרָא, מִדְּאָמַר רַחֲמָנָא שֶׁאֵין לָהּ בָּנִים מוּתֶּרֶת — הָא יֵשׁ לָהּ בָּנִים אֲסוּרָה. וְדִלְמָא: אֵין לָהּ בָּנִים — אֲסוּרָה לְעָלְמָא וְשַׁרְיָא לְיַבָּם. יֵשׁ לָהּ בָּנִים — שַׁרְיָא לְעָלְמָא וְשַׁרְיָא לְיַבָּם! אִי נַמִי: אֵין לָהּ בָּנִים — מִצְוָה, יֵשׁ לָהּ בָּנִים — רְשׁוּת, אִי נַמִי: אֵין לָהּ בָּנִים — אִין, יֵשׁ לָהּ בָּנִים — לָא, *וְלָאו הַבָּא מִכְּלַל עֲשֵׂה — עֲשֵׂה! כָּתַב קְרָא אַחֲרִינָא: (שם כ) "עֶרְוַת אָחִיו גִּלָּה". וְאֵימָא אֵשֶׁת אָח מִן הָאֵם כְּאֵשֶׁת אָח מִן הָאָב: מָה אֵשֶׁת אָח מִן הָאָב — לְאַחַר מִיתַת בַּעְלָהּ שַׁרְיָא, אַף אֵשֶׁת אָח מִן הָאֵם — לְאַחַר מִיתַת בַּעְלָהּ שַׁרְיָא! אָמַר קְרָא "הִיא" בַּהֲוָיָיתָהּ תְּהֵא. אֲחוֹתוֹ דִּכְתַב בָּהּ כָּרֵת לָמָּה לִי? לְכִדְרַבִּי יוֹחָנָן. דְּאָמַר ר' יוֹחָנָן: שֶׁאִם *עֲשָׂאָן כּוּלָּם בְּהֶעְלֵם אַחַת — חַיָּיב עַל כָּל אַחַת וְאַחַת. וּלְרַבִּי יִצְחָק, דְּאָמַר: כָּל חַיָּיבֵי כְּרֵיתוֹת בִּכְלָל הָיוּ, וְלָמָּה יָצְתָה כָּרֵת בַּאֲחוֹתוֹ — לְדוּנוֹ בְּכָרֵת וְלֹא בְּמַלְקוֹת, לְחַלֵּק מְנָלַן? נָפְקָא לֵיהּ: (שם יח) מִ"וְאֶל אִשָּׁה בְּנִדַּת טוּמְאָתָהּ" לְחַיֵּיב עַל כָּל אִשָּׁה וְאִשָּׁה. דּוֹדָתוֹ דִּכְתַב בָּהּ רַחֲמָנָא "עֲרִירִים יִהְיוּ" ל"ל? לְכִדְרַבָּה. דְּרַבָּה רָמֵי: (שם כ) כְּתִיב "עֲרִירִים יִהְיוּ" וּכְתִיב (שם) "עֲרִירִים יָמֻתוּ"! הָא כֵּיצַד? יֵשׁ לוֹ בָּנִים — קוֹבְרָן, אֵין לוֹ בָּנִים — הוֹלֵךְ עֲרִירִי. וְאִיצְטְרִיךְ לְמִכְתַּב "עֲרִירִים יִהְיוּ" וְאִיצְטְרִיךְ לְמִכְתַּב "עֲרִירִים יָמֻתוּ". דְּאִי כָּתַב רַחֲמָנָא "עֲרִירִים יִהְיוּ" ה"א: עַד חֶטְאֵיהּ, אֲבָל מֵחֶטְאֵיהּ וְאֵילָךְ — לָא כָּתַב רַחֲמָנָא "עֲרִירִים יָמֻתוּ". וְאִי כָּתַב רַחֲמָנָא "עֲרִירִים יָמֻתוּ" ה"א: מֵחֶטְאֵיהּ וְאֵילָךְ, אֲבָל מֵעִיקָּרָא — לָא, צְרִיכָא.§ הַעֲרָאָה דְּחַיָּיבֵי לָאוִין מְנָלַן? מִדְּגַלֵּי רַחֲמָנָא (שם יט) "שִׁכְבַת זֶרַע" גַּבֵּי שִׁפְחָה חֲרוּפָה — מִכְּלָל דְּחַיָּיבֵי לָאוִין בְּהַעֲרָאָה. אַדְּרַבָּה, מִדְּגַלֵּי רַחֲמָנָא הַעֲרָאָה בְּחַיָּיבֵי כְּרֵיתוֹת — מִכְּלָל דְּחַיָּיבֵי לָאוִין בִּגְמַר בִּיאָה! אָמַר רַב אַשִׁי: אִם כֵּן לִשְׁתּוֹק קְרָא מִשִּׁפְחָה חֲרוּפָה, הַעֲרָאָה דְּחַיָּיבֵי לָאוִין דִּכְהוּנָּה מְנָלַן? (שם כ) אָתְיָא "קִיחָה" (שם כא) "קִיחָה". דְּחַיָּיבֵי עֲשֵׂה מְנָלַן? אָתְיָא

רש"י

אַלְמָא אֲחוֹת אִשָּׁה בֵּין מִן הָאָב בֵּין מִן הָאֵם. דְּהָא שְׁלִישִׁית אֲחוֹתָהּ שֶׁל שְׁנִיָּה מֵאִמָּהּ הִיא. וְטַעְמָא — דִּשְׁנִיָּה לָאו אִשְׁתּוֹ הִיא, מִשּׁוּם הָכִי מוּתָּר בַּשְּׁלִישִׁית. הָא אִם הָווּ קִידּוּשֵׁי שְׁנִיָּה קִידּוּשִׁין — הָוְיָא אָסוּר בַּשְּׁלִישִׁית: אֲחוֹת אִשָּׁה קְרוֹבֵי עַצְמוֹ חָשֵׁיב לָהּ, שֶׁמֵּחֲמַת עַצְמוֹ נֶאֶסְרָה עָלָיו וְלֹא מֵחֲמַת אָבִיו. וּלְאַפּוֹקֵי דּוֹדָתוֹ, דִּקְרוֹבַת אָבִיו הִיא: ה"ג הָכָא: ת"ל עֶרְוַת אָחִיךָ הִיא. **בְּחַיֵּי בַעְלָהּ.** אִם גֵּירְשָׁהּ. **מִדְּרַב הוּנָא.** דִּכְתִיב "אֵשֶׁת אָחִיו נִדָּה הִיא" כִּדְלְעֵיל (דף נד:). **וְלָאו הַבָּא מִכְּלַל עֲשֵׂה עֲשֵׂה.** "יְבָמָהּ יָבֹא עָלֶיהָ", אֲבָל כָּרֵת לֵיכָּא. הָכִי גָּרְסִינַן: כְּתִיב קְרָא אַחֲרִינָא עֶרְוַת אָחִיו גִּלָּה. **אַף אֵשֶׁת אָח מִן הָאֵם לְאַחַר מִיתַת בַּעְלָהּ.** בְּלֹא בָּנִים שַׁרְיָא. וְא"ת: הָא יָלְפִינַן (לעיל דף יז:) "אַחֲוָה" "אַחֲוָה" מִבְּנֵי יַעֲקֹב! אִיכָּא לְמֵימַר: אַחִים מִן הָאָב — מִצְוָה, מִן הָאֵם — רְשׁוּת. **עֶרְוַת אָחִיךָ הִיא.** מֵהַאי קְרָא מְרַבִּינַן אֵשֶׁת אָח מִן הָאֵם. **אֲחוֹתוֹ דִּכְתַב בָּהּ כָּרֵת לָמָּה לִי.** כֵּיוָן דְּדָרְשַׁתְּ הַעֲרָאָה, וּקְרָאֵי יְתֵירֵי, כּוּלְּהוּ כָּרֵת דַּאֲחוֹתוֹ מַאי תִּדְרוֹשׁ בֵּיהּ? הָא כְּבָר נִכְתַּב בְּכָל הָעֲרָיוֹת "וְנִכְרְתוּ הַנְּפָשׁוֹת הָעוֹשׂוֹת". **חַיָּיב עַל כָּל אַחַת וְאַחַת.** וְאִי לָא כָּתַב אֶלָּא חַד כָּרֵת אַכּוּלְּהוּ, הֲוֵי אָמִינָא: הֵיכָא דַּעֲבַדִינְהוּ לְכוּלְּהוּ בְּהֶעְלֵם אֶחָד — לָא מִחַיֵּיב אֶלָּא חֲדָא, הַשְׁתָּא הָוֵי דָּבָר שֶׁהָיָה בַּכְּלָל וְיָצָא מִן הַכְּלָל לְלַמֵּד עַל הַכְּלָל כּוּלּוֹ; דְּמָה אֲחוֹתוֹ מְיוּחֶדֶת שֶׁהִיא עֶרְוָה וְחַיָּיבִין עָלֶיהָ בִּפְנֵי עַצְמָהּ, אַף כָּל שֶׁהִיא עֶרְוָה — חַיָּיבִין עָלֶיהָ בִּפְנֵי עַצְמָהּ. **לְכָרֵת נִתְּנָה וְלֹא לְמַלְקוֹת.** דְּאִי הִתְרוּ בּוֹ לְמַלְקוֹת אֵינוֹ לוֹקֶה, דְּלָאו שֶׁנִּיתַּן לְאַזְהָרַת כָּרֵת הוּא, לְפִיכָךְ אֵין לוֹקִין עָלָיו. °דְּלָא הֲוָה לֵיהּ לְעוֹנְשׁוֹ כָּרֵת אא"כ הִזְהִיר עָלֶיהָ, הִלְכָּךְ אַזְהָרָה לָאו לְמַלְקוֹת נִתְּנָה. **מִוְאֶל אִשָּׁה.** לְחַלֵּק עַל כָּל אִשָּׁה וְאִשָּׁה שֶׁבְּפָרָשָׁה זוֹ, דַּהֲוָה לֵיהּ לְמִכְתַּב: וְנִדָּה לֹא תִקְרַב. **עֲרִירִים.** הַיְינוּ נַמִי כָּרֵת, שֶׁאֵין זַרְעוֹ נִכְרָת. **עֲרִירִים יִהְיוּ.** לִשְׁעַת מִיתָתָן. מַשְׁמַע, סוֹפָן לָבֹא לִידֵי עֲרִירִי, דְּאִם יֵשׁ לוֹ בָּנִים — קוֹבְרָן. **עֲרִירִים יָמוּתוּ.** מַשְׁמַע דְּאִם הֵן עַכְשָׁיו עֲרִירִים — כֵּן יָמוּתוּ, וַאֲפִי' יִוָּלְדוּ לָהֶם לְאַחַר מַעֲשֶׂה. **דְּאִי כָּתַב רַחֲמָנָא עֲרִירִים יִהְיוּ הֲוֵי אָמִינָא** דַּהֲווּ לֵיהּ עַד חֶטְאֵיהּ. וְהָכִי מַשְׁמַע: סוֹפָם לִהְיוֹת עֲרִירִים, שֶׁיָּמוּתוּ בְּנֵיהֶם שֶׁיֵּשׁ לָהֶם עַתָּה, וְיִהְיוּ עֲרִירִים. אֲבָל בִּשְׁעַת מִיתָתָם לֹא יָמוּתוּ עֲרִירִים, דְּבָנִים דַּהֲווּ לֵיהּ מֵחֶטְאֵיהּ וְאֵילָךְ — לָא מַיְיתִי. **וְאִי כָּתַב רַחֲמָנָא** עֲרִירִים יָמוּתוּ הֲוֵי **אָמִינָא מֵחֶטְאֵיהּ** וְאֵילָךְ. דְּהָכִי מַשְׁמַע: מֵ"חֶטְאָם יִשָּׂאוּ" וְאֵילָךְ — עֲרִירִים יָמוּתוּ; אֲבָל בָּנִים דְּמֵעִיקָּרָא — לָא מַיְיתִי. כָּתַב רַחֲמָנָא "עֲרִירִים יִהְיוּ" — סוֹפָן לָבֹא לִידֵי עֲרִירִים, דְּמִדִּכְתִיב "עֲרִירִים יִהְיוּ" — מִכְּלָל דְּהַשְׁתָּא לָאו עֲרִירִים נִינְהוּ. **שִׁפְחָה חַיָּיבֵי לָאוִין הִיא.** דִּכְתִיב בָּהּ "לֹא יִהְיֶה קָדֵשׁ" (דברים כג). וְגַלֵּי בָּהּ רַחֲמָנָא דְּלָא מַיְיתִי אָשָׁם עַד שֶׁיִּגְמוֹר בָּהּ בִּיאָתוֹ, דִּכְתִיב "שִׁכְבַת זֶרַע". מִכְּלָל דְּחַיָּיבֵי מַלְקוֹת דְּלָאו דְּאָשָׁם, כְּגוֹן מַמְזֵר וְשִׁפְחָה שֶׁאֵין חֲרוּפָה — בְּהַעֲרָאָה מִיחַיֵּיב. **שִׁפְחָה חֲרוּפָה.** שִׁפְחָה כְּנַעֲנִית הַמְאוֹרֶסֶת לְעֶבֶד עִבְרִי, שֶׁמּוּתָּר בָּהּ, כְּדִכְתִיב (שמות כא) "אִם אֲדוֹנָיו יִתֶּן לוֹ אִשָּׁה". **לִשְׁתּוֹק קְרָא.** דְּלָא לְגַלֵּי שִׁכְבַת זֶרַע בְּשִׁפְחָה חֲרוּפָה, וַאֲנָא אָמִינָא (א) כִּשְׁאָר חַיָּיבֵי לָאוִין — בִּגְמַר בִּיאָה. **דִּכְהוּנָּה מְנָלַן.** דְּמִשִּׁפְחָה לָא גָּמְרִינַן אֶלָּא לָאו הַשָּׁוֶה בַּכֹּל, דּוּמְיָא דְּשִׁפְחָה חֲרוּפָה. **קִיחָה קִיחָה.** כְּתִיב גַּבֵּי חַיָּיבֵי כְּרֵיתוֹת (ויקרא כ) "אִישׁ אֲשֶׁר יִקַּח אֶת אֲחוֹתוֹ", וּכְתִיב בְּחַיָּיבֵי לָאוִין דִּכְהוּנָּה "לֹא יִקָּחוּ" (שם כא). **דְּחַיָּיבֵי עֲשֵׂה.** כְּגוֹן מִצְרִי וַאֲדוֹמִי עַד דּוֹר שְׁלִישִׁי, מְנָלַן הַעֲרָאָה דִּידְהוּ בְּיִשְׂרְאֵלִית? וְקָאֵי בַּעֲשֵׂה, כְּדִכְתִיב "דּוֹר שְׁלִישִׁי יָבֹא" (דברים כג) וְלֹא שֵׁנִי. וְלָאו הַבָּא מִכְּלַל עֲשֵׂה עֲשֵׂה. בִּיאָה

תוספות

מאשת אח ילפינן. ואפילו למאי דפרישית לעיל דאחות אשה לא חשיב חומרא מה שבידו לרבות, מ"מ ליכא למיפרך: מה לאשת אח שכן בידו לרבות — דהכא לא יליף, אלא דשייך אחוה מן האם באחות אשה כמו באשת אח. **דיש** לה בנים לאחר מיתת בעלה. תימה: הכא מצרכינן קרא לאסור לאחר מיתה, וכן בפ' "ד' מיתות" (סנהדרין נג. נד.) גבי אשת אב וכלתו, ופ"ק דקדושין (דף יג: ושם) קבעי: אשת איש מנלן דשריא אחר מיתת בעלה? וי"ל: דבכל הני צריך קרא לאסור, דלא נילף מאשת איש דשריא לאחר מיתה, כדיליף התם. וקשה: דב"האשה רבה" (לקמן דף צד: ושם) קאמר גבי חמותו לאחר(ב) מיתה דממעט לה רבי עקיבא מדכתיב "ישרפו אותו ואתהן" — את שתיהן, כלומר שתיהן קיימות. נהי דמעטיה קרא משרפה, מאיסורא מי מיעטיה? משמע דאי לאו קרא — היתה בשרפה! וי"ל: דבכולהו צריך קרא לאסור ולהתיר, דלא נילפו מהדדי. **בהוייתה** תהא. ומכל מקום איצטריך לעיל (דף יז:) למילף אחוה(ג) מבני יעקב, דלא נימא דבעינן דמיחדי באבא ובאימא משום דכתיב "יחדו". (ד) **דכתב** רחמנא גבי דודתו למה לי. אפילו למאי דמפרש (בה) דאין ערירי בכל חייבי כריתות אלא היכא דמפרש קרא בהדיא — אתי שפיר, כדפרישית בריש מכילתין (דף ב. ד"ה "אשת"). **לישתוק** קרא משפחה חרופה. וא"ת: השתא דחייבי לאוין בהערלה, אם כן לישתוק קרא בחייבי כריתות! ותירץ ה"ר משה כהן: דאי לאו קרא בחייבי כריתות הוה אמינא: מדגלי רחמנא בשפחה — מכלל דחייבי כריתות בהערלה, אבל חייבי לאוין — בגמר ביאה. דילפינן משפחה חרופה. אבל השתא דכתיב הערלה בחייבי כריתות, אי כל חייבי לאוין בגמר ביאה, א"כ לישתוק קרא משפחה חרופה(א).
אתיא

ס"א אינו

תוספות ישנים

ובחמישית: **מדגלי** רחמנא שכבת זרע בשפחה חרופה מכלל דחייבי לאוין בהערלה. וא"ת אדרבה נימא דניליף מינה דמה שפחה חרופה בגמר ביאה אף חייבי לאוין וכו' וא"ל א"כ לשתוק קרא משפחה חרופה דהא עדיין לא מסקינן אדעתין הך קושיא עד לקמן. וי"ל דהא מסיק אדעתיה שפיר דאם איתא דחייבי לאוין בגמר ביאה לשתוק משפחה חרופה דשפחה חרופה נמי חייבי לאוין היא דכתיב לא יהיה קדש אבל לקמן גבי חייבי כריתות לא הוה מסקינן אדעתין לומר ישתוק קרא משפחה חרופה כיון דלא ידעינן ליה רק מדיוקא מדגלי רחמנא בחייבי כריתות מכלל דחייבי לאוין בגמר ביאה. עוי"ל דאין להקשות הכא ניליף מיניה דהא ודאי מיניה בעי' למילף דהכי פירושא מדגלי רחמנא בשפחה חרופה ש"ז גבי חיוב האשם מכלל דחיוב הלאו הוי קודם גמר ביאה וא"כ חייבי לאוין הוו בהערלה: **א)** ולפי' זה קשה את שפרשתי דשמעינן מש"ז דכתיב גבי אשם דחיוב הלאו הוי משעת הערלה וא"כ אפילו אי לא כתיב הערלה בחייבי כריתות ידעינן דחייבי לאוין בהערלה ומצינן לתרץ כתירוץ שתרלתי בתי'

עין משפט נר מצוה

כא א מיי' פ"ב מהל' איסורי ביאה הל' ט סמג לאוין קח טוש"ע אה"ע סימן טו סעי' כו:
כב ב שם סעיף כב:
כג ג מיי' פ"א מהלכות יבום ה"א טוש"ע שם סי' קנז סעי' א:
כד ד ה ו מיי' פ"א מהלכות איסורי ביאה הלכה י:

מסורת הש"ס

[לעיל נד: וש"נ]

מכות יג. כריתות ב:

הגהות הב"ח

(א) רש"י ד"ה לשתוק וכו' כשאר חייבי לאוין נמי לא מיחייב בהערלה אלא בגמר ביאה: (ב) תוס' ד"ה דיש וכו' לאחר מיתת אשתו דממעט לה ר"ע: (ג) ד"ה בהוייתה וכו' למילף אחוה אחוה מבני: (ד) ד"ה דכתב כך צריך להתחיל דודתו דכתב רחמנא גבי ערירים למה לי אפי' למאן דמפרש כנ"ל:

גליון הש"ס

רש"י ד"ה לכרת ניתנה וכו' דלא הו"ל לעונשו כרת אא"כ הזהיר עליה. עיין מכות דף יג ע"ב:

עין משפט
נר מצוה

כח א מיי' פ"ג מהל' איסורי ביאה הל' טו סמג לאוין קפה טור אה"ע סי' כ:

כו ב ג מיי' שם פ"א הל' יא יב סמג שם טור אה"ע שם:

כז ד מיי' שם הלכה י וסמג שם טוש"ע אה"ע סימן כ סעיף א בהג"ה:

תוספות ישנים

הראשון: א) עוד פר"ת דאחרי שרבינו הערלה כגמר ביאה מעתה ביאה נקראת אע"ג דליכא אלא הערלה ור"ל התם תחלת הערלה קונה או סוף הערלה קונה ומסיק כל הבועל דעתו על גמר הערלה וכת"י העראה זו הכנסת העטרה דלמ"ד זו נשיקה לא שייך בה תחלה וסוף ומקשינן מהא דאמרינן לעיל אלא מן האירוסין יבא עשה וידחה ל"ת ומאי קאמר הלא [ביבמה] דעתו על גמר ביאה ממש דאי לאו הכי לא קני ליה ליבמתו דבעינן שיהא ראוי להקמת שם ומקודם שגמר ביאתו עשה בה הערלה ונקראת בעולה בהכי וא"כ איכא עשה ול"ת אף [באלמנה] מן האירוסין עשה דבתולה ולא בעולה ולאו הבא מכלל עשה עשה ולאו דאלמנה. וי"ל דלעיל ס"ל לתלמודא כמ"ד העראה זו נשיקה ולא שייך בה תחלה סוף וא"כ לא הוי א) בעולה בסוף הערלה. עוי"ל דכיון דלא הוי בעולה רק מעצמו ליכא עשה דבעולת עצמו אינה רק מדרבנן וא"ת הא אמרינן לקמן ולו תהיה לאשה פרט לאלמנה לכ"ג דכיון דלא חזיא למיקם קמיה וכו' וקאמר היכי דמי אילימא כדרכה תיפוק ליה דהויא לה בעולה. ומאי קאמר הלא אמרינן דבעולת עצמו לא הוי אלא מדרבנן וי"ל דה"ק תיפוק ליה דהויא בעולה וכחלוצה שויוה רבנן וא"כ אין לה קנס דלא חזיא למיקם קמיה. עוד יש מתרצים דהא דאמרינן הכא דהערלה קונה מקיחה קיחה הייט לאחר קדושי כסף לחשוב הערלה כחופה והא דאמרינן דעתו על גמר ביאה היינו בלא קדושי כסף. וא"ת למה לי קרא בקדושין ובעלה מלמד שניקנית בביאה תיפוק ליה מקיחה קיחה וי"ל אי לאו דשמעינן מקרא דבעילה גמור' קונה באשה לא הוה ידעינן מקיחה קיחה הערלה. ורבינו נתנאל תירץ דלפי' דלעיל מכוון הדבר הזה דובעלה דמשמע ביאה גמורה מיירי בלא קדושין דכסף ותחלת קניינו בביאה בעי' ביאה גמורה ומעתה ידעינן מקיחה קיחה הערלה לאחר קדושי כסף שמועיל כמו חופה: **פרט** לשקינא

א) נראה דל"ל וא"כ לא מקרי בעולה על ידי הערלה.

אתיא ביאה ביאה. והוי כאילו כתיב דור שלישי יערה, משמע הא דור שני – לא יערה, ולא שייך לאקשויי מהא דאמר בסוף "הנשרפין" (סנהדרין פד.) דבר הבא מן הכלל אין דנין אותו בגזירה שוה, דהכא ביאה דאתיא לגזירה שוה כתיבא בהדיא, ולא מן הכלל אתי, כי הכיא דהתם דלא ילפינן חילול חילול מתרומה כהן העובד באנינות, דלא כתיב חילול אלא דנפיק מכלל דכתב בכהן גדול "ומן המקדש לא יצא ולא יחלל" (ויקרא כא) הא אחר שעבד – חלל. **אי** למאן דאמר עשה עשה. ל"ג לי', וברוב ספרים ליתא, דבין לרב ובין לשמואל איכא לאו, כדפרישי' בסוף "החולץ" (לעיל מט: ד"ה "אי כרב"). **אשה** לבעלה מנין אתיא קיחה קיחה. פירוש: דנקנית בהערלה. הקשה ה"ר נסים: דבפ"ק דקדושין (דף י. ושם) בעי: תחלת ביאה קונה או סוף ביאה קונה? למאי נפקא מינה – שהערה בה וקבלה קידושין מאחר כו'. ומסיק רבא דכל הבועל דעתו על גמר ביאה, ולא קני בהערלה! ותירץ הר' שמעון הזקן: דהא דאמר הכא דקני בהערלה – היינו בשלא עשה כי אם הערלה ופירש מיד, ולא גמר ביאתו. אבל התם איירי כשעושה כל הביאה, דלא קני בהערלה, כיון שדעתו על גמר ביאה. וכן מוכח הלשון, דקאמר התם: כל הבועל – דעתו על גמר ביאה, ולא קאמר כל המערה. וה"ר יצחק בן ה"ר מאיר פירש: דכשמפרש שרוצה לקנות בהערלה – קני בהערלה אפי' אם גומר ביאתו, אבל בסתם – דעתו על גמר ביאה. ור"ת פירש שם בע"א, ושם פירשתיא. **קיחה** קיחה. תימה: דנפקא לן בפרק קמא דקדושין (דף ט:) דאשה נקנית בביאה מדכתיב "ובעלה", ותיפוק ליה מקיחה קיחה! וי"ל: אי לאו דכתיב ובעלה – מקיחה דעריות לא הוה גמרינן ועיקר דיאה, כיון דקיחה דעריות לא משתעי בקנין כלל, אבל לענין שתיחשב הערלה כגמר ביאה – ילפינן שפיר מהתם. ואם תאמר: ונילף מקיחה דיבמה דאיירי בקנין, דכתיב "ולקחה לו לאשה"! וי"ל: דאינו מופנה לג"ש. וא"ת: ונילף מקיחה דחייבי לאוין דכהונה, דקיחה דידהו איירי בקנין, כדאמר בפרק בתרא דקידושין (דף עח.): קדש לוקה משום "לא יקח", ודרשינן ליה נמי לג"ש! וי"ל: דלא איירי בקיחה דביאה, אלא בסתם קידושין, כדאמר התם: בעל – לוקה משום "לא יחלל", ועוד י"ל: דאי לאו "ובעלה" לא הוה גמרינן קידושי כסף מקיחה קיחה דשדה עפרון. אלא הוה מוקמינן קיחה דקרא בקידושי ביאה, משום דמסתבר למגמר טפי קיחה דאשה מקיחה דאשה. אבל השתא דכתיב "ובעלה" – ע"כ גמרינן קיחה משדה עפרון קידושי כסף, דליכא למימר דאיצטריך קיחה להערלה – דא"כ לשתוק מ"ובעלה", ונילף כולה מילתא מעריות. **לאחר** מיתה נמי שארו איקרי כו'. והא דפשיטא לן בפרק "יש נוחלין" (ב"ב דף קיד:) *דאין הבעל יורש את אשתו כשהוא בקבר, וקאמר נמי התם: כשם שאין האיש יורש את אשתו בקבר להנחיל לקרוביו, כך הבן לא יירש את אמו בקבר להנחיל לאחיו מן האב. הא דפשיטא ליה בבעל טפי מבבן – היינו מהך דרשא דהכא דאשמועינן דלאחר מיתה לא מיקרי שארו. וא"ת: דבפרק "ד' מיתות" (סנהדרין סו:) ממעט משמש מתה מקרא אחרינא. דדריש התם ומתו גם שניהם – פרט למעשה הורדוס. והיינו משמש מתה, כדאמר בבבא בתרא (דף ג:): דהטמין בדובשא יוקתא דבי חשמונאי, והיה בא עליה לייתובי יצריה! ואר"י: דאיצטריך דרשא דשמעתין למאן דדריש התם "ומתו גם שניהם" – עד שיהו שניהם שוים. והא דקאמר התם ואידך מעשה הורדוס לאו כלום הוא – המ"ל דנפקא ליה מקרא דהכא, אלא דניחא ליה לאוקמי ההוא תנא דדריש עד שיהו שניהם שוים אפילו כמ"ד משמש מת בעריות פטור. ויש ספרים דגרסי התם: פרט למעשה אידודין. וכן גורס בערוך*: ופי' רש"י שם דמעשה אידודין היינו דרך אברים, וקשה: דהכא פשיטא ליה לאביי דדרך אברים לאו כלום הוא? וי"ל: דהיינו כמ"ד התם דמעשה אידודין לאו כלום הוא, ואפילו למאן דממעט התם מקרא – איכא למימר דמקרא התם פשיטא ליה לאביי הכא. **לשקינא** לה דרך אברים. ואם תאמר: הא אפילו אמר לה אל תסתרי סתם הוי קינוי, ואם כן מה בכך אם הזכיר נמי דרך אברים? כיון דאמר לה נמי אל תסתרי! ויש לומר דהכי פירושו: שקינא לה דרך אברים, שאמר לה: איני חושדך אלא דרך אברים, וכן שלא כדרכה. **אינו** חייב אלא על ביאת מירוק. נראה דמחייב בשפחה חרופה אפילו בלא הוצאת זרע. [אלא שתהא] ביאה הראויה להזריע. כמו באשת איש, דלא בעינן הוצאת זרע, אף על גב דכתיב בה ש"ז. ולא אתא למעוטי בשפחה חרופה אלא הערלה ושלא כדרכה בספ"ב דכריתות (דף יא:). ונראה דלמ"ד הערלה זו הכנסת עטרה אין ראויה להתעבר בהערלה אלא במירוק גיד, שאם היתה ראויה להתעבר – לא הוה מוקמי קרא למעוטי הערלה שלא כדרכה.

אָתְיָא "בִּיאָה" "בִּיאָה". יְבָמָה לַשּׁוּק מְנָלַן? אִי לְמַאן דַּאֲמַר לָאו — לָאו, אִי לְמַאן דַּאֲמַר עֲשֵׂה — עֲשֵׂה. אֶלָּא יְבָמָה לַיָּבָם מְנָלַן? אָתְיָא "בִּיאָה" "בִּיאָה". אִשָּׁה לְבַעְלָהּ מְנָלַן? אָתְיָא "קִיחָה" "קִיחָה". אֲמַר רָבָא: לָמָּה לִי דִּכְתַב רַחֲמָנָא "שִׁכְבַת זֶרַע" בְּשִׁפְחָה חֲרוּפָה, "שִׁכְבַת זֶרַע" בְּאֵשֶׁת אִישׁ, "שִׁכְבַת זֶרַע" בְּסוֹטָה, דְּשִׁפְחָה חֲרוּפָה — [א]כְּדַאֲמָרַן. דְּאֵשֶׁת אִישׁ — פְּרָט לִמְשַׁמֵּשׁ מֵת. הָנִיחָא לְמַאן דַּאֲמַר *מְשַׁמֵּשׁ מֵת בַּעֲרָיוֹת [ב]פָּטוּר, אֶלָּא לְמ"ד חַיָּיב — מַאי אִיכָּא לְמֵימַר? אֶלָּא [ג]פְּרָט לִמְשַׁמֵּשׁ מֵתָה. דְּסד"א: [הוֹאִיל] לְאַחַר מִיתָה נַמִי אִיקְּרֵי שְׁאֵרוֹ, אֵימָא לִיחַיַּיב עֲלַהּ בְּאֵשֶׁת אִישׁ — קמ"ל. דְּסוֹטָה לָמָּה לִי? לִכְדְתַנְיָא: *"שִׁכְבַת זֶרַע" פְּרָט לְדָבָר אַחֵר. מַאי דָּבָר אַחֵר? אָמַר רַב שֵׁשֶׁת: פְּרָט לְשֶׁקִּינֵּא לָהּ שֶׁלֹּא כְּדַרְכָּהּ. א"ל רָבָא: "מִשְׁכְּבֵי אִשָּׁה" כְּתִיב! אֶלָּא אָמַר רָבָא: פְּרָט לְשֶׁקִּינֵּא לָהּ דֶּרֶךְ אֵבָרִים. א"ל אַבַּיֵי: פְּרִיצוּתָא אָסַר רַחֲמָנָא? אֶלָּא אָמַר אַבַּיֵי: פְּרָט לְשֶׁקִּינֵּא לָהּ בִּנְשִׁיקָה. הָנִיחָא לְמ"ד *הַעֲרָאָה זוֹ הַכְנָסַת עֲטָרָה, אֶלָּא לְמ"ד זוֹ נְשִׁיקָה — מַאי אִיכָּא לְמֵימַר? אֶלָּא, לְעוֹלָם לְשֶׁקִּינֵּא לָהּ דֶּרֶךְ אֵבָרִים, וְאִיצְטְרִיךְ: סד"א: בְּקְפִידָא דְּבַעַל תָּלָה רַחֲמָנָא, וְהָא קָא קָפֵיד, קמ"ל. אָמַר שְׁמוּאֵל: *הַעֲרָאָה זוֹ נְשִׁיקָה, מָשָׁל לְאָדָם שֶׁמַּנִּיחַ אֶצְבָּעוֹ עַל פִּיו — אִי אֶפְשָׁר שֶׁלֹּא יִדְחוֹק הַבָּשָׂר. כִּי אֲתָא רַבָּה בַּר בַּר חָנָה אָמַר רַבִּי יוֹחָנָן: גְּמַר בִּיאָה בְּשִׁפְחָה חֲרוּפָה — זוֹ הַכְנָסַת עֲטָרָה. מְתִיב רַב שֵׁשֶׁת: "שִׁכְבַת זֶרַע" אֵינוֹ חַיָּיב אֶלָּא עַל בִּיאַת הַמֵּירוּק. מַאי לָאו — מֵירוּק גִּיד? לָא, מֵירוּק עֲטָרָה. כִּי אֲתָא רַב דִּימִי א"ר יוֹחָנָן: [ד]הַעֲרָאָה — זוֹ הַכְנָסַת עֲטָרָה. אָמְרוּ לֵיהּ: וְהָא רַבָּה בַּר בַּר חָנָה לָא אֲמַר הָכִי? אֲמַר לְהוּ: אוֹ אִיהוּ שַׁקְרָאִי אוֹ אֲנָא שַׁקְרִי. כִּי אֲתָא רָבִין א"ר יוֹחָנָן: הַעֲרָאָה זוֹ הַכְנָסַת עֲטָרָה. אַדְּרַבָּה בַּר בַּר חָנָה — וַדַּאי פְּלִיג, אַדִּשְׁמוּאֵל מִי לֵימָא פְּלִיג?! לָא, מִנְּשִׁיקָה וְעַד הַכְנָסַת עֲטָרָה — הַעֲרָאָה קָרֵי לָהּ. כִּי אֲתָא רַב שְׁמוּאֵל בַּר יְהוּדָה א"ר יוֹחָנָן הַעֲרָאָה — זוֹ הַכְנָסַת עֲטָרָה, גְּמַר בִּיאָה — גְּמַר בִּיאָה מַמָּשׁ.

מִכָּאן

בִּיאָה בִּיאָה. מֵחַיָּיבֵי לָאוִין, דִּכְתִיב בְּהוּ "לֹא יָבֹא מַמְזֵר". יְבָמָה לַשּׁוּק. בְּלֹא חֲלִיצָה, מִנַּיִן דְּהַעֲרָאָה דִּידָהּ כִּגְמַר בִּיאָה? אִי לְמַאן דַּאֲמַר לָאו. דִּכְתִיב "לֹא תִהְיֶה אֵשֶׁת הַמֵּת" (דברים כה) יָלְפִינַן הַעֲרָאָה לְחַיָּיבֵי לָאוִין. אִי לְמַאן דַּאֲמַר עֲשֵׂה. דִּכְתִיב (שם) "יְבָמָהּ יָבֹא עָלֶיהָ" וְלֹא אַחֵר, וְלָאו הַבָּא מִכְּלַל עֲשֵׂה – עֲשֵׂה. וְהַאי "לֹא תִהְיֶה" מַפֵּיק לָהּ לְאֵין קִידּוּשִׁין תּוֹפְסִין בָּהּ. וְה"ק: לֹא יְהֵא בָּהּ הֲוָיָה לְזָר. וּפְלוּגְתָּא דְּרַב וּשְׁמוּאֵל הִיא בְּ"הָאִשָּׁה קַמָּא" (לקמן צב:). **אֶלָּא** יְבָמָה לַיָּבָם מְנָלַן. דְּקָנֵי לָהּ בְּהַעֲרָאָה. **אִשָּׁה** לְבַעְלָהּ. לְעִנְיַן מְקַדֵּשׁ בְּבִיאָה, מְנָלַן דִּבְהַעֲרָאָה מִתְקַדְּשָׁה? קִיחָה קִיחָה. "כִּי יִקַּח אִישׁ אִשָּׁה וּבְעָלָהּ" (דברים כד) וּמֵהָכָא יָלְפִינַן קִידּוּשֵׁי בִּיאָה: כְּתִיב הָכָא קִיחָה וּכְתִיב הָתָם בְּחַיָּיבֵי כְרֵיתוֹת קִיחָה (ויקרא כ). לָמָּה לִי לְמִיכְתַּב שִׁכְבַת זֶרַע בְּאֵשֶׁת אִישׁ. "וְאֶל אֵשֶׁת עֲמִיתְךָ לֹא תִתֵּן שְׁכָבְתְּךָ לְזָרַע" (ויקרא יח) וְהָא אִיתְרַבֵּי בָּהּ הַעֲרָאָה מֵהֶקֵּישָׁא דְּר' יוֹנָה? שִׁכְבַת זֶרַע בְּסוֹטָה. הַנִּסְתָּרָה, דְּנֶאֱסֶרֶת מִסָּפֵק, כְּתִיב "וְשָׁכַב אִישׁ אוֹתָהּ שִׁכְבַת זֶרַע" (במדבר ה). **כְּדַאֲמַרַן.** דְּבָעֵינַן גְּמַר בִּיאָה. דְּלָא תֵּימָא כִּי הֵיכִי דְּמִחַיֵּיב מַלְקוֹת בְּהַעֲרָאָה לִיחַיֵּיב נַמִי אָשָׁם בְּהַעֲרָאָה. לִמְשַׁמֵּשׁ מֵת. בְּאֵבֶר מֵת בְּלֹא קִישּׁוּי, דְּאֵין רָאוּי לְהַזְרִיעַ. **הָנִיחָא** לְמ"ד. בִּשְׁבוּעוֹת בְּפֶרֶק "יְדִיעוֹת הַטּוּמְאָה". לִמְשַׁמֵּשׁ מֵתָה. אֵשֶׁת אִישׁ לְאַחַר מִיתָתָהּ. **סד"א הוֹאִיל וּלְאַחַר** מִיתָתָהּ שְׁאֵרוֹ. דְּבַעְלָהּ מִיקְרֵי, דִּכְתִיב גַּבֵּי טוּמְאָה "כִּי אִם לִשְׁאֵרוֹ" (ויקרא כא) וְאָמְרִי': *שְׁאֵרוֹ זוֹ אִשְׁתּוֹ, לִיחַיֵּיב עָלֶיהָ. **לְשֶׁקִּינֵּא** לָהּ שֶׁלֹּא כְּדַרְכָּהּ. שֶׁהָיָה חוֹשְׁדָהּ עִמּוֹ בְּכָךְ, וּכְשֶׁאָמַר אַל תִּסָּתְרִי עִמּוֹ – יָדוּעַ לַכֹּל דְּלָדַעַת כֵּן הִזְהִירָהּ, דְּלֹא הָיָה חוֹשְׁדָהּ עִמּוֹ בְּבִיאָה אַחֶרֶת. לִישָּׁנָא אַחֲרִינָא: לְשֶׁקִּינֵּא לָהּ שֶׁלֹּא כְּדַרְכָּהּ – אַל תִּסָּתְרִי עִמּוֹ לִיבָּעֵל לוֹ שֶׁלֹּא כְּדַרְכָּהּ. **מִשְׁכְּבֵי אִשָּׁה כְּתִיב.** הוּקְשׁוּ שְׁנֵיהֶן. דֶּרֶךְ **אֵבָרִים.** מִיעוּךְ דַּדִּים, וְדָשׁ מִבַּחוּץ בִּשְׁאָר אֵבָרִים. **פְּרִיצוּתָא** קָאָסַר רַחֲמָנָא. בִּתְמִיָּה. כְּלוֹמַר, פְּשִׁיטָא דְּלָאו קִינּוּי הוּא, דְּמִשּׁוּם פְּרִיצוּתָא לָא מִיתַּסְרָא עֲלֵיהּ. **בִּנְשִׁיקָה.** אֵבֶר נוֹשֵׁק בְּמְקוֹם תַּשְׁמִישׁ. **הָנִיחָא** לְמ"ד. לְקַמָּן בִּשְׁמַעְתִּין: הַעֲרָאָה זוֹ הַכְנָסַת עֲטָרָה, אֲבָל נְשִׁיקָה לָאו הַעֲרָאָה הִיא, וְלָא מִיתַּסְרָא לְבַעְלָהּ בְּהָכִי – שַׁפִּיר קָאָמְרַתְּ (דְּלָא מִיתַּסְרָא לְבַעְלָהּ), דְּלָאו קִינּוּי הוּא. **אֶלָּא** לְמ"ד נְשִׁיקָה הַעֲרָאָה הִיא. הֵיכִי מְמַעֵט לָהּ. **גְּמַר בִּיאָה** זוֹ הַכְנָסַת עֲטָרָה. מִכְּלָל דִּנְשִׁיקָה הַעֲרָאָה הִיא, כִּשְׁמוּאֵל. **שִׁכְבַת** זֶרַע. בְּשִׁפְחָה חֲרוּפָה קָאֵי. **עֲטָרָה.** רֹאשׁ הַגִּיד הִיא, וְאֵינָהּ מִן הַגִּיד אֶלָּא בָּשָׂר. **מֵירוּק.** שֶׁמַּזְרִיעַ. **וַדַּאי פְּלִיגָא.** דְּהָא אָמַר: הַכְנָסַת עֲטָרָה זוֹ הִיא גְּמַר בִּיאָה, וְהָכָא קָרֵי לָהּ הַעֲרָאָה. **אַדִּשְׁמוּאֵל.** דְּאָמַר: נְשִׁיקָה הָוֵי הַעֲרָאָה. מִי **לֵימָא פְּלִיג.** דִּלִשְׁמוּאֵל הָוֵי הַכְנָסַת עֲטָרָה גְּמַר בִּיאָה, וּלְרָבִין נְשִׁיקָה לָאו כְּלוּם הִיא. אוֹ דִּלְמָא תַּרְוַיְיהוּ, בֵּין לְרָבִין בֵּין לִשְׁמוּאֵל הַעֲרָאָה נִינְהוּ, וּמַר אָמַר חֲדָא וּמַר אָמַר חֲדָא וְלָא פְּלִיגִי.

מִכָּאן

לדברים

[סנהדרין נה.] שבועות יח. סוטה כו: גז"ש [סנהדרין עג:] סוטה כו: [לעיל כב:] ס"א איתו [וע"ש היטב בתוס' ד"ה מה אשה] [ערך הרדוס]

תוספות חד מקמאי

לתרומה אין האשה אוכלת בתרומה עד שתכנס לחופה: אמר רבה שכבת זרע דכתב גבי שפחה חרופה למעט מינה דכל חייבי לאוין בהערלה דא"כ לישתוק קרא מיניה דשפחה חרופה. שכבת זרע דאשת איש למ"ד משמש מת בעריות חייב פרט למשמש מתה. שכבת זרע דסוטה לאו למעקרה קינא לה שלא כדרכה דהא משכבי אשה [כתיב]. אלא פרט שקנא לה דרך אבריה ואע"ג דפריצות בעלמא איצטריך ס"ד בקפידא דבעל תלה רחמנא והא קפיד קמ"ל. ולמ"ד העראה זו הכנסת עטרה פרט לשקנא לה בנשיקה מהו: רב

בח א ב מיי' פ"ח מהל' תרומות הל' ו:
בט ג מיי' שם הל' ט:
ל ד ה מיי' שם הל' י:

מכאן ואילך אינו אלא נשיקה, ופטור עליה. ופליג אדשמואל.§ "אחד המערה ואחד הגומר קנה".§ מאי קנה? *רב אמר: קנה לכל. ושמואל אמר: לא קנה אלא לדברים האמורים בפרשה: לירש בנכסי אחיו, ולפוטרה מן הייבום. אמן הנשואין לד"ה אכלה, דהא הות קאכלה מעיקרא. כי פליגי – מן האירוסין. רב אמר: אוכלת, דהא רבי רחמנא ביאת שוגג כמזיד. ושמואל אמר: כי רבי רחמנא – לאוקמיה במקום בעל, לאלומי מבעל – לא. ואזדא שמואל לטעמיה, דאמר רב נחמן אמר שמואל: כל שהבעל מאכיל – יבם מאכיל, וכל שאין הבעל מאכיל – יבם אינו מאכיל. מיתיבי: בת ישראל פקחת שנתארסה לכהן פקח, ולא הספיק לכונסה עד שנתחרש – אינה אוכלת. מת, ונפלה לפני יבם חרש – אוכלת. ובזו יפה כח היבם מכח הבעל. בשלמא לרב – ניחא, אלא לשמואל – קשיא! אמר לך שמואל: אימא הכי: ולא הספיק לכונסה עד שנתחרש – אינה אוכלת בתרומה. כנס ואח"כ נתחרש – אוכלת, מת ונפלה לפני יבם חרש – אוכלת. ומאי "בזו" דאילו בעל חרש מעיקרא – לא אוכלת, ואילו יבם חרש מעיקרא – אכלה. ואיכא דאמרי: מן האירוסין – ד"ה לא אכלה, דהא לא אכלה בחיי בעל. כי פליגי – מן הנשואין. רב אמר: באוכלת, דהא הות אכלה מעיקרא. ושמואל אמר: אינה אוכלת, כי רבי רחמנא ביאת שוגג כמזיד – לדברים האמורים בפרשה, אבל לכל מילי – לא. והאמר רב נחמן אמר שמואל: כל שהבעל מאכיל – יבם מאכיל! אימא: כל ביאה שהבעל מאכיל בה – יבם מאכיל בה – וכל ביאה שאין הבעל מאכיל בה – אין היבם מאכיל בה. מיתיבי גבת ישראל פקחת שנתארסה לכהן פקח, ולא הספיק לכונסה עד שנתחרש – אינה אוכלת. מת ונפלה לפני יבם חרש – אוכלת, ובזו יפה כח יבם מכח בעל. בשלמא לרב – מתרץ דכדתריץ מעיקרא. אלא לשמואל קשיא! קשיא.§ ת"ר: בת ישראל פקחת שנתארסה לכהן פקח, ולא הספיק לכונסה עד שנתחרש – אינה אוכלת, הנולד לה בן – אוכלת. מת הבן, רבי נתן אומר: אוכלת, וחכמים אומרים: אינה אוכלת. מאי טעמא דרבי נתן? אמר רבה: הואיל שכבר אכלה. א"ל אביי: אלא מעתה בת ישראל שניסת לכהן ומית ליה – תיכול, שכבר אכלה! אלא, כיון דמית ליה פקע ליה קדושתיה מינה – הכא נמי, כיון דמית ליה פקע קדושתיה מינה! אלא אמר רב יוסף: קסבר ר' נתן נשואי חרש מאכילין בתרומה, ולא גזרינן נשואי חרש אטו קדושי חרש. א"ל אביי: אי הכי, נולד לה בן למה לי! משום רבנן. וליפלוג רבי נתן עלייהו ברישא – שביק להו לרבנן עד דמסיימי מילתייהו, והדר פליג עלייהו. אי הכי ליתני: מת הבן אינה אוכלת, רבי נתן אומר: אוכלת! קשיא.§ "וכן הבא על אחת מכל העריות".§ *אמר רב עמרם: הא מלתא אמר לן רב ששת, ואנהרינהו

מכאן ואילך. מהכנסת עטרה ולמטה אינו אלא נשיקה, ופטור, ומדפטר בנשיקה – ודאי פליג אדשמואל, דנשיקה קרי לה הערה, והערה רבינן לה לחיובי. קנה לכל. באחד מן הביאות גרועות הללו קנה לה לכל דבר, ואוכלת בתרומה מיד אם כהן הוא, אפי' הלך למדינת הים ולא בא עליה ביאה גמורה. האמורים בפרשה. בפרשת יבמים, שכתב בה מקרא זה "יבמה יבא עליה", דדרשינן ליה: בין בשוגג בין במזיד בין באונס בין ברצון. לירש. דכתיב "יקום על שם אחיו" (דברים כה). ולפוטרה מייבום. דאם מת ולו בנים מאשה אחרת מותרת לשוק, או אם הוציאה בגט לא בעיא חליצה, או אם היתה לה צרה נפטרה בביאתו של זו. מן הנשואין. היכא דנפלה לפניו מן הנשואין שכבר היתה אוכלת בימי אחיו, וכשמת ובטל קנינו פסקה מלאכול. דכ"ע לא פליגי דקניא לה הך ביאה גרועה להאכילה. לאוקמיה במקום בעל. שאם היתה אוכלת בחייו תאכל בשביל זה. אבל לאלומי מבעל, דבחיי הבעל לא היתה אוכלת, דאין האשה אוכלת בתרומה עד שתכנס לחופה, האי נמי לא אלים מיניה. ודוקא בביאה בלא דעת קנין, אבל בביאה גמורה – אשתו גמורה היא, ואוכלת אפי' לשמואל. אין היבם מאכיל. בביאה גרועה. אינה אוכלת. (דהך חופה לאו חופה היא), דגזרינן נשואי חרש אטו קידושי חרש, כדאמרינן לקמן. מת. חרש זה לאחר שכנסה, ונפלה לפני יבם חרש. אוכלת. דלא גרעה ביאת חרש מביאת שוגג וזנות ואונס שאין מתכוין לקנות, ורבייה רחמנא לגבי יבם. לשמואל קשיא. דהא לא הוה אכלה מעיקרא, וקאכלה השתא. אימא כנסה ואח"כ נתחרש אוכלת. מת אחר שכנסה ונתחרש ונפלה כו' – אוכלת, דהא אכלה מעיקרא. ומאי בזו. יפה כחו, ומאי ייפוי כח איכא? הא בעל נמי חרש הוא, ומאכילה. חרש מעיקרא. קודם שכנסה. דהא אכלה מעיקרא. והשתא הדרא בהך ביאה, דהא רחמנא רבייה. כל ביאה שהבעל מאכיל. כגון ביאת חופה. בשלמא לרב. אע"ג דהא מתני' פריכא ליה, דקתני אכלה ואע"ג דלא אכלה מעיקרא, והויא כנופלת מן האירוסין, דאמרן לא אכלה אפי' לרב. מתרץ לה כדמתרצינן מעיקרא. אליבא דשמואל, חסורי מחסרא והכי קתני: כנסה ואח"כ נתחרש – אוכלת, מת ונפלה לפני יבם חרש – אוכלת, דהא אכלה מעיקרא. אלא לשמואל. דאפי' האוכלת בחיי בעלה אינה אוכלת בשביל היבם, בביאה גרועה. קשיא. דהא ביאת חרש כביאת שוגג ואונס היא, בלא כוונת קנין, ואכלה. נולד לה בן אוכלת. בשביל בנה, כדכתיב "ויליד ביתו הם יאכלו בלחמו" (ויקרא כב) קרי ביה: "יאכילו". מת הבן. והאב קיים. ר' נתן אומר אוכלת. בשביל בעלה. ומית ליה. בלא בן. קסבר ר' נתן נשואי חרש. דקדשה כשהוא פקח מאכילין בתרומה, דמדאורייתא משעת אירוסין אוכלת, דכתיב (שם) "וכהן כי יקנה נפש קנין כספו הוא יאכל בו" מיד, ורבנן הוא דגזרי עד שתכנס לחופה, משום גזירה, שמא ימזגו לה כוס בבית אביה ותשקה לאחיה ולאחותה, כדאמרינן בכתובות בפ' אע"פ (דף נז:). הלכך, כיון דהאי בשעת קנין הוי בן דעת, והשתא הכניסה לחופה, וליכא למיגזר *שמא תשקה – אכלה. אבל לא גזרינן נשואי חרש אטו קידושי חרש, דלאו בר קנין הוא. ורבנן דאסרי גזרי נשואי חרש דהוי בן דעת בשעת קידושין אטו היכא דקדשה כשהוא חרש, דקנינו לאו קנין. נולד לה בן למה לי. בלא בן נמי אכלה לרבי נתן. משום רבנן. לאשמועינן היכא דנולד לה בן מודו. והדר פליג עלייהו. ואוכלת דקאמר רבי נתן – אכולה מילתא קאי, בין אסיפא דמת הבן, בין ארישא קודם שנולד לה בן, דקאמרי רבנן אינה אוכלת. אי הכי. דרבי נתן ארישא נמי פליג, ומנטר הוא דנטר לרבנן עד סיומא. ליתני מת הבן אינה אוכלת רבי נתן אומר אוכלת. דתיהוי כולה מילתא דרבנן בחדא, והדר ליפלוג רבי נתן אכולה. אבל השתא – ליכא למימר דנטר להו אסיומא, ובמת הבן לחודא פליג. ואנהרינהו

לדברים האמורים. אע"ג דכל שאר דברים כתובים נמי בפרשה, כדדרשינן: כיון שלקחה – נעשית כאשתו לכל דבר – כיון דביאת שוגג לא קני בעלמא סברא הוא דלא רבייה אלא לדברים המפורשים בפרשה בהדיא, כגון לירש בנכסי אחיו, דכתיב "יקום על שם אחיו" לנחלה, ולפטור אשת אחיו מן היבום, דכתיב "לו לאשה" ולא לאחיו לאשה, דפקע מינה זיקת אחיו, ולפטור צרתה, דכתיב "בית אחיו" – בית אחד הוא בונה ואינו בונה שני בתים, דהנהו דברים הוו לאוקמיה במקום בעל. אבל בתרומה לא אכלה ע"י ביאה גרועה, ולא יורשה, ולא מיטמא לה, ולא מיפר נדריה, דהיינו לאלומי מבעל. אבל מן הנשואין – זכאי בכולהו, דלא הוי אלא לאוקמיה במקום בעל, דילפינן מהני דכתיבי, ולא פליגי אלא בביאת שוגג וכיוצא בה. אבל בהערה דקניא נמי בעלמא, וביאה היא לכל דבר – לא פליגי בה. א)ומה שקבע מחלוקתן כאן אמתני' דאחד הגומר ואחד המערה – לאו משום דעלה פליגי, אלא משום דמסיים בה "קנה", דקאי נמי אביאת שוגג. כן נראה לר"י. ובירושלמי איכא פלוגתייהו. ואיכא דמוקי פלוגתייהו בהערה.

מן הנשואין כ"ע לא פליגי דאכלה. ע"י ביאה. וה"ה דהוה מצי למינקט לענין ליורשה, ולהטמא לה, ולהפר נדריה. אלא נקט אכילת תרומה לרבותא, וכ"ש לשאר דברים. דזימנין שהיא כאשתו לכל דבר ולא אכלה בתרומה, כדאמר בכתובות בפ' "נערה" (דף מח: ושם): מסורה לכל חוץ לתרומה, גבי מסר האב לשלוחי הבעל. [וע' היטב תוס' סוטה כד: ד"ה דהאמר רב].

מת ונפלה לפני יבם חרש אוכלת. וא"ת: ואמאי אוכלת? וניחוש לסימפון, שהרי לא בדקה, שלא הספיק לכונסה עד שנתחרש, וא"כ אינה זקוקה לו! ולקמן נמי דקאמר דגזרינן נישואין דחרש אטו קידושין – תיפוק ליה משום סימפון, ולר' נתן נמי אמאי אוכלת! ואור"י דלא חיישינן לסימפון אלא כשיכול הדבר להתגלות שיש סימפון ויהיו קידושי טעות. אבל הכא, דנתחרש, לא חיישינן שמא יתפקח וימצא סימפון.

כל ביאה שהבעל מאכיל בה. אי (א) ביאה אירוסין עושה – אר"י דכל ביאה שהבעל מאכיל בה, ע"י חופה שאחריה קאמר.

*)ממזרת ונתינה לישראל פסלה. לשון פסלה נקט משום אחריני, דממזרת ונתינה הם פסולות ועומדות.

מאי

*) שייך למתני' לעיל נג:

[לקמן נח:] סוטה כד:

[כת"ס אין]

[לעיל נה.]

ס"א שמא תשקה ותאכל ולא גזרינן

הגהות הב"ח

(א) תוס' ד"ה כל וכו' אי ביאה. נ"ב בפ"ק דקדושין דף י ע"א קא מיבעיא ליה ביאה אי נישואין עושה או אירוסין עושה וע"ש:

תוספות ישנים

לה שלא כדרכה. ואין להקשות ומי גרע מקינא לה סתם דודאי גרע דגלי בדעתיה שאינו חושדה אלא בשלא כדרכה ומ"מ פריך משכבי אשה כתיב וא"כ קנוי גמור הוא: לדברים האמורים בפרשה. ואע"ג דבפרשה משמע דהויא כאשתו לכל דבר דאמרינן כיון שלקחה נעשית כאשתו לכל דבר מ"מ לא שמעינן מהתם ביאת שוגג ואונס (הא) [רק מיירי] בביאה גמורה אבל ביאת שוגג ואונס לא הוי כאשתו לכל דבר אלא לדברים האמורים בהדיא בפרשה: מן הנשואין דברי הכל אכלה ע"י ביאת שוגג דבלא ביאה לא דאמרינן ולא היבמה עד שתבעל: לאלומי מבעל לא. וה"ה דהוה מצי למימר דאיכא בינייהו ליורשה וליטמא לה לשמואל כיון דלא אלימא מבעל לא ירית לה ולא מיטמא כמו בעל גופיה באשתו ארוסה: א) ובירושלמי לא משמע כן וז"ל הירושלמי קנה ולא חילק בין ביאה לביאה מאי קנה שמואל אמר לא קנה לכל אלא לדברים האמורים בפרשה לירש בנכסי המת ולהתיר צרתה לשוק ור' יוחנן אומר קנה לכל. א"ר יצחק ב"ר אליעזר פליגין בשמערה בה אבל אם גמר הביאה כ"ע מודו וא"כ משמע דרב ושמואל דהכא קיימי אהערה וניחא שסתם התלמוד פלוגתייהו דרב ושמואל אחר מתני' אחד המערה ואחד הגומר קנה דעלה קיימי כן פירש רבינו נתנאל אך התוספות לא פירשו כן. ופירשו דקיימי אביאת שוגג וראיה לדבריהם דקאמר בסמוך כי רבי רחמנא ביאת שוגג כמזיד וכו' משמע דבביאת שוגג איירי אבל בהערה לא פליגי דביאה היא לכל דבר וקניא נמי בעלמא ואע"פ שקבע כאן מחלוקתן על משנה אחד המערה ואחד הגומר לאו משום דקאי עלה אלא משום דמסיים קנה דקאי נמי אשוגג כ"נ לר' שנ"ץ: ולא הספיק לכונסה עד שנתחרש. לקמן מפרש טעמא דגזרינן נשואי חרש אטו קדושי חרש וא"ת בלא האי טעמא לא תאכל משום סמפון דשמא יש בה מום וקדושי טעות הוו דלא ידע לבודקה הבעל לפי שלא הספיק לכונסה עד שנתחרש וי"ל טעמא מאי קדושי טעות הוו כשנמצא בה מום משום דאימר אם היה יודע שכן הוא לא היה מקדשה וזה החרש לא היה לו דעת להקפיד בדבר ולא חיישינן שמא יתפקח וימצא סמפון: נשואי חרש מאכילין בתרומה. דלא איכא משום סמפון כיון דהוה בר דעת כשקדשה ולשמא ימזגו ליכא דאינה בבית אביה ואטו קדושי חרש לא גזר רבי נתן: הבא על אחת מכל העריות האמורות בתורה או פסולות ודוקא הני אבל ביאת זנות דפנויה לא פסיל לה לכהן ולא משויא לה זונה דלית לסבר פנוי הבא על הפנויה שלא לשם אישות עשאה זונה אלא לר' אלעזר ולא ס"ל כוותיה: ממזרת ונתינה לישראל פסל לאו לפוסלה לכהונה מיירי דבלא"ה אפסלה וקיימא ולתרומה דבי נשא ליכא למימר דאינה בת כהן אלא ר"ל לענין מלקות למלקי הבא עליה אם בעל בהערה

תוספות חד מקמאי

רב אמר קנה לכל ושמואל אמר לא קנה אלא לדברים האמורים בפרשה אבל להאכילה בתרומה לא קנה באונס ובשוגג. והלכתא כרב ודוקא באונס ובשוגג דה"ל כביאה אבל בלא ביאה לא אכלה מן הנשואין אע"פ שכבר אכלה בחיי בעלה. ושמעינן מהא דהא דתנן בפ' אע"פ ובפ' אלמנה לכ"ג היבם אינו מאכיל בתרומה אע"פ שכבר אכלה בחיי בעלה ולאפוקי (מהמ"פ תוין) [מהמפרשים] שפרשוה כשלא אכלה בחיי הבעל אבל אם אכלה בחיי הבעל אוכלת שומרת יבם בתרומה. ת"ר בת ישראל פקחת שנתארסה לכהן פקח ולא הספיק לכנסה עד שנתחרש אינה אוכלת מת ונפלה לפני יבם חרש אינה אוכלת כנסה הבעל ואח"כ נתחרש אוכלת מת ונפלה לפני

עין משפט נר מצוה

לא א מיי' פי"ח מהלכו' איסורי ביאה הל' ח סמג לאוין קכא ועשין מה טוש"ע אה"ע סימן ו סעיף יא:

לב ב מיי' שם הלכה א ז סמג לאוין שם:

לג ג מיי' פכ"ד מהל' אישות הלכה יט:

לד ד מיי' שם הל' כא וסמג שם וטוש"ע שם סעיף י:

לה ה מיי' פי"ח מהל' איסורי ביאה הל' ז סמג שם:

לו ו מיי' פ"ז מהלכות תרומות הלכה כא:

לז ז מיי' שם הלכה יד:

גמרא

ואנהרינהו לעיינין ממתניתין: [א]אשת ישראל שנאנסה, אע"פ שמותרת לבעלה – פסולה לכהונה. ותנא תונא: וכן הבא על אחת מכל העריות האמורות בתורה, או פסולות. מאי "וכן"? מאי לאו: לא שנא בשוגג ולא שנא במזיד ולא שנא באונס ולא שנא ברצון. וקתני "פסלה". לא, מאי "וכן" – אהעראה. העראה דמאן? אילימא דעריות – למימרא דעריות ילפי' מיבמה? אדרבה, יבמה ילפינן מעריות, דעיקר העראה בעריות כתיב! אלא מאי "וכן" – אשלא כדרכה דעריות – אדרבה, עיקר "משכבי אשה" בעריות כתיב? אלא מאי "וכן" אשלא כדרכה דחייבי לאוין. [ב]אמר *רבא: אשת כהן שנאנסה – בעלה לוקה עליה משום זונה. משום זונה – אין, משום טומאה – לא? אימא: אף משום זונה. מתיב רבי זירא: °"והיא לא נתפשה" – אסורה, *הא נתפשה – מותרת. ויש לך אחרת שאע"פ שנתפשה – אסורה, ואי זו – זו אשת כהן, ולאו *הבא מכלל עשה – עשה! אמר רבה: הכל היו בכלל זונה, כשפרט לך הכתוב גבי אשת ישראל "והיא לא נתפשה" אסורה, הא נתפשה – מותרת, מכלל דאשת כהן – כדקיימא קיימא. ואיכא דאמרי, אמר רבה: [ג]אשת כהן שנאנסה – בעלה לוקה עליה משום טומאה. משום טומאה – אין, משום זונה – לא, אלמא: באונס לא קרינא ביה זונה, מתיב רבי זירא: "והיא לא נתפשה" – אסורה, [ג]הא נתפשה – מותרת, [ד]ויש לך אחרת שאף על פי שנתפשה אסורה, ואיזו זו – אשת כהן, ולאו הבא מכלל עשה – עשה! אמר(א) רבא: [ה]הכל היו בכלל °"אחרי אשר הטמאה", כשפרט לך הכתוב גבי אשת ישראל "והיא לא נתפשה" אסורה הא נתפשה – מותרת, מכלל דאשת כהן כדקיימא קיימא.§

מתני' [ו]אלמנה לכהן גדול, גרושה וחלוצה לכהן הדיוט מן האירוסין – לא יאכלו בתרומה, *רבי אלעזר ורבי שמעון מכשירין. *נתארמלו או נתגרשו, מן הנשואין – פסולות, מן האירוסין – כשרות.§

גמ' תניא, אמר ר"מ: ק"ו, ומה קדושי רשות – אין מאכילין, קדושי עבירה – לא כ"ש?! אמרו לו: לא, אם אמרת בקידושי רשות – שכן אין לו להאכיל במקום אחר, תאמר בקדושי עבירה – שכן יש לו להאכיל במקום אחר. א"ר אלעזר א"ר אושעיא: פצוע דכא כהן שקדש בת ישראל – באנו למחלוקת ר"מ ורבי אלעזר ור"ש. לר"מ דאמר משתמרת לביאה פסולה דאורייתא לא אכלה – [ז]הא נמי לא אכלה, לר' אלעזר ור' שמעון דאמרי משתמרת לביאה פסולה דאורייתא אכלה הא

(במדבר ה; דברים כד; תורה אור)

רש"י

ואנהרינהו לעיינין ממתניתין. ממשנתנו הביא ראיה לדבריו, והאיר עינינו בה. אע"פ שמותרת לבעלה. דכתיב (במדבר ה) "והיא לא נתפשה" – אסורה, הא נתפשה – מותרת. פסולה לכהונה. אם מת בעלה, לא תנשא לכהן. ותנא תונא. תנא דידן, כמו: חבוגא, חאוגא. מאי וכן. לאו אאונס ואשוגג דלעיל קאי, וקתני: הבא על אחת מכל העריות פסלה לכהונה, ואשת איש בכלל עריות היא. לא אהעראה. וברצון, דהויא זונה: ופרכינן עיקר העראה בעריות כתיבא. והיכי מדמה לה מתני' ליבמה, כאילו מיבמה גמר לה? אשלא כדרכה. דקתני גבי יבמה: ולא חילק בין ביאה לביאה – דהיינו בין כדרכה לשלא כדרכה, ועלה תני: וכן הבא על אחת מכל העריות פסלה לכהונה משום זונה. ולעולם ברצון, וגמר "ביאה" "ביאה" מיבמה, דרבינן בה "ולקחה" – שלא כדרכה: ה"ג. אלא מאי וכן אשלא כדרכה דחייבי לאוין. אלמנה לכ"ג, גרושה וחלוצה לכהן הדיוט, דלא כתיב בהו "משכבי אשה". אבל משום הערלה לא איצטריך למיתנייה, דהא רבינן לעיל הערלה דחייבי לאוין מ"קיחה" "קיחה" דעריות. בעלה לוקה עליה משום זונה. דכתיב "זונה לא יקחו" (ויקרא כא), וסתם זונה היינו מנאפת תחת בעלה, שטעתה מאחר בעלה לזרים. וזו, אע"ג דנאנסה, גבי כהן לא פליג רחמנא בין אונס בין רצון, כדגמרי' מ"והיא לא נתפשה". ד"היא" מיעוטא משמע: "היא" אשת ישראל – הוא דיש חילוק בין נתפשה ללא נתפשה, אבל אשת כהן אין חילוק. משום טומאה לא. בתמיה. הא אמרי' בפ"ק (דף יא:), הא מה אני מקיים "אחרי אשר הוטמאה" – לרבות סוטה שנבעלה, דכתיב "לא יוכל בעלה" (דברים כד). הכל היו בכלל זונה. כל הנבעלות תחת בעליהן, בין באונס בין ברצון, בכלל "זונה לא יקחו" הן, שהרי כולן נבעלו פעילת זנות, והוציא לך הכתוב אשת ישראל אנוסה מן הכלל, אבל אשת כהן – כדקיימא קיימא. משום טומאה. "אחרי אשר הוטמאה" – לרבות סוטה שנבעלה. **מתני'** מן האירוסין לא יאכלו בתרומה. משעה שנתקדשו לאלו קדושי עבירה – נפסלה מלאכול בתרומה דבי נשא, אם בת כהן היא. ר' אלעזר ור"ש מכשירין. עד שתבעל לו ותעשה חללה, כדכתיב "לא יחלל" – שני חלולין, אחד לה ואחד לזרעה. נתארמלו או נתגרשו. מן הכהנים הללו. מן הנשואין פסולות. דשוייה חללה בביאתו. מן האירוסין כשרות. דאפילו ר"מ לא פסיל מן האירוסין אלא בחייהן, דמשתמרת לביאה פסולה, אבל מתו – לא. **גמ'** מה קידושי רשות. כגון ישראל שקידש בת כהן, שאין קידושיה עבירה. אין מאכילין. כלומר אין מניחין אותן לאכול, דתנן לקמן: האירוסין פוסלין, בפ' אלמנה לכה"ג (דף סז:). תאמר בקידושי עבירה שיש לו. לכהן זה להאכיל במקום אחר בראויה לו. כך שמעתי, ולבי מגמגם. חדא, דאין זה לשון הש"ס, והכי איבעיא ליה למימר: ומה קידושי רשות פוסלין כו'. ועוד, מדקאמר ר' אושעיא פצוע דכא כהן שקדש בת ישראל באנו למחלוקת ר"מ ור"א, ולא קתני פצוע דכא כהן שקידש בת כהן – ש"מ דפלוגתא דמתני' לאו בבת כהן לחודה היא, דא"כ היכי מגי רבי אושעיא למימר לרבי *אליעזר ור' שמעון אכלה? אימר דאמרי ר' אלעזר ור"ש בבת כהן, בבת ישראל מי אמרי? לשון אחר, והוא עיקר: אלמנה לכ"ג גרושה וחלוצה לכהן הדיוט מן האירוסין לא יאכלו בתרומה – בין בבת כהן בין בבת ישראל קמיירי. בבת כהן – כדפרישית, בבת ישראל ואליבא דמשנה ראשונה, דאמר בכתובות (דף נז.): הגיע זמן ולא נישאו – אוכלות משלו ואוכלות בתרומה. וקאמר ר' מאיר: אלמנה לכ"ג, אע"פ דקידושיו קידושין וקנין כספו היא – לא תאכל בתרומה כשאר הארוסות לכהן שאוכלות מן התורה. מ"ט – דמשתמרת לביאת עבירה. ור' אלעזר ור"ש מכשירין, דהא קנין כספו היא. ואי משום חללה – הרי כל זמן שלא בא עליה לא נתחללה. נתארמלו או נתגרשו. מן הכהנים הללו, מן האירוסין – כשרות לינשא לכהנים אם נתאלמנו. וגבי גרושה, אם בת כהן היא – כשרה לתרומה. מן הנשואין פסולה. דשוייה חללה. ומה קידושי רשות. ישראל שקידש בת ישראל, אין מאכילה בתרומה. קידושי עבירה. כגון אלו לכ"ש. במקום אחר. אפילו נשאת, תאמר בקידושי עבירה שיש לו להאכיל בראויה לו. פצוע דכא. משתמרת לביאה פסולה דאורייתא היא. הא

(לעיל; [ג"ל רבה])

תוספות

מאי וכן מאי לאו לא שנא בשוגג כו' וקתני פסלה. וליכא למימר משום אחרים נקט פסלה ולא משום אשת איש – דעיקר חידוש דאונס ורצון לא הוי אלא באשת איש. אבל בשאר עריות – אין חידוש טפי באונס מברצון לענין פסולי כהונה(ג). **עיקר** הערלה בעריות כתיב. ואית ספרים דגרסי: אדרבה, יבמה הוא דילפינן מעריות, ויש לפרש בדוחק: דאע"ג דיבמה מחייבי לאוין הוא דילפינן, ולא מעריות – חשיב ליה כאילו ילפינן מעריות, דע"י עריות ושפחה חרופה שמעינן לה בחייבי לאוין. **וכן** אשלא כדרכה דחייבי לאוין. פי' בקונטרס: אלמנה לכ"ג, גרושה וחלוצה לכהן הדיוט. אבל משום הערלה – לא איצטריך למיתנייה, דהא מרבינן ליה לעיל מקיחה קיחה דעריות. וקשה לר"י: דאי משום חייבי לאוין דכהונה נקט לה – לשלא כדרכה נמי לא איצטריך, דאיכא למילף נמי קיחה קיחה מעריות, דכתיב בהו "משכבי אשה"! אלא נראה לר"י: דקאי אשאר חייבי לאוין דלאו דכהונה, דלא כתיב בהו קיחה, דלא שמעינן בהו שלא כדרכה אלא מג"ש ד"ביאה" "ביאה" מיבמה, כי היכי דילפינן לעיל מינייהו יבמה לענין הערלה. **ואי** זו זו אשת כהן. מ"והיא" קדריש. וא"ת: והא קדרשינן לה בכתובות בפרק "נערה" (דף נא: ושם) לדרשא אחריתי, לתחלתה באונס וסופה ברצון, דשריא! ואר"י: דהתם אסמכתא היא. דמסברא היא דשריא, דחשיב אונס, אע"ג דסופה ברצון – דיצרא אלבשה, כי היכי דהוי אסמכתא הא דקאמר (לקמן דף ק:) ואי זו זו שקדושיה טעות.

מן האירוסין לא יאכלו. פי' בקונט' בלשון שני, ונראה לו עיקר, דאיירי בין בבת כהן בין בבת ישראל. דר"מ פסיל אפי' בבת כהן, ור"א ור' שמעון מכשירין אפי' בבת ישראל. ונתארמלו או שנתגרשו מן האירוסין כשרות ולא שייך כשרות בבת ישראל אלא לינשא לכהונה, דבתרומה לא אכלה. ובנתגרשה לא שייך אפי' לינשא, ויש לפרש בנתגרשה, אם בת כהן היא – כשרה לתרומה. ובגמ' דקאמר מה קדושי רשות אין מאכילים – בישראל שקדש בת ישראל קאמר. וקשה לר"י: דמה ק"ו הוא זה? דכיון דליכא לד כהונה כלל – מאין להם להאכיל לאותם הקידושין? ועוד הקשה ה"ר משה כהן: דהיאך יאכיל בת ישראל בהגעת זמן? דבפסולות לא שייך אוכלות משלו ואוכלות בתרומה, כדאמרי' ב"יש מותרות" (לקמן פה.): "בעמוד והוצא קאי – מזוני אית לה"! א)ונראה דבבת כהן איירי, כדפי' בקונטרס בלשון ראשון. ובגמ' גרים: מה קדושי רשות פוסלין. וכן גירסת ר"ת. וגבי פצוע דכא גרסי' שקדש בת כהן, וכן ר"ת, ולא כמו שכתוב בספרים "שקידש בת ישראל". ולפי שהגירסא היתה כתובה בספר רש"י פי' כן, אבל הגירסא כתובה בספר ר"ת כמו שפירשתי.

תוספות ישנים

בהערלה לכד: **ומאי** וכן לא שנא בשוגג לא שנא במזיד ובאונס וברצון וקתני פסולות. וא"ת היכי מוכח מהכא דאשת ישראל שנאנסה אסורה לכהן דלמא הא דתני פסל באונס קאי אפסולות לכהונה ולומר שנעשות חללות באונס דע"כ פסול לא קאי אכולה מלתא דמתני' דהא ממזרת ונתינה מפסלי וקיימי וי"ל דהא לאו חדוש הוא לומר דפסולות לכהונה שמתחללות באונס דמה לנו לחלק אכן תימה אמאי לא משני דפסל לא קאי אאשת איש אלא (באשתו נאמן) [נקטיה] לענין הערלה (לקנוס) [ללקות] [וכמו] כדפ"ה גבי ממזרת ונתינה וי"ל דפסיקא ליה דקאי אאשת איש דומיא דשאר עריות דר"ל פסל לכהונה: **אדרבה** יבמה ילפינן מעריות דעיקר הערלה (ביבמה) [בעריות] כתיבא. ואע"ג דיבמה ילפינן לעיל מביאה ביאה מחייבי לאוין קאמר הכא הכי כלומר לא [illegible] **וכן** [illegible] א) ולא נהירא הך פירושה [illegible] אבל כיון דפשיטא ליה [illegible] יבמה [illegible] כי הגיע זמנו [illegible] יאכלו דקנין כספו הוא:

תוספות חד מקמאי

לפני יבם חרש אוכלת נולד לה בן אוכלת מת הבן אינה אוכלת. אמר רבה אשת כהן שנאנסה בעלה לוקה עליה משום טומאה אבל משום (אונס) [זונה] לא כל באונס לא קרינן לה זונה מסתברא דלא פליג רב' אדרב עמרם דאמר אשת ישראל שנאנסה פסולה לכהונה ע"כ לא פליגי בה אלא לענין מלקות

הגהות הב"ח

(א) גמ' אמר רבה הכל היו: (ב) תוס' ד"ה מאי וכן וכו' כהונה הס"ד ואח"כ מ"ה ה"ג אדרבה עיקר הערלה:

גליון הש"ס

גמ' אמר רבה אשת כהן שנאנסה. עיין לעיל דף לה ע"א תד"ה אע"פ:

מסורת הש"ס

[ג"ל רבה]

לקמן ק: כתובות נא: עד. נדה נב.

[לעיל נד: וש"נ]

[לקמן עה.]

[לקמן נג.]

[ג"ל אלעזר]

מיהו אם [נאנסה מודה] שפסלה לכהונה שהרי נבעלה לפסול לה דכתיב ובת איש כהן כי תהיה לאיש זר היא בתרומת הקדשים לא תאכל. ומינה ילפינן בפרק אלמנה לכ"ג כיון שנבעלה לפסול פסלה מהתרומה ומהכהונה ק"ו מגרושה שמותרת בתרומה פסלה לכהונה זו שאסורה בתרומה אינו דין שפסולה לכהונה והכי איתא בפ' אלמנה לכ"ג והיינו דתנן בפ"ק דכתובות מעשה בתינוקת שירדה למלאות מים מן המעיין ונאנסה אר"י בן נורי אם רוב העיר משיאין לכהונה תנשא זו לכהונה. ואם אין רוב העיר משיאין לכהונה פסולה מפני שנבעלה לפסול לה וכל שנבעלה לפסול לה ל"ש באונס ולא שנא ברצון פסולה לכהונה מק"ו דתרומה כדפרישנא אבל לעולם זונה לא הויא אליבא דלישנא בתרא. ולא פליג רב' אדרב עמרם ואפי' לישנא בתרא. והאי דלא אנהר רב ששת עיינין ממתני' דכתובות דתינוקת. דדלמא שאני התם דזר דמעיקרא הוא אבל באשת איש לאו זר דמעיקרא הוא. ולא כדברי בעל התוספת: הא דתנן אלמנה לכ"ג גרושה וחלוצה לכהן הדיוט מן האירוסין לא יאכלו בתרומה אפי' באלמנה כהנת שכבר אכלה כיון שמשמרת לביאה פסולה משוו לה רבנן כאילו נבעלה ונפסלה מלאכול בתרומה אבל כשנתארמלה ונתגרשה מן הנשואין פסולה שהרי נבעלה לפסול לה. מן הארוסין כשרה שהרי לא נבעלה לפסול לה ואינה משמרת לביאה פסולה. וא"א א"ר אושעיא פצוע דכא כהן שקדש בת ישראל באנו

תורה אור

הָא נַמִי אָכְלָה. מִמַּאי? דִּלְמָא עַד כָּאן לָא קָאָמְרִי רַבִּי אֶלְעָזָר וְרַבִּי שִׁמְעוֹן הָתָם אֶלָּא דְּיֵשׁ לוֹ לְהַאֲכִיל בְּמָקוֹם אַחֵר, אֲבָל הָכָא, דְּאֵין לוֹ לְהַאֲכִיל בְּמָקוֹם אַחֵר – לָא. וְכִי תֵּימָא: הָכָא נַמִי יֵשׁ לוֹ לְהַאֲכִיל בְּבַת גֵּרִים – וְהָא מִיבַּעְיָא בָּעֵי לָהּ רַבִּי יוֹחָנָן מֵרַבִּי אוֹשַׁעְיָא, וְלָא פְּשֵׁיט לֵיהּ. אִיתְּמַר, אַבַּיֵּי אָמַר: הוֹאִיל וּמַאֲכִילָהּ בְּלֹא *יְדָעָהּ, רָבָא אָמַר: הוֹאִיל וּמַאֲכִילָהּ בַּעֲבָדָיו וְשִׁפְחוֹתָיו הַכְּנַעֲנִים. אַבַּיֵּי לָא אֲמַר כְּרָבָא, קִנְיָן דְּאִישׁוּת מִקִּנְיָן דְּאִישׁוּת – יָלְפִינַן, וְלָא יָלְפִינַן קִנְיָן דְּאִישׁוּת מִקִּנְיָן דַּעֲבָדִים. וְרָבָא לָא אֲמַר כְּאַבַּיֵּי – שָׁאנֵי הָתָם שֶׁכְּבָר אָכְלָה. וְאַבַּיֵּי: *שֶׁכְּבָר אָכְלָה לָא אָמְרִינַן, דְּאִי לָא תֵּימָא הָכִי – בַּת יִשְׂרָאֵל שֶׁנִּיסֵּת לְכֹהֵן וּמֵית – תֵּיכוּל, שֶׁכְּבָר אָכְלָה. וְרָבָא: *הָתָם – פָּקַע קִנְיָנֵיהּ, הָכָא – לָא פָּקַע קִנְיָנֵיהּ. גּוּפָא, בְּעָא מִינֵּיהּ רַבִּי יוֹחָנָן מֵרַבִּי אוֹשַׁעְיָא: פְּצוּעַ דַּכָּא כֹּהֵן שֶׁנָּשָׂא בַּת גֵּרִים, מַהוּ שֶׁיַּאֲכִילֶנָּה בִּתְרוּמָה? אִישְׁתִּיק וְלָא אֲמַר לֵיהּ וְלָא מִידֵי. לְסוֹף אֲתָא גַּבְרָא רַבָּה אַחֲרִינָא, וּבְעָא מִינֵּיהּ מִילְּתָא [אַחֲרִיתָא], וּפְשַׁט לֵיהּ. וּמַנּוּ – רֵישׁ לָקִישׁ. א"ל רַבִּי יְהוּדָה נְשִׂיאָה לְרַ' אוֹשַׁעְיָא: אַטּוּ רַ' יוֹחָנָן לָאו גַּבְרָא רַבָּה הוּא? אֲמַר לֵיהּ: דְּקָבָעֵי מִינָּאי מִילְּתָא דְּלֵית לָהּ פִּתְרֵי. לְמַאן? אִי לְרַבִּי יְהוּדָה – בֵּין בִּקְדוּשָּׁתֵיהּ קָאֵי בֵּין לָאו בִּקְדוּשָּׁתֵיהּ קָאֵי – לָא אָכְלָה. אִי בִּקְדוּשָּׁתֵיהּ קָאֵי לָא אָכְלָה, דְּהָא *אֲמַר מָר: בַּת גֵּר זָכָר כְּבַת חָלָל זָכָר. אִי לָאו בִּקְדוּשָּׁתֵיהּ קָאֵי – לָא אָכְלָה, דְּהָא אָמְרִינַן: קְהַל גֵּרִים אִיקְּרֵי קָהָל, וְאִי לְרַ' יוֹסֵי, בֵּין בִּקְדוּשָּׁתֵיהּ קָאֵי בֵּין לָאו בִּקְדוּשָּׁתֵיהּ קָאֵי – אָכְלָה. בִּקְדוּשָּׁתֵיהּ קָאֵי אָכְלָה – דְּהָא אֲמַר: *אַף גֵּר שֶׁנָּשָׂא גִּיּוֹרֶת בִּתּוֹ כְּשֵׁרָה לִכְהוּנָּה. אִי לָאו בִּקְדוּשָּׁתֵיהּ קָאֵי אָכְלָה – דְּהָא אֲמַר: [א]קְהַל גֵּרִים לָא אִיקְּרֵי קָהָל. אֶלָּא אַלִּיבָּא דְּהַאי תַּנָּא. דִּתְנַן, רַבִּי אֱלִיעֶזֶר בֶּן יַעֲקֹב אוֹמֵר: *[ב]אִשָּׁה בַּת גֵּרִים לֹא תִּנָּשֵׂא לִכְהוּנָּה עַד שֶׁתְּהֵא אִמָּהּ מִיִּשְׂרָאֵל. וְהָכִי קָמִיבַּעְיָא לֵיהּ: כַּשְׁרוּת מִיתּוֹסְפָא בָהּ וְאָכְלָה, אוֹ דִּלְמָא קְדוּשָּׁה מִיתּוֹסְפָא בָּהּ וְלָא אָכְלָה? תָּא שְׁמַע: כִּי אֲתָא רַבִּי אַחָא בַּר חִינָּנָא מִדָּרוֹמָא, אֲתָא וְאַיְיתֵי מַתְנִיתָא בִּידֵיהּ: מִנַּיִן לִפְצוּעַ דַּכָּא כֹּהֵן שֶׁנָּשָׂא בַּת גֵּרִים [ג]שֶׁמַּאֲכִילָהּ בִּתְרוּמָה – שֶׁנֶּאֱמַר °"וְכֹהֵן כִּי יִקְנֶה נֶפֶשׁ קִנְיַן כַּסְפּוֹ וגו' יֹאכַל בּוֹ", לְמַאן? אִילֵימָא לְרַבִּי יְהוּדָה – הָאָמַר: בֵּין בִּקְדוּשָּׁתֵיהּ קָאֵי בֵּין לָאו בִּקְדוּשָּׁתֵיהּ קָאֵי – לָא אָכְלָה. וְאִי לְרַבִּי יוֹסֵי – ל"ל קְרָא? הָאָמַר: בֵּין בִּקְדוּשָּׁתֵיהּ קָאֵי, בֵּין לָאו בִּקְדוּשָּׁתֵיהּ קָאֵי – אָכְלָה. אֶלָּא לָאו – לְרַבִּי אֱלִיעֶזֶר בֶּן יַעֲקֹב, וש"מ: כַּשְׁרוּת אִיתּוֹסְפָא בָּהּ, וְאָכְלָה. ש"מ. אִיתְּמַר, רַב אָמַר: יֵשׁ

רש"ל (ליד "רבה אחרינא"); ויקרא כב (ליד "שמאכילה בתרומה")

רש"י

הא נמי אכלה. דקנין כספו היא, ואוכלת דבר תורה. ועד דבעיל לה דשוייה חללה – אכלה. הכא אין לו להאכיל במקום אחר. שאין לך אשה שמותרת לו. בבת גרים. דקסבר: קהל גרים לא אקרי קהל, ואינן בכלל "לא יבא פצוע דכא", ונושאה בהיתר, ומאכילה תרומה. והא בעי מיניה ר' יוחנן מרבי אושעיא. לקמן בשמעתין, ולא פשיט ליה אי מאכילה בתרומה או לא. איתמר. לשנויי קושיין אתא. הואיל ומאכילה (א) בלא ידעה. היה נשוי כהן אשה ואוכלת בתרומה, ונעשה פצוע דכא ובא עליה – לא תאכל בתרומה, דשוייה חללה, דנבעלה לפסול לה. ואם לא ידעה משנעשה פצוע דכא – הרי זו אוכלת, משנה היא בפ' "הערל" (לקמן ע.). אלמא מלינו פצוע דכא כהן מאכיל במקום אחר, הלכך, בקידושי עבירה נמי מאכיל כל זמן שלא עשאה חללה. שכבר אכלה. כשהוא בריא. דלית ליה פתרי. שאין (ג) יודע לפרשה. למאן אי לר' יהודה כו'. הש"ס הוא דקא בעי לה, ומפרש ואזיל עד סיפא, ופשטה. אבל ר' אושעיא לא פשט בה מידי, כדאמרן לעיל: הא בעא מיניה כו'. ואית דמפרשי דלית ליה פתרי – אינה צריכה לפרש. דלמאן קבעי לה, אי לר' יהודה כו' – ושבוש הוא, מפני שני דברים: חדא – דאמרן לעיל ולא פשט ליה, ואם כן, דרבי אושעיא קאמר לה לכולה מילתא – הא פשטה בהמקנא. ועוד: דקנסיב ואזיל לפרושי דלא צריכה ליה למיבעיא לן, וקא נסיב בסיפא תא שמע, אלמא צריכה רבה. בין בקדושתיה קאי כו'. לקמן בפרק "הערל" (דף עו.) מיבעיא לן: כהן פצוע דכא מהו בגיורת? בקדושתיה קאי ואסור כו'. והכא, בין בקדושתיה קאי – כהן הנעשה פצוע דכא, בין בקדושת כהן קאי – ואסור בכל האסורות לכהונה, בין לאו בקדושתיה קאי, ואינו מוזהר מלישא אשה פגומה – לא אכלה. אי בקדושתיה קאי לא אכלה דהא אמר מר בת גר זכר כבת חלל זכר. ובת חלל פסולה לכהונה, בפרק "עשרה יוחסין". וכיון דבקדושתיה קאי – לא אכלה, דאמרינן: הרי זו פסולה לו, ועשאה חללה בביאתו. ואי לאו בקדושתיה קאי. ואינה אסורה לו משום קדושת כהן – אפי' הכי לא אכלה, שאסורה לו משום פצוע דכא, דהאמרת קהל גרים איקרי קהל. פלוגתא דר' יהודה ור' יוסי בפרק "עשרה יוחסין". אליבא דהאי תנא קמיבעיא ליה. לר' יוחנן, וכגון דאמה מישראל. כשרות איתוספא בה. וראויה לכהונה, ולאו קדושה לאקרויי קהל. ומותרת לפצוע דכא, ואוכלת ממה נפשך, דאי נמי בקדושתיה קאי – הרי זו מותרת לו, ומשום פצוע דכא לא מיתסר בה, דהא לאו איקרי קהל. או דלמא קדושה נמי איתוספא בה. וקהל איקרי, ואסורה לפצוע דכא ולא אכלה.א) לישנא אחרינא מפי המורה: בת גר וגיורת קמיבעיא ליה, אליבא דראב"י מאי? כשרות איתוספא בהך דאמה מישראל לאקרויי קהל, אבל בת גר וגיורת לאו קהל היא, ואכלה, שמותרת לפצוע דכא, והאי לאו בקדושה קאי דתיתסר עליה משום כהונה. או דלמא קדושה איתוספא בה. לינשא לכהונה. והך דאין אמה מישראל, נהי דקדושה לית בה – כשרות מיהא אית בה, ובכלל קהל היא, ואסורה לפצוע דכא, ולא אכלה. ולשון ראשון נראה עיקר. לרבי יוסי. לא איצטריך נפש יתירה, כדאמר לעיל דממה נפשך אכלה.

יש

[מלשון והאדם ידע וגו' בראשית ד עוד שם יט אשר לא ידעו איש עוד שם כד ואיש לא ידעה]

[לקמן עה.]

[גז"ש]

הגהות הב"ח

(א) רש"י ד"ה הואיל ומאכילה בלא כו' נ"ב פי' כשלא בא עליה לאחר שנעשה פצוע דכא ע"ל ר"פ הערל: (ב) ד"ה דלית וכו' שאין אני יודע:

קדושין עז.

שם

בכורים פ"א מ"ה

תוספות

והא בעא רבי יוחנן מר' אושעיא ולא פשיט ליה. מדרבי אושעיא אדרבי אושעיא פריך. ותימה: דלקמן מסקינן דרבי יוחנן בעי אליבא דר' אליעזר בן יעקב, אבל אליבא דר' אלעזר ור' שמעון אפשר דמאכיל בבת גרים, דר"ש מכשיר גיורת פחותה מבת ג' לכהן, ודלמא סבר נמי דקהל גרים לא מיקרי קהל. ומיהו, בקונטרס פי' דכולה סוגיא דהש"ס מסיק לה, אבל ר' אושעיא לא פשט מידי. אביי אמר הואיל ומאכילה בלא ידעה. תימה: דבלא ידעה גופה אמאי מאכיל לאביי? דמשתמרת לביאה פסולה! היא וטעמא שכבר אכלה לית ליה לאביי, כדקאמר בסמוך. ורבא נמי, היכי קאמר שאני התם שכבר אכלה, הא אליבא דרבי *אליעזר קיימא הכא, ורבי *אליעזר אית ליה ב"הערל" (לקמן עה.) שכבר אכלה לא אמרינן, אההיא מתני' גופה דלא ידעה, דקאמר: מאן תנא משתמרת לביאה פסולה דאורייתא אכלה – אמר ר' אלעזר: במחלוקת שנויה, ור' אלעזר ור' שמעון היא. ורבי יוחנן אמר: אפילו תימא רבי מאיר, שאני התם שכבר אכלה! ויש לומר: דטעמא שכבר אכלה מהני לכ"ע לענין זה שאוכלת לרבי אלעזר ור' שמעון, אע"פ שאין מאכיל במקום אחר. ולא פליג ר"א *ורבי יוחנן אלא במאי דקאמר ר' יוחנן דאוכלת אפי' לרבי מאיר מטעם שכבר אכלה, דלא חשיבא משתמרת לביאה פסולה, כיון דתחילת אכילתה הוו נישואי כשרות והוי כאילו הן קיימין ועומדין עדיין שתאכל מכאן. ומייתי אביי אפצוע דכא שקידש, דחשיב יש לו להאכיל במקום אחר, כיון שמאכיל בלא ידעה. ורבא סבר דלא חשיב יש לו להאכיל במקום אחר, כיון דאין מאכיל התם על ידי מעשה של עכשיו אלא ע"י שכבר אכלה. אתא גברא רבה אחרינא ובעא מיניה מילתא אחריתי. כאן משמע שהיה ר"ל גדול כשבא לפני רבי יוחנן, כמו שפירש ר"ת בב"מ (דף פד. ד"ה אי), שהיה לומד תורה לפני ר' אושעיא רבו של רבי יוחנן. [וע"ע תוס' עירובין סה: ד"ה ר"ל]. ואי לאו בקדושתיה קאי לא אכלה דהא אמר קהל גרים איקרי קהל. תימה: דהוה ליה למימר בין בקדושתיה קאי בין לא קאי – לא אכלה מהני תרי טעמי, דבת גר זכר כבת חלל זכר, ועוד דקהל גרים איקרי קהל. דהא אפילו לא בקדושתיה קאי – לא אכלה נמי, מטעם דבת גר זכר כבת חלל זכר, דהרי היא כחללה, וחללה אינה אוכלת בתרומה. כדמוכח בפרק בתרא דקדושין (דף עז.) ואי הוה טעמא דר' יהודה בבת גר זכר משום דכתיב "מזרע ישראל" כדמוכח התם – הוה מצי למימר דלא הויא ממש כחללה אלא דוקא לינשא לכהונה. אבל התם משמע דעיקר טעמא דרבי יהודה מק"ו: ומה חלל שבא מטיפה כשרה כו', ולפי זה – אית לן לשוייה כחללה לגמרי. דהא אמר אף גר שנשא גיורת בתו כשרה לכהונה. אכתי צריך לטעמא, דאית ליה קהל גרים לא אקרי קהל, ולא חש להזכיר, אלא נטר עד דקאמר אי לאו בקדושתיה קאי אכלה כו'. דאי לא קאי – סגי לה בטעם דקהל גרים לא איקרי קהל למודיה. הכי גרסינן דתנן רבי אליעזר בן יעקב אומר אשה בת גרים כו'. דמשנה היא במסכת ביכורים (פ"א משנה ה). ולא קשיא דלא מייתי מתניתין דפרק בתרא דקדושין – (דף עז.) דהך נמי משנה היא.

רב

עין משפט נר מצוה

לח א מיי' פט"ו מהל' איסורי ביאה הל' ז סמג לאוין קיז טוש"ע אה"ע סימן י סעיף כב:

לט ב מיי' שם פי"ט הל' ו סמג לאוין קנג טוש"ע שם סימן ז סעיף כא:

מ ג מיי' פ"ז מהל' תרומות הלכה יג:

[אלעזר] [אלעזר]

תוספות ישנים

א) ודוחק הוא דקרי לקדושה קריאת קהל ולכשרות היתר כהונה. הלא לישנא דקדושה משמע כהונה כדאמרינן לעיל איסור קדושה אלמנה לכה"ג ופ"ה לשון אחר דבת גר וגיורת קא מיבעיא ליה ואליבא דר' אליעזר בן יעקב ובעי מאי כשרות איתוספא ביה פירוש בההיא שאמה מישראל ליקרא קהל פירוש אף כשרות דקהל עם היתר כהונה אבל בת גר וגיורת דלית בה כל כך אלא כשרות דקהל ולא קדושה לכהונה א"כ לא נקראת קהל ומותרת לפצוע דכא אם אמת הדבר דלאו בקדושתיה קאי ולא תיאסר עליו משום כהונה דאי בקדושתיה קאי אסורה ליה כדאמרינן דבת גר כבת חלל אליבא דר' אליעזר נמי כדקאמר דבת גר וגיורת לא תנשא לכהונה או דלמא קדושה אתוספא בה בההיא דאמה מישראל יותר מבת גר וגיורת דמותרת לכהונה והך דאין אמה מישראל נהי דקדושה לית בה להנשא לכהן מ"מ כשרות אית בה להיות בכלל קהל ואסירא בפצוע דכא ולא אכלה בין בקדושתי' קאי בין לאו בקדושתיה קאי ורש"י פי' דלשון עיקר:

תוספות חד מקמאי

באנו למחלוקת ר"מ ור"ש ור"א לר"מ דאמר משמרת לביאה פסולה לא אכלה הא נמי לא אכלה לר"א ור"ש אכלה. ממאי דלמא ע"כ לא אמר ר"א ורבי שמעון אלא היכא דיש לו להאכיל במקום אחר אבל פצוע דכא דאין לו להאכיל במקום אחר לא. אביי אמר הואיל ומאכיל בלא ידיעה. פירוש אליבא דר"א ור"ש אבל אליבא דר"מ אינו מאכיל בלא ידיעה שהרי משתמרת לביאה פסולה. רבא אמר הואיל ומאכיל בשפחותיו ועבדיו. רבא לא אמר כאביי שאני התם שכבר אכלה פירוש אפילו לר"מ אכלה משום טעמא שכבר אכלה והכי איתא בפ' הערל: בעא מניה רבי יוחנן מר' אושעיא פצוע דכא כהן שנשא בת גרים מהו שתאכל בתרומה ואסיקנא אליבא דרבי יוסי דקי"ל דלא בין בקדושתיה קאי בין לאו בקדושתיה קאי אכלה. דהא אמר גר שנשא

גיורת בתו כשרה לכהונה ואי לאו בקדושתיה קאי [אכלה] דהא אמר קהל גרים לא אקרי קהל ור' יוחנן דקא מיבעיא ליה אליבא דראב"י קמיבעיא ליה דאמר אשה בת גרים לא תנשא לכהונה עד שתהא אמה מישראל וקמיבעיא ליה כשרות אתוספא בה ואכלה או דלמא קדושה איתוספא בה ולא אכלה ראב"י נמי ס"ל כר' יוסי בהא דקהל גרים לא איקרי קהל וקמיבעיא ליה כשאמו מישראל כשרות לחודה איתוספא בה שכשרה לכהונה ולא קדושה וכשם שאם אין אמה מישראל לא איקרי קהל כך כשאמה מישראל לא איקרי קהל ואכלה או דלמא כשאמה מישראל קדושה נמי אתוספא דאקרי קהל ולא אכלה. ואית דמפרשי לה כשאין אמה מישראל והכי קמיבעיא ליה כשאמו מישראל כשרות אתוספא בה לאקרויי קהל אבל כשאין אמו מישראל לא אקרי קהל ואכלה או דלמא קדושה אתוספא בה למשרייא לכהונה אבל לאקרויי קהל אע"פ שאין אמו מישראל איקרי קהל ואסורה לפצוע דכא:

גרס'

[א]יש חופה לפסולות, ושמואל אמר: אין חופה לפסולות. אמר שמואל: ומודה לי אבא בתינוקת פחותה מבת שלש שנים ויום אחד, הואיל ואין לה ביאה – אין לה חופה. אמר רבא: אף אנן נמי תנינא, *[ב]בת שלש שנים ויום אחד מתקדשת בביאה [ג]ואם בא עליה יבם קנאה, [ד]וחייבין עליה משום אשת איש, [ה]ומטמאה את בועלה לטמא משכב תחתון כעליון. [ו]נשאת לכהן – אוכלת בתרומה, [ז]בא עליה אחד מכל הפסולין – פסלה. בת שלש שנים ויום אחד הוא דמפסלה בביאה – מפסלה בחופה, הא פחותה מבת שלש שנים ויום אחד, דלא מפסלה בביאה – לא מפסלה נמי בחופה, שמע מינה. אמר רמי בר חמא: יש חופה לפסולות – באנו למחלוקת רבי מאיר ורבי אלעזר ורבי שמעון, לרבי

יש חופה לפסולות. כה"ג שהכניס אלמנה בת כהן לחופה ולא בא עליה, ומעיקרא נמי לא קידשה – אפילו הכי פסלה מתרומה דבי נשא, דחופה ככניסת בעילה דמיא. **ומודה לי אבא.** משום דקשיש מיניה קרי ליה אבא, כמו לשון נשיאי ורבי. **הואיל ואין לה ביאה.** אין ביאתה פוסלתה מתרומת אביה – אין חופתה פוסלתה. **אף אנן נמי תנינא.** דאין ביאתה פוסלתה, וכיון דאין ביאתה פוסלתה – כ"ש דאין חופתה פוסלתה. דהא חשיבות חופה אינה אלא משום שהיא קרובה לביאה, והיכא דביאה לא חשיבא – כל שכן חופה. **ומטמאה את בועלה.** אם נדה היא, לטמא בועלה משכב תחתון כעליון. במסכת נדה מפרש לה: שיהא תחתון של בועל נדה כעליונו של זב, שמטמא אוכלין ומשקין. ואין מטמא אדם וכלים, כתחתון של נדה עצמה שהוא קרוי מדרס ואב הטומאה. **מן הפסולין.** כגון חלל נתין וממזר, או אלמנה לכהן גדול. **פסלה.** מתרומת בית אביה.

רב אמר יש חופה לפסולות. נראה לר"י לפרש לפי שיטת הקונטרס, דפליגי בחופה בלא כסף. דרב ושמואל סברי כרב הונא, דאית ליה בריש קידושין (דף ה.) דחופה קונה, וקאמר רב דכי היכי דקנו קידושי חופה בכשרות – הכא נמי קני בפסולות. ועדיפא מקידושי כסף, דאפי' ר"מ ור"ש דאמרי דקידושי כסף לא פסלי – בחופה דקרובה לביאה מודו, כדקאמרינן בדיחויא דמילתא דרמי בר חמא. ולא שייך כאן דיו, דהא דמשתמרת לביאה פסולה דאורייתא – לא אכלה מדרבנן, והחמירו חכמים בחופה יותר, לפי שקרובה לביאה. וטעמא דרב, משום דסבר דבפסולות נמי שייך שארו, וכי היכי דקרינן בה "שארו" על ידי חופה שאחר קידושין, לשויה נשואה לענין השקאת סוטה, דבעינן "תחת אישך" דהיינו נשואה. ולענין נערה המאורסה לאפוקי מסקילה לחנק – קויה נמי דלא רחוק לשויה ארוסה. ושמואל אמר: אין חופה לפסולות, דחופה לא מהני אלא בכשרות, דחופה קירוב ביאה הוא ולא מהניא אלא בראויות לביאה, אבל בפסולות שאין ראויות לביאה – לא. וחופה דלאחר קידושין נמי לא מהניא בפסולות לשמואל, א) דלא שייך בהו שארות וקירוב ביאה מדמייתי מההוא שלא שטיתי ארוסה כו' סייעתא לרב דמיירי בחופה שאחר הקידושין. ורמי בר חמא דקאמר דיש חופה לפסולות באנו למחלוקת כו' – פליג אדרב ושמואל, ואתא למימר דליתיה לדרב דפסל לכולי עלמא, וליתא דשמואל דאמר דלכולי עלמא לא פסלה, אלא כי היכי דפליגי בקידושין – ה"נ פליגי בחופה. כן צריך לפרש לפי שיטת הקונטרס. ב) ולא רצה לפרש דאיירי בחופה שאחר הקידושין – דא"כ לא מצי שמואל למימר דלכולי עלמא לא פסלה, דהא פסולה וקיימא משעת קידושין לר' מאיר. ואין לפרש בחופה שאחר קידושין, וכגון שלא היה הפסול בשעת קידושין, כגון שנעשה פצוע דכא אחר הקידושין, או כהן גדול שקידש קטנה ובגרה תחתיו – דבכהאי גוונא נמי מיפסלא, כדמוכח בבעיא דלקמן (דף נט.) בכהן שקידש קטנה ובגרה תחתיו לפירוש ר"י (שם ד"ה "מהו"). ומתאי דאמר ב"הערל" (לקמן עה.) דאפי' לרבי יוחנן, דמוקי מתניתין דאם לא ידעה אפילו כר"מ משמע דוקא בנשואה שכבר אכלה, אבל ארוסה לא – אין ראיה, דהתם בבת ישראל מיירי שאינה אוכלת אלא מכחו, ולכך לא תתחיל לאכול על ידי נישואין פסולין. אבל בת כהן לכהן, איכא למימר: כיון דאכלה מקודם – אוכלת נמי לאחר שנפצע. ולא מסתבר נמי לאוקמי בארוסה שכבר אכלה בהגעת זמן, כמשנה ראשונה, וכר' יוחנן דאמר היכא דכבר אכלה דלא מפסלא משום שימור ביאה פסולה לר"מ – דדוחק להעמיד פלוגתא כמשנה ראשונה. ועוד: דמשמע דאיירי רב ושמואל בפסולות דמתני': אלמנה לכהן גדול, גרושה וחלוצה לכהן הדיוט. וקשיא לר"י על פירוש הקונטרס: דלישנא דקאמר רמי בר חמא לר"מ דאמר קידושין פסלי חופה נמי פסלה – משמע דאיירי בחופה שאחר קידושין, דאי בחופה בלא כסף – הא חופה נמי קידושין היא, ולא הוה ליה למימר סתם קידושין אלא כסף ושטר. ועוד הקשה ר"ת: דלפירוש הקונטרס אתו רב ושמואל דלא כהלכה, דלא קיימא לן כרב הונא, מדאמר בריש קידושין (דף ג. ושם): מניינא דרישא למעוטי חופה, ולרב הונא דאמר חופה קונה למעוטי מאי? וקאמר נמי בגמרא התם (דף ה:): ורב הונא – כסף באישות לא אשכחן כו'. משמע דאין הלכה כמותו. ועוד הקשה ה"ר י"ט מיוני: לשמואל דאמר אין חופה לפסולות, אבל לכשרות יש חופה – ואמאי? הא רב הונא יליף דחופה קונה מהצד השוה דכסף ושטר וביאה, והשתא איכא למפרך: מה להצד השוה שכן קונין בפסולות, תאמר בחופה שאף אחר שתלמוד שקונה – אין קונה בפסולות! *דבכי האי גוונא שייכא פירכא כדאשכחן בפרק קמא דמנחות (דף ו.) גבי טריפה לגבוה ובבבא קמא (דף מ:) גבי שור האיצטדין ואין לומר דלא חשיבא פירכא משום דחופה דפסולות אינה קרויה חופה – דמכל מקום פירכא היא, כדפריך התם – מה לכסף שכן פודין בו הקדשות ומעשר שני, תאמר בביאה כו'. ונראה לר"י כפירוש ר"ת: דבחופה שאחר קידושין איירי רב ושמואל, ובנתאלמנה או נתגרשה דמתניתין קיימי. רב אמר: יש חופה לפסולות, ואם נתאלמנו או נתגרשו אחר חופה – פסולות לכולי עלמא, כיון דיש חופה, וחופה חשיבא כביאה לפסול לעולם. ושמואל אמר: אין חופה לפסולות, והוי נתאלמנו או נתגרשו מן האירוסין, דכשרות אפילו לר"מ. והא דלא קבעי ליה אמתניתין דנתאלמנו או נתגרשו – משום דאפלוגתא דר"מ ור"א ור"ש קיימי. והא דאמר רמי בר חמא לרבי מאיר דאמר קידושין פסלי – ה"פ: כיון שמחמיר כל כך, דאפי' בקידושין לא אכלה – כמו כן יחמיר בחופה בנתאלמנה או נתגרשה שלא תאכל לעולם וכו'. ולפירושו נמי רמי בר חמא פליג אדרב ושמואל. **אמר שמואל ומודה לי אבא.** לא כמו שפירש בקונטרס לשון חשיבות, אלא כך היה שמו של רב, כדפירש בערוך בערך 'אבא'. כדאמרינן בברכות (דף מז.): אילו מייתו ארדליא וגולייא לאבא. ורב כהנא דאמר (שם דף סב.): דמי פומיה דאבא כדלא טעים תבשילא, וב"ראשית הגז" (חולין קלז:) נמי אמר: מאן ריש סידרא בבבל, אמר ליה: אבא אריכא. וקצת קשיא על רב כהנא שהיה תלמידו של רב היאך היה קורא לרב בשמו? וב"חלק" (סנהדרין ק.) אמר: מפני מה נענש גחזי – מפני שקרא רבו בשמו. ושמא משום דרב כהנא תלמיד חבר דרב הוה, כדאמרינן בפרק "אחד דיני ממונות" (שם לו:): כגון רב כהנא ורב אסי, דלגמריה דרב הוו צריכי. ולסבריה דרב לא הוו צריכי ובסוף בבא קמא (דף קיז:) נמי אמר דשייליה רבי יוחנן כל ספיקי דהוו ליה*. **וחייבין** עליה משום אשת איש. פירוש: אם קבל בה אביה קידושין. ותימה: דלמאי איצטריך למתני? דמסיפא שמעינן לה, דקתני: ואם בא עליה אחד מכל העריות – מומתין על ידה, ואשת איש בכלל, כדמוכח בפרק "בן סורר ומורה" (סנהדרין דף סט. ושם). ואפילו בהמה בכלל, כדמוכח בפרק "ארבע מיתות" (שם נה: ושם) בשמעתא דתקלה וקלון! ונראה לר"י: דקאי אאם בא עליה יבם קנאה, וקמ"ל דקנאה קנין גמור מדאורייתא, ולא הוי כביאת בן תשע, דקתני בההיא משנה (נדה מה.), דהתם לא קנה אלא מדרבנן כדאמרינן (שם): עשו ביאת בן תשע כמאמר בגדול, דממעטינן לה מדאורייתא בפרק "ארבע מיתות" (סנהדרין דף נג:) ובפרק קמא דקידושין (דף יט.) מ"אשר ינאף את אשת איש" – פרט לאשת קטן. וקשה, דבפ' "בן סורר" (סנהדרין סט.) דייק מינה שהולכין בדיני נפשות אחר הרוב, דאי לא אזלינן – ניחוש דלמא אילונית היא, ואדעתא דהכי לא קדיש. ולהאי פירושא דקאי אאם בא עליה יבם – אמאי פריך ניחוש דלמא אדעתא דהכי לא קדיש – היינו אחיו הראשון. ויצטרך לומר והאי נמי אדעתא דהכי לא יבם, ה"ל למיפרך טפי: ניחוש דלמא אדעתא דהכי קדיש אחיו הראשון, דשוב אינה אשת יבם. או ה"ל להקשות בסתם: ניחוש דלמא אילונית היא, ובכל ענין בין אדעתא דהכי קדיש אחיו הראשון או לא קדיש – אינה אשת יבם! וי"ל: דנקט אדעתא דהכי לא קדיש – משום דמסיפא נמי בעי למיפרך, ואם בא עליה אחד מכל העריות כו'. דמרישא היה יודע דמצי לשנויי: מאי חייבין דקתני – קרבן, כדמשני ליה. ופריך: הא מומתין קתני. ומכח זה הקשה בתחלה, ומשני: בדקבלה עילויה. פירוש: בסיפא, אבל ברישא לעולם נ"ל מאי חייבין דקתני – קרבן. דהתם לא מהני מידי מה שקבלה עילויה, כדפירשנו. וריב"א פירש: דאצטריך וחייב עליה משום אשת איש, דאי לאו דקתני לה – הוה מוקמינן ואם בא עליה אחד מכל העריות דוקא בעריות, ולא בבהמה. אבל השתא, דקתני וחייב עליה משום אשת איש והוא הדין כל העריות – תו לא איצטריך סיפא, אלא משום בהמה. ומכח זה דייק בפרק "ד' מיתות" (שם דף נה:) דכל העריות אפילו בהמה. תדע, דבסיפא גבי בן תשע קתני כל העריות שבתורה מומתין על ידו, ואפילו הכי קתני: ונסקלת בהמה על ידו, אלמא: לא הוי בהמה בכלל כל העריות. **נשאת** לכהן אוכלת בתרומה. אבל פחותה מבת ג', כיון דלאו בת ביאה היא – לא בדיק לה, *ואיכא למיחש לסמפון, *וגם חוזר ומשלחה לבית אביה, ולהכי לא אכלה. דהכי

דהכי

תוספות ישנים

א) ותימה מאי קאמר אבל חופה דלא קני לה הלא פ"ה דכלהו סברי כרב הונא דחופה קונה ונ"ל דגרסינן אבל חופה לא קני לה בלא דלי"ת. ור"ל אבל חופה לא קני לה לפסולה דדוקא בכשרות קונה וא"ת ולשמואל למה לי קרא לומר מטמא הוא לאשתו כשרה ואינו מטמא לאשתו פסולה פשיטא שהרי אינה אשתו וי"ל דלחופה אחר ביאה אצטריך קרא דהא שמואל נמי מודה דיש ביאה לפסולות וראיה לדבר דמייתי לקמן תיובתא לשמואל מההיא דאמן אמן וקאמר אלא דקני לה כשהיא ארוסה ומסתברא וקא משקה לה כשהיא נשואה משמע דבהכי לא קשיא לשמואל ואמאי הלא אינה אשתו אם אין ביאה לפסולה אלא ודאי שמואל נמי מודה דיש ביאה: **ב)** וקשה לקמן דמייתי לאמרה אמן שלא סטיתי וכו' ומסיק אלא דקני לה כשהיא ארוסה וכו' וש"מ יש חופה לפסולות ומאי מייתי סייעתא לרב ליסני דהתם לאחר קדושין איירי דהא קאמר שלא שטיתי ארוסה וי"ל דמ"מ מייתי שפיר דכיון דמשום החופה עם הקדושין החופה חזקה כ"כ שתהא נקראת אשתו לענין שתשתה וקרינא בה והביא האיש את אשתו וגם היא חזקה כ"כ שיוצאת מדין ארוסה שהיא בסקילה ונידונת בחנק א"כ חופה בלא קדושין נמי תועיל מיהא לפסול מתרומה דבי נשא ונראה לר"י דלרב אע"ג דיש חופה לפסולות מ"מ אינו מטמא לה כדאמרינן מטמא הוא לאשתו כשרה ואינו מטמא לאשתו פסולה ומספקא ליה לר"י אם אינו יורשה. ונראה דכיון דאינו מטמא לה כדפרישית א"כ לא יירשנה דאם היה יורשה היה מטמא לה כיון דקריי' ולא עגו לה דהויא כמת מצוה דהכי אמרינן לקמן פ' האשה רבה גבי קטנה כיון דלא ירתי לה אחיה הוי קריא ולא עגו לה והויא כמת מצוה ולא נהירא דא"כ כ"ג ונזיר יטמאו לאחיהם כשמתו בלא בנים לאו ליכא דירית להו רק הם והוי מת מצוה כדפרישית וזה לא מצינו בכל התלמוד

וכ"ל דדוקא היכא שהבעל ירית לה שלא כדין כגון לקמן גבי קטנה שאין לבעל בה קדושין רק מדרבנן א"כ כיון שהוא יורשה ואין קרוביה יורשין אותה קריא ולא עגו לה והויא מת מצוה אבל היכא דבדין אית ליה אין זה מת מצוה שאינם מקפידים וקרייא שפיר ועגו לה כיון שאין מפסידים שום דבר מדינם. וא"ת הכא נמי שלא כדין ירית לה דהא ירושת הבעל דרבנן וי"ל דכיון שאין זאת האשה חלוקה מאחרות שהרי כל העולם הורגלו לירש נשותיהם אע"ג דאינן אלא מדרבנן נראה לקרובים שיורשה בדין ושפיר עגו לה קרוביה ולא הויא מת מצוה אבל בקטנה הכל יודעים כי קדושיה אינם כלום רק מפני שמא נהגו בה מנהג הפקר וא"כ לא עגו לה כיון דלא ירתי לה:

עין משפט נר מצוה

מא א מיי' פ"ז מהל' תרומות הלכה כא:
מב ב מיי' פ"ג מהל' אישות הלכה יא טוש"ע אה"ע סימן לז סעיף א:
מג ג טוש"ע שם סימן קסז סעיף ד:
מד ד מיי' פ"ג מהל' איסורי ביאה ה"ב:
מה ה מיי' פ"ג מהל' מטמא משכב ומושב הלכה ג:
מו ו מיי' פ"ו מהל' תרומות הל' ג:
מז ז מיי' פי"ח מהל' איסורי ביאה הלכה יז ופי"ט ה"ב טוש"ע אה"ע סי' ו סעיף ט וסי' ז סעיף יב:

מסורת הש"ס

קדושין י. סנהדרין נה: סט. נדה מד:

גליון הש"ס

תום' ד"ה רב אמר דבכה"ג שייכא פירכא כדאשכחן בפ' קמא דמנחות. עיין בב"מ דף מב ע"א תד"ה אמר: **ד"ה** נשאת לכהן וכו' ואיכא למיחש לסמפון וכו'. עיין לקמן דף עב ע"א תד"ה מבחוץ:

[וע"ע היטב תוס' חולין לח. ד"ה איצטריך]

ג"א אם

תוספות חד מקמאי

גרסי' בפ' עשרה יוחסין בא לימלך מורין לו כראב"י אבל אין מוציאין מידו כר' יוסי: אתמר רב אמר יש חופה לפסולות ושמואל אמר אין חופה לפסולות. פירוש חופה בלא קדושין והכי משמע לקמן דאמר רמי בר חמא יש חופה לפסולות באנו למחלוקת ר"מ ור"ש ור"א עד ודלמא לא היא ע"כ לא קאמר ר"מ אלא בקדושין דקני לה אבל חופה דלא קנה לה. אלמא בחופה בלא קידושין עסקינן והפירוש הנכון בחופה דאחר קדושי' איירי וכהן שנפצע אחר קדושין ונכנסת לחופה לאחר שנפצע. ומסתברא כיון דקי"ל הלכתא כרב באיסור ורב ששת נמי קאי כוותיה הלכתא כרב ואף על גב דרבנן דפליגי עליה דר"י בן בנו של ר"י בן ברוקה סבירא להו אין חופה לפסולות אפילו הכי הלכתא כרב ורב ששת הלכך כהנת שנכנסה לחופה עם פסול לה אע"פ שלא נבעלה כמי שנבעלה דמי ונפסלה מלאכול בתרומה ובחלה:

לְרַבִּי מֵאִיר דְּאָמַר קִדּוּשִׁין פָּסְלִי — חוּפָּה נַמִי פָּסְלָה, לְרַ' אֶלְעָזָר וְרַ' שִׁמְעוֹן דְּאָמְרִי קִדּוּשִׁין לָא פָּסְלִי — חוּפָּה נַמִי לָא פָּסְלָה. וּמִמַּאי? דִּלְמָא עַד כָּאן לָא קָאָמַר ר"מ הָתָם אֶלָּא בְּקִדּוּשִׁין דְּקָנֵי לָהּ. אֲבָל חוּפָּה דְּלָא קָנָה לָהּ — לָא. א"נ, עַד כָּאן לָא קָאָמְרִי רַבִּי אֶלְעָזָר וְרַבִּי שִׁמְעוֹן הָתָם — אֶלָּא בְּקִדּוּשִׁין, דְּלָא קְרִיבִי לְבִיאָה, אֲבָל חוּפָּה דִּקְרִיבָא לְבִיאָה — הָכִי נַמִי דְּפָסְלָה. אֶלָּא אִי אִיכָּא לְמֵימַר — בִּפְלוּגְתָּא דְּהָנֵי תַּנָּאֵי, דְּתַנְיָא: נִישְּׂאוּ זוֹ וָזוֹ, כְּשֵׁרוֹת וּפְסוּלוֹת, אוֹ שֶׁנִּכְנְסוּ לְחוּפָּה וְלֹא נִבְעֲלוּ — אוֹכְלוֹת מִשֶּׁלּוֹ וְאוֹכְלוֹת בִּתְרוּמָה. נִכְנְסוּ, מִכְּלָל דְּנִישְּׂאוּ — נִישְּׂאוּ מַמָּשׁ? אֶלָּא לָאו — כְּגוֹן שֶׁנִּכְנְסוּ לְחוּפָּה וְלֹא נִבְעֲלוּ. וְקָתָנֵי: אוֹכְלוֹת מִשֶּׁלּוֹ וְאוֹכְלוֹת בִּתְרוּמָה. רַבִּי יִשְׁמָעֵאל בְּנוֹ שֶׁל רַ' יוֹחָנָן בֶּן בְּרוֹקָה אוֹמֵר: כָּל שֶׁבִּיאָתָהּ מַאֲכִילָתָהּ — חוּפָּתָהּ מַאֲכִילָתָהּ, וְכָל שֶׁאֵין בִּיאָתָהּ מַאֲכִילָתָהּ — אֵין חוּפָּתָהּ מַאֲכִילָתָהּ. מִמַּאי? דִּלְמָא רַבִּי יִשְׁמָעֵאל בְּנוֹ שֶׁל רַבִּי יוֹחָנָן בֶּן בְּרוֹקָה כְּרַ' מֵאִיר סְבִירָא לֵיהּ, דְּאָמַר: קִדּוּשִׁין לָא אָכְלָה. הַאי "כָּל שֶׁאֵין בִּיאָתָהּ מַאֲכִילָתָהּ אֵין חוּפָּתָהּ מַאֲכִילָתָהּ"? "כָּל שֶׁאֵין בִּיאָתָהּ מַאֲכִילָתָהּ אֵין כַּסְפָּהּ מַאֲכִילָתָהּ" מִיבָּעֵי לֵיהּ! דִּלְמָא, אַיְּידֵי דְּאָמַר ת"ק חוּפָּה — אָמַר אִיהוּ נַמִי חוּפָּה. אָמַר רַב עַמְרָם: הָא מִילְּתָא אֲמַר לָן רַב שֵׁשֶׁת, וְאַנְהֲרִינְהוּ לְעַיְינִין מִמַּתְנִיתִין: יֵשׁ חוּפָּה לִפְסוּלוֹת, וְתַנָּא תּוּנָא: *"אָמֵן [א]שֶׁלֹּא שָׂטִיתִי אֲרוּסָה, וּנְשׂוּאָה, שׁוֹמֶרֶת יָבָם, וּכְנוּסָה". הַאי אֲרוּסָה הֵיכִי דָּמֵי? אִילֵימָא דְּקָנֵי לָהּ כְּשֶׁהִיא אֲרוּסָה, (א) וְקָא מַשְׁקֶה לָהּ כְּשֶׁהִיא אֲרוּסָה — אֲרוּסָה בַּת מִשְׁתְּיָא הִיא? וְהָא תְּנַן: *[ב]אֲרוּסָה וְשׁוֹמֶרֶת יָבָם לֹא שׁוֹתוֹת וְלֹא נוֹטְלוֹת כְּתוּבָּה! אֶלָּא דְּקָנֵי לָהּ כְּשֶׁהִיא אֲרוּסָה, וְאִיסְתַּתְּרָה, וְקָמַשְׁקֶה לָהּ כְּשֶׁהִיא נְשׂוּאָה — מִי בָּדְקִי לָהּ מַיָּא? וְהָתַנְיָא: *°"וְנִקָּה הָאִישׁ מֵעָוֹן" [ג]בִּזְמַן שֶׁהָאִישׁ מְנוּקֶּה מֵעָוֹן הַמַּיִם בּוֹדְקִין אֶת אִשְׁתּוֹ, אֵין הָאִישׁ מְנוּקֶּה מֵעָוֹן — אֵין הַמַּיִם בּוֹדְקִין אֶת אִשְׁתּוֹ! אֶלָּא דְּקָנֵי לָהּ כְּשֶׁהִיא אֲרוּסָה, וְאִיסְתַּתְּרָה וְנִכְנְסָה לְחוּפָּה וְלֹא נִבְעֲלָה, וּשְׁמַע מִינָּהּ: יֵשׁ חוּפָּה לִפְסוּלוֹת. אָמַר רָבָא: וְתִסְבְּרָא דְּהָא מְתָרַצְתָּא הִיא? וְהָא כִּי אֲתָא רַבִּי אַחָא בַּר חֲנִינָא מִדָּרוֹמָא, אֲתָא וְאַיְיתִי מַתְנִיתָא בִּידֵיהּ: °"מִבַּלְעֲדֵי אִישֵׁךְ" [ד]מִי *שֶׁקָּדְמָה שְׁכִיבַת בַּעַל לְבוֹעֵל, וְלֹא שֶׁקָּדְמָה שְׁכִיבַת בּוֹעֵל לְבַעַל. אָמַר רָמִי בַּר חָמָא: מַשְׁכַּחַת לָהּ כְּגוֹן שֶׁבָּא עָלֶיהָ אֲרוּסָהּ בְּבֵית אָבִיהָ. דִּכְוָותָהּ גַּבֵּי שׁוֹמֶרֶת יָבָם — שֶׁבָּא עָלֶיהָ יָבָם בְּבֵית חָמִיהָ?

שׁוֹמֶרֶת

רש"י

לְרַבִּי מֵאִיר דְּאָמַר קִידּוּשִׁין פָּסְלִי. חוּפָּה בְּלֹא קִידּוּשִׁין נַמִי פָּסְלָה. חוּפָּה. אֵינָהּ קוֹנָה בְּלֹא כֶּסֶף אוֹ שְׁטָר אוֹ קִידּוּשֵׁי בִיאָה, כִּדְאִיתָא בְּפ"ק דְּקִדּוּשִׁין (דף ה:). נִישְּׂאוּ. לְכֹהֵן זוֹ וָזוֹ, וּמַאי זוֹ וָזוֹ כְּשֵׁרוֹת וּפְסוּלוֹת. מִכְּלָל דְּנִישְּׂאוּ מַמָּשׁ. בִּבְעִילָה?! בִּתְמִיָּה: וְכִי בִּיאָה בִּפְסוּלָה מִי אִיכָּא לְמ"ד דְּלָא פָּסְלָה מִתְּרוּמָה דְּבֵי נָשָׁא? אֶלָּא פֵּירוּשֵׁי קָא מְפָרֵשׁ: נִישְּׂאוּ כֵּיצַד — כְּגוֹן שֶׁנִּכְנְסוּ לְחוּפָּה וְלֹא נִבְעֲלוּ. אוֹכְלוֹת מִשֶּׁלּוֹ כו'. דְּחוּפָּה לָא פָּסְלָה. אֵין חוּפָּתָהּ מַאֲכִילָתָהּ. אִם בַּת יִשְׂרָאֵל הִיא. וְאַלִּיבָּא דְּמִשְׁנָה אַחֲרוֹנָה, דִּתְנַן (כתובות דף נז.): ב"ד שֶׁל אַחֲרֵיהֶם אָמְרוּ: אֵין הָאִשָּׁה אוֹכֶלֶת בִּתְרוּמָה עַד שֶׁתִּכָּנֵס לַחוּפָּה. וְאָמַר ר' יִשְׁמָעֵאל: חוּפָּה פְּסוּלָה אֵינָהּ מַאֲכֶלֶת, וְה"ה בִּיאָה, מִדְּמַקִּישׁ חוּפָּה לְבִיאָה מַשְׁמַע דְּאִם בַּת כֹּהֵן הִיא חוּפָּה פּוֹסַלְתָּהּ כְּבִיאָתָהּ. מִמַּתְנִי'. דְּמַסֶּכֶת סוֹטָה. אָמֵן. אָמֵן, תְּרֵי זִימְנֵי, לְרַבּוֹת כָּל הָנֵי. שׁוֹמֶרֶת יָבָם וּכְנוּסָה. כְּלוֹמַר — וְאִם הָיְתָה יְבִמְתּוֹ וּכְנָסָהּ — הַיָּבָם מַשְׁקֶה אוֹתָהּ, וּמַשְׁבִּיעָהּ אַף עַל סְתִירָה שֶׁנִּסְתְּרָה בְּעוֹדָהּ שׁוֹמֶרֶת יָבָם, וּמַיִם בּוֹדְקִין אוֹתָהּ עַל שְׁתֵּיהֶן, דְּהָא אִי זַנַּאי בְּעוֹדָהּ שׁוֹמֶרֶת יָבָם — אֲסוּרָה עָלָיו, וּכְר' עֲקִיבָא מוֹקְמִינַן לָהּ בְּמַסֶּכֶת סוֹטָה (דף יח:), דְּאָמַר: אֵין קִידּוּשִׁין תּוֹפְסִין בְּחַיָּיבֵי לָאוִין, דִּמְשַׁוֵּי לָהּ יְבָמָה לַשּׁוּק כְּאֵשֶׁת אִישׁ. וְכִי הֵיכִי דְּאֵשֶׁת אִישׁ מִיתַּסְרָא אַגַּבְרָא בִּזְנוּת — שׁוֹמֶרֶת יָבָם נַמִי מִיתַּסְרָא אַיְּבָמָהּ. וְכֵיוָן דְּמִיתַּסְרָא עֲלֵיהּ — בַּת קִינּוּי הִיא. דְּקַנֵּי לָהּ. קִינֵּא לָהּ וְהִתְרָה בָּהּ: אַל תִּסָּתְרִי עִם אִישׁ פְּלוֹנִי. לֹא שׁוֹתוֹת. דְּבָעֵינַן "תַּחַת אִישֵׁךְ". וְלֹא נוֹטְלוֹת כְּתוּבָּה. אִם קִינֵּא לָהּ וְנִסְתְּרָה שֶׁהִיא גָּרְמָה לֶאֱסוֹר אֶת עַצְמָהּ עָלָיו. אֶלָּא דְּקַנֵּי לָהּ כְּשֶׁהִיא אֲרוּסָה וְקָא אִיסְתַּתְּרָה. בְּאֵירוּסֶיהָ, וּנְשָׂאָהּ, וּמַשְׁקֶה לָהּ. וּמִי בָּדְקִי לָהּ. וְהָתַנְיָא כו'. מְנוּקֶּה מֵעָוֹן. שֶׁלֹּא בָּא עָלֶיהָ לְאַחַר שֶׁנִּסְתְּרָה, שֶׁהַתּוֹרָה אֲסָרָהּ עָלָיו, דִּכְתִיב (במדבר ה) "וְהִיא נִטְמָאָה". וש"מ. מִדְּמַשְׁקֶה לָהּ — יֵשׁ חוּפָּה לִפְסוּלוֹת, וְקָרֵינַן בֵּיהּ "תַּחַת אִישֵׁךְ", דְּקָנֵי לָהּ חוּפָּה. וְאַף עַל גַּב דְּלָא חַזְיָא לְבִיאָה, דְּהָא אֲסוּרָה לוֹ מִשֶּׁנִּסְתְּרָה: אָמַר רָבָא וְתִסְבְּרָא דְּהָא מַתְנִי' מְתָרַצְתָּא הִיא וְהָא כִּי אֲתָא כו'. שֶׁבָּא עָלֶיהָ אֲרוּסָהּ בְּבֵית אָבִיהָ. קוֹדֶם סְתִירָה, וּלְעוֹלָם מְתָרַצְתָּא הִיא: וּפָרְכִינַן. דִּכְוָותָהּ גַּבֵּי שׁוֹמֶרֶת יָבָם שֶׁבָּא עָלֶיהָ. לְשֵׁם זְנוּת בְּבֵית חָמִיהָ בְּאַלְמְנוּתָהּ, וַהֲדַר קִינֵּא לָהּ וְאִיסְתַּתְּרָה, וְהִכְנִיסָהּ לְחוּפָּה וְלֹא נִבְעֲלָה, וּמַשְׁקֶה לָהּ, וּמַשְׁבִּיעָהּ שֶׁלֹּא שָׂטִית בַּסְּתִירָה הָרִאשׁוֹנָה.

שׁוֹמֶרֶת

תוספות

דהני תנאי. דתנא קמא סבר: אוכלות משלו ואוכלות בתרומה, דאין חופה פוסלתה מלאכול בתרומה, דאין חופה לפסולות. ורבי ישמעאל סבר: דיש חופה, דקאמר: כל שאין ביאתה מאכילתה – חופה נמי פוסלתה מן התרומה, אפילו היא בת כהן. דאי בבת ישראל קאמר *דאין חופה מאכילתה – בהא לא הוה פליג תנא קמא, לפי מה שפירשתי דמתני' איירי בבת כהן. ולפי מה שפי' בקונטרס דבבת ישראל נמי פליגי דאכלה לרבי אלעזר ורבי שמעון בהגעת הזמן אפילו היא פסולה – יש לפרש כאן שמדקדק מדמקשינן חופה לביאה, כדפי' בקונטרס, דמשמע *שאותה חופה כביאה. וא"ת: לת"ק, כיון דאין חופה לפסולות – אמאי אוכלות משלו? וי"ל: דלא גרע מהגעת זמן. ואוכלות בתרומה – כיון דנכנסה לחופה, דליכא למיחש למזיגת כוס ולסימפון. ואם תאמר: דאכתי פסולות אמאי אוכלות משלו? בעמוד והולא קאי, מזוני אית להו?! כדאמרינן בריש "יש מותרות" (לקמן פה.)! וי"ל: דלאלדדין קתני, אוכלות משלו – לאחר מיתה, ואוכלות בתרומה – מחיים.

שומרת יבם וכנוסה. וא"ת: היאך מתנה על זנות דיבמה? הא תנן (סוטה דף יח:): כל שאילו תיבעל ולא תהא אסורה לו – לא היה מתנה עמה! וי"ל דהכא נמי נאסרה כדרב המנונא, דאמר: שומרת יבם שזינתה אסורה ליבמה. ובפ' שני דסוטה (דף יח: ושם) מייתי מינה סייעתא לרב המנונא, ודחי: הא מני ר' עקיבא היא, דאמר: אין קידושין תופסין בחייבי לאוין. וא"ת: והיכי מפיק כולהו מחד "אמן" יתירא: אמן על האלה, אמן על השבועה, אמן אם מאיש זה, אמן אם מאיש אחר, וארוסה ונשואה, ושומרת יבם, וכנוסה? וי"ל: דחד "אמן" קאי אכל מה דכתיב בפרשה, ואלה ושבועה כתיב בהדיא, וכן מאיש אחר – דכתיב "מבלעדי אישך", ואמן יתירא – לשומרת יבם וארוסה קאתי*.

אלא דקני לה כשהיא ארוסה(ב) ומשקה לה כשהיא נשואה. דהשתא לא ממעטינן מ"תחת אישך", כיון דהשתא בשעת השקאה היא תחת בעלה. וא"ת: ומנלן דקרא משמע שהסתירה היא כשהיא נשואה? דטומאה "תחת אישך" כתיב! וי"ל: דכי היכי דמרבה מאיש אישך קינוי דאירוסין, בריש "ארוסה" (סוטה כד. ושם) ה"נ נרבה סתירה.

ונקה האיש מעון. וא"ת: ונוקמה כגון שבא עליה בשוגג, וכשבא עליה – לא ידע עדיין שנסתרה? דכי האי גוונא חשיב מנוקה מעון, דהא כי מוקי לה ע"י גלגול לא חשיב אין מנוקה מעון אם זינתה באירוסין! וי"ל: דהכא, כיון דבשעת השקאה יודע שבא עליה באיסור, אפילו בא עליה שוגג – לא חשיב מנוקה מעון. אבל על ידי גלגול, שאינו יודע בשעת השקאה – מנוקה מעון קרינן ביה.

דכוותה גבי שומרת יבם כו'. פי' בקונטרס בלישנא אחרינא: דמוקי לה הכי כי היכי דלא תיקשי: שומרת יבם בת משתיא היא? אבל משום קדמה שכיבת בעל לבועל לא פריך, דמה שקדמה שכיבת המת – כשכיבת בעל היא. ולשון דכוותה לא משמע הכי, דמשמע דמאותו הטעם שאנו מעמידים לארוסה – בבא עליה ארוסה בבית אביה, דהיינו: מטעם דבעינן שתקדים שכיבת בעל, יש לנו להעמיד בשומרת יבם בבית חמיה. ועוד, דבריש פרק "ארוסה" (סוטה כד: ושם) קאמר בהדיא דכוותה שומרת יבם כו' אקושיא דקדמה שכיבת בעל לבועל, דקאמר: טעמא דכתיבי הני קראי, הא לאו הכי – הוה אמינא: ארוסה שותה, והא כי אתא כו' ולא שקדמה שכיבת בועל לבעל, אמר רמי בר חמא: משכחת לה כגון שבא עליה ארוס בבית אביה, ודכוותה גבי שומרת יבם כו'. ונראה לר"י כפירוש ראשון שבקונטרס: דמטעם שתקדום שכיבת בעל קאמר דכוותה בשומרת יבם – שבא עליה יבם בבית חמיה, דכרבי יאשיה אתיא מתניתא: דשלא שטיתי שומרת יבם וכנוסה, דלדידיה שומרת יבם בת משתיא היא, כדיליף התם. ולא צריך לאוקמא כשבא עליה יבם בבית חמיה אלא משום דליקדום שכיבת בעל. דלרבי יונתן דפליג עליה התם אפילו בא עליה יבם בבית חמיה לא שתיא, כדאמרינן התם. ומוקי כוותיה ההיא דארוסה ושומרת יבם לא שותות כו'. וא"ת: וכיון דהני מתני' פליגי אהדדי, א"כ, מאי פריך לעיל אלא דקינא לה ומשקה לה כשהיא ארוסה, והתנן ארוסה ושומרת יבם כו'! ויש לומר: דלא פליגי רבי יאשיה ורבי יונתן אלא בשומרת יבם, אבל בארוסה – ליכא מאן דפליג.

שומרת

מסורת הש"ס

קדושין כז: סוטה יח.

סוטה כג: קדושין כז: ספרי פ' נשא

במדבר ה

סוטה כח. מז: שבועות ה. קדושין כז: ספרי פ' נשא

שם

סוטה כד:

עין משפט נר מצוה

מח א מיי' פ"ד מהלכ' סוטה הלכה טז:

מט ב מיי' פ"ב שם הלכה ב:

נ ג מיי' שם הל' ח ופ"ג הלכ' יז:

ס"א משום דלא קניא האי חופה כלל

נא ד מיי' שם פ"ב הלכה ה:

ס"א שעושה

תוספות ישנים

אמן שלא שטיתי ארוסה ונשואה וכו' האי ארוסה היכי דמי אלימא שקינא לה כשהיא ארוסה ואסתתרה וקא משקה לה כשהיא ארוסה והשתא ארוסה ונשואה בחד שבועה מפיק א) לאיירי דנקט איידי הקנוי בארוסים וההשקאה בנשואים והשתא לא הוי דומיא דסיפא אמן מאיש זה אמן מאיש אחר דמיירי בתרתי ולמסקנא ניחא שפיר דמוקמי' לה ע"י גלגול והוי ארוסה ונשואה בתרתי:

א) אולי צ"ל דאיידי דנקט דהיה הקינוי וההשקאה באירוסין נקט נמי הקינוי באירוסין וההשקאה בנשואים.

הגהות הב"ח

(א) גמ' כשהיא ארוסה ואיסתתרה וקא משקה לה כשהיא ארוסה: (ב) תוס' ד"ה אלא וכו' ארוסה ואיסתתרה ומשקה:

[וע"ע תוס' קדושין כז: ד"ה אמן]

נב א מיי' פ"ד מהל' סוטה הל' יז:
נג ב מיי' פ"ז מהל' תרומות הל' כב:
נד ג ד מיי' שם הל' כג:

*שׁוֹמֶרֶת יָבָם קָרֵית לָהּ?! אִשְׁתּוֹ מַעַלְיָא הִיא! דְּהָא *אָמַר רַב: קָנָה לַכֹּל. כִּשְׁמוּאֵל דְּאָמַר: לֹא קָנָה אֶלָּא לַדְּבָרִים הָאֲמוּרִים בַּפָּרָשָׁה. מִידֵי הוּא טַעְמָא — אֶלָּא לְרַב, הָא אָמַר רַב קָנָה לַכֹּל! הָכָא בְּמַאי עָסְקִינַן, כְּגוֹן דַּעֲבַד בָּהּ מַאֲמָר, וּב"ש הִיא, דְּאָמְרִי: *מַאֲמָר קוֹנֶה קִנְיָן גָּמוּר. אִי הָכִי, הַיְינוּ אֲרוּסָה! וּלְטַעֲמִיךְ, נְשׂוּאָה וּכְנוּסָה לָאו חֲדָא מִילְּתָא הִיא? אֶלָּא: נְשׂוּאָה — דִּידֵיהּ, וּכְנוּסָה — דְּחַבְרֵיהּ. הָכָא נַמִי: אֲרוּסָה — דִּידֵיהּ, וְשׁוֹמֶרֶת יָבָם — דְּחַבְרֵיהּ. רַב פַּפָּא אָמַר: הַאי תַּנָּא הוּא, דְּתַנְיָא: *אֵין מְקַנִּין לָהּ לַאֲרוּסָה לְהַשְׁקוֹתָהּ כְּשֶׁהִיא אֲרוּסָה, אֲבָל מְקַנִּין אוֹתָהּ לְהַשְׁקוֹתָהּ כְּשֶׁהִיא נְשׂוּאָה. רַב נַחְמָן בַּר יִצְחָק אָמַר: *אעַל יְדֵי גִּלְגּוּל. שָׁלַח רַב חֲנִינָא מִשְּׁמֵיהּ דְּרַבִּי יוֹחָנָן: הָעוֹשֶׂה מַאֲמָר בִּיבִמְתּוֹ, [וְיֵשׁ לוֹ אָח], אֲפִילּוּ הוּא כֹּהֵן וְהִיא כֹּהֶנֶת — פְּסָלָהּ מִן הַתְּרוּמָה. לְמַאן? אִילֵימָא לְרַבִּי מֵאִיר, אֵימַר דַּאֲמַר רַבִּי מֵאִיר מִשְׁתַּמֶּרֶת לְבִיאָה פְּסוּלָה לָא אָכְלָה — מִדְּאוֹרַיְיתָא, דְּרַבָּנַן מִי אֲמַר? וְאֶלָּא לְרַבִּי אֶלְעָזָר וְרַבִּי שִׁמְעוֹן, הַשְׁתָּא מִשְׁתַּמֶּרֶת לְבִיאָה פְּסוּלָה דְּאוֹרַיְיתָא אָכְלָה, דְּרַבָּנַן מִיבַּעְיָא? אֶלָּא כִּי אֲתָא רָבִין אֲמַר: עָשָׂה בָּהּ מַאֲמָר בִּיבִמְתּוֹ — דִּבְרֵי הַכֹּל אָכְלָה, ביֵשׁ לוֹ אָח חָלָל — דִּבְרֵי הַכֹּל אֵינָהּ אוֹכֶלֶת. לֹא נֶחְלְקוּ אֶלָּא שֶׁנָּתַן לָהּ גֵּט, רַבִּי יוֹחָנָן אָמַר: אוֹכֶלֶת, רֵישׁ לָקִישׁ אָמַר: אֵינָהּ אוֹכֶלֶת. רַבִּי יוֹחָנָן אָמַר: גאוֹכֶלֶת, אֲפִילּוּ לְרַבִּי מֵאִיר דְּאָמַר אֵינָהּ אוֹכֶלֶת — הָנֵי מִילֵּי מִשְׁתַּמֶּרֶת לְבִיאָה פְּסוּלָה דְּאוֹרַיְיתָא, דאֲבָל דְּרַבָּנַן — אָכְלָה. וְרֵישׁ לָקִישׁ אָמַר: אֵינָהּ אוֹכֶלֶת, אֲפִילּוּ לְר"א וְרַבִּי שִׁמְעוֹן דְּאָמְרִי אוֹכֶלֶת — הָנֵי מִילֵּי דְּיֵשׁ לוֹ לְהַאֲכִיל בְּמָקוֹם אַחֵר, אֲבָל הָכָא, כֵּיוָן דְּאֵין לוֹ לְהַאֲכִיל בְּמָקוֹם אַחֵר — לָא. וְכִי תֵּימָא: הָכָא נַמִי יֵשׁ לוֹ לְהַאֲכִילָהּ בְּחוֹזֶרֶת — חוֹזֶרֶת פְּסָקָהּ מִינֵּיהּ, וּקְרוֹבָה לְבֵי נָשָׁא, אֲבָל הָא אֲגִידָא בֵּיהּ.§ "נִתְאַרְמְלוּ אוֹ נִתְגָּרְשׁוּ וכו'".§ בְּעָא מִינֵּיהּ רַבִּי חִיָּיא בַּר יוֹסֵף מִשְּׁמוּאֵל: כֹּהֵן גָּדוֹל שֶׁקִּדֵּשׁ אֶת הַקְּטַנָּה וּבָגְרָה תַּחְתָּיו, מַהוּ

רש"י

שׁוֹמֶרֶת יָבָם קָרֵית לָהּ. קָנָה לַכֹּל. בְּבִיאַת שׁוֹגֵג וּמֵזִיד. מִידֵי הוּא טַעְמָא אֶלָּא לְרַב. הָא דְּמַיְיתִינַן יֵשׁ חוּפָּה לִפְסוּלוֹת — לְסַיּוּעֵהּ לְרַב מַיְיתִינַן לָהּ, דַּאֲמַר לְעֵיל: יֵשׁ חוּפָּה לִפְסוּלוֹת, וְרַב — הָאֲמַר לְעֵיל קָנָה לַכֹּל, וּלְדִידֵיהּ לָא מִיתַּרְצְתָּא הִיא. כְּגוֹן דַּעֲבַד מַאֲמָר. וְאַחַ"כ בָּא עָלֶיהָ בִּזְנוּת בְּבֵית חָמִיהָ. וּב"ש הִיא דְּאָמְרִי. בְּפֶרֶק "ד' אַחִין" (לעיל דף כט:) מַאֲמָר קוֹנֶה קִנְיָן גָּמוּר — לַעֲשׂוֹת אֲרוּסָה גְּמוּרָה, וְהִפְרִיחַ אֶת זִיקַת הַיִּבּוּם, וְתוּ לָא מִקַּנְיָא לֵיהּ בְּבִיאַת מֵזִיד אֶלָּא בִּמְסִירַת חוּפָּה כְּאִשָּׁה בְּעָלְמָא. כִּדְאָמְרִינַן בְּ"ד' אַחִין" (שם). וּמִשּׁוּם הָכִי קָרֵי לָהּ שׁוֹמֶרֶת יָבָם אֲפִילּוּ לְאַחַר בִּיאָה, דְּאָתִי לְב"ה — לָא אַלִּים מַאֲמָר לְהַפְרִיחַ זִיקַת יְבָמִין וְלֵיחוּל זִיקַת אֵירוּסִין וְנִישּׂוּאִין, וַהֲוֵי קָנֵי לָהּ בְּבִיאַת זְנוּת לְגַמְרֵי. אִי הָכִי הַיְינוּ אֲרוּסָה. גְּמוּרָה, וַאֲרוּסָה — הָא תָּנָא לָהּ. נְשׂוּאָה דִּידֵיהּ. אִשְׁתּוֹ, שֶׁלֹּא הָיְתָה יְבִמְתּוֹ. דְּחַבְרֵיהּ. אָחִיו. דְּיִבִּמְתּוֹ שַׁיָּיךְ לְשׁוֹן כְּנִיסָה. לִישָּׁנָא אַחֲרִינָא, וְעִיקָּר: דִּכְוָותָהּ גַּבֵּי שׁוֹמֶרֶת יָבָם דְּקַשְׁיָא לָךְ נַמִי בָּהּ: הָא לָאו בַּת אַשְׁקוּיֵי הִיא — מוֹקְמַתְּ לָהּ נַמִי כְּגוֹן שֶׁבָּא עָלֶיהָ, דְּהָא כְּשֶׁנִּכְנְסָה לַחוּפָּה לֵיכָּא לְאוֹקוֹמָהּ, דְּהָא חוּפָּה בִּיבָמָה לָא שַׁיְיכָא. שׁוֹמֶרֶת יָבָם קָרֵית כו'. אֶלָּא לָא תּוֹקְמָהּ לְשׁוֹמֶרֶת יָבָם כְּשֶׁבָּא עָלֶיהָ, אֶלָּא כְּגוֹן דַּעֲבַד בָּהּ מַאֲמָר. וּלְשֶׁקָּדְמָה שְׁכִיבַת בַּעַל לָא קָפְדִינַן, דְּהָא קָדְמָה שְׁכִיבַת בַּעַל הָרִאשׁוֹן שֶׁהִיא בָּאָה מִכֹּחוֹ, וּמַאֲמָר קוֹנֶה קִנְיָן גָּמוּר וְקָרֵינַן בָּהּ "תַּחַת אִישֵׁךְ". רַב פַּפָּא אָמַר. לְעוֹלָם לָא תֵּדוֹק מִינָּהּ דְּיֵשׁ חוּפָּה, וְהָכָא כְּגוֹן דְּקִינֵּא לָהּ כְּשֶׁהִיא אֲרוּסָה וּנְשָׂאָהּ וּבָא עָלֶיהָ וַהֲדַר אִיסְתַּתְּרָה, וּמַשְׁקֶה לָהּ עַל יְדֵי אוֹתוֹ קִינּוּי, וְהַאי תַּנָּא הוּא כו': לִישָּׁנָא אַחֲרִינָא: אֲמַר רַב פַּפָּא — לְעוֹלָם דְּקִינֵּא לָהּ כְּשֶׁהִיא אֲרוּסָה, וְאִיסְתַּתְּרָה, וּמַשְׁקֶה לָהּ כְּשֶׁהִיא נְשׂוּאָה. [הג"ה עַד שֶׁלֹּא נִבְעֲלָה, וּדְקַשְׁיָא לָךְ מִשֶּׁקָּדְמָה שְׁכִיבַת בַּעַל לַבּוֹעֵל, הַאי תַּנָּא וכו'. עכ"ה]. וּדְקַשְׁיָא לָךְ אֵין מְנוּקֶּה מֵעָוֹן — הַאי תַּנָּא הוּא, דְּלֵית לֵיהּ הָךְ דְּרָשָׁא. וְזֶה הוּא לְשׁוֹן מוֹרִי, וְהוּא נִרְאֶה עִיקָּר. דְּלְלִישָּׁנָא קַמָּא אִיכָּא לְמִיפְרַךְ: אִם כֵּן מַאי לֹא שָׂטִיתִי אֲרוּסָה? וְאַדְּרַבָּה, הָא לָא כְּשֶׁהִיא אֲרוּסָה אִיסְתַּתְּרָה. רַב נַחְמָן אָמַר. מַתְנִיתִין בְּדְלָא קִינֵּא וְלָא אִיסְתַּתְּרָה כְּשֶׁהִיא אֲרוּסָה, אֶלָּא קִינֵּא לָהּ מִשֶּׁנְּשָׂאָהּ וְאִיסְתַּתְּרָה, וּמַשְׁקֶה לָהּ ע"י קִינּוּי שֶׁל עַכְשָׁיו, וּמְגַלְגֵּל עָלֶיהָ שְׁבוּעָה כָּל יָמִים שֶׁהָיְתָה תַּחְתָּיו מִשֶּׁנִּתְאָרְסָה וְנִבְדְּקָה, וּמִכָּאן לְגִלְגּוּל שְׁבוּעָה מִן הַתּוֹרָה. פְּסָלָהּ מִן הַתְּרוּמָה. עַד שֶׁיִּכְנוֹס. מִשְׁתַּמֶּרֶת לְבִיאָה פְּסוּלָה. שֶׁיֵּשׁ בְּיַד אָחִיו לָבֹא עָלֶיהָ, וּבִיאָתוֹ בִּיאָה. וְכִי הֵיכִי דְּהִיא מִשְׁתַּמֶּרֶת לְבִיאָתוֹ, כָּךְ הִיא מִשְׁתַּמֶּרֶת לְבִיאַת אָחִיו, שֶׁהִיא פְּסוּלָה מִדְּרַבָּנַן, דְּיֵשׁ בִּיאָה אַחַר מַאֲמָר, כִּדְתְנַן (לעיל דף נ:): מַאֲמָר לָזוֹ וּבָעַל לָזוֹ כו', וְכֵן בְּב' יְבָמִין וִיבָמָה אַחַת. דְּאוֹרַיְיתָא. בִּיאָה שֶׁהִיא פְּסוּלָה דְּאוֹרַיְיתָא, כְּגוֹן אַלְמָנָה לְכֹהֵן גָּדוֹל. דִּבְרֵי הַכֹּל. בֵּין לְרַבִּי יוֹחָנָן בֵּין לְרֵישׁ לָקִישׁ אָכְלָה בִּתְרוּמָה דְּבֵי נָשָׁא, דְּהָא אֲפִילּוּ לְרַבִּי מֵאִיר לָא פָּסֵיל אֶלָּא בְּמִשְׁתַּמֶּרֶת לְבִיאָה פְּסוּלָה דְּאוֹרַיְיתָא. יֵשׁ. לָזֶה הַיָּבָם אָח חָלָל. לְדִבְרֵי הַכֹּל לָא אָכְלָה. אֲפִי' הִיא בַּת כֹּהֵן. וְאע"ג דַּעֲבַד בָּהּ מַאֲמָר כֹּהֵן כָּשֵׁר — אַכַּתִּי מִשְׁתַּמֶּרֶת לְבִיאָה פְּסוּלָה הִיא, לְבִיאַת הֶחָלָל, דַּהֲוָיָא פְּסוּלָה דְּאוֹרַיְיתָא וְלָא אָכְלָה. וַאֲפִי' לְרַבִּי אֶלְעָזָר וְרַבִּי שִׁמְעוֹן, כִּי מַכְשְׁרִי — בְּאַלְמָנָה לְכ"ג קָמַכְשְׁרִי, שֶׁיֵּשׁ לוֹ לְהַאֲכִיל בְּמָקוֹם אַחֵר. אֲבָל מִשְׁתַּמֶּרֶת לְיָבָם חָלָל, דְּאֵין לוֹ לְהַאֲכִיל, דְּהָא כֹּהֵן חָלָל זָר הוּא — פָּסַל לָהּ, וְלָא אָכְלָה. אֶלָּא שֶׁנָּתַן לָהּ גֵּט. כֹּהֵן לִיבִמְתּוֹ כֹּהֶנֶת. וְאַכַּתִּי, לְבִיאָתוֹ הִיא מִשְׁתַּמֶּרֶת, וּבִיאָתָהּ פְּסוּלָה מִדְּרַבָּנַן הִיא, דְּגֵט מְהַנֵּי בָּהּ מִדְּרַבָּנַן. אֲפִילּוּ לְרַבִּי אֶלְעָזָר דְּאָמַר אוֹכֶלֶת. הָנֵי מִילֵּי עַל יְדֵי קִידּוּשִׁין, דְּיֵשׁ לוֹ לְהַאֲכִיל כִּי הַאי גַּוְונָא בְּמָקוֹם אַחֵר. אֲבָל עַל יְדֵי גֵּירוּשִׁין. דְּאֵין לוֹ לְהַאֲכִיל עַל יְדֵי גֵּירוּשִׁין בְּמָקוֹם אַחֵר — לָא. וְאִם תֹּאמַר. הָכָא נַמִי יֵשׁ לוֹ לְהַאֲכִיל עַל יְדֵי גֵירוּשִׁין גְּמוּרִים בְּחוֹזֶרֶת, דְּאִם הָיָה מְגָרְשָׁהּ לְגַמְרֵי — הָיְתָה חוֹזֶרֶת לְבֵית אָבִיהָ, וְאוֹכֶלֶת בִּתְרוּמָה. וּבָגְרָה תַּחְתָּיו. בִּימֵי אֵירוּסִין. וְכ"ג אָסוּר בְּבוֹגֶרֶת, כִּדְאָמְרִינַן בְּמַתְנִיתִין, וּמִצְוָתוֹ בִּקְטַנָּה אוֹ בְּנַעֲרָה.

מַהוּ

תוספות

שומרת יבם קרית לה אשתו מעלייתא היא דהא אמר רב קנה לכל. ואע"ג דקרי לה שומרת יבם במילתיה דרבי יאשיה ורבי יונתן, דאיירו בבא עליה יבם בבית חמי', ובלא עבד בה מאמר – התם משום דלאו אשתו מעליא היא לענין השקאה קרי לה שפיר שומרת יבם, אפילו לרב דאמר קנה לכל, דהא ממעט לה רבי יונתן בברייתא מ"תחת אישך". ורבי יאשיה קרי לה נמי שומרת יבם, דקתני: יכול שאני מוציא שומרת יבם כו' – משום דאי לאו רבויא ד"איש איש" הוה ממעט לה. וכן מסיק התם. אבל הכא לא הזכיר שום טעם שהיה ראוי לקרותה על ידו שומרת יבם. ועוד: כיון דקונה לכל – לא הוה ליה למימר שומרת יבם וכנוסה, דהך נמי כנוסה היא.

דהא אמר רב קנה לכל. ונפל מן הגג ונתקע, או בנתכוון להטיח בכותל, ליכא לאוקמה – ד"ויתן איש בך את שכבתו מבלעדי אישך" דמשמע מבלעדי אישך שנתן בך את שכבתו, משמע דבעינן בבעל כוונת שכיבה.

רב פפא אמר האי תנא. פי' בקונטרס בלשון שני: לעולם דקינא לה ואיסתתרה כשהיא ארוסה, והאי תנא הוא דלית ליה הך דרשא ד"ונקה האיש מעון" ולית ליה הך דרשא שקדמה שכיבת בעל. וקש' לר"י: דבריש שבועות (דף ה. ושם) ובסוטה (דף כח.) ובכמה דוכתי פריך: ומי בדקי לה מיא, והתניא: ונקה האיש וכו'. ולא משני: האי תנא הוא. משמע דליכא מאן דפליג. ועוד: מנא ליה דהאי תנא לא בעי שתקדום שכיבת בעל? דלמא כשבא עליה ארוסה בבית אביה איירי! ונראה כלשון ראשון שבקונטרס, ושלא שטית ארוסה דקאמר – לא שנסתרה באירוסין קאמר, אלא ה"ק: שלא שטית להיות נבדקת עליה בקינוי דאירוסין. מיהו, גם ללשון זה קצת קשה: כיון שצריך להביא ראיה על זה שמועיל קינוי דאירוסין להשקותה בסתירה דנישואין – מנא ליה דהאי תנא אית ליה האי סברא? הא איכא לפרושי מקנין לארוסה להשקותה כשהיא נשואה – היינו דקינא לה כשהיא ארוסה ואיסתתרה ונכנסה לחופה ולא נבעלה, כדפי' מתניתין דלעיל.

על ידי גלגול. לא בעי*) לאפוקי גלגול מגלגול דאיש אחר, דלא דמי, דגלגול דאיש אחר ראוי להשקות על ידו אם היה מקנא על ידו, אבל קרקעות – לאו בנות שבועה נינהו כלל. אבל מגלגול דארוסה יליף שפיר, דלאו בת השקאה היא כלל – ואפי' הכי מגלגל זנות דאירוסין. וא"ת: ולמאי דדייקינן מיניה לעיל דיש חופה לפסולות, ולא מוקמינן על ידי גלגול – מנלן גלגול שבועה? וי"ל: דנפקא ליה מ"איש אחר" ולא הוה מפליג בין קרקעות לאיש אחר. אי נמי דמשמע ליה מ"איש אחר" – אפילו קטן, דדמי לקרקעות, שאין מקנין על ידו, כדתנן בסוף פרק "ארוסה" (סוטה דף כו: וכן בריש פ' שם כד.).

אימור דאמר רבי מאיר כו'. גם מכאן ראיה דחשיב משתמרת לביאה פסולה, אף על פי שלא היו הקידושין בעבירה.

*) ס"א לאתויי

תוספות ישנים

שומרת יבם קרית לה אשתו מעלייתא היא. הכא פריך משום דקאמר בתר הכי וכנוסה [אבל] בסוטה לא נוכל לפרש כן וא"ת ולוקמה שנתכוון להטיח בכותל והטיח ביבמתו דאמרינן לעיל לא קנה וי"ל דא"כ הדרא קושיא לדוכתין דלא קדמה שכיבת בעל לבועל דלאו שכיבה מקרייא: **דעבד** בה מאמר והשתא פרחה מינה זיקת יבמין וחלה עליו זיקת ארוסין ונשואין דמאמר קונה קנין גמור לב"ש והשתא לא קנאה בביאה דמחסרא מסירה לחופה ולעולם מיירי שבא עליה יבם בבית חמיה: **ע"י** גלגול פי' ומיירי דקינא לה בנשואין ומשקה לה בנשואין אבל על ידי גלגול נשבעת שלא זנתה בארוסין והשתא נימא דארוסה ונשואה תרתי מילי נינהו והוי כמו אמן מאיש זה אמן מאיש אחר וא"ת מ"מ תקשי דאם אמת הדבר שזנתה כשהיא ארוסה היכי בדקי לה מיא בנשואין הלא אינו מנוקה מעון וי"ל דמ"מ כיון שאינו מזיד בדבר בדקי ליה שפיר מיא. וא"ת א"כ לעיל כי פריך ומי בדקי לה מיא והלא אין האיש מנוקה מעון ליטני דמיירי כשבא עליה בשוגג וי"ל דלעיל לא מצי לשנויי הכי דכיון דמיירי דקני לה בארוסין יש לו להשמר שלא יבא עליה וכאשר בא עלי' קרוב למזיד ואינו מנוקה מעון שהרי חשדה מזנות מדקני לה אבל הכא לא קני לה בארוסין כלל והוי האיש מנוקה מעון אפילו אם זנתה כי לא [עלה] על דעתו שזנתה א"כ הוי האיש מנוקה מעון: **כ"ג** שקדש את הקטנה ובגרה תחתיו מהו בתר אירוסין אזלינן ושריא ליה או בתר נשואין אזלינן ואסורה. ופשיט מן האירוסין כשרות אלמא מדלא פסלינן מאירוסין דבתר נשואין אזלינן ותימה דהשתא פשיטא ליה דבתר נשואין אזלינן ולקמן פשיטא ליה דבתר אירוסין אזלינן מההיא דנתמנה להיות כ"ג יכנוס. וע"ק דקאמר לשווייה חללה לא קא מבעיא ליה משמע דר' יוחנן היה סבור דרבי חייא בעי לשווייה חללה ולפ"ה הלא לא מיירי כלל לשווייה חללה אלא לענין אם אסורה לו או מותרת אכן שהיה מדמה איסור חללות לאיסור קיחה והול"ל שאני איסור חללה מאיסור קיחה ונראה דודאי ס"ד לר' יוחנן דר' חייא קא בעי לענין חללות ופשיטא ליה לאסור לכונסה. אכן דכאן קבעי לר' מאיר דאמר משמרת לביאה פסולה לא אכלה ולכך קבעי היכא דקדשה קטנה ובגרה אי בתר נשואין אזלי' והויא ביאה פסולה ותשבינן לה מעת אירוסין משמרת לביאה פסולה ולא אכלה או דלמא לא. ופשיט לה מגופה דמתני' דאזלינן בתר נשואין וקא"ל לשווייה חללה לא קא מיבעיא ליה א) כיון דס"ד דפשיטא ליה שאסור לכונסה דודאי בזה אנכי מסופק אי שרי לכונסה אי לא אי קיחה דאירוסין או קיחה דנשואין ופשיט ליה מההוא דיכנוס דקיחת אירוסין קאמר קרא וא"כ מ"מ הדרן קושיין לדוכתא דמעיקרא פשיט לה ר' יוחנן מההיא דמתני' דבתר נשואין אזלינן ולכן פשיט ליה לאסור לכונסה והשתא קא פשיט מההיא דיכנוס דשרי לכונסה וי"ל דלעיל לא קא פשיט אלא לדבריו דאשר עלה בדעתו דרבי חייא היה שואלו ממנו לשווייה חללה ועל כן היה ר' יוחנן סבור שהיה פשוט לר' חייא שאסור לכונסה ועל כן היה משיב לו לפי דעתך שפשוט לך לאסור לכונסה ומיבעיא לך אי חשבינן לה לפסול מתרומה כיון דהאירוסין הוו

א) נראה דצ"ל ולא כס"ד דפשיטא ליה שאסור לכונסה אלא דבזה אנכי מסופק.

תוספות חד מקמאי

כי אתא רבין אמר כהן שעשה מאמר ביבמתו לר"ג אכלה ואפי' לר"מ דאמר משמרת לביאה פסולה לא אכלה ה"מ ביאה פסולה מדאוריי' אבל ביאה פסולה מדרבנן כגון זה שאם בא עליה אחר אין בה פסולות אלא מדרבנן אכלה. יש לו אח חלל ד"ה אינה אוכלת לא נחלקו אלא בנתן לה גיטה ר"י אומר אוכלת אע"פ שאינו מאכיל במקום אחר אפילו לר"מ דאמר אינה אוכלת ה"מ דיש לו להאכיל במקום אחר אבל הכא כיון דאינו מאכיל במקום אחר לא. וכ"ת להאכיל בחוזרת חוזרת פסקה מניה וחזרה לבי נשא הוא איננה גביה והלכתא כר' יוחנן:

מסורת הש"ס

סוטה כד:
[לעיל נו.]
[לעיל כט: וש"נ]
סוטה כה.
קדושין כז:

מַהוּ? בָּתַר נִישּׂוּאִין אָזְלִינַן, אוֹ בָּתַר אֵירוּסִין אָזְלִינַן? א"ל: תְּנֵיתוּהָ, *נִתְאַרְמְלוּ אוֹ נִתְגָּרְשׁוּ, מִן הַנִּשּׂוּאִין — פְּסוּלוֹת, מִן הָאֵירוּסִין — כְּשֵׁרוֹת. אֲמַר לֵיהּ: לְשַׁוּוֹיָהּ חֲלָלָה — לָא קָמִיבָּעֲיָא לִי דְּבִיאָה הִיא דִּמְשַׁוְּיָא חֲלָלָה. כִּי קָמִיבָּעֲיָא לִי °"וְהוּא אִשָּׁה בִבְתוּלֶיהָ יִקָּח" מַאי? קִיחָה דְּקִדּוּשִׁין בָּעֵינַן, אוֹ קִיחָה דְּנִישּׂוּאִין בָּעֵינַן? אֲמַר לֵיהּ, הָא נַמִי תְּנֵיתוּהָ: *אאֵירֵס אֶת הָאַלְמָנָה וְנִתְמַנָּה לִהְיוֹת כֹּהֵן גָּדוֹל — יִכְנוֹס. שָׁאנֵי הָתָם, דִּכְתִיב °"יִקַּח אִשָּׁה". הָכָא נַמִי כְּתִיב "אִשָּׁה". אַחַת וְלֹא שְׁתַּיִם. וּמָה רָאִיתָ? בהָא אִישְׁתַּנֵּי גּוּפָהּ, וְהָא לָא אִישְׁתַּנֵּי גּוּפָהּ.§ **מתני'** גכֹּהֵן גָּדוֹל לֹא יִשָּׂא אַלְמָנָה, דבֵּין אַלְמָנָה מִן הָאֵירוּסִין בֵּין אַלְמָנָה מִן הַנִּישּׂוּאִין. הוְלֹא יִשָּׂא אֶת הַבּוֹגֶרֶת, רַ' אֶלְעָזָר וְרַ' שִׁמְעוֹן מַכְשִׁירִין בְּבוֹגֶרֶת. [וְלֹא יִשָּׂא אֶת מוּכַּת עֵץ].§ **גמ'** תָּנוּ רַבָּנַן: °"אַלְמָנָה לֹא יִקָּח", בֵּין אַלְמָנָה מִן הָאֵירוּסִין, בֵּין אַלְמָנָה מִן הַנִּישּׂוּאִין. פְּשִׁיטָא! מַהוּ דְּתֵימָא: לֵילַף אַלְמָנָה אַלְמָנָה מִתָּמָר, מַה לְּהַלָּן — מִן הַנִּישּׂוּאִין, אַף כָּאן — מִן הַנִּישּׂוּאִין, קמ"ל. וְאֵימָא הָכִי נַמִי! דּוּמְיָא דִּגְרוּשָׁה, מַה גְּרוּשָׁה ובֵּין *מִן הַנִּישּׂוּאִין בֵּין מִן הָאֵירוּסִין, אַף אַלְמָנָה בֵּין מִן הָאֵירוּסִין בֵּין מִן הַנִּישּׂוּאִין.§ "וְלֹא יִשָּׂא אֶת הַבּוֹגֶרֶת".§ *תָּנוּ רַבָּנַן: "וְהוּא אִשָּׁה בִבְתוּלֶיהָ יִקָּח", פְּרָט לְבוֹגֶרֶת שֶׁכָּלוּ לָהּ בְּתוּלֶיהָ, דִּבְרֵי רַ' מֵאִיר. רַ' אֶלְעָזָר וְרַ' שִׁמְעוֹן מַכְשִׁירִין בְּבוֹגֶרֶת. בְּמַאי קָא מִיפַּלְגִי? *רַבִּי מֵאִיר סָבַר: "בְּתוּלָה" אֲפִילּוּ מִקְצָת בְּתוּלִים מַשְׁמַע, "בְּתוּלֶיהָ" עַד דְּאִיכָּא כָּל הַבְּתוּלִים, "בִּבְתוּלֶיהָ" בִּכְדַרְכָּהּ אִין, שֶׁלֹּא כְּדַרְכָּהּ לָא. וְרַבִּי אֶלְעָזָר וְרַבִּי שִׁמְעוֹן סָבְרִי: "בְּתוּלָה" בְּתוּלָה שְׁלֵימָה מַשְׁמַע, "בְּתוּלֶיהָ" וַאֲפִי' מִקְצָת בְּתוּלִים, "בִּבְתוּלֶיהָ" עַד שֶׁיִּהְיוּ כָּל בְּתוּלֶיהָ קַיָּימִין, בֵּין בִּכְדַרְכָּהּ בֵּין שֶׁלֹּא כְּדַרְכָּהּ. אָמַר רַב יְהוּדָה אָמַר רַב: זנִבְעֲלָה שֶׁלֹּא כְּדַרְכָּהּ — פְּסוּלָה לִכְהוּנָּה. מְתִיב רָבָא: °"וְלוֹ תִהְיֶה לְאִשָּׁה" חבְּאִשָּׁה הָרְאוּיָה לוֹ, פְּרָט לְאַלְמָנָה לְכֹהֵן גָּדוֹל, גְּרוּשָׁה וַחֲלוּצָה לְכֹהֵן הֶדְיוֹט. הֵיכִי דָּמֵי? אִלֵימָא בִּכְדַרְכָּהּ — מַאי אִירְיָא מִשּׁוּם אַלְמָנָה? תֵּיפּוֹק לֵיהּ מִשּׁוּם דַּהֲוְיָא לָהּ בְּעוּלָה. אֶלָּא לָאו שֶׁלֹּא כְּדַרְכָּהּ. וּמִשּׁוּם אַלְמָנָה — אִין, מִשּׁוּם בְּעוּלָה — לָא.
הָא

[ויקרא כא] [שם] [שם] [דברים כב]

רש"י

מַהוּ. לְכוֹנְסָהּ מִשֶּׁבָּגְרָה, אוֹ לֹא. בָּתַר קִיחָה דְּאֵירוּסִין אָזְלִינַן וְשַׁרְיָא לֵיהּ, אוֹ בָּתַר נִישּׂוּאִין אָזְלִינַן, וְכֵיוָן דְּבָגְרָה — אֲסִירָא לֵיהּ. מִן הָאֵירוּסִין כְּשֵׁרוֹת. אַלְמָא בִּפְסוּל כְּהוּנָּה בָּתַר נִישּׂוּאִין אָזְלִינַן מִדְּלָא פָּסֵיל אַלְמָנָה שֶׁנִּתְאָרְסָה לְכ"ג וּמֵת. יִכְנוֹס. אַלְמָא בָּתַר אֵירוּסִין אָזְלִינַן. שָׁאנֵי הָתָם דִּכְתִיב אִשָּׁה. "כִּי אִם בְּתוּלָה מֵעַמָּיו יִקַּח אִשָּׁה", וְהַאי אִשָּׁה קְרָא יְתֵירָא הוּא, וּמִינֵּיהּ מְרַבִּינַן לְקַמָּן בְּפִירְקִין (דף סא.) דְּאִם אֵירֵס אַלְמָנָה וְנִתְמַנָּה לִהְיוֹת כֹּהֵן גָּדוֹל יִכְנוֹס. אַחַת וְלֹא שְׁתַּיִם. אֵירוּלָא הוּא: אַחַת יֵשׁ לְךָ לְרַבּוֹת, וְלֹא שְׁתַּיִם. הָא אִישְׁתַּנֵּי גּוּפָהּ. בּוֹגֶרֶת נִשְׁתַּנָּה גוּפָהּ מִן אֵירוּסִין לְנִישּׂוּאִין, אַלְמָנָה לֹא נִשְׁתַּנֵּית. **מתני'** וְלֹא יִשָּׂא אֶת הַבּוֹגֶרֶת. פְּלוּגְתַּיְיהוּ מְפָרֵשׁ בַּגְּמָ'. **גמ'** פְּשִׁיטָא. אַלְמָנָה סְתָמָא מַשְׁמַע. מִתָּמָר. "שְׁבִי אַלְמָנָה" (בראשית לח). דּוּמְיָא דִּגְרוּשָׁה. וּבִגְרוּשָׁה פְּשִׁיטָא לֵיהּ; דִּסְתָמָא הִיא, דְּלֵית לָךְ לְמֵילַף כִּדְיָלְפִינַן ג"ש בְּאַלְמָנָה. בְּתוּלָה. אִי הֲוָה כְּתִיב "בְּתוּלָה יִקָּח" — מִקְצָת בְּתוּלִים מַשְׁמַע, וַהֲוַאי מִישְׁתְּרֵי בּוֹגֶרֶת. הַשְׁתָּא דִּכְתִיב "בְּתוּלֶיהָ" — מִיתַּסְרָא בּוֹגֶרֶת, דְּמַשְׁמַע דְּבָעֵינַן כָּל בְּתוּלֶיהָ. בִּבְתוּלֶיהָ. בֵּי"ת יְתֵירָא, דְּמַשְׁמַע הָכִי: לְמִדְרַשׁ בִּמְקוֹם בְּתוּלֶיהָ, דְּהַיְינוּ כְּדַרְכָּהּ, אִם נִבְעֲלָה — נִפְסְלָה לְכ"ג, אֲבָל בִּבְעִילָה שֶׁלֹּא כְּדַרְכָּהּ — לֹא. דִּלְמֵיסַר בְּעוּלָה שֶׁלֹּא כְּדַרְכָּהּ לֵיכָּא לְמֵימַר מֵהַאי קְרָא, וּלְמִידְרַשׁ עַד שֶׁיִּהְיוּ כָּל בְּתוּלֶיהָ קַיָּימִין, וַאֲפִילּוּ שֶׁלֹּא כְּדַרְכָּהּ, כִּדְדָרְשִׁינַן לֵיהּ אַלִּיבָּא דְּרַבִּי אֶלְעָזָר — כֵּיוָן דִּ"בְתוּלָה" מְמַעֵט בּוֹגֶרֶת, כ"ש בְּעוּלָה שֶׁלֹּא כְּדַרְכָּהּ. הִלְכָּךְ, כִּי אָתָא קְרָא — לְמִישְׁרֵי אָתָא, וְכִדְדָרְשִׁינַן. וְרַבִּי אֶלְעָזָר וְרַבִּי שִׁמְעוֹן סָבְרִי. אִי הֲוָה כְּתִיב בְּתוּלָה — שְׁלֵימָה מַשְׁמַע, וּמִיתַּסְרָא בּוֹגֶרֶת. הַשְׁתָּא דִּכְתִיב "בְּתוּלֶיהָ" — אֲפִילּוּ מִקְצָת בְּתוּלִים מַשְׁמַע, לְרַבּוֹת בּוֹגֶרֶת. בִּבְתוּלֶיהָ. ב' יְתֵירָא מַשְׁמַע שֶׁתְּהֵא בִּבְתוּלֶיהָ, שֶׁלֹּא אָבְדָה מֵהֶם כְּלוּם עַל יְדֵי בְעִילָה, בֵּין כְּדַרְכָּהּ בֵּין שֶׁלֹּא כְּדַרְכָּהּ. וְכֵיוָן דְּאִיתְרַבַּאי בּוֹגֶרֶת לְהֶיתֵּירָא, אִיצְטְרִיךְ לְמֵיסַר בְּעוּלָה שֶׁלֹּא כְּדַרְכָּהּ. פְּסוּלָה לִכְהוּנָּה. לְכ"ג שֶׁמְּצוּוֶּה עַל הַבְּתוּלָה. אֲבָל לְהֶדְיוֹט אֲפִילּוּ כְּדַרְכָּהּ כְּשֵׁרָה. וְאֵין זוֹנָה אֶלָּא הַנִּבְעֶלֶת לְאָסוּר לָהּ. וְלוֹ תִהְיֶה לְאִשָּׁה. בִּמְאַנֵּס נַעֲרָה בְּתוּלָה כְּתִיב. פְּרָט לְאַלְמָנָה. מִן הָאֵירוּסִין, וְזֶה הַמְאַנֵּס כ"ג הוּא. אוֹ גְּרוּשָׁה אוֹ חֲלוּצָה מִן הָאֵירוּסִין הִיא, אִם כֹּהֵן הֶדְיוֹט הוּא. הֵיכִי דָּמֵי. הָךְ בִּיאַת אוֹנֶס, שֶׁבָּא עָלֶיהָ כֹּהֵן גָּדוֹל זֶה. תֵּיפּוֹק לֵיהּ דַּהֲוְיָא לָהּ בְּעוּלָה. וְתַנְיָא לְקַמָּן: אֲנוּסַת עַצְמוֹ וּמְפוּתַּת עַצְמוֹ – לֹא יִשָּׂא.
הָא

[לעיל נו:] [לקמן סא.] רש"ל וס"א [נ"ל מן האירוסין בין מן הנישואין אף וכו' וכ"א בילקוט] כתובות לז: [לקמן ס.]

תוספות

מהו בתר נישואין אזלינן. מתוך פירוש הקונטרס משמע דשמואל ידע דמיבעיא ליה אם מותר לכונסה משבגרה או לא, אע"ג דמתניתין לא איירי באיסור קיחה – מ"מ שמואל הוה מדמי איסור קיחה לאיסור חללה. וקשה לר"י: דמעיקרא פשט ליה שמואל דבתר נישואין אזלינן, ובתר הכי פשט ליה דבתר אירוסין אזלינן? ועוד: דלא הוה ליה למימר לשוויה חללה לא קמיבעיא לי, כיון דאיהו נמי ידע דלא קמיבעיא ליה אלא לענין קיחה, אלא שהיה מדמה זה לזה. והכי הוה ליה למימר: שאני איסור קיחה מאיסור חללה! ונראה לר"י: דשמואל היה סבר דמיבעיא ליה אי חשיב ליה לר"מ משתמרת לביאה פסולה, כיון שהקידושין היו בהיתר, או לא. והיה יכול להשיבו דזו ביאה כשרה היא, דמותר לכנוס, כדקאמר בסמוך. אלא לפי דבריו, שסבור דאסור לכנוס, משיב לו: תנינא דמן הנישואין פסולות. וכיון דעיקר חללות מן הנשואין – סברא הוא דבתר נישואין אזלינן. אפי' הוי הקידושין בהיתר. **הא** לא אישתני גופה. קודם נישואין, אחר שנתמנה להיות כ"ג. וה"ה אם אירס בוגרת, או קטנה ובגרה, ואח"כ נתמנה להיות כ"ג. דדוקא נתמנה ואח"כ בגרה הוא דלא יכנוס, דנשתנה הגוף אחר שנתמנה. וצ"ע אם אחר שנתמנה נעשית מוכת עץ או בעולה, אי הוי נשתנה הגוף ולא יכנוס, או לא? וקצת משמע בפ"ק דקדושין (דף י.) דלא חשיבא בעולה אישתני גופה, דקאמר: אי תחלת ביאה קונה יכול כ"ג לקדש בביאה, ואי חשוב כאישתני גופה – היאך יכנוס? והלא בעולה היא בשעת נישואין, אם תאמר דביאה אירוסין (א) עושה! ומיהו, בפ' "אלו נערות" (כתובות לח: ושם) חשיב בעולה שינוי הגוף, גבי הא דפריך: אדרבה "בתולה" "בתולה" לגזירה שוה, שהרי אני קורא בה "נערה אשר לא אורסה", ומשני: הא – אישתני גופה, הא – לא אישתני גופה. והא דאמרי' בפ' "נערה" בכתובות (דף מה. ושם) ודלמא כי חדית רחמנא – היכא דלא אישתני גופה, שלא בגרה – התם שהיתה כבר בעולה מן הבועל, לא חשיב שינוי הגוף בבעילת בעל. ובעילת בועל, אע"ג דהוי שינוי הגוף – התם לא איירי אלא בנשתנה הגוף אחר העבירה. [וע"ע תוס' כתובות מה. ד"ה דלמא]. **דומיא** דגרושה. וא"ת: אדרבה, גרושה דומיא דאלמנה, דדוקא מן הנשואין! וי"ל: דלחומרא מקשינן. ועוד אר"י: דגרושה הויא אף מן האירוסין, כמו גרושה דכהן הדיוט, ואע"ג דב"השולח" (גיטין מא. ושם) אמרי': לא, דכולי עלמא ג"ש עדיפא מהקישא – שאני התם, דעיקר שטר נפקא לן מגזרה שוה. [וע"ע תוס' זבחים מח. ד"ה דכ"ע]. **פרט** לבוגרת שכלו בתוליה. לאו דוקא כלו, אלא כלומר: נתמעטו קצת. לא מצי למימר: לרבי מאיר בתולה שלימה משמע, בין כדרכה בין שלא כדרכה "בתוליה" – להכשיר שלא כדרכה, "בבתוליה" – למעוטי בוגרת – דלא משמע ליה למדרש מבי"ת אלא לענין שלא כדרכה, "בבתוליה" – במקום בתוליה. ועוד: דע"כ לר"מ "בתולה" – מקצת בתולה, דשמעינן ליה לר"מ בפרק "אלמנה ניזונת" (כתובות צז: ושם) דאמר: מקצת כסף ככל כסף. ועוד: דאי אפשר דבתולה – שלימה משמע, למעוטי שלא כדרכה, דמ"בתולה" ליכא למעוטי שלא כדרכה, דהא בקנס של נערה כתיב בתולה, ואפילו הכי יש לה קנס, כדאמר בפרק קמא דקידושין (דף י.): מודה רבי לענין קנס דכולהו משלמי. וכן לענין סקילה בנערה המאורסה – לא פליג רבי אלא משום דכתיב "לבדו". ומיהו קשה לר"י: למאן דאמר "בתולה" שלימה משמע, אמאי איצטריך גבי קנס למעוטי בוגרת? תיפוק ליה מדכתיב "בתולה" דמשמע שלימה. וכן גבי נערה המאורסה. ומיהו, בתולה דגבי קנס איכא למימר דאיצטריך לכדדרשינן בפרק "אלו נערות" (כתובות לח: ושם). **אילימא** בכדרכה תיפוק ליה דהויא בעולה. משמע דאסירא ליה, אע"פ שהיא בעולת עצמו. והא דקאמר בריש "אלו נערות" (שם ל. ושם): איכא בינייהו בעולה לכהן גדול – היינו בעולה מאותה בעילה עצמה שנאנסה בה. וכן פירש ר"ח. ולא כמו שדוחק שם בקונטרס לפרש שנבעלה לאחר שלא כדרכה. ועוד: דא"כ הוה ליה למיפרך: הניחא לר"א דאמר נבעלה שלא כדרכה פסולה, אלא לר"מ – מאי איכא למימר. **אלא** לאו שלא כדרכה. משמע דמשלם קנס אביאה שלא כדרכה. וכן בפ"ק דקידושין (דף י. ושם) דקאמר: מודה רבי לענין קנס, דכולהו משלמין. הקשה ריב"א מכאן על פירוש רש"י בפ' "בן סורר ומורה" (סנהדרין עג. ושם), גבי רדף אחר חייבי לאוין ואחר חייבי כריתות, דניתן להציל בנפשו, ופריך: ואלו נערות שיש להם קנס
הבא

עין משפט נר מצוה

נה א מיי' פי"ז מהל' איסורי ביאה הל' יב סמג לאוין קכה ועשין כו:
נו ב מיי' שם הל' יז:
נז ג מיי' שם הלכה א:
נח ד מיי' שם הל' יא:
נט ה מיי' שם הל' יג:
ס ו מיי' שם הל' יח טוש"ע אה"ע סימן ו סעיף א:
סא ז מיי' שם הלכה יד:
סב ח מיי' פ"א מהל' נערה בתולה הל' ה סמג לאוין פל טוש"ע אה"ע סי' קעז סעיף ד:

תוספות חד מקמאי

אמר רב יהודה אמר רב נבעלה שלא כדרכה פסולה לכהונה פי' לכ"ג מתיב רבה ולו תהיה לאשה באשה הראויה לו פרט לאלמנה לכ"ג גרושה וחלוצה לכהן הדיוט ה"ד אלימא כדרכה מאי איריא משום אלמנה תיפוק ליה דה"ל בעולה. פירוש הא תניא לקמן אנוסת עצמו ומפותת עצמו לא (תצא) [ישא אלא] לאו בשלא כדרכה ומשום אלמנה אין משום בעולה לא. הא מני ר"מ היא ורב דאמר כר"א ושמעינן מהא מתניתא שלא כדרכה יש לה קנס. ואקשינן אי כר"א מאי איריא משום בעולה. וקשה לן ומאי קושיא דלמא רב ס"ל כר"א בשלא כדרכה ופליג עליה בפנוי הבא על הפנויה. ועוד לישני ליה רב דאמר כר"ש. ועוד לישני ליה דבאנס מיירי דבכה"ג לא עשה זונה בפנוי הבא על הפנויה (ועוד לישני ליה) דאלת"ה קשיא דרב אדרב דהא אמר רב בפ"ק דכתובות הלכה כר' יוסי דאמר אם רוב העיר משיאין לכהונה ה"ז תנשא לכהונה א) דראב"י גבי אנוסת עצמו ומפותת עצמו הולד חלל. ב)ואוקימנא דראב"י במפותה אבל באנוסה ליכא משום זונה בפנוי הבא על הפנויה (ואנוסת חברו דקתני משום לה דאמר לא ישא) לכך נראה מה שפירש הראב"ד דהכי פריך אי רב ביחידאה ס"ל ה"ל לאשמועינן הא דר"א אלא לאו ש"מ דאליבא דר"ה אמר למילתיה ושני ליה בממאנת ודכ"ע בעל א' עושה אותה בעולה שלא כדרכה כדאית' בפ"ק דקידושין: אמר רב שימי בר חייא נבעלה לבהמה כשרה לכהונה ואפי' לכ"ג דאין זנות לבהמה. וקטנה שנתפתתה תחת בעלה אסורה לבעלה כהן ומותרת לבעלה ישראל דפיתוי קטנה אונס הוא ואונס בישראל משרא שרי. הא דתניא אי אתה עושה חלל מנדה ה"ק אפילו בא עליה ב' פעמים דאילו ראשונה לא צריך דהא [אין חלל אלא] מאסור כהונה אלא כגון שחזר ובא עליה ביאה שניה כיון דנדה שכיב לבעלה בתר יומי נדותה אינה מתחללת. ג) נראה בפרק עשרה יוחסין אמר רב אסי הלכך כהן שבא על אחותו זונה עשה לה חללה לא עשה לה חזר ובא עליה עשאה חללה:
והא

א) נראה דל"ל ועוד דלקמן פסק רב הלכה כראב"י גבי אנוסת חבירו ומפותת חבירו הולד חלל כו'. ב) לפנינו בגמ' לא אמרינן שום חילוק בין מפותה לאנוסה אליבא דר"א וצ"ע. ג) נראה דל"ל גרסינן בפ' עשרה יוחסין דף עז ע"ב.

הגהות הב"ח

(א) תום' ד"ה הא לא אישתני וכו' דביאה אירוסין. נ"ב בפ"ק דקידושין קא מיבעיא ליה וע"ש דף י ע"א:

הָא מַנִּי — רַ' מֵאִיר הִיא, וְרַב דְּאָמַר כְּרַ' אֶלְעָזָר. אִי כְּרַבִּי אֶלְעָזָר, מַאי אִירְיָא מִשּׁוּם בְּעוּלָה? תֵּיפּוֹק לֵיהּ דְּהָוְיָא לָהּ זוֹנָה, דְּהָא א"ר אֶלְעָזָר: *פָּנוּי הַבָּא עַל הַפְּנוּיָה שֶׁלֹּא לְשֵׁם אִישׁוּת עֲשָׂאָהּ זוֹנָה! אָמַר רַב יוֹסֵף: כְּגוֹן שֶׁנִּבְעֲלָה לִבְהֵמָה, דְּהָתָם, מִשּׁוּם בְּעוּלָה — אִיכָּא, מִשּׁוּם זוֹנָה — לֵיכָּא. אֲמַר לֵיהּ אַבַּיֵי: מִמָּה נַפְשָׁךְ, אִי בְּעוּלָה הָוְיָא — זוֹנָה נַמִי הָוְיָא, וְאִי זוֹנָה לָא הָוְיָא — [א]בְּעוּלָה נַמִי לָא הָוְיָא. וְכִי תֵּימָא: מִידֵּי דְּהָוְיָא אַמּוּכַּת עֵץ שֶׁלֹּא כְּדַרְכָּהּ — אִם כֵּן אֵין לְךָ אִשָּׁה שֶׁכְּשֵׁרָה לִכְהוּנָּה שֶׁלֹּא נַעֲשֵׂית מוּכַּת עֵץ עַל יְדֵי צְרוֹר. אֶלָּא אֲמַר רַבִּי זֵירָא: [ב]בִּמְמָאֶנֶת. אָמַר רַב שִׁימִי בַּר חִיָּיא: [ג]נִבְעֲלָה לִבְהֵמָה — כְּשֵׁרָה לִכְהוּנָּה. תַּנְיָא נַמִי הָכִי: [ד]נִבְעֲלָה לְמִי שֶׁאֵינוֹ אִישׁ, אע"פ שֶׁבִּסְקִילָה — כְּשֵׁרָה לִכְהוּנָּה. כִּי אֲתָא רַב דִּימִי אֲמַר: מַעֲשֶׂה בְּרִיבָה אַחַת בְּהִיתְלוּ שֶׁהָיְתָה מְכַבֶּדֶת אֶת הַבַּיִת, וּרְבָעָהּ כֶּלֶב כּוּפְרִי מֵאַחֲרֶיהָ, וְהִכְשִׁירָהּ רַבִּי לִכְהוּנָּה. אֲמַר שְׁמוּאֵל: וּלְכֹהֵן גָּדוֹל. בִּימֵי רַבִּי כֹּהֵן גָּדוֹל מִי הֲוָה? אֶלָּא: רְאוּיָה לְכֹהֵן גָּדוֹל. א"ל רָבָא *מִפַּרְקִין לְרַב אַשִׁי: מְנָא הָא מִילְּתָא דַּאֲמוּר רַבָּנַן *אֵין זְנוּת לִבְהֵמָה — דִּכְתִיב °"לֹא תָבִיא אֶתְנַן זוֹנָה וּמְחִיר כֶּלֶב", דברים כג וּתְנַן: *[ה]אֶתְנַן כֶּלֶב וּמְחִיר זוֹנָה מוּתָּרִין, (מִשּׁוּם) שֶׁנֶּאֱמַר °"גַּם שְׁנֵיהֶם" שְׁנַיִם וְלֹא אַרְבָּעָה. שם ת"ר: [ו]אֲנוּסַת עַצְמוֹ וּמְפוּתַּת עַצְמוֹ — לֹא יִשָּׂא, וְאִם נָשָׂא — נָשׂוּי. אֲנוּסַת חֲבֵירוֹ וּמְפוּתַּת חֲבֵירוֹ — לֹא יִשָּׂא, וְאִם נָשָׂא, רַ' אֱלִיעֶזֶר בֶּן יַעֲקֹב אוֹמֵר: [ז]הַוָּלָד חָלָל, וַחֲכָמִים אוֹמְרִים: הַוָּלָד כָּשֵׁר. § "אִם נָשָׂא — נָשׂוּי". § אָמַר רַב הוּנָא אָמַר רַב: [ח]וּמוֹצִיא בְּגֵט. וְאֶלָּא הָא דְּקָתָנֵי: "אִם נָשָׂא — נָשׂוּי"! אָמַר רַב אַחָא בַּר יַעֲקֹב: לוֹמַר שֶׁאֵין

תורה אור

הָא מַנִּי ר"מ. דְּאָמַר: "בְּתוּלֶיהָ" – עַד שֶׁיְּהוּ כָּל בְּתוּלֶיהָ קַיָּימִין, פְּרָט לְבוֹגֶרֶת. וְאַיְּיתַר לֵיהּ "בִּבְתוּלֶיהָ" לְמַעוּטֵי בְּעוּלָה שֶׁלֹּא כְּדַרְכָּהּ, דִּשְׁרְיָא. וְרַב. דְּאָמַר פְּסוּלָה – כְּרַבִּי אֶלְעָזָר, דְּאָמַר לְעֵיל: "בְּתוּלֶיהָ" – מִקְצָת בְּתוּלִים, לְרַבּוּיֵי בּוֹגֶרֶת. וְאָתָא "בִּבְתוּלֶיהָ" לְמַעוּטֵי בְּעוּלָה שֶׁלֹּא כְּדַרְכָּהּ, כִּדְלְעֵיל. דְּהָוְיָא לָהּ זוֹנָה. וַאֲפִי' לְכֹהֵן הֶדְיוֹט אֲסוּרָה. דְּהָא אָמַר רַבִּי אֶלְעָזָר כו'. לְקַמָּן בְּפִירְקִין (דף סא:). אִיסּוּר זוֹנָה לֵיכָּא. דְּיָלְפִינַן לְקַמָּן בִּשְׁמַעְתִּין: אֵין זְנוּת לִבְהֵמָה. אִי זוֹנָה לָא הָוְיָא. א"כ לָאו בִּיאָה הִיא, וַאֲפִי' לְכֹהֵן גָּדוֹל תִּשְׁתְּרֵי. וְכ"ת מִידֵּי דְּהָוְיָא אַמּוּכַּת עֵץ. דְּהָא רַבִּי אֶלְעָזָר קָאָמַר בְּמַתְנִי', לֹא יִשָּׂא אֶת מוּכַּת עֵץ, וְתִיבָּעֵי לְמֵימַר דַּאֲפִי' בְּמוּכַּת עֵץ שֶׁלֹּא כְּדַרְכָּהּ פְּסוּלָה. א"כ אֵין לְךָ אִשָּׁה שֶׁכְּשֵׁרָה לִכְהוּנָּה גְּדוֹלָה שֶׁלֹּא נַעֲשֵׂית מוּכַּת עֵץ עַל יְדֵי צְרוֹר. שֶׁל קִינּוּחַ בֵּית הַכִּסֵּא. אֶלָּא א"ר זֵירָא. מַשְׁכַּחַתְּ לָהּ לְהָא דְּרַב אַלִּיבָּא דְּרַבִּי אֶלְעָזָר דְּהָוְיָא בְּעוּלָה, וְלֹא זוֹנָה וְלֹא אַלְמָנָה וְלֹא גְּרוּשָׁה – בִּקְטַנָּה יְתוֹמָה הַמִּשֶּׂאֶת לְבַעַל, וּבְעָלָהּ שֶׁלֹּא כְּדַרְכָּהּ וּמֵיאֲנָה בּוֹ. דְּאֵין כָּאן פְּסוּל זְנוּת וְאַלְמְנוּת וְגֵירוּשִׁין, וְאַשְׁמְעִינַן רַב דְּיֵשׁ כָּאן פְּסוּל בְּעוּלָה לְכֹהֵן גָּדוֹל. כְּשֵׁרָ' לִכְהוּנָּה. אֲפִי' לְכֹהֵן גָּדוֹל, דְּמוּכַּת עֵץ בְּעָלְמָא הִיא. וּמַאן דְּשָׁרֵי בְּמוּכַּת עֵץ – שָׁרֵי בָּהּ. לְמִי שֶׁאֵינוֹ אִישׁ. בְּהֵמָה. שֶׁבִּסְקִילָה. אִם יֵשׁ עֵדִים וְהַתְרָאָה – הֵיכָא דְּלֵיכָּא עֵדִים וְהַתְרָאָה – כְּשֵׁרָה לִכְהוּנָּה. בְּהִיתְלוּ. שֵׁם מָקוֹם. כּוּפְרִי. כְּלָבִים גְּדוֹלִים שֶׁצָּדִין בָּהֶן חַיּוֹת*. מֵאַחֲרֶיהָ. שֶׁלֹּא כְּדַרְכָּהּ. דְּאִי כְּדַרְכָּהּ – לָא גָּרְעָה מִמּוּכַּת עֵץ: רַבִּי. לְאַחַר חוּרְבַּן הַבַּיִת הָיָה כַּמָּה דּוֹרוֹת, שֶׁהוּא סוֹף הַתַּנָּאִים, וּבִימֵי רַבָּן יוֹחָנָן בֶּן זַכַּאי חָרַב הַבַּיִת, דִּתְנַן (ר"ה דף כט:): מִשֶּׁחָרַב בֵּית הַמִּקְדָּשׁ הִתְקִין רַבָּן יוֹחָנָן בֶּן זַכַּאי וכו'. אֶתְנַן כֶּלֶב.(א) שֶׁאִם אָמַר אָדָם לְזוֹנָה הֵילָךְ טָלֶה זֶה וְהִבָּעֲלִי לְכַלְבִּי, וּמְחִיר זוֹנָה שֶׁהֶחֱלִיף זוֹנָה בְּטָלֶה – מוּתָּרִים לַמִּזְבֵּחַ. וּמִדְּשָׁרֵי אֶתְנַן כֶּלֶב – אַלְמָא לָאו זְנוּת הוּא. לֹא יִשָּׂא. כֹּהֵן גָּדוֹל, דִּכְתִיב "בְּתוּלָה יִקָּח" (ויקרא כא) – בִּשְׁעַת לִיקּוּחִין תְּהֵא בְּתוּלָה. שֶׁאֵין

הבא על אחותו – ומשני: משעת הערלה הוא דפגמה, איפטר ליה מקטלא, ממונא לא משלם עד גמר ביאה. ופירש בקונטרס: דאין משלם קנס עד גמר ביאה, שיש שם הסרת בתולים. ומפרש ר"ת וריב"א: דודאי משלם קנס אהערלה ואשלא כדרכה, אע"ג דאין מסיר בתולים. והתם דוקא קאמר דלא משלם עד גמר ביאה – משום דמעיקרא קם לי' בדרבה מיניה, דניתן להצילה בנפשו. והא דנקט התם כגון שבא עליה שלא כדרכה וחזר ובא עליה בכדרכה – הוה מצי למינקט וחזר ובא עליה שלא כדרכה, כיון דחייב קנס אשלא כדרכה. ועוד נראה לר"י: דאע"ג דיש קנס בשלא כדרכה – בהערלה אין קנס, לפי שלא נתרבתה הערלה להיות כגמר ביאה לענין קנס. דהא לעריות וחייבי לאוין וחייבי עשה ואשה לבעלה ויבמה מרבינן קראי לעיל (דף נה.) לרבות הערלה וכן משמע מתוך הך דשמעתין, דאי יש קנס בהערלה – הוה ליה לשנויי כגון שלא עשה אלא נשיקה ובנשיקה אינו מסיר בתולים כדמשמע בפרק בן סורר (סנהדרין דף עג: ושם) וא"ת ואי אין קנס בהערלה היאך איש מתחייב קנס למאן דאמר הערלה זו הכנסת עטרה? דבהכנסת עטרה הוא מסיר בתוליה, כדמוכח ב"בן סורר" (ג"ז שם), ואז היא כבר בעולה, ורחמנא אמר "בתולה" ולא בעולה! וי"ל: דבהכי חייב רחמנא, הואיל ובבעילה זו נעשית בעולה, אע"ג דלא מתחיל חיוב קנס עד אח"כ. דאי לא תימא הכי – למה ליה למכתב הערלה כלל? לילף הערלה מנערה המאורסה בכל העריות, דאיתקוש כולם להדדי, כדאמרי' בריש פירקין (דף נה.)! ובנערה המאורסה ע"כ מיחייב בהערלה, דאי בגמר ביאה – כבר הסיר בתוליה בהכנסת עטרה, ורחמנא אמר "בתולה" ולא בעולה, כדדרשינן בפ' "ד' מיתות" (סנהדרין סו:) אלא ע"כ, אפי' לא מחייב אלא עד גמר ביאה, כיון דבביאה זו נעשית בעולה – חייב רחמנא. אבל קשה: אי לא מחייב קנס בהערלה, א"כ מאי פריך ב"בן סורר": הניחא למ"ד הערלה זו נשיקה, אלא למאן דאמר הערלה זו הכנסת עטרה – מאי איכא למימר? הא לדידיה נמי אתי שפיר, דהא לא מיחייב קנס בהכנסת עטרה אלא בגמר ביאה ממש!

הא מני ר' מאיר. – אע"ג דלר' מאיר חייבי לאוין וכריתות בני קנס, דרב גופיה מוקי מתניתין דריש "אלו נערות" (כתובות דף כט.) כרבי מאיר – הכא לאו מקנס ממעט להו, אלא לענין שאין ראויה לקיימה. כדקתני נמי סיפא ד"אלו נערות" (שם לט.): אם לא היתה ראויה לבא בישראל אינו רשאי לקיימה, שנאמר "ולו תהיה לאשה" – באשה הראויה לו. תימה: דהתם (דף מ.) פריך עלה וליתי עשה ולידחי לא תעשה, ומאי פריך? שאני הכא דגלי קרא! וי"ל, דפריך הכי: וניתי עשה, וכי תימא שאני הכא דגלי קרא – אם כן נגמר מהכא בכל מקום דלא דחי! א"נ, פריך: דלא הוה ליה לאוקמי קרא בחייבי לאוין אלא בחייבי כריתות דוקא, דהוה אמינא שמותר לקיימה הואיל ואיתרבו לקנס מהבתולות ומנערות, בריש "אלו נערות" (שם דף כט:) דקראי משתמעי דהיכא דאיכא קנס איכא נישואין. אבל בחייבי לאוין – נימא דאתי עשה ודחי לא תעשה. אבל קשה: דמשני, היכא אמרינן דדחי – כגון מילה בצרעת, אבל הכא אי אמרה לא בעינא ליה – מי איתיה לעשה כלל. א"כ למה לי קרא למעוטי שלא ישאנה? ונראה לר"י: דהכא לאו מיתורא קדריש, אלא הכי פירושו: "ולו תהיה לאשה" – באשה הראויה לו, פרט לאלמנה. משום דדרשינן ב"אלו נערות" (שם דף לט.) "תהיה" – מדעתה, וכיון דבעינן מדעתה – א"כ בעינן אשה הראויה לו, דלא חשיב עשה, דהא אי אמרה לא בעינא ליה – מי איתיה לעשה כללו! ומעיקרא דפריך וניתי עשה ונדחי לא תעשה – סלקא דעתך דכי אמרה: מיהא בעינא ליה – ידחה עשה את לא תעשה, דלא מסיק אדעתיה דלא אתי עשה ודחי לא תעשה אלא כגון מילה בצרעת כו'. א"נ: מעיקרא ס"ד כדפי', דמייתורא קא דריש. **ורבי** דאמר כרבי אלעזר. לא שסבר רב כרבי אלעזר, דהא רב ושמואל דאמרי תרוייהו: בוגרת ומוכת עץ לא ישא, ורבי אלעזר מכשיר בוגרת. אלא הכי קאמר: דרב דאמר לרבי אלעזר נבעלה שלא כדרכה פסולה לכהונה, כיון דמכשיר בוגרת, וליה לא סבירא ליה. והשתא ניחא דפריך: אי כר' אלעזר – מאי איריא משום בעולה, תיפוק ליה דהויא זונה, דהא אמר רבי אלעזר פנוי כו'. ואי אליבא דנפשיה קאמר – מאי פריך? דלמא משום דסבר לה כר' אלעזר במדא סבר לה כוותיה בכל מילי?! דאין שני הדברים הללו תלויין זה בזה, דמה ענין זה אצל זה? ועוד: דעל כרחך לא סבר כוותיה בהא, דאמר: "פנוי הבא על הפנויה עשאה זונה" מדפריך ארב בסמוך, ובהא אמר רב עמרם, דאין הלכה כר' אלעזר; ובסוף פ"ק דכתובות (דף טו. ושם) גבי תינוקת שנאנסה – פסיק לשם כר' יוסי, דמכשיר. והיכי הוה מכשיר, אפילו בתרי רובי, אי סבר "פנוי הבא על הפנויה עשאה זונה"! ודוחק לומר, דלא אצטריך לפסוק אלא לבא עליה לשום אישות, אלא אליבא דר' אלעזר קאמר, וליה לא סבירא ליה. **שנים** ולא ארבעה. וא"ת: ומהיכא תיסק אדעתיה למיסר דאיצטריך קרא למעוטי. וי"ל, דסלקא דעתך לאסור משום דאיתקוש, וכי תימא: אם איתא דהני נמי אסור, לכתוב רחמנא: "אתנן ומחיר כלב וזונה"! – א"כ הוה אמינא דכל חד לחוד שרי. ומיהו,(ב) למאן דאמר (ב"מ לד: ובשאר דוכתי) "משמע שניהם כאחד ומשמע אחד בפני עצמו, עד שיפרוט לך הכתוב: 'יחדו'" – ה"ל למכתב הכי. ובפ' "כל האסורין" (תמורה דף ל: ושם) מהאי דרשה דשנים ולא ד', נפקא לן דאין זנות לבהמה. שאינו

סג א מיי' פי"ז מהל' איסורי ביאה הל' יד:

סד ב מיי' שם הל' יח:

סה ג ד מיי' פי"ח שם הל' א סמג לאוין קפא טוש"ע אה"ע סימן ו סעיף ח:

סו ה מיי' פ"ד מהל' איסורי מזבח הל' יח:

סז ו מיי' פ"א מהל' נערה בתולה הל' ו ופי"ז מהלכות איסורי ביאה הל' טו טז:

סח ז מיי' פי"ט מהל' איסורי ביאה הל' ז טוש"ע אה"ע סימן סעיף יב:

סט ח מיי' שם פי"ז הל' טו טז ופ"א מהלכות נערה בתולה הלכה ו:

לקמן סא: עו. סנהדרין נח. תמורה ל.

תמורה ל: סוטה כו:

[מפרזקיא]

[ובערוך פי' כלב קטן שטות בלילה במדברות מן כפריס]

[תמורה ל. ע"ש ל: וגם בסוטה כו:]

הגהות הב"ח

(א) רש"י ד"ה אתנן כלב. נ"ב ובמסכת תמורה דף ל' פרש"י הילך טלה זה ותלין כלבתך אצלי אלא דסוגיא דהכא ורבעה כלב כופרי כו' משמע דמיירי בנבעלת לכלב וכן בסוטה דף טו ע"ב: (ב) תוס' ד"ה שנים וכו' ומיהו ודאי למאן דאמר משמע וכו' ובפ' כל האיסורין בלאו האי דרשה:

גליון הש"ס

גמ' ורב דאמר כרבי אלעזר. עיין תשובת הרשב"א סי' אלף רל"ח:

תוספות ישנים

הוו בכשרות הא ודאי בתר נשואין אזלינן והוו נשואי פסולות אבל ר' יוחנן אליבא דנפשיה סבר דקרי לכונסה כמו שהשיב לו לבסוף דקיחה דאירוסין קאמר קרא: **אי** כר"א מאי איריא. ותימה דאטו משום דס"ל כרבי אלעזר במלתי' דשלא כדרכה יסבור כמותו מכל וכל. וא"כ מאי פריך מאי איריא משום בעולה תיפוק לי' דהוה לה זונה דאמר ר"א פנוי הבא על הפנויה עשאה זונה דלמא לא סבר לה כוותיה במילתא דפנוי הבא על הפנויה עשאה זונה וע"ק דהלכה כרב באיסורי וא"כ הלכה כר' אלעזר דבתולה שלימה משמע וא"כ היכי הוי מנהג שאנו כותבין בכתובות בוגרת כסף זוזי מאתן דחזו ליכי מדאורייתא הלא כתיב כי יפתה איש נערה בתולה דבתולה שלימה משמע ומינה שמעינן מוהר הבתולות שהוא מאתים וא"כ אין בוגרת כבתולה. וע"ק דודאי רב לא מצי סבר כרבי אלעזר דבפ"ק דכתובות פסק רב כר' יוסי דאמר אם רוב העיר משיאין לכהונה תנשא לכהונה ולא אמרינן עשאה זונה משום פנוי הבא על הפנויה שלא לשם אישות ועוד דלקמן קאמר רב בוגרת לא ישא אלמא לאו כר' אלעזר ס"ל דמכשר בבוגרת וע"ק דהלכה כרב ולקמן פסקינן הלכה כראב"י דלא ס"ל כר"א בההיא דפנוי הבא על הפנויה וא"כ קשה הלכתא אהלכתא לכנ"ל דרב כר"א ר"ל דאליבא דר"א קאמר אבל לא סבר כן ולהכי פריך לר' אלעזר מאי אריא משום בעולה תיפוק ליה דהויא לה זונה: **גם** שניהם שנים ולא ארבעה. מפורש במרובה:

שֶׁאֵין מְשַׁלֵּם קְנָס בִּמְפוּתָּה. אֲזַל רַב גְּבִיהָה מִבֵּי כְּתִיל, אֲמָרָהּ לִשְׁמַעְתָּא קַמֵּיהּ דְּרַב אַשִׁי. אֲמַר לֵיהּ: וְהָא רַב וְרַ' יוֹחָנָן דְּאָמְרִי תַּרְוַיְיהוּ: [א]בּוֹגֶרֶת [ב]וּמוּכַּת עֵץ — לֹא יִשָּׂא, [ג]וְאִם נָשָׂא — נָשׂוּי. אַלְמָא: סוֹפָהּ לִהְיוֹת בּוֹגֶרֶת תַּחְתָּיו, סוֹפָהּ לִהְיוֹת מוּכַּת עֵץ תַּחְתָּיו, הָכָא נַמִי — סוֹפָהּ לִהְיוֹת בְּעוּלָה תַּחְתָּיו! קַשְׁיָא. § "אֲנוּסַת חֲבֵירוֹ וּמְפוּתַּת חֲבֵירוֹ — לֹא יִשָּׂא, וְאִם נָשָׂא, רַ' אֶלְעָזָר בֶּן יַעֲקֹב אוֹמֵר: הַוָּלָד חָלָל, וַחֲכָמִים אוֹמְרִים: הַוָּלָד כָּשֵׁר". § אָמַר רַב הוּנָא אָמַר רַב: *הֲלָכָה כְּרַ' אֱלִיעֶזֶר בֶּן יַעֲקֹב. וְכֵן אָמַר רַב גִּידֵּל אָמַר רַב: הֲלָכָה כְּרַבִּי אֱלִיעֶזֶר בֶּן יַעֲקֹב. אִיכָּא דְּאָמְרִי, אָמַר רַב הוּנָא אָמַר רַב: מַאי טַעְמָא דְּרַבִּי אֱלִיעֶזֶר בֶּן יַעֲקֹב — סָבַר לָהּ כְּרַבִּי אֶלְעָזָר. וּמִי סָבַר לָהּ כְּוָתֵיהּ? וְהָא קַיְימָא לָן: *מִשְׁנַת רַ' אֱלִיעֶזֶר בֶּן יַעֲקֹב קַב וְנָקִי, וְאִילּוּ בְּהָא *אָמַר רַב עַמְרָם (א) אָמַר רַב: אֵין הֲלָכָה כְּרַבִּי אֶלְעָזָר! קַשְׁיָא. רַב אַשִׁי אֲמַר: בְּיֵשׁ חָלָל מֵחַיָּיבֵי עֲשֵׂה קָמִיפַּלְגִי. רַבִּי אֱלִיעֶזֶר בֶּן יַעֲקֹב סָבַר: *יֵשׁ חָלָל מֵחַיָּיבֵי עֲשֵׂה, וְרַבָּנַן סָבְרִי: אֵין חָלָל מֵחַיָּיבֵי עֲשֵׂה. מ"ט דְּרַאבַּ"י — דִּכְתִיב (ויקרא כא) "אַלְמָנָה וּגְרוּשָׁה וַחֲלָלָה זוֹנָה אֶת אֵלֶּה לֹא יִקָּח כִּי אִם בְּתוּלָה וגו'", וּכְתִיב "וְלֹא יְחַלֵּל זַרְעוֹ בְּעַמָּיו" אַכּוּלְּהוּ. וְרַבָּנַן "אֵלֶּה" הִפְסִיק הָעִנְיָן. וְרַבִּי אֱלִיעֶזֶר בֶּן יַעֲקֹב — אָמַר "אֵלֶּה" [ד]לְמַעוּטֵי נִדָּה. כְּמַאן אָזְלָא הָא דְּתַנְיָא: מֵ"אֵלֶּה" אַתָּה עוֹשֶׂה חָלָל, וְאִי אַתָּה עוֹשֶׂה חָלָל מִנִּדָּה, כְּמַאן — כְּרַבִּי אֱלִיעֶזֶר בֶּן יַעֲקֹב. וְרַבִּי אֱלִיעֶזֶר בֶּן יַעֲקֹב, נִכְתְּבֵיהּ לְ"אֵלֶּה" לְבַסּוֹף! קַשְׁיָא. תָּנוּ רַבָּנַן: אֲחוֹתוֹ אֲרוּסָה, רַבִּי מֵאִיר וְרַ' יְהוּדָה אוֹמְרִים: מִטַּמֵּא לָהּ, רַבִּי יוֹסֵי וְרַבִּי שִׁמְעוֹן אוֹמְרִים: [ה]אֵין מִטַּמֵּא לָהּ. אֲנוּסָה וּמְפוּתָּה — ד"ה אֵין מִטַּמֵּא לָהּ, וּמוּכַּת עֵץ — אֵין מִטַּמֵּא לָהּ, דִּבְרֵי רַ' שִׁמְעוֹן. שֶׁהָיָה רַ' שִׁמְעוֹן אוֹמֵר: רְאוּיָה לְכ"ג מִטַּמֵּא לָהּ, שֶׁאֵין רְאוּיָה לְכ"ג — אֵין מִטַּמֵּא לָהּ. וּבוֹגֶרֶת מִטַּמֵּא לָהּ — דִּבְרֵי כָּל אָדָם. מַאי טַעְמָא דְּר"מ וְרַ' יְהוּדָה? דְּדָרְשִׁי הָכִי: (שם) "וְלַאֲחוֹתוֹ הַבְּתוּלָה" [ה]פְּרָט לַאֲנוּסָה וּמְפוּתָּה. יָכוֹל שֶׁאֲנִי מוֹצִיא אַף מוּכַּת עֵץ — ת"ל (שם) "אֲשֶׁר לֹא הָיְתָה לְאִישׁ", מִי שֶׁהֲוָיָיתָהּ עַל יְדֵי אִישׁ, [ו]יָצְאָה זוֹ שֶׁאֵין הֲוָיָיתָהּ עַל יְדֵי אִישׁ. "הַקְּרוֹבָה" לְרַבּוֹת הָאֲרוּסָה. [ז]"אֵלָיו" לְרַבּוֹת הַבּוֹגֶרֶת. הָא לָמָּה לִי קְרָא? וְהָאָמַר *רַבִּי מֵאִיר: "בְּתוּלָה" אֲפִילּוּ מִקְצָת בְּתוּלָה מַשְׁמַע! אִיצְטְרִיךְ, סָלְקָא דַּעְתָּךְ אָמִינָא: נֵילַף "בְּתוּלָה" "בְּתוּלָה" מֵהָתָם, מַה לְּהַלָּן נַעֲרָה — אַף כָּאן נַמִי נַעֲרָה, קָא מַשְׁמַע לָן. וְרַבִּי יוֹסֵי וְרַבִּי שִׁמְעוֹן, מַאי טַעֲמַיְיהוּ? דָּרְשִׁי הָכִי: "וְלַאֲחוֹתוֹ הַבְּתוּלָה" פְּרָט לַאֲנוּסָה וּמְפוּתָּה וּמוּכַּת עֵץ, "אֲשֶׁר לֹא הָיְתָה" פְּרָט לַאֲרוּסָה, "הַקְּרוֹבָה" [ח]לְרַבּוֹת אֲרוּסָה שֶׁנִּתְגָּרְשָׁה, "אֵלָיו" לְרַבּוֹת אֶת הַבּוֹגֶרֶת. "הַקְּרוֹבָה" לְרַבּוֹת אֲרוּסָה שֶׁנִּתְגָּרְשָׁה? וְהָא

רש"י

שֶׁאֵין מְשַׁלֵּם קְנָס בִּמְפוּתָּה. שֶׁאִם מְפוּתָּה הִיא, אַהֲנוּ לֵיהּ נִשּׂוּאִין לְמִפְטְרֵיהּ מִקְּנָסָא. שֶׁהַמְפַתֶּה אֵין מְשַׁלֵּם קְנָס אֶלָּא כְּשֶׁאֵין כּוֹנְסָהּ, דִּכְתִיב "אִם מָאֵן יְמָאֵן" (שמות כב). אֲבָל אִם מָהוֹר יִמְהָרֶנָּה לּוֹ לְאִשָּׁה – לֹא יִתֵּן כְּלוּם. אֲבָל אוֹנֵס נוֹתֵן מִיָּד, אֲפִילּוּ הוּא כּוֹנְסָהּ, דִּכְתִיב (דברים כב) "וְנָתַן הָאִישׁ הַשּׁוֹכֵב עִמָּהּ... תורה אור וְלוֹ תִהְיֶה לְאִשָּׁה". אֲמָרָהּ לִשְׁמַעְתָּא. לְהָא דְּרַב הוּנָא דְּאָמַר וּמוֹצִיאָהּ בְּגֵט. סוֹפָהּ לִהְיוֹת מוּכַּת עֵץ תַּחְתָּיו. כְּלוֹמַר: סוֹפָהּ לִיבָּעֵל לוֹ, וּלְאַבֵּד בְּתוּלֶיהָ. סוֹפָהּ לִהְיוֹת בְּעוּלָה תַּחְתָּיו. וְאִם נָשָׂא נָשׂוּי דְּקָתָנֵי – לְגַמְרֵי קָאָמַר, דְּמוּתָּר לְקַיְּימָהּ, הוֹאִיל וּלְעַצְמוֹ נִבְעֲלָה, וְסוֹפָהּ לִהְיוֹת בְּעוּלָה לוֹ. סָבַר לָהּ כְּר' אֶלְעָזָר. דְּאָמַר (לקמן דף סא:): פָּנוּי הַבָּא עַל הַפְּנוּיָה שֶׁלֹּא לְשֵׁם אִישׁוּת – עֲשָׂאָהּ זוֹנָה, וְקַיְּימָה עֲלֵיהּ בְּלָאו. וּמֵחַיָּיבֵי לָאוִין דִּכְהוּנָּה הָוֵי הַוָּלָד חָלָל. [עי' תוספות בכורות כג: ד"ה משנת] דְּרַב עַמְרָם. לְקַמָּן בְּפִירְקִין (שם). בְּיֵשׁ חָלָל מֵחַיָּיבֵי עֲשֵׂה. *ר' אֱלִיעֶזֶר ב"י לָא כְּר' אֶלְעָזָר סְבִירָא לֵיהּ, וְלָאו [נ"ל ורבי אליעזר ס' מהרש"ל] זוֹנָה הִיא, וְלָא קַיְּימָא עֲלֵיהּ בְּלָאו אֶלָּא בַּעֲשֵׂה, דִּכְתִיב "בְּתוּלָה יִקָּח" וְלֹא בְּעוּלָה, [לעיל מט. וש"נ] וְלָאו הַבָּא מִכְּלַל עֲשֵׂה – עֲשֵׂה. וּכְתִיב לֹא יְחַלֵּל אַכּוּלְּהוּ. וַאֲפִי' אַ"בְּתוּלָה יִקָּח [לקמן סא: וע"ש] וְלֹא בְּעוּלָה", דַּעֲשֵׂה הוּא. אֵלֶּה הִפְסִיק הָעִנְיָן. דִּכְתִיב "אֵלֶּה" בָּתַר חַיָּיבֵי לָאוִין, לְאַשְׁמוּעִינַן: אֵלֶּה שֶׁהֵן חַיָּיבֵי לָאוִין [לקמן עז: פה:] חֲלוּקִין מִדִּין חַיָּיבֵי עֲשֵׂה. לְמַעוּטֵי נִדָּה. שֶׁאִם בָּא כֹּהֵן עַל אִשְׁתּוֹ נִדָּה – אֵין הַוָּלָד חָלָל. וְלִכְתְּבֵיהּ לְבַסּוֹף. הוֹאִיל וְלָאו לְפַלּוּגִינְהוּ אָתֵי. קַשְׁיָא. לְרַב אַשִׁי דְּמוֹקֵי פְּלוּגְתַּיְיהוּ בְּטַעְמָא דְּהָנֵי קְרָאֵי. אֲחוֹתוֹ אֲרוּסָה. שֶׁל כֹּהֵן הֶדְיוֹט. אֲבָל נְשׂוּאָה – פְּשִׁיטָא לָן דְּאֵין מִטַּמֵּא, דִּכְתִיב "וְלַאֲחוֹתוֹ הַבְּתוּלָה". אֲנוּסָה וּמְפוּתָּה. אֲחוֹתוֹ שֶׁנֶּאֶנְסָה אוֹ שֶׁנִּתְפַּתְּתָה. דִּבְרֵי הַכֹּל אֵין מִטַּמֵּא לָהּ. וְטַעְמָא דְּכוּלְּהוּ מְפָרֵשׁ לְקַמָּן. וּמוּכַּת עֵץ אֵין מִטַּמֵּא לָהּ דִּבְרֵי ר"ש. ר"ש לְטַעְמֵיהּ, דְּאָמַר בְּמַתְנִיתִין: מוּכַּת עֵץ אֲסוּרָה לְכ"ג, אַלְמָא: לָאו בִּכְלַל בְּתוּלָה הִיא. שֶׁאֵינָהּ רְאוּיָה לְכ"ג אֵין מִטַּמֵּא לָהּ. דְּהָכָא וְהָכָא "בְּתוּלָה" כְּתִיב. דִּבְרֵי כָּל אָדָם. וַאֲפִי' לְרַבִּי מֵאִיר, דְּפָסֵיל בּוֹגֶרֶת לְכֹהֵן גָּדוֹל – הָכָא לְעִנְיַן טוּמְאָה אִיתְרַבֵּי, כִּדְלְקַמָּן. פְּרָט לַאֲנוּסָה וּמְפוּתָּה. שֶׁאֵינָהּ בְּתוּלָה. יָכוֹל שֶׁאֲנִי מוֹצִיא אַף מוּכַּת עֵץ. שֶׁאֵינָהּ בְּתוּלָה. לְרַבּוֹת אֶת הָאֲרוּסָה. וְאִיצְטְרִיךְ לְרַבּוּיָא, דְּלָא תֵּימָא "אֲשֶׁר לֹא הָיְתָה" – פְּרָט לַאֲרוּסָה שֶׁהָיְתָה לְאִישׁ, דַּהֲוָיָה לְשׁוֹן קִידּוּשִׁין הִיא: ה"ג. לָמָּה לִי קְרָא וְהָא אָמַר ר"מ בְּתוּלָה מִקְצָת בְּתוּלִים מַשְׁמַע. [לעיל נט.] לְעֵיל אֲמַר הָכִי: מִדְּאִיצְטְרִיךְ לְמִכְתַּב "בִּבְתוּלֶיהָ" לְגַבֵּי כ"ג לְהוֹצִיא אֶת הַבּוֹגֶרֶת לר"מ – מִכְּלַל דִּבְתוּלָה – בּוֹגֶרֶת נַמִי מַשְׁמַע. מֵהָתָם. "כִּי יִמְצָא אִישׁ נַעֲרָה בְּתוּלָה" (דברים כב). מִדְּשָׁבְקֵיהּ

תוספות

שאינו משלם קנס במפותה. ואם תאמר: וכיון דבעיא גט, ואית לה כתובה, כמו אלמנה לכ"ג דיש לה כתובה, כדאמרינן ב"יש מותרות" (לקמן דף פה. ושם) אע"ג דאסורה מן התורה, וא"כ – מאי נפקא מינה דאין משלם קנס? הרי יש לה כתובה, ומה לי קנס ומה לי כתובה! ואומר ר"י: דנפקא מינה אם מחלה לכתובה. ועוד נפקא מינה: דלא משלם מן העידית כדין קנס, אלא מן הזיבורית כדין כתובת אשה. ועוד: דכתובת בעולה דרבנן. ועוד נראה: דהא דאמר רב מוציא בגט – היינו מדרבנן. ולהכי נקט פלוגתא *דרבי באנוסת חבירו, דבאנוסת עצמו – מודה דלא הוי חלל. ומיהו, אלינן למימר דנקט אנוסת חבירו להודיעך כוחן דרבנן דמכשרי. **סופה** להיות בעולה תחתיו. ואין לומר דמוציאה בגט דקאמר רב – היינו לרבי אלעזר, דאמר: פנוי הבא על הפנויה עשאה זונה. דהא רב אברייתא קאי, וברייתא דלא כרבי אלעזר, דהא אמרי רבנן הולד כשר. **חלל** מחייבי עשה. תימה: כיון ד"לא יחלל" קאי נמי אבעולה לרבי אליעזר בן יעקב, אם כן אין זה חייבי עשה גרידא, ד"לא יחלל" לאו הוא, כדקאמר בפרק [בתרא] דקידושין (דף עח.): בעל – לוקה משום "לא יחלל"!. **אלה** הפסיק הענין. ולא מוקמינן "לא יחלל" אבעולה, אע"ג דמינה סליק – משום דמיסתבר טפי לאוקמי אחייבי לאוין. **ואי** אתה עושה חלל מנדה. בתורת כהנים מפרש, דאיצטריך דלא נילף דליהוי חלל מקל וחומר מהני שהם חייבי לאוין. תימה: דמה לאלמנה וכיוצא בה – שכן הן עצמן מתחללות? וכי תימא ה"נ, כיון דבא עליה עשאה זונה – הא לא הוי זונה, כיון דתפסי בה קידושין!. **אלין** לרבות הבוגרת. וא"ת: למה לי "אליו"? נרבי בוגרת מ"ולא היתה לאיש" כדמרבינן מיניה מוכת עץ! וי"ל: דאי לאו "אליו" הוה מוקמינן "לא היתה" לבוגרת גרידא, דבוגרת מסתבר לרבות טפי ממוכת עץ. משום דמוכת עץ איתעביד בה מעשה, ולהכי מוקי "אליו" דכתיב ברישא לרבות בוגרת, ו"לא היתה לאיש" דכתיב בסוף מוקי למוכת עץ. וכן משמע דבוגרת עדיפא ממוכת עץ, דהא בבוגרת לא פליגי, כדקתני: ובוגרת מטמא לה דברי כל אדם. ועוד נראה: דממשמעות "בתולה" מימעטא מוכת עץ אפילו לרבי מאיר, מדפריך גבי בוגרת: והא למה לי קרא. וגבי מוכת עץ לא פריך הכי, ולהכי מוקי קרא קמא בבוגרת. וניחא נמי השתא הא דדרשינן דרשא ד"אשר לא היתה לאיש" ברישא, אע"ג דכתיב בסוף – משום דממשמעות "בתולה" הוה לן למעוטי מוכת עץ, הוצרך לפרש דמתרבי מ"אשר לא היתה לאיש". **נילף** "בתולה" "בתולה" מהתם. אומר ר"ת: מהתם – היינו מכ"ג, ולא כמו שפירש בקונטרס דמ"בתולה" דאונס ומפתה קאמר. וכן נראה לר"י, דהא בכולה שמעתא לא איירי באונס ומפתה, ולא ה"ל למימר מהתם, אלא מהתם – היינו כ"ג, כדפירש ר"ת, דאיירי ביה, ומשום דרבי שמעון גמרה מהתם, קא סלקא דעתך נילף מהתם, כדקאמר: ראויה לכהן גדול מטמא לה כו', ועל כרחך לא לסימנא בעלמא נקטיה, מדפריך בסמוך: והא אמר רבי שמעון ראויה לכ"ג כו'. ואי פריך משום דאין הכלל אמת – מהא לא הוה משני מידי, אלא ודי פריך דמכ"ג ה"ל למילף. ומוכת עץ מהתם גמר לה רבי שמעון, כדקתני בהדיא בברייתא: הראויה לכ"ג כו', דאי לאו דמיעטיה רחמנא מוכת עץ מ"בבתוליה" עד שיהו כל בתוליה קיימין, וגמר מהתם – ה"ל למידרש הכא: מי שהווייתה על ידי איש, יצתה מוכת עץ, והוה ילפינן התם מהכא. והא

עין משפט נר מצוה

ע א מיי' פי"ז מהל' איסורי ביאה הלכ' יג:

עא ב מיי' שם הלכ' יד:

עב ג מיי' שם הלכה טו:

עג ד מיי' שם פי"ט הל' ו סמג לאוין קנב טוש"ע אה"ע סימן ו סעיף ח:

עד ה ו ז ח מיי' פ"ב מהל' אבל הלכה י יא סמג עשין נח ולאוין רלה טוש"ע יו"ד סימן שעג סעיף ז:

עה [ה] מיי' שם הלכה י טוש"ע שם:

[נ"ל דר"א בן יעקב]

תוספות ישנים

אלה למעוטי נדה. כמאן אזלא כר' אליעזר בן יעקב. משמע אבל לרבנן לא מצי אתי וסברי דיש חלל מנדה וא"ת ומהיכא נילף לומר דעושה חלל מנדה אי מק"ו דגרושה שאין בה לאו שאני גרושה שהיא עצמה מתחללת ופסלה בביאתו מתרומה דבי נשא תאמר בנדה דלא פסלה דהא אית בה הויה וא"ל כיון דבעלה עשאה זונה דהא כיון דתפסי בה קדושי לא הויא כשאר חייבי כריתות ואי מאלמנה לכה"ג מה לאלמנה שכן היא עצמה מתחללת כדלעיל דא"ל היא עצמה תתחלל מק"ו דלימא איסור כהונה שאני כדפרישית לעיל וי"ל יליף מאלמנה ומגרי שני שפוסלים ובנו פגום אף אני אביא נדה. וקסבר האי תנא דעבדינן שפיר צד השוה היכא דחדא הוי איסור כהונה ואידך אינו איסור כהונה כדפרישית לעיל. ולר"א בן יעקב ניחא דאצטריך קרא למימר דאי אתה עושה חלל מנדה דס"ד דניליף מחייבי עשה דיש חלל מהם אליבא דידיה: **אליו** לרבות הבוגרת. תימה למה לי קרא כיון דרבינן מוכת עץ משום שאין הווייתה ע"י איש ה"ה בוגרת דבוגרת נמי אין הווייתה ע"י איש. וגם כי עדיפא יותר בוגרת ממוכת עץ משום דלא אתעביד בה מעשה וא"כ כיון דחזינן מוכת עץ כ"ש בוגרת וי"ל דס"ד דבוגרת גריעא ממוכת עץ משום דאשתני גופה ומלא היתה לאיש לא נפקא דשמא קרא לא איירי אלא בדבר שבא ע"י מעשה:

הגהות הב"ח

(א) גמ' בהא אמר רב עמרם אין הלכה כצ"ל ותיבות אמר רב נמחק:

גליון הש"ס

גמ' אמר ר"ה אמר רב הלכה כראב"י. עיין תוס' בכורות דף כג ע"ב ד"ה משנת: **שם** ואילו בהא אמר רב עמרם אמר רב. מדברי תוס' לעיל דף נט ע"ב ד"ה ורב מבואר דל"ג כאן אמר רב וכן הוא לקמן סא ע"ב: **שם** ראב"י סבר יש חלל מחייבי עשה. עיין לקמן דף עז ע"ב תד"ה מחלל:

עה א מיי' פי"ח מהל' איסורי ביאה הלכה ג סמג לאוין קנא טוש"ע אה"ע סימן ו סעיף ח:

תורה אור

וְהָא אָמַר רַבִּי שִׁמְעוֹן: רְאוּיָה לְכֹהֵן גָּדוֹל — מְטַמֵּא לָהּ, שֶׁאֵין רְאוּיָה לְכֹהֵן גָּדוֹל — אֵין מְטַמֵּא לָהּ! שָׁאנֵי הָתָם דְּרַבֵּי רַחֲמָנָא "קְרוֹבָה". א"ה מוּכַּת עֵץ נַמִי [רַבֵּי]! "קְרוֹבָה" אַחַת וְלֹא שְׁתַּיִם. וּמָה רָאִיתָ? הָא אִתְעֲבִיד בָּהּ מַעֲשֶׂה, הָא לָא אִתְעֲבִיד בָּהּ מַעֲשֶׂה. וְרַבִּי יוֹסֵי, *מִדְּשָׁבְקֵיהּ(א) לְבַר זוּגֵיהּ — מִכְּלָל דִּבְמוּכַּת עֵץ כְּרַבִּי מֵאִיר סְבִירָא לֵיהּ, מְנָא לֵיהּ? מִ"לֹּא הָיְתָה לְאִישׁ". וְהָא אַפִּיקְתֵּיהּ! חַד מִ"לֹּא הָיְתָה" וְחַד מִ"לְּאִישׁ". "אֵלָיו" לְרַבּוֹת הַבּוֹגֶרֶת. וְהָא אָמַר ר' שִׁמְעוֹן: "בְּתוּלָה" בְּתוּלָה שְׁלֵימָה מַשְׁמַע! טַעֲמָא דִּידֵיהּ נַמִי הָתָם מֵהָכָא, דְּדָרֵישׁ הָכִי: מִדְּ"אֵלָיו" לְרַבּוֹת הַבּוֹגֶרֶת, מִכְּלָל דְּ"בְתוּלָה" בְּתוּלָה שְׁלֵימָה מַשְׁמַע. *תַּנְיָא, ר' שִׁמְעוֹן בֶּן יוֹחַי אוֹמֵר: גִּיּוֹרֶת פְּחוּתָה מִבַּת שָׁלֹשׁ שָׁנִים וְיוֹם אֶחָד כְּשֵׁירָה לִכְהוּנָּה, שֶׁנֶּאֱמַר °"וְכֹל הַטַּף בַּנָּשִׁים אֲשֶׁר לֹא יָדְעוּ מִשְׁכַּב זָכָר הַחֲיוּ לָכֶם" וַהֲרֵי פִּנְחָס עִמָּהֶם. וְרַבָּנַן: לַעֲבָדִים וְלִשְׁפָחוֹת. — אִי הָכִי — בַּת שָׁלֹשׁ שָׁנִים וְיוֹם אֶחָד נַמִי! כִּדְרַב הוּנָא. דְּרַב הוּנָא רָמֵי: כְּתִיב °"כָּל אִשָּׁה יֹדַעַת אִישׁ לְמִשְׁכַּב זָכָר הֲרֹגוּ". הָא אֵינָהּ יוֹדַעַת — קַיְּימוּ, מִכְּלָל דְּהַטַּף בֵּין יָדְעוּ בֵּין לֹא יָדְעוּ — קַיְּימוּ, וּכְתִיב °"וְכֹל הַטַּף בַּנָּשִׁים אֲשֶׁר לֹא יָדְעוּ מִשְׁכַּב זָכָר הַחֲיוּ לָכֶם", הָא יָדְעֵי — הֲרוֹגוּ. הֱוֵי אוֹמֵר: בִּרְאוּיָה לִיבָּעֵל הַכָּתוּב מְדַבֵּר. תַּנְיָא נַמִי הָכִי: "וְכָל אִשָּׁה יוֹדַעַת אִישׁ" בִּרְאוּיָה לִיבָּעֵל הַכָּתוּב מְדַבֵּר. אַתָּה אוֹמֵר בִּרְאוּיָה לִיבָּעֵל, אוֹ אֵינוֹ אֶלָּא נִבְעֲלָה מַמָּשׁ? כְּשֶׁהוּא אוֹמֵר "וְכֹל הַטַּף בַּנָּשִׁים אֲשֶׁר לֹא יָדְעוּ מִשְׁכַּב זָכָר" הֱוֵי אוֹמֵר בִּרְאוּיָה לִיבָּעֵל הַכָּתוּב מְדַבֵּר. מְנָא יָדְעֵי? אָמַר רַב *הוּנָא בַּר בִּיזְנָא אָמַר ר' שִׁמְעוֹן חֲסִידָא: הֶעֱבִירוּם לִפְנֵי הַצִּיץ, כׇּל שֶׁפָּנֶיהָ מוֹרִיקוֹת — בְּיָדוּעַ שֶׁהִיא רְאוּיָה לִיבָּעֵל, כׇּל שֶׁאֵין פָּנֶיהָ מוֹרִיקוֹת — בְּיָדוּעַ שֶׁאֵינָהּ רְאוּיָה לִיבָּעֵל. אָמַר רַב נַחְמָן: *סִימָן לַעֲבֵירָה הִדְרוֹקָן. כַּיּוֹצֵא בַּדָּבָר אַתָּה אוֹמֵר: °"וַיִּמְצְאוּ מִיּוֹשְׁבֵי יָבֵישׁ גִּלְעָד אַרְבַּע מֵאוֹת נַעֲרָה בְתוּלָה אֲשֶׁר לֹא יָדְעוּ אִישׁ לְמִשְׁכַּב זָכָר". מְנָא יָדְעֵי? אָמַר רַב כָּהֲנָא: הוֹשִׁיבוּם עַל פִּי חָבִית שֶׁל יַיִן, *בְּעוּלָה — רֵיחָהּ נוֹדֵף, בְּתוּלָה — אֵין רֵיחָהּ נוֹדֵף. וְנַעַבְרִינְהוּ לִפְנֵי צִיץ! אָמַר רַב כָּהֲנָא בְּרֵיהּ דְּרַב נָתָן: °"לְרָצוֹן לָהֶם" כְּתִיב, לְרָצוֹן וְלֹא לְפוּרְעָנוּת. אִי הָכִי בְּמִדְיָן נַמִי! אָמַר רַב אַשִׁי: "לָהֶם" כְּתִיב, לָהֶם לְרָצוֹן וְלֹא לְפוּרְעָנוּת, וּלְגוֹיִם — אֲפִילּוּ לְפוּרְעָנוּת. אָמַר רַבִּי יַעֲקֹב בַּר אִידִי אָמַר רַבִּי יְהוֹשֻׁעַ בֶּן לֵוִי: הֲלָכָה כְּרַבִּי שִׁמְעוֹן בֶּן יוֹחַאי. אֲמַר לֵיהּ רַבִּי זֵירָא לְרַבִּי יַעֲקֹב בַּר אִידִי: *בְּפֵירוּשׁ שְׁמִיעַ לָךְ, אוֹ מִכְּלָלָא שְׁמִיעַ לָךְ? מַאי כְּלָלָא? דַּאֲמַר ר' יְהוֹשֻׁעַ בֶּן לֵוִי: עִיר אַחַת הָיְתָה בְּאֶרֶץ יִשְׂרָאֵל שֶׁקָּרָא עָלֶיהָ עַרְעָר, וְשִׁגֵּר רַבִּי אֶת רַבִּי רוֹמָנוּס וּבְדָקָהּ, וּמָצָא בָּהּ בַּת גִּיּוֹרֶת פְּחוּתָה מִבַּת שָׁלֹשׁ שָׁנִים וְיוֹם אֶחָד — וְהִכְשִׁירָהּ רַבִּי לִכְהוּנָּה. אֲמַר לֵיהּ: בְּפֵירוּשׁ שְׁמִיעַ לִי. *וְאִי מִכְּלָלָא מַאי? דִּלְמָא שָׁאנֵי הָתָם, הוֹאִיל וְאִנְסִיב — אִנְסִיב. דְּהָא רַב וְרַבִּי יוֹחָנָן דְּאָמְרִי תַּרְוַיְיהוּ: בּוֹגֶרֶת וּמוּכַּת עֵץ — לֹא יִשָּׂא, וְאִם נָשָׂא — נָשׂוּי. הָכִי הַשְׁתָּא?! בִּשְׁלָמָא הָתָם — סוֹפָהּ לִהְיוֹת בּוֹגֶרֶת תַּחְתָּיו, סוֹפָהּ לִהְיוֹת בְּעוּלָה תַּחְתָּיו. הָכָא — סוֹפָהּ לִהְיוֹת זוֹנָה תַּחְתָּיו?! רַב סַפְרָא מַתְנֵי לָהּ מִכְּלָלָא, וְקַשְׁיָא לֵיהּ, וּמְשַׁנֵּי לֵיהּ הָכִי. הַהוּא כָּהֲנָא דְּאִנְסִיב גִּיּוֹרֶת פְּחוּתָה מִבַּת שָׁלֹשׁ שָׁנִים וְיוֹם אֶחָד. אֲמַר לֵיהּ ר"נ בַּר יִצְחָק: מַאי הַאי? אֲמַר לֵיהּ: דַּאֲמַר רַבִּי יַעֲקֹב בַּר אִידִי אָמַר ר' יְהוֹשֻׁעַ בֶּן לֵוִי: הֲלָכָה כר"ש בֶּן יוֹחַאי. אֲמַר לֵיהּ: [א]זִיל אַפֵּיק, וְאִי לָא — מַפֵּיקְנָא לָךְ רַ' יַעֲקֹב בַּר אִידִי מֵאוּנָךְ. תַּנְיָא וְכֵן הָיָה ר"ש בֶּן יוֹחַאי אוֹמֵר

קִבְרֵי

(במדבר לא) (שם) (שם) (שופטים כא) (שמות כח)

מִדְּשָׁבְקֵיהּ (ב) לְבַר זוּגֵיהּ. דְּגַבֵּי מוּכַּת עֵץ לָא פָּלֵיג אֶלָּא ר' שִׁמְעוֹן לְחוּדֵיהּ, וְשָׁבְקֵיהּ ר' יוֹסֵי דַּהֲוָה בַּר זוּגֵיהּ בַּאֲרוּסָה. מִכְּלָל דִּבְמוּכַּת עֵץ כְּר' מֵאִיר סְבִירָא לֵיהּ לְר' יוֹסֵי, דִּמְטַמֵּא לָהּ. מִ"לֹּא הָיְתָה". דְּדָרֵישׁ לֵיהּ לְר' מֵאִיר: מִי שֶׁהֲוָיָיתָהּ עַל יְדֵי אִישׁ. וְהָא אַפְּקֵיהּ. ר' יוֹסֵי לְהוֹצִיא אֶת הָאֲרוּסָה. חַד מִ"לֹּא הָיְתָה". לְהוֹצִיא אֶת הָאֲרוּסָה. מִ"לְּאִישׁ". לְמִישְׁרֵי מוּכַּת עֵץ, שֶׁאֵין מְקוּלְקֶלֶת עַל יְדֵי אִישׁ. וְהָא אָמַר ר' שִׁמְעוֹן. לְעֵיל: "בְּתוּלָה" — שְׁלֵימָה מַשְׁמַע, מִדְּאִיצְטְרִיךְ "בְּתוּלֶיהָ" לְמִישְׁרֵי בּוֹגֶרֶת לְכ"ג. כְּשֵׁרָה לִכְהוּנָּה. לָא מַחְזְקִינַן לָהּ כְּזוֹנָה. אִי הָכִי אֲפִילּוּ בַּת ג' שָׁנִים. נַמִי לִיתַּכְשַׁר לְרַבִּי שִׁמְעוֹן, וּבִלְבַד שֶׁלֹּא תְּהֵא נִבְעֶלֶת. דְּהָא קְרָא אַנִּבְעֲלָה הוּא דְּקָא קָפֵיד לֵיהּ, וְקָאָמַר: כׇּל שֶׁאֵין נִבְעֶלֶת — הַחֲיוּ לָכֶם. כִּדְרַב הוּנָא. לָא מָצֵית אָמְרַתְּ דְּבַת ג' שָׁנִים לֵימָא קְרָא "הַחֲיוּ". דְּרַב הוּנָא רָמֵי. "אִשָּׁה" מַשְׁמַע גְּדוֹלָה, וְקָאָמַר קְרָא: יוֹדַעַת — הֲרוֹגוּ, וְשֶׁאֵינָהּ יוֹדַעַת — הַחֲיוּ, מִכְּלָל דְּטַף, לָא שְׁנָא הָכִי וְלָא שְׁנָא הָכִי — הַחֲיוּ, וּכְתִיב וְכׇל הַטַּף וגו'. הֱוֵי אוֹמֵר. מִדְּקָשׁוּ קְרָאֵי אַהֲדָדֵי עַל כׇּרְחָךְ "יוֹדַעַת" דִּקְרָא וַ"אֲשֶׁר לֹא יָדְעוּ" — לָאו יְדִיעָה מַמָּשׁ קָאָמַר, דְּאִם כֵּן — לָא מִיתָּרְצָא דּוּקְיָא דִּקְרָא. אֶלָּא בִּרְאוּיָה לִיבָּעֵל הַכָּתוּב מְדַבֵּר — דְּכׇל אִשָּׁה הָרְאוּיָה לֵידַע — הֲרוֹגוּ, וְהָשְׁתָּא מַשְׁמַע: אִשָּׁה — אֲפִילּוּ טַף בַּת ג' דִּרְאוּיָה לֵידַע. וְלָא תֵּידוֹק: הָא טַף בֵּין יָדְעִי בֵּין לָא יָדְעִי — הַחֲיוּ, דְּהָא בִּרְאוּיָה קָא מִישְׁתַּעֵי קְרָא. אֶלָּא "הַחֲיוּ לָכֶם" דְּקָאָמַר רַחֲמָנָא — בִּפְחוּתָה מִבַּת שָׁלֹשׁ קָאָמַר. בִּרְאוּיָה לִיבָּעֵל. אע"פ שֶׁלֹּא נִבְעֲלָה. כְּשֶׁהוּא אוֹמֵר וְכׇל הַטַּף אֲשֶׁר לֹא יָדְעוּ הַחֲיוּ. הָא אִשָּׁה, אע"פ שֶׁלֹּא יָדְעָה — הֲרוֹגוּ הֱוֵי בִּרְאוּיָה לִיבָּעֵל קָמִשְׁתָּעֵי קְרָא. פָּנֶיהָ מוֹרִיקוֹת. נֵס הָיָה. הִדְרוֹקָן. פְּנֵיהֶן שֶׁל עוֹבְרֵי עֲבֵירָה מוֹרִיקִין. מֵאַנְשֵׁי יָבֵשׁ גִּלְעָד. בִּימֵי פִּלֶגֶשׁ בַּגִּבְעָה, שֶׁנֶּהֶרְגוּ כׇּל אַנְשֵׁי יָבֵשׁ גִּלְעָד לְפִי שֶׁלֹּא בָּאוּ לְהִלָּחֵם בְּשֵׁבֶט בִּנְיָמִין כְּשְׁאָר אַחִים. וְהֶחֱיוּ כׇּל שֶׁלֹּא נִבְעֲלָה, וּנְתָנוּם לַנּוֹתָרִים מִשֵּׁבֶט בִּנְיָמִין לְנָשִׁים. בְּפֵירוּשׁ שְׁמִיעַ לָךְ. מִינֵּיהּ דְּרַבִּי יְהוֹשֻׁעַ בֶּן לֵוִי. אוֹ מִכְּלָלָא. דְּשָׁמְעַתְּ מִינֵּיהּ מִילְּתָא דְּדָיְיקַתְּ מִינֵּיהּ דִּסְבִירָא לֵיהּ כְּר' שִׁמְעוֹן. מַאי כְּלָלָא. מֵאֵיזֶה כְּלָל הָיָה לוֹ לוֹמַר. עַרְעָר. לִפְסוֹל מִשְׁפַּחַת הָעִיר. רוֹמָנוּס גָּרְסִינַן. וְהִכְשִׁירָהּ. הַנִּיחָהּ תַּחַת בַּעְלָהּ כֹּהֵן. וְאִי מִכְּלָלָא מַאי. וְאִי מֵהַאי כְּלָלָא שְׁמִיעַ לֵיהּ לְר' יַעֲקֹב, מַאי אִית לֵיהּ לְרַבִּי זֵירָא לְאוֹתְבֵיהּ, דְּקָא בָּעֵי מִינֵּיהּ: בְּפֵירוּשׁ שְׁמִיעַ לָךְ אוֹ מִכְּלָלָא? הָכָא סוֹפָהּ לִהְיוֹת זוֹנָה תַּחְתָּיו? בִּתְמִיָּה. אִי סְבִירָא לֵיהּ דְּפָסוּל — מִשּׁוּם זְנוּת סְבִירָא לֵיהּ, וְאִם כֵּן — לָא שְׁנָא לְכַתְּחִלָּה וְלָא שְׁנָא דִּיעֲבַד — אֲסִירָא. וְקַשְׁיָא לֵיהּ. כִּדְאַקְשֵׁי: דִּלְמָא הָתָם הוֹאִיל וְאִינְסִיב אִינְסִיב. וּמְשַׁנֵּי הָכִי. כִּדְשַׁנֵּינַן: בִּשְׁלָמָא הָתָם סוֹפָהּ לִהְיוֹת בְּעוּלָה תַּחְתָּיו כו'. מַפֵּיקְנָא לָךְ ר' יַעֲקֹב מֵאוּנָךְ. כְּלוֹמַר: מְשַׁמְּתִינַן לָךְ, וְתַפֵּיק עַל כׇּרְחָךְ.

אֵין

[לקמן סג.] קידושין [עח:] עח. נ"ל חנא שבת לג. [כתובות י:] [שבת לג: עירובין מו. ועי' ברכות ע.] [ברכות יב. וש"נ]

והא אמר רבי שמעון בתולה שלימה משמע. תימה: דלעיל פריך: למה לי לרבות הבוגרת — והא אמר רבי מאיר "בתולה" — אפילו מקצת בתולים [משמע]. משמע דאי הוה סבר בתולה שלימה — לא הוה קשה לן מידי. והשתא פריך איפכא! ואומר ר"י: דהכא פריך הכי: והאמר רבי שמעון בתולה שלימה משמע, ולהכי מכשיר התם בכהן גדול בוגרת — ואם כן למה לי הכא "אליו" לרבות בוגרת? נילף "בתולה" "בתולה" מהתם! ומשני: טעמא דידיה נמי מהכא. ואם תאמר: מאחר דמרבינן הכא בוגרת, למה לי יו"ד ד"בתוליה" לעיל להכשיר בוגרת? נילף מהכא! ואמר ר"י: דצריך למכתב התם בתוליה ביו"ד, משום דבענין אחר לא אפשר למכתב יתור של בי"ת, דבבתוליה, למדרש מיניה עד שיהו כל בתוליה קיימין, למעוטי שלא כדרכה ומוכת עץ, כדפרישית לעיל. **הא** אינה יודעת יקיימוה. לא היה צריך למידק הכי, אלא: הא טף, אפי' יודעת — יקיימו כו'. אלא שרוצה להקשות משניהם ד"כל אשה יודעת" משמע: דאינה יודעת — קיימו, וטף נמי, אפילו יודעת — קיימו. ובאידך קרא ד"טף אשר לא ידעו" משמע הא ידעו, או גדולה ואפי' לא ידעה — הרוגו. **בראויה** ליבעל הכתוב מדבר. ו"יודעת איש" היינו ראויה לדעת איש. והא דכתיב "אשה" דמשמע דוקא גדולה — היינו משום דליקשו קראי, ומתוך כך מוקמינן דבראויה ליבעל הכתוב מדבר. דאי לא כתיב אשה אלא סתם וכל "יודעת איש" הוה אמינא דהאי קרא נמי בטף איירי. ובטף, יודעת — הרוגו, ושאינה יודעת — יקיימו. אבל גדולה — אפילו אין יודעת הרוגו. **סימן** לעבירה הדרוקן. ע"י העבירה בא הדרוקן, כדאמרינן ב"במה מדליקין" (שבת דף לג.) והדרוקן לאו היינו ירקון, כדאמר ב"הרואה" (ברכות דף סב:) אבל קצת יש להדרוקן ירוקת פנים, כדאמר. דכל שפניה מוריקות*.

קברי

[ועי' בתוספות בכורות מד: ד"ה לידי כו']

תוספות ישנים

והאמר ר' שמעון בתולה שלמה משמע. וא"ת ומאי פריך אדרבה היא הנותנת דסד"א בתולה שלמה משמע אילטריך אליו לרבות בוגרת. דהכי משמע לעיל הך סברא דפריך לר"מ האמר [בתולה] מקצת בתולה משמע הא אי אמרינן בתולה שלמה משמע ניחא דאצטריך אליו לרבות בוגרת ונראה לפרש דה"ק והאמר ר"ש בתולה שלמה משמע ואינו מייתי [רק] תחלת דבר ור"ל בתולה שלמה משמע ובבתולה מקצת בתולים דהיינו מלתיה דלעיל וא"כ למה לי אליו לרבות בוגרת תיפוק ליה דניליף מהתם ודוחק הוא דהא לא מייתי קרא דבבתוליה. ונ"ל דה"ק והאמר רבי שמעון בתולה שלמה משמע ואמאי קאמר ר' שמעון כן הו"ל למגמר מהכא דלאו שלמה משמע דהא אמרינן אליו לרבות את הבוגרת: **טעמא** דידי נמי מהכא מדאצטריך אליו לרבות את הבוגרת א"כ בתולה משמע בתולה שלמה והקשה הר' ידידיה היכי קאמר ר"ש מדאצטריך לרבות הבוגרת א"כ בתולה משמע בתולה שלמה דלמא לעולם אימא לך מקצת בתולים משמע ומ"מ אינטריך אליו לרבות בוגרת דלא ניליף בתולה בתולה מהתם דלדריש בתולה מקצת בתולים משמע בבתוליה עד שיהיו כל בתוליה קיימין כמו דאמר ר"מ לעיל ונראה לרשב"י דהא לא קשה מידי דהכי מני להקשות אמאי לא קאמר ר"ש כר"מ בהדיא ובהא ודאי מצינו שפיר למימר טעם דדלמא ר' שמעון ניחא ליה א) שפיר לומר בתולה שלמה ואצטריך אליו למעט ממשמעותיה דקרא משנאמר כר' מאיר דבתולה משמע ואצטריך דלא ניליף בתולה מהתם דהתם נמי משמע בתולה מקצת בתולים רק דמפקינן מבתוליה עד דאיכא כל בתולים. ועוד ב) מדקא"ל לר' שמעון למצוא טעם להעמיד דבתולה שלמה משמע מלומר מקצת בתולים ועוד אינו ר"ל בתולים משמע בבתוליה עד שיהיו כל בתוליה קיימין דא"כ לא מצינו לאסור שלא כדרכה דלא מצינו למדרש בבתוליה בין בכדרכה בין שלא כדרכה דא"כ לשתוק קרא מיניה ומבתוליה שמעינן לה דבעינן לעולם כל בתולים לעיל לר' מאיר וא"כ היינו צריכים לדרוש בבתוליה כדרכה אין שלא כדרכה לא בעינן כל בתולים ור' שמעון לא ניחא לדורשה שלא כדרכה כיון דמצינו לומר איפכא ולפסול שלא כדרכה:

א) אולי צ"ל ניחא ליה טפי לומר בתולה שלמה משמע מדאיצטריך אליו למעט ממשמעותיה דקרא משנאמר כר"מ דבתולה מקצת בתולה משמע כו'. ב) אולי צ"ל ועוד דניחא ליה טפי למצוא טעם לר"ש להעמיד דבתולה וכו'.

הגהות הב"ח

(א) גמ' ורבי יוסי מדשבקיה בר זוגיה כצ"ל ואות ל' נמחק: (ב) רש"י ד"ה מדשבקיה בר זוגיה וכו' ושבקיה לרב יוסי דהוה:

קברי *[א]גוים אינן מטמאין באהל, שנא' °"ואתן צאני צאן מרעיתי אדם אתם" ⊕אתם קרויין "אדם", ואין הגוים קרויין "אדם". מיתיבי: °"ונפש אדם ששה עשר אלף"! משום בהמה. °"אשר יש בה הרבה משתים עשרה רבוא אדם אשר לא ידע בין ימינו לשמאלו (ובהמה רבה)". משום בהמה. °"כל הורג נפש וכל נוגע בחלל תתחטאו"! דלמא איקטיל חד מישראל. ורבנן: "לא נפקד ממנו איש". ור' שמעון בן יוחי: "לא נפקד ממנו איש" לעבירה. רבינא אמר: [ב]נהי דמעטינהו קרא מאטמויי באהל, דכתיב °"אדם כי ימות באהל", ממגע ומשא מי מעטינהו קרא?. § **מתני'** *⊕[ג]אירס את האלמנה ונתמנה להיות כהן גדול — יכנוס. ומעשה ביהושע בן גמלא שקידש את מרתא בת ביתוס, ומנהו המלך להיות כה"ג, וכנסה. שומרת יבם שנפלה לפני כהן הדיוט, ונתמנה להיות כה"ג, אע"פ שעשה בה מאמר — הרי זה לא יכנוס. § **גמ'** ת"ר: מנין שאם אירס את האלמנה ונתמנה להיות כהן גדול שיכנוס — ת"ל °"יקח אשה". א"ה שומרת יבם נמי! "אשה ולא יבמה". § "מעשה ביהושע וכו'". § מנהו — אין, נתמנה — לא. אמר רב יוסף: ⊕קטיר קחזינא הכא. *דאמר רב אסי: תרקבא דדינרי עיילה ליה מרתא בת ביתוס לינאי מלכא, עד דמוקי ליה ליהושע בן גמלא בכהני רברבי. § **מתני'** [ד]כהן גדול שמת אחיו — חולץ ולא מייבם. § **גמ'** *קא פסיק ותני, [ה]לא שנא מן האירוסין ולא שנא מן הנשואין. בשלמא מן הנשואין — עשה ולא תעשה הוא, [ו]ואין עשה דוחה לא תעשה ועשה. אלא מן האירוסין, [ז]יבא עשה וידחה את לא תעשה! [ח]גזירה ביאה ראשונה אטו ביאה שניה. § **מתני'** [ט]כהן הדיוט לא ישא אילונית, אלא א"כ יש לו *אשה ובנים. רבי יהודה אומר: אע"פ שיש לו אשה ובנים — *לא ישא אילונית, שהיא זונה האמורה בתורה. וחכמים אומרים: [י]אין זונה אלא גיורת, ומשוחררת, ושנבעלה בעילת זנות. § **גמ'** א"ל ריש גלותא לרב הונא: מ"ט — משום פריה ורביה, אפריה ורביה כהנים הוא דמפקדי, וישראל לא מפקדי?! אמר ליה: משום דקא בעי למיתני סיפא, רבי יהודה אומר: אע"פ שיש לו אשה ויש

(מראי מקומות בגליון: יחזקאל לד; במדבר לא; יונה ד; במדבר לא; שם יט; ויקרא כא; לקמן סא.)

אין מטמאין. את המאהיל עליהם. אתם קרוים אדם. וגבי טומאת אהל כתיב "אדם כי ימות באהל" (במדבר יט). נפש אדם. במדין כתיב. ומשני: הא דקרי להו אדם — משום דבעי למכתב בהמה גבייהו, כדכתיב "ומחמורים ובקר", וגבי בהמה מיקרו אדם. אבל אדם סתמא — לא מיקרו: אנשי נינוה גוים היו. תורה אור כל הורג נפש. במדין כתיב, ומדבעו טומאת שבעה — אלמא מיטמו. ממגע ומשא מי מעטינהו. וגבי מגע אשכחן נוגע בעצם או בחלל דלא כתיב אדם. הלכך, אע"ג דלא מיקרו אדם מטמו במגע ובמשא. ת"ל בתולה מעמיו יקח אשה. האי "אשה" לא איצטריך אלא לדרשא. מינהו אין. כלומר: המלך מינהו, אבל אחיו הכהנים וסנהדרין לא מנוהו. נתמנה לא. נתמנה לא קתני, דהוי משמע דראוי היה לכך. קטיר קחזינא הכא. קשר של רשעים אני רואה כאן, שלא היה ראוי לכך, אלא שנתן ממון ומינוהו. **מתני'** חולץ. כהן גדול. ולא מייבם. דאלמנה היא ואסורה לו. **גמ'** לא תעשה ועשה. "אלמנה לא יקח", "בתולה יקח" (ויקרא כא) ולא בעולה. **מתני'** אלא אם כן יש לו בנים. משום דמצווה על פריה ורביה, וה"ה לישראל. וגמרא מפרש אמאי נקט כהן. שהיא זונה האמורה בתורה. וגמרא מפרש לה. אלא הגיורת והמשוחררת. דביאת עכו"ם ועבד פסלה. ושנבעלה בעילת זנות. כגון ישראלית הנבעלת לפסול לה. גמ'

קברי גוים אינן מטמאין באהל. תימה: למה ליה לרבי בנאה לציוני מערתא דאברהם אבינו ואדם הראשון (ב"ב נח.)? אף דאיקרו "אדם" אדם ואברהם, או אפי' לרבנן דאמרי קברי גוים מטמאין באהל — הא לא מטמא באהל אפילו קברי ישראל אלא אותם שמתו משעה שנאמרה אותה פרשה ד"אדם כי ימות באוהל", דכי ימות משמע באותם העתידים למות עדיין, ומדאיצטריך נמי בנזיר (דף נד. ושם) קרא לרבות קבר שלפני הדבור למגע — מכלל דבאהל לא מטמא*. **ואין** הגוים קרוים אדם. תימא: דבריש מס' ע"ז (ג. ושם) ופ' "ד' מיתות" (סנהדרין דף נט. ושם) דרשינן: דגוי העוסק בתורה הרי הוא ככהן גדול, שנאמר "אשר יעשה אותם האדם" וגו', כהנים לוים וישראלים — לא נאמר, אלא: "האדם", ופי' בקונטרס בסנהדרין (ג"ז שם ד"ה "האדם") דההוא לית ליה הך דר"ש דהכא? ויתכן לפי ספרים דגרסי התם רבי ירמיה, אבל לספרים דגרסי התם ר' מאיר — קשיא, דשמעינן ליה לר"מ בפ' קמא דכריתות (דף ו:) דסך שמן המשחה לגוי — פטור, ומשמע דטעמא משום דכתיב "על בשר אדם" ואין גוי קרוי אדם! ומיהו, מצי למימר דטעמא דרבי מאיר דפטור הוי מטעם דכל שהוא בסך — הרי הוא בלא ייסך, וכל שאין בסך — אין בלא ייסך. ור"ת מפרש: ⊕דיש חילוק בין "אדם" ל"האדם", דגוים בכלל "האדם" נינהו, והא דקאמר כהנים לוים וישראלים לא נאמר — ה"ק: אדם לא נאמר, דהוי משמע כהנים לוים וישראלים, אלא "האדם". וכל הני קראי דמייתי כתיב "אדם". דלא פריך מקראי דכתיב "האדם". וה"ר משולם היה אומר: דגבי פורענות דוקא קאמר "אתם קרוין אדם" דלא רצה לכתוב ישראל בהדיא גבי פורענות, אבל גבי "האדם וחי" — הוה ליה למכתב בהדיא כהנים לוים וישראלים, כמו שרגיל בכל מקום. והא דפריך מהני קראי, אע"ג דגוים נמי קרויין אדם — מ"מ פריך, כיון דגבי פורענות ישראל קרוין אדם, היכא דלא איירי אלא בגוים דוקא — לא הוה ליה למיקרינהו אדם. והא דכתיב (תהלים קכד) "בקום עלינו אדם" — היינו לפי שהזכיר השם, וכן "ואתה אדם ולא אל" גבי חירם (יחזקאל כח). והא דכתיב "ואתן אדם תחתיך" (ישעיה מג) — הא דרשינן בברכות (דף סב:) אל תקרי אדם וכו'. והא דכתיב "והארץ נתן לבני אדם" (תהלים קטו) ודרשינן מיניה (גיטין מז.) דיש קנין לגוים — ⊕היינו בני אדם הראשון*. **ממגע** ומשא מי מעטינהו. ואע"ג דכתיב "וכל אשר יגע על פני השדה וגו' או בעצם אדם" (במדבר יט) — הא דרשינן בנזיר פרק "כ"ג" (דף נג. ושם) לענין אהל. ואר"י: דאין הלכה כר"ש, דרשב"ג פליג עליה. כדתנן במס' אהלות (פרק יח מ"ט, כתובות עז.), והלכה כמותו במשנתנו. ואריכים כהנים ליזהר מקברי גוים. ובפרק "המקבל" (ב"מ קיד:) בעובדא דאליהו דהשיב לרבה בר אבוה כר' שמעון בן יוחי דהכא — לחויי קא מדחי לה. ועיקר טעמא שהיה סומך על רוב ארונות שיש בהן פותח טפח. וכן היה רגיל בכל מקום לדחות, כמו שמצינו כשהיה קובר רבי עקיבא ואמר ליה: לאו כהן ניהו מר? אמר ליה: צדיקים אינם מטמאים. ועיקר טעמא לפי שהיה מת מצוה, שהיה מהרוגי מלכות והיו יראים לקברו. ומיהו, בבתי גוים מותרים ליכנס, כדתניא בתוספתא דאהלות: מדורות הגוים — טמאים, בחוצה לארץ — טהורים: **עיילה** ליה מרתא בת ביתוס לינאי מלכא. לאו היינו ינאי כ"ג דבפרק "האומר" בקידושין (דף סו.), דאם כן — לא היה מושיב אחר במקומו[א]. **כהן** גדול שמת אחיו חולץ ולא מייבם. [ב] וא"ת: מרישא שמעי' לה, דקתני שומרת יבם[א] לכהן הדיוט ונתמנה להיות כ"ג לא יכנוס? ואר"י: דהכא — חולץ אתא לאשמועינן, דס"ד משום בזיון דכ"ג שרוקקת לפניו לא תחלוץ. אע"ג דכבר תנן לה לעיל[ג] ובפרק "כ"ג" בסנהדרין (דף יח.). **אין** זונה אלא גיורת ומשוחררת. אפי' נתגיירה פחותה מבת ג' שנים אסורה מטעם זונה, כדאמר לעיל (דף ס:) גבי עיר אחת שהיתה בא"י כו'. וטעמא — לפי שבאה מן הגוים השטופים בזימה. אע"ג דבפרק בתרא דקידושין (דף עח.) דריש לה מקרא דיחזקאל, למר כדאית ליה ולמר כדאית ליה, מ"מ, בין למר ובין למר אסירא מטעם זונה, ואתא יחזקאל ואסמכה אקראי. והקשה ה"ר משה מפונטייש"א: דהכא משמע דגיורת אסורה לכהן מדאורייתא מטעם זונה, ובפרק "אין מעמידין" (ע"ז דף לו:) אמר: דב"ד של חשמונאי גזרו דהבא על הגויה חייב משום "נשג"ז". פי': אם הוא כהן חייב משום זונה. ואיכא למ"ד משום "נש"ג", אבל משום זונה — לא, דנשייהו לא מפקרי? ולאביי (בתמורה כט:) ניחא, דאגויה לא מחייב משום דכתיב "לא יקח ולא יחלל", ובגויה לא קרינן בה "לא יקח" דלא תפסי בה קידושין, ולא שייך נמי בה חלול זרע, שאין הזרע מתייחס אחריו, אבל לרבא דפליג עליה וקאמר: אחד זה ואחד זה, פירוש בין זונה גויה בין זונה ישראלית אתננה אסור, וכהן הבא עליה לוקה משום זונה — קשה! ויש לומר: דרבא לא פליג אלא היכא דזינתה, דיליף לה מזונה ישראלית, כדקאמר רבא. אבל לא זינתה — מודה דלא מיתסרא משום זונה. כדקאמר אביי, משום דכתיב "לא יחלל". והיכא דלא זינתה הוצרכו לגזור. אבל גיורת דשייך בה קיחה וחילול — אסורה משום זונה, אע"ג דלא זינתה. **שנבעלה** בעילת זנות. פירוש בקונטרס: ישראלית שנבעלה לפסול לה. וא"א לומר כן, דמחייבי לאוין דתפסי בה קידושין לא הוי זונה, ⊕אלא מחייבי כריתות, כדפי' ב"החולץ" (לעיל דף מט.).

כל

תוספות ישנים

ואין הגוים כו'. פרשתי בב"ק בפרק שור שנגח: **דלמא** אקטיל חד מישראל. י"מ דר"ש מוכיח מכאן דכל קבוע כמחצה על מחצה מדקאמר תתחטאו דלמא אקטיל חד מישראל אע"ג דגוים רובא אכן לא נהירא דלמסקנא אין הדבר מיושב דקאמר ממגע ומשא מי מעטינהו קרא וש"מ הוצרכו חטוי משום טומאת מגע ומשא ועוי"ל דאין ראיה מכאן דדלמא הכי פירושא דלמא אקטיל חד מישראל והם היו פושטים ידיהם על החללים ונמצא שנגעו בכולם א) האהלות ואפי' אי ליכא אלא חד מישראל אטמו מחמתיה. ובכתובות פי' דנפקא ליה מוארב לו וקם עליו והקשינו מנא ליה לר' שמעון דמפיק לדרשא אחרינא בפרק ואלו הן הנשרפים (דף ע"ט) מנליה ופי' שם ור"ת פסק דלא כר"ש דאמר קברי ישמעאלים אין מטמאים באהל דכל מקום ששנה רשב"ג הלכה כמותו ורשב"ג פליג עליה דר"ש דאמר ב) מדורות גוים מטמאין באהל מפני שקוברין שם נפליהם. ובמסכת אהלות (פי"ח מ"ט) נמי רשב"ג פליג עליה דקאמר עיר גוים שחרבה אין בה משום מדורות הגוים משמע אבל ישובה אית בה ומטמאה באהל: **ממגע** ומשא מי אמעיט. וא"ת הא כתיב נמי או בעצם אדם דמשמע ישראל ולא גוים וי"ל דבנזיר מוקמינן לכולי קרא בטומאת אהל אבל ממגע ומשא לא אמעוט גוים: **א)** וגם אין זה יהושע בן גמלא ג) שהיה בב"ב שתקן כמה תקנות שאותו צדיק היה אלא אחר הוא זה ד): **ב)** וא"ת והא כבר תנינא לעיל אלמנה לכה"ג חולצת ולא מתייבמת גבי איסור מצוה ואיסור קדושה וי"ל דהכא עיקר ולעיל תנייא שום כללא דכייל ותני:

א) נראה דצ"ל או שבאהילו בכולם. ב) לפנינו במשנה דאהלות פי"ח משנה ז' תנן סתמא ולא הוזכר שם רשב"ג. ג) נ"ל שהוזכר בב"ב (דף כ"א). ד) ועי' תוס' ב"ב שם ד"ה זכור.

עין משפט נר מצוה

עו א ב מיי' פ"ג מהל' אבל הלכה ג ופ"א מהל' טומאת מת הלכה יג סמג לאוין רלא טוש"ע י"ד סימן שעב סעי' ב:

עז ג מיי' פי"ז מהל' איסורי ביאה הל' יג:

עח ד מיי' שם ופ"ה מהלכות כלי המקדש הלכה י:

[ועי' תוס' ב"ב נח. כתבו ישוב לזה ותוס' נדה ע: ד"ה ואין נגיב]

עט ה מיי' פי"ז מהל' איסורי ביאה הלכה יב:

פ ו מיי' פ"ו מהלכות יבום הלכה יא:

פא ז ח מיי' שם הלכ' י:

פב ט מיי' פט"ו מהלכות אישות הלכה ז סמג עשין מט טוש"ע אה"ע סי' א סעי' ח:

פג י מיי' פי"ח מהל' איסורי ביאה הלכה ב סמג לאוין קכא טוש"ע שם סי' ו סעי' ח:

מסורת הש"ס

ב"מ קיד: [כריתות ו:]

רש"ל מ"ז

[לעיל נט.]

יומא יח.

סנהדרין יח: לעיל כ.

[פי' או אשה לפרות ולרבות עמה או בנים תו"ע בשם הרמב"ם ומתוך פרש"י משמע דגרס אא"כ יש לו בנים ולא היה בגרסתו אשה כלל]

[ועי' תוספות נזיר נד. ב"ק לח. ב"ב נח. מס' ע"ז ג. סנהדרין נט: ובנדה ע:]

הגהות הב"ח

(א) תוס' ד"ה כהן וכו' שומרת יבם שנפלה לפני כהן הדיוט: (ב) בא"ד תנן לה לעיל. נ"ב בפרק ב' דף כ:

גליון הש"ס

גמ' אתם קרוין אדם. עי' מתני' רפ"ג דנגעי' ובתוי"ט שם רפי"ב: **מתני'** אירס את האלמנה. עי' לעיל דף כ ע"ב תד"ה אטו ביאה: **גמ'** קטיר קחזינא הכא. עיין ב"ב דף כ"א ע"א תד"ה זכור: **תוס'** ד"ה ואין וכו' דיש חילוק בין אדם להאדם. עי' ירמיה לב כ' ובישראל ובאדם: **בא"ד** בסוף הדבור היינו בני אדם הראשון. עיין ברמב"ן סימן שי"ז: **ד"ה** שנבעלה וכו' אלא מחייבי כריתות וכו'. עיין גיטין ד' פט ע"א תד"ה בעולה ובמהרש"א שם:

עין משפט נר מצוה

פד א מיי' פ"א מהלכות יבום הלכה טז יח סמג עשין נא טוש"ע אה"ע סי' קסז סעי' ג ד:
פה ב ג מיי' פי"ז מהל' איסורי ביאה הלכ' יג:
פו ד מיי' פט"ו מהל' אישות הלכה א סמג עשין מט טוש"ע אה"ע סימן א סעיף א:
פז ה מיי' שם הלכה ד טוש"ע שם סעיף ה:
פח ו ז ח מיי' שם הלכ' טז ופר"א מהל' איסורי ביאה הלכה כו טוש"ע שם סעי' ח:

וְיֵשׁ לוֹ בָּנִים לֹא יִשָּׂא אַיְלוֹנִית, שֶׁהִיא זוֹנָה הָאֲמוּרָה בַּתּוֹרָה. דְּאַזּוֹנָה כֹּהֲנִים הוּא דְּמִפַּקְדִי, וְיִשְׂרָאֵל לָא מִפַּקְדִי, מִשּׁוּם הָכִי קָתָנֵי כֹּהֵן. אֲמַר רַב הוּנָא: מַאי טַעְמָא דְּרַ' יְהוּדָה — דִּכְתִיב °"אָכְלוּ וְלֹא יִשְׂבָּעוּ הִזְנוּ וְלֹא יִפְרֹצוּ", כָּל בִּיאָה שֶׁאֵין בָּהּ[א] (א) פִּירְצָה — אֵינָהּ אֶלָּא בְּעִילַת זְנוּת. תַּנְיָא, רַבִּי אֱלִיעֶזֶר אוֹמֵר: כֹּהֵן לֹא יִשָּׂא אֶת הַקְּטַנָּה. אֲמַר לֵיהּ רַב חִסְדָּא לְרַבָּה: פּוּק עַיֵּין בָּהּ, דִּלְאוּרְתָּא בָּעֵי לָהּ רַב הוּנָא מִינָּךְ. נְפַק עַיֵּין בָּהּ: רַבִּי אֱלִיעֶזֶר סָבַר לָהּ כְּרַבִּי מֵאִיר, וְסָבַר לָהּ כְּרַבִּי יְהוּדָה. סָבַר לָהּ כְּרַבִּי מֵאִיר — *דְּחָיֵישׁ לְמִיעוּטָא, וְסָבַר לָהּ כְּרַבִּי יְהוּדָה — דְּאָמַר: אַיְלוֹנִית זוֹנָה הָוְיָא. וּכְרַבִּי מֵאִיר מִי סָבַר לָהּ? וְהָתַנְיָא: *קָטָן וּקְטַנָּה — לֹא חוֹלְצִין וְלֹא מְיַבְּמִין, דִּבְרֵי רַבִּי מֵאִיר. אָמְרוּ לוֹ לְרַבִּי מֵאִיר: [א]יָפֶה אָמַרְתָּ שֶׁאֵין חוֹלְצִין °"אִישׁ" כְּתִיב בַּפָּרָשָׁה, *וּמַקְשִׁינַן אִשָּׁה לְאִישׁ. אֶלָּא מַאי טַעְמָא אֵין מְיַבְּמִין? [א"ל]: קָטָן — שֶׁמָּא יִמָּצֵא סָרִיס, קְטַנָּה — שֶׁמָּא תִּמָּצֵא *אַיְלוֹנִית, וְנִמְצְאוּ פּוֹגְעִין בָּעֶרְוָה, וְתַנְיָא: קְטַנָּה — מִתְיַיבֶּמֶת וְאֵינָהּ חוֹלֶצֶת, דִּבְרֵי רַבִּי אֱלִיעֶזֶר. וּכְרַבִּי יְהוּדָה מִי סָבַר לָהּ? וְהָתַנְיָא: "זוֹנָה" זוֹנָה כִּשְׁמָהּ, דִּבְרֵי רַבִּי אֱלִיעֶזֶר. •רַבִּי עֲקִיבָא אוֹמֵר: "זוֹנָה" זוֹ מוּפְקֶרֶת. רַבִּי מַתְיָא בֶּן חָרָשׁ אוֹמֵר: אֲפִי' *הָלַךְ בַּעְלָהּ לְהַשְׁקוֹתָהּ, וּבָא עָלֶיהָ בַּדֶּרֶךְ — עֲשָׂאָהּ זוֹנָה. רַבִּי יְהוּדָה אוֹמֵר: "זוֹנָה" זוֹ אַיְלוֹנִית. וַחֲכָמִים אוֹמְרִים: אֵין זוֹנָה אֶלָּא גִּיּוֹרֶת וּמְשׁוּחְרֶרֶת וְשֶׁנִּבְעֲלָה בְּעִילַת זְנוּת. רַ' *אֱלִיעֶזֶר [צ"ל אלעזר] אוֹמֵר: *פָּנוּי הַבָּא עַל הַפְּנוּיָה שֶׁלֹּא לְשֵׁם אִישׁוּת — עֲשָׂאָהּ זוֹנָה. אֶלָּא אָמַר רַב אַדָּא בַּר אַהֲבָה: הָכָא בְּכֹ"ג עָסְקִינַן, לְאֵימַת קָנֵי לָהּ — לְכִי גָּדְלָה, בְּעוּלָה הִיא. אֲמַר רָבָא: מְכַלֵּי לֵב! אִי דְּקִדְּשָׁהּ אֲבוּהָ — מֵהַהִיא שַׁעְתָּא הוּא דְּקָנֵי לָהּ, וְאִי דְּקִדְּשָׁה נַפְשָׁהּ — הָא רַבִּי אֱלִיעֶזֶר הִיא וְלָא רַבָּנַן! אֶלָּא אָמַר רָבָא: לְעוֹלָם בְּכֹהֵן הֶדְיוֹט, וְחָיְישִׁינַן שֶׁמָּא תִּתְפַּתֶּה עָלָיו. א"ה יִשְׂרָאֵל נָמֵי! • *פִּתּוּיֵי קְטַנָּה אוֹנֶס הוּא, וְאוֹנֶס בְּיִשְׂרָאֵל מִישְׁרָא שָׁרֵי. רַב פָּפָּא אָמַר: בְּכֹ"ג, וְהַאי תַּנָּא הוּא, דְּתַנְיָא: °"בְּתוּלָה" [ב]יָכוֹל קְטַנָּה — ת"ל "אִשָּׁה". אִי "אִשָּׁה" יָכוֹל בּוֹגֶרֶת — ת"ל "בְּתוּלָה". [ג]הָא כֵּיצַד? יָצְתָה מִכְּלַל קְטַנּוּת, וְלִכְלַל בַּגְרוּת לֹא בָּאתָה. רַב נַחְמָן בַּר יִצְחָק אָמַר: הַאי תַּנָּא הוּא, דְּתַנְיָא "בְּתוּלָה" אֵין בְּתוּלָה אֶלָּא נַעֲרָה, וְכֵן הוּא אוֹמֵר °"וְהַנַּעֲרָה טֹבַת מַרְאֶה מְאֹד בְּתוּלָה". רַ' אֶלְעָזָר אוֹמֵר: פָּנוּי הַבָּא עַל הַפְּנוּיָה שֶׁלֹּא לְשֵׁם אִישׁוּת — עֲשָׂאָהּ זוֹנָה. *אָמַר רַב עַמְרָם: אֵין הֲלָכָה כְּרַבִּי אֶלְעָזָר.§

מתני' [ד]לֹא יְבַטֵּל אָדָם מִפְּרִיָּה וּרְבִיָּה אֶלָּא א"כ יֵשׁ לוֹ בָּנִים. ב"ש אוֹמְרִים: שְׁנֵי זְכָרִים, וּב"ה אוֹמְרִים: [ה]זָכָר וּנְקֵבָה, שֶׁנֶּאֱמַר °"זָכָר וּנְקֵבָה בְּרָאָם".§

גמ' הָא יֵשׁ לוֹ בָּנִים, מִפְּרִיָּה וּרְבִיָּה — בָּטֵיל, מֵאִשָּׁה — לָא בָּטֵיל. מְסַיְּיעָא לֵיהּ לְרַב נַחְמָן אָמַר שְׁמוּאֵל, דְּאָמַר: [ו]אע"פ שֶׁיֵּשׁ לוֹ לָאָדָם כַּמָּה בָּנִים — אָסוּר לַעֲמוֹד בְּלֹא אִשָּׁה, שֶׁנֶּאֱמַר °"לֹא טוֹב הֱיוֹת הָאָדָם לְבַדּוֹ". וְאִיכָּא דְּאָמְרִי: הָא יֵשׁ לוֹ בָּנִים — בָּטֵיל מִפְּרִיָּה וּרְבִיָּה, וּבָטֵיל נָמֵי מֵאִשָּׁה. נֵימָא תֶּיהֱוֵי תְּיוּבְתָּא דְּרַב נַחְמָן אָמַר שְׁמוּאֵל! לָא, [ז]אֵין לוֹ בָּנִים — נוֹשֵׂא אִשָּׁה בַּת בָּנִים, יֵשׁ לוֹ בָּנִים — נוֹשֵׂא אִשָּׁה דְּלָאו בַּת בָּנִים. [ח]נָפְקָא מִינַּהּ — לִמְכּוֹר סֵפֶר תּוֹרָה בִּשְׁבִיל בָּנִים.§ "בֵּית שַׁמַּאי אוֹמְרִים שְׁנֵי זְכָרִים".§ מַאי טַעֲמַיְיהוּ דְּבֵית שַׁמַּאי — יָלְפִינַן מִמֹּשֶׁה, דִּכְתִיב °"בְּנֵי מֹשֶׁה גֵּרְשׁוֹם וֶאֱלִיעֶזֶר", וּבֵית הִלֵּל — יָלְפִינַן מִבְּרִיָּיתוֹ שֶׁל עוֹלָם. וּבֵית שַׁמַּאי, לִילְפֵי מִבְּרִיָּיתוֹ שֶׁל עוֹלָם! *אֵין דָּנִין אֶפְשָׁר

מִשֶּׁאִי

תורה אור: הושע ד | דברים כה | ויקרא כא | בראשית כד | בראשית ה | שם ב | ד"ה א כג

רש"י

גמ' פּוּק עַיֵּין בָּהּ. אַמַּאי לֹא יִשָּׂא אֶת הַקְּטַנָּה. רַבִּי מֵאִיר חָיֵישׁ לְמִיעוּטָא. כִּדְתַנְיָא לְקַמָּן: קָטָן שֶׁמָּא יִמָּצֵא כו' — ה"נ חָיֵישׁ רַבִּי אֱלִיעֶזֶר דְּשֶׁמָּא תִּמָּצֵא קְטַנָּה זוֹ אַיְלוֹנִית. קָטָן וּקְטַנָּה. אוֹ קָטָן אוֹ קְטַנָּה. אִישׁ כְּתִיב. בְּפָרָשַׁת חֲלִיצָה "וְאִם לֹא יַחְפֹּץ הָאִישׁ לָקַחַת אֶת יְבִמְתּוֹ". פּוֹגְעִים בָּעֶרְוָה. כֵּיוָן דְּלָאו בְּנֵי הֲקָמַת שֵׁם נִינְהוּ — פָּגַע בְּאֵשֶׁת אָח שֶׁלֹּא בִּמְקוֹם מִצְוָה, דְּרַחֲמָנָא פְּטָרֵיהּ, דִּכְתִיב "אֲשֶׁר תֵּלֵד" (דברים כה) — פְּרָט לְאַיְלוֹנִית. וְאֵינָהּ חוֹלֶצֶת. דְּאֵינָהּ נִפְטֶרֶת לַשּׁוּק בַּחֲלִיצָתָהּ, דְּאֵין מַעֲשֵׂה קְטַנָּה כְּלוּם. אֲבָל מִתְיַיבֶּמֶת, וְתִגְדַּל אֶצְלוֹ, וְתִתְקַיֵּים מִצְוַת יִבּוּם. כִּשְׁמָהּ. לְשׁוֹן טוֹעָה, שֶׁטּוֹעָה מִתַּחַת בַּעְלָהּ לַאֲחֵרִים. דִּלְרַבִּי אֱלִיעֶזֶר אֵין זוֹנָה אֶלָּא אֵשֶׁת אִישׁ. מוּפְקֶרֶת. וַאֲפִי' פְּנוּיָה, מֵאַחַר שֶׁהִפְקִירָה עַצְמָהּ לַכֹּל — קְרוּיָה זוֹנָה. אֲבָל מִשּׁוּם בְּעִילָה אַחַת — לָא הָוְיָא זוֹנָה הַפְּנוּיָה. הָלַךְ בַּעְלָהּ. לְבֵ"ד הַגָּדוֹל, וְהוֹלִיכָהּ לְהַשְׁקוֹתָהּ מֵי הַמָּרִים, שֶׁקִּינֵּא לָהּ וְנִסְתְּרָה, וַאֲסוּרָה לוֹ עַד שֶׁתִּשְׁתֶּה — עֲשָׂאָהּ זוֹנָה, הוֹאִיל וְנִבְעֲלָה לְפָסוּל לָהּ. וְאִם מֵת — אֲסוּרָה לְכֹהֵן. אֶלָּא גִּיּוֹרֶת. דְּנִבְעֲלָה בְּגַיּוּתָהּ לְגוֹיִם, וְכֵן מְשׁוּחְרֶרֶת. דְּגוֹי וְעֶבֶד, הוֹאִיל וְלָאו בְּנֵי קִדּוּשִׁין נִינְהוּ — פָּסְלֵי. וְשֶׁנִּבְעֲלָה. לְפָסוּל לָהּ, כְּגוֹן א' מִכָּל הָעֲרָיוֹת, וּכְגוֹן בַּת יִשְׂרָאֵל לְנָתִין וּמַמְזֵר. לְכִי גָּדְלָה. דְּקִידּוּשֵׁי קְטַנָּה לָאו כְּלוּם הֵן, וְהָוְיָא לֵיהּ כִּמְכוּנֶּסֶת עִמּוֹ וּמְפוּתַּת עִמּוֹ. מְכַלֵּי לֵב. כְּמוֹ מְכַלֵּי לֵב. [אִי דְּקִדְּשָׁהּ אֲבוּהָ כו']. הָאָב זַכַּאי לְקַדֵּשׁ בִּתּוֹ קְטַנָּה, בְּפ"ק דְּקִידּוּשִׁין (דף ג:): "אֶת בִּתִּי נָתַתִּי לָאִישׁ הַזֶּה". הָא רַבִּי אֱלִיעֶזֶר הִיא וְלָא רַבָּנַן. בִּתְמִיָּה, דְּקָתָנֵי לְעֵיל: רַבִּי אֱלִיעֶזֶר אוֹמֵר כֹּהֵן לֹא יִשָּׂא אֶת הַקְּטַנָּה, וְנַשְׁמַע דִּפְלִיגִי רַבָּנַן עֲלֵיהּ, וכה"ג מִי פְּלִיגִי רַבָּנַן (ב)? תִּתְפַּתֶּה. וְתִזְנֶה עָלָיו, לְפִי שֶׁאֵין בָּהּ דַּעַת (ג) כְּלוּם. רַב פָּפָּא אָמַר בְּכֹהֵן גָּדוֹל וְהַאי תַּנָּא הוּא. דְּאָסַר קְטַנָּה מִגְּזֵירַת הַכָּתוּב. בְּתוּלָה. "מֵעַמָּיו יִקַּח אִשָּׁה". [מֵאִשָּׁה לָא בָּטֵיל]. מִדְּקָתָנֵי לֹא יְבַטֵּל אָדָם מִפְּרִיָּה וּרְבִיָּה אֶלָּא א"כ יֵשׁ לוֹ בָּנִים, וְלָא קָתָנֵי לֹא יְבַטֵּל אָדָם מֵאִשָּׁה אֶלָּא אִם כֵּן יֵשׁ לוֹ בָּנִים — שְׁמַע מִינַּהּ: הָא יֵשׁ לוֹ בָּנִים, מֵאִשָּׁה לָא בָּטֵיל, דְּצָרִיךְ לִישָּׂא אִשָּׁה, אֲבָל אֵין צָרִיךְ לַחֲזוֹר אַחַר רְאוּיָה לְבָנִים. לִמְכּוֹר ס"ת. כְּדֵי לִישָּׂא בַּת בָּנִים, וְאִם יֵשׁ לוֹ בָּנִים — לֹא יִמְכּוֹר, אֶלָּא יִשָּׂא עֲקָרָה אוֹ זְקֵנָה. ב"ש אוֹמְרִים שְׁנֵי זְכָרִים. אֲבָל לֹא זָכָר וּנְקֵבָה. יָלְפִינַן מִמֹּשֶׁה. שֶׁכֵּיוָן שֶׁהָיוּ לוֹ שְׁנֵי בָנִים — פֵּירֵשׁ מִן הָאִשָּׁה. מִבְּרִיָּיתוֹ שֶׁל עוֹלָם. אָדָם וְחַוָּה.

מִשֶּׁאִי

תוספות

כל ביאה שאין בה פירצה. קטנה אתיא לכלל פירצה לכשתתגדל, ולא ממעט אלא היכא דלא אתיא לעולם לכלל פירצה. **אין** בתולה אלא נערה. קשה: דלהאי תנא אמאי איצטריך בשום מקום לכתוב נערה בתולה?. **וכן** הוא אומר והנערה טובת מראה מאד. תימה: דהכא משמע דרבקה נערה היתה, ובסדר עולם (פ"א) תניא בהדיא: שהיתה בת שלש כשנשאה יצחק. ואי אפשר להגיה, דהא תניא התם יצחק אבינו כשנעקד על גבי המזבח היה בן שבעה ושלשים שנה, ובו בפרק נולדה רבקה, וכתיב "ויהי יצחק בן ארבעים שנה וגו'" — נמצאת שהיתה בת ג'. וה"ר שמואל חסיד משפיר"א הוכיח שהיתה בת י"ד. מדתניא בספרי: ו' זוגות שנותיהן שוות: וקחשיב קהת ורבקה. וקהת חיה קל"ג, כדכתיב בקרא. ואם היתה בת י"ד כשנשאה — אז החשבון מכוון, דכשנולד יעקב היתה בת ל"ד, (א) ויעקב היה בן צ"ט כשמתה רבקה — הרי קל"ג. שהרי כשנתברך היה בן ס"ג, שאז מת ישמעאל, וכל שנותיו של ישמעאל קל"ז, כדכתיב וישמעאל (גדול מיצחק י"ד שנה, ויצחק בן ס' שנה בלדת אותם, א"כ ישמעאל) בן ע"ד. ונשאר מלידת יעקב עד סוף שני ישמעאל ס"ג, וי"ד נטמן בבית עבר, כדאמרינן במגילה (דף יז.). ועשרים שנה בבית לבן, ושתי שנים בדרך, ואז מתה רבקה כדדרשינן (מדרש רבה קהלת פ"ג): אלון בכות — שתי בכיות, של רבקה ומניקתה — הרי צ"ט! וצריך לומר דמדרשות חלוקים זה על זה. **פנוי** הבא על הפנויה כו'. לאו דוקא נקט פנוי, דכ"ש נשוי שמזנה על אשתו דחשובה זונה. **לא** יבטל אדם מפריה ורביה. אע"ג דמרישא שמעינן לה, דקתני: כהן הדיוט לא ישא אילונית, ולאו דוקא כהן, כדאמרינן לעיל — מ"מ איצטריך הכא להנך דיוקי דגמרא. או משום פלוגתא דבית שמאי ובית הלל הדר תני לה. **מאשה** לא בטיל. פירש בקונטרס: מדלא קתני לא יבטל מאשה. **א"ד** מאשה בטיל. להאי לישנא דייק מדלא קתני "לא ישא אדם אשה שאינה בת בנים" אלא אם כן יש לו בנים. **נפקא** מינה למכור ספר תורה בשביל בנים. כלומר, להאי מילתא נמי נפקא מינה. ול"ג למאי נפקא מינה — דהא טובא נפקא מינה, כדקאמר בהדיא: אין לו בנים — נושא אשה בת בנים, יש לו בנים — נושא אשה דלאו בת בנים. ועוד אר"י: דמאי למימר דאפילו יש לו בנים לעולם מצוה לישא בת בנים, אלא מודו היכא דצריך למכור ספר תורה בשביל בת בנים, כיון דיש לו בנים — לא ימכור, מאחר שמוצא שאינה בת בנים, ולא יצטרך למכור.

מלעתיה

תוספות ישנים

פנוי הבא על הפנויה שלא לשם אישות עשאה זונה. ואיכא בינו לרבי עקיבא דר' עקיבא אומר זונה זו מופקרת רגילה בזנות כמה פעמים אבל בביאה ראשונה לא עשאה זונה ולר' אליעזר עשאה זונה בפעם אחת: **א)** ובזה ניחא דפריך לקמן ולילף מיצחק פי' שנשאה כ' שנה ואי כפ"ה שבת ג' שנים היתה א"כ משעה שהיתה ראויה להריון דהיינו מי"ג (בסמוך) [שנה] לא שהתה רק עשר שנים אלא ודאי בת י"ד שנה כדפרישית ומ"מ קשה להכא דמשמע שלא היתה בוגרת ופרשנו שהיתה בת י"ד שנה ושמא יש הרבה מדרשים חלוקים זה מזה: **הא** יש לו בנים בטיל מפריה ורביה בטיל נמי מאשה מדקאמר הכי ולא קאמר לא יבטל אדם מאשה בת בנים אבל אשה בעלמא נסיב מדלא קאמר הכי משמע דאף מאשה נמי בטיל כי יש לו בנים:

תוספות חד מקמאי

והא דתנן וב"ה אומרים זכר ונקבה. וב"ש בשני זכרים מקיים מצות פריה ורביה דזכרים עדיפי מנקבות מדאמר לקמן בני בנים הרי הם כבנים סבר אביי למימר ברא לברא וברתא לברתא אבל ברתא לברא לא וכו' אלמא זכרים עדיפי מנקבות.

גליון הש"ס

גמ' א"ל רב חסדא לרבה פוק. עיין גיטין דף כז ע"א: **שם** ר"ע אומר זונה זו מופקרת. עי' סנהדרין דף נ ע"ב תד"ה ת"ל ובת כהן: **שם** פתויי קטנה אונס הוא. וכן הוא בירושלמי פ"א דסוטה הובא בתוס' בסוטה דף כ"ה ע"א ד"ה מכאן עיין כתובות דף ט ע"א תד"ה ואב"א ושם דף מ ע"ב תד"ה לא:

הגהות הב"ח

(א) גמ' כל ביאה שאין בה פירצה אינה: (ב) רש"י ד"ה הא רבי אליעזר וכו' רבנן עליה הס"ד: (ג) ד"ה תתפתה וכו' דעת אלים:

הגהות מהר"ב רנשבורג

א] גמ' כל ביאה שאין בה פירצה. נ"ב מלשון ופרצת ימה וקדמה:

מסורת הש"ס: [לקמן קיט. וש"נ] | לקמן קיח: קיט. כתובות יט: נדה לב: | [לקמן קה: קיט.] | [עי' תוס' נדה לב: ד"ה שמא ותוס' לעיל ב: ד"ה או ותוס' גיטין מו: ד"ה המוציא] | לקמן פה: | [לעיל נט: וש"נ] | [לעיל לג:] | [לעיל ס: ע"ש] | [לעיל מו. וש"נ]

מִשַּׁמַּאי אֶפְשָׁר. וּבֵית הִלֵּל נַמִי, לֵילְפוּ מִמֹּשֶׁה! אָמְרִי לָךְ: מֹשֶׁה מִדַּעְתֵּיהּ הוּא דַּעֲבַד. דְּתַנְיָא: *שְׁלֹשָׁה דְּבָרִים עָשָׂה מֹשֶׁה מִדַּעְתּוֹ, וְהִסְכִּימָה דַּעְתּוֹ לְדַעַת הַמָּקוֹם: פֵּירַשׁ מִן הָאִשָּׁה, וְשִׁיבֵּר הַלּוּחוֹת, וְהוֹסִיף יוֹם אֶחָד. פֵּירַשׁ מִן הָאִשָּׁה, מַאי דְּרַשׁ? אָמַר: וּמָה יִשְׂרָאֵל שֶׁלֹּא דִּבְּרָה עִמָּהֶם שְׁכִינָה אֶלָּא לְפִי שָׁעָה, וְקָבַע לָהֶם זְמַן — אָמְרָה תּוֹרָה °"אַל תִּגְּשׁוּ אֶל אִשָּׁה", אֲנִי שֶׁמְּיוּחָד לְדִבּוּר בְּכָל שָׁעָה וְשָׁעָה, וְלֹא קָבַע לִי זְמַן — עַל אַחַת כַּמָּה וְכַמָּה. וְהִסְכִּימָה דַּעְתּוֹ לְדַעַת הַמָּקוֹם, שֶׁנֶּאֱמַר °"לֵךְ אֱמוֹר לָהֶם שׁוּבוּ לָכֶם לְאָהֳלֵיכֶם וְאַתָּה פֹּה עֲמוֹד עִמָּדִי". שִׁיבֵּר אֶת הַלּוּחוֹת, מַאי דְּרַשׁ? אָמַר: וּמָה פֶּסַח, שֶׁהוּא אֶחָד מִשֵּׁשׁ מֵאוֹת וּשְׁלֹשׁ עֶשְׂרֵה מִצְוֹת, אָמְרָה תּוֹרָה °"כָּל בֶּן נֵכָר לֹא יֹאכַל בּוֹ", הַתּוֹרָה כּוּלָּהּ וְיִשְׂרָאֵל מְשׁוּמָּדִים — עַל אַחַת כַּמָּה וְכַמָּה. וְהִסְכִּימָה דַּעְתּוֹ לְדַעַת הַמָּקוֹם, דִּכְתִיב °"אֲשֶׁר שִׁבַּרְתָּ", וְאָמַר רֵישׁ לָקִישׁ: אָמַר לֵיהּ הקב"ה לְמֹשֶׁה: *יִישַׁר כֹּחֲךָ שֶׁשִּׁבַּרְתָּ. הוֹסִיף יוֹם אֶחָד מִדַּעְתּוֹ, מַאי דְּרַשׁ? דִּכְתִיב °"וְקִדַּשְׁתָּם הַיּוֹם וּמָחָר" הַיּוֹם כְּמָחָר, מַה מָּחָר לֵילוֹ עִמּוֹ — אַף הַיּוֹם לֵילוֹ עִמּוֹ. וְלַיְלָה דְּהָאִידָּנָא נָפַק לֵיהּ. ש"מ: תְּרֵי יוֹמֵי, לְבַר מֵהָאִידָּנָא. וְהִסְכִּימָה דַּעְתּוֹ לְדַעַת הַמָּקוֹם — דְּלָא שָׁרְיָא שְׁכִינָה עַד שַׁבְּתָא. תַּנְיָא, *רַבִּי נָתָן אוֹמֵר, ב"ש אוֹמְרִים: שְׁנֵי זְכָרִים וּשְׁתֵּי נְקֵבוֹת, וּבה"א: זָכָר וּנְקֵבָה. א"ר הוּנָא: מ"ט דְּרַבִּי נָתָן אַלִּיבָּא דְּב"ש — דִּכְתִיב °"וַתֹּסֶף לָלֶדֶת אֶת אָחִיו אֶת הָבֶל" הֶבֶל וַאֲחוֹתוֹ, •קַיִן וַאֲחוֹתוֹ. וּכְתִיב °"כִּי שָׁת לִי אֱלֹהִים זֶרַע אַחֵר תַּחַת הֶבֶל כִּי הֲרָגוֹ קָיִן". וְרַבָּנַן אוֹדוּיֵי הוּא דְּקָא מוֹדֵית. תַּנְיָא אִידָךְ, *ר' נָתָן אוֹמֵר: ב"ש אוֹמְרִים: זָכָר וּנְקֵבָה, וּבה"א: אוֹ זָכָר אוֹ נְקֵבָה. אָמַר רָבָא מ"ט דְּר' נָתָן אַלִּיבָּא דְּב"ה — *שֶׁנֶּאֱ' °"לֹא תֹהוּ בְרָאָהּ לָשֶׁבֶת יְצָרָהּ" וְהָא עֲבַד לָהּ שֶׁבֶת. אִיתְּמַר, *הָיוּ לוֹ בָּנִים בְּגֵיוּתוֹ וְנִתְגַּיֵּיר, •רַ' יוֹחָנָן אָמַר: [א]קִיֵּים פְּרִיָּה וּרְבִיָּה, וְרֵישׁ לָקִישׁ אָמַר: לֹא קִיֵּים פְּרִיָּה וּרְבִיָּה. רַבִּי יוֹחָנָן אָמַר: קִיֵּים פְּרִיָּה וּרְבִיָּה, דְּהָא הָווּ לֵיהּ. וְרֵישׁ לָקִישׁ אָמַר: לֹא קִיֵּים פְּרִיָּה וּרְבִיָּה — *גֵּר שֶׁנִּתְגַּיֵּיר כְּקָטָן שֶׁנּוֹלַד דָּמֵי. וְאָזְדוּ לְטַעֲמַיְיהוּ, דְּאִיתְּמַר, *הָיוּ לוֹ בָּנִים בְּגֵיוּתוֹ וְנִתְגַּיֵּיר, רַבִּי יוֹחָנָן אָמַר: [ב]אֵין לוֹ בְּכוֹר לְנַחֲלָה, דְּהָא הֲוָה לֵיהּ "רֵאשִׁית אוֹנוֹ". וְרֵישׁ לָקִישׁ אָמַר: יֵשׁ לוֹ בְּכוֹר לְנַחֲלָה, גֵּר שֶׁנִּתְגַּיֵּיר כְּקָטָן שֶׁנּוֹלַד דָּמֵי. וּצְרִיכָא, דְּאִי אַשְׁמְעִינַן בְּהַהִיא קַמַּיְיתָא — בְּהַהִיא קָאָמַר רַבִּי יוֹחָנָן, מִשּׁוּם דְּמֵעִיקָּרָא נַמִי בְּנֵי פְּרִיָּה וּרְבִיָּה נִינְהוּ, אֲבָל לְעִנְיַן נַחֲלָה, דְּלָאו בְּנֵי נַחֲלָה נִינְהוּ, אֵימָא מוֹדֵי לֵיהּ לְרֵישׁ לָקִישׁ. וְאִי אִיתְּמַר בְּהָא — בְּהָא קָאָמַר רֵישׁ לָקִישׁ, אֲבָל בְּהַהִיא — אֵימָא מוֹדֶה לֵיהּ לְרַ' יוֹחָנָן, צְרִיכָא. אֵיתִיבֵיהּ רַ' יוֹחָנָן לר"ל: °"בָּעֵת הַהִיא שָׁלַח בְּרֹאדַךְ בַּלְאֲדָן בֶּן בַּלְאֲדָן מֶלֶךְ בָּבֶל וגו'"! א"ל: בְּגֵיוּתָן — אִית לְהוּ חַיִּים, נִתְגַּיְּירוּ — לֵית לְהוּ חַיִּים. אָמַר *רַב: [ג]הַכֹּל מוֹדִין בְּעֶבֶד שֶׁאֵין לוֹ חַיִּים, דִּכְתִיב °"שְׁבוּ לָכֶם פֹּה עִם הַחֲמוֹר", עַם *הַדּוֹמֶה לַחֲמוֹר. מֵיתִיבֵי: •°"וּלְצִיבָא חֲמִשָּׁה עָשָׂר בָּנִים וְעֶשְׂרִים עֲבָדִים"! אָמַר רַב אַחָא בַּר יַעֲקֹב: כְּ"פַר בֶּן בָּקָר". א"ה, ה"נ! שָׁאנֵי הָתָם דְּיַחְסִינְהוּ בִּשְׁמַיְיהוּ וּבִשְׁמָא דַּאֲבוּהוֹן, וְהָכָא לָא מְפָרֵשׁ. וְאִיבָּעֵית אֵימָא: יַחְסִינְהוּ בְּדוּכְתָּא אַחֲרִיתֵי בַּאֲבוּהוֹן וּבְאַבָּא דַּאֲבוּהוֹן, דִּכְתִיב °"וַיִּשְׁלָחֵם הַמֶּלֶךְ אָסָא אֶל בֶּן הֲדַד בֶּן טַבְרִימוֹן בֶּן חֶזְיוֹן מֶלֶךְ אֲרָם הַיּוֹשֵׁב בְּדַמֶּשֶׂק לֵאמֹר". אִיתְּמַר, הָיוּ לוֹ בָּנִים וּמֵתוּ, רַב הוּנָא אָמַר: קִיֵּים פְּרִיָּה וּרְבִיָּה, [ד]רַבִּי יוֹחָנָן אָמַר: לֹא קִיֵּים. רַב הוּנָא אָמַר: קִיֵּים — מִשּׁוּם דְּרַב אַסִּי, דְּאָמַר *רַב אַסִּי: *) אֵין בֶּן דָּוִד בָּא עַד שֶׁיִּכְלוּ כָּל נְשָׁמוֹת שֶׁבַּגּוּף, שֶׁנֶּאֱמַר °"כִּי רוּחַ מִלְּפָנַי יַעֲטוֹף וגו'". וְרַבִּי יוֹחָנָן אָמַר: לֹא קִיֵּים פְּרִיָּה וּרְבִיָּה, "לָשֶׁבֶת יְצָרָהּ" בָּעֵינַן — וְהָא לֵיכָּא. מֵיתִיבֵי בְּנֵי

*) ע"ז ה. נדה יג: לקמן סג:

רש"י

מִשַּׁמַּאי אֶפְשָׁר. דְּאִי לָא אִיבְּרַאי חַוָּה — לָא הֲוָה נְקֵבָה אַחֲרִיתִי. אֲבָל הָכָא, מִי שֶׁיֵּשׁ לוֹ שְׁנֵי זְכָרִים — נְקֵבוֹת הַרְבֵּה בָּעוֹלָם. מִדַּעְתֵּיהּ. מִשּׁוּם שְׁכִינָה, וְאָסוּר לִשְׁאָר כָּל אָדָם לַעֲשׂוֹת כֵּן. הוֹסִיף יוֹם אֶחָד. הקב"ה אָמַר לוֹ "וְקִדַּשְׁתָּם הַיּוֹם וּמָחָר", וְהוּא אָמַר "הֱיוּ נְכוֹנִים לִשְׁלֹשֶׁת יָמִים". וְלֹא קָבַע לִי זְמַן. אֵימָתַי יְדַבֵּר עִמִּי, שֶׁאֶפְרוֹשׁ יוֹם אֶחָד קוֹדֶם. לְאָהֳלֵיכֶם. לִנְשֵׁיכֶם. אֲשֶׁר. לְשׁוֹן יִישַׁר. עַד שַׁבְּתָא. בְּמַסֶּ' שַׁבָּת, בְּפֶרֶק ר"ע (דף פו.) גָּמְרִינַן לָהּ, דַּעֲבוּד פְּרִישָׁה בְּאַרְבַּע בְּשַׁבְּתָא, וּפֵירְשׁוּ חֲמִישִׁי וְשִׁשִּׁי שְׁלֵימִים, וּבְשַׁבְּתָא שַׁרְיָא שְׁכִינָה וְהוּא שְׁלִישִׁי לַיָּמִים הַשְּׁלֵמִים, וְיוֹם רִאשׁוֹן לָא חָשֵׁיב, שֶׁלֹּא הָיָה לֵילוֹ עִמּוֹ. אֶת קַיִן אֶת הֶבֶל. אֶתִין רִבּוּיִין *[הֵן], לוֹמַר: נְקֵבוֹת הָיוּ עִמָּהֶן. כִּי שָׁת לִי זֶרַע אַחֵר תַּחַת הֶבֶל. אַלְמָא תַּשְׁלוּמִין בָּעֵי, וְלָא סַגְיָא בְּלָא שְׁנֵי זְכָרִים וּשְׁתֵּי נְקֵבוֹת. תְּרֵי תַנָּאֵי. אַלִּיבָּא דְּר' נָתָן. מ"ט דְּר' נָתָן אַלִּיבָּא דְּב"ה. אוֹ זָכָר אוֹ נְקֵבָה, וְלָא מִבְּרִיַּית עוֹלָם יָלֵיף, וְלָא מִמֹּשֶׁה. לֹא תֹהוּ בְרָאָהּ. לֹא בָּרָא עוֹלָמוֹ לְתוֹהוּ, אֶלָּא לָשֶׁבֶת — לִהְיוֹת עֲסוּקִים בְּיִישּׁוּבוֹ שֶׁל עוֹלָם. אֵין לוֹ בְּכוֹר לְנַחֲלָה. בֵּן בְּכוֹר שֶׁיִּוָּלֵד לוֹ מִשֶּׁיִּתְגַּיֵּיר — אֵינוֹ נוֹטֵל פִּי שְׁנַיִם. בְּנֵי נֹחַ. בְּנֵי פְּרִיָּה וּרְבִיָּה נִינְהוּ — דִּכְתִיב "וַיֹּאמֶר לָהֶם פְּרוּ וּרְבוּ" (בראשית ט). בְּגֵיוּתָן. לָאו בְּנֵי דִּין נַחֲלָה נִינְהוּ, דְּבַת כְּבֵן, וּבְכוֹר כְּפָשׁוּט. אֲבָל יְרוּשָּׁה — נָהֲגָא בְּהוּ, כִּדְאָמְרִינַן בְּקִדּוּשִׁין (דף יז:): גּוֹי יוֹרֵשׁ אָבִיו דְּבַר תּוֹרָה. בַּלְאֲדָן בֶּן בַּלְאֲדָן. אַלְמָא: בָּנִים מִיקְרוּ. חַיִּים. מִתְיַיחֲסִין אַחֲרֵי אֲבִיהֶם. נִתְגַּיְּירוּ אֵין לָהֶם חַיִּים. מֵרִאשׁוֹנִים, דְּקָטָן שֶׁנּוֹלַד דָּמֵי. שְׁבוּ לָכֶם פֹּה. אֱלִיעֶזֶר עֶבֶד אַבְרָהָם הֲוָה. צִיבָא. עֶבֶד כְּנַעֲנִי שֶׁל מְפִיבֹשֶׁת הֲוָה. שָׁאנֵי הָכָא דְּיַחְסִינְהוּ בִּשְׁמַיְיהוּ. שֶׁהִזְכִּיר שְׁמוֹ [וּשְׁמוֹ] שֶׁל אָבִיו "בַּלְאֲדָן בֶּן בַּלְאֲדָן", אַלְמָא בָּנִים אִיקְרוּ, אֲבָל הָכָא לֹא הוּזְכְּרוּ בִּשְׁמוֹתָן. מִשּׁוּם דְּרַב אַסִּי. כְּלוֹמַר, טַעְמָא דִּפְרִיָּה וּרְבִיָּה מִשּׁוּם דְּרַב אַסִּי. וְהָאִי, כֵּיוָן דִּנְטָלוּ עַל יָדוֹ מִנְּשָׁמוֹת שֶׁבְּאוֹתוֹ אוֹצָר שֶׁשְּׁמוֹ גּוּף — הֲרֵי קִיֵּים מִצְוַת פְּרִיָּה וּרְבִיָּה.

תוספות

מדעתיה הוא דעבד. אע"ג דק"ו קאמר – אין זה ק"ו גמור. דאטו מפני שלוה פעס אחד לבטל יבטל לעולס פרו ורבו? אי נמי דוקא אז אמר לבטל, משוס עשרת הדברות.

וקבע להם זמן. וא"ת: אדרבה, משוס דקבע להס זמן (א) וידבר עמהס – בודאי יש לפרוש יותר מעל הספק? ויש לומר: *דהכא פי' וקבע להס זמן (*משה) שלשה ימיס ולא היו לריכים לפרוש אלא יוס אחד משוס קרי, אלא משוס ספק פליטה הוזקקו לפרוש שלשה ימיס. ק"ו אני, שלא קבע לי זמן, ויש ספק שיתיחד הדבור בשעת תשמיש או ביוס תשמיש.

דכתיב אמור להם. וא"ת: ומנלן שפירש מדעתו? והלא משעה שנאסר במתן תורה עס ישראל – שוב לא הותר לו, כדכתיב "ואתה פה עמוד עמדי"! ויש לומר: דאי לאו דפירש מדעתו – למה כעסו עליו אהרן ומריס? אלא ודאי כששמע מפי הגבורה "אל תגשו אל אשה" נשא ק"ו בעלמו. וגלה לה דעתו, ועשה לה אהל בפני עלמו או נתן לה גט – ולפיכך כעסו עליו. וא"ת: ולמה המתינו כל כך, שלא כעסו עליו אלא בחלרות שהוא זמן גדול אחר מתן תורה? וי"ל: שלא נתגלה להס אלא באותה שעה. כדתניא בסיפרי: שבשעה שאמר הקב"ה למשה ליקח ע' זקניס מישראל, אמרה מריס: אשרי נשותיהן של אלו שנתבקשו לגדולה. אמרה לפורה: אוי להן לנשותיהן של אלו, שמיוס שדברה השכינה עס אחיך פירש ממני. וא"ת: ולמה כעסו עליו, מאחר שהסכים לו המקוס? וי"ל: משוס דאמרינן (במכות דף י:) בדרך שאדס רולה לילך מוליכין אותו, וסייעוהו בבא לטהר.

התורה כולה וישראל משומדים כו'. אין זה ק"ו *גמור, דשאני פסח משוס דקדשיס. אבל כל התורה כולה – אדרבה, יש לו ללמדס ולהחזירס בתשובה.

אף היום לילו עמו. אין זו דרשה גמורה, ד"היוס" משמע: היוס ממש.

רבי יוחנן אמר קיים פריה ורביה. אע"ג דלענין כמה דבריס אמרינן (לעיל כב.) גר שנתגייר כקטן שנולד דמי, מכל מקוס מסתברא ליה לר' יוחנן הכא, כיון דבגויותו קייס דזרעו מיוחס אחריו באותה שעה – מפטר נמי כשנתגייר.

בני פריה ורביה נינהו. וא"ת: דבפ' "ד' מיתות" (סנהד' נט: ושס) משמע דבני נח לא מיפקדו אפריה ורביה! וי"ל: דהכא לאו בני חיוב אפריה ורביה קאמר, אלא כלומר שבניהס נקראיס על שמס, כדאמרינן בסמוך.

דלאו בני נחלה נינהו. כלומר: נחלת בכורה. אבל גוי יורש את אביו דבר תורה, כדאמרינן בפ"ק דקדושין (דף יז:).

הכל מודים בעבד שאין לו חיים כו'. ואס נשתחרר לא קייס פריה ורביה. וא"ת: הא דאמרינן גבי חליו עבד וחליו בן חורין לישא שפחה אינו יכול, משמע דאס היה יכול לישא שפחה – הוה סגי ליה בהכי, ואמאי? והא לא *מיפקד אפריה ורביה, ולא מיפטר בהכי? ויש לומר: דאס היה יכול לישא שפחה – לא הוה כפינן לרבו לשחררו, כיון דשבת מיהא היה יכול לקייס, אף על גב דפריה ורביה לא מקייס בהכי. ואף על גב דלעיל משמע דפריה ורביה תלי בשבת, דקאמר רבא מאי טעמא דרבי נתן אליבא דבית הלל – "לא תהו בראה לשבת יצרה" והא עבד ליה שבת – מכל מקוס לא הוה כפינן לרבו, כיון דיכול לקייס כל דהו.

וכל

עין משפט נר מצוה

פט א מיי' פט"ו מהל' איסות הלכה ו סמג עשין מט טוש"ע אה"ע סימן א סעיף ז:

צ ב מיי' פ"ב מהלכות נחלות הלכה יב סמג עשין נו טוש"ע ח"מ סי' רעז סעיף ט:

צא ג מיי' שס ופט"ו מהל' איסות הל' ו סמג שס (וסימן ט') טור ש"ע שס וטוש"ע אה"ע סימן א סעיף ז:

צב ד מיי' פט"ו מהל' איסות הלכה ה סמג עשין מח טוש"ע אה"ע סימן א סעיף ו:

נ"ל דהכי

רש"ל מ"ז

תוספות ישנים

אין בן דוד בא עד שיכלו נשמות שבגוף. תימה דאמרי' (שבת קי"ט) אלמלא ישראל משמריס שתי שבתות מיד נגאלין והלא לריך שיכלו כל הנשמות שבגוף וי"ל שהיו יולדות ששה בכרס אחד ויכלו הנשמות שבגוף מיד:

עיין אדר"נ פ"ב איתא ק"ו אחר

תוספות חד מקמאי

והא דמקשינן בגמרא וב"ה לילפו ממשה. ומאי קושיא דהא ב"ה ילפי מברייתו של עולם זכר ונקבה בראם ובזכר ונקבה נמי קיים מצות פריה ורביה. ה"ק כיון דמשה אשכחן שהיו לו שני זכרים לילפי ממשה ולא מברייתו של עולם דהא אי אפשר: **הא** דאמר אין ישיבה בחו"ל עולה לו ה"מ למי שדר בארץ אבל למי שלא דר בא"י כגון בשאר ארצות ודאי ישיבת ח"ל עולה לו וכ"כ הראב"ד ז"ל:

[כתובות קיא. קדושין סח. ב"ק מט. נדה יז.]

נ"ל לא מיפטר מפ"ו מהרש"ל

גליון הש"ס

גמ' קין ואחותו. עיין סנהדרין דף לח ע"ב תד"ה וילדו ובסוטה דף ט ע"ב רש"י ד"ה קין ובב"ב דף קכג ע"א ובמהרש"א חדושי אגדות שם: **שם** ר' יוחנן אמר קיים כו'. עיין טורי אבן ר"ה דף כח ע"א תד"ה אילימא: **שם** מיתיבי ולציבא. עיין טורי אבן חגיגה דף ב ע"א ד"ה כאן כמשנה ראשונה.

הגהות הב"ח

(א) תוס' ד"ה וקבע וכו' זמן לדבר עמהם:

מסורת הש"ס

שבת פז.

כ"ה בדפו"י

שבת פז. ב"ב יז: מנחות נט.

[תוס' פ"ח ע"ש נ"ע]

[תוספתא שם]

עדיות פ"א מי"ג

[בכורות מז.]

לעיל כב. וש"נ

[בכורות מז.]

מ"ב כ

[נ"ל רבי אבא כך איתא בהלפס ובהרא"ש] בראשית כב

מ"א טו

[בע"ז ה. ובנדה יג: איתא ר' יוסי]

צג א מיי' פט"ו מהל' אישות הלכה ב וסמג עשין מח טוש"ע אה"ע סימן א סעיף ו:
צד ב מיי' שם הלכה ד טוש"ע שם ס"ה:
צה ג ד מיי' שם הלכה ה טור שו"ע שם סעיף ו:
צו ה טוש"ע שם סי' א סעיף ח בהג"ה:
צז ו ז טוש"ע א"ח סי' רמ סעי' א וטוש"ע י"ד סימן קפד סעיף י:
צח ח מיי' פ"ד מהל' איסורי ביאה הלכה יב וס"ח הלכה ג טוש"ע י"ד סימן קפד סעיף ב:
צט ט (טור) שו"ע שם סעיף י [בהג"ה] וטוש"ע א"ח סימן רמ סעיף א:
ק י מיי' פט"ו מהלכות אישות הלכה יט:
קא כ מיי' פ"ב מהל' איסורי ביאה הלכה כה סמג לאוין קכו טור אה"ע סימן ב:
קב ל מיי' פ"ב מהלכות איסורי ביאה הי"ד:

וכל שכן ברא לברתא. אע"ג דאמרינן לעיל אין שני זכרים חשובים כבן ובת! הכא שבא מכח מי שפטרתו מפריה ורביה – פשיטא דקאי שפיר הבן במקום הבת. **חייב** אדם לפקוד את אשתו. אומר ר"ת: דפקידה זו אינו תשמיש, אלא כשהוא רוצה לצאת בדרך, אם הוא רחוק ממנה – לא יצא לדרך אא"כ ישוב אליה ויפקדנה, (ב) או בתשמיש או בשאר דברים, וידבר על לבה. ופריך: מהתם נפקא ליה, מלמד שהאשה משתוקקת על בעלה כשיוצא לדרך, ומסתמא כיון שמתאוה לו – יש לו לפוקדה, דהמכבד אשתו עליו הכתוב אומר "אז תקרא וגו'"! ומשני, אמר רב יוסף: לא נצרכה אלא לאשתו נדה. ה"ג בכל הספרים ישנים. והכי פי': דחד קרא אתא דאפילו באשתו נדה יש לו לפוקדה, וכמה – עונה. אע"פ שאסור לשמש, מ"מ שמחה ותענוג הוא לה, הואיל ורוצה לצאת בדרך. והכי אמרי' בריש "הדר" (עירובין סג: ושם): הישן בקילעא שאיש ואשתו ישנים – שם עליו הכתוב אומר "נשי עמי תגרשון מבית תענוגיה". ואמר רב יוסף התם: ואפילו אשתו נדה. ומה שהגיהו בספרים "לא נצרכה אלא סמוך לוסתה" – אין נראה כלל. דהגיהו כן לפי שרוצין לפרש דפקידה היינו תשמיש, ובשבועות (דף יח: ושם) מוכיח דסמוך לוסתה מדאורייתא, מ"והזרתם את בני ישראל וגו'" ועוד: דמוקי לה ביוצא לדבר הרשות, וא"כ, אפילו למאן דאמר (נדה דף טו.) ווסתות דרבנן – אם כן סמוך לווסתה נמי דרבנן – מכל מקום למה יהא מותר ביוצא לדבר הרשות?. **סמוך** לפירקן. אבניו נמי קאי, כדאמרי' ב"הנשרפין" (סנהד' דף עו: ושם) ואע"ג דקטן לא תקינו ליה רבנן נשואין, כדאמרינן לקמן (ג) בפרק "אלמנה" (דף סח.) מ"מ להכי תקינו ליה נשואין, דלא הויא בעילתו בעילת זנות*. **והנושא** את בת אחותו. פירש רשב"ם: דה"ה בת אחיו. אבל אחותו נקט לפי שמשדלתו בדברים, ושכיח שנושא בתה. ור"ת אומר: דדוקא נקט בת אחותו, לפי שהיא בת מזלו כדאמרי': *רוב בנים דומין לאחי האם*):

[ועי' היטב תוס' לקמן נו: ד"ה נשא ותוספות סנהדרין עו: ד"ה סמוך]
[כ"ב קי. מס' סופרים ספט"ו]
*) [עיין תוס' לקמן נט. ד"ה ספק]

*בְּנֵי בָנִים הֲרֵי הֵן כְּבָנִים! כִּי תַנְיָא הַהִיא – לְהַשְׁלִים. מֵיתִיבֵי: *אבְּנֵי בָנִים הֲרֵי הֵם כְּבָנִים, מֵת אֶחָד מֵהֶם, באוֹ שֶׁנִּמְצָא סָרִיס, לֹא קִיֵּים פְּרִיָּה וּרְבִיָּה. תְּיוּבְתָּא דְּרַב הוּנָא! תְּיוּבְתָּא.§ "בְּנֵי בָנִים הֲרֵי הֵם כְּבָנִים".§ סְבַר אַבַּיֵי לְמֵימַר: בְּרָא לִבְרָא [א] וּבְרַתָּא לִבְרַתָּא, וְכ"ש בְּרָא לִבְרַתָּא, אֲבָל בְּרַתָּא לִבְרָא – לָא. א"ל רָבָא: ג"לָשֶׁבֶת יְצָרָהּ" בָּעֵינָא, וְהָא אִיכָּא. דְּכוּלֵּי עָלְמָא מִיהַת דתְּרֵי מֵחַד לָא. וְלָא?! וְהָא אָמְרִי לֵיהּ רַבָּנַן *לְרַב שֵׁשֶׁת: נְסֵיב אִיתְּתָא וְאוֹלֵיד בְּנֵי! וַאֲמַר לְהוּ: בְּנֵי בְּרַתִּי בָּנַי נִינְהוּ. הָתָם דַּחוּיֵי קָמַדְחֵי לְהוּ, *דְּרַב שֵׁשֶׁת אִיעֲקַר מִפִּירְקֵיהּ דְּרַב הוּנָא. [לקמן סד:] אֲמַר לֵיהּ רַבָּה לְרָבָא בַּר מָארִי: המְנָא הָא מִילְּתָא דַּאֲמוּר רַבָּנַן בְּנֵי בָנִים הֲרֵי הֵן כְּבָנִים? אִילֵימָא מִדִּכְתִיב °"הַבָּנוֹת בְּנוֹתַי וְהַבָּנִים בָּנַי" (בראשית לא) אֶלָּא מֵעַתָּה, "וְהַצֹּאן צֹאנִי" הָכִי נַמִי? אֶלָּא – דְּקָנֵית מִינַּאי, הָכָא נַמִי – דְּקָנֵית מִינַּאי! אֶלָּא מֵהָכָא: °"וְאַחַר בָּא חֶצְרוֹן אֶל בַּת מָכִיר אֲבִי גִלְעָד (דה"א ב) וַתֵּלֶד לוֹ אֶת שְׂגוּב", וּכְתִיב: °"מִנִּי מָכִיר יָרְדוּ (שופטים ה) מְחוֹקְקִים" וּכְתִיב °"יְהוּדָה מְחוֹקְקִי" (תהלים ס וקח). מַתְנִיתִין דְּלָאו כְּרַבִּי יְהוֹשֻׁעַ. דְּתַנְיָא, רַבִּי יְהוֹשֻׁעַ אוֹמֵר: נָשָׂא אָדָם אִשָּׁה בְּיַלְדוּתוֹ – יִשָּׂא אִשָּׁה בְּזִקְנוּתוֹ, הָיוּ לוֹ בָנִים בְּיַלְדוּתוֹ – יִהְיוּ לוֹ בָנִים בְּזִקְנוּתוֹ, שֶׁנֶּאֱ' °"בַּבֹּקֶר זְרַע אֶת זַרְעֶךָ וְלָעֶרֶב אַל תַּנַּח יָדֶךָ (קהלת יא) כִּי אֵינְךָ יוֹדֵעַ אֵי זֶה יִכְשַׁר הֲזֶה אוֹ זֶה וְאִם שְׁנֵיהֶם כְּאֶחָד טוֹבִים". ר"ע אוֹמֵר: לָמַד תּוֹרָה בְּיַלְדוּתוֹ – יִלְמוֹד תּוֹרָה בְּזִקְנוּתוֹ, הָיוּ לוֹ תַּלְמִידִים בְּיַלְדוּתוֹ – יִהְיוּ לוֹ תַּלְמִידִים בְּזִקְנוּתוֹ, שֶׁנֶּאֱ' "בַּבֹּקֶר זְרַע אֶת זַרְעֶךָ וגו'". אָמְרוּ: שְׁנֵים עָשָׂר אֶלֶף זוּגִים תַּלְמִידִים הָיוּ לוֹ לְרַבִּי עֲקִיבָא מִגְּבַת עַד אַנְטִיפְרַס, וְכוּלָּן מֵתוּ בְּפֶרֶק אֶחָד, מִפְּנֵי שֶׁלֹּא נָהֲגוּ כָּבוֹד זֶה לָזֶה. וְהָיָה הָעוֹלָם שָׁמֵם, עַד שֶׁבָּא ר"ע אֵצֶל רַבּוֹתֵינוּ שֶׁבַּדָּרוֹם וּשְׁנָאָהּ לָהֶם: ר"מ, וְר' יְהוּדָה, וְר' יוֹסֵי, וְרַבִּי שִׁמְעוֹן, וְרַבִּי אֶלְעָזָר בֶּן שַׁמּוּעַ. וְהֵם הֵם הֶעֱמִידוּ תוֹרָה אוֹתָהּ שָׁעָה. תָּנָא: כּוּלָּם מֵתוּ מִפֶּסַח וְעַד עֲצֶרֶת. אָמַר רַב חָמָא בַּר אַבָּא וְאִיתֵימָא ר' חִיָּיא בַּר אָבִין: כּוּלָּם מֵתוּ מִיתָה רָעָה. מַאי הִיא? א"ר נַחְמָן: אַסְכָּרָה. א"ר מַתְנָא: הֲלָכָה כְּרַבִּי יְהוֹשֻׁעַ. אָמַר רַבִּי תַּנְחוּם א"ר חֲנִילַאי: הכָּל אָדָם שֶׁאֵין לוֹ אִשָּׁה שָׁרוּי בְּלֹא שִׂמְחָה, בְּלֹא בְרָכָה, בְּלֹא טוֹבָה. בְּלֹא שִׂמְחָה – דִּכְתִיב °"וְשָׂמַחְתָּ אַתָּה וּבֵיתֶךָ", בְּלֹא בְרָכָה – דִּכְתִיב °"לְהָנִיחַ בְּרָכָה אֶל בֵּיתֶךָ" (יחזקאל מד), בְּלֹא טוֹבָה – דִּכְתִיב °"לֹא טוֹב הֱיוֹת הָאָדָם לְבַדּוֹ" (בראשית ב). בְּמַעַרְבָא אָמְרִי: בְּלֹא תוֹרָה, בְּלֹא חוֹמָה. בְּלֹא תוֹרָה – דִּכְתִיב °"הַאִם אֵין עֶזְרָתִי בִי וְתֻשִׁיָּה נִדְּחָה מִמֶּנִּי" (איוב ו), בְּלֹא חוֹמָה – דִּכְתִיב °"נְקֵבָה תְּסוֹבֵב גָּבֶר" (ירמיה לא). רָבָא בַּר עוּלָּא אָמַר: בְּלֹא שָׁלוֹם, דִּכְתִיב °"וְיָדַעְתָּ כִּי שָׁלוֹם אָהֳלֶךָ וּפָקַדְתָּ נָוְךָ וְלֹא תֶחֱטָא" (איוב ה). אָמַר ריב"ל: כָּל הַיּוֹדֵעַ בְּאִשְׁתּוֹ שֶׁהִיא יִרְאַת שָׁמַיִם, וְאֵינוֹ פּוֹקְדָהּ – נִקְרָא חוֹטֵא, שֶׁנֶּאֱמַר "וְיָדַעְתָּ כִּי שָׁלוֹם אָהֳלֶךָ וגו'". וְאָמַר ריב"ל: יחַיָּיב אָדָם לִפְקוֹד אֶת אִשְׁתּוֹ בְּשָׁעָה שֶׁהוּא יוֹצֵא לַדֶּרֶךְ שֶׁנֶּאֱ' "וְיָדַעְתָּ כִּי שָׁלוֹם אָהֳלֶךָ וגו'". הָא מֵהָכָא נָפְקָא? מֵהָתָם נָפְקָא: "וְאֶל *אִישֵׁךְ תְּשׁוּקָתֵךְ" מְלַמֵּד שֶׁהָאִשָּׁה מִשְׁתּוֹקֶקֶת עַל בַּעְלָהּ בְּשָׁעָה שֶׁהוּא יוֹצֵא לַדֶּרֶךְ! א"ר יוֹסֵף: כלֹא נִצְרְכָה אֶלָּא *) סָמוּךְ לְוֶוסְתָּהּ (עירובין סג:). וְכַמָּה? חאֲמַר **) רָבָא: עוֹנָה. טוְהָנֵי מִילֵּי – לִדְבַר הָרְשׁוּת, אֲבָל לִדְבַר מִצְוָה – מִיטְרִידִי. *ת"ר: יהָאוֹהֵב אֶת אִשְׁתּוֹ כְּגוּפוֹ, וְהַמְכַבְּדָהּ יוֹתֵר מִגּוּפוֹ, וְהַמַּדְרִיךְ בָּנָיו וּבְנוֹתָיו בְּדֶרֶךְ יְשָׁרָה, כוְהַמַּשִּׂיאָן סָמוּךְ לְפִירְקָן – עָלָיו הַכָּתוּב אוֹמֵר "וְיָדַעְתָּ כִּי שָׁלוֹם אָהֳלֶךָ". *הָאוֹהֵב אֶת שְׁכֵנָיו, וְהַמְקָרֵב אֶת קְרוֹבָיו, לוְהַנּוֹשֵׂא אֶת בַּת אֲחוֹתוֹ, (סנהדרין עו:) (ג"ז שם)
וְהַמַּלְוֶה

*) שבועות יח: נדה סג: **) [נ"ל רבה]

בְּנֵי בָנִים הֲרֵי הֵן כְּבָנִים. קס"ד שֶׁמֵּת הַזָּכָר אוֹ הַנְּקֵבָה, וְהָיָה לוֹ בֵּן, שֶׁיִּצְטָרֵף עִם אֲחוֹת אָבִיו אוֹ עִם אֲחִי אִמּוֹ – אֵין אֲבִי הָאָב חַיָּיב עוֹד בִּפְרִיָּה וּרְבִיָּה. וְטַעְמָא, שֶׁהָיָה לוֹ לַמֵּת בֵּן, הָא לָאו הָכִי לָא קִיֵּים, דְּשֶׁבֶת בָּעֵינַן, וְקַשְׁיָא לְרַב הוּנָא. כִּי תַנְיָא הַהִיא לְהַשְׁלִים. כְּגוֹן שֶׁלֹּא הָיָה לוֹ לַזָּקֵן אֶלָּא בֵּן אֶחָד, וְנָשָׂא הַבֵּן אִשָּׁה וְהוֹלִיד בַּת – פָּטוּר הַזָּקֵן, שֶׁהֲרֵי הִשְׁלִים זֶה אֶת חוֹבָתוֹ. אֲבָל אִי הֲוָה לֵיהּ מֵעִיקָּרָא זָכָר וּנְקֵבָה, וַאֲפִילּוּ מֵתוּ בְּלֹא בָנִים – קִיֵּים פְּרִיָּה וּרְבִיָּה. דְּכוּלֵּי עָלְמָא. בֵּין לְאַבַּיֵי בֵּין לְרָבָא. תְּרֵי מֵחַד. וְהַשֵּׁנִי מֵת בְּלֹא בָנִים – לֹא קִיֵּים הַזָּקֵן פְּרִיָּה וּרְבִיָּה. אִיעֲקַר מִפִּרְקֵיהּ דְּרַב הוּנָא. שֶׁהָיָה מַאֲרִיךְ בִּדְרָשָׁיו, וּצְרִיכִים לְמֵי רַגְלַיִם, וּמַעֲמִידִים עַצְמָן וְנֶעֱקָרִים, (א) כִּדְתַנְיָא בִּבְכוֹרוֹת (דף מד:). מְנָא הָא מִילְּתָא כו'. אַבְּנֵי בִתּוֹ קָאֵי, דִּבֶן בְּנוֹ פְּשִׁיטָא לָן. מִנִּי מָכִיר יָרְדוּ מְחוֹקְקִים. וְלֹא מָצִינוּ לְמֵימַר מִבְּנֵי בָנָיו אֶלָּא מִבְּנֵי בִתּוֹ, דְּהָא כְּתִיב קְרָא אַחֲרִינָא "יְהוּדָה מְחוֹקְקִי", וְלָא מַשְׁכַּחַתְּ לָהּ דְּלֵיתוֹ מִתַּרְוַיְיהוּ אֶלָּא הָכִי, דְּנָפְקוּ מְחוֹקְקִים מֵחֶצְרוֹן מִבִּתּוֹ שֶׁל מָכִיר, אַלְמָא: בְּנֵי בִתּוֹ כְּבָנָיו. מַתְנִיתִין. דְּקָתָנֵי אא"כ כו', הָא אִם יֵשׁ לוֹ – יִבָּטֵל, דְּלָא כְּר' יְהוֹשֻׁעַ. לָעֶרֶב. לְעֵת זִקְנָתוֹ. אֵי זֶה יִכְשַׁר. אֵיזֶה זֶרַע יְהֵא הָגוּן וִירֵא שָׁמַיִם, וּמִתְקַיֵּים. מִגְּבַת עַד אַנְטִיפְרַס. [בֵּין הָעֲיָירוֹת הַלָּלוּ הָיוּ כּוּלָּם]. שָׁמֵם. שֶׁנִּשְׁתַּכְּחָה תּוֹרָה. בֵּיתֶךָ. אִשָּׁה. הַאִם אֵין עֶזְרָתִי בִי. אִשְׁתִּי, דִּכְתִיב (בראשית ב) "עֵזֶר כְּנֶגְדּוֹ", מִיָּד "תּוּשִׁיָּה נִדְּחָה מִמֶּנִּי", שֶׁצָּרִיךְ לַעֲסוֹק בְּצָרְכֵי בֵיתוֹ, וְתַלְמוּדוֹ מִשְׁתַּכֵּחַ. וְיָדַעְתָּ כִּי שָׁלוֹם אָהֳלֶךָ. בִּזְמַן שֶׁיֵּשׁ לְךָ אֹהֶל, וְאֵין אָהֳלוֹ אֶלָּא אִשְׁתּוֹ,* שֶׁנֶּאֱמַר "שׁוּבוּ לָכֶם לְאָהֳלֵיכֶם". וְאֵין פּוֹקְדָהּ. בְּתַשְׁמִישׁ, בְּעֵת עוֹנָתָהּ. כִּי שָׁלוֹם אָהֳלֶךָ. שֶׁלֵּימָה בְּיִרְאַת שָׁמַיִם. בְּשָׁעָה שֶׁיּוֹצֵא לַדֶּרֶךְ. מִשּׁוּם שֶׁמִּתְאַוָּה לוֹ בְּאוֹתָהּ שָׁעָה יוֹתֵר. תְּשׁוּקָתֵךְ. תַּאֲוָתֵךְ. ה"ג. לֹא נִצְרְכָה אֶלָּא סָמוּךְ לְוֶוסְתָּהּ. [אע"ג] דַּאֲמוּר רַבָּנַן (שבועות דף יח:) חַיָּיב אָדָם לִפְרוֹשׁ מֵאִשְׁתּוֹ וכו', וַאפ"ה כְּשֶׁיּוֹצֵא לַדֶּרֶךְ – יִפְקְדֶנָּה. עוֹנָה. אִם רְגִילָה לִרְאוֹת בַּיּוֹם – אֲסוּרָה כָּל הַיּוֹם, וְאִם רְגִילָה לִרְאוֹת בַּלַּיְלָה – אֲסוּרָה כָּל הַלַּיְלָה. וה"מ. דְּחַיָּיב לְפוֹקְדָהּ, כִּי אָזֵל לִדְבַר הָרְשׁוּת. אֲבָל לִדְבַר מִצְוָה – לָא, מִשּׁוּם דְּטָרִיד בְּמִצְוָה, אִי נַמִי: מִיטְרִיד בְּתַשְׁמִישׁ, וִיבַטֵּל מִמִּצְוָה. יוֹתֵר מִגּוּפוֹ. דְּזִילוּתָא דְּאִיתְּתָא קָשָׁה מִדְּגַבְרָא. וְהַנּוֹשֵׂא בַּת אֲחוֹתוֹ. גַּעְגּוּעֵי אָדָם רַבִּין עַל אֲחוֹתוֹ יוֹתֵר מִן אָחִיו, וּמִתּוֹךְ כָּךְ נִמְצָא מְחַבֵּב אֶת אִשְׁתּוֹ.

תורה אור

[לקמן ע. קדושין ז.]
[תוספתא פ"ח]
[בשאלתות פרשת הברכה איתא לר' אבא בר זבדא]
[מ"ק ז:]

הגהות הב"ח

(א) רש"י ד"ה איעקר וכו' ונעקרים כדאיתא לקמן דף סד ע"ב הס"ד: (ב) תוס' ד"ה חייב וכו' ויפקדנה (או בתשמיש או) תא"מ. ונ"ב ס"א אינו ואפשר לייחד דה"פ זה אינו תשמיש עכ"פ ואפילו סמוך לווסתה אלא או בתשמיש כשהווסת רחוק או בשאר דרכיה וחיבוק ונשיקה: (ג) ד"ה סמוך וכו' כדאמרינן לקמן ג"ב דף סט ע"ב והטיקר בר"פ חרש דף קיג כל"ה שמא:

הגהות הגר"א

[א] גמ' וברתא לברתא. נ"ב גי' הרמב"ם אבל ברתא לברתא וברתא לברא לא א"ל כו' ובזה מתורץ קושיות תוס' ד"ה וכ"ש:

גליון הש"ס

גמ' מנא הא מילתא דאמור רבנן בני בנים הרי הן כבנים. עיין יומא דף סו ע"ב ולעיל דף יז ע"א וכפרי רש"י בחומש בראשית כ י"ב ובמ"ב ח כו ובדק"ט בראשית טו י ול"ע ובראשית כ"ט ש"ב יט כה ובמהרש"א ח"א סוף סוטה ד"ה אל תקרין:

תוספות ישנים

חייב אדם לפקוד אשתו בשעה שיוצא לדרך. פ"ה שהפקידה היא בתשמיש ולא נהירא לה דהא מוקי לה תלמודא בסמוך לווסתה ...

לאשתו נדה וא"כ אין יכול להיות תשמיש לכן נ"ל לפוקדה בדברי ריצוי והכי ר"ל וכמה יש לפוקדה עונה וכ"מ (בנדרים) [בעירובין ס"ג] דשייך פקידה בדברים אפילו באשתו נדה דקאמר כל הישן בקילעא שאיש ואשתו ישנים עליו הכתוב אומר ואת נשי עמי תגרשון מבית תענוגיה ומוקים לה תלמודא אפילו באשתו נדה דסד"א דחיישינן שמא ירגילנו בדבר עבירה קמ"ל דלא חיישינן וגם ר"ל [כאן] הכי אע"ג דאמור רבנן חייב אדם לפרוש מאשתו סמוך לווסתה וסד"א שמא יבעול מתוך רבוי דברים ויעבור על דת מצות חכמים [קמ"ל]: **והמלוה** סלע לעני בשעת דחקו פירשתי בסנהדרין פרק אלו הנשרפין: **והנושא** בת אחותו לפי שהיא בת גילו כדאמרינן רוב בנים דומין לאחי

והמלוה סלע לעני בשעת דחקו — עליו הכתוב אומר "אז תקרא וה' יענה תשוע ויאמר הנני".§ סי' אש"ה וקרק"ע עז"ר זא"ת שת"י הברכו"ת תגר"י פחת"י.§ א"ר אלעזר: כל אדם שאין לו אשה — אינו אדם, שנאמר "זכר ונקבה בראם ויקרא את שמם אדם". ואמר רבי אלעזר: כל אדם שאין לו קרקע — אינו אדם, שנא' "השמים שמים לה' והארץ נתן לבני אדם". ואמר רבי אלעזר: מאי דכתיב "אעשה לו עזר כנגדו", *זכה — עוזרתו, לא זכה — כנגדו. ואיכא דאמרי: ר' אלעזר רמי, כתיב "כנגדו" וקרינן "כניגדו", זכה — כנגדו, לא זכה — מנגדתו. אשכחיה רבי יוסי לאליהו, א"ל: כתיב "אעשה לו עזר", במה אשה עוזרתו לאדם? א"ל: אדם מביא חיטין — חיטין כוסס? פשתן — פשתן לובש? לא נמצאת מאירה עיניו ומעמידתו על רגליו?! וא"ר אלעזר: מאי דכתיב "זאת הפעם עצם מעצמי ובשר מבשרי" מלמד שבא אדם על כל בהמה וחיה ולא נתקררה דעתו עד שבא על חוה. ואמר ר' אלעזר: מאי דכתיב "ונברכו בך כל משפחות האדמה" אמר ליה הקב"ה לאברהם: שתי ברכות טובות יש לי להבריך בך: רות המואביה ונעמה העמונית. "כל משפחות האדמה" אפילו משפחות הדרות באדמה אין מתברכות אלא בשביל ישראל. "כל גויי הארץ" — אפילו ספינות הבאות מגליא לאספמיא אינן מתברכות אלא בשביל ישראל. ואמר רבי אלעזר: עתידים כל בעלי אומניות שיעמדו על הקרקע, שנאמר "וירדו מאניותיהם כל תופשי משוט מלחים כל חבלי הים *על הארץ יעמדו". ואמר ר' אלעזר: אין לך אומנות פחותה מן הקרקע, שנאמר "וירדו". רבי אלעזר חזיא להההיא ארעא דשדי ביה כרבא לפותיא, א"ל: אי תשדייה לאורכיך — הפוכי בעיסקא טב מינך. רב על לביני שיבלי, חזנהו דקא נייפן. אמר להו: אי נייפת איתנופי, הפוכי בעיסקא טב מינך. אמר רבא: מאה זוזי בעיסקא — כל יומא בשרא וחמרא, מאה זוזי בארעא — מילחא וחפורה. ולא עוד אלא מגניא ליה אארעא ומרמיא ליה תיגרי. אמר רב פפא: זרע ולא תזבין. אע"ג דכי הדדי נינהו — הני מברכן. זבין ולא *תיזול, הני מילי — ביסתרקי. אבל גלימא — לא מיתרמיא ליה. (א) טום ולא תשפיץ, שפוץ ולא תיבני, *שכל העוסק בבנין מתמסכן. קפוץ זבין ארעא, מתון נסיב איתתא, נחית דרגא נסיב איתתא, סק דרגא בחר שושבינא. א"ר אלעזר *בר אבינא: *אין פורענות באה לעולם אלא בשביל ישראל, שנאמר "הכרתי גוים נשמו פנותם החרבתי חוצותם" וכתיב "אמרתי אך תיראי אותי תקחי מוסר". רב הוה מיפטר מרבי חייא, אמר ליה: רחמנא ליצלך ממידי דקשה ממותא. ומי איכא מידי דקשה ממותא? נפק, דק ואשכח "ומוצא אני מר ממות את האשה וגו'". רב הוה קא מצערא ליה דביתהו, כי אמר לה "עבידי לי *טלופחי" עבדא ליה חימצי, "חימצי" — עבדא ליה טלופחי. כי גדל חייא בריה, אפיך לה. אמר ליה: איעליא לך אמך! אמר ליה: אנא הוא דקא אפיכנא לה. אמר ליה: היינו דקא אמרי אינשי: דנפיק מינך — טעמא מלפך. את לא תעביד הכי, *שנאמר "למדו לשונם דבר שקר העוה וגו'". רבי חייא הוה קא מצערא ליה דביתהו. כי הוה משכח מידי — צייר ליה בסודריה, ומייתי ניהלה. אמר ליה רב: והא קא מצערא ליה למר! א"ל: דיינו שמגדלות בנינו, ומצילות אותנו מן

תורה אור: ישעיה נח; בראשית ה; תהלים קטו; בראשית ב; שם ב; שם יב; שם יח; יחזקאל כז; צפניה ג; שם; קהלת ז; ירמיה ט

רש"י

אז תקרא. לעיל מיניה כתיב "כי תראה ערום וכסיתו" — היינו דוחק העני. "ומבשרך לא תתעלם" — היינו אוהב את שכניו שהן כקרוביו, ומקרב את קרוביו, ונושא בת אחותו. כנגדו. חלוקה עליו וסותרת דבריו. מנגדתו. מדלא כתיב יו"ד, לשון נגדא דמלקות(ב). חטים כוסס. בתמיה(ג). זאת הפעם. מכלל דפעמים אחרים שמש, ולא עלו בדעתו. שתי ברכות. כמו: מבריך את הגפן (כלאים פ"ז מ"א). רות המואביה ונעמה העמונית. יצאו מהם מלכים ונביאים. נעמה — אמו של רחבעם, ויצא ממנה חזקיה ואסא ויהושפט דהוו צדיקים גמורים, וישעיהו הנביא. דאמר מר: אמוץ ואמציה אחים הוו (מגילה דף י:). שיעמדו על הקרקע. יניחו אומנותם לעסוק בחריש ובקציר: וירדו מאניותיהם כל תופשי משוט אל הארץ יעמדו. וירדו. לשון ירידת עניות. דשדי בה כרבא. זרע כרוב. לישנא אחרינא: כרבא — חרישה, כמו: כרוב ותני (ב"ב דף יב.), כמה דמסיק תעלא מבי כרבא (נדה דף סה:). לפותיא. לרוחב הערוגה. אי תשדייה לאורכיך. כלומר: אפילו תחזור ותחרשנה — לא יועיל כלום לפי עסקא. דהפוכי בעסקא טוב. להרויח יותר. דקא נייפן. הרוח מנשבת זו בזו. אי תניפנו. כמה שתרצו תנופפו, אין תועלת בהן לפי פרקמטיא. תניפנו — לשון הניפי לי במניפה (ב"מ דף פו.). חפורה. שחת שעכרה מועט ואוכל עשבים וחזיז במלח. חפורה. ירק מן התבואה עד שלא הביאה שליש. מגניא ליה אארעא. [משכבת אותו על הארץ], לשמור כל הלילה: [ומרמיא ליה תיגרי. בשבילה מתקוטט עם בני אדם]. זרע. תבואה לאכילת ביתך. ולא תזבון. לא תקנה תבואה מן השוק. ואע"ג דכי הדדי נינהו. אפילו חיטין בזול וקרקעך אינו חשוב, ואין לך שכר(ד) לפי השעה — אפ"ה הני מתברכין, ברכה מצויה בדבר שאין לוקח בדמים ואין כלה מהר. ברכה. פליסו"ן בלע"ז. זבן ולא תיזול. מכור כלי תשמישך והשתמש בדמים בפרקמטיא, קודם שתבא לידי עניות. ביסתרקי. כלי הבית, טאפי"ט בלע"ז. אבל גלימא. שהיא להתכבד בלבישתה — לא ימכור, דלמא כי הדר בעי לה לא מתרמיא ליה הגונה כמותה. טום. תרגום של סתום, כמו "סתמום פלשתים" (בראשית כו) — טומינון פלשתאי טום ולא תשפוץ אם יש לך חור קטן בכותל רעוע — סתום אותו מיד, ולא תרחיב בנקב לשפץ בו טיט ולבנים הרבה ליפותו. שפוץ. פלסטי"ר בלע"ז. ואם בעל נפש אתה להנאות בנייניך — הרחב הנקב ושפציהו להיות יפה. ולא תיבני. לא תפיל את כל הכותל ותבנהו. מתון נסיב איתתא. המתן עד שתבדוק מעשיה, שלא תהא רעה וקנטרנית. נחית דרגא ונסיב איתתא. לא תקח אשה חשובה ממך, שמא לא תתקבל עליה. שושבינא. אוהב טוב, בחר לך אדם חשוב להדבק אחריו. בשביל ישראל. ליראם, כדי שיחזרו בתשובה. חימצי. מין קטנית. אפיך לה. היה אומר האב לבנו: אמור לאמך לעשות עדשים, והוא אומר לה: עשי חימצי, והיא עושה עדשים. טעמא מלפך. פעמים שהבן מחכים את אביו, אני היה לי לעשות כן(ה). אבל אתה. דבר שקר הוא, וכתיב "למדו לשונם דבר שקר". כי הוה משכח מידי. דבר הראוי לה. מן

תוספות

המלוה סלע לעני בשעת דחקו. מקשה ר"ת: דבפ"ק דחגיגה (דף ה. ושם) אמר "ומצאוהו (ו) צרות רבות ורעות" — זה הממציא מעות לעני בשעת דחקו? ואומר ר"ת: דהתם מיירי ששואל ממנו המושל מס, וזקוק למכור ביתו או שדהו על כך, וזה ממציא לו מעות. ואם לא היה מוצא למכור היו מקילין מעליו. והיינו צרות רבות, שצריך למכור בזול ומפסיד הכל. ומסיק עלה: דהיינו דאמרי אינשי: זוזא לעצלא לא שכיח, כלו': לקנות תבואה אין ממציאין לו מעות, לתליתא שכיח — כשדוחקין אותו למכור, כמו תליוהו וזבין (ב"ב דף מז:). ורש"י פירש שם בענין אחר.

אפילו ספינות הבאות מגליא לאספמיא. מ"כל" דריש, שבא לרבות אפילו הנך שאין עומדים אלא מעט בארץ. **שאין** לך אומנות פחותה כו'. אף על גב דרבי אלעזר גופיה קאמר לעיל כל אדם שאין לו קרקע אינו אדם — צריך לומר קרקע לבנות עליו, שידור בו, וגם לצורך מזונותיו, כדאמר רב פפא בסמוך: זרע ולא תזבון והכא מיירי באדם שעיקר אומנותו בקרקע. **זבין** ולא תיזול. פי' בקונטרס לשון דלות, כלומר: מכור כלי תשמישך קודם שתעני. וקשה: דמאי שנא דנקט ביסתרקי טפי משאר מילי? ונראה לר"ת כפירוש ר"ח: דתיזול ענין אריגה, כמו סתר זוללי בשוקא (חולין ס.) כלומר: קנה בגדים ולא תארוג, כי יותר תרויח בקנין מבאריגה. אבל גלימא — טוב לארוג, דאימור לא מיתרמי ליה כרצונו.

תוספות ישנים

לאחי האם י"מ [דנקט אחותו] דלאחותו לא מציא למטרח להשיאה אבל לא נקט בת אחיו דלאחיו טרח ומשיאה וי"מ דווקא בת אחותו אבל לא בת אחיו דאתי להפקיע מצות יבום: **אין** לך [אומנות] פחותה מקרקע וא"ת והא איהו קאמר לעיל כל אדם שאין לו קרקע אינו אדם י"ל לדירתו יש לו לקנות או גם להשתכר למזונות (בנין) [ביתו] אבל להיות בה כל אומנתו אינו עושה כהוגן שאין לך אומנות פחותה מקרקע להיות בה כל עיקר מלאכתו: **זבין** ולא תידול. פי' מכור כלי תשמישך קודם שתהיה עני ולא נהירא דמאי קאמר ה"מ ביסתרקי אבל גלימא לא הרי יש לו למכור כל אשר לו קודם שיהיה עני ונראה לפרש כדאמרינן באלו טרפות סתר דולי בשוקא ור"ל זבין ולא תידול כלומר קנה בגדים ארוגים ולא תארוג שרגילות יותר למצוא בזול לקנות מלארוג וה"מ ביסתרקי אבל גלימא לא דודאי גלימא יש לו לארוג בביתו דלמא לא מתרמיא לה עשויה כתיקנה היטב כפי מדתו:

עין משפט נר מצוה

קג א טוש"ע אה"ע סי' א סעיף א בהג"ה:
קד ב מיי' פ"ה מהלכות דעות הלכה י:

הגהות הב"ח

(א) גמ' לא מתרמיא ליה כדבעי טום ולא: (ב) רש"י ד"ה מנגדתו וכו' דמלקות הוא הס"ד: (ג) ד"ה חיטין כוסס בתמיה וכי אדם אוכל חיטין כמות שהן ולובש פשתן כמות שהוא הס"ד: (ד) ד"ה ואע"ג וכו' שכר (לפי השעה) תא"מ ונ"ב ס"א בעבודת הקרקע לפי השער: (ה) ד"ה טעמא וכו' אבל וכו' שקר הוא לך וכתיב כצ"ל והד"א: (ו) תוס' ד"ה המלוה וכו' ומצאוהו רעות רבות וצרות זה:

[בערובין סג. פרש"י ד"ה זכה אם יש לו מזל טוב]

[ג"ל אלו]

[גירסת הערוך תידול ע"ש דמבואר ראיה כמו דוללא בשוקא חולין ס.]

[סוטה יא.]

[בילקוט ליתא ואם כן שפיר כולל הך מימרא דרבי אלעזר בהדי הנך מימרות דר"א לעיל וג"ל ואמר ר"א אין וכו']

[שבת קלט. ע"ש ב"ב ח. ע"ש]

[ונזיר עדשים תרגום ותבשיל דטלופחין]

סוכה מו:

עין משפט
נר מצוה

קה א טוש"ע אה"ע סי' א סעיף א בהג"ה:
קו ב ג שם סעיף א:
קז ד מיי' פט"ו מהלכות אישות הלכה ג טור ש"ע שם סעיף ד:

מסורת הש"ס

מן החטא. הרהור עבירה. עבורי מיעברא במלה. נוחה לרצות, ומעברת על מדותיה. פומא. לקלל ולגדף עד זמן סעודה, כדי לצערו. ומהדרא ליה גבא. שלא לאכול עמו, ולצערו. מתפקקין. נסתמין. לשון "ויפק", כמו "פוקקין הנקבים" (שבת דף קכה:). צרתה בצדה. ישא אחרת עליה. בחברתה. מקבלת תוכחה יותר. בסילתא. קוץ. סגריר. יום גשם ורוח. דלף טורד וגו' ואשת מדינים נשתוה. שוין הן. תלוין בכספו. שאין לו זריעה בקרקע, דכל שעה מיצר ודואג שמא תייקר התבואה או ינעלו שערי שבר. אין אלהים. מי שאמר "אין אלהים" קרי תורה אור נבל. חברי. פרסיים רשעים ומבזין, ואינם מכירים כבודם של ישראל. שגא. כסף נסל, מרוב צער שהיו בני הישיבה מסורים בידם. אמרו ליה מקבלי שוחדא. לבטל גזירתא. תריץ. יתיב, *ושמח. אמרו ליה על שלשה גזרו. אמר להם: מפני שלשה עבירות שהיו ביד בני בבל. גזרו על הבשר. שלא יאכלו בשר שחוטה: אמר להם – מפני עבירה שבידם, שהיו גוזלים מתנות כהונה, זרוע ולחיים וקיבה. [ועל המרחצאות מפני הטבילה. שלא היו זהירין בה. מחטטי שכבי. מוציאים הנקברים מקבריהם]. ששמחים ביום אידם. באה עליהם זו הגזרה להתחבל בה. בכם ובאבותיכם. ואבותם כבר מתו, ומה מכה יש בהן? [אלא] חטוטי שכבי. וכתיב ונבחר מות מחיים. בתריה דהאי קרא, דהואיל ואין ניתנים לקבורה – היאך יבחרו החיים למות? א"ל. האי נבחר לא קאמר שיהו הן בוחרין מות מחיים, אלא נביא הוא דקאמר להו: מוטב להן לרשעים שימותו ממה שיחטאו ויחיו. מספר ימיו כפלים. כלומר: שמח בחלקו, ודומה לו כאילו ימיו כפלים. מאשת חן. של אחרים. רוכל. המוכר בשמים לנשים להתקשט בהן, ומצוי בו ניאוף, ובא בעלה ופלעו. כניצוץ אש המבעיר גחלת. כן יצרו מבעירו. ככלוב. קן עופות. מחר מת. ואיננו בעולם, ולא ירצה אותה דאגה שהוא מיצר ויגרא ודואג עליה, ונמצא שנצטער אתמול על עולם שאין שלו. גוף. פרגוד שחוצץ בין שכינה למלאכים, ושם רוחות ונשמות נתונות, שנבראו מששת ימי בראשית העתידות להנתן בגופים העתידים להבראות. שנאמר כי רוח מלפני יעטוף. הגאולה, ונשמות שאני עשיתי(ג). יעטוף. לשון עכבה, כדכתיב (בראשית ל) "והיה העטופים ללבן". ורישיה משתעי בגאולה – "כי לא לעולם אריב" וגו'. ואתם פרו ורבו. בתריה דתרוייהו כתיב, הלכך – כמו שעשה שתיהן הוא.

מתני'

צרתה בצדה. רבא לטעמיה דאמר בסוף פירקין (לקמן סה.): נושא אדם כמה נשים על אשתו.

שיתקיים ע"י אחרים. אע"ג דמשמע בפרק "אע"פ" (כתובות דף סג. וסח) אגנא דחו של ר"ע. דקאמר התם ברתיה של ר"ע עבדא ליה לבן עזאי הכי – הא אמר בפ"ק דסוטה (דף ד:) דנשא וגירש. יוליא

תוספות ישנים

אתו חברי לבבל שגא פל מפורש בשבת (פ"ק) [דף מה:]

מן החטא. *מקרי ליה רב יהודה לרב יצחק בריה: °"ומוצא אני מר ממות את האשה". א"ל: כגון מאן? כגון אמך. (א) והא *מתני ליה רב יהודה לרב יצחק בריה: אין אדם מוצא קורת רוח אלא מאשתו ראשונה, שנאמר °"יהי מקורך ברוך ושמח מאשת נעוריך". וא"ל: כגון מאן? כגון אמך. מתקיף תקיפא, ועבורי מיעברא במלה. היכי דמי אשה רעה? אמר אביי: מקשטא ליה תכא, ומקשטא ליה פומא. רבא אמר: מקשטא ליה תכא, ומהדרא ליה גבא. אמר רבי חמא בר חנינא: אכיון שנשא אדם אשה – עונותיו מתפקקין, שנאמר °"מצא אשה מצא טוב ויפק רצון מה'". *במערבא, כי נסיב אינש איתתא אמרי ליה הכי: מצא או מוצא? מצא – דכתיב "מצא אשה מצא טוב", "מוצא" – דכתיב "ומוצא אני מר ממות את האשה". אמר רבא: אשה רעה מצוה לגרשה, דכתיב °"גרש לץ ויצא מדון וישבות דין וקלון". ואמר רבא: אשה רעה וכתובתה מרובה – צרתה בצדה, דאמרי אינשי: בחברתה ולא בסילתא. ואמר רבא: קשה אשה רעה כיום סגריר, שנאמר °"דלף טורד ביום סגריר ואשת מדינים נשתוה". ואמר רבא: בא וראה כמה טובה אשה טובה – וכמה רעה אשה רעה. כמה טובה אשה טובה – דכתיב "מצא אשה מצא טוב". אי בגופה משתעי קרא – כמה טובה אשה טובה שהכתוב משבחה, אי בתורה משתעי קרא – כמה טובה אשה טובה שהתורה נמשלה בה. כמה רעה אשה רעה – דכתיב "ומוצא אני מר ממות את האשה". אי בגופה משתעי קרא – כמה רעה אשה רעה שהכתוב מגנה, אי בגיהנם משתעי קרא – כמה רעה אשה רעה, שגיהנם נמשלה בה. °"הנני מביא רעה אשר לא יוכלו לצאת ממנה". אמר רב נחמן אמר רבה בר אבוה: זו אשה רעה וכתובתה מרובה. °"נתנני ה' בידי לא אוכל קום" אמר רב חסדא אמר מר עוקבא בר חייא: זו אשה רעה וכתובתה מרובה. במערבא אמרו: זה שמזונותיו תלוין בכספו. °"בניך ובנותיך נתונים לעם אחר" *אמר רב חנן בר רבא אמר רב: זו אשת האב. °"בגוי נבל אכעיסם" אמר רב חנן בר רבא אמר רב: זו אשה רעה וכתובתה מרובה. רבי אליעזר אומר: אלו המינים. וכן הוא אומר °"אמר נבל בלבו אין אלהים וגו'". במתניתא תנא: אלו אנשי ברבריא ואנשי מרטנאי, שמהלכין ערומים בשוק. שאין לך משוקץ ומתועב לפני המקום יותר ממי שמהלך בשוק ערום. רבי יוחנן אמר: אלו חברים. אמרו ליה לר' יוחנן: אתו חברי לבבל, שגא נפל. אמרו ליה: מקבלי שוחדא. תריץ יתיב. גזרו על ג' מפני ג'; גזרו על הבשר – מפני המתנות, גזרו על המרחצאות – מפני הטבילה, קא מחטטי שכבי – מפני ששמחים ביום אידם, שנאמר °"והיתה יד ה' בכם ובאבותיכם", אמר רבה בר שמואל: זו חטוטי שכבי, דאמר מר: בעון חיים – מתים מתחטטין. א"ל רבא לרבה בר מארי: כתיב °"לא יאספו ולא יקברו לדומן על פני האדמה יהיו" וכתיב °"ונבחר מות מחיים". אמר ליה: נבחר מות לרשעים, שלא יחיו בעולם הזה ויחטאו ויפלו בגיהנם. *כתוב בספר בן סירא: "אשה טובה – מתנה טובה(ב) לבעלה". וכתיב "טובה בחיק ירא אלהים תנתן. אשה רעה – צרעת לבעלה". מאי תקנתיה – יגרשנה ויתרפא מצרעתו. "אשה יפה אשרי בעלה, מספר ימיו כפלים". "העלם עיניך מאשת חן פן תלכד במצודתה. אל תט אצל בעלה למסוך עמו יין ושכר, כי בתואר אשה יפה רבים הושחתו, ועצומים כל הרוגיה". "רבים היו פצעי רוכל המרגילים לדבר ערוה, כניצוץ מבעיר גחלת, ככלוב מלא עוף כן בתיהם מלאים מרמה", "אל תצר צרת מחר כי לא תדע מה ילד יום, שמא מחר בא ואיננו, נמצא מצטער על העולם שאין שלו". "מנע רבים מתוך ביתך, ולא הכל תביא ביתך. רבים יהיו דורשי שלומך, גלה סוד לאחד מאלף". *אמר רבי אסי: אין בן דוד בא עד שיכלו כל הנשמות שבגוף שנאמר °"כי רוח מלפני יעטוף ונשמות אני עשיתי". תניא, רבי אליעזר אומר: בכל מי שאין עוסק בפריה ורביה – כאילו שופך דמים שנאמר °"שופך דם האדם באדם דמו ישפך" וכתיב בתריה "ואתם פרו ורבו". רבי *יעקב אומר: גכאילו ממעט הדמות, שנאמר °"כי בצלם אלהים עשה את האדם" וכתיב בתריה "ואתם פרו וגו'". בן עזאי אומר: כאילו שופך דמים, וממעט הדמות, שנאמר "ואתם פרו ורבו". אמרו לו לבן עזאי: יש נאה דורש ונאה מקיים, נאה מקיים ואין נאה דורש. ואתה – נאה דורש ואין נאה מקיים! אמר להן בן עזאי: ומה אעשה דשנפשי חשקה בתורה, אפשר לעולם שיתקיים על ידי אחרים. תניא אידך, רבי אליעזר אומר: כל מי שאין עוסק בפריה ורביה – כאילו שופך דמים, שנאמר "שופך דם האדם" וסמיך ליה "ואתם פרו וגו'". רבי אלעזר בן עזריה אומר: כאילו ממעט הדמות, בן עזאי אומר: וכו'. אמרו לו לבן עזאי יש נאה דורש וכו'. *ת"ר: °"ובנחה יאמר שובה ה' רבבות אלפי ישראל" מלמד

הגהות הב"ח

(א) כגון אמך איני והא מתני: (ב) שם מתנה טובה בחיק ירא כצ"ל ותיבות לבעלה וכתיב טובה נמחק: (ג) רש"י ד"ה שנאמר כי רוח וכו' שאני עשיתי יעטוף ומסיפא לרישיה מידרש:

[סנהדרין כב:] קהלת ז
שם. משלי ה
ס"א וסמך שם יח
ברכות ח. שם כב
שם כז
ירמיה יח
איכה א
דברים כח
שם נז. ע"ש שם לב
תהלים יד
ש"א יב
ירמיה ח
שם
[סנהדרין ק: ע"ש]
לעיל סב. ע"ז ה. נדה יג: ישעיה נז
[בילקוט ובע"י איתא רבי עקיבא וכן איתא בשאלתות פ' נח סימן ה וע"ע תוספתא פ"ח] בראשית ט
שם
[ב"ק פג. ע"ש] במדבר י

מלמד שאין השכינה שורה על פחות משני אלפים ושני רבבות מישראל. הרי שהיו ישראל שני אלפים ושני רבבות חסר אחד, וזה לא עסק בפריה ורביה — לא נמצא זה גורם לשכינה שתסתלק מישראל?! אבא חנן אמר משום רבי אליעזר: חייב מיתה, שנאמר "ובנים לא היו להם" הא היו להם בנים — לא מתו. אחרים אומרים: גורם לשכינה שתסתלק מישראל, שנאמר "להיות לך לאלהים ולזרעך אחריך", בזמן שזרעך אחריך — שכינה שורה, אין זרעך אחריך — על מי שורה, על העצים ועל האבנים?!.§

מתני' [א]נשא אשה ושהה עמה עשר שנים ולא ילדה — אינו רשאי לבטל. [ב]גירשה — מותרת לינשא לאחר, ורשאי השני לשהות עמה י' שנים. ואם הפילה — מונה משעה שהפילה.§

גמ' ת"ר: *נשא אשה ושהה עמה עשר שנים ולא ילדה — יוציא ויתן כתובה, שמא לא זכה להבנות ממנה. אע"פ שאין ראיה לדבר — זכר לדבר: "מקץ עשר שנים לשבת אברם בארץ כנען" ללמדך שאין ישיבת חו"ל עולה לו מן המנין. [ג]לפיכך, חלה הוא או שחלתה היא, או שניהם חבושים בבית האסורים — אין עולין לו מן המנין. א"ל רבא לרב נחמן: ולילף מיצחק, דכתיב "ויהי יצחק בן ארבעים שנה בקחתו את רבקה וגו'" וכתיב "ויצחק בן ששים שנה בלדת אותם"! א"ל: יצחק עקור היה. — א"ה, אברהם נמי עקור היה! ההוא מיבעי ליה לכדר' חייא בר אבא. *דא"ר חייא בר אבא א"ר יוחנן: למה נמנו שנותיו של ישמעאל — כדי לייחס בהן שנותיו של יעקב. אמר רבי יצחק: יצחק אבינו עקור היה, שנאמר "ויעתר יצחק לה' לנכח אשתו", "על אשתו" לא נאמר, אלא "לנוכח" מלמד ששניהם עקורים היו. א"ה "ויעתר לו" "ויעתר להם" מיבעי ליה! לפי שאינו דומה תפלת צדיק בן צדיק לתפלת צדיק בן רשע. א"ר יצחק: מפני מה היו אבותינו עקורים — *מפני שהקב"ה מתאוה לתפלתן של צדיקים. *א"ר יצחק: למה *) נמשלה תפלתן של צדיקים כעתר — מה עתר זה מהפך התבואה ממקום למקום, כך תפלתן של צדיקים מהפכת מדותיו של הקב"ה ממדת רגזנות למדת רחמנות. אמר רבי אמי: אברהם ושרה טומטמין היו, שנאמר "הביטו אל צור חצבתם

*) סוכה יד. ע"ש

רש"י

מתני' אינו רשאי לבטל. אלא: או יגרשנה, או ישא אחרת עמה. מותרת לינשא לאחר. ולא אמרינן עקרה היא, דשמא הראשון לא זכה ליבנות ממנה. **גמ'** מקץ עשר שנים. בא על הגר. והאי דלא נסיב לה בהנך שני קמאי, עד שלא בא לארץ כנען שהיו שנים מרובות בפדן ארם — ללמדך שאין ישיבת חוצה לארץ עולה לו, דלמא משום עון חוצה לארץ הם עקורים. לפיכך. הואיל וקא חזינן שאין ישיבת חוצה לארץ מן המנין, דתלינן בכל דבר המונען מן ההריון תלה הוא או תלתה היא כו'. ולילף מיצחק. ששהה עשרים שנה ולא נשא אחרת. עקור היה. ויודע שמחמת עצמו הוא, ולקמן נפקא לן דעקור היה. אברהם נמי עקור היה. כדאמרינן לקמן, והיכי ילפת מיניה? ההוא מיבעי ליה כו'. כלומר: יצחק עקור היה, משום הכי לא נסיב אחריתי. וקרא דיצחק בן ששים שנה לא יתירא הוא, דתימא להכי כתביה רחמנא למיגמר מיניה שהיית עשרים שנה, דההוא מיבעי ליה כו'. אבל מקץ עשר שנים דאברהם, אע"ג דעקור הוה — ילפינן מיניה. דאי לאו לדרשא, למאי הלכתא קמשמעינן קרא "מקץ עשר שנים"? לייחס בהן. לידע שנותיו של יעקב, בן כמה שנים היה כשהלך לבית עבר, וכשעמד על הבאר. ובשלהי *גמרא דמגילה (דף יז.) מפרש לה. והאי קרא ד"יצחק בן ששים שנה" מייתי ליה התם, דילפינן מיניה דגדול תלמוד תורה מכיבוד אב ואם, שכל אותן שנים שהיה יעקב בבית עבר לא נענש עליהם. ויעתר להם מיבעי ליה. בשלמא אי אמרת תפלת יצחק על אשתו היתה — היינו דכתיב "ויעתר לו" כמו שהיה מתפלל עליה, "ותהר רבקה אשתו". אלא אי אמרת על עצמו היה מתפלל, ו"לנוכח אשתו" משמע ששניהם היו צועקים זה מול זה, ויעתר להם מיבעי ליה. לפי שאינו דומה. תפלתו, שהיה צדיק בן צדיק, לתפלתה, שהיתה צדקת בת רשע. לפיכך תלה בו הכתוב. עתר. פל"א (א) בלע"ז. [מ]ושפם

תוספות

יוציא ויתן כתובה. בסוף "המדיר" (כתובות עז. ושם) איכא פלוגתא דאמוראי כשנשא אשה ושהה עמה עשר שנים, אם כופין אותו להוציא אם לאו. וקשה: דלמ"ד אין כופין — תקשי ליה מהכא דקתני "יוציא", ולשון יוציא — משמע בכפיה, כדמשמע התם, דאמר רב: האומר איני זן ואיני מפרנס — יוציא ויתן כתובה. ופריך עליה שמואל: עד שכופין אותו להוציא יכפוהו לזון.(א) ונראה דלא משמע יוציא *לכפיה — אלא היכא שעושה לאשה שלא כדין, אבל הכא שאינו אלא משום דאינו רשאי לבטל מפריה ורביה — לא משמע לשון כפיה. וכל הנהו ד"המדיר" (ג"ז ש) דתנן בהו: יוציא ויתן כתובה — בכפיה קאמר, כיון שמתנהג עמה שלא כדין. ולעיל ב"החולץ" (דף לט.) נמי אמרי' כשאין רוצה לא לייבם ולא לחלוץ דחוזרין אצל גדול למיכפייה, לפי שמתנהג עמה שלא כדין, שאינו רוצה לא לכנוס ולא לפטור. ונראה דכופין אותו בשוטים. דאי במילי — הא אמר בסוף "המדיר" (כתובות עז. ושם) ד"בדברים לא יוסר עבד". ותימה: דכי פריך ב"המדיר" למאן דאמר כופין בנשא אשה ושהה עמה עשר שנים, דלתניי' בהדי אלו שכופין אותו להוציא — תקשי ליה נמי מכל הנהו דתנן ב"המדיר" (ג"ז שם), והיא ד"נערה שנתפתתה" (שם מח.) דהאומר אי אפשי אלא אני בבגדי והיא בבגדה — יוציא ויתן כתובה, וההוא דסוף פירקין (לקמן דף סה.) דאמר ר' אמי: הנושא אשה על אשתו — יוציא ויתן כתובה? וי"ל: דלא קתני הנך דאתייה כפייה דידהו על ידי פשיעת בעל, אלא הנהו דאתיין ממילא, כגון מוכה שחין ובעל פוליפוס. והא דקתני מצרף ומקמץ ובורסי, אע"פ שנעשו אחר שנשאו — הנהו אין מתכוונים להקניט ולצער את האשה. ומיהו, קשיא: דליתני בזה מחמת טענה, דאמר בסוף פרקין (שם:) דכופין אותו להוציא, אע"פ שאין פושע — דמה יכול לעשות שהוא עקור? ונראה לפרש: דקתני סיפא בין שהיו עד שלא נישאו בין משנישאו, בכולן אמר ר' מאיר יכולה היא שתאמר: סבורה הייתי לקבל כו'. והכא לא שייך למיתני בה סבורה הייתי שאני יכולה לקבל. ורובן מיתרצי בההיא שנויא. ובירושלמי משמע דאין כופין *בהנהו דתנן ב"המדיר" (כתובות עז.) ור"ח הביאו בשילהי "אע"פ" (שם סג:) *וזה לשונו: בירושלמי דסוף "אלמנה ניזונית" תנינן: גט המעושה, בישראל כשר, בגוים פסול. אמר שמואל: פסול ופוסל לכהונה. ואמר שמואל: אין מעשים אלא לפסולות. *(אמר שמואל) והתנינן המדיר אשתו מלהנות כו', ומשני: שמעגו שמואלא, שמעגו שכופין? בתמיה. ש"מ דאין כופין אלא היכא דקתני כופין, אבל היכא דאמור רבנן יוציא, ולא פירשו כופין — אומרים לו: חייבוך רבנן להוציא, ואם לא הוציא — מותר לקרותו עבריינא, אבל לכפותו בשוטים — לא. וגר"ח כדברי האומר איני זן ואיני מפרנס — כופין אותו להוציא, ויתן כתובה. והיא ד"החולץ" (לעיל לט.) דחוזרים אצל גדול למכפייה — היינו טעמא דכופין לפי שמונעה מכל ענייני אישות, בין תשמיש המטה לחודיה, או משום מזונות לחודייהו — אין כופין. ומההוא עובדא דבי נשיאה בקיסרי דסוף פירקין (לקמן סה:), דקאמר רבי יוחנן: יוציא ויתן כתובה, דמשמע התם דכופין ליה — אין ראיה דכופין כל היכא דקאמר יוציא, דהתם לאו מימרא היא, אלא כשבא מעשה לפניו צוה להם שיוציא. משמע שאמר להם לכפותו, וכל היכא דלא קאמר בהדיא כופין — אין כופין, שלא יהא גט מעושה בישראל שלא כדין, ופסול. **יוציא** ויתן כתובה. נראה דבכל הנהו דתנן (כתובות עז.) שכופין אותו להוציא — שנותן כתובה אע"פ שמגרש בעל כרחו. מדפריך התם דליתני בהדייהו הך דשהה י' שנים, וקאמר הכא דאית לה כתובה. ומשמע נמי התם (שם) דהוה תני בהדייהו אלמנה לכ"ג גרושה וחלוצה לכהן הדיוט אי לאו משום דאורייתא לא קתני. והנהו אית להו כתובה, כדאמר ב"יש מותרות" (לקמן פה.) ובאה מחמת טענה אמרינן לקמן (שם) דיש לה כתובה, אע"פ שכופין אותו לגרש. ורבינו גרשום כתב בתשובה דמוכת שחין אין לה כתובה. ודקדק מדקתני גבי בורסי שנשא אשה, יכולה שתאמר כסבורה הייתי לקבל ועכשיו איני יכולה לקבל. ואם היו כופין ליתן כתובה — אם כן כל שעה תעריס ותנשא ותאמר כן כדי לגבות כתובה לאלתר? וי"ל: דשמא אותה אין לה כתובה. כיון שיכולה להעריס. אבל אחריני — יש להם כתובה. ובהדיא תני בתוספתא יוציא ויתן כתובה. **אע"פ** שאין ראיה לדבר. ראיה גמורה אינה, דמשם אין ללמוד שיהא זקוק לגרש אשתו אפילו אם אי אפשר בלא גירושין. ואדרבה, ראוי ללמוד מכאן דאפי' את"ל בעלמא הנושא אשה על אשתו יוציא ויתן כתובה — היכא דשהה עמה י' שנים שרי להכניס צרתה, כמו שמצינו באברהם, אולי ירחמו מן השמים ויזכה עדיין ליבנות ממנה, כמו שלבסוף זכה אברהם משרה. **ולילף** מיצחק. ואם תאמר: יצחק נמי לא שהה יותר מי', לפי מה שפי' שלא היתה רבקה אלא בת ג' כשנשאה, ועד שהיתה בת י"ג לא היתה ראויה להוליד? ויש לומר: דמדרשים חלוקין, כדפרישי' לעיל.* ועוד: דמוכח בפרק "בן סורר ומורה" (סנהדרין סט:) שדורות הראשונים היו ראוין להוליד הרבה קודם הזמן הזה. **אי** הכי אברהם נמי עקור היה. כדאמר לקמן אברהם ושרה טומטמים היו. ואע"פ שמסתמא כבר נקרע כשנשא שרה הכא אליבא דרבי יהודה פריך, דאמרינן ב"הערל" (לקמן פא.) טומטום שנקרע — אין מוליד. ועוד: דאפי' לרבנן נמי דפליגי עליה — לא שכיח שיוליד.

ימי

[תוספתא פ"ח]

[נ"ל פ"ח]

מגילה יז.

ישעיה נא

[חולין ס: ע"ש]

[נ"ל ואמר רבי]

[רש"ל מ"ז]

[דף סא: ד"ה וכן]

במדבר ג · בראשית יז · שם טז · שם כה · שם

הגהות הב"ח

(א) רש"י ד"ה עתר פל"א בלע"ז. נ"ב רחת והתוספות פ"ק דסוכה השיגו על פירושו וכתבו דהעיקר כמו שפי' רש"י לכאן עתר פורק"א בלע"ז דהיינו שופי"ל בלשון אשכנז שיש לו שוקלים וע"ש בדף יד ע"א:

עין משפט נר מצוה

קח א מיי' פט"ו מהל' אישות הלכה ז סמג עשין מט טוש"ע אה"ע סימן קנד סעיף י:

קט ב ג מיי' שם הלכה יא יב יד טוש"ע שם סעיף יא יב יז:

בכפיה כצ"ל. יעב"ץ

[ליתא שם]

תוספות ישנים

א) וא"ת ומאי א) מקשה התם לרב תחליפא ליתיב מהך ברייתא דתני נשא אשה ושהה עמה וכו' יוציא ויתן כתובה וכל יוציא ר"ל כופין. לכ"נ דודאי יוציא לא משמע כופין אם לא שהתלמוד מפרש בהדיא [ונראה דאין כופין] אלא בדבר שמתנהג עם האשה שלא כדין. אבל הכא אינו מתנהג שלא כדין דטעמא דאמרינן יוציא היינו משום דנכריח אותו משום שאינו רשאי ליבטל מפריה ורביה וגם ניחא דהתם פליגי אי ר"ל כופין אי לאו. ב) דודאי הכא לא ידעינן דיוציא ר"ל טופין כדפרישית ובהכי פליגי דחד אמר אין כופין ורב תחליפא אמר כופין א"נ י"ל דלכ"ע לא אמרינן יוציא כופין בשום מקום אם אינו מפרש בהדיא וגרסי' באיני זן ואיני מפרנס כופין וניחא הכל וכן משמע בירושלמי גבי גט המעושה תמן תנינן כו' עי' בתוס' מעו"ך: **מה** עתר זה מהפך את התבואה. פ"ה עתר פילא. ולא נהירא ג) דאמרי' שמהפכת הקש מעל התבואה וא"כ הוי פורקא ורחת היינו פיל"א:

א) נראה דצ"ל ועוד קשה דמאי מקשה התם לרב תחליפא ממתני' ליתיב מהך ברייתא אמתני' דתני הכא דיוציא ויתן כתובה וכו'. ב) אולי צ"ל הרי דהכא לא ידעינן אי ר"ל טופין ובהכי פליגי וכו'. ג) אולי צ"ל ולא נהירא דאמרינן בסוכה (י"ד) דעתר מהפך את התבואה כגורן וכו' וא"כ היינו פורק"א

תוספות חד מקמאי

והא דתניא שמא [לא] זכה להבנות ממנה. מקשי' עלה בגמ' ודילמא איהי היא דלא זכיא כלומר לא יתן לה כתובה ומשני איהי כיון דלא מפקדה אפריה ורביה לא מיענשא. משמע דלר' יוחנן בן ברוקא דאמר מפקדה לית לה כתובה ובשלהי פירקין גרסינן עובדא הוה קמיה ר"י בבנישתא דקסרין ואמר יוציא ויתן כתובה ואי ס"ד דלא מפקדה כתובה מאי עבידתה אלמא אי מפקדה יש לה כתובה קשיא הך. י"ל ולפרש דההיא דהבעל היה עקור תליה בדידיה ולא בדידה ואי מפקדה יש לה כתובה אבל היכא דאין הבעל עקור דאיכא למיתלא בדידה ובדידיה אמרי' אוקי ממונא בחזקת מריה ואיהי היא דלא זכאי ואין לה כתובה אי הוה מפקדה ואי לא מפקדה לא מענשא ואית לה כתובה והראב"ד פירש בהגהת ספריו דהא דמקשינן הכא ודלמא איהי היא דלא זכאי לישנא בעלמא הוא דקשיא ליה דקתני שמא לא זכה ליבנות הימנה ולא משום כתובה אקשי ליה: הוא אמר מינה והיא אמרה מיניה א"ר אמי דברים שבינו לבינה היא נאמנת מ"מ איהו קים לה בגוה כחץ איהו לא קים ליה. ה"ר אלפס פרשה בבאין לדון על עסקי כתובה וכן פרש"י ז"ל. הוא אמר מינה ולית לה כתובה והיא אמרה מיניה ואית לי כתובה (והא) וא"ר אמי היא נאמנת ויש לה כתובה. והקשה עליו הרב ר' אברהם אב"ד ואבא מרי וב"ה למה ליה למימר לאנתתיה מיניה דאינו יורה כחץ אפי' יורה כחץ יש לה כתובה שמא לא זכה ליבנות הימנה ואיהו דמפקיד מענש איהי דלא מפקדה לא מענשא וכתב הראב"ד ז"ל איכא דמתריץ דהאי גברא הוה ליה בני וכיון דאית ליה ליכא למימר לא זכה ליבנות הימנה ואיהי כיון דלא מפקדה לא מענשה בהא דכיון דלא מפקדה לא איכפת ליה ולא ענשינן ליה במידי דלא איכפת ליה. לכך פי' אבא מארי ז"ל דבבאה מחמת טענה מיירי כגון ששהתה עמו עשר שנים ולא ילדה לו והבעל יש לו בנים ולא מפקינן מניה מידי. אלא היא בעיא למיפק מיניה דבעינא חוטרא לידה ומרה לקבורה ובעיא למיפק בלא כתובה דליכא למימר שמא עיניה נתנה באחר ולפיכך אמר ר' אמי איהי מהימנא ומפקינן לה מיניה בלא כתובה. אבל כתובה לא יהבין לה שמא עיניה נתנה באחר ובלא כתובה נמי לא מפקינן מיניה אלא לאחר ששהתה עשר שנים אבל בתוך עשר שנים אע"פ שבאה מחמת טענה לא מפקינן מיניה אפי' בלא כתובה שמא עיניה נתנה באחר. ורב אחא משבחא פירש אפילו בתוך עשר שנים כיון שבאת מחמת טענה מפקינן לה מיניה בכתובה ולא מסתברא כותיה

עין משפט נר מצוה

קי א מיי' פט"ו מהל' אישות הלכה יד טוש"ע אה"ע סימן קנד סעיף יז:

קיא ב מיי' פ"א מהלכות מילה הלכה יח סמג עשין כח טוש"ע י"ד סימן רסג סעיף ב:

קיב ג טוש"ע שם סעיף ג:

קיג ד מיי' פכ"א מהל' איסורי ביאה הלכה ל טוש"ע אה"ע סי' ב סעי' ז:

קיד ה ו מיי' שם הל' לא סמג לאוין קכו טוש"ע שם סעיף ז וסעיף ח:

קטו ז מיי' פי"ח מהל' סנהדרין הלכה ד:

קטז ח מיי' פ"ח מהל' איסורי ביאה הלכה ה סמג לאוין קיא טוש"ע י"ד סימן קפט סעיף ב:

תוספות

ימי שנותינו בהם שבעים שנה. אע"ג דהאי קרא בתפלת משה כתיב – מסתמא דוד אמרו, שמצינו שחי כך, אבל משה מצינו שחי יותר:

בעי מיניה מרב יוסף. פר"י: דנראה ששאלו: הלכה כרבי או כרשב"ג, והשיבו דהלכה כשניהם.

דתנן מי שלקה ושנה כו'. הקשה ה"ר משה: דב"הנשרפים" (סנהדרין פא: ושם) מוקי לה אפילו כרשב"ג, ועבירות מחזקות! ואמר ר"י: דאע"ג דאיכא תנא התם דאמר עבירות מחזקות, מתוך לשון התוספה משמע ליה לרב יוסף דקסבר מלקיות מחזקות. דנראה לו דוחק דלא נקט מי שלקה ושנה אלא לאשמועינן דאיירי בעבירה שיש בה מלקות. ואפי' את"ל דקסבר עבירות מחזקות – שמא סבר רב יוסף דכיפה צריכה התראה.

ושור

גמרא

חצבתם ואל מקבת בור נקרתם" וכתיב "הביטו אל אברהם אביכם ואל שרה תחוללכם". (ישעיה נא) אמר רב נחמן אמר רבה בר אבוה: שרה אמנו *אילונית היתה, שנאמר "ותהי שרי עקרה אין לה ולד" (בראשית יא) אפי' בית ולד אין לה. אמר רב יהודה בריה דרב שמואל בר שילת משמיה דרב: לא שנו אלא בדורות הראשונים, ששנותיהן מרובות. אבל בדורות האחרונים ששנותיהן מועטות – שתי שנים ומחצה, כנגד שלשה עיבורים. רבה אמר רב נחמן: שלש שנים, כנגד שלש פקידות. *דאמר מר: בר"ה נפקדו שרה רחל וחנה. אמר רבה: ליתנהו להני כללי. מכדי מתני' מאן תקין – רבי, והא בימי דוד אימעוט שני, דכתיב "ימי שנותינו בהם שבעים שנה". (תהלים צ) והאי "שמא לא זכה להבנות הימנה" ודלמא איהי דלא זכיא! איהי, כיון דלא מפקדא אפריה ורביה – לא מיענשה. איני? והא אמרו ליה רבנן לר' אבא בר זבדא: נסיב איתתא ואוליד בני! ואמר להו: אי זכאי – הוו לי מקמייתא. התם דחוי קא מדחי להו לרבנן. דר' אבא בר זבדא איעקר מפרקיה דרב הונא, רב גידל איעקר מפרקיה דרב הונא, רבי חלבו איעקר מפרקיה דרב הונא, *רב ששת איעקר מפרקיה דרב הונא. רב אחא בר יעקב אחדתיה *סוסכינתא, תליוה בארזא דבי רב ונפק מיניה כהוצא ירקא. אמר רב אחא בר יעקב: שיתין סבי הוינא, וכולהו איעקור מפרקיה דרב הונא, לבר מאנא דקיימי בנפשאי "החכמה תחיה בעליה". (קהלת ז) § גירשה מותרת וכו'. [א]שני – אין, שלישי – לא. מתניתין מני – *רבי היא. דתניא: [ב]מלה הראשון ומת, שני ומת, שלישי – לא תמול, דברי רבי. רבן שמעון בן גמליאל אומר: *שלישי – תמול, רביעי – לא תמול. והתניא איפכא, *הי מינייהו אחרינתא? ת"ש, דאמר ר' חייא בר אבא א"ר יוחנן: [ג]מעשה בארבע אחיות בצפורי, שמלה ראשונה ומת, שניה ומת, שלישית ומת, רביעית באת לפני רבן שמעון בן גמליאל, אמר לה: אל תמולי. ודלמא אי אתיא שלישית – נמי הוה אמר לה? א"כ מאי אסהדותיה דר' חייא בר אבא. ודלמא הא קמ"ל דאחיות מחזקות! אמר רבא: השתא דאמרת אחיות מחזקות – [ד]לא ישא אדם אשה לא ממשפחת נכפין, ולא ממשפחת מצורעים, והוא דאתחזק תלתא זימני. מאי הוה עלה? כי אתא רב יצחק בר יוסף אמר: עובדא הוה קמיה דר' יוחנן בכנישתא דמעון ביוה"כ שחל להיות בשבת, ומלה ראשונה ומת, שניה ומת, שלישית באה לפניו. – אמר לה: לכי ומולי. א"ל אביי: חזי דקשרית איסורא וסכנתא! סמך עלה אביי, ואזל נסבה לחומה ברתא דאיסי בריה דרב יצחק בריה דרב יהודה. דנסבה רחבא דפומבדיתא ושכיב, רב יצחק בריה דרבה בר בר חנה ושכיב, ונסבה הוא ושכיב. אמר רבא: ומי איכא דעביד עובדא בנפשיה כי האי, והא איהו דאמר: אבין – דסמכא, יצחק סומקא – לאו בר סמכא. אבין – ישנו בחזרה, יצחק סומקא – אינו בחזרה. ועוד: אימר דפליגי לענין מילה, בנישואין מי פליגי? אין, והתניא: *[ה]ניסת לראשון ומת, לשני ומת, לשלישי – לא תנשא, דברי רבי. רבן שמעון בן גמליאל אומר: לשלישי תנשא, לרביעי לא תנשא. בשלמא גבי מילה – איכא משפחה דרפי דמא ואיכא משפחה דקמיט דמא. אלא נישואין מ"ט? א"ל רב מרדכי לרב אשי, הכי אמר אבימי מהגרוניא משמיה דרב הונא: מעין גורם. ורב אשי אמר: [ו]מזל גורם. מאי בינייהו? *איכא בינייהו דאירסה ומית, אי נמי דנפל מדיקלא ומית. א"ל רב יוסף בריה דרבא לרבא: בעי מיניה מרב יוסף, הלכה כרבי? ואמר לי: אין. הלכה כרבן שמעון בן גמליאל? ואמר לי: אין. אחוכי אחיך בי? א"ל: לא, סתמי *היא, ופשיט לך: נישואין ומלקיות – כרבי, וסתות ושור המועד כרבן שמעון בן גמליאל. נישואין – הא דאמרן, מלקיות – דתנן: *[ז]מי שלקה ושנה – ב"ד כונסין אותו לכיפה, ומאכילין אותו שעורים עד שתהא כריסו נבקעת. וסתות – דתנן: *[ח]אין האשה

קובעת

רש"י

חוצבתם. נעשה לו זכרות. נוקרתם. נעשה לה נקבות, כמו "אני קרתי ושתיתי מים" (ישעיהו לז). אין לה ולד. קרא יתירא הוא, דהא כתיב עקרה. לא שנו. דשוהה עשר שנים. שלשה עיבורים. כ"ז חדשים לימי הולד, וחדש לכל עיבור ועיבור לימי טומאה וטהרה, דאשה מתעברת סמוך לוסתה. שלש פקידות. שהקב"ה פוקד העקרות לשמוע תפלתן בר"ה, וגוזר עליהן הריון. להני כללי. דקאמר כל דורות של עכשיו שתי שנים ומחצה שהייתן. ודלמא איהי דלא זכיא. ולא תטול כתובה. כיון דלא מיפקדא אפריה ורביה. לא איכפת לה, ולא ענש לה קודשא בריך הוא על עונותיה. איני והא אמרו ליה כו'. אמתני' פריך, דקתני: ישא אחרת שמא לא זכה להבנות ממנה, ויזכה להבנות מן השניה. סוסכינתא. חולי מעופר השטן, ואדם נעקר הימנו. כהוצא ירקא. ירוק ככף תמר. שלישי לא. דהוחזקה עקרה. הי מינייהו אחרינתא. איזו מהמשניות נשנית אחרונה, דנסמוך עלה אמילתא דמר ודמר? דכל חד וחד הדר משיטתיה קמייתא ונקט שיטתיה דחבריה, ובתרייתא עיקר, דההדור בהו מקמייתא. אמר לה אל תמולי. אלמא: מתניתא קמייתא אחרינתא, דהאי מעשה בסוף ימיו של רשב"ג הוה, מדקא מסהיד עליה ר' יוחנן שהיה אמורא, וסוף התנאים, והוא ראה את המעשה. דאחיות מחזקות. דכי היכי דאשה מוחזקת בג' פעמים – כך היא מוחזקת בשלש אחיותיה. נכפין. חולין. איסורא וסכנתא. שאם חזקה בשני פעמים והשלישי ניתן לדחות ממנה – הויא מילה שלא בזמנה, ואינה דוחה את השבת. וסכנתא. סכנת נפשות. סמך עלה אביי. על הא דרב יצחק, דאמר משמיה דרבי יוחנן: בתלת זימני הוא דהויא חזקה. בנפשיה. בסכנת נפשו. אבין דסמכא. מה שאמר אבין משום רבי יוחנן – יש לסמוך עליו. ישנו בחזרה. חוזר על תלמודו. לשון אחר: מצוי כל שעה לפני רבי יוחנן, ואם חזר בו רבי יוחנן משום דבר שאמר תחלה – שומע אבין וחוזר גם הוא בו. אבל רב יצחק אינו מצוי לפניו, ופעמים ששמע דבר מרבי יוחנן ולמחר חזר בו רבי יוחנן, והוא אינו יודע. דאירסה. השלישי ומת. אי נמי. דנסבה וסליק לדיקלא ונפל ומת. למ"ד מעין גורם – לא הוחזקה זו, שהרי מעיינה לא גרם לו שימות, שהרי לא מת מחולי: ה"ג. בעי מיניה מרב יוסף הלכה כרבי ואמר לי אין הלכה כרשב"ג ואמר לי אין אחוכי אחיך בי. שאלתי מרב יוסף אם הלכה כרבי, ואמר לי: הלכה, ופעם אחרת שאלתיו אם הלכה כרשב"ג, ואמר לי: הלכה. וכמדומה אני שמשחק בי: ה"ג. אמר ליה סתמי הוא ופשיט לך. לא שיחק בך, סתומות של משנה הן: יש שסתמה כרבן שמעון בן גמליאל, ויש שסתמה כרבי. דאיכא מילתא דמחזקינן לה בתרי זימני, ואיכא מילתא דבעינן תלתא זימני. ומשום הכי פשט לך כמר וכמר, *כסתומים. נישואין הא דאמרן. דסתם לן תנא דידן כרבי, דקתני: רשאי השני, שני – אין, שלישי – לא. כונסין אותו לכיפה. אם חזר וחטא בשלישית, דמחזקינן ליה ברשיעא מתרי זימני שלקה.

קובעת

תוספות ישנים

אבין ישנו בחזרה. פי' שהיה תדיר חוזר תלמודו ומתקיים בידו אבל יצחק סומקא לא היה בקי כל כך א"נ י"מ אבין ישנו בחזרה פי' שהיה תמיד אצל ר' יוחנן ויודע כשהיה ר' יוחנן חוזר מדבריו אבל יצחק לא היה תמיד אצל רבו ולא ידע כשר' יוחנן מתחרט מדבורו: **מלקיות** דתנן מי שלקה ושנה ב"ד מכניסין אותו לכיפה. וא"ת למ"ד עבירות מחזיקות היכי מייתי דסתם לן תנא כר' דלמא היינו משום שעבר ג' פעמים והוחזק בעבירות וי"ל דדייק מדנקט מי שלקה ושנה משמע דבתרי הויא חזקה שנראה לו דוחק לפרש דלא נקט לקה אלא לאשמעינן דאיירי בעבירה שיש בה מלקות. ואפי' את"ל דקסבר עבירות מחזיקות שמא ס"ל כמ"ד כיפה צריכה התראה ומייתי שפיר דהא התרינו לו משום כיפה אחרי ב' מלקיות א"כ משמע דבתרי זמני הויא חזקה:

תוספות חד מקמאי

וב"ה פירש דלאחר עשר שנים דמפקינן לה מיניה היינו בכתובה ולאבא מרי ז"ל מסתברא דלא מפקינן בכתובה לעולם ואפי' לאחר כמה שנים ואפי' באה מחמת טענה. ואע"ג דאמרי' לקמן בשמעתי' אתא עובדא קמיה דר' יוחנן בבי כנשתא דקסרי ואמר יוציא ויתן כתובה ומסקנא מוקמי' לה בבא מחמת טענה א) ההיא לאו טענה כגון דידעינן בבעל שהוא עקור ולא שייך למימר בה שמא עיניה נתנה באחר אבל הכא דבעינא למיפק מתותיה בטענה דאינו יורה כחץ לא מהמנינן לה למיפק מיניה בכתובה דאמרי' שמא עיניה נתנה באחר ומשקרה במאי דטענה. הרי כאן ג' סברות בבאה מחמת טענה דלדעת ר' אחא מפקינן מיניה אפי' בתוך עשר ובכתובה ולדעת הרב בעל (התוספות) [הלכות] ב) לאחר עשר שנים מפקינן לה מיניה ובכתובה ולדעת אבא מרי ז"ל לא מפקינן לה מיניה לעולם בכתובה אפילו לאחר עשר אבל בלא כתובה מפקינן לה מיניה בעל כרחו בבא מחמת טענה ולאחר עשר שנים ויש לדחוק ולפ' בפי' הרב אלפס ג) ובודאי אי לא הוא הוא דמר איהו מינה לא הוה איהי צריכה למימר מיניה. אלא כגון דאמר איהו בודאי מינה שהיא עקרה ווסתותיה ומעיינה שאינה כשאר נשים ומשום הכי איצטריכה איהי למי' שאינו יורה כחץ אבל בודאי אם היתה אילונית ידועה ואמרה איהי שאינו יורה כחץ לא מהמנינן לה. ויש דמפרשי' דאשלישית וארביעית לרשב"ג קאי דאמר תצא בלא כתובה ואמרה איהי מיניה אית לה כתובה וא"ר אמי היא נאמנת ולא נהירא דא"כ לא משכחת לה שתצא בלא כתובה אם תרצה לטעון מיניה. אלא ודאי במקרה אי אמרה מיניה לא מהימנא ואין לה כתובה. והא דא' אם נשאת לג' [אנשים] לרשב"ג תצא בלא כתובה. איכא מאן דאמר בתוך עשר אם שהתה עמו כדי שלש עיבורין. ומסתברא בלאחר עשר אבל בתוך עשר יש לה כתובה שמא עדיין יזכה ליבנות הימנה. והראב"ד פירש אפי' בתוך עשר אם שהה כדי עבור תצא משלישי בלא כתובה. ודאתן עלה מיהת דאשה לא מפקדה אפריה ורבי'. איכא לעיוני מה ששנינו בנדרים [השמים] ביני לבינך למשנה ראשונה יוצאה בכתובה למשנה אחרונה יעשו דרך בקשה שמא עיניה נתנה באחר והא לא מפקדה וי"ל משנה ראשונה ודאי ס"ל דמפקדה ומשנה אחרונה דקא' שמא עיניה נתנה באחר לדברי המשנה ראשונה קאמ' שמא עיניה נתנה באחר ולמשנה אחרונה אטמאה אני לך ואנטולה אני לך מן היהודים קאי אבל השמים ביני ובינך לא היה צריך לטעם שמא עיניה נתנה באחר דבלאו הכי נמי אינה יוצאה אליבא דהלכתא דלא מפקדה. ועוד יש להעמיד משנת נדרים כבאת מחמת טענה ולפיכך היה צריך לטעם שמא עיניה נתנה באחר וזה שלא כדברי רב אחא משבחה. ויש לפרש שיש מי שאומר שכיון שאינו יורה כחץ כמי שאינו יכול להזקק עמה דמי ולפיכך אי לאו משום טעמא דשמא עיניה נתנה באחר כופין אותו להוציא ולאו מילתא היא והראב"ד פי' השמים ביני ובינך שאינו נזקק עמה ומאמינין לה מגו דאי בעיא אמרה אינו יורה כחץ. ומאי דאתמר עלה בגמ' בנדרים צריך הביאור למדחק להאי פירושה ודוק ותשכח:

א) אולי צ"ל ההיא לאו בטענה דבעינא תוערא לידה אלא כגון וכו'. ב) הוא בבה"ג בהלכות כתובות סי' ל"ז. ג) נראה דצ"ל דוודאי אי לאו דאמר איהו דמינה לא הוה איהי וכו'.

מסורת הש"ס

[עי' תוס' גיטין מו: ד"ה המוציא וכו']

ר"ה יא. [ברכות כט.]

[לעיל סב:]

[גירס' הערוך סוסכינתא פי' שנצטייר בשרו כגוון מן החולי]

[עירובין ו:. לעיל כו. כתובות מג:] ב"מ קו: סנהדרין פא: [מנחות נב. חולין פו:]

נדה סד.

נ"ל נינהו. יעב"ץ

סנהדרין פא:

נדה סג:

נ"ל כסתמי. יעב"ץ

גליון הש"ס

שם א"ב דאירסה ומית. עיין לקמן קח ע"א וכתו' שם ד"ה קטנה.

קוֹבַעַת לָהּ וֶסֶת עַד שֶׁתִּקְבָּעֶנָּה שָׁלֹשׁ פְּעָמִים, וְאֵין מְטַהֶרֶת מִן הַוֶּסֶת עַד שֶׁתֵּעָקֵר מִמֶּנָּה שָׁלֹשׁ פְּעָמִים. וְשׁוֹר הַמּוּעָד – דִּתְנַן: *אאֵין הַשּׁוֹר נַעֲשֶׂה מוּעָד עַד שֶׁיָּעִידוּ בּוֹ שְׁלֹשָׁה פְּעָמִים.§ ת"ר: בנִיסֵּת לָרִאשׁוֹן וְלֹא הָיוּ לָהּ בָּנִים, לַשֵּׁנִי וְלֹא הָיוּ לָהּ בָּנִים, לַשְּׁלִישִׁי – לֹא תִּנָּשֵׂא אֶלָּא לְמִי שֶׁיֵּשׁ לוֹ בָּנִים. נִישֵּׂאת לְמִי שֶׁאֵין לוֹ בָּנִים – תֵּצֵא בְּלֹא כְּתוּבָּה. אִיבַּעְיָא לְהוּ: נִישֵּׂאת לַשְּׁלִישִׁי וְלֹא הָיוּ לָהּ בָּנִים, מַהוּ דְּלִיתְבְּעוּהָ הָנָךְ קַמָּאֵי? מִי מָצוּ אָמְרִי לָהּ: אִיגַּלַּאי מִילְּתָא דְּאַתְּ הוּא דְּגָרְמַתְּ, אוֹ דִּלְמָא מָצֵית אָמְרָה לְהוּ: הַשְׁתָּא הוּא דְּכָחֲשִׁי? גמִסְתַּבְּרָא מָצֵית אָמְרָה לְהוּ: הַשְׁתָּא הוּא דְּכָחֲשִׁי. אִיבַּעְיָא לְהוּ: נִישֵּׂאת לָרְבִיעִי וְהָיוּ לָהּ בָּנִים, מַהוּ דְּתִיתְבְּעֵיהּ לַשְּׁלִישִׁי? אָמְרִינַן לָהּ: שְׁתִיקוּתִיךְ יָפָה מִדִּיבּוּרֵיךְ, דְּמָצֵי אָמַר לָהּ: אֲנָא אַדַּעְתָּא דְּהָכִי לָא גֵּרַשְׁתִּיךְ. מַתְקִיף לָהּ רַב פַּפָּא: אִי אִיהִי שָׁתְקָא אֲנַן מִי שָׁתְקִינַן? נִמְצָא גֵּט בָּטֵל וּבָנֶיהָ מַמְזֵרִין! דאֶלָּא אָמְרִינַן: הַשְׁתָּא הוּא דְּבִרְיָיתָא.§ ההוּא אָמַר: מִינַּהּ, וְהִיא אָמְרָה: מִינֵּיהּ – אָמַר רַבִּי אַמִּי: דְּבָרִים שֶׁבֵּינוֹ לְבֵינָהּ נֶאֱמֶנֶת. וְטַעְמָא מַאי? והִיא – קַיְימָא לָהּ בְּיוֹרֶה כְּחֵץ, הוּא – לָא קִים לֵיהּ בְּיוֹרֶה כְּחֵץ. זאֲמַר אִיהוּ: אֵיזִיל אִינְסִיב אִיתְּתָא וְאִיבְדּוֹק נַפְשַׁאי. אָמַר רַבִּי אַמִּי: אַף בְּזוֹ יוֹצִיא וְיִתֵּן כְּתוּבָּה, שֶׁאֲנִי אוֹמֵר: כָּל הַנּוֹשֵׂא אִשָּׁה עַל אִשְׁתּוֹ – יוֹצִיא וְיִתֵּן כְּתוּבָּה. רָבָא אָמַר: חנוֹשֵׂא אָדָם כַּמָּה נָשִׁים עַל אִשְׁתּוֹ, וְהוּא דְּאִית לֵיהּ לְמֵיזַיְינִינְהִי.

הוא

רש"י

קובעת לה וסת. לסמוך עליה להיות דייה שעתה, דתנן (נדה דף ב.): כל אשה שיש לה וסת – דייה שעתה, ולא מטמאינן לה למפרע מעת לעת. ועוד: דאם קובעת לה וסת והגיע זמן וסתה ולא בדקה – טמאה, דאורח בזמנו בא. ואינה מטהרת מן הוסת. אפילו נעקרה פעמים, שבדקה בב' וסתות ולא ראתה, ושינתה ראייתה ליום אחר ב' פעמים – אפילו הכי מחזקינן וסתה לכשיגיע, ואם לא בדקה – טמאה, דאורח בזמנו בא. אדעתא דהכי לא גרשתיך. אילו הייתי יודע שאת בת בנים – לא גרשתיך, ונמצא גט בטל למפרע. מתקיף לה רב פפא. ואי מצי בעלה לבטולי גט בהכי, כי שתק מאי הוי? אנן מי שתקינן? הא ודאי אדעתא דהכי לא גירשה. אלא מדשתקינן – ודאי לא מצי לבטולי, דאמרינן ליה: מספיקא קא מגרשת לה, ולא איכפת לך בה, וגמרת בדעתיך לגרושין. אלא. אי איכא למפטריה, הכי פטרינן ליה; דאמרינן ליה: השתא היא דאיברית, שחזרה להיות בריאה מחולייה. מינה. יודע אני שממתמה הוא שאין לי בנים, ולא אתן כתובה: כל שכבת זרע שאינו יורה כחץ אינה מזרעת*.

תוספות

ושור המועד. רבי לא פליג אקרא, אלא כלומר: התם מתקיימין דברי רשב"ג דלא מיתחזיק אלא בתלת זימני*: נישאת למי שאין לו בנים תצא בלא כתובה. משמע דמן השני יש לה כתובה. וכן משמע בסמוך. דקאמר: נישאת לשלישי ולא היו לה בנים מהו דליתבעוה הנך קמאי? משמע שהשני נתן לה כתובה. ותימה לר"י: דלמאי יש לה כתובה מן השני? הא כיון דאסר לה לשלישי – א"כ סבר דבתרי זימני הויא חזקה? וכ"ת משום דאמרה ליה השתא הוא דכחשי ונסתחפה שדהו – אם כן מאי קבעי נישאת לשלישי כו', מי מצי אמרי לה דאיגלאי מילתא דאת גרמת, או דלמא מציא אמרה השתא הוא דכחשי, הלא אע"ג דלא נישאת לשלישי – אין לה כתובה מן השני אלא מטעם דמצי אמרה השתא הוא דכחשי! ואר"י: דלענין ממון מודה רבי דלא הוי חזקה עד דאיתחזיק בג' זימני, כדאשכחן בשור המועד. דבשור המועד לא פליג, כדפירשתי לעיל. ומיהו, תימה: דהשתא לענין איסורא לא סמכינן ארוב נשים דחזיין לבנים – משום דאיתרע רובא ע"י דאיתחזק בתרי זימני, ולענין ממון סמכינן אהאי רובא אע"ג דאיתרע בתרי זימני? ובעלמא* אמרי' איפכא: דאזלינן בתר רובא לענין איסורא, ולענין ממונא לא אזלינן א). תצא בלא כתובה. לכאורה נראה דוקא בשהתה עם השלישי, דומיא דנשאת לשלישי ולא היו לה בנים דבסמוך. וטעמא, דלענין ממון לא מחזקינן לה בעקרה עד דאיתחזק בתלת זימני. וא"ת: מן השלישי נמי לא תפסיד כתובה, דתימא ליה: השתא הוא דכחשי, כמו שאומרת לראשון ולשני! י"ל: דטענה דהשתא הוא דכחשי לא מהני להוציא, אלא לענין שלא תחזיר מה שגבתה מראשון ומשני. אבל קשה: דאי בשהתה עמה י' שנים – היכי קאמר בסמוך גבי נישאת לרביעי והיו לה בנים, או דלמא מצי אמר לה אדעתא דהכי לא גרשתיך, והא אע"ג שהיא בת בנים – על כרחו הוא צריך לגרשה, כיון דלא זכה ליבנות ממנה! לכך נראה לר"י דלאלתר תצא שלא בכתובה, ולא משום קנס, דקנסוה כמו בשניות לפי שניסאת באיסור, מדקבעי בסמוך נישאת לרביעי והיו לה בנים מהו דתיתבעיה לשלישי. ואי קנס הוא – היכי תיתבע לשלישי? אלא נראה לר"י דבשלא הכיר בה איירי, ותצא שלא בכתובה – משום דהוי מקח טעות. ומ"מ, כשיש לה בנים מן הרביעי – חוזרת ותובעת לשלישי, דאיגלאי מילתא דלאו מקח טעות הוא. וכן מלא ר"י בהלכות דרב יהודאי גאון דבלא הכיר בה איירי. אבל הכיר בה – יש לה כתובה. והא דקתני בתוספתא ניסאת למי שאין לו בנים תצא שלא בכתובה, מפני שניסואיה ניסואי מינות – נראה שהסופרים טעו וכתבו מינות במקום טעות, דלא שייך כאן לשון מינות כלל. אי איהי שתקא אנן מי שתקינן. וא"ת: דתנן ב"השולח" (גיטין מו: ושם): המוציא אשתו משום אילונית, רבי יהודה אומר לא יחזיר כו'. נשאת לאחר והיו לה בנים, והיא תובעת כתובתה, א"ר יהודה, אומר לה: שתיקותיך יפה מדבוריך. והשתא תקשה התם: אי היא שתקה – אנן מי שתקינן? וי"ל: דהתם, כיון דתקינן לרבי יהודה דלא יחזיר – ליכא למיחש לקלקולא. ורבנן, אע"ג דיחזיר – לא חיישינן התם לקלקולא, כיון דלא(א) חשיב לבדוק יפה בסימני אילונית – גמר בדעתו לגרש בכל ענין, ולהכי שתקינן. וכי תובעת כתובתה – מצי אמר לה: אדעתא למיתב כתובה לא גירשתיך. אבל הכא, דליכא תקנה דלא יחזיר – פריך שפיר: היכי שתקינן. ואפי' רבנן דלא חיישי התם לקלקולא – היינו דוקא בספק אילונית, דכיון דלא חשש לבדוק יפה – גמר לגרש בכל ענין. אבל הכא – אין בידו לבדוק ומוכיח הדבר שמשום בנים מוציאה, שכבר נישאת לשנים ולא היו לה בנים – איכא קילקולא, ולהכי פריך לכ"ע: אנן מי שתקינן. ואתי נמי שפיר הא דמשמע ב"השולח" דלא מצי מקלקל לה אלא כשאמר לה משום שם רע ונדר ואילונית אני מוציאך. והכא אע"ג דלא אמר לה משום עקרות אני מוציאך – מצי מקלקל לה, כדפי'. ומשני: דהכא לא שייך קילקולא, דאמרינן: השתא הוא דבריית, ובשעה שגירשה לא היתה ראויה. אבל בשם רע ונדר ואילונית – איכא קלקולא כשנתגלה לבסוף שהשם רע היה שקר, ולא היתה אילונית גם מתחלה. דאם – היתה לא הוה בריאה לעולם. ונדר נמי, כיון שיכול להפר – כאילו לא היה נדר. ואם תאמר: דפ"ק דנדה (דף יב: ושם) אמר גבי אשה שאין לה וסת לא יחזיר אפי' הדר ואיתקן – משום קלקולא, והשתא והא אין יכול לקלקלה, דלאמר השתא הוא דבריאת, כדאמרי' הכא? ואר"י: דלא דמי, דקלקול בנים – אין רפואה מועלת כ"כ, ולכך בשעה שגירשה לא היתה בת בנים, דלא שכיח(ב) שתרפא – לגמרי מגרש לה. אבל קלקול דוסת – שכיח להתרפאות ולא גמר ומגרש, דיאמר אילו הייתי יודע שסם מועיל לה – לא הייתי מגרשה. וה"ר שלמה מדריו"ש תירץ: דהתם יש לחוש שתקבע וסת, כמו שהתחילה לקבוע סמוך לגירושין. דליכא למימר השתא הוא דבריאת – דהא איגלאי מילתא למפרע דבעוד שהיתה תחתיו איבריאת. שבינו לבינה היא נאמנת. תימה: דבמאי איירי? דאי בשהתה עשר שנים עמו – למה לי טעמא דאין יורה כחץ? אפילו יורה כחץ נמי יוציא ויתן כתובה, לפי שלא זכה ליבנות ממנה. ואי לא שהה – ניחוש שמא עיניה נתנה באחר, כמשנה אחרונה דסוף נדרים (דף צ:) דתנן: בראשונה היו אומרים ג' נשים יוצאות ונוטלות כתובה: השמים ביני לבינך, פי': גלוי לשמים שאין יורה כחץ. דהכי משמע התם בגמרא כו', חזרו לומר: שלא תהא אשה נותנת עיניה באחר ומקלקלת על בעלה, אלא השמים ביני לבינך – יעשו דרך בקשה: יבקשו שיכנס רחמים. או כמו שפר"ת: שיעשו סעודה ויתפייסו. וכ"ת: דהתם באינה באה מחמת טענה, והכא בבאה מחמת טענה – מ"מ ניחוש שמא נתנה עיניה באחר! ועוד: דהתם אם אין באה מחמת טענה – מאי נפקא לה מיניה. ובמשנה ראשונה למה אמרו יוציא ויתן כתובה? והיא דסוף שמעתין דכופין בבאה מחמת טענה, ולא חיישי' שמא עיניה נתנה באחר – איכא לאוקמא בידוע שהוא עקור, או בשהתה עמו י' שנים ויש לו בנים מאשה אחרת. דאי לאו דבאה מחמת טענה – לא היו כופין משום ביטול פריה ורביה, כיון דיש לו בנים. והך דהכא – ליכא לאוקמה בשהה י' שנים ויש לו בנים ובאה מחמת טענה – דא"כ אפי' יורה כחץ נמי כופין, כיון דלא זכה ליבנות ממנה. ומיהו, י"ל קצת: דכיון דיש לו בנים – אין לתלות *)באונס שלו, אלא אית לן למימר לאדרבה: איהי היא דלא זכתה, כדאמר לעיל. ולכך צריכה טעם דיורה כחץ. ואע"פ שיש לו בנים מאשה אחרת – שמא אח"כ נתקלקל. ויש להאמינה, דמוכח מילתא דשהה י' שנים ולא ילדה. ומה שלא אמרה מיד – משום דעד י' שנים לא הייתו חוששין לדבריה, דהוה תלינן בעיניה נתנה באחר. א"נ: איכא לאוקמא בדלא שהה עמה י' שנים ובבאה מחמת טענה, דכיון שיש לה טענה מעליא – לא רצו להפסידה, ואוקמוה אדין משנה ראשונה, דלא חשו לעיניה נתנה באחר. והיא דנדרים – באינה באה מחמת טענה, ומ"מ, למשנה ראשונה – יוציא ויתן כתובה משום דשמא אין לה הנאת תשמיש כ"כ כשאין יורה כחץ. שטוענת שרוצה שיהא לה זכר, דמי שאין לו בנים חשוב כמת. והר"ר יצחק בן רבינו מאיר פירש: דהכא אניסת לשלישי קאי, דאמרו תצא בלא כתובה, וקמ"ל דאי אמרה דאין יורה כחץ דנאמנת ולא תפסיד כתובתה ממנו, דחזיא ליה כיון דאין דאין ראוי לבנים. וקשה לר"י: דמתוך הלשון משמע דהוא אמר מינה והיא אמרה מיניה, דמחמת שהיו יחד הרבה ולא הולידו מחמת כן באים לב"ד. ועוד ק"ק: דלמה אין לחוש שטוענת כן ומשקרת בשביל כתובה? וה"ר שמואל ב"ר חיים פירש: דהכא איירי כששהתה עם השלישי י' שנים, וכרשב"ג דאמר בתלת זימני הויא חזקה, דמסקנא דשמעתין כוותיה אתיא, כדקאמר: הוא אומר אפילה

*) אולי צ"ל בעונם.

תוספות ישנים

שור מועד דתנן. וא"ת היאך יחלוק רבי על זה הלא מקראי שמעינן לה בפרק כילד הרגל וליכא מאן דפליג גבי תמול חד שלשום תרי וכו' דמשמעות דורשים איכא בינייהו וי"ל אה"נ ומ"מ מייתי ראיה ומוכח מקרא כרשב"ג דבתלתא זמני הויא חזקה. וא"כ יש לנו לומר דהדין עמו בכל מקום דבג' זמני הויא חזקה: א) ומסופק הר"י אם הא דקאמר תצא ר"ל לאלתר או לאחר עשר שנים. ונראה דר"ל לאלתר מדאמרינן לקמן דאמר לה אדעתא דהכי לא גרשתיך. ואי מיירי לאחר עשר שנים מאי קאמר אדעתא דהכי לא גרשתיך הלא בעל כרחו מגרש לה כדאמרינן במתני' אלא ודאי לאלתר תצא וטעמא משום דכיון שעברה על דברי חכמים שאסרוה לינשא לו קנסינן לה. א"נ מ"ה אמרינן תצא משלישי בלא כתובה דמקח טעות דמצי למימר אני לא ידעתי שהיתה עם שני אנשים עשר שנים ולא ילדה ואילו הייתי יודע כן לא נשאתיה. וקשה דאמר לקמן את הוא דגרמת ואי לאלתר מאי קאמר דלמא אם תשהה עמו עשר שנים תלד. לכ"נ דלאחר עשר שנים קאמר תצא. והא דקאמר לקמן דאמר לה אדעתא דהכי לא גרשתיך. ה"ק אם יבא אליהו ויאמר דבת בנים היא לא הייתי מגרשה וכל אשר כפוהו ב"ד להוציא כפיית טעות היתה. ור"ל תצא בלא כתובה ובלא תוספת דנשים שאמרו חכמים דיוצאות ואין להם כתובה אין להם תוספת: השתא הוא דכחשי. ואין להקשות א"כ משלישי נמי אמאי אין לה כתובה תאמר השתא הוא דכחשי וי"ל דטענת השתא הוא דכחשי מועלת לענין שלא יוציאו שני בעליה את הכתובה שנתנו בידה אבל אינה מועלת להוציא הכתובה מיד השלישי: שתיקותיך יפה ליך מדבוריך. משום דאמר לה אילו הייתי יודע שכן הוא אפי' אם נותנים לי מאה מנה לא הייתי מגרשך ונמצא גט בטל ובניה ממזרים ותימה דבגיטין משמע דלא מצי אמר לה הכי אלא כשאומר לה משום שם רע אני מוציאך. אבל הכא לא פירש לה דמשום עקרות הוא מוציאה וא"כ מציא אמרה ליה לא גרשתני משום עקרות כי לא פירשת כשנתת לי גט דמשום עקרות אתה נותן גט דודאי משום שנאה גרשתני. וי"ל דה"נ מיירי שפי' דמשום עקרות הוא מוציאה ועוי"ל דמיירי שפיר שלא פירש ואעפ"כ יש הוכחה בדבר דמשום עקרות הוציאה שהרי יצתה בלא כתובה ויכול לומר אילו הייתי יודע שלא היתה עקרה לא הייתי מוציאה אבן לא הייתי יכול לבודקה. אבל המוציא אשתו משום שם רע צריך לפרש דאם לא

תוספות חד מקמאי

אמר אזול ואנסיב אתתא ואבדוק נפשאי אמר רב [אמי] אף בזו יוציא ויתן כתובה לפי' רב אחא משבחא ולפי' המאור איכא לפרושי דאמילתא דלעיל קאי דאמרה איהי מיניה ואמר איהו אזול ואבדוק נפשאי דאנסיב אתתא ואם יהיה לו בנים ממנה נמצאו דבריה בדאים. אבל לפי אבא מרי ז"ל לאו אמילתא דלעיל קאי דא"כ היכי קאמר ר' אמי אף בזו יוציא ויתן כתובה דהא במילתי' דלעיל לית לה כתובה אלא אמתני' קאי דקתני שהה עמה עשר שנים אינו רשאי ליבטל ויוציא ויתן כתובה. אמר הבעל לא אגרשנה אלא אזול ואבדוק נפשאי ואם יהיו לו בנים ממנה א"ר [אמי] יוציא ויתן כתובה. הוא אומ' הפילה בתוך עשר ולא אוציא והיא אומרת לא הפלתי ויש לב"ד לכופו ולהוציא מידו א"ר אמי אף בזו היא נאמנת דאם איתה דאפלה נפשה בעקרתא לא מחזקא ואם נשאת לשלישי ואמרה איהי אפילי' ויש לי כתובה והוא אומר לא הפילה ולית לה כתובה בכה"ג מאי בעל מהימן. א)ואי אמרת נמי הפילת כלומר ויש לה כתובה והוא אומר לא הפילה כלל מסת' דאיהו נאמן ולא אמרי' בהא נפשה בנפלנית לא מחזקה להוציא כתובה מידו. ומאי דפי' הרב אלפס בהיא אמרה מיניה לענין כתובה קא' כדין מנה לי בידך והלה אומר איני יודע. לא נהיר דהיכא דאמר הוא מינה דבעי לאפוקי בלא כתובה ודאי כגון דאומר מינה קודם נישואין דאי בשעת נישואין היתה ראויה לבנים ולבתר הכי אינה ראויה לא מפסדה כתובה בהם דנסתחפה שדהו [וא"כ] איכא לעיוני דהא קי"ל כרב נחמן ור' יוחנן דאמרי מנה לי בידך והלה אמר איני יודע פטור אע"ג דקי"ל כר"ג גבי מוכת עץ אני והוא אומר לא כי אלא דרוסת איש את דאיהו מהימנא דברי ושמא ברי עדיף. הא אסיקנא בפ"ק דכתובות שאני התם דאיכא חזקה מגופיה אי נמי משום דאיכא למימר מיגו אבל הכא כי היכי דאיכא חזקה לדידיה דבת בנים איכא חזקה לדידיה דיורה כחץ הוא ואמאי מפקי' מיניה כתובה. וגבי מתני' דנדרים נמי דשלש נשים יוצאות ונוטלות כתובה איכא לעיוני הכי דאפי' משנה אחרונה לא פליג למשנה ראשונה אלא משום עיניה נתנה באחר הא לאו הכי כייפי' לאפוקי ויהיב לה כתובה ומ"ש מנה לי בידך והלה או' איני יודע פטור. וי"ל כיון דנתחייב לו בשעת נשואין בכתובה

א) נראה דצ"ל בכה"ג מאי אי בעל מהימן או דהיא מהימנה ומסתבר דאיהו מהימן וכו'.

עין משפט נר מצוה

[עי' בתוספות בדיבור שלאחר זה ד"ה נשאת כו' דבשור המועד לא פליג כדפרישית לעיל כו']

קיז א מיי' פ"ו מהלכות נזקי ממון הלכה א:

קיח ב מיי' פט"ו מהלכות אישות הלכה יד סמג עשין מט טוש"ע אה"ע סימן קנד סעיף יז [וברב אלפס עוד סוף פ"ז דכתובות דף קב.]

קיט ג טוש"ע שם סעיף יח:

קכ ד שם סעיף יט:

קכא ה ו מיי' שם טוש"ע שם סעיף ו:

קכב ז מיי' פי"ד שם סמג שם טוש"ע אה"ע סימן א סעיף ט וסימן עו סעיף ז:

גליון הש"ס

גמ' היא קיימא לה ביורה כחץ. עיין נדה דף מג ע"א תד"ה ברגווה:

[ב"ק מו: ב"ב לב:]

מסורת הש"ס

ב"ק כג: ע"ש

[חגיגה טו.]

הגהות הב"ח

(א) תום' ד"ה אי איהי וכו' כיון דלא חשש לבדוק יפה: (ב) בא"ד דלא שכיח שתתרפא וגמר ומגרש לה:

הוא אמר: אפלת בגו עשר, והיא אמרה: לא אפלית. א"ר אמי: אף בזו היא נאמנת, דאם איתא דהפילה – נפשה בעקרתה לא מחזקה. הפילה, וחזרה והפילה, וחזרה והפילה – הוחזקה לנפלים. הוא אמר: אפילה תרי, והיא אמרה: תלת. אמר רבי יצחק בן אלעזר: עובדא הוה בי מדרשא, ואמרו: היא מהימנא, דאם איתא דלא אפלה – נפשה בניפלי לא מחזקה.§

מתני' האיש מצווה על פריה ורביה, אבל לא האשה. רבי יוחנן בן ברוקה אומר: על שניהם הוא אומר "ויברך אותם אלהים ויאמר להם [אלהים] פרו ורבו".§

גמ' מנא הני מילי? אמר ר' אילעא משום ר' אלעזר בר' שמעון: אמר קרא "ומלאו את הארץ וכבשוה" איש דרכו לכבש, ואין אשה דרכה לכבש. אדרבה, "וכבשוה" תרתי משמע! אמר רב נחמן בר יצחק: "וכבשה" כתיב. רב יוסף אמר: מהכא, "אני אל שדי פרה ורבה" ולא קאמר "פרו ורבו". ואמר רבי אילעא משום ר' אלעזר בר' שמעון: כשם שמצוה על אדם לומר דבר הנשמע – כך מצוה על אדם שלא לומר דבר שאינו נשמע. רבי אבא אומר: חובה, שנאמר "אל תוכח לץ פן ישנאך הוכח לחכם ויאהבך". וא"ר אילעא משום רבי אלעזר בר' שמעון: מותר לו לאדם לשנות בדבר השלום, שנאמר "אביך צוה וגו' כה תאמרו ליוסף אנא שא נא וגו'". ר' נתן אומר: מצוה, שנאמר "ויאמר שמואל איך אלך ושמע שאול והרגני וגו'". דבי רבי ישמעאל תנא: גדול השלום שאף הקדוש ברוך הוא שינה בו. דמעיקרא כתיב "ואדוני זקן" ולבסוף כתיב "ואני זקנתי".§ "רבי יוחנן בן ברוקה אומר".§ איתמר, רבי יוחנן ור' יהושע בן לוי, חד אמר: הלכה כרבי יוחנן בן ברוקה, וחד אמר: אין הלכה כרבי יוחנן בן ברוקה. תסתיים דרבי יוחנן הוא דאמר "אין הלכה" דיתיב ר' אבהו וקאמר משמיה דרבי יוחנן הלכה, ואהדרינהו רבי אמי ורבי אסי לאפייהו. ואיכא דאמרי: רבי חייא בר אבא אמר, ואהדרינהו רבי אמי ורבי אסי לאפייהו. אמר רב פפא: בשלמא למאן דאמר רבי אבהו אמרה – משום כבוד בי קיסר לא אמרו ליה ולא מידי, אלא למאן דאמר רבי חייא בר אבא אמרה – לימרו ליה: לא אמר רבי יוחנן הכי! מאי הוה עלה? ת"ש, דאמר ר' אחא בר חנינא אמר ר' אבהו אמר ר' אסי: עובדא הוה קמיה דרבי יוחנן בכנישתא דקיסרי, ואמר: "יוציא ויתן כתובה". ואי ס"ד לא מפקדה – כתובה מאי עבידתה? דלמא בבאה מחמת טענה. כי ההיא דאתאי לקמיה דר' אמי, אמרה ליה: הב לי כתובה. אמר לה: זיל, לא מיפקדת. אמרה ליה: מסיבו דילה מאי תיהוי עלה דהך אתתא? אמר: כי הא – ודאי כפינן. ההיא דאתאי לקמיה דרב נחמן, אמר לה: לא מיפקדת. אמרה ליה: לא בעיא הך אתתא חוטרא לידה ומרה לקבורה? אמר: כי הא – ודאי כפינן. יהודה וחזקיה תאומים היו, אחד נגמרה צורתו לסוף תשעה ואחד נגמרה צורתו לתחלת שבעה. יהודית, דביתהו דר' חייא, הוה לה צער לידה, שנאי מנא ואתיא לקמיה דר' חייא, אמרה: אתתא מפקדא אפריה ורביה? אמר לה: לא. אזלא אשתיא סמא דעקרתא. לסוף איגלאי מילתא. אמר לה: איכו ילדת לי חדא כרסא אחריתא! דאמר מר: יהודה וחזקיה – אחי, פזי וטוי – אחוותא.

רש"י

הוא אמר אפלת בגו עשר. כשהנו באין לכופו להוציא, הוא אומר: "הפילה בתוך עשר", ועדיין אין זמן להוציא, דתנן: מונה משעה שהפילה. והיא אמרה לא אפלית. אלא עקרה אני. הוחזקה לנפלים. ויוציא ויתן כתובה, שמא לא זכה ליבנות ממנה. אפילה תרי. ולא אוציא. היא מהימנא. וכופין אותו. ולא שהיא תובעת גירושין, אלא שעלינו לכופו לקיים פריה ורביה. מתני' אבל לא האשה. וטעמא מפרש בגמרא. גמ' לומר דבר הנשמע. דכתיב (ויקרא יט) "הוכח תוכיח" – להוכיח מי שמקבל הימנו. אביך צוה. יעקב לא צוה, אלא הם שינו מפני דרכי שלום. איך אלך. וכתיב "ויאמר ה' עגלת בקר תקח בידך ואמרת לזבוח" וגו' – הקב"ה צוה לשנות. ואדוני זקן. שרה אמרה לשון בזוי, וכשגלה הקב"ה הדבר לאברהם, כתיב: "למה זה צחקה שרה וגו' ואני זקנתי", ושינה הדבר מפני השלום. משמיה דרבי יוחנן. הלכה כר' יוחנן בן ברוקה. ואהדרינהו לאפייהו. דלא אמרה רבי יוחנן מעולם. וחלקו לו כבוד, ולא רצו להכחישו: רבי אבהו קרוב למלכות הוה, כדאמר בסנהדרין (דף יד.) ובכתובות (דף יז.): דמשרן אמהתא דבי קיסר: רבא דעמיה, מדברנא דאומתיה. עובדא הוה. והיא תובעתו לגרשה, לפי שלא היו לה בנים. דאתאי לקמיה דרבי אמי. ותובעתו לגרשה. לא מפקדת. ואם רוצה את לצאת – אין לך כתובה. מסיבו דילה. בזקנתה מה תהא עליה? חוטרא לידה. עד שתשען עליו לעת זקנתה, ואם תמות יקברנה. איכו ילדת לי חדא כרסא. ומי יתן שלא שתית, ותלדי לי עוד כרס אחד, שני בנים. אחי. תאומים. אחוותא

תוספות

אפילה תרי, והיא אמרה תלתא. והשתא ניחא הא דקאמר הוא אומר מינה, שהרי עכשיו הוחזקה בתלת זימני, ויש לה להפסיד כתובתה. והיא אמרה מיניה. ומסיק דנאמנת. ואם טוענת דאין יכול להזקק – פסקו רבותינו דנאמנת אפילו למשנה אחרונה. דדוקא כשטוענת שאין יורה כחץ חיישינן שמא משקרת, לפי שבעלה לא ידע בה דמשקרת, כדאמרי' בסוף נדרים (דף צא.). אבל במילתא דידע בה דמשקרא – נאמנת מדרב המנונא, *לפי שאין האשה מעיזה פניה בפני בעלה א).

ולא קאמר פרו ורבו. אע"ג דלאדם הראשון קאמר "פרו ורבו" – ההוא ברכה בעלמא, ולא למצוה*.

ואי סלקא דעתך דלא מיפקדא כתובה מאי עבידתה. משמע דאי מיפקדא – ניחא דיש לה כתובה. ותימה: דאי מפקדא, א"כ מיענשא אפריה ורביה, ואית לן למימר לאדרבה: איהי היא דלא זכתה, כדמוכח לעיל! ותירץ ר"י בן ר' מאיר: דהכא בידוע שהוא עקור. אבל ק"ק: אמאי פריך כתובה מאי עבידתה, ולא פריך נמי: אמאי יוציא.

כי הא ודאי כפינן. פר"ח: דכל הנך דכופין מחמתה – דוקא מנה ומאתים אית לה, אבל תוספת – לית לה, דאדעתא למיפק לא אוסיף לה. ודייק מהא דאמר בריש "אע"פ" (כתובות דף נד:) תנאי כתובה ככתובה, נפקא מינה למורדת כו', ולא קאמר נפקא מינה לבאה מחמת טענה, והיוצא בה. והא דלא קאמר נ"מ לשהה עמה עשר שנים, שיש לה נמי תוספת, דלא גרעה מאילונית, דאמר בסוף "אלמנה ניזונת" (שם ד' קא.) דיש לה תוספת – מילתא דפשיטא היא, כיון דלא מחמתה כופין, דמה היא יכולה אם ב"ד כופין אותו משום פריה ורביה. ור"ת מפרש: דלכל מילי הוי תנאי כתובה [ככתובה]. וממאנת וחברותיה דאין להם כתובה אע"פ שיש להם תוספת – התם משום דאיגלאי מילתא דלא נתקדשה מעולם. ולא יתכן דלענין "פרעתי" לא הוי תנאי כתובה ככתובה, דאכתובה – לא אמר כלום, ובתוספת – נאמן לומר "פרעתי", כדמוכח בעובדא דשבתאי בריה דרבי מרינוס (ב"מ יז.) ויש לדחות: דהתם לא הוסיף חתן עצמו, כ"א שבתאי אביו, ולא חשיב כשאר תוספת. ואין להאריך כאן. כן מצאתי בתשובה אחת שפסק ריצב"א על אשה שהיתה טוענת על בעלה כי אין לאיש גבורתו. והאיש היה טוען כי היה לו גבורת אנשים, אך היא בועטת וגורמת שאין יכול לבעול, דלא מהימנא מדרב המנונא*, כיון שהיתה תובעת כתובה. והיכא שהודה הבעל שאין יכול לבעול – פסק דצריך ליתן גט וכתובה אפילו אינה באה מחמת טענה, כיון דאין יכול כלל לקיים לה עונה. ודוקא מנה ומאתים, אבל תוספת – לא יתן. דהא נכנסה לחופה ולא נבעלה עמד בתיקו בריש ""אע"פ" (כתובות דף ט. ושם) דשמא לא כתב אלא ע"מ תיבת ביאה. ולרב האי גאון, דכל תיקו חולקין – שייך כאן דין חולקין. אבל נדוניתה שהכניסה לו – יחזיר הכל מה שידעו שהכניסה לו אבל מה שכותבין נדוניא גדולה לכבוד הכלה – נראה לו דהוי כעין תוספת. ומיהו, אם יכול להתקשות, ויש(א) כאן לכל הפחות הכנסת עטרה. אבל אין לו כח למרק – על זה נראה לו דיש תוספת, דיש כאן תיבת ביאה בהכנסת עטרה. ואם אין יכול לבעול מחמת שרתתה לו – כתב דאם המתין ג' שנים – דימתין עוד שנה. ואף על הקשוי כתב שאין לה למהר לסתור בנינה, כי רחמי שדי מרובים. ומטעם דפסק ר"ת דאין תוספת בבאה מחמת טענה משום דאדעתא למיפק לא כתב לה – זה הטעם אין שייך באין יכול ליבעול, דמידע ידיע דנישאת לו מתחילה לכך:

הדרן עלך הבא על יבמתו

עין משפט נר מצוה

קכג א מיי' פט"ו מהל' אישות הלכה יג טוש"ע אה"ע סימן קנד סעיף יג:

קכד ב מיי' שם טוש"ע שם סעיף יד:

קכה ג מיי' שם הלכה ב טוש"ע שם סימן א סעיף א:

קכו ד מיי' שם טוש"ע שם סעיף יג:

[לקמן קטז.]

קכז ה ו מיי' שם הלכה י טוש"ע שם סימן קנד סעיף ז:

[עיין רש"א סנהדרין נט: סד"ה גמרא והרי פריה ורביה]

[בנדרים צא. ועי' בהר"ן שם ובתוספות שם]

מסורת הש"ס

שבת קיא. גיטין מג: קדושין לה.

סוף מס' ד"א [ב"מ פז.]

בראשית יח

[כתובות סד.]

[נדה כז.]

תוספות חד מקמאי

בכתובה ה"ל כהלויתני ואיני יודע אם פרעתיך שחייב לדברי הכל כדתנן ההוא בהגוזל זוטא אבל במלתא דר"ג גבי מוכת עץ טוען הבעל שמעולם לא נתחייב לה בכתובה ולפום הכי אי לאו משום מגו א"נ משום חזקת דגופה הוה איהו מהימן:

תוספות ישנים

לא אמר משום שם רע אני מוציאה לא מצי אמר לה אילו הייתי יודע וכו' שהרי היה יכול לבודקה. ומדלא בדקה כאשר אנחנו רואים לבסוף כי שקר היה ודאי אמרינן שמחמת שנאה נתן לה גט ואפילו היה יודע בודאי שהשם רע שקר היה מגרשה. וגם כי לשם גרשה מדעתו. אבל הכא ב"ד נוו אותו לגרשה: **אי** איהי שתקה אנן מי שתקינן. וא"ת התם גבי המוציא את אשתו משום שם רע ואיילונית דאמרינן ר"י אומר אומרין לה שתיקותיך יפה ליך מדבוריך כי נשאת לאחר והיו לה בנים והיא תובעת כתובתה. אמאי לא פריך תלמודא אי איהו שתיק אנן מי שתקינן וי"ל דודאי הא דקאמר גט בטל ובניה ממזרים לא הוי אלא לעז בעלמא. וגם קשה אמאי לא קאמרי רבנן התם השתא הוא דבריאת כדאמרינן הכא וגם ר' יהודה למה לי טעמא דאמרינן שתיקותיך יפה ליך מדבוריך תיפוק לי דשמא השתא הוא דבריאת ומעיקרא הוות איילונית כשיגרשה ואין לה כתובה וצ"ל דבאיילונית לא מצי למימר השתא הוא דבריאת דלא שכיח לאיילונית תתרפא: **א)** אכן הכא קשה דלא מיירי בעקר מדקאמר איהי קים לה ביורה כחץ א"כ אין אנו יודעין כלל שהוא עקר וי"ל דהכא קאי אהא דאמרינן לעיל נשאת לשלישי ולא היו לה בנים ושהתה עם שני אנשים עשר שנים עם כל אחד והיא אומרת מיניה ואין לו להוציאה בלא כתובה אע"פ שיש לו לגרשה בדין מ"מ לא הוחזקתי לעקרה כי לא שהיתי כי אם שתי פעמים עשר שנים וזאת הפעם אינה מן המספר כי בשבילך הוא וכתובה אין לי להפסיד בשתי פעמים כדפרישנא דדוקא להנשא אסירה והוא אומר מינה והויא הוחזקה לעקרה ואין לה כתובה. אכן בהלכות גדולות איתא דהכא מיירי בתוך עשר שנים ובבאה מחמת טענה והיא לנדרים מיירי באינה באה מחמת טענה ולאי תקשי א"כ היכי הוה אמרינן מתחלה יוצאת ונוטלת כתובה לימא לה זיל לא מפקדת ומה לנו לדבריה. וי"ל דהתם מיירי דקאמרה שאין זרע יורה כחץ ולא נהניתי מביאתו: **לשנות** בדבר השלום. **א)** י"מ דאין זה שנוי גמור שהרי אמרה אחרי בלותי היתה לי עדנה בניחותא כלומר איני נבהלת אם אלד כי פרסתי נדה וחזרתי לנעורי אבן ואדוני זקן יוליד בנים. והמפרשים שאין זה שנוי גמור לפי שטח לומר כן מפני כבוד שכינה. וגם גבי שמואל י"ל דאין זה שנוי גמור שהרי היה הולך למשוח לדוד ולזבוח זבח זבחים כאשר קרא לדוד. והשם אמר לו שלא יגלה לשאול שהולך למשוח ולזבוח רק אזבוח לבד: **ואי** ס"ד לא מפקדא כתובה מאי עבידתה. פי' הרי אמר לה אם תרצי להיות עמי הרי זה טוב ואם אין את רוצה להיות אצלי ה"ז גיטיך בלא כתובה ומשמע אבל אי מיפקדא ניחא [ותימה] דאדרבה אז תיקשי אמאי יתן לה כתובה דלמא איהי לא [זכתה] דלעיל פריכינן הכי ומשני כיון דלא מפקדא **ב)** מיענשא ולא יתן כתובה וי"ל דהא דפרישית לעיל ניחא דמיירי הכא דידעינן ביה שהוא עקור וא"כ אי מיפקדא יתן לה כתובה דמיניה הוא מסתמא כיון שידוע הוא לעקור אבל פריך שפיר דאי לא מיפקדא כתובה מאי עבידתה הרי לא יבנה לעולם מאחרת ומשום האשה אין קפידא דהא לא מיפקדא:

א) נראה דצ"ל י"מ דהיה שינוי גמור שהרי אמרה וכו' ויש מפרשים שאין זה שינוי גמור לפי שטח וכו' ועי' היטב בתוס' על התורה ובדברי הריב"א שם מה שהביא בשם תוס'. ב) נ"ל כיון דלא מפקדא לא יענשא אבל אי מפקדא א"ל ליתן כתובה וי"ל לפי מאי דפרישית וכו'.

הגהות הב"ח

(א) תוס' סד"ה כי הא וכו' אם יכול להתקשות ויש לו כח לכל הפחות וכו' דיש לה תוספת:

אחוותא. תאומות ובנותיו היו. ועשאה בת חורין. כדי שתהא מותרת לינשא ומדכפינן לרבה אלמא מפקדא. מנהג הפקר נהגו בה. לפי שלא היתה יכולה לינשא היתה מפקרת עצמה ומוטאים בה לפיכך כפו את רבה לשחררה.

הדרן עלך הבא על יבמתו

אחוותא. ולא מיפקדי? והאמר רב אחא בר רב קטינא א"ר יצחק: *מעשה באשה אחת שחציה שפחה וחציה בת חורין, וכפו את רבה ועשאה בת חורין! אמר רב נחמן בר יצחק: [א]מנהג הפקר נהגו בה.§

הדרן עלך הבא על יבמתו

אלמנה [ב]לכהן גדול, גרושה וחלוצה לכהן הדיוט, הכניסה לו עבדי מלוג ועבדי *צאן ברזל, עבדי מלוג – לא יאכלו בתרומה, עבדי צאן ברזל – יאכלו. [ג]ואלו הן עבדי מלוג: אם מתו – מתו לה, ואם הותירו – הותירו לה, אע"פ [ד]שהוא חייב במזונותן הרי אלו לא יאכלו בתרומה. [ה]ואלו הן עבדי צאן ברזל: אם מתו – מתו לו, ואם הותירו – הותירו לו, הואיל והוא חייב באחריותן הרי אלו יאכלו בתרומה. [ו]בת ישראל שניסת לכהן והכניסה לו עבדים, בין עבדי מלוג בין עבדי צאן ברזל, הרי אלו יאכלו בתרומה. [ז]ובת כהן שניסת לישראל והכניסה לו עבדים, בין עבדי מלוג בין עבדי צאן ברזל, הרי אלו לא יאכלו בתרומה.§ **גמ'** ועבדי מלוג לא יאכלו בתרומה, אמאי? להוי כקנינו שקנה קנין! דתניא: מנין לכהן [ח]שנשא אשה [ט]וקנה עבדים שיאכלו בתרומה – שנאמר °"וכהן כי יקנה נפש קנין כספו הוא יאכל בו". [י]ומנין לאשה שקנתה עבדים, •ועבדיו שקנו עבדים, שיאכלו בתרומה – שנאמר "וכהן כי יקנה נפש קנין כספו הוא יאכל בו". קנינו שקנה קנין – אוכל! כל האוכל – מאכיל, כל שאין אוכל – אינו מאכיל. ולא? והרי ערל וכל הטמאים, שאינן אוכלין ומאכילין! התם פומייהו כאיב להו. והרי ממזר, שאין אוכל – ומאכיל! אמר רבינא: [כ]קנין אוכל קאמר, קנין אוכל – מאכיל, שאינו אוכל – אינו מאכיל. ורבא אמר: מדאורייתא מיכל אכלי, ורבנן הוא דגזרי בהו, כדי שתאמר: אני איני אוכלת, עבדי אינן אוכלין, זונה היא אצלו! הלכך אתי לאפוקה. רב אשי אמר: גזירה שמא תאכיל לאחר מיתה. אלא מעתה, בת ישראל שנשאת לכהן לא תאכיל גזירה שמא תאכיל לאחר מיתה! אלא אמר רב אשי: באלמנה כהנת דאתיא לאורויי: מעיקרא אכלי בתרומה דבי נשא, אינסבי ליה להאי – אכלי בתרומה דגבראי, והשתא הדרי לי למילתיה קמייתא, ולא ידעה דמעיקרא לא שויתה לנפשה חללה, השתא שויתה לנפשה חללה. תינח אלמנה כהנת, אלמנה בת ישראל מאי איכא למימר – באלמנותה *לא פליגי רבנן. איתמר: המכנסת שום לבעלה, היא אומרת: כלי אני נוטלת, והוא אומר: דמים אני נותן, הדין עם מי? רב יהודה אמר: הדין

(ויקרא כב)

רש"י

אלמנה לכהן גדול: הכניסה לו עבדי מלוג. מה שהאשה מכנסת לבעלה, ושמה לו לקבלם עליו באחריות כתובתה, כמו שכותבין: ודא נדוניא דהנעלת ליה. והוא מוסיף כנגדן וכותב: סך הכל קבל עליו פלוני כך וכך בכתובתה – קורין צאן ברזל. ויש שמכנסת ממון הרבה ואינה כותבת כולו בכתובתה, ומשיירת לעצמה – הן נכסי מלוג. והבעל אוכל פירות, והקרן שלה קיים. ואם מתו – מתו לה, *או פחתו – פחתו לה. לשון צאן ברזל – קרן קיים שאין פוחת ונפסד, שאפילו מתו כולן – אחריותן עליו לשלם לה כשימות או יגרשנה. עבדי מלוג לא יאכלו. לפי שהן שלה, והיא חללה. ולקמן בגמרא מפרש טעמא. בת ישראל שניסת לכהן. אפילו עבדי מלוג שאינן שלו – יאכלו, דהיינו קנינו שקנה קנין. וילפינן בגמרא דקנינו שקנה קנין אוכל. **גמ'** שנשא אשה וקנה עבדים. או קנה עבדים. ומנין לאשה. בת ישראל לכהן, שקנתה עבדים מנכסי מלוג שלה, או עבדיו של כהן שקנו עבדים. ועבדיו שקנו עבדים. גרסי'. וא"ת: מה שקנה עבד קנה רבו, ולמאי איצטריך קרא לרבוייהו? משכחת לה כגון שנתנו לו לעבד מנה על מנת שאין לרבו רשות בו. וכהן כי יקנה נפש קנין כספו. "קנין כספו" קרא יתירא, ודרשינן דלהכי אתא. והכי משמע: כהן כי יקנה קנין כספו נפש, שעבדו יקנה עבד – הוא יאכל בו. הערל. כהן ערל אינו אוכל, ועבדיו אוכלין, כדתנן לקמן (דף ע.). פומייהו כאיב להו. כלומר, מחוסרי תקנתא הם, אבל עומדים ליתקן ולאכול. אבל זו שהיא נעשית חללה – אין לה תיקון עולמית. והרי ממזר. בת ישראל שניסת לכהן וילדה בת, והבת ניסת לממזר וילדה בן ומתה, והבן קיים, והרי אם אמו אשת כהן אוכלת בשבילו תרומה לאחר מיתת בעלה – לפי שיש לה זרע מן הכהן, כדתנן בסיפא בפרקין (דף סט:), והוא אינו אוכל – דזר הוא. והוא הדין נמי אי כשר הוה, שנולד מישראל כשר, נמי אין אוכל, ומאכיל אם אמו. והא דנקט לאתויי ממזר – משום דמתניתין היא. שמא תאכיל. עבדי מלוג שלה לאחר מיתת הכהן בעלה. אבל בעבדי צאן ברזל ליכא למגזר, דהשתא לאו משום דידה אכלי אלא משום כהן שהוא רבן. אלא מעתה בת ישראל שנישאת לכהן לא תאכיל. עבדי מלוג בתרומה. גזירה שמא תאכיל לאחר מיתה. אלמה תנן במתניתין: בין עבדי מלוג בין עבדי צאן ברזל יאכלו. באלמנה כהנת. בת כהן ששבה לתרומת אביה ממיתת בעלה. ואי אמרינן יאכלו עבדי מלוג בתרומה בחיי בעלה כהן גדול זה, משום קנינו שקנה קנין, דלא גרעה הך חללה מעבד שקנה עבדים – אתיא לאורויי היתירא אחר מיתתו, להאכילם בתרומה מחמת אביה, דאמרה: מעיקרא באלמנותי הראשון היו עבדי אוכלין בתרומה דבי נשא. אינסבי ליה. לכ"ג, אכלי עבדי בתרומה דגבראי. השתא, כשמת, הדרי למילתא קמייתא, ויאכלו עבדי בתרומה דבי נשא כמעיקרא, באלמנותי הראשון. אלמנה בת ישראל. דלא אתיא לאורויי, מאי איכא למימר? מאי טעמא לא אכלי בחייו, הא לא גרעה מעבד שקנה עבדים! לא פליגי. לא חילקו בין אלמנה לאלמנה. המכנסת שום לבעלה. נכסי צאן ברזל ששמה לו בכתובתה, והיו בהן כלים ודבר המסויים, וכשגירשה ובאתה ליטול כתובתה. היא אומרת כלי אני נוטלת והוא אומר דמים אני נותן. כמו שקבלתי עלי בשומא, ומאחר הן באחריותי, ושלי הן. הדין

תוספות

אלמנה לכהן גדול: עבדי מלוג לא יאכלו. אפילו למ"ד(א) (גיטין דף מז:) קנין פירות כקנין הגוף דמי – לא חשיב בהכי קנין כספו, כיון שאין הגוף שלו, כמו שאין יוצאין בשן ועין לאיש, אפילו למ"ד קנין פירות כקנין הגוף דמי, כדאמר ב"החובל" (ב"ק דף פט: ושם). וקצת יש להביא ראיה דבתרומה אזלינן בתר קנין הגוף, דבריש פרק בתרא דכריתות (דף כד:) אמר, גבי המפקיר עבדו יצא לחירות, דמעוכב גט שחרור אוכל בתרומה, אע"פ שאין לרב פירות, אלא הגוף. ואפילו למ"ד קנין פירות כקנין הגוף דמי אתיא. **מנין** לכהן כו'. ממתניתין דקתני בסיפא "בת ישראל שניסת לכהן דעבדי מלוג שלה אוכלין" לא בעי למפרך – דה"א דאכלי מכח האשה עצמה שאוכלת, ולא מכח הבעל, משום קנינו שקנה קנין, להכי פריך מברייתא דקתני: קנינו שקנה קנין אוכל. וא"כ, אפילו אינה אוכלת – יש להם לאכול: **לכהן** שנשא אשה כו'. ה"ה שאירס, אלא נקט נשא משום דארוסה מדרבנן לא אכלה משום דעולא (כתובות דף נז:) או משום סמפון. **שנאמר** וכהן כי יקנה נפש. והא דדרשינן לעיל בפ' "הבא על יבמתו" (דף נז.) פצוע דכא כהן שנשא בת גרים – היינו מ"נפש" יתירא. **ועבדיו** שקנו עבדים. אפילו לרבי מאיר, דאמר (בקדושין דף כג:) אין קנין לעבד בלא רבו אפילו ע"מ שיצא בו לחירות, משכחת לה עבדים שקנו עבדים – במפקיר עבדו, דאוכל בתרומה, כדאמרינן בפרק בתרא דכריתות (ד' כד:). **גזירה** שמא תאכיל לאחר מיתה. ובעבדי צאן ברזל לא שייך למגזר, אפי' למ"ד (בסמוך) הדין עמה – דכל זמן שלא גבתה אותם בב"ד אוכלין מכחו, ואחר שגבתה ושמו לה ב"ד – הרי כאילו קנתה עבדים לאחר מיתת בעלה. **אלא** מעתה בת ישראל שניסת לכהן לא תאכיל שמא כו'. תימה: דלא דמי, דהתם ליכא למיטעי, דהא בחיי הבעל היתה אוכלת בעצמה ועכשיו אינה אוכלת. אבל כאן, אם יאכלו עבדים בחיי הבעל, אע"פ שבעצמה אינה אוכלת – איכא למגזר שמא תאכיל גם לאחר מיתה! ואית ספרים דגרסי: בת ישראל שניסת לכהן לא תאכל. ופריך: דהיא עצמה לא תאכל, שמא תאכל אחר מיתה. ולספרים דגרסי "נמי לא תאכיל" – איכא למימר דאכולי מילתא פריך: שלא תאכל ולא תאכיל, אלא דנקט לא תאכיל משום דניחא ליה לאקשויי מעבדים אעבדים. כרשיני

תוספות ישנים

עבדי מלוג לא יאכלו בתרומה. וא"ת למ"ד קנין פירות כקנין הגוף דמי אמאי לא יאכלו הא אית ליה בגווייהו פירות וי"ל דגבי תרומה כיון דהויא מן התורה בעינן קנין הגוף דכתיב כי יקנה נפש. וה"נ אמרינן מחוסר גט שחרור אוכל בתרומה אע"ג דאין (לבעל) [להאדון] בו שום פירות שפחררו מ"מ כיון דגופו קנוי דצריך גט אוכל בתרומה: **ועבדים** שקנו עבדים. פ"ה וא"ת הא למה לי קרא מה שקנה עבד קנה רבו וי"ל דאצטריך היכא שנתנו לו ע"מ שאין לרבו רשות בו וא"ת לר"מ דאמר (איהו) בקדושין (כ"ד) דאפ"ה לא קני ליה עבד דקני ליה רבו משום דאין קנין לעבד בלא רבו מאי איכא למימ' וי"ל דלר"מ נימא דעיקר קרא לאשה שקנתה עבדים ואגב אשה נקט עבדים שקנו עבדים וא"ת והא אשה נמי אמרינן מה שקנתה אשה קנה בעלה וי"ל דהכא מיירי שנתנו לה במתנה ע"מ שאין לבעלה רשות בהן ובמתנה זכתה ואין הבעל אוכל פירות. וא"ת ואמאי לא פריך מגופה דמתני' בת ישראל שנשאת לכהן והכניסה לו בין עבדי מלוג בין עבדי צאן ברזל אלמא קנינו שקנה קנין אוכל וי"ל דאי מהתם הוה ידע תלמודא שפיר דמשנינן דשאני התם שהיא אוכלת ולכך עבדיה אוכלין מכחה. אבל הכא שאינה אוכלת לא אכלי עבדיהם דהיינו כדמשני כל האוכל מאכיל וכו' אבל פריך מהא דקאמר מכח הפסוק דקנין כהן שקנה קנין אוכל וכיון דמקרא נפיק ס"ד דאין חילוק בין אוכלת לאינה אוכלת דמכח הכהן יש להם לאכול ומ"מ משני דווקא האוכל קאמר קרא דמאכיל אבל קנין שאינו אוכל אינו מאכיל: ת"ל וכהן כי יקנה נפש קנין כספו דדרשינן וכהן כי יקנה כספו נפש יאכל וכו'. וא"ת והא אצטריך לקמן לפצוע דכא כהן שנשא בת גרים. וי"ל דמיתורא דנפש קא דריש:

תוספות חד מקמאי

אלמנה. הא דתנן אלמנה לכ"ג גרושה וחלוצה לכהן הדיוט והכניסה לו (נכסי) [עבדי] מלוג לא יאכלו אסקוה רבא ורב אשי בתראי דמדרבנן היא אבל מדאורייתא אכלי דלא גרע מקניינו שקנה קנין דתניא מנין לכהן שנשא אשה וקנה עבדים שיאכלו בתרומה שנאמר וכהן כי יקנה נפש קנין וכו' אפילו קניינו שקנה קנין אוכל ומיהו רבינא ס"ל דמדאורייתא נמי לא אכלה דכל קנין שאוכל מאכיל קנין שאינו אוכל אינו מאכיל אבל מידי דלא קנין הוא אע"פ שאינו אוכל מאכיל שהרי ישראל אע"פ שאין אוכלים ומאכילין אם אמו שהיתה בת ישראל לכהן כדאיתא במתני':

הגהות הב"ח

(א) תום' ד"ה עבדי וכו' למ"ד קנין כ"ב פרק החולץ דף לו:

גליון הש"ם

גמ' ועבדיו שקנו עבדים. עי' נזיר ד' סא ע"ב תד"ה אי הכי בעבדים נמי:

מסורת הש"ם

גיטין לח. [סג: ע"ש]

ס"א ואם הותירו הותירו

[לקמן קז. כתובות נב: ב"מ נג.]

עין משפט נר מצוה

קכח א מיי' פ"ט מהל' עבדים ה"ו סמג עשין פב טוש"ע יו"ד סי' רסז סעיף עט:

א ב מיי' פ"ז מהל' תרומות הל' כ טוי"ד סי' שלב:

ב ג מיי' פט"ז מהל' אישות הל' א סמג עשין מח טוש"ע אה"ע סי' פה סעי' ב:

ג ד מיי' שם פכ"ב הל' כה סמג שם טוש"ע שם סעי' טז:

ד ה מיי' שם פט"ז הל' א טוש"ע שם סעי' ב:

ה ו מיי' פ"ז מהל' תרומות הל' יח טוי"ד סי' שלב:

ו ז מיי' שם הלכה יט:

ז ח מיי' שם פ"ו הל' ג טור שם:

ח ט מיי' שם הל' א:

[וז"ל רש"י ב"מ סט: ד"ה אין מקבלין צאן ברזל וכו' ונראה לי שרוב המקבלים כך היו נוהגים לקבל בהמה דקה להכי קרי להו צאן]

ט י ב מיי' פ"ז שם הל' יח טור שם:

גמרא

א הַדִּין *עִמָּהּ, וְרַ' אַמִּי אָמַר: הַדִּין עִמּוֹ. רַב יְהוּדָה אָמַר: הַדִּין עִמָּהּ, מִשּׁוּם *שֶׁבַח בֵּית אָבִיהָ – דִּידָהּ הָוֵי. רַ' אַמִּי אָמַר: הַדִּין עִמּוֹ, כֵּיוָן דַּאֲמַר מָר: אִם מֵתוּ – מֵתוּ לוֹ, וְאִם הוֹתִירוּ – הוֹתִירוּ לוֹ, הוֹאִיל וְחַיָּיב בְּאַחֲרָיוּתָן – יֹאכְלוּ. אֲמַר רַב סַפְרָא: מִי קָתָנֵי "וְהֵן שֶׁלּוֹ"? "הוֹאִיל וְחַיָּיב בְּאַחֲרָיוּתָן" קָתָנֵי, וּלְעוֹלָם לָאו דִּידֵיהּ נִינְהוּ. וְכָל הֵיכָא דְּחַיָּיב בְּאַחֲרָיוּתָן אָכְלֵי בִּתְרוּמָה? וְהָתְנַן: ב יִשְׂרָאֵל *שֶׁשָּׂכַר פָּרָה מִכֹּהֵן – הֲרֵי זֶה יַאֲכִילֶנָּה כַּרְשִׁינֵי תְרוּמָה. כֹּהֵן שֶׁשָּׂכַר פָּרָה מִיִּשְׂרָאֵל, אע"פ שֶׁמְּזוֹנוֹתֶיהָ עָלָיו – לֹא יַאֲכִילֶנָּה כַּרְשִׁינֵי תְרוּמָה! וְתִסְבְּרָא? נְהִי נַמִי דִּמְחַיֵּיב בִּגְנֵבָה וַאֲבֵדָה – בַּאֲוֹנָסֶיהָ, בְּכַחֲשָׁהּ, וּבִפְחָתַת דָּמִים מִי מִיחַיֵּיב! הָא לָא דָּמְיָא אֶלָּא לְסֵיפָא: ג יִשְׂרָאֵל שֶׁשָּׁם פָּרָה מִכֹּהֵן – לֹא יַאֲכִילֶנָּה כַּרְשִׁינֵי תְרוּמָה, אֲבָל כֹּהֵן שֶׁשָּׁם פָּרָה מִיִּשְׂרָאֵל – יַאֲכִילֶנָּה כַּרְשִׁינֵי תְרוּמָה. יָתֵיב רַבָּה וְרַב יוֹסֵף בְּשִׁילְהֵי פִּרְקֵיהּ דְּרַב נַחְמָן, וְיָתְבֵי וְקָאָמְרִי: תַּנְיָא כְּוָותֵיהּ דְּרַב יְהוּדָה, וְתַנְיָא כְּוָותֵיהּ דְּרַבִּי אַמִּי. תַּנְיָא כְּוָותֵיהּ דְּרַ' אַמִּי: ד עַבְדֵי צֹאן בַּרְזֶל יוֹצְאִין בְּשֵׁן וָעַיִן לְאִישׁ, אֲבָל לֹא לְאִשָּׁה. תַּנְיָא כְּוָותֵיהּ דְּרַב יְהוּדָה: ה הַמַּכְנֶסֶת שׁוּם לְבַעְלָהּ, אִם רָצָה הַבַּעַל לִמְכּוֹר – לֹא יִמְכּוֹר, וְלֹא עוֹד אֶלָּא אֲפִילּוּ הִרְוִיחַ לָהּ שׁוּם מִשֶּׁלּוֹ, אִם רָצָה הַבַּעַל לִמְכּוֹר – לֹא יִמְכּוֹר. מָכְרוּ שְׁנֵיהֶם לְפַרְנָסָה, זֶה הָיָה מַעֲשֶׂה לִפְנֵי רשב"ג, וְאָמַר: הַבַּעַל מוֹצִיא מִיַּד הַלָּקוֹחוֹת. אָמַר רָבָא אָמַר רַב נַחְמָן: הֲלָכָה כְּרַב יְהוּדָה. א"ל רָבָא לְרַב נַחְמָן: וְהָתַנְיָא כְּוָותֵיהּ דְּרַ' אַמִּי! אע"ג דְּתַנְיָא כְּוָותֵיהּ דְּרַ' אַמִּי, מִסְתַּבְּרָא טַעֲמָא דְּרַב יְהוּדָה, מִשּׁוּם שֶׁבַח בֵּית אָבִיהָ. הַהִיא אִיתְּתָא דְּעַיְּילָה לֵיהּ לְגַבְרָא אִיצְטְלָא דְּמֵילְתָא בִּכְתוּבְּתָהּ, שְׁכֵיב, שְׁקַלוּהָ יַתְמֵי וּפְרָסוּהָ אַמִּיתְנָא. אָמַר רָבָא: ו קַנְיֵיהּ מִיתְנָא. אֲמַר לֵיהּ נָאנַאי, בְּרֵיהּ דְּרַב יוֹסֵף, בְּרֵיהּ דְּרָבָא, לְרַב כָּהֲנָא: וְהָאָמַר רָבָא אָמַר רַב נַחְמָן: הֲלָכָה כְּרַב יְהוּדָה! אֲמַר לֵיהּ: מִי לָא מוֹדֶה רַב יְהוּדָה דִּמְחוּסַּר גּוּבַיְינָא? וְכֵיוָן דִּמְחוּסַּר גּוּבַיְינָא – בִּרְשׁוּתֵיהּ קָאֵי. רָבָא לְטַעְמֵיהּ, דְּאָמַר רָבָא: *הֶקְדֵּשׁ, חָמֵץ, וְשִׁחְרוּר

רש"י

הַדִּין עִמָּהּ. וְתִטּוֹל כֵּלֶיהָ. יֹאכְלוּ. וּמִדְּאָכְלֵי בִּתְרוּמָה – ש"מ דִּידֵיהּ נִינְהוּ. שֶׁשָּׂכַר פָּרָה מִיִּשְׂרָאֵל. וְהָא שׂוֹכֵר חַיָּיב בְּאַחֲרָיוּתָהּ אִם נִגְנְבָה אוֹ נֶאֶבְדָה, וְקָתָנֵי לֹא יַאֲכִילֶנָּה כַּרְשִׁינֵי תְרוּמָה: ה"ג. וְתִסְבְּרָא נְהִי נַמִי דְּחַיָּיב בִּגְנֵבָה וַאֲבֵדָה בַּאֲוֹנָסֶיהָ וּבְכַחֲשָׁהּ וּבְנִפְחַת דָּמֶיהָ מִי מִיחַיֵּיב. שׂוֹכֵר פָּטוּר מִן הָאוֹנָסִין, וְכֵן אִם כָּחֲשָׁה וְאִם הוּזַל דָּמֶיהָ. הָא. מַתְנִיתִין לָא דָּמְיָא אֶלָּא לְסֵיפָא. אֲבָל כֹּהֵן שֶׁשָּׁם פָּרָה מִיִּשְׂרָאֵל. בְּדָמִים, כְּשֶׁשְּׂכָרָהּ הֶעֱמִידוּהָ שׁוּמָא לוֹ, *וְהִתְנָה עִמּוֹ לְהַחֲזִירָהּ לוֹ בְּדָמִים הַלָּלוּ, שֶׁאִם תִּכְחַשׁ אוֹ תָּמוּת אוֹ יוּזְלוּ פָּרוֹת בָּעוֹלָם יִתֵּן הַדָּמִים. יַאֲכִילֶנָּה כַּרְשִׁינֵי תְרוּמָה. הוֹאִיל וְקִבְּלָהּ בְּאַחֲרָיוּתוֹ, וְאַף עַל פִּי שֶׁחוֹזֶרֶת בְּעֵינֶיהָ אִם לֹא יִפְחֲתוּ דָּמֶיהָ – כָּל כַּמָּה דְּלָא הָדְרָה דִּידֵיהּ הוּא. וְגַבֵּי עֲבָדִים נַמִי, אע"ג דְּהָדְרִי בְּעֵינַיְיהוּ, כֵּיוָן דִּלְעִנְיַן יוּקְרָא וְזוּלָא קָיְימֵי בִּרְשׁוּתֵיהּ – אָכְלֵי. בְּשִׁילְהֵי פִּירְקֵיהּ. כְּשֶׁסִּיֵּים הַדְּרָשָׁה. בְּשֵׁן וָעַיִן לְאִישׁ. אִם סִימֵּא הַבַּעַל אֶת עֵינוֹ. אֲבָל לֹא לְאִשָּׁה. אִם סִימְּתָה עֵינוֹ, דְּלָאו דִּידָהּ הוּא. לֹא יִמְכּוֹר. שֶׁאִם יְגָרְשֶׁנָּה תִּטּוֹל כֵּלֶיהָ. מָכְרוּ שְׁנֵיהֶם. אוֹ זֶה אוֹ זֶה. לְפַרְנָסָה. אוֹרְחָא דְּמִילְּתָא נָקַט, שֶׁאֵין אָדָם מוֹכֵר כְּלֵי תַּשְׁמִישָׁיו אֶלָּא לִמְזוֹנוֹת. הַבַּעַל מוֹצִיא. לָא מִיבַּעְיָא דְּאִם מָכַר הוּא בְּלֹא דַּעְתָּהּ, וּמֵת אוֹ גֵּרְשָׁהּ – דְּהִיא מוֹצִיאָה מִיַּד הַלָּקוֹחוֹת, אֶלָּא אֲפִילּוּ מֵתָה הִיא הוּא מוֹצִיא מִיַּד הַלָּקוֹחוֹת, דִּמְכִירָה לָאו מְכִירָה הֲוַאי(א), *(שֶׁמָּא יָמוּת הוּא בְּחַיֶּיהָ וְנִמְצֵאת מְכִירָה שֶׁלֹּא כַּדִּין) כָּל זְמַן שֶׁהִיא קַיֶּימֶת. קַנְיֵיהּ מִיתְנָא. תַּכְרִיכֵי הַמֵּת אִיסּוּרֵי הֲנָאָה הֵן כְּהֶקְדֵּשׁ, דְּגָמַר "שָׁם" "שָׁם" מֵעֶגְלָה עֲרוּפָה, בְּפֶ' "נִגְמַר הַדִּין" (סנהדרין דף מז:). מִי לָא מוֹדֶה רַב יְהוּדָה דִּמְחוּסַּר גּוּבַיְינָא. אע"ג דְּהַדִּין עִמָּהּ, מוֹדֶה הוּא דְּכָל כַּמָּה דְּלָא גָּבְתִינְהוּ מִינֵּיהּ – לָאו בִּרְשׁוּתָהּ קָיְימֵי, אֶלָּא שִׁיעְבּוּדָא בְּעָלְמָא אִית לָהּ עֲלַיְיהוּ. דְּהָא אִם נֶאֶנְסוּ אוֹ נֶאֶבְדוּ – חַיָּיב בְּאַחֲרָיוּתָן. וְכֵיוָן דְּבִרְשׁוּת יַתְמֵי נִינְהוּ – אָתֵי הֶקְדֵּשׁ דְּאַקְדְּשׁוּהּ יַתְמֵי וּמַפְקַע לָהּ לְשִׁיעְבּוּדַיְיהוּ, וְיָהֲבֵי דְּמֵי. רָבָא לְטַעְמֵיהּ כו'. הֶקְדֵּשׁ – דַּוְקָא קְדוּשַּׁת הַגּוּף, כִּי הַאי גַּוְונָא. אֲבָל קְדוּשַּׁת דָּמִים – לָא, כִּדְתְנַן (ערכין דף כג:): מוֹסִיף עוֹד דִּינָר וּפוֹדֶה הַנְּכָסִים הַלָּלוּ כו'. חָמֵץ. גּוֹי שֶׁהִלְוָה אֶת יִשְׂרָאֵל עַל חֲמֵצוֹ אַחַר הַפֶּסַח – אָסוּר בַּהֲנָאָה, דְּאָתֵי אִיסּוּר חָמֵץ וּמַפְקַע לֵיהּ לְשִׁיעְבּוּדָא דְּגוֹי. וְהָא דִּתְנַן בְּפֶרֶק "כָּל שָׁעָה" (פסחים דף ל.): מוּתָּר בַּהֲנָאָה – רָבָא מוֹקֵי לָהּ הָתָם כְּשֶׁהִרְהִינוֹ אֶצְלוֹ, שֶׁנְּתָנוֹ יִשְׂרָאֵל בְּבֵיתוֹ שֶׁל גּוֹי, דְּהַהוּא לָא מִיחַסַּר גּוּבַיְינָא. וְשִׁחְרוּר

תוספות

כרשיני תרומה. אר"י: דעיקרס קיימי למאכל בהמה. דאם היו עיקרם לאדם – היה אסור ליתנם לבהמה, משום הפסד תרומה. ומ"מ חזו לאדם, דאי לא חזו כלל לאדם – פטורין מתרומה ומעשר, כדאמר בריש "כלל גדול" (שבת דף סח. ושם).

לא יאכילנה כרשיני תרומה. והא דתנן (עירובין דף כו:) מערבין לישראל בתרומה, דשרי בהנאה! אר"ת דהיינו דוקא הנאה שאין של כילוי, אבל הנאה של כילוי כגון להאכיל לבהמתו – אסור. וכן להדליקה ולהסיקה תחת תבשילו, כדתנן במסכת תרומות (פי"א מ"י) מדליקין בשמן של תרומה(ג) במבואות האפילות ע"ג כהן, ברשות כהן. פי': כשיש שם כהן שצריך לאותה אורה, דנר לאחד נר למאה, אבל לא ברשות ישראל. והא דאמר ב"כל שעה" (פסחים דף לד.) אבא שאול גבל של בית רבי הוה והיה מחמם חמין *בשמן של תרומה שנטמאה – אמר ר"ת: דהיינו לכהנים שבבית רבי. וטעמא דלא אסור אלא הנאה של כילוי מפרש ר"י: משום דדרשינן בפ' "במה מדליקין" (שבת דף כו. ושם) גבי אין מדליקין בטבל טמא "את משמרת תרומותי" – בשתי תרומות הכתוב מדבר, אחת תרומה טמאה ואחת תרומה טהורה. מה תרומה טהורה – אין לך בה אלא משעת הרמה ואילך, פירוש: עיקר הנאתה, דהיינו אכילה – אף תרומה טמאה אין לך בה עיקר הנאה, דהיינו הדלקה, אלא משעת הרמה ואילך. ומהכא יליף דאין מדליקין בטבל טמא. ובטבל טהור נמי(ג) משמע גבי עובדא דרבי פנחס בן יאיר (חולין דף ז.) דאסור הנאה של כלוי, היינו משום דהדר ילפינן תרומה טהורה מטמאה. ולא כמו שפירש שם בקונטרס *דכ"ש בטבל טהור. דכל שכן לא הוי, דטהור מטמא הוא דילפינן, וכי היכי דילפינן לאסור טבל בהנאה של כילוי – הכי נמי ילפינן לאסור זו בתרומה, דמשעת הרמה לא הותרה אלא לכהנים ולא לישראל*א).

***ישראל** ששכר פרה מכהן שמאכילה כרשיני תרומה אע"פ שמזונותיה עליו. אר"י: היינו משום דבהמה האוכלת היא קנין כספו של כהן, וישראל אין נהנה אלא הדמים, והרי הוא כמוכר תרומה לכהן והדמים שלו. אבל כהן ששכר פרה מישראל – לא יאכילנה, דלאו קנין כספו דכהן הוא, דשכירות לא קניא.

דמחייב בגניבה ואבדה כו'. כאן משמע דהלכתא כמ"ד דשוכר כנושא שכר דמי ב"האומנים" (ב"ב דף פ:) וכן הלכה, כדמשמע בריש "המפקיד" (שם דף לו.) גבי שוכר ושואל פעמים שניהם באנס כו', ובפרק "השואל" (שם דף נז.) גבי ההוא דאגר כודני לבי חוזאי*. **אבל** כהן ששם פרה מישראל. פירש בקונטרס: כששכרה הימנו התנה להחזיר לו דמים אלו אם תכחש או תאנס או יוזלו הפרות. ואר"י, דאסור לעשות כן משום רבית, כדמוכח בפרק "איזהו נשך" (שם דף סד.*) אלא איירי בשואל. **עבדי** צאן ברזל יוצאין בשן ועין. תימה לר"י: מה ראיה מייתי מהכא לרבי אמי? דהא רב יהודה נמי מודה דיוצאין בשן ועין לאיש, דחשיב כעבדו, כי היכי דחשיב כספו לענין תרומה, דתנן: עבדי צאן ברזל יאכלו בתרומה, דתרומה ושן ועין ענין אחד הוא, כדפי' במתני'. ועוד הקשה הר' משה כהן: דמי לא מודה רב יהודה דמיחסרי גוביינא, וא"כ ברשותיה קיימי, ושחרור מפקיע מידי שעבוד, כדאמר לקמן גבי איצטלא דמילתא דפרסוה אמיתנא, דאפי' לרב יהודה מפקיעין מידי שיעבוד. דאפי' שחרור דשן ועין, דממילא, אמרינן ב"החובל" (ב"ק דף פט: ושם) דמפקיע מידי שיעבוד? ואין לומר דרבה ורב יוסף דדייקי מהכא תניא כוותיה דרבי אמי לית להו דרבא, דאמר שיחרור מפקיע מידי שיעבוד – דהא ממתני' ד"השולח" (גיטין דף מ: ושם) דייק לה. ואין לומר לית להו ההוא טעמא דלקמן כיון דמיחסרי גוביינא ברשותיה קיימי, דהא רבא אית ליה ההוא טעמא בסמוך ואפ"ה קאמר רבא לרב נחמן: והא תניא כוותיה דרבי אמי! ותירץ ה"ר שמואל בר' חיים מוורדי"ש: דדייק מאבל לא לאשה. ומחיים לא איצטריך, דפשיטא, אלא לאחר מיתה קאמר דאין יוצאין לאשה – משום דהדין עמו. **הבעל** מוציא מיד הלקוחות. פי' בקונטרס: דאפילו מתה היא, מוציא הוא מיד הלקוחות. משמע מתוך פירושו דכל זמן שהאשה חיה – אין הבעל יכול להוציאם כשמכר הוא עצמו, אלא כשמתה האשה, דאז יורש כחה, והיא היתה יכולה למחות בחיים. ותימה הוא: דכיון שהמכירה קיימת כל זמן שהאשה שותקת – למה תוכל לבטל מכירתו במחאתה על חנם? דמחיים אין לה בהם כלום. ועוד: דאפילו אם האשה תוכל להוציא מחיים – נראה דאין הבעל יכול להוציא אחר מיתה, ולא אמרינן דבמקום אשתו קאי – כיון שמכר בעצמו, כדמשמע בפרק "מי שהיה נשוי" (כתובות דף נא:) גבי ההוא גברא דזבין כתובתה דאימיה בטובת הנאה, אמר: אי אתיא אם ומערערה – לא מפלינא לך. שכיבא אימיה, אתא איהו וקא מערער. סבר רמי בר חמא: איהו במקום אימיה קאי, א"ל רבא: נהי דלאחריות דאימיה לא קביל עילויה – אחריות דידיה קביל עילויה, ונראה כפר"ח: דאין המקח קיים כלל אפי' שעה אחת, דתקון רבנן שלא תהא אשה צריכה לטרוח ולחזור להוציא מיד הלקוחות אחר מיתת הבעל. דלא דמי לאשה הטורפת מנכסים משועבדים לכתובה – דהתם הויא מכירה, דשמא לא תהא אשה צריכה לטרוח שיפרעו לה כתובתה, או תטרוף מבני חרי. אבל היכא שאין יכולים לסלקה בשאר נכסים – תקנו שהמקח בטל לאלתר.

פוסל

עין משפט נר מצוה

י א טוש"ע אה"ע סימן פה סעי' ג:
יא ב מיי' פ"ט מהל' תרומות הל' ז טוי"ד סי' שלא:
יב ג מיי' שם הל' ח:
יג ד מיי' פ"ה מהל' עבדים הל' טו טוש"ע יו"ד סי' רכז סעיף לח:
יד ה מיי' פכ"ב מהל' אישות הל' ופכ"ב מכירה הל' טו סמג עשין פא טוש"ע אה"ע סי' צ סעי' יד:
טו ו מיי' פי"ד מהלכות אבל הל' כב סמג עשין מד"ע ג טוש"ע יו"ד סי' שמט סעי' ג:

מסורת הש"ס

גיטין מד:
[כתובות עט:]
נ"ל התנה להחזיר לו דמים אלו אם תכחש או הוזל דמיה שיאכילנה כרשיני תרומה, רש"ל
ע"ז טו. [תרומות פי"א מ"ט]
[וצ"ל בחיטין]
רח"ח אין זה
[שבת כו.]
לעיל מו. כתובות נט: גיטין מ: נדרים פו: ב"ק פט:
[וע"ע תוספות פסחים לג: ד"ה אמר קרא ותוספות מנחות סז: ד"ה כדין]
יזקלת נראה שצייך כל דיבור זה לדלעיל והכל בדיבור אחד נאמרו וכן מגלתי אח"כ ברש"ל
[וע"ע תוספות ב"ק מז: ד"ה סברוה]
[וע"ע כתוס' ד"ה אי תקפה]

הגהות הב"ח

(א) רש"י ד"ה הבעל וכו' לאו מכירה הואי כל זמן שהיא קיימת שמא ימות הוא בחייה ונמצאת מכירה שלא כדין כצ"ל: (ב) תוס' ד"ה לא וכו' בשמן של תרומה שנטמאה במבואות האפלות וגבי החולים בשבת כהן: (ג) בא"ד ובטבל טהור נמי אין מדליקין כדמשמע גבי עובדא:

תוספות ישנים

הואיל וחייב באחריותן יאכלו. והיינו דלא כרב יהודה. ותימה דהא כרב יהודה מאי ספיר אתיא לרב יהודה נמי מודה שהם ברשותו של בעל קודם שיגרשנה ומ"ה אכלי בתרומה וי"ל דלרב יהודה כיון דלאחר מיתה וגירושין יהיו שלה דקאמר הדין עמה וגם מחיים קאמר רב יהודה לקמן אם רצה הבעל למכור לאו כדידיה דמו ולא היה להם לאכול בתרומה דאין גופן קנוי לו: **א)** וה"ר משה תירץ דכל הנאות של תרומה מותרו' לישראל רק להאכיל לבהמתו משום דהויא בכלל נפש כדדרשינן על כל נפשות מת לא יבא שומע אני אפילו נפש בהמה כשהוא אומר לאביו ולאמו וכו' משמע דבהמה הויא בכלל נפש ולהכי אמרי' הכא דהיכא שספרה של ישראל אין להאכילה תרומה כדכתיב וכהן כי יקנה נפש קנין כספו דבעינן שהנפש יהיה קנין כספו כשאוכל בתרומה: **יוצאין** בשן ועין לאיש. וא"כ הדין עמו דאי הדין עמה לא היה יכול להוציאם לחרות דאע"ג דרב יהודה מודה לאוכלין בתרומה מ"מ לא קאמר דמצי להוציאם לחרות דכיון דקאמר לקמן אם רצה הבעל למכור לא ימכור כמו כן אינו יכול למכור העבד לעצמו להיות מגן ועין בן חורין: **ורבא** לטעמיה דאמר הקדש חמץ ושחרור מפקיע מידי שעבוד. ותימה מאי מדמה התם הוא טעמא משום שיכול הלוה לסלק למלוה בזוזי אבל הכא כיון דהדין עמה אין היורשין יכולים לסלקה בדמים. וי"ל דדוקא התם שהקנה הגוף העבד למלוה בעינן שיוכל הלוה לסלקו בזוזי דאי לאו הכי לא הוי השחרור מפקיע מידי שעבוד אבל הכא דאף על גב דהדין עמה כ"ז שלא גבתה ברשותא דבעל קאי והגוף קנוי לו עתה שהרי משתעבד הוא ממנו וא"כ יכול הקדשו ושחרורו להפקיע שעבוד האשה וא"ת אמאי לא אמרינן אלמוה רבנן לשעבודא דאשה כדאמרינן פרק אע"פ י"ל דהיינו דווקא כשאינו אוסר לכל העולם אבל הכא דאסר לכולי עלמא משום דפרסוה על המת [לא] אמרינן אלמוה:

תוספות חד מקמאי

איתמר המכנסת שום לבעלה הוא אומר (כלי) [דמים] אני נותן והיא אומרת כלי אני נוטלת רב יהודה אומר הדין עמה משום שבח בית אביה והלכתא כותיה וכ"ש אם אמרה דמים אני נוטלת שהדין עמה משום דינא ולא משום שבח בית אביה תניא כותיה דרב יהודה המכנסת שום לבעלה אם רצה הבעל למכור לא ימכור מכרו שניהם לפרנסה היה מעשה לפני ר"ג ואמר הבעל מוציא מיד הלקוחות. כתב הרב אלפס הא מילתא דר"ג בעיא ולא אפשטא שפיר ולא עבדי' בה עובדא ואבא מרי ז"ל כתב מכרו שניהם לפרנסה כיון שלקחה מן האיש וחזר ולקח האשה. וכ' רש"י לא מבעיא אשה עצמה שמוציאה מן הלקוחות אפי' בחיי בעלה כיון שיכולה לומר בשעת גביית כתובה כלי אני

וְשִׁחְרוּר — מַפְקִיעִין מִידֵי שִׁעְבּוּד. א"ר יְהוּדָה: אהִכְנִיסָה לוֹ שְׁנֵי כֵּלִים בְּאֶלֶף זוּז, וְשָׁבְחוּ וְעָמְדוּ עַל שְׁנֵי אֲלָפִים — אֶחָד נוֹטַלְתּוֹ בִּכְתוּבָּתָהּ, וְאֶחָד נוֹתֶנֶת דָּמִים וְנוֹטַלְתּוֹ, מִפְּנֵי שֶׁשֶּׁבַח בֵּית אָבִיהָ. מַאי קָא מַשְׁמַע לָן, שֶׁבַח בֵּית אָבִיהָ דִּידַהּ הָוֵי — הָא אֲמָרָהּ רַב יְהוּדָה חֲדָא זִימְנָא! מַהוּ דְּתֵימָא: ה"מ — הֵיכָא דְּמָטְיָא לְמִשְׁקַל בִּכְתוּבָּתָהּ, אֲבָל מֵיתַן דָּמֵי וּמִישְׁקַל לָא — קמ"ל.§

מתני' בבַּת יִשְׂרָאֵל שֶׁנִּיסֵּת לְכֹהֵן וָמֵת, וְהִנִּיחָהּ מְעוּבֶּרֶת, לֹא יֹאכְלוּ עֲבָדֶיהָ בִּתְרוּמָה, מִפְּנֵי חֶלְקוֹ שֶׁל עוּבָּר. *שֶׁהָעוּבָּר פּוֹסֵל, וְאֵינוֹ מַאֲכִיל, דִּבְרֵי רַ' יוֹסֵי. אָמְרוּ לוֹ: מֵאַחַר שֶׁהֵעַדְתָּ לָנוּ עַל בַּת יִשְׂרָאֵל לְכֹהֵן — אַף בַּת כֹּהֵן לְכֹהֵן וָמֵת, וְהִנִּיחָהּ מְעוּבֶּרֶת — לֹא יֹאכְלוּ עֲבָדֶיהָ בִּתְרוּמָה, מִפְּנֵי חֶלְקוֹ שֶׁל עוּבָּר.§

גמ' אִיבַּעְיָא לְהוּ: טַעֲמָא דְּרַבִּי יוֹסֵי מִשּׁוּם דְּקָסָבַר עוּבָּר בִּמְעֵי זָרָה זָר הוּא, אוֹ דִּלְמָא: יָלוּד — מַאֲכִיל, שֶׁאֵינוֹ יָלוּד — אֵינוֹ מַאֲכִיל? לְמַאי נָפְקָא מִינָּהּ — לְעוּבָּר בִּמְעֵי כֹּהֶנֶת, מַאי? אֲמַר רַבָּה: הַיְינוּ טַעֲמָא דְּרַבִּי יוֹסֵי: דְּקָסָבַר עוּבָּר בִּמְעֵי זָרָה — זָר הוּא. רַב יוֹסֵף אֲמַר: גיָלוּד — מַאֲכִיל, שֶׁאֵין יָלוּד — אֵינוֹ מַאֲכִיל. מֵיתִיבֵי, אָמְרוּ לוֹ לְרַ' יוֹסֵי: מֵאַחַר שֶׁהֵעַדְתָּ לָנוּ עַל בַּת יִשְׂרָאֵל לְכֹהֵן — בַּת כֹּהֵן לְכֹהֵן מַהוּ? אָמַר לָהֶם: זוֹ שָׁמַעְתִּי, וְזוֹ לֹא שָׁמַעְתִּי. אִי אָמְרַתְּ בִּשְׁלָמָא עוּבָּר בִּמְעֵי זָרָה זָר הוּא — הַיְינוּ דְּקא"ל: "זוֹ שָׁמַעְתִּי, וְזוֹ לֹא שָׁמַעְתִּי". אֶלָּא, אִי אָמְרַתְּ יָלוּד — מַאֲכִיל, שֶׁאֵין יָלוּד — אֵין מַאֲכִיל, מַאי "זוֹ שָׁמַעְתִּי וְזוֹ לֹא שָׁמַעְתִּי" אִידִי הִיא! קַשְׁיָא. אָמַר רַב יְהוּדָה אָמַר שְׁמוּאֵל: זוֹ דִּבְרֵי רַ' יוֹסֵי, אֲבָל חֲכָמִים אוֹמְרִים: יֵשׁ לוֹ בָּנִים — אוֹכְלִים מִשּׁוּם בָּנִים, אֵין לוֹ בָּנִים — אוֹכְלִים מִשּׁוּם אַחִים. אֵין לוֹ אַחִים — אוֹכְלִים מִשּׁוּם מִשְׁפָּחָה כּוּלָּהּ. "זוֹ" וְלָא ס"ל?! הָא א"ל שְׁמוּאֵל לְרַב חָנָא בַּגְדָתָאָה: *פּוּק אַיְיתִי לִי בֵּי עֲשָׂרָה, דְּאֵימָא לָךְ בְּאַנְפַּיְיהוּ: הַמְזַכֶּה לְעוּבָּר — קָנָה! אֶלָּא: *"זוֹ" וְס"ל. מַאי קמ"ל, דִּפְלִיגִי רַבָּנַן עֲלֵיהּ דְּרַבִּי יוֹסֵי — וּמִי פְּלִיגִי? (א) מְתִיב רַבִּי זַכַּאי: זוֹ עֵדוּת הֵעִיד רַ' יוֹסֵי מִפִּי שְׁמַעְיָה וְאַבְטַלְיוֹן, וְהוֹדוּ לוֹ. אָמַר רַב אַשִׁי: מִי קָתָנֵי "וְקִבְּלוּ"? "וְהוֹדוּ לוֹ" קָתָנֵי, דְּמִסְתַּבֵּר טַעְמֵיהּ. ת"ר:* דהִנִּיחַ בָּנִים — אֵלּוּ וְאֵלּוּ אוֹכְלִים. הִנִּיחָהּ מְעוּבֶּרֶת — אֵלּוּ וְאֵלּוּ אֵין אוֹכְלִים. הִנִּיחַ בָּנִים וְהִנִּיחָהּ מְעוּבֶּרֶת, עַבְדֵי מְלוֹג אוֹכְלִים, כְּדֶרֶךְ שֶׁהִיא אוֹכֶלֶת. עַבְדֵי צֹאן בַּרְזֶל לֹא יֹאכְלוּ, מִפְּנֵי חֶלְקוֹ שֶׁל עוּבָּר, שֶׁהָעוּבָּר פּוֹסֵל וְאֵינוֹ מַאֲכִיל, דִּבְרֵי רַ' יוֹסֵי. רַבִּי יִשְׁמָעֵאל בְּרַבִּי יוֹסֵי אוֹמֵר מִשּׁוּם אָבִיו: הַבַּת — מַאֲכֶלֶת, הַבֵּן — אֵינוֹ מַאֲכִיל. הר"ש בֶּן יוֹחַי אוֹמֵר: זְכָרִים — יֹאכְלוּ כּוּלָּן, נְקֵבוֹת — לֹא יֹאכְלוּ, שֶׁמָּא יִמָּצֵא עוּבָּר זָכָר, וְאֵין לְבָנוֹת בִּמְקוֹם הַבֵּן כְּלוּם. מַאי אִירְיָא שֶׁמָּא יִמָּצֵא עוּבָּר זָכָר? תֵּיפוֹק לֵיהּ דִּנְקֵבָה נַמִי פָּסְלָה! חֲדָא וְעוֹד קָאָמַר; חֲדָא — דִּנְקֵבָה נַמִי פָּסְלָה, וְעוֹד: שֶׁמָּא יִמָּצֵא עוּבָּר זָכָר, וְאֵין לְבָנוֹת בִּמְקוֹם הַבֵּן כְּלוּם. זְכָרִים יֹאכְלוּ? וְהָאִיכָּא עוּבָּר! קָסָבַר: אֵין

וְשִׁחְרוּר. יִשְׂרָאֵל שֶׁשִּׁיעְבֵּד עַבְדּוֹ לְבַ"ח, וְשִׁחְרְרוֹ הַלֹּוֶה – יָצָא לְחֵירוּת, וְהַמַּלְוֶה גּוֹבֶה מִלֹּוֶה* מִמָּקוֹם אַחֵר. בִּכְתוּבָּתָהּ. שֶׁהִיא אֶלֶף זוּז, דְּהָא מַאי דְּאַשְׁבְּחוּ – בִּרְשׁוּתֵי' אַשְׁבְּחוּ. אֲבָל לְמֵיתַן דְּמֵי וּמִשְׁקַל לָא. אֶלָּא שֶׁלּוֹ הֵן עוֹלָמִי', קמ"ל. **מתני'** וְהִנִּיחָהּ מְעוּבֶּרֶת. אע"פ שֶׁיֵּשׁ לָהּ בָּנִים הֵימֶנּוּ וְהִיא אוֹכֶלֶת בִּתְרוּמָה – לֹא יֹאכְלוּ עַבְדֵי צֹאן בַּרְזֶל בִּתְרוּמָה, לְפִי שֶׁהֵן שֶׁל יוֹרְשִׁים, וְיֵשׁ לָעוּבָּר בָּהֶן חֵלֶק, וְאֵין לָעוּבָּר כֹּחַ לְהַאֲכִילָן בִּתְרוּמָה. אִי מִשּׁוּם דְּקָסָבַר: עוּבָּר בִּמְעֵי זָרָה זָר הוּא, אִי מִשּׁוּם דְּקָסָבַר: יָלוּד – מַאֲכִיל, שֶׁאֵין יָלוּד – אֵין מַאֲכִיל, שֶׁנֶּאֱמַר (ויקרא כב) "וִילִיד בֵּיתוֹ הֵם יֹאכְלוּ בְּלַחְמוֹ", קְרֵי בֵּיהּ: יַאֲכִילוּ. שֶׁהָעוּבָּר פּוֹסֵל. אִם בַּת כֹּהֵן נִישֵּׂאת לְיִשְׂרָאֵל, וְהִנִּיחָהּ מְעוּבֶּרֶת, וְאֵין לָהּ בֵּן אַחֵר – פּוֹסְלָהּ מִלָּשׁוּב לְבֵית אָבִיהָ כִּנְעוּרֶיהָ. וְאֵינוֹ מַאֲכִיל. אִם בַּת יִשְׂרָאֵל לְכֹהֵן הִיא, וּמֵת וְהִנִּיחָהּ מְעוּבֶּרֶת – אֵין בָּעוּבָּר כֹּחַ לְהַאֲכִילָהּ, וְה"ה לַעֲבָדִים. אַף בַּת כֹּהֵן לְכֹהֵן. כֵּיוָן דְּאָמְרַתְּ שֶׁאֵין יָלוּד אֵינוֹ מַאֲכִיל, הֵיאָךְ הָעֲבָדִים אוֹכְלִין בִּתְרוּמָה מִפְּנֵי חֶלְקוֹ שֶׁל עוּבָּר? שֶׁהֲרֵי עֲבָדָיו הֵן, וְאֵין אוֹכְלִים אֶלָּא בִּשְׁבִילוֹ, וְהוּא אֵין בּוֹ כֹּחַ לְהַאֲכִיל. **גמ'** בִּמְעֵי כֹּהֶנֶת. בַּת כֹּהֵן מְעוּבֶּרֶת מִכֹּהֵן. אִי אָמְרַתְּ מִשּׁוּם זָרוּת – לֵיכָּא, וְאִי מִשּׁוּם שֶׁאֵין יָלוּד – אִיכָּא. וְזוֹ לֹא שָׁמַעְתִּי. לְאִיסּוּר, אֶלָּא לְהֶיתֵּרָא. יֵשׁ לוֹ בָּנִים אֲחֵרִים. לְבַד מֵעוּבָּר זֶה. אוֹכְלִים. הָעֲבָדִים בִּשְׁבִיל בָּנִים, דְּעוּבָּר לֵית לֵיהּ זְכִיָּה. בִּשְׁבִיל מִשְׁפָּחָה. שֶׁאֵין אֶחָד מִיִּשְׂרָאֵל שֶׁאֵין לוֹ יוֹרְשִׁין, וְכָל זְמַן שֶׁלֹּא נוֹלַד הָעוּבָּר זוֹכֶה הַקָּרוֹב לִירוּשַּׁת כֹּהֵן, וְאוֹכְלִים בְּגִינוֹ. זוֹ דִּבְרֵי רַבִּי יוֹסֵי. וְלָא סְבִירָא לֵיהּ לִשְׁמוּאֵל דְּעוּבָּר אִית לֵיהּ זְכִיָּה. בַּגְדָתָאָה. בַּעַל אַגָּדָה. לָ"א: שֵׁם מָקוֹם שֶׁהוּא בְּבָבֶל שֶׁשְּׁמוֹ בַּגְדָּד*. בֵּי עֲשָׂרָה. לְפָרְסֵם אֶת הַדָּבָר. הִנִּיחַ בָּנִים. הַכֹּהֵן, וְלֹא הִנִּיחָהּ מְעוּבֶּרֶת. אֵלּוּ וְאֵלּוּ. עַבְדֵי מְלוֹג וְעַבְדֵי צֹאן בַּרְזֶל אוֹכְלִין. דְּעַבְדֵי מְלוֹג אוֹכְלִין בִּשְׁבִילָהּ, שֶׁהִיא אוֹכֶלֶת בִּשְׁבִיל בָּנֶיהָ, וְעַבְדֵי צֹאן בַּרְזֶל אוֹכְלִין בִּשְׁבִיל בָּנִים. הִנִּיחָהּ מְעוּבֶּרֶת. וְלֹא הִנִּיחַ לָהּ בָּנִים. אֵלּוּ וְאֵלּוּ אֵין אוֹכְלִין. שֶׁהָעוּבָּר אֵינוֹ מַאֲכִיל לֹא אֶת אִמּוֹ וְלֹא אֶת הָעֲבָדִים. הִנִּיחַ בָּנִים וְהִנִּיחָהּ מְעוּבֶּרֶת עַבְדֵי מְלוֹג אוֹכְלִים. שֶׁהֵם שֶׁלָּהּ וְאֵין לָעוּבָּר חֵלֶק בָּהֶן, וְהִיא אוֹכֶלֶת בִּשְׁבִיל בָּנֶיהָ. עַבְדֵי צֹאן בַּרְזֶל לֹא יֹאכְלוּ מִפְּנֵי חֶלְקוֹ שֶׁל עוּבָּר. שֶׁיֵּשׁ לוֹ חֵלֶק בָּהֶן, דְּאִית לֵיהּ זְכִיָּה, וְלָא יָדְעִינַן הֵי מִתְרַמֵּי לְחֶלְקוֹ. לְפִיכָךְ עֲבָדִים אֲסוּרִים לֶאֱכוֹל. שֶׁהָעוּבָּר פּוֹסֵל. בַּת כֹּהֵן הַמְעוּבֶּרֶת מִיִּשְׂרָאֵל. וְאֵינוֹ מַאֲכִיל. בַּת יִשְׂרָאֵל הַמְעוּבֶּרֶת מִכֹּהֵן, וְלֹא אֶת עֲבָדָיו. הַבַּת מַאֲכֶלֶת. לְקַמָּן מְפָרֵשׁ לָהּ. כּוּלָּן זְכָרִים. לָ"ג "כּוּלָּן", אֶלָּא ה"ג: זְכָרִים יֹאכְלוּ כּוּלָּן נְקֵבוֹת לֹא יֹאכְלוּ אִם יֵשׁ זָכָר בַּבָּנִים – אוֹכְלִים הָעֲבָדִים בִּשְׁבִילוֹ, וְלָא חָיְישִׁינַן לְחֶלְקוֹ שֶׁל עוּבָּר, דְּשֶׁמָּא נְקֵבָה הִיא וְאֵין לָהּ חֵלֶק בִּמְקוֹם בֵּן, וְאת"ל זָכָר הוּא – שֶׁמָּא תַּפִּיל, שֶׁכָּל הַיּוֹלְדוֹת – מֶחֱצָה זְכָרִים וּמֶחֱצָה נְקֵבוֹת, וְיֵשׁ שֶׁמַּפִּילוֹת – סְמוֹךְ מִיעוּטָא דְּמַפִּילוֹת לְמֶחֱצָה דִּנְקֵיבוֹת, הָווּ לְהוּ זְכָרִים הָרְאוּיִם לִירַשׁ מִיעוּטָא, וּלְמִיעוּטָא לָא חָיְישִׁינַן. כּוּלָּן נְקֵבוֹת – לֹא יֹאכְלוּ, שֶׁמָּא יְהֵא עוּבָּר זָכָר כו'. תֵּיפוֹק לֵיהּ. דְּאִ"נ הָוְיָא נְקֵבָה פָּסְלָה, דְּכֵיוָן שֶׁכָּל אוֹתָן שֶׁלְּפָנֵינוּ נְקֵבוֹת – יֵשׁ לָעוּבָּר חֵלֶק בָּהֶן, אֲפִילּוּ הִיא נְקֵבָה. אֵין

פוסל ואין מאכיל. נראה לפרש שהעובר פוסל בעבדי אביו, ואין מאכיל את אמו. דתרווייהו אעבדים ליכא למימר: פוסל בעבדי אביו ואין מאכיל בעבדי אביו, דכיון דאשמועינן דפוסל – היכי משכחת שיאכיל. ובקונטרס פירש כולה מילתא אאמו, ואע"ג דאעבדים קאי – ה"ק: שהעובר פוסל ואין מאכיל את אמו וה"ה לעבדיו דפוסל. **למאי** נפקא מינה לעובר במעי כהנת. אע"ג דע"כ דרשינן ההיא דרשא דילוד מאכיל, דמהאי טעמא אמרינן לקמן דבת ישראל לכהן והניחה מעוברת דלא מאכיל, דהתם לא שייך טעמא דעובר במעי זרה זר הוא, דאפילו זר מאכיל את אמו, ואפילו ממזר, כדאמרינן לקמן (ד' סט:), – מ"מ מיבעיא ליה לענין עבדים, דאיכא למימר דוקא לענין אמו דכתב בה קרא "ויליד ביתו הם יאכלו", דמינה דרשינן שמאכיל את אמו, דרשינן ילוד מאכיל. אבל עבדים שאוכלים מטעם קנין כספו – לא קאמר קרא ילוד מאכיל, שאינו ילוד לא.

היינו דקאמר זו שמעתי כו'. ורבנן שהיו אומרים לו כן הוו סברי דטעמא משום דילוד מאכיל.

אוכלין בשביל כל המשפחה כולה. ה"מ למימר דטעמא דרבנן משום דלא סבירא להו דרשא דשאין ילוד אין מאכיל לגבי עבדים, ולית להו נמי דעובר במעי זרה זר הוא. אלא קבלה היתה בידו דטעמא משום דלא זכי בהו עובר. וקצת תימה: דהא מסתמא מעשה ידיהם עד שיולד הוא לעובר ולא לבני משפחה, קשה לר"י: דתנן בפרק "יוצא דופן" (נדה ד' מד.) דבן יום אחד פוסל מן התרומה, ופריך בגמרא: מאי איריא בן יום אחד? אפי' עובר נמי! ומשני רב ששת: מתניתין בכהן שיש לו ב' נשים, אחת גרושה ואחת שאינה גרושה, ויש לו בנים משאינה גרושה ובן יום אחד מן הגרושה פוסל בעבדי אביו. ולאפוקי מדרבי יוסי, דאמר: עובר נמי פוסל, קמ"ל: בן יום אחד – אין, עובר – לא. והשתא, למה ליה לאוקמי כשיש לו שתי נשים? אפי' אין לו אלא אחת גרושה, ודוקא בן יום אחד אבל עובר – לא, דאוכלין בשביל כל המשפחה כולה לרבנן! ואר"י: דרב ששת לטעמיה, דאית ליה ב"מי שמת"* המזכה לעובר קנה, ולא אכלי בשביל המשפחה. ולהכי מוקי בשיש לו בנים משאינה גרושה, ואין העובר שבמעי גרושה פוסל, משום דלא חיישינן למיעוטא, דסמוך מיעוטא דמפילות למחצה דנקבות והוו להו זכרים מיעוטא, כדלקמן, ולאפוקי מדר' יוסי, דרבי יוסי חייש למיעוטא. ואתי שפיר דבפרק "מי שמת" (ב"ב קמב. ושם) פריך למ"ד המזכה לעובר קנה מדתנן "יוצא דופן" (נדה דף מד. ושם) בן יום אחד נוחל ומנחיל, אבל עובר לא – ולא פריך מרישא דבן יום אחד פוסל, דאיכא לאוקמא בשתי נשים כו'. **זו** וסבירא ליה. אע"ג דשמואל פסיק ב"אע"פ" (כתובות דף נט.) כרבי יוחנן הסנדלר, דאין אדם מקנה דשלב"ל – שמואל חשיב עובר כבא לעולם.

טז א מיי' פכ"ב מהל' איסורי ביאה הלכה כו טוש"ע אה"ע סי' פח סעיף ג:
יז ב ג מיי' פ"ח מהל' תרומות הל' ד טור יו"ד סי' שלא:
יח ד ה מיי' שם טור שם:

תוספות ישנים

רב יוסף אמר ילוד מאכיל שאינו ילוד אינו מאכיל אבל לא ס"ל שיהא הטעם משום דעובר במעי זרה זר הוא דא"כ מאי קא מיבעיא להו לרבנן מאחר שהעדת מה ענין זה לזה בת ישראל שנשאת לכהן עובר במעי זרה [הוא] ולא אכלי אבל במעי כהנת לא פסיל. [ורבה אמר לך אין] טעמא דר' יוסי משום דילוד מאכיל שאינו ילוד אינו מאכיל א"כ מה בעו מיניה רבנן בכהן במעי כהנת הלא ההיא היא כדקאמר תלמודא אלא טעמא משום דעובר במעי זרה הוא: ואימא קמייהו המזכה לעובר קנה. וא"ת והא אמר שמואל הלכה כר' יוחנן הסנדלר דאמר אין אדם מקנה דבר שלא בא לעולם וי"ל שאני הכא שהמתנה הויא בעולם ולא נהירא דהא אמרינן בגיטין דלדבר שלא בא לעולם לא קנה אף דבר שישנו בעולם. וי"ל דעובר חשוב כדבר שהוא בעולם ומיירי הכא בהוכר עוברה. וא"ת ומאי האי דקאמר זו ולא ס"ל וכו' והאמר ליה שמואל וכו' המזכה לעובר קנה ואת אמרת דהלכה כחכמים דאין לעובר זכיה דלמא דגם רבנן [ס"ל] דמזכה לעובר קנה דאית ליה לעובר [זכיה] ובתוספתין למיעוט קמיפלגי דהרבה תנאי פליגי בהא ונפרש דר' יוסי סבר חוששין למיעוט שמא יהיה (לה) זכר קיים ורבנן לא חיישי דסמוך מיעוטא דמפילות למחצה זכרים ומחצה נקבות והו"ל זכרים מיעוטא וי"ל דא"א לומר כן מדקאמר שמואל לעיל אליבא דרבנן אין לו אחין אוכלין בשביל כל המשפחה א"כ טעמייהו משום דאין מזכה לעובר קונה דא"ל משום דאין חוששין למיעוט דהא לאו מיעוט איכא דבין יהיה הולד זכר או נקבה יהיה הולד חלק בעבדים שאף נקבה תירש קודם לאחיו ולמשפחה: **כולם** זכרים יאכלו. הקונטרס לא גרים כולם זכרים דאפי' אי ליכא אלא חד זכר יאכלו בגללו ולא חיישינן למיעוט שמא

הגהות הב"ח

(א) גמ' ומי פליגי והאמר ר' זכאי א' עדות:

נ"ל מלוה שלו. יעב"ץ

ב"ב קמא: נדה מד.

[ואתנס בסוכה כג: משמע כפי' הערוך ער' מערכי לשון ערך דיגלת סוף הערה לא]

ב"ב קמב: כתובות ז: [זבחים לב.] [ב"ב קה.]

תוספות חד מקמאי

אני נוטלת אשתכח דדילה נינהו ומצי למימר נחת רוח עשיתי לבעל אלא אפילו הבעל עצמו במקום אשה קאי ומוציא מיד הלקוחות מכח האשה. ומכרו שניהם לפרנסה ורבותא נקט אפילו לפרנסה שניהם צריכין לו אפ"ה הבעל מוציא מיד הלקוחות ולא מבעי' מה שהכניסה לו מטלטלין שהאשה מוציאה מיד הלקוחות אפי' בחיי בעלה אלא אפי' קרקעות דלא מבעיא הבעל מכוחו אלא אפי' הכניסה לו קרקעות וקבלם עליו הבעל נמי שיכולה לומר בשעת גבית כתובה קרקעותי אני נוטלת אשתכח דדילה נינהו ואם מכרם הבעל האשה מוציאה מיד הלקוחות אפי' בחיי בעלה וכן אם לקח מן האיש וחזר ולקח מן האשה מה שלקח מן האשה הוא בטל מיד שיכולה לומר נחת רוח עשיתי לבעלי כיון שנטל הבעל עליו. (אבל נכסי מלוג שהגוף שלה אמרי' בפ' ח"ה שאינה יכולה לומר נחת רוח עשיתי לבעלי). ואפי' בחיי הבעל מוציאה מיד הלקוחות ולכך נהגו בנרבונה לכתוב בכתובה הוא נתן לה קרקע פלוני והיא הביאה לו בנדונייתה כדי שתוכל לטרוף מן הלקוחות בחיי הבעל אם מכרן. וכן אם לקח מן האיש וחזר ולקח מן האשה כיון שיכולה לומר נחת רוח עשיתי לבעלי נמי א)שלקח מן האשה היא ותוציא מהלקוחות אפלו בחיי בעלה ולפיכך אמר רשב"ג שהבעל מוציא מיד הלקוחות מכח האשה. ופ' השולח פי' בדין נכסי האיש והאשה ודין אפותיקי סתם ודין אפותיקי מפורש. ומיהו מילתא פשיטא היא דנכסי הבעל אינה מוציאה מיד הלקוחות אם מכרם הבעל עד שעת גבית כתובה והיינו דאמר פ' האשה שנפלו לה. אבעי לזבוני מי לא מזבין. ורש"י פי' ל"מ אם מת הוא או גרשה שהאשה מוציאה מיד הלקוחות אם מכר הוא בלא דעתה אלא אפי' מתה היא הוא מוציא מיד הלקוחות דשעת מכירה לאו מכירה ודאית היא שמא ימות הוא ונמצאת מכירה שלא כדין והראב"ד פי' מכרו שניהם לפרנסה כגון שמכר האחד בפני חברו וקא' רשב"ג שאם מכרה האשה בפני בעלה הבעל מוציא מיד הלקוחות. וזהו לשונו מה שפסק הרב אלפס דרבנן דאמרי עובר לית ליה זכייה מסתברא כוותייהו דרבא קאי כרבנן בפ' מי שמת ואביי פליג עליה וכו' וקי"ל אביי ורבא הלכה כרבא וכבר כתבתי דבר זה בפרק מי שמת. מצאתי כתוב בחדושי שחדשתי לפני אבא מארי ז"ל שמעשה היה בלוניל לפני הראב"ד ז"ל ולפני זקני הרב ר' משולם ולפני הרב ר' שמואל ב"ר משה ע"ה באחד שנתן מתנה לבנו קודם ארבעים יום ליצירתו והיה מחלוקת ביניהם יש מהם שאמרו שהמתנה מתנה הואיל ודעתו של אדם קרובה אצל העובר ויש מהם שאמרו שאין המתנה מתנה דכיון דארבעים יום קודם ליצירתו מיא בעלמא הוא וכמו דלא עיברה כלל דמיא וגמר הדין ע"פ רובם שהמתנה מתנה ולאבא מארי ז"ל היה מסתברא כדברי היחיד שאין המתנה מתנה:

א) נראה דל"ל נמי שלה שלקח מן האשה בטל הוא ומוציא מן הלקוחות.

ימצא עובר זכר. אבל בנקבות לא יאכלו נ"ל כולם נקבות דאי איכא חד זכר אכלי ודוחק הוא למחוק גרסת הספרים. ונראה לה"ר נתנאל לייסב גרסת הספרים כולם זכרים יאכלו פי' כולם פי' [בין] עבדי מלוג בין עבדי צאן ברזל לאי ליכא זכר אבל נקבות לא יאכלו כולם. פי' עבדי צאן ברזל אלא עבדי מלוג בלבד לפי שמכח האשה הם באים ולא מכח הבנות:

עין משפט נר מצוה

יט א ב מיי׳ פ״י מהל׳ נחלות הלכה ד סמג עשין נו טוש״ע חו״מ סימן רפט סעי׳ א:
כ ג מיי׳ פי״ט מהל׳ אישות הלכה יז סמג עשין כו טוש״ע אה״ע סימן קיב סעי׳ יא:
כא ד מיי׳ שם הל׳ יט סמג עשין פא טוש״ע שם סעיף יד:
כב ה מיי׳ פ״ח מהל׳ תרומות הל׳ א טוי״ד סי׳ שלא:
כג ו מיי׳ שם הל׳ יא:
כד ז מיי׳ פ״ו מהלכות יבוס סמג עשין נא טוש״ע אה״ע סי׳ קעג סעי׳ א:
כה ח מיי׳ פ״ח מהל׳ תרומות הל׳ ב טוי״ד סי׳ שלא:
כו ט מיי׳ שם הלכה ה:
כז י מיי׳ שם הלכה ז:

אין חוששין למיעוטא. ואיבעית אימא: לעולם קסבר חוששין למיעוטא, דעבדינן ליה תקנתא כרב נחמן אמר שמואל. דאמר *רב נחמן אמר שמואל: [א]יתומים שבאו לחלוק בנכסי אביהם, ב"ד מעמידין להם אפוטרופוס ובורר להם חלק יפה. הגדילו — יכולין למחות. ורב נחמן דידיה אומר: [ב]הגדילו — אין יכולין למחות. דא"כ — מה כח ב"ד יפה? לימא, דרב נחמן תנאי היא! לא, דכ"ע אית להו דרב נחמן, והכא *בחוששין למיעוטא קמיפלגי. ר' ישמעאל בר' יוסי אומר משום אביו. הבת — מאכיל, הבן — אינו מאכיל. מ"ש בן דלא מאכיל — משום חלקו של עובר, בת נמי לא תאכיל — מפני חלקו של עובר! אמר אביי: הכא בנכסים מועטים עסקינן, וכגון דאיכא בן בהדי בת, מה נפשך: אי האי דמעברא בן הוא — לא עדיף מהאי דקאי, אי בת היא — אמאי אכלה, בתקנתא דרבנן — כמה דלא נפק לאויר העולם לא תקינו רבנן. במאי אוקימתא — בנכסים מועטים, אימא סיפא: שמא ימצא העובר זכר, ואין לבנות במקום בן כלום, אדרבה, [ג]נכסים מועטים דבנות נינהו! סיפא אתאן לנכסים מרובין. ונכסים מועטים דבנות נינהו? *והאמר רבי אסי א"ר יוחנן: [ד]יתומין שקדמו ומכרו בנכסים מועטים, מה שמכרו מכרו! ואלא מאי בת דקתני — אם — א"ה, היינו ר' יוסי! כולה ר' ישמעאל בר' יוסי קתני לה.§ **מתני׳** [ה]העובר, והיבם, והאירוסין, והחרש, ובן תשע שנים ויום אחד — פוסלין ולא מאכילין. [ו]ספק שהוא בן ט' שנים ויום אחד ספק שאינו, ספק הביא ב' שערות וספק שלא הביא, *נפל הבית עליו ועל בת אחיו ואין ידוע אי זה מת ראשון — [ז]צרתה חולצת ולא מתייבמת.§ **גמ׳** "העובר".§ [ח]אי בת כהן לישראל היא פסיל לה, °"כנעוריה" — פרט למעוברת. אי בת ישראל לכהן היא לא מאכיל לה, ילוד מאכיל, שאינו ילוד אינו מאכיל.§ "היבם".§ [ט]אי בת כהן לישראל היא פסיל לה, °"ושבה אל בית אביה" פרט לשומרת יבם, אי בת ישראל לכהן היא לא מאכיל לה, °*"קנין כספו" אמר רחמנא, והא קנין דאחיו הוא.§ "והאירוסין".§ [י]אי בת כהן לישראל היא פסיל לה, דהא

רש"י

אין חוששין למיעוטא. לשמא יהא זכר, ויש לו חלק בהן. דבתר רובא אזלינן, ורובא יולדות או נקבות או מפילות, כדפרישית לעיל. דעבדינן ליה תקנתא. בוררין לעובר שאר נכסים לחלקו, ונמצאו העבדים כולן לחלק הנולדים. אבל היכא דכולן נקבות — לא מלינו למיעבד תקנתא, שמא יהא העובר זכר ויהא הכל שלו. יתומים. קטנים שבאו לחלוק, מעמידין אפוטרופוס לכל אחד ואחד, ובורר כל אפוטרופוס חלק אחד יפה לחלקו. הגדילו. היתומים יכולים למחות, ומהניא חלוקה לפירות דעד מחאה. לימא דרב נחמן תנאי היא. מדקאמר ר' שמעון זכרים יאכלו משום תקנתא דרב נחמן — מכלל דת"ק דקאמר עבדי צאן ברזל לא יאכלו, אפי' בתקנתא קאמר. ולית ליה דרב נחמן, ואינן רשאין לחלוק עד שהגדילו. לא דכולי עלמא איתא להו דרב נחמן. ואי דעבד להו תקנתא, הכי נמי דאכלי אפילו לתנא קמא. והכא בדלא עבוד תקנתא פליגי, וקאמר רבי שמעון — יאכלו, ולא חייש למיעוטא. ותנא קמא חייש למיעוטא. הבת מאכיל. קס"ד ה"ק: אם יש כאן בת ולא בן — מאכיל עבדים, אבל אם זכרים הם — לא יאכלו העבדים. בנכסים מועטים. דתקון רבנן הבנות יזונו והבנים ישאלו על הפתחים. וכגון דאיכא בן בהדה. דהך בת, דהוו כולהו בחזקת הבן מדאורייתא. דהשתא ממה נפשך: אי עובר זכר הוא — לא עדיף מהאי דשקלינהו רבנן מיניה, ואוקמינהו ברשות בת. ואי עובר בת היא — כיון דיש בן זכר לפנינו, אין לעובר נקבה חלק בהן אלא בתקנתא דרבנן, וכמה דלא נפק כו'. ולהכי נקט בן בהדה, דאי לא הוה בן — אית ליה זכייה לעובר נקבה מדאורייתא בנכסים בתורת ירושה בהדי הך בת. והכי מפרש מילתא דר' ישמעאל: הבת עם הבן מאכלת, אבל אם יש בן בלא בת — אינו מאכיל. מה שמכרו מכרו. וכיון דלענין מכירה ברשותייהו קיימי, היכי אכלי? אלא מאי הבת דקתני אם. והכי קאמר: האם מאכלת עבדי מלוג שלה כדרך שהיתה אוכלת, והבן אינו מאכיל את עבדי צאן ברזל מפני חלקו של עובר. **מתני׳** העובר פוסל. בת כהן שניסת לישראל ומת, והניחה מעוברת. ואינו מאכיל. בת ישראל שנשאת לכהן ומת והניחה מעוברת. והיבם. בת כהן שומרת ליבם ישראל — פוסלה מתרומת אביה, ובת ישראל שומרת ליבם כהן — אינו מאכילה. והאירוסין. בת כהן מאורסת לישראל — פוסלה, ובת ישראל מאורסת לכהן — אינו מאכילה. ובן ט' שנים. בגמרא מפרש לה. ספק שהוא בן ט' ספק שאינו. הוי נמי כבן ט', ופוסל. ואמילתא דלעיל קאי. ספק שהביא שתי שערות כו'. לעיל קאי, לענין האירוסין, דקתני פוסלין. והכי קאמר: קטן שקידש האשה, ספק הביא שתי שערות וקידושיו קידושין, ספק שלא הביא — פוסל בת כהן המאורסת לו מן התרומה. נפל הבית עליו ועל בת אחיו. שהיא אשתו, ספק הוא מת תחלה ונפלו שתיהן לפני אחיו, ופוטרת צרתה משום צרת הבת, ספק בת אחיו מתה ראשונה, ובשעת נפילה ליבם לא הואי צרתה צרת ערוה, דתנן (לעיל דף ג:): וכולן אם מתו או מיאנו — צרותיהן מותרות. צרתה חולצת ולא מתייבמת. איידי דאיירי בספק לחומרא תני לה בהדייהו. **גמ׳** ושבה אל בית אביה כנעוריה. משמע בזמן שהיא דומה לנעוריה. ילוד מאכיל. ישראלית האוכלת בשביל בנה — אינה אוכלת אלא אם כן ילוד. בן מאכיל את אמו נפקא לן בתורת כהנים (ויקרא כב) מ"ויליד ביתו הם יאכלו בלחמו" — קרי ביה יאכילו. ומהכא ילוד הוא דמשתמע. ושבה פרט לשומרת יבם. שאינה ברשותה לשוב, דהא אגידא ביה. דקנייה

תוספות

אין חוששין למיעוטא כו'. הקשה הר"ר שמואל בר' חיים: הא כי הוי נמי נפל פסיל, כדמוכח בפ' "מי שמת" (ב"ב דף קמב. ושם) דלמאן דאמר המזכה לעובר קנה — זוכה העובר בנכסי אביו עד שתפיל האשה, דתניא (שם), גבי גר שמת ובזבזו ישראל נכסיו ושמעו שאשתו מעוברת, והחזירו, ואחר כך שמעו שהפילה והחזיקו, המחזיק בשניה זכה, בראשונה — לא זכה! ואר"י: דהכא יש להסתפק שמא כבר הוא נפל. וא"ת: דהכא חייש רבי יוסי למיעוטא, ובפ' "מצות חליצה" (לקמן דף קה:) קאמר דקטנה חולצת, ואמאי? הא אין עולה לייבום, כיון דחייש למיעוטא, דחיישינן שמא תמצא אילונית, וכיון דאין עולה לייבום אין עולה לחליצה! ♦וי"ל: דחשיב עולה לייבום, כיון דאם יבא אליהו ויאמר דאינה אילונית היתה יכולה להתייבם. ולא דמיא לחולצת תוך ג' חדשים, *(א) דאפי' יבא אליהו ויאמר דלא מיעברא לא משגחינן ביה. וא"ת: דבפ"ק דכתובות (דף יד:) לא חייש ר' יוסי למיעוטא בתינוקת שנאנסה! ואר"י: דברובא דאיתיה קמן כ"ע מודו דלא חיישינן למיעוטא. ומיהו, ל"ע בריש "המוכר פירות" (ב"ב דף צג:) דאזיל רבי יוסי בתר רובא דזריעה להוציא ממון, ואייתי מינה ראיה לרב דאמר הולכין בממון אחר הרוב, אלמא לא חייש רבי יוסי למיעוט לענין ממונא, וכל שכן לענין איסורא! ♦ויש לחלק. **יתומים** שבאו לחלוק כו'. מפורש "בהשולח" (גיטין דף לד.). **מועטים** עסקינן. אע"ג דפסקינן בפ' "נערה" בכתובות (דף נא.) דמזון האשה והבנות ממקרקעי ולא ממטלטלי — סוגיא דהכא סברא דעבדא כמקרקעי דמי, כרבי אלעזר דאמר בס"ק דב"ק (דף יא: ושם) הלכה, גובין מן העבדים. ומיהו, אין הלכה כן, אלא כרב נחמן דפליג עלי', דקי"ל ככל הני שמעתא דשלח ליה ר' אבא לרב יוסף בר חמא פרק "יש נוחלין" (ב"ב דף קכח.), דמסיק התם דשלח ליה: אין גובין, אבל אין לומר דחשיב עבדא כמטלטלי, וסבר כרבי דאמר בפרק "נערה" (כתובות דף נא.) מזון האשה והבנות בין ממקרקעי בין ממטלטלי — דא"כ, בסמוך דפריך במאי אוקימתא בנכסים מועטים, ודוחק לומר דסיפא אתא לנכסים מרובין, ה"ל למימר: דסבר לה ר"ש בן יוחאי כר"ש בן אלעזר, דקי"ל (שם) כוותיה, דמזוני מקרקעי ולא ממטלטלי. **שקדמו** ומכרו כו'. מלשון קדמו משמע דאיירי שקדמו למכור קודם שהחזיקו בהן בית דין לצורך בנות. אבל אין נראה לר"י, דא"כ, הוה ליה לאוקמי כגון שכבר החזיקו בהן בנות ע"פ ב"ד, אלא אין שום חזקה מועלת, אלא קדמו קודם שיאכלו הבנות קאמר. ומיהו אר"י דיש לדחות: דמשמע ליה דבת אוכלת מיד אחר מיתת הבעל, בלא החזקה על פי ב"ד.
מה שמכרו מכרו. והדמים שלהם, דאם לא כן — בחזקת הבנות הן. וכן משמע בסוטה (דף כא:) דחשיב ליה רשע ערום — זה המשיא עצה למכור בנכסים מועטים. **קנין** כספו אמר רחמנא והאי קנין דאחיו הוא. אמר ר"ת: דאסמכתא בעלמא הוא דמדאורייתא מיכל אכלה.א) דהא למשנה ראשונה דפרק "אף על פי" (כתובות דף נז. ושם) היכא דאכלה בחיי הבעל אכלה נמי בחזקת היבם. ודייק ר"ת מדקתני התם ואפילו כולם בפני הבעל חסר יום אחד, משמע הא כולן בפני הבעל — אוכלת. ועוד: דתניא בתוספתא (דכתובות פ"ה) זו משנה ראשונה, אבל רבותינו אמרו: אין האשה אוכלת בתרומה עד שתיכנס לחופה, ולא היבמה עד שתיבעל, משמע דלמשנה ראשונה — אוכלת. ובירושלמי דפרק "אע"פ" הגיע זמן ולא נישאו, או שמתו בעליהן — אוכלות משלו ואוכלות בתרומה. והיינו בלא ביאה, דאי אחר ביאה — פשיטא דאשתו גמורה היא, והיינו טעמא דמשנה ראשונה

תוספות ישנים

יתומים שקדמו ומכרו בנכסים מועטים מה שמכרו מכרו. פ"ה קדמו קודס שהגבו ב"ד לבנות ולא נהירא דא"כ מה פריך הכא לוקמה כשכבר הגבו ב"ד הנכסים לבנות ולכן נ"ל קדמו ומכרו קודם שאכלו הבנות הנכסים: **א)** ור' יצחק בר' אברהם פי' דודאי דרשה גמורה היא והאי דמשמע התם דלמשנה ראשונה אוכלת כי הגיע זמנה בפני הבעל היינו דווקא בתרומ' דרבנן אבל בתרומה דאורייתא לא אכלה אפי' למשנה ראשונה דקנין כספו אמרה רחמנא והאי קנין דאחיו הוא. וכן משמע פרק נערה המאורסה (דף עג) גבי בוגרת ששהתה י"ב חדש וכו' וקאמר ר' אליעזר ומשנה ראשונה אמרו דבר אחד דתנן היבם אינו מאכיל וכו' וקאמר אביי ודלמא לא היא עד כאן לא אשמעי' משנה ראשונה אלא להאכילה בתרומה דרבנן משמע דבכתובות בתרומה דרבנן מיירי: **אי** בת כהן לישראל פסל לה דהא קניה בהאי הויה ולא נהירא לגרום כן שהרי אצטריך כי תהיה לומר בת כהן שנבעלה לפסול לה פסלה וי"ל דטעמא משום דכתיב ושבה אל בית אביה וזו עומדת בבית בעלה ואוכלת ביה:

מסורת הש"ם

כתובות ק: קידושין מב. גיטין לד.
לקמן קיט. וש"נ
כתובות קג. סוטה כח: ב"ב קמ.
לעיל לה.
[כתובות נח.]
[לעיל לה:]
ויקרא כב
שם
שם

הגהות הב"ח

(א) תוס' ד"ה אין וכו' לאפוקי יבא אליהו. נ"ב ע"ל בפרק החולץ דף מא ע"ב:

גליון הש"ס

תוס' ד"ה אין חוששין וכו'. וי"ל דחשיב עולה ליבום. עיין לעיל דף מא ע"ב: באה"ד כמו שכתבו ויש לחלק. עי' בר"ן שבת דף יט ע"ב ובנב"י יו"ד סי' קלא בשם תשובת הר"ן ודו"ק:

תורה אור

דְּהָא קָנְיָהּ בַּהֲוָיָה, וְאִי בַּת יִשְׂרָאֵל לְכֹהֵן הִיא — לָא מַאֲכִיל לָהּ מִשּׁוּם דְּעוּלָּא.§ "וְהַחֵרֵשׁ".§ [א]אִי בַּת כֹּהֵן לְיִשְׂרָאֵל הִיא — פָּסֵיל לָהּ, דְּהָא קָנְיָהּ בְּתַקַּנְתָּא דְּרַבָּנַן, וְאִי בַּת יִשְׂרָאֵל לְכֹהֵן הִיא — לָא מַאֲכִיל, "קִנְיַן כַּסְפּוֹ" אָמַר רַחֲמָנָא, וְהַאי לָאו בַּר קִנְיָן הוּא.§ "וּבֶן תֵּשַׁע שָׁנִים וכו'".§ קס"ד בְּשׁוֹמֶרֶת יָבָם לְבֶן תֵּשַׁע וְיוֹם אֶחָד. לְמַאי? אִי לְמִיפְסַל — קָטָן נַמִי מִיפְסַל פָּסֵיל, אִי לַאֲכוּלֵי — גָּדוֹל נַמִי לָא מַאֲכִיל! אָמַר אַבָּיֵי: הָכָא בְּיָבָם בֶּן תֵּשַׁע שָׁנִים וְיוֹם אֶחָד הַבָּא עַל יְבִמְתּוֹ עָסְקִינַן, דְּמִדְּאוֹרַיְיתָא קָנְיָא לֵיהּ. סד"א: הוֹאִיל וּמִדְּאוֹרַיְיתָא קָנְיָא לֵיהּ, וּבִיאָתוֹ בִּיאָה, אֵימָא לוֹכִיל — קמ"ל: *עָשׂוּ [ב]בִּיאַת בֶּן ט' שָׁנִים וְיוֹם אֶחָד כְּמַאֲמָר בְּגָדוֹל. א"ל רָבָא: אִי הָכִי, סֵיפָא דְּקָתָנֵי: סָפֵק בֶּן ט' שָׁנִים וְיוֹם אֶחָד סָפֵק שֶׁאֵינוֹ, הַשְׁתָּא וַדַּאי בֶּן ט' לָא מַאֲכִיל — סָפֵק מִיבַּעְיָא?! אֶלָּא אָמַר רָבָא: [ג]בְּבֶן תֵּשַׁע שָׁנִים וְיוֹם אֶחָד דְּהָנָךְ פְּסוּלִים קָתָנֵי, דְּפָסְלֵי בְּבִיאָתָן. וְכִדְתַנְיָא: *[ד]בֶּן תֵּשַׁע שָׁנִים וְיוֹם אֶחָד גֵּר עַמּוֹנִי וּמוֹאָבִי, מִצְרִי וַאֲדוֹמִי, כּוּתִי, נָתִין, חָלָל וּמַמְזֵר, שֶׁבָּאוּ עַל כֹּהֶנֶת לְוִיָּה וְיִשְׂרְאֵלִית — פְּסָלוּהָ. וְהָא מִדְּקָתָנֵי סֵיפָא: אִם אֵינָן רְאוּיִן לָבֹא בְּיִשְׂרָאֵל הֲרֵי אֵלּוּ פּוֹסְלִים, מִכְּלָל דְּרֵישָׁא לָאו בִּפְסוּלִים עָסְקִינַן! רֵישָׁא פְּסוּלֵי קָהָל, סֵיפָא פְּסוּלֵי כְהוּנָּה.§ גּוּפָא, *בֶּן ט' שָׁנִים וְיוֹם א' גֵּר עַמּוֹנִי וּמוֹאָבִי מִצְרִי וַאֲדוֹמִי כּוּתִי נָתִין חָלָל וּמַמְזֵר שֶׁבָּאוּ עַל כֹּהֶנֶת לְוִיָּה וְיִשְׂרְאֵלִית(א) — פְּסָלָן. רַבִּי יוֹסֵי אוֹמֵר: כָּל שֶׁזַּרְעוֹ פָּסוּל — פּוֹסֵל, כָּל שֶׁאֵין זַרְעוֹ פָּסוּל — אֵינוֹ פּוֹסֵל. רשב"ג אוֹמֵר: כָּל שֶׁאַתָּה נוֹשֵׂא בִּתּוֹ — אַתָּה נוֹשֵׂא אַלְמָנָתוֹ, וְכָל שֶׁאֵין אַתָּה נוֹשֵׂא בִּתּוֹ — אִי אַתָּה נוֹשֵׂא אַלְמָנָתוֹ.§ מְנָא הָנֵי מִילֵּי? אָמַר רַב יְהוּדָה אָמַר רַב: אָמַר קְרָא °"וּבַת כֹּהֵן כִּי תִהְיֶה לְאִישׁ זָר", [ה]כֵּיוָן שֶׁנִּבְעֲלָה לְפָסוּל לָהּ — פְּסָלָהּ. הַאי מִיבְּעֵי לֵיהּ דְּקָאָמַר רַחֲמָנָא: בַּת כֹּהֵן דְּמִינַּסְבָא לְזָר [ו]לָא תֵּיכוּל! הַהִיא °מִ"וְשָׁבָה אֶל בֵּית אָבִיהָ כִּנְעוּרֶיהָ מִלֶּחֶם אָבִיהָ תֹּאכֵל" נָפְקָא, מִדְּקָאָמַר רַחֲמָנָא: "וְשָׁבָה אֶל בֵּית אָבִיהָ תֹּאכֵל" מִכְּלָל דְּמֵעִיקָּרָא לָא אָכְלָה! אִי מֵהַהִיא הֲוָה אָמֵינָא *לָאו הַבָּא מִכְּלַל עֲשֵׂה — עֲשֵׂה, כָּתַב רַחֲמָנָא הַאי לְלָאו. [לָאו] °מִ"וְכָל זָר לֹא יֹאכַל קֹדֶשׁ" נָפְקָא. הַהוּא

ויקרא כב / שם / שם

רש"י

דְּקָנְיָהּ בַּהֲוָיָה. וּמִשְּׁעַת הֲוָיָה אִיפְּסִילָה, כִּדְכְתִיב "וּבַת כֹּהֵן כִּי תִהְיֶה לְאִישׁ זָר". מִשּׁוּם דְּעוּלָּא. בְּמַסֶּ' כְּתוּבּוֹת, בְּפֶרֶק אַע"פ (דף מ:): דְּבַר תּוֹרָה אֲרוּסָה בַּת יִשְׂרָאֵל אוֹכֶלֶת בִּתְרוּמָה, דִּכְתִיב "קִנְיַן כַּסְפּוֹ הוּא יֹאכַל בּוֹ", וּמַה טַּעַם אָמְרוּ אֵינָהּ אוֹכֶלֶת, גְּזֵירָה שֶׁמָּא יִמְזְגוּ לָהּ כּוֹס בְּבֵית אָבִיהָ וְתֵלֵךְ וְתַשְׁקֶה לְאָחִיהָ וְלַאֲחוֹתָהּ. בְּתַקַּנְתָּא דְּרַבָּנַן. דְּחֵרֵשׁ, אע"ג דְּלָאו בַּר דַּעַת הוּא — תַּקִּינוּ בֵּיהּ רַבָּנַן נִשּׂוּאִין, לְקַמָּן בְּפֶ' "חֵרֵשׁ שֶׁנָּשָׂא" (דף קיב:). קס"ד בְּשׁוֹמֶרֶת יָבָם לְבֶן ט'. וְלֹא בָּא עָלֶיהָ, וּלְמַאי הִלְכְתָא נָקַט בֶּן ט', אִי לְמִיפְסַל, לְאַשְׁמוּעִינַן דְּכֵיוָן דַּחֲזִי לְבִיאָה פָּסֵיל לָהּ בִּזִּיקַת יְבָמִין — מַאי אִירְיָא בֶּן ט', אֲפִילּוּ קָטָן נַמִי, דְּלָא קָרֵינַן בָּהּ "וְשָׁבָה אֶל בֵּית אָבִיהָ", וּלְשַׁמְעִינַן בָּצִיר מִבֶּן ט'. וְאִי לַאֲכוּלֵי כו'. וְאִי לְהָכִי נָקַט בֶּן ט' לְאַשְׁמוּעִינַן רְבוּתָא, דְּאע"ג דַּחֲזִי לְבִיאָה לֹא מַאֲכִיל יְבִמְתּוֹ בִּזִּיקָתוֹ — אֲפִילּוּ גָּדוֹל מַמָּשׁ לֹא מַאֲכִיל, דְּלָאו קִנְיָנוֹ הוּא, דְּהָא אַשְׁמְעִי' בְּגָדוֹל בְּרֵישָׁא דְּמַתְנִי'. הַבָּא עַל יְבִמְתּוֹ. דְּאִילּוּ גָּדוֹל הֲוָה אָכְלִי, וְאַשְׁמוּעִינַן רְבוּתָא דְּאע"ג דְּבִיאָתוֹ בִּיאָה — לֹא מַאֲכִיל, וּפוֹסְלִין דְּקָתָנֵי בְּמַתְנִיתִין — אַשְּׁמָרָא קָאֵי, אַעוּבָּר וְיָבָם בְּלֹא בִּיאָה וְאֵירוּסִין וְחֵרֵשׁ, אֲבָל בֶּן ט' — לֹא נָקַט לֵיהּ אֶלָּא מִשּׁוּם וְאֵין מַאֲכִילִין. אִי הָכִי. דְּמִשּׁוּם אֵינוֹ מַאֲכִיל נָקַט לֵיהּ, לָמָּה לִי לְמִיתְנֵי סֵיפָא, דְּקָתָנֵי סָפֵק שֶׁהוּא בֶּן תִּשְׁעָה סָפֵק שֶׁאֵינוֹ — הָוֵי נַמִי כְּבֶן ט', הַשְׁתָּא וַדַּאי בֶּן ט' כו'. פּוֹסְלִין. כְּגוֹן מַמְזֵר וְנָתִין. וּמִשּׁוּם פּוֹסְלִין נָקַט לֵיהּ. וְלֹא מַאֲכִילִין — לֹא אַבֶּן ט' קָאֵי, אֶלָּא אַשְּׁמָרָא: עוּבָּר וְיָבָם אֵירוּסִין וְחֵרֵשׁ. בֶּן תִּשְׁעָה. שֶׁהוּא גֵּר עַמּוֹנִי וּמוֹאָבִי וכו' — דַּאֲסוּרִין לָבֹא בַּקָּהָל. מִצְרִי וַאֲדוֹמִי. עַד דּוֹר שְׁלִישִׁי בַּעֲשֵׂה. כּוּתִי וְנָתִין. בְּ"לֹא תִתְחַתֵּן בָּם", דְּקָסָבַר:(ב) גֵּירֵי אֲרָיוֹת הֵן. חָלָל. פָּסוּל לִכְהוּנָּה. פְּסָלוּהָ. אִם בַּת כֹּהֵן — מִן הַתְּרוּמָה, וּלְוִיָּה וְיִשְׂרְאֵלִית — לִינָּשֵׂא לִכְהוּנָּה עוֹלָמִית. מִדְּקָתָנֵי סֵיפָא. דְּמַתְנִיתִין. סֵיפָא פְּסוּלֵי כְהוּנָּה. חָלָל. וְאע"ג דְּקָתָנֵי שֶׁאֵינָן רְאוּיִן לָבֹא בְּיִשְׂרָאֵל — לָא מַיְירֵי אֶלָּא בִּכְהוּנָּה. דְּמֵרֵישָׁא הֲוָה אָמֵינָא פְּסוּלֵי קָהָל הוּא דְּפָסְלִי, אֲבָל בִּיאַת חָלָל — לָא. לְהָכִי תָּנֵי סֵיפָא מִשְׁנָה יְתֵירָה, לְאַשְׁמוּעִינַן חָלָל. פְּסָלוּהָ. כֹּהֶנֶת מִתְּרוּמָה דְּבֵי נָשָׁא וּמִן הַכְּהוּנָּה, לְוִיָּה וְיִשְׂרְאֵלִית מִן הַכְּהוּנָּה. רַבִּי יוֹסֵי אוֹמֵר כו'. טַעְמָא דְּרַבִּי יוֹסֵי וְרַבָּן שִׁמְעוֹן מְפָרֵשׁ לְקַמָּן בִּשְׁמַעְתִּין, מַאי קָאָמְרִי וּמַאי פְּלוּגְתַּיְיהוּ. לָאו מִ"וְכָל זָר" נָפְקָא. "וְכָל זָר לֹא יֹאכַל קֹדֶשׁ". וְהַשְׁתָּא סָלְקָא דַעְתָּךְ דְּקָסָבַר דְּהָךְ בַּת כֹּהֵן נַמִי מִשְׁתַּמַּע מִינֵּיהּ, הוֹאִיל וְנִיסֵּת לְיִשְׂרָאֵל. הַאי

תוספות

ראשונה דאינה אוכלת היכא דלא אכלה, משום דאין חייב במזונותיה אלא היכא דעמד בדין וברח, כדאמרינן ב"החולץ" (לעיל דף מא: ושם) ולא מייחד לה דוכתא. ומשום סימפון נמי איכא למיחש, דשמא יש סימפון ולא היתה אשתו מעולם, כיון שלא הגיע זמן בחיי הבעל ולא ברח. ואין להקשות: לעולא דאמר (כתובות דף נז:) טעמא משום שמא תשקה — כי אכלה בחיי הבעל נמי לא תיכול, כיון דאין יבם חייב במזונותיה לא מייחד לה דוכתא! — דאיכא למימר: כיון דזכתה — זכתה. אבל קשה: דא"כ מאי פריך בפרק "אע"פ" (שם דף נז: ושם) אלא מעתה לקיט כהן בבית ישראל לא יאכל בתרומה — שאני לקיט דכבר אכל כל ימי חייו! וי"ל: דכיון דהגיע זמן, וייחד לה דוכתא בבית אביה — שוב אינה זזה משם, ולא דמיא ללקיט כהן בבית ישראל. וא"ת: ומאחר דאכלה מדאורייתא — מפני מה אסרוה למשנה אחרונה עד שתבעל, אפילו נפלה מן הנשואין, הא ליכא למיחש תו לסימפון! ויש לומר: דכיון דאסורה ארוסה בהגעת זמן למשנה אחרונה — אסרו נמי יבמה, משום דמיחלפא בה, ששתיהן זמן כניסתן לאחר. ומיהו, הא דדרשינן לעיל (דף סו.) בת ישראל לכהן דאכלה בתרומה מ"קנין כספו" — דרשא גמורה היא. דהא לעיל (דף נז.) דרשינן מהתם פלוע דכא כהן שנשא בת גרים שמאכילה בתרומה. ואע"ג דבפ"ק דקדושין (ד' י: ושם) מייתי לה מק"ו דבן בג בג, ונשואה דריש בספרי מ"כל טהור בביתך", ואית דמפיק לה מ"אתם וביתכם" — ההיא דספרי אסמכתא הוא. וכמה דרשות יש בגמרא שדורש בתורת כהנים ובספרי מפסוקים אחרים. ומיהו, לא יתיישב הא דמייתי הך אסמכתא דהאי קנין דאחיו הוא התם בפרק "אע"פ" (כתובות דף נח. ושם*) דמייתי לה על משנה ראשונה, דקתני: היבם אין מאכיל, לפי מה שפירשנו, דהיינו דוקא היכא דלא אכלה, דמהך דרשא אפי' אכלה בחיי הבעל — לא תאכל בחיי היבם! ואמר רבינו תם: דהתם ה"פ: קנין כספו אמר רחמנא שאוכלת בתרומה, ורבנן הוא דתקון משנים עשר חדש ולהלן דאוכלת. והאי קנין דאחיו הוא, ולא תקון רבנן שתאכל מחמת היבם אלא עד שתבעל, אם לא שכבר אכלה בחיי הבעל.

אי בת כהן לישראל היא פסיל לה דהא קניה בהא הויה. מתוך הלשון משמע דמקרא דמ"כי תהיה לאיש זר" נפקא, כדפירש בקונטרס. ומיהו, לקמן מפיק ליה מ"ושבה אל בית אביה" — מכלל דמעיקרא לא אכלה, ו"כי תהיה לאיש זר" מוקמינן לנבעלה לפסול לה פסלה. והכא הך דרשא הפשוטה נקט, דאי לאו דנפקא לן מ"ושבה" הוה מוקמינן לאירוסין דפסלי. וכן דרך הגמרא בכמה מקומות*. ועוד אמר ר"י: דמשום דמהאי קרא ד"כי תהיה" דרשינן נמי דאינה חוזרת בהויה דאירוסין לחזה ושוק, להכי נקטיה נמי הכא. **קניא** ליה. לאו דוקא, אלא כלומר: זקוקה לו, דביאת בן תשע לא הוי אלא כמאמר בעלמא, ובפרק קמא דקדושין (דף יט.) ממעטין ליה דלא קניא מקרא ד"אשת איש", פרט לאשת קטן. ויש ספרים דגרסי: חזיא ליה. והכי פירושו: כיון דמדאורייתא זקוקה, וביאתו ביאה, ולא בעינן כוונה ביבמה — קס"ד דקני לה מדאורייתא, ולוכיל. קא משמע לן דלא, משום דלא קני לה.

רישא פסולי כהונה סיפא פסולי קהל. וכן גירסת ר"ת, ולא כספרים דגרסי איפכא. דהא קתני סיפא: ואם אינו ראוי לבא בישראל. וא"ת: וכיון דתנא רישא פסול כהונה, למה לי למיתני בסיפא פסול קהל? דכ"ש הוא! ויש לומר: דתנא סיפא לגלויי ארישא, שלא תאמר רישא פסולי קהל דוקא. ואם תאמר: וספק בן ט' היאך פוסל בביאתו, נוקמיה אחזקה קמייתא דהוה פחות מבן תשעה ונוקי איתתא בחזקת כשרות! ומיהו, לכהונה ניחא, דלא אזלינן בתר חזקה ליוחסין, כדקאמר רבי יהושע בפרק קמא דכתובות (דף יג.): לא מפיה אנו חיין, אלא היא בחזקת בעולה לנתין וממזר, ואפי' ברוב כשרים אצלה, כדאמר התם. ולא מוקמינן לה אחזקה. ואפילו לרבן גמליאל ורבי אליעזר דמכשרי — היינו משום דאמרה לכשר נבעלתי. אבל הכא, דלא ידעה אם הוא בן תשעה — לא. אבל לתרומה — קשיא, אמאי לא מוקמינן להו אחזקה? דאפילו לענין תרומה איירי כמו לענין *עבדים, ולתרומה מוקמינן אחזקה, דהא בכתובות בפ"ב (דף כו. ושם) גבי מוחזק לן באבוה דהאי דכהן הוא, ונפק עליה קלא דבן גרושה הוא כו', ומוקי לה בתרי ותרי. משמע דאי לאו משום זילותא דבי דינא הוה מסקי ליה לכולי עלמא. והיינו לענין תרומה, דאי לכהונה — לא מסקינן ליה בתרי ותרי, כדמוכח בקידושין ב"האומר" (דף סו.) גבי עובדא דינאי המלך! ויש לומר: דהכא כגון דהשתא דאתי קמן הוי ודאי בן תשעה, אף על פי שהיה ספק כשבא עליה — לא מוקמינן ליה אחזקה קמייתא, אלא אזלינן בתר השתא, שהוא ודאי בן תשעה, דחזקה קמייתא איתרע ליה.

לימא

עין משפט נר מצוה

כח א מיי' פ"ט מהל' תרומות הלכה ט:
כט ב מיי' פ"א מהל' יבום הל' טז ופ"ה הל' יח סמג עשין נא נב טוש"ע אה"ע סימן קסז סעי' א:
ל ג מיי' פ"ח מהל' תרומות הל' יא טוי"ד סי' שלא:
לא ד מיי' פי"ח מהל' איסורי ביאה הל"ג סמג לאוין קכ טוש"ע אה"ע סי' ו סעי' ח וע"ש בטור ובב"י:
לב ה מיי' פ"ז מהל' תרומות הל' ז והל' י:
לג ו מיי' שם הלכה ה:

מסורת הש"ס

לקמן ע. [נדה מה.]
קדושין עד:
[תוספתא נדה פ"ו]
[לעיל נד: וש"נ]
[ד"ה ואפילו]
[וע' תוס' עירובין טו: ד"ה כתיבה]
נ"א שכר ויכס מהרש"א וע"ש

תוספות ישנים

ספק בן תשע. וא"ת אמאי פסל אוקמיה אחזקתיה דלא הוה בן תשע וא"ל דמעלה עשו ביוחסין דהיינו דווקא לכהונה אבל לתרומה מאי איכא למימר וי"ל כיון דסופו ליגדל אין החזקה כלום א):

א) עי' בתוס' ד"ה רישא ובקדושין ע"ט.

הגהות הב"ח

(א) גמ' וישראלית פסלוה ר' יוסי: (ב) רש"י ד"ה כותי וכו' דקסבר כותים גירי:

לד א מיי׳ פ״ו מהל׳ תרומות הלכה ט:
לה ב מיי׳ שם הל׳ ז:
לו ג מיי׳ שם הל׳ ח:

ההוּא מִיבָּעֵי לֵיהּ לְגוּפֵיהּ! תְּרֵי "וְכָל זָר" כְּתִיבִי. וְאַכַּתִּי מִיבָּעֵי לֵיהּ לְכִדְרַ׳ יוֹסֵי בְּרַ׳ חֲנִינָא. דְּא״ר יוֹסֵי בְּרַבִּי חֲנִינָא: "וְכָל זָר" – *זָרוּת אָמַרְתִּי לְךָ, וְלֹא אֲנִינוּת! דְּרַבִּי יוֹסֵי בְּרַבִּי חֲנִינָא מִן "זָר" "וְכָל זָר" נָפְקָא, – וְאַכַּתִּי מִיבָּעֵי לֵיהּ לְכִדְתַנְיָא: אכְּשֶׁהִיא חוֹזֶרֶת – *חוֹזֶרֶת לִתְרוּמָה, וְאֵינָהּ חוֹזֶרֶת לְחָזֶה, וָשׁוֹק וַאֲמַר רַב חִסְדָּא אֲמַר רָבִינָא בַּר רַב שֵׁילָא: מַאי קְרָא? דִּכְתִיב: °"וּבַת כֹּהֵן כִּי תִהְיֶה לְאִישׁ זָר הִיא בִּתְרוּמַת הַקֳּדָשִׁים לֹא תֹאכֵל" – לֹא תֹאכַל בַּמּוּרָם *מִן הַקֳּדָשִׁים. – •א״כ לִכְתּוֹב קְרָא "הִיא בַּקֳּדָשִׁים לֹא תֹאכֵל", מַאי "בִּתְרוּמַת הַקֳּדָשִׁים" – בשָׁמְעַתְּ מִינַּהּ תַּרְתֵּי. אַשְׁכַּחַן כֹּהֶנֶת, לְוִיָּה וְיִשְׂרְאֵלִית מְנָלַן? *כְּדא״ר אַבָּא אֲמַר רַב: "בַּת" "וּבַת", הָכָא נַמִי "בַּת" "וּבַת". – כְּמַאן – כְּר״ע, *דְּדָרֵישׁ וָוִין! אֲפִילּוּ תֵּימָא רַבָּנַן, כּוּלֵּיהּ "וּבַת" קְרָא יְתֵירָא הוּא. אַשְׁכַּחַן לִתְרוּמָה, לִכְהוּנָּה מְנָלַן? אַטּוּ לְוִיָּה וְיִשְׂרְאֵלִית לָאו לִכְהוּנָּה מְרַבֵּינַן לְהוּ? דְּאִי לִתְרוּמָה – בְּנוֹת מֵיכַל תְּרוּמָה נִינְהוּ? אַלְמָנָה לָא? מַשְׁכַּחַתְּ לָהּ דְּקָאָכְלָה בִּשְׁבִיל בְּנָהּ! בִּשְׁבִיל בְּנָהּ – ק״ו: וּמַה כֹּהֶנֶת, דְּבִקְדוּשָּׁה דְּנַפְשַׁהּ אָכְלָה, פָּסֵיל לָהּ, לְוִיָּה וְיִשְׂרְאֵלִית דְּלָא אָכְלָה אֶלָּא בִּשְׁבִיל בְּנָהּ – לֹא כ״ש?! וְהִיא הַנּוֹתֶנֶת: כֹּהֶנֶת דְּקָדֵישׁ גּוּפָהּ – פָּסֵיל לָהּ, הָא דְּלָא קָדֵישׁ גּוּפָהּ – לָא פָּסֵיל לָהּ. אֶלָּא לִכְהוּנָּה, ק״ו מִגְּרוּשָׁה! וּמַה גְּרוּשָׁה גשֶׁמּוּתֶּרֶת בִּתְרוּמָה – אֲסוּרָה לִכְהוּנָּה, זוֹ שֶׁאֲסוּרָה בִּתְרוּמָה – אֵינוֹ דִּין שֶׁפְּסוּלָה לִכְהוּנָּה? וְכִי מַזְהִירִין מִן הַדִּין? •*גַּלּוֹיֵי מִילְּתָא בְּעָלְמָא הוּא. וְאֵימָא: נִבְעֲלָה לְפָסוּל לָהּ – חַיָּיבֵי כָּרֵיתוֹת! "כִּי תִהְיֶה" אֲמַר רַחֲמָנָא, הָנָךְ דְּאִית בְּהוּ הֲוָיָה, חַיָּיבֵי כָּרֵיתוֹת – לָאו בְּנֵי הֲוָיָה. אִי הָכִי, גּוֹי וְעֶבֶד לָא לִיפְסְלוּ! הָנָךְ פָּסְלֵי מִדְּרַבִּי יִשְׁמָעֵאל. דְּא״ר יוֹחָנָן *מִשּׁוּם רַבִּי יִשְׁמָעֵאל: מִנַּיִן לְגוֹי וְעֶבֶד שֶׁבָּא עַל בַּת יִשְׂרָאֵל, וְעַל כֹּהֶנֶת וּלְוִיָּה, שֶׁפְּסָלוּהָ – שֶׁנֶּאֱמַר °"וּבַת כֹּהֵן כִּי תִהְיֶה אַלְמָנָה וּגְרוּשָׁה וגו׳". מִי

תורה אור: ויקרא כב; שם

האי מִיבָּעֵי לֵיהּ לְגוּפֵיהּ. לְזָר גָּמוּר, אֲבָל הָךְ דְּלָאו זָרָה הִיא – אִיצְטְרִיכָא "וּבַת כֹּהֵן" לְאָסְרָהּ. תְּרֵי וְכָל זָר כְּתִיבִי. "וְכָל זָר לֹא יֹאכַל קֹדֶשׁ" (ויקרא כב), וְעוֹד גַּבֵּי בַּת כֹּהֵן כְּתִיב "וְשָׁבָה אֶל וגו׳ מִלֶּחֶם אָבִיהָ תֹּאכֵל וְכָל זָר לֹא יֹאכַל בּוֹ" (שם). וּמֵהָכָא תֵּיפּוֹק לָאו לְבַת כֹּהֵן הַנְּשׂוּאָה לְיִשְׂרָאֵל, לְאוֹסְרָהּ תַּחַת בַּעְלָהּ לִתְרוּמָה. דְּרַבִּי יוֹסֵי בְּרַ׳ חֲנִינָא. בְּפֶרֶק "הֶעָרֵל", לְהַתִּיר אוֹנֵן בִּתְרוּמָה. וְאַכַּתִּי. הַאי דְ"בַת כֹּהֵן כִּי תִהְיֶה" מִיבָּעֵי לֵיהּ לְלִיקּוּחִין גְּמוּרִים, וּלְאַשְׁמוּעִינַן כְּשֶׁהִיא חוֹזֶרֶת לְבֵית אָבִיהָ בְּמִיתַת הַבַּעַל וְזֶרַע אֵין לָהּ – אֵינָהּ חוֹזֶרֶת לְחָזֶה וְשׁוֹק שֶׁל שְׁלָמִים לֶאֱכוֹל כִּשְׁאָר אֲחָיוֹת הָאוֹכְלוֹת, כְּדִכְתִי׳ "אַתָּה וּבָנֶיךָ וּבְנוֹתֶיךָ" (ויקרא י). אַשְׁכַּחַן כֹּהֶנֶת. דְּמִיפַּסְלָא לִתְרוּמָה בְּבִיאַת פָּסוּל. כְּדא״ר אַבָּא. בְּפֶ׳ "יֵשׁ מוּתָּרוֹת". ר׳ עֲקִיבָא דּוֹרֵשׁ וָוִין. בְּסַנְהֶדְרִין בְּפֶרֶק "ד׳ מִיתוֹת" (ד׳ נא:): יִשְׁמָעֵאל אָחִי, "בַּת" "וּבַת" אֲנִי דּוֹרֵשׁ. כּוּלֵּיהּ וּבַת קְרָא יְתֵירָא הוּא. דְּהָא כְּתִיב לְעֵיל מִינֵּיהּ "וְכֹהֵן כִּי יִקְנֶה נֶפֶשׁ וגו׳ וִילִיד בֵּיתוֹ", וּמָצֵי לְמִכְתַּב בַּתְרֵיהּ "וְכִי תִהְיֶה לְאִישׁ זָר". לִכְהוּנָּה מְנָלַן. שֶׁלֹּא תִּנָּשֵׂא עוֹד לְכֹהֵן מִשֶּׁבָּא עָלֶיהָ פָּסוּל. אַלְמָנָה לָא. בִּתְמִיָּה, וְהָא מַשְׁכַּחַתְּ לָהּ דְּקָאָכְלָה בִּשְׁבִיל בְּנָהּ – וְאִיצְטְרִיךְ לְאַשְׁמוּעִינַן דְּאִם תִּיבָּעֵל לְפָסוּל לָהּ תֵּיאָסֵר. ק״ו. וְלָא אִיצְטְרִיךְ "וּבַת" לְרַבּוּיֵיהּ. וְהִיא הַנּוֹתֶנֶת. קוּשְׁיָא הִיא. כְּלוֹמַר: אִיצְטְרִיךְ לְרַבּוּיֵיהּ, דְּק״ו הַהוּא דְּקָיָלְפַתְּ מִינֵּיהּ אִיסּוּרָא – הִיא הַמִּדָּה נוֹתֶנֶת הַדִּין לְהַתִּיר וְלֹא לֶאֱסוֹר. כֹּהֶנֶת דְּקָדֵישׁ גּוּפָהּ כו׳. וְכִי מַזְהִירִים מִן הַדִּין. מִדִּין ק״ו, לְאוֹקְמֵיהּ בְּלָאו גָּמוּר? הָא קיי״ל (מכות דף יז:) דְּאֵין מַזְהִירִין מִן הַדִּין! גִּלּוּיֵי מִילְּתָא בְּעָלְמָא הוּא. וְלָאו מֵילָף מִינֵּיהּ יָלְפִינַן לָאו לִכְהוּנָּה מִתְּרוּמָה, דְּמִמֵּילָא כֵּיוָן דְּאִיפַּסְלָה לִתְרוּמָה – אִיפַּסְלָה לִכְהוּנָּה, דִּתְרוּמָה הַיְינוּ קְדוּשַּׁת כְּהוּנָּה. וְאֵימָא נִבְעֲלָה לְפָסוּל לָהּ חַיָּיבֵי כָּרֵיתוֹת. שֶׁאִם בָּא עָלֶיהָ אָחִיהָ פְּסָלָהּ מִתְּרוּמָה דְּבֵי נָשָׁא. אֲבָל חַיָּיבֵי לָאוִין, כֵּיוָן דְּתָפְסִי לְהוּ בָּהּ קִידּוּשֵׁי – לָא פָּסְלֵי לָהּ. וְכוּתִי וְנָתִין וּמַמְזֵר דְּפָסְלִי, מְנָלָן? הָנָךְ דְּאִית בְּהוּ הֲוָיָה. מִדְּאַפְּקָהּ לְהָךְ בִּיאָה בִּלְשׁוֹן הֲוָיָה, שְׁמַע מִינֵּיהּ בִּבְנֵי קִידּוּשִׁין מִשְׁתָּעֵי קְרָא, וְאַפ״ה פָּסְלֵי: לְאַפּוֹקֵי חַיָּיבֵי כָּרֵיתוֹת ל״ג. אִי הָכִי. אֵימָא קְרָא דַּוְקָא בְּנֵי קִידּוּשִׁין נָקַט, וְגוֹי וְעֶבֶד לָא פָּסְלֵי. וה״ה דְּמָצֵי נַמִי לְמֵימַר חַיָּיבֵי כָּרֵיתוֹת לָא לִיפְסְלֵי. אֶלָּא מִשּׁוּם דְּאַיְירֵי בְּהוּ לְעֵיל, דְּקָתָנֵי כּוּתִי, הַיְינוּ גּוֹי. וּבְמַתְנִיתִין (לקמן דף סט:) תְּנַן: הָעֶבֶד פּוֹסֵל מִשּׁוּם בִּיאָה: עֶבֶד כְּנַעֲנִי לֵית לֵיהּ קִידּוּשִׁין, דִּכְתִיב (בראשית כב) "עִם הַחֲמוֹר" – עַם הַדּוֹמֶה לַחֲמוֹר. גּוֹי לֵית לֵיהּ קִידּוּשִׁין – דְּאָמְרִינַן (סנהדרין דף נב:) "אֵשֶׁת רֵעֵהוּ" – פְּרָט לְאֵשֶׁת(א) אֲחֵרִים. וּבִשְׁאִלְתּוֹת דְּרַב אַחַאי *יָלֵיף לָהּ מִדְּתָנֵי רַב חֲנַנְיָא (שם מ:): בְּעוּלַת בַּעַל – יֵשׁ לָהֶן, מִידֵּי אַחֲרִינָא – לָא. וְגַבֵּי יִשְׂרָאֵל מַקִּישׁ הֲוָיוֹת לַהֲדָדֵי, מַאן דְּאִית לֵיהּ קִידּוּשֵׁי כֶּסֶף וּשְׁטָר – אִית לֵיהּ בָּהּ קִידּוּשֵׁי בִּיאָה, אֲבָל גּוֹי דְּלֵית לֵיהּ קִידּוּשֵׁי כֶּסֶף וּשְׁטָר – לֵית לֵיהּ קִידּוּשֵׁי בִּיאָה, *וּמְשַׁנֵּי: פָּסֵיל מִדְּרַבִּי יוֹחָנָן – וּמֵהַאי קְרָא גּוּפֵיהּ מִשְׁתַּמְּעֵי חַיָּיבֵי כָּרֵיתוֹת לִפְסוּלָא. וְאִית דִּמְפָרְשֵׁי: וְאֵימָא נִבְעֲלָה לְפָסוּל לָהּ חַיָּיבֵי כָּרֵיתוֹת נַמִי מ״ש דְּלָא תָּנֵי לְהוּ לְעֵיל? וּמְשַׁנֵּי: "כִּי תִהְיֶה" כְּתִיב – מִדְּאַפְּקָהּ רַחֲמָנָא לִבְעִילָה בִּלְשׁוֹן הֲוָיָה – לָא פָּסֵיל מִתְּרוּמָה אֶלָּא בַּר קִידּוּשֵׁי דַּוְקָא. דִּבְנֵי הֲוָיָה לְאַפּוֹקֵי חַיָּיבֵי כָּרֵיתוֹת דְּלָאו בְּנֵי הֲוָיָה נִינְהוּ כו׳ וּסְבִירָא לְהוּ דְּחַיָּיבֵי כָּרֵיתוֹת לָא פָּסְלֵי. וְקַשְׁיָא לִי בְּגַוָּהּ טוּבָא: חֲדָא, (דִּתְמִיָּה הִיא, דְּהָא חֲמִירֵי חַיָּיבֵי כָּרֵיתוֹת מֵחַיָּיבֵי לָאוִין. וְעוֹד) דִּתְנַן בְּפֶ׳ "ד׳ אַחִין" (לעיל דף לג:): אִם הָיוּ כֹּהֲנוֹת – נִפְסְלוּ מִתְּרוּמָה, בִּבְעִילַת אֵשֶׁת אִישׁ. וְעוֹד, ק״ו: חַיָּיבֵי לָאוִין פָּסְלֵי – חַיָּיבֵי כָּרֵיתוֹת לָא(ב) פָּסְלֵי? וְעוֹד: הָא אָמְרִינַן בַּ"עֲשָׂרָה יוֹחֲסִין" (קדושין דף עז:) דְּכֹהֵן הַבָּא עַל אֲחוֹתוֹ עֲשָׂאָהּ זוֹנָה. וְכֵיוָן דְּזוֹנָה הִיא, בְּעִילָתוֹ פּוֹסַלְתָּהּ, דְּתַנְיָא (לקמן דף נח.): לְוִיָּה שֶׁנִּשְׁבֵּית אוֹ שֶׁנִּבְעֲלָה בְּעִילַת זְנוּת נוֹתְנִים לָהּ מַעֲשֵׂר וְאוֹכֶלֶת. לְוִיָּה – אִין, אֲבָל תְּרוּמָה לְכֹהֶנֶת – לָא. וְעוֹד: הָא תְּנַן בְּמַתְנִיתִין (לקמן דף סט:): מַמְזֵר פּוֹסֵל וּמַאֲכִיל, וְלָא מַשְׁכַּחַת לָהּ אֶלָּא בְּאִם אִמּוֹ. וְאִי חַיָּיבֵי כָּרֵיתוֹת לָא פָּסְלֵי בְּבִיאָתָם, מַשְׁכַּחַתְּ לָהּ דְּמַמְזֵר פּוֹסֵל וּמַאֲכִיל אֶת אִמּוֹ. כֵּיצַד? בַּת כֹּהֵן שֶׁבָּא עָלֶיהָ אָחִיהָ מֵאִמָּהּ, וְהוּא יִשְׂרָאֵל, וְיָלְדָה לוֹ בֵּן – פּוֹסֵל מִן הַתְּרוּמָה. וּבַת יִשְׂרָאֵל שֶׁבָּא עָלֶיהָ אָחִיהָ מֵאִמָּהּ כֹּהֵן, וְיָלְדָה לוֹ בֵּן – הֲרֵי זֶה מַמְזֵר, וּמַאֲכִילָהּ. אֶלָּא מִדְּלָא נָקַט אִמּוֹ – ש״מ בִּיאַת אָחִיהָ, אֲפִי׳ בְּלֹא יָלְדָה, נַמִי פּוֹסַלְתָּהּ. חַיָּיבֵי כָּרֵיתוֹת לָאו בְּנֵי הֲוָיָה נִינְהוּ. בְּקִידּוּשִׁין, בְּפֶרֶק "הָאוֹמֵר לַחֲבֵירוֹ" (ד׳ סז:). שֶׁפְּסָלוּהָ. מִן הַתְּרוּמָה. מִי שֶׁיֵּשׁ לוֹ אַלְמְנוּת וְגֵירוּשִׁין בָּהּ. אֲנִי קוֹרֵא בָּהּ: "וְשָׁבָה אֶל בֵּית אָבִיהָ, מִלֶּחֶם אָבִיהָ תֹּאכֵל", וְלֹא מִגּוֹי וְעֶבֶד. אַשְׁכַּחַן

לימא קרא היא בקדשים לא תאכל. פי׳: דאי לתרומה לחודה אתא – א״כ לימא קרא "היא בקדשים". דכולה פרשתא לתרומה קדריש. ומדכתיב ב"תרומת הקדשים" – שמע מינה דלמורם מן הקדשים נמי אתא. ואם תאמר: ולימא דכוליה להכי אתא, לומר שאין חוזרת לחזה ושוק! ואמר רבינו יצחק: דפשטא דקרא איירי בתרומה, דאיירי בה בכל הפרשה.

רבי עקיבא דדריש ווין. בסנהדרין פרק "ארבע מיתות" (דף נא.) (רבי) ישמעאל אחי, בת ובת אני דורש.

כמאן כר׳ עקיבא דדריש ווין. הק׳ הר׳ משה מריגנשבור״ג: דמאן תנא דפליג עליה דר׳ עקיבא התם גבי בת ובת בפ׳ "ארבע מיתות" (שם דף נא:) – רבי ישמעאל, והתם בההיא שמעתא גופא אמרינן: ור׳ ישמעאל האי "בת ובת" מאי דריש ביה – לרבות בת בעלי מומין, אלמא דר׳ ישמעאל נמי דריש ווי! ותירץ, דה״פ: כמאן כרבי עקיבא דדריש ווי דמוקי ויו ד"ובת" לרבות נשואה, ולא מצריך לרבות בת בעלי מומין. והוא הדין דמרבה הכא לויה וישראלית. אבל רבי ישמעאל דמצריך התם לרבות בת בעלי מומין, כדקאמר, לפי שמצינו שחילק הכתוב בין תמימים לבעלי מומין – יכול נחלוק בבנותיהן, ה״נ יהא צריך כאן לרבות בת בעלי מומין, ולא נוקמיה לרבות לויה וישראלית. וק״ק: בסמוך, דקאמר ר׳ יוחנן משום ר׳ ישמעאל: מנין לגוי ועבד שבאו על כהנת לויה וישראלית כו׳, ומרבינן *(ליה) לויה וישראלית מ"ובת". ופריך: כמאן – כרבי עקיבא, דדריש ווי, טפי הוה ליה לאקשויי דר׳ ישמעאל אדר׳ ישמעאל, דהיכי דריש מ"ובת" לויה וישראלית והא איצטריך לבת בעלי מומין, כדדריש התם! ואר״י: דלא נקט הכא ר׳ עקיבא לאפוקי ר׳ ישמעאל, דהא ר׳ ישמעאל נמי דריש ווי, אלא לאפוקי שאר תנאי דלא דרשי ווי בעלמא. תדע, דלא קאמר אפי׳ תימא רבי ישמעאל, אלא אפילו תימא רבנן. ועוד יש לומר: דר׳ ישמעאל לא דריש ווי, והא דקאמר בסנהדרין (שם:) ורבי ישמעאל האי "בת ובת" מאי עביד ליה – לא מסיק הכי אלא ליישב דרשא דרבי ישמעאל למאן דדריש ווי.

גוי ועבד דלאו בני הויה נינהו לא ליפסלו. פירש בקונטרס: דה״ה דה״מ למימר נמי חייבי כריתות לא ליפסלו, אלא נקט גוי ועבד משום דאיירי בהו לעיל, דקתני כותי דהיינו גוי ובמתני׳ (לקמן דף סט:) תנן: העבד פוסל משום ביאה. ומשני דפסלי מדר׳ יוחנן כו׳. ומהאי קרא משתמעי נמי חייבי כריתות. וק׳ לר״י: דכל היכא דקתני כותי – לאו בתורת גוי נקיט ליה, אלא לפסולא בעלמא. כי ההיא דתנן (קדושין דף עד.) אלו הספקות: שתוקי ואסופי וכותי. וב"אלו נערות" (כתובות דף כט. ושם) דתנן: הבא על הממזרת והנתינה והכותית – יש להן קנס. ודייקינן בפ׳ "שור שנגח ד׳ וה׳" (ב״ק דף לח: ושם) דקסבר כותים גירי אמת הן, מדיש להן קנס. ועוד: ר׳ יוחנן משום ר׳ ישמעאל דנקט גוי ועבד, אמאי לא נקט חייבי כריתות? ונראה לר״י: דפשיטא ליה להש״ס דעיקר קרא ד"לאיש זר" איירי בחייבי כריתות, כדאמר פ׳ "עשרה יוחסין" (קדושין דף עה:) גבי גוי ועבד: השתא ממזר הוי – מיפסל בביאתו מיבעיא? ואפילו לר׳ יהושע דלא הוי ממזר מחייבי כריתות, מ״מ כיון דחמירי – חשיבי "לאיש זר". ואפי׳ אותם חייבי כריתות דלא הוו זר אלא מעיקרא, כיון דעיקר קרא בחייבי כריתות איירי. והכי פריך: ואימא נבעלה לפסול לה חייבי כריתות דוקא, ולא חייבי לאוין! ומשני: "כי תהיה" אמר רחמנא, לרבות חייבי לאוין. ומיהו, חייבי לאוין כיון דלא חמירי בעינן דליהוי זר אלא מעיקרא, כדלקמן. ופריך: גוי ועבד דלאו בני הויה נינהו לא ליפסלו, דלא אתרבו מ"כי תהיה", וחרש נמי לא איקרו דאין בהם ממזרות, ולא חמירי דאין בהם אלא לאו בעלמא? ומשני: דפסלי מדרבי ישמעאל. אבל חייבי כריתות לא נפקי מהתם. דבני אלמנות וגירושין הוו לאחריני, אלא מ"לאיש זר", ועיקר קרא בדידהו משתעי.

גוי ועבד. וא״ת: והא איצטריך למכתב "אלמנה וגרושה" לומר שחוזרת כשנתאלמנה או נתגרשה! וי״ל: דא״כ לכתוב חד מינייהו, דלית ליה צריכותא דר׳ עקיבא דבסמוך. ומדכתב תרוייהו – דריש: למי שיש לו אלמנות וגירושין, יצאו כו׳. ואימא

הגהות הב״ח
(א) רש״י ד״ה עבד וכו׳ פרט לאשת גוי ובשאלתות וכו׳: (ב) בא״ד חייבי כריתות לא כל שכן ושוד הא אמרי:

יעב״ץ מ״ז

גליון הש״ס
גמ׳ א״כ לכתוב קרא היא. עיין לעיל דף ח ע״ב תד״ה ויבמה: **שם** גלוי מילתא בעלמא הוא. עיין בר״ש פ״ב מ״ג דטבול יום ועיין סנהדרין דף טו ע״א:

לקמן ע: עא.
לקמן פז.
ג״ז שם כתובות כה. קדושין סט:
[לקמן סט. פז.]
[ג״ז שם סט. עב: סנהדרין כא: נא. יומא מה. סוטה כח. מנחות נא: פז:]
[סנהדרין עו.]
לעיל מה. סוטה כו: קדושין עה:
[פ׳ וישלח סימן כה]
[וע׳ היטב רש״י לעיל מה. ד״ה חייבי]
בס״א איט

תורה אור

מִי שֶׁיֵּשׁ לוֹ אַלְמְנוּת וְגֵירוּשִׁין בָּהּ, יָצְאוּ גּוֹי וְעֶבֶד שֶׁאֵין לוֹ אַלְמְנוּת וְגֵירוּשִׁין. אַשְׁכַּחַן כֹּהֶנֶת, לְוִיָּה וְיִשְׂרְאֵלִית מְנָא לָן? כְּדַאֲמַר *ר' אַבָּא אֲמַר רַב: "בַּת" "וּבַת" ה"נ "בַּת" "וּבַת". כְּמַאן, כְּרַבִּי עֲקִיבָא, *דְּדָרֵישׁ וָוֵי? אֲפִילּוּ תֵּימָא רַבָּנַן, כּוּלֵּהּ "וּבַת" קְרָא יְתֵירָא הוּא. וְאֵימָא: מִי שֶׁיֵּשׁ לוֹ אַלְמְנוּת וְגֵירוּשִׁין בָּהּ, כִּי לֵית לֵיהּ זֶרַע — קָאָכְלָה, כִּי אִית לֵיהּ זֶרַע — לָא אָכְלָה, מִי שֶׁאֵין לוֹ אַלְמְנוּת וְגֵירוּשִׁין בָּהּ, אע"ג דְּאִית לֵיהּ זֶרַע — נַמִי תֵּיכוּל! אִם כֵּן רִבּוּיֵי לְוִיָּה וְיִשְׂרְאֵלִית לָמָּה לִי? וּלְרַבִּי עֲקִיבָא, דְּאָמַר: *אֵין קִדּוּשִׁין תּוֹפְסִין בְּחַיָּיבֵי לָאוִין, וּמַאי "כִּי תִהְיֶה לְאִישׁ זָר" כִּי תִּיבָּעֵל, "אַלְמָנָה וּגְרוּשָׁה" לָמָּה לִי? אַלְמָנָה לְהַחְמִיר עָלֶיהָ, וּגְרוּשָׁה לְהָקֵל עָלֶיהָ. וּצְרִיכָא, דְּאִי אַשְׁמַעִינַן אַלְמָנָה — אַלְמָנָה הוּא דְּכִי לֵית לָהּ זֶרַע אָכְלָה, מִשּׁוּם דְּחַזְיָא לִכְהוּנָּה, אֲבָל גְּרוּשָׁה דְּלָא חַזְיָא לִכְהוּנָּה — אֵימָא אע"ג דְּלֵית לָהּ זֶרַע לָא אָכְלָה. וְאִי אַשְׁמַעִינַן גְּרוּשָׁה — גְּרוּשָׁה הוּא דְּכִי אִית לָהּ זֶרַע לָא אָכְלָה, מִשּׁוּם דְּלָא חַזְיָא לִכְהוּנָּה, אֲבָל אַלְמָנָה, דְּחַזְיָא לִכְהוּנָּה, אֵימָא: אע"ג דְּאִית לָהּ זֶרַע נַמִי תֵּיכוּל — צְרִיכָא. וְאֵימָא: נִבְעֲלָה לְפָסוּל לָהּ — אַף מַחֲזִיר גְּרוּשָׁתוֹ! "לְאִישׁ זָר" אָמַר רַחֲמָנָא, מִי שֶׁזָּר אֶצְלָהּ מֵעִיקָּרָא, לְאַפּוֹקֵי הַאי דְּלָא זָר אֶצְלָהּ מֵעִיקָּרָא הוּא. אִי הָכִי, חָלָל דְּלָאו זָר הוּא(א) מֵעִיקָּרָא, לָא לִפְסוֹל! אָמַר קְרָא: °"לֹא יְחַלֵּל זַרְעוֹ בְּעַמָּיו", *מַקִּישׁ זַרְעוֹ לוֹ: מַה הוּא פּוֹסֵל [א]אַף זַרְעוֹ נַמִי פּוֹסֵל. וְאֵימָא: מִשְּׁעַת הֲוָיָה? דּוּמְיָא דְּכֹהֵן גָּדוֹל בְּאַלְמָנָה, מַה כֹּהֵן גָּדוֹל בְּאַלְמָנָה — בְּבִיאָה, אַף הַאי נַמִי — בְּבִיאָה. וְאֵימָא: עַד דְּאִיכָּא הֲוָיָה וּבִיאָה! דּוּמְיָא דְּכ"ג בְּאַלְמָנָה, [ב]מַה כֹּהֵן גָּדוֹל בְּאַלְמָנָה — בְּבִיאָה לְחוּדָהּ, אַף הַאי נַמִי בְּבִיאָה לְחוּדָהּ. "וְרַבִּי יוֹסֵי אוֹמֵר: כָּל *שֶׁזַּרְעוֹ פָּסוּל — פּוֹסֵל, וְכָל שֶׁאֵין זַרְעוֹ פָּסוּל — אֵינוֹ פּוֹסֵל". *מַאי אִיכָּא בֵּין ת"ק לְרַבִּי יוֹסֵי? אֲמַר ר' יוֹחָנָן: מִצְרִי שֵׁנִי וַאֲדוֹמִי שֵׁנִי אִיכָּא בֵּינַיְיהוּ. וּשְׁנֵיהֶם לֹא לְמָדוּהָ אֶלָּא מִכֹּהֵן גָּדוֹל בְּאַלְמָנָה. ת"ק סָבַר: מַה כ"ג בְּאַלְמָנָה, שֶׁבִּיאָתוֹ בַּעֲבֵירָה — וּפוֹסֵל, אַף הַאי נַמִי פּוֹסֵל. וְרַבִּי יוֹסֵי סָבַר: כְּכֹהֵן גָּדוֹל, מַה כֹּהֵן גָּדוֹל — שֶׁזַּרְעוֹ פָּסוּל וּפוֹסֵל, אַף כָּל שֶׁזַּרְעוֹ פָּסוּל פּוֹסֵל, לְאַפּוֹקֵי מִצְרִי שֵׁנִי [ג]דְּאֵין זַרְעוֹ פָּסוּל, דִּכְתִיב: °"בָּנִים אֲשֶׁר יִוָּלְדוּ לָהֶם דּוֹר שְׁלִישִׁי יָבֹא לָהֶם בִּקְהַל ה'". § "רשב"ג אוֹמֵר: כָּל שֶׁאַתָּה נוֹשֵׂא בִּתּוֹ אַתָּה נוֹשֵׂא אַלְמָנָתוֹ וכו'". § מַאי אִיכָּא בֵּין ר' יוֹסֵי לְרַבָּן שִׁמְעוֹן בֶּן גַּמְלִיאֵל? אֲמַר עוּלָּא: גֵּר עַמּוֹנִי וּמוֹאָבִי אִיכָּא בֵּינַיְיהוּ. וּשְׁנֵיהֶם לֹא לְמָדוּהָ אֶלָּא מִכֹּהֵן גָּדוֹל בְּאַלְמָנָה. רַבִּי יוֹסֵי סָבַר: מַה כֹּהֵן גָּדוֹל בְּאַלְמָנָה — שֶׁזַּרְעוֹ פָּסוּל וּפוֹסֵל, אַף כָּל שֶׁזַּרְעוֹ פָּסוּל — פּוֹסֵל. רשב"ג סָבַר: מַה כֹּהֵן גָּדוֹל בְּאַלְמָנָה — שֶׁכָּל זַרְעוֹ פָּסוּל וּפוֹסֵל, אַף שֶׁכָּל זַרְעוֹ פָּסוּל וּפוֹסֵל, לְאַפּוֹקֵי עַמּוֹנִי וּמוֹאָבִי דְּאֵין כָּל זַרְעוֹ פָּסוּל, דַּאֲמַר מָר: *[ד]עַמּוֹנִי וְלֹא עַמּוֹנִית, מוֹאָבִי וְלֹא מוֹאָבִית. §

מתני' [ה]הָאוֹנֵס וְהַמְפַתֶּה וְהַשּׁוֹטֶה — לֹא פּוֹסְלִין וְלֹא מַאֲכִילִין, וְאִם אֵינָן רְאוּיִין לָבֹא בְּיִשְׂרָאֵל — הֲרֵי אֵלּוּ פּוֹסְלִין. כֵּיצַד? (ב) (הָיָה) יִשְׂרָאֵל שֶׁבָּא עַל בַּת כֹּהֵן — תֹּאכַל בִּתְרוּמָה. עִיבְּרָה

רש"י

אַשְׁכַּחַן כֹּהֶנֶת. דְּפָסֵיל לָהּ עֶבֶד. כּוּלָּהּ וּבַת קְרָא יְתֵירָא הוּא. דְּהָא כְּתִיב בִּקְרָא דִּלְעֵיל מִינֵּיהּ "וּבַת כֹּהֵן", וּמָצֵי לְמִכְתַּב אַבַּתְרֵיהּ "וְכִי תִהְיֶה אַלְמָנָה וּגְרוּשָׁה". אע"ג דְּאִית לָהּ זֶרַע תֵּיכוּל. וְכִבְהֵמָה בְּעָלְמָא חֲשִׁיב. אִם כֵּן. דְּהַאי קְרָא לְקוּלָּא כְּתִיב, וּלְאַשְׁמוּעִינַן דְּזֶרַע דְּגוֹי וְעֶבֶד לָא פָּסֵיל — רִבּוּיֵי לְוִיָּה וְיִשְׂרְאֵלִית דִּכְתִיב בֵּיהּ לָמָּה לִי דִּכְתַב, "וּבַת" קְרָא יְתֵירָא? הַשְׁתָּא כֹּהֶנֶת גּוּפַהּ אַשְׁמוּעִינַן דְּלָא מִיפַּסְלָא בְּזֶרַע גּוֹי וְעֶבֶד, לְוִיָּה וְיִשְׂרְאֵלִית מִיבַּעְיָא?! וְאִי מִשּׁוּם לְאַשְׁמוּעִינַן דְּמִי שֶׁיֵּשׁ לוֹ אַלְמְנוּת וְגֵירוּשִׁין, אֲפִי' הָכִי כִּי אִית לָהּ זֶרַע מִינֵּיהּ לָא תֵּיכוּל, וְאִיצְטְרִיךְ לְמֵיסַר לְוִיָּה וְיִשְׂרְאֵלִית הָאוֹכֶלֶת בִּתְרוּמָה בִּשְׁבִיל בְּנָהּ כֹּהֵן, דְּכִי תִּינָּשֵׂא לְזָר וִיהֵא לָהּ זֶרַע מִמֶּנּוּ לֹא תָּשׁוּב לִתְרוּמָה בְּמִיתַת בַּעְלָהּ — הָא פְּשִׁיטָא לָן; דְּכֵיוָן דְּכֹהֶנֶת גּוּפַהּ מִיפַּסְלָא בְּזֶרַע יִשְׂרָאֵל מִתְּרוּמָה דְּבֵי נָשָׁא, כָּל שֶׁכֵּן יִשְׂרְאֵלִית הָאוֹכֶלֶת בִּשְׁבִיל בְּנָהּ. אֶלָּא וַדַּאי, כִּי רַבִּי קְרָא לְוִיָּה וְיִשְׂרְאֵלִית — לְהָכִי רַבְּיֵיהּ, שֶׁאִם אוֹכֶלֶת בִּשְׁבִיל בְּנָהּ, וְנִבְעֲלָה לְגוֹי וְעֶבֶד, אֲפִי' אֵין לָהּ זֶרַע — נִפְסְלָה, דְּלָא נָפְקָא לָן מִכֹּהֶנֶת, כִּדְאָמְרִינַן לְעֵיל (דף סח:): כֹּהֶנֶת הִיא דְּקָדֵישׁ גּוּפַהּ כו'. וּלְרַבִּי עֲקִיבָא דְּאָמַר אֵין קִדּוּשִׁין תּוֹפְסִין. לְאָדָם פָּסוּל, וְהַאי "כִּי תִהְיֶה לְאִישׁ זָר" דִּלְעֵיל — לָאו מִשּׁוּם הֲוָיָה נָקַט, וּלְמֵימְרָא דְּאֵין בִּיאַת פָּסוּל פּוֹסֶלֶת אֶלָּא בְּמִי שֶׁרָאוּי לְקַדֵּשׁ, דְּהָא אֵין קִדּוּשִׁין לְשׁוּם פָּסוּל. וְהַאי "כִּי תִהְיֶה" אִם בָּא לְלַמֵּד עַל בִּיאַת פְּסוּלִין — אֵינוֹ אֶלָּא לְשׁוֹן בְּעִילָה, וְכָל הַזָּרִים אֶלָּלָהּ בְּמַשְׁמַע שֶׁתְּהֵא בִּיאָתָם פּוֹסֶלֶת, אֲפִילּוּ גּוֹי וְעֶבֶד. אַלְמָנָה וּגְרוּשָׁה. לְאַשְׁמוּעִינַן גּוֹי וְעֶבֶד, לָמָּה לִי? אַלְמָנָה לְהַחְמִיר כו'. כְּלוֹמַר, לָאו לְמַעוּטֵי מִי שֶׁיֵּשׁ לוֹ אַלְמְנוּת וְגֵירוּשִׁין. אֶלָּא לְגוּפֵיהּ אִיצְטְרִיךְ, אַלְמָנָה — כְּדֵי לְהַחְמִיר עָלֶיהָ. דְּאִי לָא כְּתִיב, ה"א אַלְמְנַת יִשְׂרָאֵל וְהִיא בַּת כֹּהֵן תֵּיכוּל, וְאע"ג דְּאִית לָהּ זֶרַע. וּגְרוּשָׁה אִיצְטְרִיךְ לְכַתְבֵיהּ רַחֲמָנָא לְהָקֵל עָלֶיהָ, וּלְמֵימַר (דְּכִי נִתְגָּרְשָׁה מִיִּשְׂרָאֵל לְהָקֵל) דְּכִי לֵית לָהּ זֶרַע מִיִּשְׂרָאֵל — תֵּיכוּל, דְּאִי לָא כְּתָבֵיהּ ה"א אע"ג דְּלֵית לָהּ זֶרַע לָא תֵּיכוּל, דְּכֵיוָן דְּאִיפַּסְלָה מִכְּהוּנָּה — מִתְּרוּמָה נַמִי מִיפַּסְלָה. וְאֵימָא נִבְעֲלָה לְפָסוּל לָהּ אַף מַחֲזִיר גְּרוּשָׁתוֹ. מִשֶּׁנִּישֵּׂאת לְאַחֵר, דְּהָא זָר הוּא אֶצְלָהּ, וְתָפְסֵי לוֹ בָּהּ קִידּוּשִׁין, אַלְמָּה תַּנְיָא בְּ"הַחוֹלֵץ" (לעיל מד:) הִיא כְּשֵׁרָה וּוְלָדָהּ כָּשֵׁר, וְאוֹקִימְנָא כְּשֵׁרָה לִכְהוּנָּה — וְכ"שׁ לִתְרוּמָה! ה"ג. חָלָל דְּלָאו זָר אֶצְלָהּ הוּא לָא לִיפְסוֹל. דְּהָא חָלָל מוּתָּר אֲפִילּוּ בְּכֹהֶנֶת. מַקִּישׁ זַרְעוֹ. שֶׁל כֹּהֵן גָּדוֹל מִן הָאַלְמָנָה לוֹ, מַה הוּא פּוֹסֵל הָאַלְמָנָה בְּבִיאָתוֹ מִן הַתְּרוּמָה, כִּדְיָלֵיף בְּפֶרֶק "עֲשָׂרָה יוֹחֲסִין" (קדושין דף עז.) "וְלֹא יְחַלֵּל" — מִי שֶׁהָיָה כָּשֵׁר וְנִתְחַלֵּל, וְזוֹ הִיא הָאַלְמָנָה, אַף זַרְעוֹ הֶחָלָל פּוֹסֵל אִשָּׁה בְּבִיאָתוֹ מִן הַתְּרוּמָה. וְאֵימָא. מִדְּמַסְפְּקֵהּ רַחֲמָנָא בִּלְשׁוֹן "כִּי תִהְיֶה", מִשְּׁעַת הֲוָיָה, אִי קִידֵּשׁ פָּסוּל אֶת הָאִשָּׁה — פְּסוּלָה עוֹלָמִית, וַאֲפִי' מֵת, כְּאִילּוּ בָּא עָלֶיהָ. כֹּהֵן גָּדוֹל בְּבִיאָה הוּא דְּפָסֵיל. כִּדְכְתִיב (ויקרא כא) "לֹא יְחַלֵּל זַרְעוֹ", כְּשֶׁיֵּשׁ זֶרַע חִילֵּל, וְהָכִי נַמִי תְּנַן בְּ"הַבָּא עַל יְבִמְתּוֹ" (לעיל דף ט:) נִתְאַרְמְלוּ אוֹ נִתְגָּרְשׁוּ מִן הַנִּישּׂוּאִין — פְּסוּלוֹת, מִן הָאֵירוּסִין — כְּשֵׁרוֹת. מִצְרִי שֵׁנִי. פָּסוּל, וְזַרְעוֹ כָּשֵׁר לְת"ק, כֵּיוָן דְּהוּא פָּסוּל פּוֹסְלָהּ בְּבִיאָה, לְרַבִּי יוֹסֵי — לָא פָּסֵיל: הָכִי גָּרְסִינַן: מַה כֹּהֵן גָּדוֹל בְּאַלְמָנָה בִּיאָתוֹ בַּעֲבֵירָה וּפוֹסֵל כו'. מִצְרִי וַאֲדוֹמִי שֵׁנִי. בִּיאָתָן בַּעֲבֵירָה, דִּכְתִיב (דברים כג) "שְׁלִישִׁי" וְלֹא שֵׁנִי. כָּל שֶׁאַתָּה. כֹּהֵן נוֹשֵׂא בִּתּוֹ, אַתָּה כֹּהֵן נוֹשֵׂא אַלְמְנָתוֹ. גֵּר עַמּוֹנִי. הוּא וּבְנוֹ וּבֶן בְּנוֹ עַד סוֹף הָעוֹלָם פְּסוּלִין, אֲבָל בִּתּוֹ כְּשֵׁרָה, דְּקַיְימָא לָן (לקמן דף עו:): עַמּוֹנִי וְלֹא עַמּוֹנִית. לְרַבִּי יוֹסֵי דְּתָלֵי טַעְמָא בְּכָל שֶׁזַּרְעוֹ פָּסוּל, הוֹאִיל וְיֵשׁ בְּזַרְעוֹ פָּסוּל — פּוֹסֵל, וּלְרַבִּי שִׁמְעוֹן דְּתָלֵי טַעְמָא בְּבִתּוֹ — לָא פָּסֵיל. **מתני'** וְהַשּׁוֹטֶה. אֲפִי' עַל יְדֵי חוּפָּה וְקִידּוּשִׁין — לֹא פּוֹסֵל וְלֹא מַאֲכִיל, דְּאֵין קִנְיָנוֹ קִנְיָן. הֲרֵי אֵלּוּ פּוֹסְלִין. שֶׁהֲרֵי נִתְחַלְּלָה בְּבִיאַת פָּסוּל לָהּ. בְּאוֹנֶס אוֹ בְּפִיתּוּי, שֶׁלֹּא לְשֵׁם קִידּוּשִׁין. יִשְׂרָאֵל שֶׁבָּא עַל בַּת כֹּהֵן. עִיבְּרָה

תוספות

ואימא מי שיש לו אלמנות וגירושין בה כו'. תימה: דבכל דוכתא לחומרא מקשינן והכא פריך דנקיט לקולא:

אם כן רבויי לויה וישראלית. תימה: דהא איצטריך לרבויי לויה וישראלית לאשמועינן דחוזרת בשביל בנה, כדאמרינן בסוף "יש מותרות" (לקמן דף פז.)? ויש לומר: דמשמע ליה דאיצטריך לויה וישראלית לכל מילי דאיירי קרא, ולאשמועינן דכי אית לה זרע נמי מן הגוי תיכול בשביל בנה — לא איצטריך, כיון דאשמעינן בכהנת דקדיש גופה.

כי תהיה כי תבעל. ואם תאמר: לדידיה נמי איכא לאוקומי באלמנה לכהן גדול לרבי סימאי, ובבעולה לכהן גדול אפי' לרבי ישבב? ויש לומר: דכל פסולי כהונה נפקא לן דמיפסלי בתרומה מ"לא יחלל". אי נמי: לא משמע ליה לאוקמי "לאיש זר" גבי כהן. וא"ת: ולוקמא בסוטה שבא עליה בעלה בדרך, דליכא אלא עשה ד"ונטמאה"? ויש לומר: דזר אללה מעיקרא בעינן, אפילו לרבי עקיבא, כיון דלא הוי ממזר. ומיהו, קשה: דלמה ליה למימר מאי "כי תהיה" כי תבעל — בפשיטות הוה מצי למיפרך, דאמאי איצטריך קרא לרבי עקיבא לגוי ועבד? דהשתא ממזר הוי, מיפסלא בביאתו מיבעיא?! כדאמר בפרק "עשרה יוחסין" (קדושין עה: ושם).

כהן גדול באלמנה בביאה לחודה. כדאמר בפ' "עשרה יוחסין" (שם דף עח. ושם) בעל — לוקה משום "לא יחלל". ואם תאמר: היא גופה מנלן דלא בעינן תרתי? הא כתיב "לא יקח ולא יחלל"? ויש לומר: דלגבי *כהן אין להצריך קידושין, דכ"ש בלא קידושין. וכיון שהבן נפסל — גם היא נפסלת.

ושניהם לא למדוה אלא מאלמנה לכהן גדול. עיקר טעמא הוי מ"לאיש זר", אלא דמכ"ג באלמנה ילפינן במאי מסתבר לאוקמי קרא. ואי לאו קרא ד"לאיש זר" ליכא למילף מקל וחומר דאלמנה שנתחלל, כדפירשתי לעיל (דף טו: ד"ה מה).

והמפתה והשוטה. הא דלא תנן קטן בהדייהו, דלא תקינו ליה רבנן נישואין, כדקתני בגמרא (לקמן דף קו:) שוטה וקטן שנשאו כו', — אמר רבי יצחק: דהיינו משום דבעי למיתני בסיפא וילדה, דלא מיתני ליה בקטן.

לא פוסלין ולא מאכילין. לא איצטריך לאשמועינן באונס ומפתה דאין מאכילין, ומשום לא פוסלין נקטיה, ואפילו לרבי אלעזר דאמר *פנוי הבא על הפנויה שלא לשם אישות עשאה זונה — נראה דלא מיפסלה בתרומה, דאין זה לאיש זר. ונשאת

עין משפט נר מצוה

לז א מיי' פי"ח מהל' איסורי ביאה הל' א סמג לאוין קפא טוש"ע אה"ע סימן ו סעי' ח:

לח ב מיי' פי"ז שם הל' ג סמג לאוין קכה:

לט ג מיי' פי"ב שם הל' יט סמג לאוין קיב קטז טוש"ע שם סי' ד סעי' ג:

מ ד מיי' שם הי"ח טוש"ע שם סעי' ב:

מא ה מיי' פ"ח מהל' תרומות הל' יג טוי"ד סי' שלא:

מסורת הש"ס

[לעיל סח: לקמן פז.]

[לעיל סח: וש"נ]

[לעיל י: וש"נ]

[שזרעו עם הכנוי חשיב ב' תיבות דלא הל"ל אלא לא יחלל זרע בעמיו שבשעת הליווי עדיין אינו זרעו שיכונה בו ומדכתיב זרעו הוא כאילו אמר זרע לו והו מקיש זרעו לו כ"כ בעלי סוגיות ע' של"ה דף שנג ד"ה ענין היקש]

[לקמן עו: עז. פח. קידושין סז: עח. כתובות ז: חולין סב:]

נ"ל בן רש"ל

קידושין עז:

[שם עה.]

[לעיל נט:]

ויקרא כא

דברים כג

ס"א ל"ג

הגהות הב"ח

(א) גמ' אי הכי חלל דלאו זר הוא לא ליפסול כצ"ל ותיבת מעיקרא נמחק: (ב) שם במשנה כיצד הרי ישראל:

גליון הש"ס

תום' ד"ה כי תהיה וכו' דליכא אלא עשה. עיין לעיל דף יא ע"ב תד"ה מאי נסתפקה:

[א]עִיבְּרָה — לֹא תֹּאכַל בִּתְרוּמָה, נֶחְתַּךְ הָעוּבָּר בְּמֵעֶיהָ — תֹּאכַל. (א) הָיָה כֹּהֵן שֶׁבָּא עַל בַּת יִשְׂרָאֵל — לֹא תֹּאכַל בִּתְרוּמָה, עִיבְּרָה — לֹא תֹּאכַל, יָלְדָה — תֹּאכַל. נִמְצָא כֹּחוֹ שֶׁל בֵּן גָּדוֹל מִשֶּׁל אָב. [ב]הָעֶבֶד פּוֹסֵל מִשּׁוּם בִּיאָה, וְאֵינוֹ פּוֹסֵל מִשּׁוּם זֶרַע. כֵּיצַד? בַּת יִשְׂרָאֵל לְכֹהֵן, בַּת כֹּהֵן לְיִשְׂרָאֵל, וְיָלְדָה הֵימֶנּוּ בֵּן, וְהָלַךְ הַבֵּן וְנִכְבַּשׁ עַל הַשִּׁפְחָה, וְיָלְדָה הֵימֶנּוּ בֵּן — הֲרֵי זֶה עֶבֶד. הָיְתָה אֵם אָבִיו בַּת יִשְׂרָאֵל לְכֹהֵן — לֹא תֹּאכַל בִּתְרוּמָה, בַּת כֹּהֵן לְיִשְׂרָאֵל — תֹּאכַל בִּתְרוּמָה. [ג]מַמְזֵר פּוֹסֵל וּמַאֲכִיל. כֵּיצַד? בַּת יִשְׂרָאֵל לְכֹהֵן, וּבַת כֹּהֵן לְיִשְׂרָאֵל, וְיָלְדָה הֵימֶנּוּ בַּת, וְהָלְכָה הַבַּת וְנִישֵּׂאת לְעֶבֶד אוֹ לְגוֹי וְיָלְדָה הֵימֶנּוּ בֵּן — הֲרֵי זֶה מַמְזֵר. הָיְתָה אֵם אִמּוֹ בַּת יִשְׂרָאֵל לְכֹהֵן — תֹּאכַל בִּתְרוּמָה. בַּת כֹּהֵן לְיִשְׂרָאֵל — לֹא תֹּאכַל בִּתְרוּמָה. [ד]כֹּהֵן גָּדוֹל, פְּעָמִים שֶׁהוּא פּוֹסֵל, כֵּיצַד? בַּת כֹּהֵן לְיִשְׂרָאֵל וְיָלְדָה הֵימֶנּוּ בַּת, וְהָלְכָה הַבַּת וְנִיסֵּת לְכֹהֵן וְיָלְדָה הֵימֶנּוּ בֵּן — ה"ז רָאוּי לִהְיוֹת כֹּהֵן גָּדוֹל עוֹמֵד וּמְשַׁמֵּשׁ עַל גַּבֵּי הַמִּזְבֵּחַ, מַאֲכִיל אֶת אִמּוֹ, וּפוֹסֵל אֵם אִמּוֹ. זֹאת אוֹמֶרֶת: לֹא כִּבְנִי כ"ג שֶׁהוּא פּוֹסְלֵנִי מִן הַתְּרוּמָה.§ **גמ'** תָּנֵינָא לְהָא דְּת"ר: *[ה]שׁוֹטֶה וְקָטָן שֶׁנָּשְׂאוּ נָשִׁים וָמֵתוּ — נְשׁוֹתֵיהֶן פְּטוּרוֹת מִן הַחֲלִיצָה וּמִן הַיִּיבּוּם.§ כֵּיצַד? (ב) הָיָה יִשְׂרָאֵל שֶׁבָּא עַל בַּת כֹּהֵן — תֹּאכַל בִּתְרוּמָה. עִיבְּרָה — לֹא תֹּאכַל.§ כֵּיוָן דְּעִיבְּרָה לֹא תֹּאכַל — לֵיחוּשׁ שֶׁמָּא עִיבְּרָה! מִי לָא תְּנַן: *מַפְרִישִׁין אוֹתָן ג' חֳדָשִׁים שֶׁמָּא מְעוּבָּרוֹת הֵן! אָמַר רַבָּה בַּר רַב הוּנָא: לְיוּחֲסִין חָשְׁשׁוּ, לִתְרוּמָה לֹא חָשְׁשׁוּ. וְלִתְרוּמָה לֹא חָשְׁשׁוּ? וְהָתַנְיָא: *[ו]"הֲרֵי זֶה גִּיטֵּיךְ שָׁעָה אַחַת קוֹדֶם לְמִיתָתִי" — אֲסוּרָה לֶאֱכוֹל בִּתְרוּמָה מִיָּד! אֶלָּא אָמַר רַבָּה בַּר רַב הוּנָא: בְּנִישּׂוּאִין — חָשְׁשׁוּ, בִּזְנוּת — לֹא חָשְׁשׁוּ. וּבְנִישּׂוּאִין מִי חָשְׁשׁוּ? וְהָתַנְיָא: [ז]בַּת כֹּהֵן שֶׁנִּישֵּׂאת לְיִשְׂרָאֵל וָמֵת — טוֹבֶלֶת וְאוֹכֶלֶת בִּתְרוּמָה לָעֶרֶב! אָמַר רַב חִסְדָּא: [ח]טוֹבֶלֶת וְאוֹכֶלֶת עַד אַרְבָּעִים, דְּאִי לָא מִיעַבְּרָא — הָא לָא מִיעַבְּרָא, וְאִי מִיעַבְּרָא — עַד אַרְבָּעִים מַיָּא בְּעָלְמָא הִיא. אֲמַר לֵיהּ אַבַּיֵי: אִי הָכִי, אֵימָא סֵיפָא: הוּכַּר עוּבָּרָהּ בְּמֵעֶיהָ — תְּהֵא מְקוּלְקֶלֶת לְמַפְרֵעַ! מַאי [ט]מְקוּלְקֶלֶת: עַד אַרְבָּעִים. אִיתְּמַר, הַבָּא עַל אֲרוּסָתוֹ בְּבֵית חָמִיו. רַב אָמַר: הַוָּלָד מַמְזֵר, וּשְׁמוּאֵל אָמַר: הַוָּלָד שְׁתוּקִי. אָמַר רָבָא: מִסְתַּבְּרָא מִילְּתֵיהּ דְּרַב — דְּדַיְימָא מֵעָלְמָא, אֲבָל לָא דַּיְימָא מֵעָלְמָא — בָּתְרָא דִּידֵיהּ שָׁדֵינַן לֵיהּ. אָמַר רָבָא: מְנָא אָמִינָא לָהּ — דְּקָתָנֵי: יָלְדָה תֹּאכַל. הֵיכִי דָּמֵי? אִילֵימָא דְּדַיְימָא מֵעָלְמָא — יָלְדָה אַמַּאי תֹּאכַל? אֶלָּא לָאו — מִינֵּיהּ דַּיְימָא וְלָא דַּיְימָא מֵעָלְמָא. וּמָה הָתָם, דִּלְהַאי אִיסּוּרָא וּלְהַאי אִיסּוּרָא — בָּתְרָא דִּידֵיהּ שָׁדֵינַן לֵיהּ, הָכָא, דִּלְהַאי אִיסּוּרָא וּלְהַאי הֶיתֵּירָא — לֹא כׇּל שֶׁכֵּן?! א"ל אַבַּיֵי: לְעוֹלָם אֵימָא לָךְ: כׇּל הֵיכָא דְּדַיְימָא מִינֵּיהּ אע"ג דְּלָא דַּיְימָא מֵעָלְמָא — אָמַר רַב הַוָּלָד מַמְזֵר, מ"ט? דְּאָמְרִינַן: מִדְּאַפְקְרָא נַפְשַׁהּ לְגַבֵּי אָרוּס — אַפְקְרָא נַפְשַׁהּ לְעָלְמָא. וּמַתְנִי' — שֶׁהָיוּ שְׁנֵיהֶם חֲבוּשִׁים בְּבֵית הָאֲסוּרִין. אִיכָּא דְּאָמְרִי: *בְּבָא עָלֶיהָ — כ"ע לָא פְּלִיגִי דְּבָתְרֵיהּ דִּידֵיהּ שָׁדֵינַן לֵיהּ, וְהָכִי אִיתְּמַר: *אֲרוּסָה שֶׁעִיבְּרָה, רַב אָמַר: הַוָּלָד מַמְזֵר, וּשְׁמוּאֵל אָמַר: [י]הַוָּלָד שְׁתוּקִי. אָמַר רָבָא: *מִסְתַּבְּרָא מִילְּתֵיהּ דְּרַב — דְּלָא דַּיְימָא מִינֵּיהּ וְדַיְימָא מֵעָלְמָא, אֲבָל

רש"י

עִיבְּרָה לֹא תֹּאכַל. כִּדְיָלְפִינַן לְעֵיל (דף סז:) עוּבָּר פּוֹסֵל, דִּכְתִיב "כִּנְעוּרֶיהָ" – פְּרָט לִמְעוּבֶּרֶת. נֶחְתַּךְ הָעוּבָּר בְּמֵעֶיהָ תֹּאכַל. מִיָּד. וְה"ה נַמִי אִם יְלָדַתּוּ וָמֵת. עִיבְּרָה לֹא תֹּאכַל. שֶׁהָעוּבָּר אֵינוֹ מַאֲכִיל אֶת אִמּוֹ יִשְׂרְאֵלִית עַד שֶׁיֵּצֵא לַאֲוִיר הָעוֹלָם, כִּדְכְתִיב (ויקרא כב) "וִילִיד בֵּיתוֹ... יֹאכְלוּ" – יָלוּד מַאֲכִיל, שֶׁאֵין יָלוּד אֵין מַאֲכִיל. גָּדוֹל מִשֶּׁל אָב. שֶׁהַבּוֹעֵל לֹא יָכוֹל לְהַאֲכִילָהּ, מִפְּנֵי שֶׁלֹּא בָּא עָלֶיהָ לְשֵׁם קִידּוּשִׁין וְלָאו קִנְיָנוֹ הוּא, וּבְנוֹ מַאֲכִילָהּ. הָעֶבֶד פּוֹסֵל מִשּׁוּם בִּיאָה. אִם בָּא עַל כֹּהֶנֶת פְּסָלָהּ מִן הַתְּרוּמָה, כִּדְאָמְרִינַן בַּגְּמָרָא לְעֵיל (דף סח:). וְאֵין פּוֹסֵל מִשּׁוּם זֶרַע. אִם יֵשׁ לָהּ זֶרַע לְבַת כֹּהֵן מִיִּשְׂרָאֵל כָּשֵׁר שֶׁהוּא עֶבֶד, וּמֵת בַּעְלָהּ יִשְׂרָאֵל וְנִשְׁאַר זֶה, לָא אָמְרִינַן הֲרֵי זֶרַע יֵשׁ לָהּ מִיִּשְׂרָאֵל, וְלֹא תָּשׁוּב לִתְרוּמַת אָבִיהָ. דְּעֶבֶד וַדַּאי לָאו זֶרַע הוּא, וּמְפָרֵשׁ וְאָזֵיל הֵיכִי מַשְׁכַּחַתְּ לָהּ שֶׁיְּהֵא בֶּן יִשְׂרָאֵל כָּשֵׁר עֶבֶד. וְנִכְבַּשׁ עַל הַשִּׁפְחָה. נִדְחַק וְנִדְבַּק עָלֶיהָ. לְשׁוֹן מַכְבֵּשׁ = פריש"א בְּלַעַ"ז, וּלְשׁוֹן גְּנַאי הוּא. הֲרֵי זֶה עֶבֶד. שֶׁוָּלָד שִׁפְחָה כָּמוֹהָ, דִּכְתִיב "הָאִשָּׁה וִילָדֶיהָ" (שמות כא). הָיְתָה אֵם אָבִיו. בַּת כֹּהֵן לְיִשְׂרָאֵל, תֹּאכַל בִּתְרוּמָה אִם מֵת אָבִיו וְהוּא קַיָּים. אע"ג דְּוָלָד וָלָד בְּעָלְמָא פָּסֵיל, כִּדְאָמְרַן (לקמן דף ע.) זֶרַע זַרְעָהּ תְּנַן כו' — הַאי לָא פָּסֵיל, דְּהָא לָאו בָּתַר אֲבוּהּ אָזֵיל, וְלָאו זַרְעוֹ הוּא. בַּת יִשְׂרָאֵל לְכֹהֵן, וּמֵת בְּנָהּ מִכֹּהֵן, וּבְנוֹ בֶּן בְּנָהּ קַיָּים וְהוּא עֶבֶד – לֹא תֹּאכַל בִּתְרוּמָה. דְּלָאו זֶרַע הוּא. כ"ג פְּעָמִים שֶׁהוּא פּוֹסֵל. אֶת בַּת כֹּהֵן מִן הַתְּרוּמָה, מִשּׁוּם זַרְעָהּ מִיִּשְׂרָאֵל. מַאֲכִיל אֶת אִמּוֹ.(ג) לְאַחַר מִיתַת אָבִיו. וּפוֹסֵל אֶת אֵם אִמּוֹ. אֲפִילּוּ לְאַחַר מִיתַת אִמּוֹ דְּאִי לָאו הוּא הֲוָה הָדְרָה אֵם אִמּוֹ לִתְרוּמָה דְּבֵי נָשָׁא לְאַחַר מִיתַת בִּתָּהּ, כִּדְאָמַר בְּ"יֵשׁ מוּתָּרוֹת" (לקמן ד' פז.): מֵת בְּנָהּ מִיִּשְׂרָאֵל – תֹּאכַל בִּתְרוּמָה. וְזֹאת. הָאִשָּׁה, אוֹמֶרֶת: לֹא כִּבְנִי כ"ג, כְּלוֹמַר לֹא יִרְבּוּ כְּמוֹתוֹ. **גמ'** נְשׁוֹתֵיהֶן פְּטוּרוֹת. אַלְמָא: אֵין קִנְיָן לְשׁוֹטֶה. כֵּיוָן. דְּאִי פְּשִׁיטָא לָן דְּעִיבְּרָה אָמְרִינַן לָהּ לֹא תֹּאכַל – אַמַּאי קָתָנֵי מַתְנִיתִין יִשְׂרָאֵל הַבָּא עַל בַּת כֹּהֵן בְּאוֹנֶס וּפִיתּוּי תֹּאכַל? לֵיחוּשׁ שֶׁמָּא עִיבְּרָה! מִי לָא תְּנַן. בְּפֶ' "ד' אַחִין" גַּבֵּי נָשִׁים שֶׁהוּחְלְפוּ בִּשְׁעַת כְּנִיסָתָן לַחוּפָּה: מַפְרִישִׁין אוֹתָן מִבַּעֲלֵיהֶן ג' חֳדָשִׁים, שֶׁמָּא מְעוּבָּרוֹת הֵן וְהַוְּלָדוֹת מַמְזֵרִין, וּבָעֵינַן הַבְחָנָה בֵּין וָלָד כָּשֵׁר לְוָלָד פָּסוּל. אַלְמָא: לַחֲדָא בִּיאָה חָיְישִׁינַן. לְיוּחֲסִין חָשְׁשׁוּ. מַעֲלָה עָשׂוּ לְיוּחֲסִין לָחוּשׁ לְבִיאָה אַחַת וּלְסָפֵק. הֲרֵי זֶה גִּיטֵּיךְ. כֹּהֵן לְבַת יִשְׂרָאֵל. אֲסוּרָה לֶאֱכוֹל בִּתְרוּמָה מִיָּד. דְּכׇל שַׁעְתָּא אָמְרִינַן הַשְׁתָּא מָיֵית, אַלְמָא: חָסְרִי לָהּ מִסָּפֵק. אֶלָּא אָמַר רַבָּה. לָא תֵּימָא לִתְרוּמָה לֹא חָשְׁשׁוּ, דְּוַדַּאי חָיְישִׁינַן לִסְפֵיקָא, אֶלָּא תָּרֵיץ לְפִירְכָא דִּלְעֵיל הָכִי. בְּנִישּׂוּאִין. כְּגוֹן שֶׁנִּתְחַלְּפוּ בִּכְנִיסָתָן לַחוּפָּה – חָשְׁשׁוּ לְשֶׁמָּא נִתְעַבְּרוּ, דְּהָא לֹא הִפְכּוּ. אֲבָל בִּזְנוּת לֹא חָשְׁשׁוּ. כִּדְקַיְימָא לָן: *אִשָּׁה מְזַנָּה מִתְהַפֶּכֶת כְּדֵי שֶׁלֹּא תִּתְעַבֵּר, הִלְכָּךְ לֵיכָּא סָפֵק. וָמֵת. בַּעְלָהּ בּוֹ בַּיּוֹם. טוֹבֶלֶת. מִשּׁוּם בִּיאָה, דִּכְתִיב "וְאִשָּׁה אֲשֶׁר יִשְׁכַּב אִישׁ אוֹתָהּ שִׁכְבַת זֶרַע" וגו' (ויקרא טו): יְצִירַת הַוָּלָד אַרְבָּעִים יוֹם. תְּהֵא מְקוּלְקֶלֶת לְמַפְרֵעַ. לְשַׁלֵּם תְּרוּמָה שֶׁאָכְלָה קֶרֶן וָחוֹמֶשׁ, דְּאִשְׁתַּכַּח דְּזָרָה הַוְיָא וְאָכְלָה תְּרוּמָה בְּשׁוֹגֵג. וְאִי כִּדְקָאָמְרַתְּ – מַאי מְקוּלְקֶלֶת? הָא וַדַּאי כׇּל מ' לָאו זָרָה הָוְיָא. עַד מ'. אִם אָכְלָה לְאַחַר מ' תְּהֵא מְקוּלְקֶלֶת לְמַפְרֵעַ עַד יוֹם אַרְבָּעִים. וּמִדִּמְתָרֵץ רַב חִסְדָּא אוֹכֶלֶת עַד אַרְבָּעִים – שְׁמַע מִינַּהּ: מֵת בַּעְלָהּ דְּקָתָנֵי בְּבָרַיְיתָא הָוֵי דְּמֵת בּוֹ בַּיּוֹם שֶׁנִּשֵּׂאת, דְּאִי שָׁהָה אֶלָּא זְמַן מְרוּבֶּה – לְאַלְתַּר אֲסוּרָה, דִּלְמָא מְעוּבֶּרֶת הִיא, דַּהֲרֵי כְּבָר אַרְבָּעִים יוֹם. הַוָּלָד מַמְזֵר. אע"פ שֶׁשְּׁנֵיהֶם מוֹדִים שֶׁבָּא עָלֶיהָ, חָיְישִׁינַן: הוֹאִיל וּפְרוּצָה הִיא – אַחֵר נַמִי בָּא עָלֶיהָ, וְאִיעַבְּרָה מִינֵּיהּ. שְׁתוּקִי. סָפֵק מַמְזֵר. דְּהָא מְסַפְּקָא לָן אִי מֵאָרוּס הוּא, וְכָשֵׁר, אִי מֵאִינִישׁ אַחֲרִינָא הוּא, הִלְכָּךְ מַמְזֵר סָפֵק הוּא. מִסְתַּבְּרָא מִילְּתֵיהּ דְּרַב. דְּמַשְׁוֵי לֵיהּ מַמְזֵר וַדַּאי. דְּדַיְימָא מֵעָלְמָא. שֶׁחֲשׁוּדָה מֵאֲחֵרִים, דְּלֵיכָּא לְאַכְשׁוּרֵי כִּשְׁאָר בְּנֵי דוֹמָה שֶׁהֵם כְּשֵׁרִים. דְּהָתָם, כֵּיוָן דִּנְשׂוּאָה הִיא, רוֹב בְּעִילוֹת הוֹלֵךְ אַחַר הַבַּעַל. אֲבָל הָכָא, לָאו אוֹרְחֵיהּ לְמִיבְעַל כּוּלֵּי הַאי בְּלֹא חוּפָּה. דְּקָתָנֵי בְּמַתְנִי' יָלְדָה. אֲנוּסָה וּמְפוּתָּה בַּת יִשְׂרָאֵל מִכֹּהֵן תֹּאכַל בִּתְרוּמָה מִשּׁוּם בְּנָהּ, דְּמַחְזְקִינַן לֵיהּ בְּכֹהֵן. הֵיכִי דָּמֵי אִי דַּיְימָא. נַמִי מֵעָלְמָא, אַמַּאי תֹּאכַל? אֶלָּא לָאו דְּדַיְימָא מִינֵּיהּ לְחוּדֵיהּ, וְקָשָׁדֵינַן לֵיהּ אַבַּתְרֵיהּ. וְאע"ג דִּלְדִידֵיהּ אִיסּוּרָא כְּכוּלֵּי עָלְמָא, דְּגָזְרוּ עַל יִחוּד שֶׁל פְּנוּיָה, וְכׇל שֶׁכֵּן אֲרוּסָה, דִּלְגַבֵּי אָרוּס הֵיתֵּר וּלְעָלְמָא בְּאִיסּוּרָא – וַדַּאי הֵיכָא דְּדַיְימָא מִינֵּיהּ לְחוּדֵיהּ אָמְרִינַן בַּתְרֵיהּ שָׁדֵינַן לֵיהּ לַוָּלָד. **בְּבָא** עָלֶיהָ כּוּלֵּי עָלְמָא **לָא פְּלִיגֵי**. הֵיכָא דְּמוֹדֶה שֶׁבָּא עָלֶיהָ. הַוָּלָד מַמְזֵר. וַדַּאי, דְּבָתַר רוּבָּא דְּעָלְמָא שָׁדֵינַן לֵיהּ, וּמֵאִינִישׁ אַחֲרִינָא הָוֵי. הָכִי

תוספות

ונשאת לעבד. תימה: דלא קתני ונכבשה עם העבד, כדקתני ונכבש עם השפחה – דנישואין לא שייכי בה:

בזנות לא חששו. כדפי' בקונטרס, דאשה מזנה מתהפכת כדי שלא תתעבר. ושוטה נמי, אע"פ שנשאת לו – מתהפכת, ואין רוצה להתעבר ממנו, לפי שיראה שלא תוכל לסובלו, כדאמרינן בפרק "חרש" (לקמן דף קיג: ושם) דאין אדם דר עם נחש בכפיפה אחת.

רב אמר הולד ממזר כו'. בפ' "עשרה יוחסין" (קדושין דף עה.) מפרש פלוגתייהו בג' גווני.

אמר ליה אביי לעולם אימא לך אע"ג דלא דיימא מעלמא אמר רב הולד ממזר. ולהאי לישנא הא דקאמר בפ"ק דכתובות (דף יג:) ההוא ארוס וארוסתו דאתו לקמיה דרב יוסף, היא אמרה: מיניה, והוא אמר:(ד) אין, מינאי. אמר רב יוסף: למאי ניחוש להו? חדא דהא קא מודה, ועוד: האמר רב יהודה כו'. לאביי דאית ליה הכא דלרב הולד ממזר, אע"ג דלא דיימא מעלמא – לא סגי התם בטעמא קמא בלא "ועוד".

איכא דאמרי בבא עליה כ"ע לא פליגי כו'. פירוש: היכא דלא דיימא מעלמא – מודה אביי דאין הולד ממזר. אלא הכי איתמר כו', ופליגי אביי ורבא בדיימא מיניה ודיימא מעלמא.

אבל

עין משפט נר מצוה

מב א מיי' פ"ח מהל' תרומות הי"ד:

מג ב מיי' פ"ו שם הל' טז טוי"ד סי' שלא:

מד ג מיי' שם הל' יג יד:

מה ד מיי' שם הל' טו:

מו ה מיי' פ"ו מהלכות יבום הל' ח סמג עשין נא נב טוש"ע אה"ע סי' קעב סעי' טז:

מז ו מיי' פ"ט מהל' תרומות הל' א סמג לאוין רכח טוי"ד סי' שלא:

מח ז ח ט מיי' שם פ"ח הל"ג טוי"ד שם:

מט י מיי' פט"ו מהל' איסורי ביאה הי"ז סמג לאוין קכה טוש"ע אה"ע סי' ד סעי' כז:

הגהות הב"ח

(א) גמ' נחתך העובר במעיה תאכל הרי כהן: (ב) שם ומן הייבום כילד הרי ישראל שבא: (ג) רש"י ד"ה מאכיל את אמו אפי' לאחר מיתת אביו: (ד) תוס' ד"ה אמר וכו' אמר מינאי כצ"ל ותיבת אין נמחק:

מסורת הש"ס

[תוס' ספי"א] לקמן נו: קיב:

לעיל לג:

סוכה כג: גיטין כח. נדרים ג:

קדושין עה:

[ע' תוס' סוטה כז ד"ה רוב בעילות.]

[ע' תוס' שם]

[לעיל לה.]

הָכִי גָּרְסִינַן: ה"ד אִילֵימָא דְּדַיְימָא מִנֵּיהּ וְלָא דַּיְימָא מֵעָלְמָא צְרִיכָא לְמֵימַר דְּתֵיכוֹל אֶלָּא לָאו דְּדַיְימָא נָמֵי מֵעָלְמָא. לא כ"ש. דְּאִי דַּיְימָא מִנֵּיהּ וּמֵעָלְמָא, דְּבַתְרֵיהּ דִּידֵיהּ שָׁדֵינַן לֵיהּ. וּמַתְנִי' בִּדְלָא דַּיְימָא כְּלָל. מִקַּמֵּי הָכִי, לָאו מִנֵּיהּ וְלָאו מֵעָלְמָא. הִלְכָּךְ אִיצְטְרִיךְ לְאַשְׁמוּעִינַן דְּתֹאכַל, דְּאָמְרִינַן בְּסָפֵק בִּיאָה נִתְעַבְּרָה. בְּנֵי בָנִים הֲרֵי הֵן כְּבָנִים. כְּפָ' "הַבָּא עַל יְבִמְתּוֹ" (לעיל סב:). כְּמַאן כר"ע. מַתְנִיתִין דְּקָתָנֵי גּוֹי וְעֶבֶד הַבָּא עַל בַּת יִשְׂרָאֵל הַוָּלָד מַמְזֵר. מִשּׁוּם רַבֵּינוּ. רַבִּי, וְאע"ג דְּשָׁמְעִינַן דִּפְלִיג אַדְּר"ע בְּפָ' ר"ג (לעיל נג:), דְּאָמַר: אֵין דְּבָרִים הַלָּלוּ אֲמוּרִים אֶלָּא לְדִבְרֵי ר"ע, וְלֵיהּ לָא ס"ל, אפ"ה, בְּגוֹי וְעֶבֶד מוֹדֶה, כִּדְאָמַר בְּ"הַחוֹלֵץ" (לעיל מה.): גּוֹי "לֹא תִתְחַתֵּן", וְעֶבֶד "לֹא תִהְיֶה קְדֵשָׁה". כּוּזָא. כְּלִי קָטָן. כְּלוֹמַר, מַמְזֵר שֶׁהוּא גָּרוּעַ. כַּדָּא. כְּלִי חָשׁוּב. כְּלוֹמַר, כֹּהֵן גָּדוֹל.

אֲבָל דַּיְימָא מַנֵּיהּ, אע"ג דְּדַיְימָא מֵעָלְמָא, בַּתְרֵיהּ דִּידֵיהּ שָׁדֵינַן לֵיהּ, אָמַר רָבָא: מְנָא אָמִינָא לָהּ, דְּקָתָנֵי: יָלְדָה – תֹּאכַל. הֵיכִי דָּמֵי? אִילֵימָא דְּדַיְימָא מַנֵּיהּ וְלָא דַּיְימָא מֵעָלְמָא – צְרִיכָא לְמֵימַר דְּתֵיכוֹל?! אֶלָּא לָאו – דְּדַיְימָא נָמֵי מֵעָלְמָא, וּמָה הָתָם, דִּלְהַאי אִיסּוּרָא וּלְהַאי אִיסּוּרָא, בַּתְרֵיהּ דִּידֵיהּ שָׁדֵינַן לֵיהּ, הָכָא דִּלְהַאי אִיסּוּרָא וּלְהַאי הֶיתֵּירָא – לֹא כׇּל שֶׁכֵּן?! א"ל אַבָּיֵי: לְעוֹלָם אֵימָא לָךְ, כׇּל הֵיכָא דְּדַיְימָא מֵעָלְמָא, אע"ג דְּדַיְימָא מַנֵּיהּ אָמַר רַב הַוָּלָד מַמְזֵר, וּמַתְנִי' בִּדְלָא דַּיְימָא כְּלָל. "הָעֶבֶד פּוֹסֵל מִשּׁוּם בִּיאָה כו'". מ"ט? אָמַר קְרָא "הָאִשָּׁה וִילָדֶיהָ תִּהְיֶה וגו'". "מַמְזֵר פּוֹסֵל וּמַאֲכִיל". ת"ר: "וְזֶרַע אֵין לָהּ", אֵין לִי אֶלָּא זַרְעָהּ, זֶרַע זַרְעָהּ מִנַּיִן? ת"ל "וְזֶרַע אֵין לָהּ", מִכׇּל מָקוֹם, אֵין לִי אֶלָּא זֶרַע כָּשֵׁר, זֶרַע פָּסוּל מִנַּיִן? ת"ל "וְזֶרַע אֵין לָהּ" – עַיֵּין עָלֶיהָ. וְהָא אַפִּיקְתֵּיהּ לְזֶרַע זַרְעָהּ! זֶרַע זַרְעָהּ לָא אִיצְטְרִיךְ קְרָא, בְּנֵי בָנִים הֲרֵי הֵן כְּבָנִים, כִּי אִיצְטְרִיךְ קְרָא – לְזֶרַע פָּסוּל. א"ל ר"ל לְרַבִּי יוֹחָנָן: כְּמַאן, כר"ע, דְּאָמַר: יֵשׁ מַמְזֵר מֵחַיָּיבֵי לָאוִין? אֲפִילּוּ תֵּימָא רַבָּנַן, בְּעוֹבֵד כּוֹכָבִים וְעֶבֶד מוֹדוּ. דְּכִי אֲתָא רַב דִּימִי א"ר יִצְחָק בַּר אֲבוּדִימִי מִשּׁוּם רַבֵּינוּ: גּוֹי וְעֶבֶד הַבָּא עַל בַּת יִשְׂרָאֵל – הַוָּלָד מַמְזֵר. "כ"ג פְּעָמִים שֶׁפּוֹסֵל". ת"ר: הֲרֵינִי כַּפָּרַת בֶּן בְּתִי כּוּזָא – שֶׁמַּאֲכִילַנִי בִּתְרוּמָה, וְאֵינִי כַּפָּרַת בֶּן בְּתִי כַּדָּא – שֶׁפּוֹסְלַנִי מִן הַתְּרוּמָה.

אבל דיימא מיניה אע"ג דדיימא נמי מעלמא בתר דידיה שדינן ליה. פי': דיימא מיניה – שבא עליה ודאי, ודיימא מעלמא – היינו שם רע, דאי דיימא מיניה נמי שם רע בעלמא – א"כ מאי מייתי רבא ממתני'? דהתם בא עליה ודאי, משום הכי בתר דידיה שדינן ליה.

הדרן עלך אלמנה

הדרן עלך אלמנה

הדרן עלך אלמנה

הֶעָרֵל וְכׇל הַטְּמֵאִים לֹא יֹאכְלוּ בִּתְרוּמָה, נְשֵׁיהֶן וְעַבְדֵיהֶן יֹאכְלוּ בִּתְרוּמָה. פְּצוּעַ דַּכָּא וּכְרוּת שָׁפְכָה, הֵן וְעַבְדֵיהֶן – יֹאכְלוּ, נְשֵׁיהֶן – לֹא יֹאכְלוּ, וְאִם לֹא יְדָעָהּ מִשֶּׁנַּעֲשָׂה פְּצוּעַ דַּכָּא וּכְרוּת שָׁפְכָה – הֲרֵי אֵלּוּ יֹאכְלוּ. וְאֵי זֶהוּ פְּצוּעַ דַּכָּא – כׇּל שֶׁנִּפְצְעוּ הַבֵּיצִים שֶׁלּוֹ, וַאֲפִילּוּ אַחַת מֵהֶן. וּכְרוּת שָׁפְכָה – כׇּל שֶׁנִּכְרַת הַגִּיד. וְאִם נִשְׁתַּיֵּיר מֵעֲטָרָה אֲפִילּוּ כְּחוּט הַשַּׂעֲרָה – כָּשֵׁר. **גמ'** תַּנְיָא, א"ר אֱלִיעֶזֶר: מִנַּיִן לְעָרֵל שֶׁאֵין אוֹכֵל בִּתְרוּמָה – נֶאֱמַר "תּוֹשָׁב וְשָׂכִיר" בְּפֶסַח, וְנֶאֱמַר "תּוֹשָׁב וְשָׂכִיר" בִּתְרוּמָה, מָה "תּוֹשָׁב וְשָׂכִיר" הָאָמוּר בְּפֶסַח עָרֵל אָסוּר בּוֹ, אַף "תּוֹשָׁב וְשָׂכִיר" הָאָמוּר בִּתְרוּמָה עָרֵל אָסוּר בּוֹ. רַבִּי עֲקִיבָא אוֹמֵר: אֵינוֹ צָרִיךְ, הֲרֵי הוּא אוֹמֵר "אִישׁ אִישׁ" לְרַבּוֹת הֶעָרֵל. אָמַר מָר: ר"א אוֹמֵר נֶאֱמַר "תּוֹשָׁב וְשָׂכִיר" בְּפֶסַח וְנֶאֱמַר "תּוֹשָׁב וְשָׂכִיר" בִּתְרוּמָה, מָה "תּוֹשָׁב וְשָׂכִיר" הָאָמוּר בְּפֶסַח עָרֵל אָסוּר בּוֹ, אַף "תּוֹשָׁב וְשָׂכִיר" הָאָמוּר בִּתְרוּמָה עָרֵל אָסוּר בּוֹ. מוּפְנֶה, דְּאִי לָאו מוּפְנֶה – אִיכָּא לְמִיפְרַךְ: מָה לְפֶסַח – שֶׁכֵּן חַיָּיבִין עָלָיו מִשּׁוּם פִּיגּוּל וְנוֹתָר וְטָמֵא. לְאֵי, אַפְנוּיֵי מוּפְנֶה. הֵי מוּפְנֶה? אִי דִּתְרוּמָה – מִצְרָךְ צְרִיכִי, דְּתַנְיָא: "תּוֹשָׁב" זֶה קְנוּי קִנְיַן עוֹלָם, "שָׂכִיר" זֶה קְנוּי קִנְיַן שָׁנִים. וְיֹאמַר "תּוֹשָׁב" וְאַל יֹאמַר "שָׂכִיר", וַאֲנִי אוֹמֵר: קְנוּי קִנְיַן עוֹלָם אֵינוֹ אוֹכֵל, קְנוּי קִנְיַן שָׁנִים – לֹא כׇּל שֶׁכֵּן?! אִילּוּ כֵּן, הָיִיתִי אוֹמֵר: "תּוֹשָׁב" זֶה קְנוּי קִנְיַן שָׁנִים, אֲבָל קְנוּי קִנְיַן עוֹלָם אוֹכֵל – בָּא "שָׂכִיר" וְלִימֵּד עַל תּוֹשָׁב, שֶׁאַף עַל פִּי שֶׁקָּנוּי קִנְיַן עוֹלָם – אֵין אוֹכֵל. אֶלָּא דְּפֶסַח מוּפְנֶה. הַאי "תּוֹשָׁב וְשָׂכִיר" דִּכְתַב רַחֲמָנָא בְּפֶסַח מַאי נִיהוּ? אִי נֵימָא תּוֹשָׁב וְשָׂכִיר מַמָּשׁ – מִשּׁוּם דַּהֲוָה לֵיהּ תּוֹשָׁב וְשָׂכִיר אִיפְּטַר לֵיהּ מִפֶּסַח?! וְהָא קַיְימָא לַן גַּבֵּי תְּרוּמָה דְּלָא אָכֵיל, אַלְמָא

תוספות ישנים

הדרן עלך אלמנה